CARLING

PUB QUIZ BOOK

PAUL DREW

ILLUSTRATIONS BY PETER COUPE

ARCTURUS

Arcturus Publishing Limited
1–7 Shand Street, London SE1 2ES

for:
Bookmart Limited
Registered Number 2372865
Desford Road
Enderby
Leicester LE9 5AD

This edition published 2001

Printed and bound by Omnia Books Limited

ISBN 1-84193-072-5

Cover design by Paul Ashby

CARLING

PUB QUIZ BOOK

PAUL DREW

FOREWORD

There is something for everyone in these entertaining quizzes, with questions that range from the relatively straightforward to others that will stump the most accomplished pub quiz masterminds. The quizzes cover the spectrum of popular subjects and are not just confined to the modern day, thus giving this giant collection great appeal to both young and old. So if you are not too sure about Britney, you can always boast about your Beethoven.

Just when you think you have grasped the ability to answer all the questions, along will come one that will totally floor you. A little voice will call out from the deep recesses of your mind, "I know this! I know the answer!" Yet no matter how hard you try, no matter how much you struggle and strain, you cannot unlock it from the depths of your memory. All that comes is an anguished groan as you are forced to look at the answer at the foot of the page and cry. "I knew it! I knew it all along!" This is the time to take a deep breath and go onto the next challenge, battered, bruised, but unbowed.

Best of luck!

GENERAL KNOWLEDGE

ENTERTAINMENT

SPORT

POP MUSIC

ART AND LITERATURE

GEOGRAPHY

WORDS

SCIENCE

PEOPLE

HISTORY

GENERAL KNOWLEDGE

1. Which jazz band leader once had a piano teacher called Mrs. Clinkscales?
2. Of which country is the letter L the international car index mark?
3. In which country is the skiing resort of Megeve?
4. Which long-running film character first made his appearance in *All-Story* magazine in October, 1912?
5. In which year did Amazon.com begin business?
6. In which year was the fluted Coca-Cola bottle first designed?
7. Which writer's skull was found during work on St. Peter's Church, Carmarthen in 2000?
8. What nationality is the composer Albert Roussel?
9. The roadrunner is the state bird of which of the United States of America?

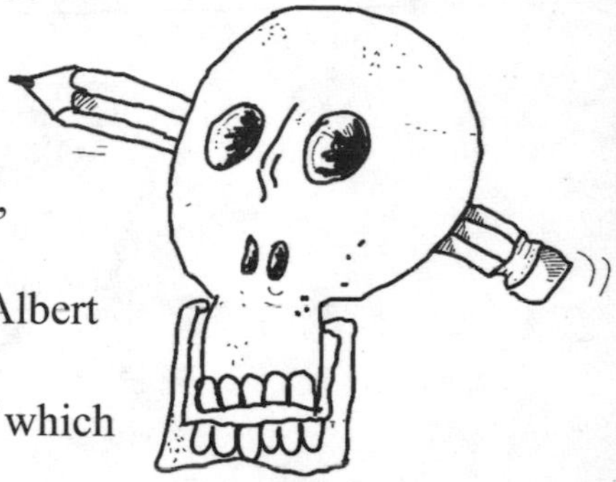

10. What is the name of the food colouring numbered E120?
11. Of what is basophobia the fear?
12. What, in slang used by Heathrow customs officers, is a frost box?
13. The space probe Beagle 2 plans to land on which planet in 2003?
14. For which beer was the *Whassup* advertising campaign in 2000?
15. Which British car ceased production in 2000 after 5,387,862 had been built?

ANSWERS **1.** Duke Ellington **2.** Luxembourg **3.** France **4.** Tarzan of the Apes **5.** 1994 **6.** 1915 **7.** Richard Steele **8.** French **9.** New Mexico **10.** Cochineal **11.** Walking **12.** A special see-through lavatory**13.** Mars **14.** Budweiser **15.** Mini Cooper.

ENTERTAINMENT

1. What was the name of Spinal Tap's manager, played by Tony Hendra, in the film *This Is Spinal Tap?*
2. Who plays Father Brian Kilkenny in the 2000 film *Keeping the Faith*?
3. What age was Stephen Daldry when appointed artistic director of the Royal Court theatre?
4. How much was Jim Carrey paid for the film *Ace Ventura: Pet Detective?*
5. What is the middle name of the comedian Paul Tonkinson?
6. Which duo wrote the 2000 sitcom *Black Books*?
7. Which comedian performed a tribute show to the singer Leonard Cohen at the 2000 Edinburgh Fringe Festival?
8. In which city in England is the Mercury Theatre?
9. Which comedian's guises include Sir Les Patterson?
10. What was Christopher Walken's character name in the film *King of New York*?
11. Which character in *Coronation Street* was born on the 13 April, 1983?
12. The bowling alley in the 2000 film *Wonder Boys* also features in which film by the Farrelly Brothers?
13. Who played Dr. Watson in the 1965 film *A Study in Terror*?
14. In which Mozart opera does the aria *E Amore Un Ladroncello* appear?
15. Who played John Watson in the 1985 film *Young Sherlock Holmes*?

ANSWERS **1.** Ian Faith **2.** Edward Norton **3.** 32 **4.** $350,000 **5.** Robert **6.** Dylan Moran and Graham Linehan **7.** Arthur Smith **8.** Colchester **9.** Barry Humphries **10.** Frank White **11.** Mark Baldwin **12.** Kingpin **13.** Donald Houston **14.** Cosi Fan Tutte **15.** Alan Cox.

SPORT

1. From which football club did Chelsea buy Celestine Babayaro in 1997?
2. Who did Mike Tyson, the former world heavyweight boxing champion, defeat in October, 2000?
3. Who was a silver medal winner for Britain at the 2000 Olympics in the men's single trap shooting event?
4. Which Barcelona footballer moved to Real Madrid in July, 2000 for £37m?
5. Which athlete was the 1986 Commonwealth men's 5,000m champion?
6. Which British athlete took bronze in the 2000 Olympic women's 800m final?
7. Who was Britain's bronze medal winner in the women's Modern Pentathlon at the 2000 Olympics?
8. To what did the American Football team the Tennessee Oilers change their name in 1999?
9. Which horse won the 1977 and 1978 Prix de l'Arc de Triomphe?
10. Who was the losing finalist in the 1988 Olympic men's singles tennis event?
11. Against which cricket team did Alex Tudor make his England Test debut in November, 1998?
12. What nationality is the boxer Eric Lucas?
13. Who was the 1996 Olympic decathlon champion?
14. Who was the 1997 U.S. Open tennis women's singles champion?
15. Who was the world matchplay golf champion from 1994-96?

ANSWERS **1.** Anderlecht **2.** Andrew Golota **3.** Ian Peel **4.** Luis Figo **5.** Steve Ovett **6.** Kelly Holmes **7.** Kate Allenby **8.** Tennessee Titans **9.** Alleged **10.** Tim Mayotte **11.** Australia **12.** Canadian **13.** Dan O'Brien **14.** Martina Hingis **15.** Ernie Els.

POP

1. Which pop star served time in HMP Stocken in 1999 as Prisoner AV8786?
2. Tjinder Singh and Ben Ayres comprise which offshoot of the group *Cornershop*?
3. *Good Boys...when They're Asleep* is a 'Best Of' compilation record of which band's music?
4. In which year was Lemmy fired from the rock group *Hawkwind* for drug-taking?
5. Which associate of Elvis Presley was born Andreas Cornelis Van Kujik?
6. Which pop star set up *Rocket Pictures* in 1996?
7. Which pop star made the album *Music In Colors* with the violinist Nigel Kennedy?
8. Andrew Victor Wood is the lead singer of which Wakefield group?
9. In which year did Bernard Butler leave the pop group *Suede*?
10. Which 1979 pop festival in Leeds was billed as 'The World's First Science Fiction Music Festival'?
11. Which member of the pop group New Kids on the Block is actor Mark Wahlberg's brother?
12. Which pop star does Noel Gallagher call *Captain Rock*?
13. From which northern town does the musician Damon Gough, a.k.a. Badly Drawn Boy hail?
14. The father of which musician played football for Celtic and was nicknamed 'The Black Arrow'?
15. In which year was Merle Haggard inducted into the Country Music Hall of Fame?

ANSWERS 1. Mark Morrison **2.** Clinton **3.** The Faces **4.** 1975 **5.** Colonel Tom Parker **6.** Elton John **7.** Stephen 'Tin Tin' Duffy **8.** Ultrasound **9.** 1994 **10.** Futurama **11.** Donnie Wahlberg **12.** Richard Ashcroft **13.** Bolton **14.** Gil Scott-Heron **15.** 1994.

ART AND LITERATURE

1. Who founded the magazine Tatler?
2. Who wrote the 2000 novel *Sleeping Cruelty*?
3. Whose paintings include 1961's *Movement in Squares*?
4. For what art form is the Stirling Prize awarded?
5. Who wrote the books *Fight Club* and *Survivor*?
6. The character Berma in Proust's *Á la recherche du temps perdu* was based on which actress?
7. Which Frenchman authored the 2000 novel *Strange Ways*?
8. The 2000 book *Speaking with the Angels*, edited by Nick Hornby, is named after a song by which singer?
9. Who wrote the novel *Any Woman's Blues*?
10. Who wrote children's book *The Day The Sea Rolled Back*?
11. Who authored the 1999 novel *The Plato Papers*?
12. Who is author of novel *Girlfriend 44*?
13. What is unusual about the novel *La Disparition* by Georges Perec?
14. In which Welsh city did the Centre for Visual Art open in 1999?
15. Who painted *Beach at Trouville* and *Towing of a Boat at Honfleur*?

ANSWERS 1. Richard Steele **2.** Lynda La Plante **3.** Bridget Riley **4.** Architecture **5.** Chuck Palahniuk **6.** Sarah Bernhardt **7.** Luc Lang **8.** Ron Sexsmith **9.** Erica Jong **10.** Mickey Spillane **11.** Peter Ackroyd **12.** Mark Barrowcliffe **13.** It doesn't contain the letter 'e' **14.** Cardiff **15.** Claude Monet.

GENERAL KNOWLEDGE

1. What was the name of the Russian nuclear submarine which sank in August, 2000?
2. According to a survey by consultants Atwood SB in 2000, how many hours does a British consumer spend queuing each year?
3. Who replaced Charles Dickens on the back of a £10 note in 2000?
4. Which car manufacturer makes the Ignis model?
5. Which theme park is near Ripon, North Yorkshire?
6. In which year was France's 'Minitel' system launched?
7. What was the subject of Kenneth Irvine's 1987 pamphlet *The Right Lines*, published by the Adam Smith Institute?
8. In which country is the skiing resort of St. Anton?
9. In which year did the first Tarzan comic strip appear?
10. What were the names of the two mynah birds in the foyer of the cinema chosen for the London premiere of Alfred Hitchcock film *The Birds*?
11. Which former ITN political editor authored the autobiography *A Ringside Seat*?
12. What is the state bird of Oklahoma in the United States of America?
13. What is the name of the food colouring numbered E123?
14. Who played the villainess Olga, Queen of the Cossacks in the 1960's *Batman* television series?
15. Of what is linonophobia the fear?

ANSWERS **1.** Kursk **2.** 73 **3.** Charles Darwin **4.** Suzuki **5.** Lightwater Valley **6.** 1982 **7.** Railway privatization **8.** Austria **9.** 1929 **10.** Tippi and Alfred **11.** Michael Brunson **12.** Scissor-tailed flycatcher **13.** Amaranth **14.** Anne Baxter **15.** String.

ENTERTAINMENT

1. Who directed 1999 film *The Faculty*?
2. In which city is the 1999 film *Bedrooms and Hallways* set?
3. Which silent movie star lost half his right hand in an explosion in August 1919?
4. Who plays gardener Clay Boone in the 1999 film *Gods and Monsters*?
5. Who directed the 1999 film *Tea With Mussolini*?
6. Which Best Actor Oscar nominee made his film debut in the 1981 film *Carbon Copy*?
7. Who played the title role in the 1952 film *Carrie*?
8. In which the 1971 film did Carol Kane make her screen debut?
9. Who plays Nick Leeson in the 1999 biopic *Rogue Trader*?
10. Who played Dorothy Parker in the film *Mrs.Parker and the Vicious Circle*?
11. Which brothers run the film production company Miramax?

12. Which comedian made his screen debut as 'Parking Valet' in the 1987 film *Beverly Hills Cop II*?
13. With which art form is Angelis Prejocaj associated?
14. How much did Eddie Murphy get to star in the film *Nutty Professor II: The Klumps*?
15. Which cast member of the television show *Auf Wiedersehen, Pet* died in 1986?

ANSWERS **1.** Robert Rodriguez **2.** London **3.** Harold Lloyd **4.** Brendan Fraser **5.** Franco Zeffirelli **6.** Denzel Washington **7.** Jennifer Jones **8.** Carnal Knowledge **9.** Ewan McGregor **10.** Jennifer Jason Leigh **11.** Bob and Harvey Weinstein **12.** Chris Rock **13.** Dance **14.** $20m **15.** Gary Holton

SPORT

1. Who was the super-heavyweight boxing champion at the 2000 Olympics?
2. Which darts player was whitewashed 6-0 in the 1994 BDO world professional championship final by John Part?
3. Who was the world heavyweight boxing champion from 1962-64?
4. From which football club did Aston Villa sign David Ginola in July, 2000?
5. Which British athlete won a bronze medal in the 2000 Olympic women's 400m final?
6. Who was the 1992 world Formula 1 motor racing champion?
7. Which dog won the 1999 greyhound derby?
8. Which horse won the 1947 Grand National?
9. Which team won the 2000 University Boat Race?
10. Which side won the 2000 rugby union Six Nations championship?
11. Where was baseball player Hank Aaron born?
12. Who was the French Open men's singles tennis champion in 1991?
13. Which American Football team won Super Bowl XXX?
14. In which country were the 1982 football World Cup finals held?
15. How many women competed at the 1896 Olympics?

ANSWERS 1. Audley Harrison **2.** Bobby George **3.** Sonny Liston **4.** Tottenham Hotspur **5.** Katharine Merry **6.** Nigel Mansell **7.** Chart King **8.** Caughoo **9.** Oxford **10.** England **11.** Mobile, Alabama **12.** Jim Courier **13.** Dallas Cowboys **14.** Spain **15.** None.

POP

1. Who produced Patti Smith's 1979 album *Wave*?
2. Which song did television D-I-Y man Andy Kane release as a single in summer, 1999?
3. In which month of 1940 was John Lennon born?
4. Which singer became an ordained monk in 1996 taking the name Jikan?
5. From which U.S. town are the band 15-60-75?
6. Björn Again are a tribute band to which group?
7. *New Forms* was the debut album of which group?
8. Which female singer's nickname is *Thunder Bitch*?
9. Which punk rocker worked as a maintenance man at the English National Opera in 1974?
10. David Bowie's debut L.P. was released on the same day as which L.P. by *The Beatles*?
11. Which rock star had a starring role in the 1980 film *Carny*?
12. Which singer-actor was born O'Shea Jackson?
13. What nationality is singer Ian Brown's wife Fabiola?
14. Which rock singer did Daryl Hannah date before going out with John F. Kennedy?
15. The centenary of the birth of which jazz band leader was celebrated on April 29, 1999?

ANSWERS 1. Todd Rundgren **2.** If I Had A Hammer **3.** October **4.** Leonard Cohen **5.** Kent, Ohio **6.** Abba **7.** Roni Size and Reprazent **8.** Kelis **9.** Joe Strummer **10.** Sgt. Pepper's Lonely Hearts Club Band **11.** Robbie Robertson **12.** Ice Cube **13.** Mexican **14.** Jackson Browne **15.** Duke Ellington.

GEOGRAPHY

1. In which country is the skiing resort of Engelberg?
2. On which Mediterranean island is the city of Catania?
3. Baracaldo is an industrial suburb of which Spanish town?
4. In which African country are the towns of Monrovia and Buchanan?
5. Which is the most westerly country of Africa through which the Tropic of Capricorn runs?
6. In which European country are the towns of Sion and Chur?
7. In which African country are the towns of Sfax and Bizerte?
8. Monastir is the former name of which city in Macedonia?
9. On which river is the town of Upington in South Africa?
10. In which Asian country is the seaport of Moulmein?
11. In which African country is the town of Meknès?
12. In which European country are the towns of Durrës and Vlorë?
13. Off which African country does the Gulf of Gabes lie?
14. Which European capital city was formerly known as Ledra?
15. In which U.S. state is the county of Volusia?

ANSWERS **1.** Switzerland **2.** Sicily **3.** Bilbao **4.** Liberia **5.** Namibia **6.** Switzerland **7.** Tunisia **8.** Bitola **9.** Orange River **10.** Myanmar **11.** Morocco **12.** Albania **13.** Tunisia **14.** Nicosia **15.** Florida.

GENERAL KNOWLEDGE

1. What is the dominant religion in Liberia?
2. The greenish-blue colour 'Alice blue' takes its name from the daughter of which U.S. president?
3. In which year did 'The El', New York's elevated railway, close down?
4. What sort of creature is a bobolink?
5. What was CAMRA's champion beer of the year in 1982 & 1983?
6. Which author won the 1984 Guardian Children's Fiction Award?
7. From the young of which animal is the leather chevrette made?
8. How many seats did the Liberal Party win in the 1945 election?
9. For which party did Gwynfor Evans win a 1966 by-election in Carmarthen?
10. In which year was the Torrey Canyon oil disaster?
11. Which London hotel won the Egon Ronay Hotel of the Year award in 1992?
12. In which year did Salman Rushdie win the 'Booker of Bookers'?
13. What is the main ingredient of chewing gum?
14. Who did sculptor F.A. Bartholdi use as a model for the Statue of Liberty?
15. In which Canadian province is the village of Grand Pré?

ANSWERS **1.** Christianity **2.** Theodore Roosevelt **3.** 1955 **4.** Bird **5.** Taylor Landlord **6.** Dick King-Smith **7.** A goat **8.** 12 **9.** Plaid Cymru **10.** 1967 **11.** The Dorchester **12.** 1993 **13.** Chicle **14.** His mother **15.** Nova Scotia.

ENTERTAINMENT

1. Who directed the 1963 film *The Cardinal*?
2. Who played Mary Shelley in the 1990 film *Frankenstein Unbound*?
3. What is Brendan Foster's character name in the 1999 film *The Mummy*?
4. What is Julia Ormond's job in the 1995 film *Captives*?
5. Which actress plays a famous television chef in the 1999 film *Playing by Heart*?
6. The film *Simon Birch* is based on which novel by John Irving?
7. Which former presenter of television show *Magpie* was the executive producer on film *Mrs. Brown*?
8. Who played Sherlock Holmes in the 1929 film *The Return of Sherlock Holmes*?
9. What was the character name of Jeffrey DeMunn in the film *Ragtime*?
10. Who directed the 1964 film *Seven Days in May*?
11. Who does Paula Tilbrook play in the television show *Emmerdale*?
12. Who directed the 1999 film *Made in Hong Kong*?
13. The 1946 film *The Captive Heart* is set during which war?
14. Which cartoonist created the Channel 4 animated series *Pond Life*?
15. Who directed the 1999 film *Happiness*?

ANSWERS 1. Otto Preminger **2.** Bridget Fonda **3.** Rick O'Connell **4.** Dentist **5.** Gena Rowlands **6.** A Prayer for Owen Meany **7.** Douglas Rae **8.** Clive Brook **9.** Houdini **10.** John Frankenheimer **11.** Betty Eagleton **12.** Fruit Chan **13.** World War II **14.** Candy Guard **15.** Todd Solondz.

SPORT

1. Which football team won the 1994/5 European Champions Cup?
2. How many times have Dundee been Scottish League champions?
3. Who won the Olympic men's 100m in 1956?
4. Which team won the 1995 world series in baseball?
5. Who was the 1997 world men's indoor bowls champion?
6. Which football team won the 1995/6 F.A. Cup?
7. Who won the Olympic women's 100m in 1968?
8. Who were the 1999 cricket county champions?
9. Who was the 1995 British Open golf champion?
10. Which football team won the 1998/9 U.E.F.A. Cup?
11. Who did Liverpool play in the quarter finals of the 2001 F.A. Cup?
12. Which boxer took the WBA light flyweight crown in March, 2001 from Beibis Mendoza?
13. Which team won the 1994/5 Scottish F.A. Cup?
14. Which American Football team won Super Bowl XXXIV?
15. Who was the manager of the Bournemouth side that knocked Manchester United out of the F.A. Cup in January 1984?

ANSWERS 1. Ajax **2.** Once **3.** Bobby Morrow **4.** Atlanta Braves **5.** Hugh Duff **6.** Manchester United **7.** Wyomia Tyus **8.** Surrey **9.** John Daly **10.** Parma **11.** Tranmere **12.** Rosendo Alvarez **13.** Celtic **14.** St. Louis Rams **15.** Harry Redknapp.

POP

1. In which year was singer Lou Reed born?
2. Who recorded the 1969 album *Songs from a Room*?
3. In which city did the Rezillos form in 1976?
4. In which year was guitarist Ry Cooder born?
5. Who produced the 1976 album *The Modern Lovers*?
6. Which group's 1995 album was called *Showbusiness*?
7. Who is the drummer in The Rolling Stones?
8. Who recorded the 1995 album *20 Mothers*?
9. In which year was David Lee Roth born?
10. In which city were the group The Comsat Angels formed?
11. What was Roxy Music's first single?
12. Which group's debut L.P. was 1985's *Virgins and Philistines*?
13. Which group recorded the 1979 album *The Crack*?
14. In which year was Bootsy Collins born?
15. Which group had a hit in 1977 with the single *Black Betty*?

ANSWERS 1. 1942 **2.** Leonard Cohen **3.** Edinburgh **4.** 1947 **5.** John Cale **6.** Chumbawamba **7.** Charlie Watts **8.** Julian Cope **9.** 1955 **10.** Sheffield **11.** Virginia Plain **12.** The Colourfield **13.** The Ruts **14.** 1951 **15.** Ram Jam.

HISTORY

1. In which month of 1963 did Harold Macmillan resign as prime minister?
2. In which month of 1960 did the *Lady Chatterley's Lover* trial begin?
3. What title did Cardinal Albino Luciani take in 1978?
4. Brigadier Murtala Mohammed became the head of which African state following a military coup in 1975?
5. Who won the Jamaican general election in December 1976?
6. Austria joined the E.U. on January 1st of which year?
7. How old was Red Rum when he died in 1995?
8. In which year was Yitzhak Rabin assassinated?
9. How did Louis XVI of France die?
10. In which year did Beethoven die?
11. In which year did Chaucer die?
12. In which century did the Venerable Bede die?
13. Who was deselected as Tory M.P. for Reigate in January 1997?
14. How many seats did the Liberal Democrats win at the 1997 election?
15. Which Tory M.P. for Beaconsfield resigned in 1997 over the cash-for-questions affair?

ANSWERS **1.** October **2.** October **3.** Pope John Paul I **4.** Nigeria **5.** Michael Manley **6.** 1995 **7.** 30 **8.** 1995 **9.** He was beheaded **10.** 1827 **11.** 1100 **12.** 8th **13.** Sir George Gardiner **14.** 46 **15.** Tim Smith.

GENERAL KNOWLEDGE

1. In which year of the 1960s did Nova magazine first appear?
2. Which two journalists comprised the 'City Slickers' in the Mirror newspaper in 1999?
3. In which country is the skiing resort of Arabba?
4. What, in slang used by Heathrow customs officers, is queening?
5. In which year did the space shuttle Challenger explode?
6. Which group of islands have been called 'Darwin's Eden'?
7. How old was Elizabeth Buttle when she gave birth in 1997?
8. In which year was murderer Rosemary West given ten life sentences?
9. In which year did Prince Albert, husband of Queen Victoria, die?
10. For how many years did Louis XIV of France reign?
11. Which car manufacturer makes the Diablo VT?
12. As what is Australian Les Hiddins better known?
13. Which firm took over The Suit Company in 1987?
14. Of which union was Jack Jones the general secretary in the 1970's?
15. In which year did the Duke and Duchess of York divorce?

ANSWERS 1. 1965 **2.** James Hipwell and Anil Bhoyrul **3.** Italy **4.** Burning seized drugs **5.** 1986 **6.** Galapagos **7.** 60 **8.** 1995 **9.** 1861 **10.** 72 **11.** Lamborghini **12.** The Bush Tucker Man **13.** Moss Bros **14.** Transport & General Workers' Union **15.** 1996.

ENTERTAINMENT

1. What was Jennifer Jason Leigh's character name in the film *Last Exit to Brooklyn*?
2. Who plays composer Mr. Kinsky in the 1999 film *Beseiged*?
3. Who directed the film *American History X*?
4. In which the 1981 film starring Sylvester Stallone was Elton John offered a cameo role?
5. Who directed the 1999 film *Plunkett and Macleane*?
6. Who was the original director of the film *A Simple Plan*?
7. How much was Jim Carrey paid to star in the film *The Mask*?
8. Which pair wrote the 2000 stage musical *The Beautiful Game*?
9. What does Lon Chaney play in the 1924 film *He Who Gets Slapped*?
10. Which actress/model was killed prior to the release of the film *They All Laughed*, in which she starred?
11. Who played Duane, brother of *Annie Hall* in the film by Woody Allen?
12. In television show *Clarissa and the Countryman*, who is *the Countryman*?
13. Who wrote the 2000 television drama *Never Never*?
14. Who directed the films *Alice in the Cities* and *Kings of the Road*?
15. What is Mark Wahlberg's character name in the film *Boogie Nights*?

ANSWERS **1.** Tralala **2.** David Thewlis **3.** Tony Kaye **4.** Escape to Victory **5.** Jake Scott **6.** John Boorman **7.** $540,000 **8.** Andrew Lloyd Webber and Ben Elton **9.** A circus clown **10.** Dorothy Stratten **11.** Christopher Walken **12.** Sir John Scott **13.** Tony Marchant **14.** Wim Wenders **15.** Dirk Diggler.

SPORT

1. Who was the first Welsh world professional snooker champion?
2. Which horse won the 1994 Irish Derby?
3. Who won the 1994 French Open golf title?
4. Which golfers entered the three-way play-off in the 1994 U.S. Open?
5. Who scored the first goal in the 1994 World Cup Finals?
6. Who won the 1994 Le Mans 24-hour race?
7. Who won the 1994 Stanley Cup?
8. Who did Andre Agassi defeat in the 1994 U.S. Open men's singles tennis final?
9. Who did Linfield play in the first round of the 1994/5 UEFA Cup?
10. Who won the 1994 Minor Counties cricket title?
11. From which country are the football side Bodoe Glimt?
12. Which cyclist won the 1994 Paris-Brussels classic?
13. Who won golf's 1994 European Open?
14. Who won the 1994 Italian Grand Prix in Formula 1?
15. In which year was Ossie Ardiles born?

ANSWERS 1. Ray Reardon **2.** Balanchine **3.** Mark Roe **4.** Colin Montgomerie, Loren Roberts & Ernie Els **5.** Jürgen Klinsmann **6.** Yannick Dalmas, Hurley Haywood & Mauro Baldi **7.** The New York Rangers **8.** Michael Stich **9.** Odense BK **10.** Devon **11.** Norway **12.** Rolf Sorenson **13.** David Gilford **14.** Damon Hill **15.** 1952.

POP

1. In which year was singer Patti Smith born?
2. Who recorded the 1976 album *Troubadour*?
3. In which year did The Smiths disband?
4. About which musician was the 1976 play *The Stars That Play With Laughing Sam's Dice*?
5. Which group recorded the 1988 album *Daydream Nation*?
6. What was Bill Harkleroad called in Captain Beefheart's Magic Band?
7. Which group recorded the 1988 album *A Little Man And a House And the Whole World Window*?
8. Which group recorded the 1980 album *Underwater Moonlight*?
9. In which city were the Soup Dragons formed?
10. What was the debut album of Nick Cave and the Bad Seeds?
11. What is guitarist Pete Kember better known as?
12. Bob 'the Bear' Hite and Al 'Blind Owl' Wilson formed which group in 1966?
13. Who recorded the album *Journeys to Glory*?
14. Which German group recorded the 1971 album *Tago Mago*?
15. Which group recorded the 1974 album *Kimono My House*?

ANSWERS 1. 1946 **2.** J.J. Cale **3.** 1987 **4.** Jimi Hendrix **5.** Sonic Youth **6.** Zoot Horn Rollo **7.** The Cardiacs **8.** The Soft Boys **9.** Glasgow **10.** From Her to Eternity **11.** Sonic Boom **12.** Canned Heat **13.** Spandau Ballet **14.** Can **15.** Sparks.

WORDS

1. What might you do with a saithe - wear it or eat it?
2. What in the England of the 18th and 19th centuries was rappee?
3. What might you do in Polynesia with a pareu - spend it or wear it?

4. Is the Japanese instrument a samisen a brass instrument or string instrument?
5. What in Malaysia is a padang?
6. What type of meat is pancetta?
7. What in ancient Rome were velites?
8. What is verglas?
9. What in New Zealand might you do with a paua - drink it or eat it?
10. Where might you wear a pantofle?
11. What in geology is a ventifact?
12. To which meat does the adjective vituline refer?
13. What is Pali - an ancient language or an old woodworking tool?
14. What is a piagle - a flower or a fortress?
15. What is a coyotillo in the U.S. and Mexico - a bush or a snake?

ANSWERS 1. Eat it - it's another name for a coalfish **2.** Snuff **3.** Wear it, it's a loincloth **4.** String **5.** A playing field **6.** Bacon **7.** Light-armed troops **8.** A thin film of ice on rock **9.** Eat it - it's an edible mollusc **10.** On the foot, it's a slipper **11.** A pebble shaped by wind-blown sands **12.** Veal **13.** A language **14.** A flower **15.** A bush.

GENERAL KNOWLEDGE

1. What nationality was novelist Pär Lagerkvist?
2. In which year was the first by-election victory for the S.D.P.?
3. Of which country was Joseph Chifley prime minister from 1945-49?
4. Who wrote the science fiction novel *Ringpull*?
5. To whom did the Crime Writers' Association award the Diamond Dagger in 1993?
6. Which book won the William Hill Sports Book of the Year award in 1992?
7. What do you do if you grangerize a book?
8. Which entertainer was voted Young Magician of the Year 1981 by the Magic Circle?
9. What is the name given to the world memory championships organized by the Brains Trust?
10. Which national award did Irene Hall of Blackburn win in 1993?
11. What was awarded the Museum of the Year title in 1974?
12. Which writer coined the word 'chortle'?
13. Who directed the film *Star Wars*?
14. In which year was the Ballet Rambert founded?
15. What type of fruit is named after Maria Ann Smith?

ANSWERS 1. Swedish **2.** 1981 **3.** Australia **4.** Jeff Noon **5.** Ellis Peters **6.** Fever Pitch by Nick Hornby **7.** Illustrate it by inserting drawings taken from other works **8.** Andrew O'Connor **9.** Memoriad **10.** Milkwoman of the Year **11.** National Motor Museum in Beaulieu **12.** Lewis Carroll **13.** George Lucas **14.** 1930 **15.** An apple (Granny Smith).

ENTERTAINMENT

1. What film, in 2000, became the most expensive to be shot in Sweden?
2. Sweet Sue and her Syncopaters are an all-girl band in which film?
3. Which pub regularly featured in 2000 BBC drama series *The Sins*?
4. Which criminal did Michael Badalucco play in the film *O Brother, Where Art Thou?*
5. Who directed the film *The Original Kings of Comedy*?
6. Who wrote the 1993 film *True Romance*?
7. Which actress made the short film *The Last Summer*, which won a prize at the Berlin film festival?
8. Who plays two brothers in the 1926 film *The Blackbird*?
9. Which film director plays an analyst in television show *The Sopranos*?
10. Who plays barristers' clerk Peter McLeish in Channel Four drama series *North Square*?
11. Who plays Jenny in the television drama *Cold Feet*?
12. Who plays the title role in the 1999 film *The Mummy*?
13. Which comedienne plays a cop in the 1999 film *Goodbye Lover*?
14. What is Kevin Kline's character name in the 1999 film *Wild Wild West*?
15. Which actor is an uncle of actor Ewan McGregor?

ANSWERS 1. Dancer in the Dark **2.** Some Like It Hot **3.** Sir Robert Peel **4.** George 'Babyface' Nelson **5.** Spike Lee **6.** Quentin Tarantino **7.** Daryl Hannah **8.** Lon Chaney **9.** Peter Bogdanovich **10.** Phil Davis **11.** Fay Ripley **12.** Arnold Vosloo **13.** Ellen DeGeneres **14.** Artemus Gordon **15.** Denis Lawson.

SPORT

1. Which horse won the British Triple Crown in 1970?
2. Before 1994, when was the last time there was no baseball World Series?
3. What did Indian Joe win in 1980?
4. Who succeeded Allan Border as Australian Test cricket captain?
5. From which club did Aston Villa sign Shaun Teale in 1991?
6. In which Australian state was cricketer Merv Hughes born?
7. What were the forenames of the cricketer C.B. Fry?
8. At what sport did Rollie Fingers achieve prominence?
9. Who won the British Open golf tournament in 1947?
10. In which year was Martina Navratilova born?
11. What nationality was the 1991 British Open golf tournament winner?
12. How many times did Jacky Ickx win the Le Mans 24 hour race?
13. Which baseball player was nicknamed 'Mr. October'?
14. What is Kevin Keegan's first name?
15. In which city was Hana Mandlikova born?

ANSWERS 1. Nijinsky **2.** 1904 **3.** The Greyhound Derby **4.** Mark Taylor **5.** Bournemouth **6.** Victoria **7.** Charles Burgess **8.** Baseball **9.** Fred Daly **10.** 1956 **11.** Australian **12.** Six **13.** Reggie Jackson **14.** Joseph **15.** Prague.

POP

1. Which former punk rocker fronts a band called *The Mescaleros*?
2. Which late singer and politician developed the Palm Springs Film Festival in the 1980's?
3. Lupine Howl are a splinter group from which pop group?
4. Who in 1999 became the oldest artist to have a No. 1 single in Japan?
5. Rene Angelil is the husband and manager of which singer?
6. Which rock groups albums include 1989's *Pump* and 1993's *Get A Grip*?
7. Which group released 1998 single *Solomon Bites the Worm*?
8. Which group recorded 1997 album *Stupid, Stupid, Stupid* ?
9. On which studio album by The Fall do the tracks *I'm A Mummy* and *Jungle Rock* appear?
10. The Blizzard of Oz were the backing band of which heavy metal star?
11. A t-shirt promoting which Todd Rundgren album was worn by Mark Chapman when he was picked up after shooting John Lennon?
12. Bonnie Prince Billy is an alias of which songwriter?
13. What is the surname of Scritti Politti's singer Green?
14. Which singer recorded the 1977 album *The Idiot*?
15. Which group recorded the 1986 album *Life's Rich Pageant*?

ANSWERS **1.** Joe Strummer **2.** Sonny Bono **3.** Spiritualized **4.** Ryuichi Sakamoto **5.** Celine Dion **6.** Aerosmith **7.** The Bluetones **8.** Black Grape **9.** Levitate **10.** Ozzie Osbourne **11.** The Hermit of Mink Hollow **12.** Will Oldham **13.** Gartside **14.** Iggy Pop **15.** R.E.M.

SCIENCE

1. How many light years from Earth are the Pleiades?
2. What is the most common sedimentary rock?
3. The rudimentary classification of particles is divided into four groups:- gauge bosons, baryons, leptons and which other?
4. Does a tapeworm have a gut?
5. In which year was the Omega Particle discovered?
6. During which period of geological time was the Pliocene epoch?
7. To which phylum do sponges belong?
8. Which element's symbol is W?
9. How many grains are there in a pennyweight?
10. What measurement is equal to 7.92 inches?
11. What is a rognon?
12. How many grams of fibre per 100 grams are there in butter beans?
13. Of what is pteronophobia a fear?
14. Which vitamin is also called pyridoxine?
15. Of what is emerald a green transparent variety?

ANSWERS **1.** 410 **2.** Sandstone **3.** Mesons **4.** No **5.** 1964 **6.** Tertiary **7.** Porifera **8.** Tungsten **9.** 24 **10.** A link **11.** An isolated island of rock in a glacier **12.** 22 **13.** Feathers **14.** Vitamin B6 **15.** Beryl.

GENERAL KNOWLEDGE

1. Which car manufacturer makes the Focus Zetec model?
2. What is the name of David Beckham and Victoria Adams's first child?
3. How did politician Slobodan Milosevic's parents die?
4. Approximately what percentage of Britain's population are blood group type O?
5. Regarding illegal immigration in the U.S.A., what does the abbreviation UDA stand for?
6. How many million people worldwide did the flu virus kill in 1919?
7. In which year was auction house Tattersalls founded?
8. *The Housekeeper's Diary* is a memoir by which former member of Prince Charles's household?
9. Which theme park is near Windsor, Berkshire?
10. In which country is the skiing resort of Vail?
11. In which year was the Royal Photographic Society founded in Bath?
12. What, to a cowboy, are 'can openers'?
13. What was the date of the Housing Act which gave council tenants the right to buy their own homes?
14. Which author famously went into hiding on the 14 February, 1989?
15. Which Hollywood actor played the Cowardly Lion in a 1953 school production of *The Wizard of Oz*?

ANSWERS 1. Ford **2.** Brooklyn **3.** They both committed suicide **4.** 45% **5.** Undocumented aliens **6.** 12m **7.** 1766 **8.** Wendy Berry **9.** Legoland **10.** U.S.A. **11.** 1853 **12.** Spurs **13.** 1980 **14.** Salman Rushdie **15.** Robert De Niro.

ENTERTAINMENT

1. Film makers Chris and Paul Weitz are sons of which Oscar nominee?
2. Who plays therapist Dr. Ben Sobel in the film *Analyze This*?
3. Who directed the Bond films *Moonraker* and *You Only Live Twice*?
4. Who directed the 1967 film *Privilege*?
5. What is Robert Carlyle's character name in the 2000 film *The Beach*?
6. *Water and Power* was the original title of which the 1974 film?
7. Who directed film *The Green Mile* which starred Tom Hanks?
8. Who plays Cardinal Richelieu in the 1935 film?
9. Which rock singer starred in the 1994 film *Car 54, Where Are You?*?
10. Which playwright directed the 1995 film *Carrington*?
11. Which French director's first major film was 1943's *Angels of Sin*?
12. Who plays tennis ace Guy Haines in the Hitchcock film *Strangers on a Train*?
13. Which film won the 1999 Guardian 'Rosebud' award at the Edinburgh Film Festival?
14. Who plays a child-abusing father in the 1999 film *The War Zone*?
15. Who plays a female insurance investigator in the 1999 film *The Thomas Crown Affair*?

ANSWERS **1.** Susan Kohner **2.** Billy Crystal **3.** Lewis Gilbert **4.** Peter Watkins **5.** Daffy **6.** Chinatown **7.** Frank Darabont **8.** George Arliss **9.** David Johansen **10.** Christopher Hampton **11.** Robert Bresson **12.** Farley Granger **13.** Ratcatcher **14.** Ray Winstone **15.** Rene Russo.

SPORT

1. What relationship is Christy O'Connor Jr. to Christy O'Connor?
2. Who was world archery champion in 1979?
3. Who was the first Spaniard to win a tennis Grand Slam singles title?
4. In which county was snooker player Dennis Taylor born?
5. With whom did Marco van Basten begin his soccer career?
6. Who was men's Olympic 100m champion in 1980?
7. Where were the first 12 British Open golf tournaments held?
8. How many times have Ipswich Town won the F.A. Cup?
9. What nationality was the first individual speedway world champion?
10. For which Japanese football team did Gary Lineker play?
11. Who did Yorkshire sign as their overseas player in the 1995 cricket season?
12. Which man won the 1994 Berlin marathon?
13. Who won snooker's 1994 Regal Masters title?
14. Which golfer won the 1994 Lancôme Trophy?
15. Who was the 1980 Olympic men's 800m champion?

ANSWERS 1. Nephew **2.** Darrell Pace **3.** Manuel Santana **4.** County Tyrone **5.** Ajax **6.** Allan Wells **7.** Prestwick **8.** Once **9.** Australian **10.** Nagoya Grampus Eight **11.** Michael Bevan **12.** Antonio Pinto **13.** Ken Doherty **14.** Vijay Singh **15.** Steve Ovett.

POP

1. Which group recorded the 1972 album *Caravanserai*?
2. In which year were the group The Cocteau Twins formed?
3. From which country do the group Shonen Knife come?
4. What was Cockney Rebel's follow-up single to *Judy Teen* in the U.K. charts?
5. What nationality is Jane Siberry?
6. Which singer recorded the 1974 album *I Can Stand a Little Rain*?
7. In which year did Phil Lynott die?
8. What was the second album by The Clash?
9. To whom is singer Siouxsie Sioux married?
10. In which year was Eric Clapton born?
11. What was the title of the debut L.P. by the Slits?
12. Which group recorded the 1979 album *Half Machine Lip Moves*?
13. Which group recorded the 1969 album *Stand!*?
14. What was the Edgar Broughton Band's debut L.P.?
15. Who was the bass player in the group The Small Faces?

ANSWERS **1.** Santana **2.** 1982 **3.** Japan **4.** Mr. Soft **5.** Canadian **6.** Joe Cocker **7.** 1986 **8.** Give 'Em Enough Rope **9.** Budgie **10.** 1945 **11.** Cut **12.** Chrome **13.** Sly and the Family Stone **14.** Wasa Wasa **15.** Ronnie Lane.

PEOPLE

1. In which year was politician Slobodan Milosevic born?
2. Of where was Frank 'Boss' Hague mayor from 1917-47?
3. In which year did Richard and Lynda La Plante divorce?
4. Which queen of England was known as the 'Virgin Queen'?
5. Which Hollywood actress made her stage debut in a 2000 West End production of play *The Seven Year Itch*?
6. What is rower Steve Redgrave's wife called?
7. In which year did actor Christopher Walken marry his wife Georgianne?
8. In which year was actor Lon Chaney born?
9. Of which drinks company was Roberto Goizueta the chief executive before his death in 1997?
10. In which year was nightclub owner Peter Stringfellow born?
11. What did actor Michael Douglas buy Catherine Zeta Jones for her 31st birthday?
12. Which French actress unveiled the Millennium Star in London in 1999?
13. In which year was artist and poet William Blake born?
14. Howard Schultz is chairman of which coffee shop chain?
15. Which member of the Cabinet opened a Henry Moore exhibition in Beijing in October, 2000?

ANSWERS **1.** 1941 **2.** Jersey City, U.S. **3.** 1996 **4.** Queen Elizabeth I **5.** Daryl Hannah **6.** Ann **7.** 1969 **8.** 1883 **9.** Coca-Cola **10.** 1940 **11.** A sapphire and diamond necklace **12.** Sophie Marceau **13.** 1757 **14.** Starbucks **15.** John Prescott

GENERAL KNOWLEDGE

1. In which country is the skiing resort of Heavenly?
2. Which actress is also known as Lady Haden-Guest?
3. In which year did Lev Termen invent the instrument the theremin?
4. What is the name of the preservative numbered E220?
5. In which of the United States of America is the loon the state bird?
6. Of what is hodophobia the fear?
7. In which year did Queen Victoria become queen of England?
8. In which city was film composer Lalo Schifrin born in 1932?
9. Which tunnel builder was known as 'the Mole of Edge Hill'?
10. In which year was former Labour MP Denis Healey born?
11. What age was model Caprice when she won the Miss Teen California Beauty Pageant?
12. Which comedian launched the 'Nobody for President' campaign in 1976?
13. What car was pop star Richey Edwards driving when he disappeared in 1995?
14. In the U.S.A. how old do you have to be to watch an *R* rated film?
15. Burger chain Wimpy was named after a character in which strip cartoon?

ANSWERS **1.** U.S.A. **2.** Jamie Lee Curtis **3.** 1917 **4.** Sulphur dioxide **5.** Minnesota **6.** Travel **7.** 1837 **8.** Buenos Aires **9.** Joseph Williamson **10.** 1917 **11.** 16 **12.** Wavy Gravy **13.** Vauxhall Cavalier **14.** 17 **15.** Popeye.

ENTERTAINMENT

1. Who plays villain Dr. Arliss Loveless in the 1999 film *Wild Wild West*?
2. Who directed the 1999 film *Buena Vista Social Club*?
3. Who play sisters Cora and Camille in the 1999 film *Cookie's Fortune*?
4. Which comedian plays Rayford Gibson in the 1999 film *Life*?
5. What is the character name of Noël Coward in the film *The Italian Job*?
6. In which year is the 1999 film *Ravenous* set?
7. Who played Vietnam War veteran Ron Kovic in the 1989 film *Born on the Fourth of July*?
8. Who is Fred Astaire's dancing partner in the 1938 film *Carefree*?
9. Who directed the 1996 film *Carla's Song*?
10. Who directed the 1942 film *Casablanca*?
11. What was Bob Hoskins's character name in the film *The Long Good Friday?*
12. Which actress produced and starred in the 1999 film *The Love Letter*?
13. Who plays Oberon in the 1999 film *William Shakespeare's A Midsummer Night's Dream*?
14. What is Toby Maguire's character name in the film *The Cider House Rules*?
15. Who took over from Simon Rattle as principal conductor of the City of Birmingham Symphony Orchestra?

ANSWERS 1. Kenneth Branagh **2.** Wim Wenders **3.** Julianne Moore and Glenn Close **4.** Eddie Murphy **5.** Mr. Bridger **6.** 1847 **7.** Tom Cruise **8.** Ginger Rogers **9.** Ken Loach **10.** Michael Curtiz **11.** Harold Shand **12.** Kate Capshaw **13.** Rupert Everett **14.** Homer Wells **15.** Sakari Oramo.

SPORT

1. Which baseball team won the 1990 World Series?
2. When was cricket's Benson and Hedges Cup first held?
3. In which year was the Tour de France first won by a non-Frenchman?
4. For which Premier League club did footballer Karl-Heinz Riedle play in the 1998/9 season?
5. Who did Great Britain play in the 1995 Davis Cup first round?
6. From which club did Wimbledon sign Efan Ekoku?
7. Who finished in the top 15 of both the 1994 bowling and batting averages?
8. Which horse won the 1994 Cesarewitch?
9. Which horse won the 1994 Prix de l'Arc de Triomphe?
10. Which horse won the 1990 St. Leger?
11. From what country do the team Trabzonspor hail?
12. Where were the 25th Summer Olympics held?
13. Who were the last British winners of the UEFA Cup?
14. What did *Reliance*, in 1903 and *Weatherly*, in 1962, win?
15. Who was women's World Cup Alpine skiing champion from 1971-75?

ANSWER **1.** Cincinnati Reds **2.** 1972 **3.** 1909 **4.** Liverpool **5.** Slovakia **6.** Norwich **7.** Chris Lewis **8.** Captain's Guest **9.** Carnegie **10.** Snurge **11.** Turkey **12.** Barcelona **13.** Tottenham Hotspur **14.** The America's Cup **15.** Annemarie Moser-Pröll

POP

1. Which group recorded the 1973 album *Dixie Chicken*?
2. Which city has *The The*'s Matt Johnson been living in since 1994?
3. Which group recorded the 1974 album *Warehouse: Songs and Stories*?
4. Which musician recorded the 1982 album *Music For A New Society*?
5. What, in 1998, became the top-selling form of music in the U.S.?
6. Which pop star is married to poet Ingrid Chavez?
7. Which group recorded the album *The Dirty Boogie*?
8. Which group released the single *Denis* in 1978?
9. Which punk group recorded the single *Skank Bloc Bologna*?
10. Which group recorded the 1986 album *Raising Hell*?
11. Simone Johnson is the real name of which rapper?
12. Which musician recorded the 1973 album *A Wizard, A True Star*?
13. Which singer recorded the 1974 album *Rock Bottom*?
14. Which singer recorded the 1985 album *Rain Dogs*?
15. Which veteran pop singer's films include 1959's *Expresso Bongo*?

ANSWERS 1. Little Feat **2.** New York **3.** Hüsker Dü **4.** John Cale **5.** Rap **6.** David Sylvian **7.** The Brian Setzer Orchestra **8.** Blondie **9.** Scritti Politti **10.** Run DMC **11.** Monie Love **12.** Todd Rundgren **13.** Robert Wyatt **14.** Tom Waits **15.** Cliff Richard.

ART AND LITERATURE

1. Who wrote the children's book *The Ship That Never Was*?
2. Which film director and playwright wrote 1994 novel *The Village*?
3. 1999 film *The 13th Warrior* is based on a story by which best-selling author?
4. Which cartoonist pens strip cartoon *The Boondocks*?
5. VTO is a band in which 1999 novel?
6. Film *Point Blank* was based on which novel by Donald Westlake?
7. Which artist's show became, in 1999, the best attended at London's Serpentine Gallery?
8. Who wrote the 2000 book *Invisible Monsters*?
9. Whose books include *The Love Machine* and *Once is Not Enough*?
10. Which writer created Nottingham cop Charlie Resnick?

11. Which crime writer authored children's book *Miranda the Panda is on the Veranda*?
12. Which video artist twin sisters' works include *Stasi City* and *Parliament*?
13. Which sculptor designed the Holocaust Memorial in Vienna's Judenplatz?
14. Which writer created Edinburgh cop Inspector Rebus?
15. Which author directed 1999 film *The Trench*?

ANSWERS 1. Mickey Spillane **2.** David Mamet **3.** Michael Crichton **4.** Aaron McGruder **5.** *The Ground Beneath Her Feet* by Salman Rushdie **6.** The Hunter **7.** Bridget Riley **8.** Chuck Palahniuk **9.** Jacqueline Susann **10.** John Harvey **11.** Patricia Highsmith **12.** Jane and Louise Wilson **13.** Rachel Whiteread **14.** Ian Rankin **15.** William Boyd.

GENERAL KNOWLEDGE

1. How many seats did the Liberals get in the 1979 election?
2. Which artist won the Melody Maker Jazz Musician of the Year award 1949-52?
3. Henri Christophe was king of which country from 1811-20?
4. What, in Australian slang, is a 'John Hop'?
5. Who won the Member to Watch award at the 1984 Parliamentarian of the Year luncheon?
6. What was awarded the Museum of the Year accolade in 1977?
7. Which world title did Magnus Ver Magnusson win in 1991?
8. Who won the Pipe Smoker of the Year award in 1993?
9. What type of fruit is an amarelle?
10. Which award did Graeme Witty win from 1988-92?
11. In which century did lexicographer Dr. Johnson live?
12. Which bird's Latin name is *Bubo bubo*?
13. Who won the 1974 Queen's Gold Medal for Poetry?
14. To whom did the Crime Writer's Association award the Diamond Dagger in 1992?
15. What would you do with a bobotie?

ANSWERS 1. 11 **2.** Johnny Dankworth **3.** Haiti **4.** A policeman **5.** Malcolm Rifkind **6.** The Ironbridge Gorge Museum in Telford **7.** World's Strongest Man **8.** Rod Hull **9.** Cherry **10.** British National Champion Ploughman (Conventional Ploughing) **11.** 18th **12.** Eagle owl **13.** Ted Hughes **14.** Leslie Charteris **15.** Eat it - it's a dish of curried mincemeat.

ENTERTAINMENT

1. Which director has a cameo role as a judge in the 1993 film *Carlito's Way*?
2. Who produced the 1993 film *Carnosaur*?
3. Who plays gypsy girl *Venus* in the 1964 film *Cartouche*?
4. Who played Hilary in the 1996 film *Hilary and Jackie*?
5. Which comic actor starred as Steve Rubell in the 1998 film *54*?
6. What is Albert Finney's profession in the 1997 film *Washington Square*?
7. Who played *The Mighty Man of Valour* in D.W. Griffiths's film *Intolerance*?
8. Who plays Percy Shelley in the 1990 film *Frankenstein Unbound*?
9. Who played Milo Vladek in the film *The Dirty Dozen?*
10. Who plays *Big Boy Matson* in the 1999 film *The Hi-Lo Country*?
11. Which U.S. comedian stars in the 1999 film *Big Daddy?*
12. Who plays English master Mr. Farthing in the film *Kes*?
13. What is the subtitle of the 1988 film *An Alan Smithee Film*?
14. In which film does George Clooney play Major Archie Gates?
15. Who directed the 2000 film *The Big Tease*?

ANSWERS 1. Paul Mazursky **2.** Roger Corman **3.** Claudia Cardinale **4.** Rachel Griffiths **5.** Mike Myers **6.** A doctor **7.** Elmo Lincoln **8.** Michael Hutchence **9.** Tom Busby **10.** Woody Harrelson **11.** Adam Sandler **12.** Colin Welland **13.** Burn Hollywood Burn **14.** Three Kings **15.** Kevin Allen.

SPORT

1. Who won golf's 1994 Solheim Cup?
2. Who won the 1994 Skoda Grand Prix in snooker?
3. Who won the 1974 World Cup in football?
4. Which golfer won the 1994 Volvo Masters?
5. Which aborigine won a world boxing title in 1968?
6. Which U.S. basketball player was known as 'Dr. J'?
7. Which jockey's first classic ride was on High Top in 1972?
8. Which Olympic showjumper was arrested for drug smuggling in 1972?
9. How many metres wide is a basketball court?
10. Which American boxer was known as 'the Toy Bulldog'?
11. From what does the game 'pelota' take its name?
12. In which year were the first table tennis world championships held?
13. Who was the first American Professional Football Association president?
14. What is the less familiar name of the Davis Cup?
15. What were the names of the five losing yachts in the Americas Cup from 1899 to 1930?

ANSWERS 1. United States **2.** John Higgins **3.** West Germany **4.** Bernhard Langer **5.** Lionel Rose **6.** Julius Erving **7.** Willie Carson **8.** Humberto Mariles **9.** 15 **10.** Mickey Walker **11.** The Spanish word for ball **12.** 1927 **13.** Jim Thorpe **14.** The International Lawn Tennis Challenge Trophy **15.** Shamrock I, Shamrock II, Shamrock III, Shamrock IV and Shamrock V.

POP

1. In which city did The Specials form in 1977?
2. Which funk group's debut single was *Rigor Mortis*?
3. In which year was Phil Spector born?
4. In which city did Cabaret Voltaire form?
5. In which year did Squeeze form?
6. Which two members of the Byrds left to form the Flying Burrito Brothers?
7. Who recorded the 1971 album *Please to See the King*?
8. Which punk group recorded the single *Orgasm Addict*?
9. Who recorded the 1970 album *Gasoline Alley*?
10. On which studio album does Kate Bush's song *Breathing* appear?
11. What is singer Gordon Sumner better known as?
12. What was the title of Buffalo Tom's debut album in 1989?
13. Which songwriter had a Top 40 hit in 1992 with *God's Great Banana Skin*?
14. In which country was Jackson Browne born?
15. In which year was Bruce Springsteen born?

ANSWERS **1.** Coventry **2.** Cameo **3.** 1940 **4.** Sheffield **5.** 1974 **6.** Chris Hillman and Gram Parsons **7.** Steeleye Span **8.** The Buzzcocks **9.** Rod Stewart **10.** Never Forever **11.** Sting **12.** Buffalo Tom **13.** Chris Rea **14.** Germany **15.** 1949.

GEOGRAPHY

1. In which European country are the towns of Dobrich and Khaskovo?
2. Which river separates Romania and Moldova?
3. On which island in Asia is the port of Pontianak?
4. On which lake does the town of Mwanza, Tanzania stand?
5. In which African country are the towns of Bonthe and Kabala?
6. In which European country are the towns of Pecs and Baja?
7. Which African country is sandwiched between Ghana and Benin?
8. Which is the most easterly country of Africa through which the Tropic of Cancer runs?
9. Hospitalet is a suburb of which Spanish city?
10. Off the coast of which African country does the Bijagos Archipelago lie?
11. In which African country is the town of Fdérik?
12. In which European country are the towns of Bendery and Tiraspol?
13. In which African country are the towns of Nakuru and Eldoret?
14. In which European country are the towns of Nitra and Kosice?
15. Which African country is sandwiched between Cameroon and Gabon?

ANSWERS **1.** Bulgaria **2.** Prut **3.** Borneo **4.** Lake Victoria **5.** Sierra Leone **6.** Hungary **7.** Togo **8.** Egypt **9.** Barcelona **10.** Guinea-Bissau **11.** Mauritania **12.** Moldova **13.** Kenya **14.** Slovakia **15.** Equatorial Guinea.

GENERAL KNOWLEDGE

1. Approximately what percentage of Britain's population are blood group type A?
2. Regarding illegal immigration in the U.S.A., what is a 'coyote'?
3. How many copies of Anthea Turner's autobiography, *Fools Rush In*, sold in the first week of its U.K. publication?
4. In which sea did a Russian nuclear submarine sink in August, 2000?
5. In which Texas city was writer Patricia Highsmith born?
6. In which county are the Clipstone, Harworth, Thoresby, and Welbeck coalfields?
7. What is the name of the preservative numbered E230?
8. Of what is genophobia the fear?
9. In the United States of America, what is the state flower of California?
10. In which city was geneticist Willaim Hamilton, who died in 2000, born?
11. On which ancient army do the Gloucester-based Ermine Street Guard model themselves?
12. In which city did the American Bar Association hold their annual conference in July, 2000?
13. Which U.S. president was known as 'The Great Emancipator'?
14. By what name is vcriminal Theodore John Kacynski better known?
15. What is hoisin?

ANSWERS 1. 43% **2.** A guide helping people to cross borders **3.** 451 **4.** Barents Sea **5.** Fort Worth **6.** Nottinghamshire **7.** Biphenyl **8.** Sex **9.** Golden poppy **10.** Cairo **11.** The Roman Army **12.** London **13.** Abraham Lincoln **14.** Unabomber **15.** A soya bean-based sauce used in Chinese cookery.

ENTERTAINMENT

1. What is the profession of Ian Hart's character in the 2000 film *The End of the Affair*?
2. James Coburn got his part in the film *The Magnificent Seven* after a chance meeting with which actor?
3. Who plays fairground ride impressario Stephen Price in the 2000 film *House on Haunted Hill*?
4. Who dubbed Dorothy Dandridge's role as *Carmen Jones* in the 1954 film?
5. What is the forename of *Bulworth* in the film starring Warren Beatty?
6. In which Tarzan film do Sean Connery and Anthony Quayle appear?
7. Who directed the 1957 film *Nights of Cabiria*?
8. Which film composer scored *Zulu* and *The Ipcress File*?
9. Who plays male lead Adam in the 1999 film *Blast From the Past*?
10. The Mel Gibson film *Payback* is a remake of which 1967 film?
11. Which former world champion boxer appears in the 2000 film *Black and White*?
12. Which criminal does Michael Badalucco play in the film *Summer of Sam*?
13. Who wrote the song *When She Loved Me* in the film *Toy Story 2*?
14. Who played actress Sarah Bernhardt in the 1928 film *The Divine Woman*?
15. Who is the female star of 1937 Fritz Lang film *You Only Live Once*?

ANSWERS **1.** Private detective **2.** Robert Vaughn **3.** Geoffrey Rush **4.** Marilyn Horne **5.** Jay **6.** Tarzan's Greatest Adventure **7.** Federico Fellini **8.** John Barry **9.** Brendan Fraser **10.** Point Blank **11.** Mike Tyson **12.** David Berkowitz a.k.a. Son of Sam **13.** Randy Newman **14.** Greta Garbo **15.** Sylvia Sidney.

SPORT

1. At what sport is Ross Norman a former world champion?
2. How many fours did Brian Lara hit in his record breaking 375 Test score?
3. How many horses finished in the 1994 Aintree Grand National?
4. Which former Chelsea boss was a coach of the Zambian football team?
5. Who won the 1994 U.S. Masters golf tournament?
6. At what sport did Betty Snowball play for England?
7. Who won cycling's 1994 Grand Prix de L'Escaut?
8. Who rode Minnehoma in the 1994 Aintree Grand National?
9. Who won the 1994 African Nations Cup in football?
10. Who won the 1994 Japan Open Tennis Tournament?
11. Who won the 1994 British Open snooker tournament?
12. Who won the 1994 Hong Kong Open tennis men's singles title?
13. What is a mashawi?
14. How many times have Liverpool won football's European Champions Cup?
15. In which sport is the Iroquois Cup competed for?

ANSWERS **1.** Squash **2.** 45 **3.** Six **4.** Ian Porterfield **5.** Jose-Maria Olazabal **6.** Cricket **7.** Peter van Petegem **8.** Richard Dunwoody **9.** Nigeria **10.** Pete Sampras **11.** Ronnie O'Sullivan **12.** Michael Chang **13.** A sumo wrestler's fighting belt **14.** Four **15.** Lacrosse.

POP

1. Singer Kool Herc started which musical form in 1973?
2. Which musician recorded the 1974 album *On the Beach*?
3. Which singer recorded the 1974 album *Court and Spark*?
4. Which singer recorded the 1970 album *Bryter Layter*?
5. Which singer-songwriter was born Ralph May in 1944?
6. Which musician recorded the 1974 album *No Other*?
7. Singer Townes Van Zandt died on New Year's Day of which year?

8. Hull University drop out Neil Megson formed the punk group Throbbing Gristle using what alias?
9. Which singer was born Veronica Bennett?
10. Which former member of The Beatles recorded the 1970 album *All Things Must Pass*?
11. Which group recorded the 1990 album *Fear of a Black Planet*?
12. What is hip-hop producer Tim Mosley known as?
13. Which musician recorded the 1972 album *Something/Anything*?
14. What is musician Mark Ramos-Nishita better known as?
15. Which pop star grew up as David Batt in Lewisham?

ANSWERS 1. Rap **2.** Neil Young **3.** Joni Mitchell **4.** Nick Drake **5.** Ralph McTell **6.** Gene Clark **7.** 1997 **8.** Genesis P-Orridge **9.** Ronnie Spector **10.** George Harrison **11.** Public Enemy **12.** Timbaland **13.** Todd Rundgren **14.** Money Mark **15.** David Sylvian.

HISTORY

1. Which island was originally named after a governor-general of the Dutch East India Company?
2. Who was king of France from 1774-92?
3. Of which country was Le Duc Anh president from 1992-97?
4. With whom did Jerry Rubin form the Yippies in 1968?
5. In which year did Margaret Roberts marry Denis Thatcher?
6. Who was president of the Republic of Ireland from 1973-74?
7. Who succeeded Michael Foot as leader of the Labour Party?
8. In which U.S. city did Franklin Pierce live after he left the White House?
9. Who was Chancellor of the Exchequer from 1964-67?
10. Who was prime minister of the Republic of Ireland from 1982-87?
11. Under which U.S. president was Hamilton Fish vice-president from 1869-77?
12. John Grey Gort was prime minister of which country from 1968-71?
13. Who was British Prime Minister from 1970-74?
14. In which year did Hugh Gaitskell become Labour Party leader?
15. In which year did the Soviet *Lunik 1* satellite become the first to escape earth's gravity?

ANSWERS 1. Tasmania **2.** Louis XVI **3.** Vietnam **4.** Abbie Hoffman **5.** 1951 **6.** Erskine Childers **7.** Neil Kinnock **8.** Concord **9.** James Callaghan **10.** Garret FitzGerald **11.** Ulysses S. Grant **12.** Australia **13.** Edward Heath **14.** 1955 **15.** 1959.

GENERAL KNOWLEDGE

1. Who won the Melody Maker British Male Jazz Vocalist of the Year award 1962-65?

2. What nationality was the actress Eleonora Duse?
3. Who won the Pipe Smoker of the Year award in 1992?
4. The name of which island in the Bristol Channel derives from the Norse 'Puffin Island'?
5. Who became Great Britain's prime minister in 1979?
6. What was awarded the Museum of the Year title in 1991?
7. Who won 1972's *Mastermind* title?
8. What type of bird is a chukar?
9. In what year did pianist Scott Joplin die?
10. Who won the Member to Watch award at the 1985 Parliamentarian of the Year luncheon?
11. Who authored *The Lady of Shalott*?
12. Which river in England is known locally as the Granta?
13. What is the Indo-European language of modern Iran?
14. Who invented the saxophone?
15. Who won the 1965 Queen's Gold Medal for Poetry?

ANSWERS 1. Matt Monroe **2.** Italian **3.** Tony Benn **4.** Lundy **5.** Margaret Thatcher **6.** The National Railway Museum, York **7.** Nancy Wilkinson **8.** A partridge **9.** 1917 **10.** Simon Hughes **11.** Tennyson **12.** Cam **13.** Farsi **14.** Adolphe Sax **15.** Philip Larkin.

ENTERTAINMENT

1. Who starred as a plane manufacturer in the 1964 film *The Carpetbaggers*?
2. Who plays an aspiring concert pianist in the 1978 film *Fingers*?
3. What is the name of the obese Scot in the film *Austin Powers: The Spy Who Shagged Me*?
4. Which French actor plays a vagabond in the 1934 musical *Caravan?*
5. Which comic actor plays Herman Blume in the 1999 film *Rushmore*?
6. Which Spanish director made the 1999 film *All About My Mother*?
7. The actor Jason Schwartzman is a nephew of which director?
8. Which 58 year-old builder famously left B.B.C.'s *Castaway 2000* programme prematurely?
9. Who won an Emmy in 1999 for her role as Carmela in television show *The Sopranos*?
10. Which actress played Miss Havisham in a 1999 television production of *Great Expectations*?
11. Who plays psychiatrist Dr. Fritz Fassbender in the 1965 film *What's New, Pussycat?*?
12. What is Lon Chaney's character name in the 1927 film *The Unknown*?
13. In which year did Daniel Barenboim become artistic director of Berlin's Staatsoper?
14. Who voices the character Stinky Pete the Prospector in the film *Toy Story 2*?
15. Ralph Fiennes plays Maurice Bendix in which 2000 film?

ANSWERS 1. George Peppard **2.** Harvey Keitel **3.** Fat Bastard **4.** Charles Boyer **5.** Bill Murray **6.** Pedro Almodovar **7.** Francis Coppola **8.** Ray Bowyer **9.** Edie Falco **10.** Charlotte Rampling **11.** Peter Sellers **12.** Alonzo the Armless **13.** 1991 **14.** Kelsey Grammer **15.** The End of the Affair.

SPORT

1. Which was the first horse to win two English Classics in the same season?
2. Who was 1993's top earning British sportsman?
3. Which horse won the 1994 Whitbread Gold Cup?
4. Who won the 1994 South Korean Open men's singles tennis tournament?
5. Who won the 1994 Monte Carlo Open men's singles tennis title?
6. Who knocked James Wattana out of the 1994 World professional snooker tournament?
7. Which golfer won the 1988 US PGA title?
8. How many teams comprised the first English football league in 1888?
9. Who won the first British Open golf title in 1860?
10. In which year did Steffi Graf win her first Grand Slam title?

11. Who won snooker's first Pot Black tournament on BBC TV?
12. Who refereed the 1994 F.A. Cup Final at Wembley?
13. Which sidc won the 1994 Middlesex Sevens competition?
14. Who won the 1994 Tennents Irish Cup in hockey?
15. Who scored twice for Milan in their 1994 European Champions Cup final win?

ANSWERS 1. Champion **2.** Lennox Lewis **3.** Ushers Island **4.** Jeremy Bates **5.** Andrei Medvedev **6.** Steve Davis **7.** Jeff Sluman **8.** 12 **9.** Willie Park, Snr. **10.** 1987 **11.** Ray Reardon **12.** David Elleray **13.** Bath **14.** Lisnagarvey **15.** Daniele Massaro.

POP

1. Which Jamaican singer featured on the 1991 single *She's a Woman* by Scritti Politti?
2. In which year was singer Arthur Brown of *Fire* fame born?
3. Who was the drummer with the group The Stone Roses?
4. Who was the vocalist in the Manchester band The Chameleons?
5. Who is the drummer in the Stranglers?
6. In which year was singer Tracy Chapman born?
7. Who was the keyboard player in The Style Council?
8. What was the debut album of the group Cheap Trick?
9. In which city did Super Furry Animals form in 1993?
10. Which songwriter recorded the 1995 album *Is the Actor Happy*?
11. Who is the drummer in the group Supergrass?
12. From which country did the group The Chills come?
13. Which group recorded the 1987 album *Children of God*?
14. What is Big Star's *Third Album* also called?
15. Which group recorded the 1973 album *Bursting at the Seams*?

ANSWERS 1. Shabba Ranks **2.** 1944 **3.** Reni **4.** Mark Burgess **5.** Jet Black **6.** 1964 **7.** Mick Talbot **8.** Cheap Trick **9.** Cardiff **10.** Vic Chesnutt **11.** Danny Goffey **12.** New Zealand **13.** Swans **14.** Sister Lovers **15.** The Strawbs.

ART AND LITERATURE

1. In which year did *The New Yorker* magazine celebrate its 75th anniversary?
2. Who authored the 2001 novel *Gabriel's Gift*?
3. Who wrote children's book *Spellfall*?
4. Whose first novel is entitled *The Second Prison*?
5. Who wrote 1952 novel *The Price of Salt* under the pseudonym Claire Morgan?
6. Artist Bridget Riley is a descendant of which British prime minister?
7. Who draws the *Clare in the Community* cartoon strip in *The Guardian* newspaper?
8. Which Florida-based author's books include *Lucky You*?
9. Who wrote the novel *The Golden Bowl*?
10. Which visual artist presented the teach-in *The Che Gavara Story* in London in 2001?
11. Who wrote the play *Bouncers*?
12. Who authored 2001 play *Mouth to Mouth*?
13. Which author's memorial service was attended by Salman Rushdie on 14 February, 1989?
14. Which architect designed Berlin's Jewish Museum?
15. Which film director designed the poster for the 1983 Cannes Film Fesitval?

ANSWERS 1. 2000 **2.** Hanif Kureishi **3.** Katherine Roberts **4.** Ronan Bennett **5.** Patricia Highsmith **6.** Gladstone **7.** Harry Venning **8.** Carl Hiaasen **9.** Henry James **10.** Gavin Turk **11.** John Godber **12.** Kevin Elyot **13.** Bruce Chatwin **14.** Daniel Libeskind **15.** Akira Kurosawa.

GENERAL KNOWLEDGE

1. In which novel does the character Yossarian appear?
2. What would you do with a hanepoot in South Africa?
3. What is the largest of all living arthropods?
4. Which horse won the 1943 Epsom Derby?
5. What nationality was author André Malraux?
6. Who is the patron saint of Portugal?
7. Which jazz musician was nicknamed 'Prez'?
8. In which European country is the resort of Bergenz?
9. Who wrote the novel *I, Robot*?
10. What type of creature was captured by Hercules as his fourth labour?
11. In which U.S. state is the city of Akron?
12. In which year did Jack the Ripper kill seven prostitutes?
13. Who was British prime minister from 1970-74?
14. What is the major religion of Malta?
15. With which woodwind instrument is Evelyn Rothwell associated?

ANSWERS **1.** Catch-22 **2.** Make wine - it's a grape **3.** Lobster **4.** Straight Deal **5.** French **6.** St. George **7.** Lester Young **8.** Austria **9.** Isaac Asimov **10.** Boar **11.** Ohio **12.** 1888 **13.** Edward Heath **14.** Roman Catholic **15.** Oboe.

ENTERTAINMENT

1. What is Gordon MacRae's character name in the 1956 film *Carousel*?
2. Who plays New York newspaperman Ike Graham in the 1999 film *Runaway Bride*?
3. Which comedian presents 'Jazz Club' on television sketch show *The Fast Show*?
4. Which director produced the 1999 film *The Last Days* about Hungarian Holocaust survivors?
5. Who plays catering manager Hilditch in the 1999 film *Felicia's Journey*?
6. In what year did children's TV series *Grange Hill* start showing?
7. Who plays Puck in the 1999 film *William Shakespeare's A Midsummer Night's Dream*?
8. Who played the title role in the 1976 film *Carrie*?
9. In which country is film *The Cars That Ate Paris* set?
10. Which director plays a petrol company executive in the 1999 film *Last Night*?
11. Which two former screen Tarzans appear in the 1950 film *Captive Girl*?
12. Which real life husband and wife play Bill and Alice Harford in the 1999 film *Eyes Wide Shut*?
13. Who plays Mrs. Cheveley in the 1999 film *An Ideal Husband* starring Rupert Everett?
14. Who played Tiffany in the soap *EastEnders*?
15. Which ex-barrister writes television drama *North Square*?

ANSWERS **1.** Billy Bigelow **2.** Richard Gere **3.** John Thomson **4.** Steven Spielberg **5.** Bob Hoskins **6.** 1978 **7.** Stanley Tucci **8.** Sissy Spacek **9.** Australia **10.** David Cronenberg **11.** Buster Crabbe and Johnny Weissmuller **12.** Tom Cruise and Nicole Kidman **13.** Julianne Moore **14.** Martine McCutcheon **15.** Peter Moffat.

SPORT

1. Who did Everton beat in their last Premier League fixture of 1993/94?
2. For how many years did Bob Beamon's long jump record stand?
3. At what sport was Joe Hagan the first world champion?
4. Who was the 1964 Olympic women's 100m champion?
5. Who was the world amateur snooker champion in 1984 & '85?
6. Who won the 1994 Italian Open men's singles tennis title?
7. Which horse won the 1994 Irish 2,000 Guineas?
8. Which team won the 1994 Welsh Cup Final in football?
9. Who was the 1994 women's USP GA golf champion?
10. In how many Tests did Allan Border captain Australia?
11. Who were the 1993/94 Spanish Football League champions?
12. Which Spanish golf course hosted the 1997 Ryder Cup?
13. Which team were 1993/94 Portuguese Football League champions?
14. Which horse finished second in the 1994 Epsom Derby?
15. Which teams contested the 1994 Stanley Cup Final?

ANSWERS 1. Wimbledon **2.** 23 years **3.** Croquet **4.** Wyomia Tyus **5.** Paul Mifsud **6.** Pete Sampras **7.** Turtle Island **8.** Barry Town **9.** Laura Davies **10.** 93 **11.** Barcelona **12.** Valderrama **13.** Benfica **14.** King's Theatre **15.** New York Rangers and Vancouver Canucks.

POP

1. In which year did U.S. group The Stray Cats move to London?
2. Which dancer played bass guitar for group *The Fall* at a gig at London's Dingwall's in April 1998?
3. Which group recorded the 1979 album *Eat To The Beat*?
4. Which singer recorded the 1970 album *Starsailor*?
5. Which group recorded the 1973 album *For Your Pleasure*?
6. An album by which British rock group entered at No. 1 in the Billboard chart in October, 2000?
7. Which group's debut CD album is called *Hybrid Therapy*?
8. In which year did the group the *New York Dolls* split?
9. Which five singers were chosen as band members in the 2001 show *Popstars*?
10. Which group recorded the 1971 album *Maggot Brain*?
11. Which group recorded the 1993 album *Giant Steps*?
12. Which Liverpool-born singer recorded the albums *Dog Leap Stairs* and *Little Black Numbers*?
13. Which group recorded the 1995 album *CrazySexyCool*?
14. What was the surname of the pop duo Mel & Kim?
15. Who sang lead vocals on the songs *Da Doo Ron Ron* and *Then He Kissed Me* by the Crystals?

ANSWERS 1. 1980 **2.** Michael Clark **3.** Blondie **4.** Tim Buckley **5.** Roxy Music **6.** Radiohead's *Kid A* **7.** Linkin Park **8.** 1975 **9.** Danny, Noel, Suzanne, Myleene, and Kym **10.** Funkadelic **11.** The Boo Radleys **12.** Kathryn Williams **13.** TLC **14.** Appleby **15.** Lala Brooks.

SCIENCE

1. What is the SI unit of magnetic flux?
2. What in meteorology is the name given to the place where a cold front has overtaken a warm front?
3. Which Whitby-born scientist is known as the 'father of genetics'?
4. What in geology is a grike?
5. What do the letters RH stand for in meteorology?
6. How many grams of fibre per 100 grams are there in apples?
7. The element rhodium is named after the Greek word for which flower?
8. What is the name given to the igneous rocks that form on the Earth's surface?
9. Approximately what percentage of the atmosphere is formed by the gas argon?
10. What is the name given to the ratio of power to area in light?
11. What in mathematics do the initials LCM stand for?
12. What are nimbostratus and cirrocumulus?
13. How many arms does a starfish usually have?
14. How many satellites does Venus have?
15. Of what is dendrophobia a fear?

ANSWERS 1. Weber **2.** An occluded front **3.** William Bateson **4.** A cleft in a limestone pavement **5.** Relative humidity **6.** Two **7.** Rose **8.** Extrusive rocks **9.** 1% **10.** Intensity **11.** Lowest common multiple **12.** Cloud types **13.** Five **14.** None **15.** Trees.

GENERAL KNOWLEDGE

1. The film *The Night of the Hunter* was based on a novel by which author?
2. In which country is the skiing resort of Astun?
3. Above what type of shop was film director Alfred Hitchcock born?
4. How much did tickets for the first Oscar ceremony in 1929 cost?
5. Which member of the pop group All Saints has a daughter called Lilyella?
6. In 1999, how many people were caught trying to cross from Canada into the U.S.?
7. Approximately what percentage of Britain's population are blood group type AB?
8. In which year did M.P. Alan Howarth defect from the Conservative Party to the Labour Party?
9. Who wrote the self-help manual *The Joy of Sex*?
10. In which of the United States of America is the ruffed goose the state bird?
11. Of what is eretephobia the fear?
12. What is the name of the preservative numbered E203?
13. In which Shakespeare play does the character Viola appear?
14. What was the profession of artist J.M.W. Turner's father?
15. Who did Gaetano Bresci assassinate in 1900?

ANSWERS 1. Davis Grubb **2.** Spain **3.** A fruit and veg shop **4.** $10 **5.** Mel Blatt **6.** 11,660 **7.** 3% **8.** 1995 **9.** Dr. Alex Comfort **10.** Pennsylvania **11.** Pins **12.** Calcium sorbate **13.** Twelfth Night **14.** Barber **15.** Umberto I of Italy.

ENTERTAINMENT

1. In which year did *Bill and Ben* first appear on television?
2. Who wrote the play *Rita, Sue, and Bob Too*?
3. Who plays killer Riddick in the 2000 film *Pitch Black*?
4. Who provides the singing voice of captain Li Shang in the Disney cartoon *Mulan*?
5. Who plays the captain in the 1960 film *The Captain's Tale*?
6. What is the name of Terrence and Phillip's film in the 1999 film *South Park: Bigger, Longer, and Uncut*?
7. Who plays Warrant Officer Brenner in the 1999 film *The General's Daughter*?
8. How did Victor Meldrew die in the sitcom *One Foot in the Grave*?
9. Which presenter on *The Big Breakfast* was in singing duo *Those Two Girls*?
10. Who created *Captain Pugwash*?
11. In which year did the children's show *Teletubbies* arrive on television?
12. Who plays the title role in the 2000 film *A Room for Romeo Brass*?
13. Mike Leigh's film *Topsy-Turvy* is centered around which operetta by Gilbert and Sullivan?
14. What is Kevin Spacey's character name in the film *American Beauty*?
15. Who directed the 2000 film *Double Jeopardy* starring Tommy Lee Jones?

ANSWERS 1. 1952 **2.** Andrea Dunbar **3.** Vin Diesel **4.** Donny Osmond **5.** John Gregson **6.** Asses of Fire **7.** John Travolta **8.** He was killed by a hit-and-run driver **9.** Denise van Outen **10.** John Ryan **11.** 1997 **12.** Andrew Shim **13.** The Mikado **14.** Lester Burnham **15.** Bruce Beresford.

SPORT

1. What did The Duke win in 1836 & '37?
2. Who won the 1992 Olympic men's 400m title?
3. Who won cycling's 1993 Milk Race?
4. In which year was the Ryder Cup first held in Britain?
5. Which horse won the 1993 Prix de l'Arc de Triomphe?
6. Who was the 1993 world 500c.c. motor cycling champion?
7. Who won the 1994 Spanish Grand Prix in Formula 1?
8. Who won the 1994 women's world snooker championship?
9. Which jockey won the 1994 Oaks?
10. In which year did Hanif Mohammad score his record innings of 499?
11. What nationality is motor racing driver David Coulthard?
12. Which rugby union side are known as 'the Pumas'?
13. What was the name of the mascot in the 1994 Football World Cup?
14. Which golfer won the 1994 Buick Classic in New York?
15. Who were the top male and female seeds in the 1994 Wimbledon tennis tournament?

ANSWERS 1. The Grand National **2.** Quincy Watts **3.** Chris Lillywhite **4.** 1929 **5.** Subotica **6.** Kevin Schwantz **7.** Damon Hill **8.** Allison Fisher **9.** Frankie Dettori **10.** 1958 **11.** Scottish **12.** Argentina **13.** Striker **14.** Lee Janzen **15.** Pete Sampras and Steffi Graf.

POP

1. What was Suzi Quatro's last solo Top Ten hit, in 1978?
2. Under which name did Elvis Costello and T-Bone Burnett release the single *The People's Limousine*?
3. Which group had Top 20 hits in 1992 with *Hold it Down* and *Easy to Smile*?
4. Which punk singer wrote the song *Texas Chainsaw Manicurist*?
5. From which country do the group Sepultra hail?
6. Which singer recorded the 1973 album *Marjory Razorblade*?
7. Who had a Top Ten single in 1997 with *Even After All*?
8. What was the second single of 1960s group The Creation?
9. Which group had a 1975 Top 20 hit with *Let Me Be the One*?
10. Which group recorded the 1993 album *Black Sunday*?
11. Which reggae star had a 1993 hit with *Oh Carolina*?
12. Which band's only album was 1984's *The Waking Hour*?
13. Jeffrey Daniel, Jody Whatley and Howard Hewitt comprised which group?
14. Which group's albums included 1979's *Machine Gun Etiquette*?
15. Which group charted in 1998 with the single *Tell Me Ma*?

ANSWERS **1.** If you can't give me love **2.** The Coward Brothers **3.** Senseless Things **4.** Jayne County **5.** Brazil **6.** Kevin Coyne **7.** Finley Quaye **8.** Painter Man **9.** The Shadows **10.** Cypress Hill **11.** Shaggy **12.** Dali's Car **13.** Shalamar **14.** The Damned **15.** Sham Rock.

PEOPLE

1. Who owns the dance venue Ministry of Sound?
2. Politician Al Gore is a distant cousin of which author?
3. Which barrister co-founded the Matrix Chambers with Cherie Blair?
4. In which year did the actress Sarah Bernhardt die?
5. Under what name does French clothes designer Agnès Troublé trade?
6. In which year did the film director Preston Sturges die?
7. Which dairy farmer was chairman of the People's Fuel Lobby in 2000?
8. Who replaced Michael Faraday on the back of a £20 note in 1999?
9. With which burger chain is Ray Kroc associated?
10. The author of book *My Father's Daughter* is the daughter of which singing legend?
11. What are television presenter Loyd Grossman's middle names?
12. What did Sir Edward Elgar call editor August Johannes Jaegar?
13. Which manager of rock groups formerly appeared as wrestler Count Bruno Alassio?
14. Which popular drink did John S. Pemberton invent?
15. Which science fiction writer grew up on a farm in Minehead?

ANSWERS **1.** James Palumbo **2.** Gore Vidal **3.** Rabinder Singh **4.** 1923 **5.** Agnès b. **6.** 1959 **7.** David Handley **8.** Edward Elgar **9.** McDonalds **10.** Frank Sinatra **11.** Daniel Gilman **12.** Nimrod **13.** Peter Grant **14.** Coca-Cola **15.** Arthur C. Clarke.

GENERAL KNOWLEDGE

1. How old was film producer Howard Hughes when he arrived in Hollywood in 1928?
2. Where was television chef Ken Hom born in 1949?
3. In which country is the skiing resort of Davos?
4. From what metal was the first 'Oscar' made?
5. Donald Spoto's book *The Dark Side of Genius* is about which film director?
6. Approximately what percentage of Britain's population are blood group type B?
7. In which Shakespeare play does the character Fortinbras appear?
8. What would you do with avruga?
9. Which architect built the monastery of Sainte-Marie de la Tourette, near Lyon?
10. What is orange pekoe?
11. What is the name of the chalk figure on Windover Hill?
12. Which football team does violinist Nigel Kennedy support?
13. Which London street runs south from Regents Park to Cavendish Square?
14. Which chain of frozen food stores was founded by two trainee managers from Woolworths?
15. Which musician played 'The Narrator' in jazz musical *The Keaton Bar & Grill* in London in 2000?

ANSWERS 1. 20 **2.** Tucson, Arizona **3.** Switzerland **4.** Bronze **5.** Alfred Hitchcock **6.** 9% **7.** Hamlet **8.** Eat them they're herring eggs **9.** Le Corbusier **10.** A type of tea **11.** The Long Man of Wilmington **12.** Aston Villa **13.** Harley Street **14.** Iceland **15.** Elvis Costello.

ENTERTAINMENT

1. Which two actors co-star with a talking duck in the 1961 film *Everything's Ducky*?
2. Which film director plays the head of a medical review board in the 1996 film *Extreme Measures*?
3. Who plays the title role in the 1958 film *Auntie Mame*?
4. Which film director designed the poster for the 1982 Cannes Film Fesitval?
5. Who is the male lead in the 1999 film *Forces of Nature*?
6. 1980 horror film *The Awakening* is based on whose novel?
7. Who played the villain The Bookworm in the 1960s *Batman* television series?
8. Who directed the 1989 film *Glory*?
9. What is film actor Michael Keaton's real name?
10. Who directed the 1998 film *Pecker*?
11. What is Danny DeVito's job in the film *Living Out Loud*?
12. Who directed the 1982 film *Evil Under the Sun*?
13. Who plays the female lead in the 1996 revenge film *Eye For an Eye*?
14. What age was Sam Raimi when he directed film *The Evil Dead*?
15. Which film legend lodged with director Peter Bogdanovich for two years in the 1970s?

ANSWERS 1. Mickey Rooney and Buddy Hackett **2.** David Cronenberg **3.** Rosalind Russell **4.** Federico Fellini **5.** Ben Affleck **6.** Bram Stoker **7.** Roddy McDowall **8.** Ed Zwick **9.** Michael Douglas **10.** John Waters **11.** Elevator man **12.** Guy Hamilton **13.** Sally Field **14.** 20 **15.** Orson Welles.

SPORT

1. Who won the 1994 men's French Open tennis singles title?
2. At what sport did Olympic gold medal winner Eric Liddell win seven caps?
3. At what sport was Karl Maier a world champion in the 1980s?
4. What nationality is the golfer Vijay Singh?
5. On which course was the 1994 US Open golf tournament held?
6. Which baseball player was known as 'the Yankee Clipper'?
7. Who knocked Zena Garrison-Jackson out of the 1994 Wimbledon women's singles tennis tournament?
8. Who scored five goals for Russia against Cameroon in the 1994 World Cup Finals?
9. When did Martina Navratilova win her first Wimbledon singles title?
10. Where was the 1994 French Grand Prix in Formula 1 held?
11. In which city was Gary Lineker born?
12. Which horse won the 1979 Epsom Derby?
13. Who won Group A in the 1994 World Cup Finals?
14. In motor racing, which is the oldest of the Grand Prix races?
15. In which country did real tennis originate?

ANSWERS **1.** Sergi Bruguera **2.** Rugby **3.** Speedway **4.** Fijian **5.** Oakmont **6.** Joe DiMaggio **7.** Gigi Fernandez **8.** Oleg Salenko **9.** 1978 **10.** Magny-Cours **11.** Leicester **12.** Troy **13.** Romania **14.** French Grand Prix **15.** France.

POP

1. Who recorded the song *The Late Great Johnny Ace* on the 1983 album *Hearts and Bones*?
2. Which jazz man was crowned 'The King of Zulus' at the 1949 New Orleans Mardi Gras?
3. Which group released the album *Jungle Marmalade*?
4. What was the nickname of the rhythm and blues guitarist Buddy Ace?
5. Which group recorded the 1980 album *Searching for the Young Soul Rebels*?
6. Which singer recorded the 1969 album *Five Leaves Left*?
7. Which group recorded the 1973 album *Countdown to Ecstasy*?
8. What is the singer Eithne Ni Bhraonain better known as?
9. Who was the original drummer in group *Lush*?
10. Who replaced Dave Alexander in group The Stooges?
11. In which city did the ska legend Roland Alphonso die?
12. Which group recorded the 1967 album *The Piper At The Gates Of Dawn*?
13. Which singer recorded the 1995 album *To Bring You My Love*?
14. Which group recorded the 1969 album *The Gilded Palace of Sin*?
15. Who was the original leader of San Francisco rock band The Mojo Men?

ANSWERS 1. Paul Simon **2.** Louis Armstrong **3.** The Lemon Pipers **4.** The Root Doctor **5.** Dexy's Midnight Runners **6.** Nick Drake **7.** Steely Dan **8.** Enya **9.** Chris Acland **10.** James Williamson **11.** Los Angeles **12.** Pink Floyd **13.** P.J. Harvey **14.** The Flying Burrito Brothers **15.** Sly Stone.

ART AND LITERATURE

1. In the National Gallery's 2000 exhibition *Encounters: New Art From Old* which artist reinterpreted John Constable's painting *The Hay Wain*?
2. Which British poet authored the collection 'The Book of Demons'?
3. Alan Moore's comic book *From Hell* is about which criminal?
4. Which French architect wrote the novel *If Only It Were True*?
5. Who wrote the book on which 1953 film *The Big Heat* is based ?
6. Whose 1996 show at the National Gallery was called *Now We Are 64*?
7. In the National Gallery's 2000 exhibition *Encounters: New Art From Old*, which artist did the photographer Jeff Wall chose to reinterpret?
8. Who painted the 1975 work *After Lunch* which features a mural of a Swiss lake?
9. Ted Lewis's book *Jack's Return Home* became which 1970 film?
10. In which Shakespeare play does the character Belarius appear?
11. Which animal painter's works include *Baron de Robeck Riding a Bay Cob*?
12. Which comedian authored novel *The Stars' Tennis Balls*?
13. John Gielgud's last film *Catastrophe* is a filmed work of which writer's play?
14. With which art form would you associate the name Brassaï?
15. Who wrote the book *Sex and the City*?

ANSWERS 1. Frank Auerbach **2.** Barry MacSweeney **3.** Jack the Ripper **4.** Marc Levy **5.** William P. McGivern **6.** Peter Blake **7.** George Stubbs **8.** Patrick Caulfield **9.** Get Carter **10.** Cymbeline **11.** George Stubbs **12.** Stephen Fry **13.** Samuel Beckett **14.** Photography **15.** Candace Bushnell

GENERAL KNOWLEDGE

1. In which year did the word game *Countdown* start on Channel Four?

2. In which children's show did the quiz *Double or Drop* appear?

3. Which Victorian detective did Alan Dobie play in the early 1980s on TV?

4. Which comedian narrated *The Wombles* on TV in the 1970s?

5. What was Victor's wife called in the show *One Foot in the Grave*?

6. In which city was the comedian Barry Cryer born?

7. Which comedian played Kevin O'Grady in the 1969 sitcom *Curry and Chips*?

8. Who did Colin Bean play in *Dad's Army*?

9. Which actress married director Renny Harlin in 1983?

10. Which writer was played by Daniel Day-Lewis in the film *My Left Foot*?

11. Which actor voiced the cartoon character *Mr. Magoo*?

12. Which actress is the older sister of Joan Fontaine?

13. What does the initial B stand for in the name of director Cecil B. De Mille?

14. *Stop Making Sense* was a film of a concert given by which pop group?

15. In which film did Robert De Niro play Rupert Pupkin?

ANSWERS **1.** 1982 **2.** Crackerjack **3.** Sergeant Cribb **4.** Bernard Cribbins **5.** Margaret **6.** Leeds **7.** Spike Milligan **8.** Private Sponge **9.** Geena Davis **10.** Christy Brown **11.** Jim Backus **12.** Olivia de Havilland **13.** Blount **14.** Talking Heads **15.** The King of Comedy.

ENTERTAINMENT

1. What is Woody's horse called in the film *Toy Story 2*?
2. What is Mark Wahlberg's character name in the film *Three Kings*?
3. Who plays humorist George Grossmith in the 2000 film *Topsy-Turvy*?
4. Who played the title role in the 2000 film *Julian Po*?
5. Who played Dr. Danny Nash in television drama series *Psychos*?
6. In which year did the children's show *Andy Pandy* first appear on television?
7. Who plays Father Jack in the sitcom *Father Ted*?
8. What was Ronnie Barker's character name in sitcom *Open All Hours*?
9. Who directed the 1957 film *Attack of the Crab Monsters*?
10. Who plays a blind detective in the 1942 film *Eyes in the Night*?
11. What was the only film shown at the 1939 Cannes Film Festival?
12. Which actor directed the 1998 film *Star Trek: Insurrection*?
13. Who play the Mitchell brothers in the 1999 film *A Simple Plan*?
14. In which country is the 1999 film *Hideous Kinky* set?
15. Who stars as a snowman in the 1998 film *Jack Frost*?

ANSWERS 1. Bullseye **2.** Sgt. Troy Barlow **3.** Martin Savage **4.** Christian Slater **5.** Douglas Henshall **6.** 1950 **7.** Frank Kelly **8.** Arkwright **9.** Roger Corman **10.** Edward Arnold **11.** The Hunchback of Notre Dame **12.** Jonathan Frakes **13.** Billy Bob Thornton and Bill Paxton **14.** Morocco **15.** Michael Keaton.

SPORT

1. Which horse won the 1994 Cheltenham Gold Cup?
2. With what sport would you associate Doggett's Coat and Badge?
3. With what sport would you associate 'The Bourda'?
4. For which team did Jos Verstappen drive in the 1994 Grand Prix season?
5. Which team finished bottom in the 1998/99 Serie A in Italy?
6. Which football team won the 1998/99 Spanish league title?
7. Which football team won the 1998/99 German league title?
8. Which referee was pushed to the ground by footballer Paulo Di Canio in 1998?
9. Who did Lennox Lewis defeat in September 1998 to retain the WBC world heavyweight title?
10. Who did Herbie Hide defeat in September 1998 to retain his WBO world heavyweight title?
11. Who finished third in the 1994 Brazilian Grand Prix in Formula 1?
12. In which year did snooker player Joe Davis die?
13. Who won golf's 1994 Lyon Open?
14. Which former athlete was the 1994 London Marathon race organiser?
15. With which sport would you associate Otilia Badescu?

ANSWERS 1. The Fellow **2.** Rowing **3.** Cricket **4.** Benetton **5.** Empoli **6.** Barcelona **7.** Bayern Munich **8.** Paul Alcock **9.** Zeljko Mavrovic **10.** Willi Fischer **11.** Jean Alesi **12.** 1978 **13.** Stephen Ames **14.** David Bedford **15.** Table tennis.

POP

1. In which year did Queen chart with the single *Seven Seas of Rhye*?
2. Who was the drummer in The Spencer Davis Group?
3. Which group had a 1995 hit with *Transamazonia*?
4. Which group recorded the 1990 album *Stay Sick!*?
5. Which duo had a 1996 Top 30 single with *Girl Power*?
6. Whose debut L.P. was 1987's *Introducing the Hardline*?
7. Which singer featured on the 1998 hit *Move Mania* by Sash!?
8. Who was the lead singer in the group Curve?
9. In which year was singer Helen Shapiro born?
10. In which city did Southern Death Cult form in 1982?
11. In which year was the singer Sandie Shaw born?'
12. Which group recorded the 1971 album *Cosmo's Factory*?
13. Which group's debut chart single was 1994's *Dolphin*?
14. What is drummer Ginger Baker's real first name?
15. Who had a 1998 Top Ten single with *Searchin' my Soul*?

ANSWERS **1.** 1974 **2.** Pete York **3.** Shamen **4.** The Cramps **5.** Shampoo **6.** Terence Trent D'Arby **7.** Shannon **8.** Toni Halliday **9.** 1946 **10.** Bradford **11.** 1947 **12.** Creedence Clearwater Revival **13.** Shed Seven **14.** Peter **15.** Vonda Shepard.

GEOGRAPHY

1. Where in New Zealand is the city of Dunedin - North Island or South Island?
2. In the U.S., is Nashville north-east or north-west of Houston?
3. In which U.S. state are Anchorage and Fairbanks?
4. In which African country are the towns of Inhambane and Tete?
5. Which river flows from France into Belgium joining the Meuse at Namur?
6. In which European country is the River Salambria?
7. Into which bay does the Sacramento River of California flow?
8. Of which state of India is Jaipur the capital?
9. On which Mediterranean island is the city of Ragusa?
10. Which Italian town houses the tomb of St. Augustine?
11. On which river is the Indian city of Patna?
12. In which South American country is the city of Salta?
13. In which African country are the towns of Gweru and Mutare?
14. Of which country was Rabaul the capital until 1941?
15. In which country is the volcano Paricutin?

ANSWERS **1.** South Island **2.** North-east **3.** Alaska **4.** Mozambique **5.** Sambre **6.** Greece **7.** San Francisco Bay **8.** Rajasthan **9.** Sicily **10.** Pavia **11.** Ganges **12.** Argentina **13.** Zimbabwe **14.** The Teritory of New Guinea **15.** Mexico.

GENERAL KNOWLEDGE

1. What acid is also called 2-hydroxypropanoic acid?
2. Yakubu Gowon was head of state of which African country from 1966-75?
3. In which year was the Battle of Leyte Gulf in World War II?
4. What type of farmyard animal is a saddleback?
5. What in Russia were the Okhrana in the late 19th century and early 20th century?
6. In law, what is 'chance-medley'?
7. Which U.S. state is known as the 'Sagebrush State'?
8. In which film is a string quartet by Boccherini used by a group of crooks to provide cover?
9. Which fictional character's symbol is a haloed pin-man?
10. What is the Hungarian name for the River Danube?
11. What does the French firm St-Gobain specialize in making?
12. Over what distance is the Ebor Handicap run at York in August?
13. Who wrote the 1912 play *Hindle Wakes*?
14. Which 1943 musical includes the song *Oh, What a Beautiful Mornin'*?
15. What is the American songbird a crow blackbird also called?

ANSWERS **1.** Lactic acid **2.** Nigeria **3.** 1944 **4.** A pig **5.** Russian Imperial secret police **6.** A sudden quarrel in which one party kills another **7.** Nevada **8.** The Ladykillers **9.** The Saint **10.** Duna **11.** Glass **12.** 1 and three-quarter miles **13.** Stanley Houghton **14.** Oklahoma! **15.** Grackle.

ENTERTAINMENT

1. What was Heather Graham's character name in the film *Boogie Nights*?
2. Who wrote and directed the 1999 film *eXistenZ*?
3. Which actress directed and starred in the 2000 film *Agnes Browne*?
4. Which film festival is held in the ski resort of Park City, Utah?
5. Who created the children's programmes *Rosie and Jim* and *Teletubbies*?
6. In which year did the children's programme *Play School* first appear on television?
7. With which field of the arts would you associate Max Stafford-Clark?
8. Who played the villain Clock King in the 1960's *Batman* television series?
9. Who played the android Bishop in the film *Aliens*?
10. Which comedian released the 1997 live video *Twin Squeaks*?
11. Which television soap actress played Princess Jasmine in a production of *Aladdin* at Tunbridge Wells at Christmas, 1997?
12. Who plays Juan Peron in the 1996 film *Evita*?
13. Who is the female lead in the 1997 film *Excess Baggage*?
14. In which city is the 1995 film *An Awfully Big Adventure* set?
15. What is the 1933 sequel to the film *King Kong*?

ANSWERS 1. Rollergirl **2.** David Cronenberg **3.** Anjelica Huston **4.** Sundance **5.** Anne Wood **6.** 1964 **7.** Drama **8.** Walter Slezak **9.** Lance Henriksen **10.** Joe Pasquale **11.** Isla Fisher **12.** Jonathan Pryce **13.** Alicia Silverstone **14.** Liverpool **15.** The Son of Kong.

SPORT

1. Who won the 1998 Luxembourg Grand Prix in Formula 1?
2. Who defeated the United States in the semi-final of the 1998 Davis Cup?
3. Who succeeded Christian Gross as the manager of Tottenham Hotspur?
4. Which former England cricket captain of the 1980s became director of coaching at Middlesex CCC?
5. Which horse won the 1998 Prix de l'Arc de Triomphe?
6. Who succeeded George Graham as manager of Leeds United?
7. Who won the 1998 men's Swiss Indoor tennis singles title?
8. Which golfer won the 1998 World Matchplay title?
9. By what score did the New York Yankees beat the San Diego Padres in the 1998 World Series in baseball?
10. Who did Naseem Hamed outpoint in October, 1998 to retain his WBO featherweight boxing title?
11. Who won the 1994 Boat Race?
12. Which horse won the 1994 William Hill Lincoln Handicap?
13. Who scored Manchester United's goal in the 1994 Coca-Cola Cup Final?
14. Who won the men's 1994 Salem Open tennis title in Osaka?
15. Which Italian world heavyweight boxing champion worked as a strongman in a circus?

ANSWERS 1. Mika Hakkinen **2.** Italy **3.** George Graham **4.** Mike Gatting **5.** Sagamix **6.** David O'Leary **7.** Tim Henman **8.** Mark O'Meara **9.** 4-0 **10.** Wayne McCullogh **11.** Cambridge **12.** Our Rita **13.** Mark Hughes **14.** Pete Sampras **15.** Primo Carnera.

POP

1. Which song by pop singer Dido was sampled by Eminem on his song *Stan*?
2. Who replaced Chris Norman as lead singer in the group Smokie?
3. Which member of the group The Supremes was nicknamed 'Blondie'?
4. Which former manager of the group Abba died in 1997 following a heart attack?
5. Under what name did the group The Stooges debut in 1967?
6. *Are You Ready?* was the third album of which West Coast rock group?
7. Whose albums include *A Day Without Rain* and *The Memory of Trees*?
8. Which R & B singer was nicknamed 'Mr. Google Eyes'?
9. Which member of cover-band Ice Water co-founded the group Big Star?
10. Which rock group's albums include *Moseley Shoals*?
11. Which member of The Beatles recorded the solo album *Electronic Sounds*?
12. Stephen Malkmus is the former lead singer and guitarist with which cult band?
13. Who was the drummer in 1960s group The Youngbloods?
14. Which brothers formed reggae group The Hippy Boys in 1967?
15. Which brothers joined the rock group Hour Glass in 1967?

ANSWERS 1. Thank You **2.** Alan Barton **3.** Florence Ballard **4.** Stig Andersson **5.** The Psychedelic Stooges **6.** Pacific Gas & Electric **7.** Enya **8.** Joseph August **9.** Chris Bell **10.** Ocean Colour Scene **11.** George Harrison **12.** Pavement **13.** Joe Bauer **14.** Carlie and Aston Barrett **15.** Duane and Gregg Allman.

HISTORY

1. Who was the Conservative prime minister from 1937-40?
2. In which year was the Exxon Valdez oil disaster?
3. What is the standard monetary unit of Uzbekistan?
4. Which place houses the Ulster American Folk Park?
5. What sort of creature is a dowitcher - a fish or a bird?
6. What are the Church of Jesus Christ of Latter-Day Saints also called?
7. John Heathcoat and John Levers designed machinery to manufacture which material?
8. Which city is home to the University of Kentucky?
9. Alcala is the main street of which European capital city?
10. Who is the heroine of the novel *Gone with the Wind*?
11. What type of performer might use a blocked shoe?
12. What is the name of the chief Belgian airline?
13. What was the Roman name for the River Severn?
14. What is the name given to a score of nought in cricket?
15. In which European capital is the Hotel Sacher?

ANSWERS **1.** Neville Chamberlain **2.** 1989 **3.** Sum **4.** Omagh **5.** A bird **6.** Mormons **7.** Lace **8.** Lexington **9.** Madrid **10.** Scarlett O'Hara **11.** A ballet dancer **12.** Sabena **13.** Sabrina **14.** Duck **15.** Vienna.

GENERAL KNOWLEDGE

1. In which country is the skiing resort of Crested Butte?
2. In which Shakespeare play does the character Touchstone appear?
3. Which president of the United States was nicknamed 'Old Hickory'?
4. Which European capital city was formerly known as Triaditsa?
5. In which year was the Central Line on the London Underground opened?
6. What book is set on June 16, 1904 in Dublin?
7. Whose books include *Lord Edgware Dies*?

8. In which opera is Cio-Cio-San the Japanese name of the central character?
9. What, in a city centre, would you do in a KX100?
10. From which country does the energy drink Red Bull originate?
11. For which club did the footballer Bruce Grobbelaar score his only league goal?
12. Who is the proprietor of the Daily Express and Sunday Express?
13. Which car manufacturer makes the VX220?
14. Who wrote the memoir *Moab is my Washpot*?
15. What is the name of the dog in the painting *Dog Looking at and Listening to a Phonograph*?

ANSWERS 1. U.S.A. **2.** As You Like It **3.** Andrew Jackson **4.** Sofia **5.** 1900 **6.** Ulysses by James Joyce **7.** Agatha Christie **8.** Madama Butterfly by Puccini **9.** Make a phone call - it is a phone box **10.** Austria **11.** Crewe Alexandra **12.** Richard Desmond **13.** Vauxhall **14.** Stepgen Fry **15.** Nipper.

ENTERTAINMENT

1. Who plays a murderer turned sculptor in the 1999 film *The Debt Collector*?
2. Who is the male lead in the 1999 film *Croupier*?
3. Who directed the 1977 film *Exorcist II: The Heretic*?
4. What is William Shatner's profession in the 1961 film *The Explosive Generation*?
5. Who directed the 1977 thriller *Audrey Rose*?
6. Who plays the amnesiac lead in the 1932 film *As You Desire Me*?
7. Which actor awakens after a 30-year coma in the 1990 film *Awakenings*?
8. What is Ingrid Bergman's profession in the 1978 film *Autumn Sonata*?
9. What profession does film director Sam Raimi have in the film *The Hudsucker Proxy*?
10. What is Lee Remick's profession in the 1962 film *Experiment in Terror*?
11. Who plays the title role in the 1975 film *Autobiography of a Princess*?
12. Who directed the 1955 film *The Night My Number Came Up*?
13. Who plays Jenny Agutter's brother in the 1970 film *Walkabout*?
14. For which agency did *Lancelot Link: Secret Chimp* work in a 1960's television series?
15. Which Canadian actress made her screen debut in the film *Love and Human Remains*?

ANSWERS **1.** Billy Connolly **2.** Clive Owen **3.** John Boorman **4.** High school teacher **5.** Robert Wise **6.** Greta Garbo **7.** Robert De Niro **8.** Concert pianist **9.** An adman **10.** Bank clerk **11.** Madhur Jaffrey **12.** Leslie Norman **13.** Lucien John **14.** APE (The Agency to Prevent Evil) **15.** Mia Kirshner.

SPORT

1. Which team won the 1990 University Boat Race?
2. In which year did the cyclist Jacques Anquetil die?
3. Who did Leicester play in the quarter finals of the 2001 F.A. Cup?
4. Which animal was the official mascot of the 1972 Summer Olympics at Munich?
5. Who was the 1996 British Open golf champion?
6. Who won the Olympic men's 100m in 1952?
7. How many times have Motherwell been Scottish League champions?
8. Which football team won the 1998/9 European Champions Cup?
9. Which football team won the 1996/7 F.A. Cup?
10. In which country were the 1994 football World Cup finals held?
11. Which boxer won the vacant WBA super-middleweight crown in March, 2001?
12. Who was the 2000 world men's indoor bowls champion?
13. Which dog won the 1998 greyhound derby?
14. Which horse won the 1950 Epsom Derby?
15. In which year was the runner Said Aouita born?

ANSWERS 1. Oxford **2.** 1987 **3.** Wycombe **4.** Waldi the Dachshund **5.** Tom Lehman **6.** Lindy Remingino **7.** Once **8.** Manchester United **9.** Chelsea **10.** U.S.A. **11.** Byron Mitchell **12.** Robert Weale **13.** Tom's the Best **14.** Galcador **15.** 1960.

POP

1. What was Pluto Shervington's 1976 Top 10 single?
2. In which city did The Cowboy Junkies form in 1985?
3. On which record label did Showaddywaddy have a No. 1 single in 1976?
4. Which group's second album was *I-Feel-Like-I'm-Fixin'-To-Die*?
5. Which group had a 1979 No. 2 single with *Some Girls*?
6. In which year was guitarist Elvin Bishop born?
7. In which city did The Dylans form in 1989?
8. Who was the songwriter in the 1980s group Black?
9. Which group recorded the 1974 album *On the Border*?
10. Who was the original bass player in the group Blondie?
11. Which group recorded the 1996 album *Don Solaris*?
12. What is David Bowie's real name?
13. Which Chicago guitarist formed the group the Electric Flag in 1967?
14. In which year was blues singer Bobby Bland born?
15. Which group recorded the 1973 album *Brain Salad Surgery*?

ANSWERS 1. Dat **2.** Toronto **3.** Bell **4.** Country Joe and the Fish **5.** Racey **6.** 1942 **7.** Sheffield **8.** Colin Vearncombe **9.** The Eagles **10.** Fred Smith **11.** 808 State **12.** David Jones **13.** Mike Bloomfield **14.** 1930 **15.** E.L.P.

WORDS

1. What, politically, does UDI stand for?
2. What would you do with a scrod in the U.S. - cook it or cook with it?
3. What is a gamin?
4. What is mazuma a slang word for ?
5. What is hoya - a plant or a bird?
6. What in nautical slang is burgoo?
7. What type of birds' nests are used to make bird's-nest soup?
8. How many strokes under par is a birdie on a golf hole?
9. What does SWALK mean on the back of an envelope?
10. For what is the Australian word 'ocker' slang?
11. What food is also called garbanzo?
12. To which part of the body does the adjective gnathic relate?
13. What would you do with ugali - write with it or eat it?
14. What does 'entre nous' mean?
15. Of which country is ukiyoe a school of painting?

ANSWERS 1. Unilateral declaration of independence **2.** Cook it - it's a fish **3.** A street urchin or waif **4.** Money **5.** A plant **6.** Porridge **7.** Swifts **8.** One **9.** Sealed with a loving kiss **10.** An uncultivated or boorish person **11.** Chick-pea **12.** The jaw **13.** Eat it - it's cornmeal and water **14.** Between you and me **15.** Japan.

GENERAL KNOWLEDGE

1. What is the nickname of Southampton F.C.?
2. What was the pen-name of writer H.H. Munro?
3. In which year was the Battle of Edgehill?
4. In which year did the German Protestant theologian Martin Luther die?
5. What sort of creature is a bluetongue?
6. In which month is Bampton Fair, in Devon, usually held?
7. What is the name of the donkey in the *Winnie-the-Pooh* tales?
8. Herm, Jethou and Lihou are part of which island group?
9. Which award given by RIBA did Woodlea Primary School win in 1993?
10. In which year did Wyoming join the Union?
11. Which artist won the 1994 B.P. Portrait Award?
12. Who was Miss United Kingdom in 1992?
13. What is the weedy plant charlock also called?
14. How would you detain someone using jougs?
15. Which was CAMRA's champion beer of Britain in 1993?

ANSWERS 1. The saints **2.** Saki **3.** 1642 **4.** 1546 **5.** A lizard **6.** October **7.** Eeyore **8.** The Channel Islands **9.** Building of the Year **10.** 1908 **11.** Peter Edwards **12.** Claire Smith **13.** Wild mustard **14.** By the neck - it's an iron ring attached to a wall **15.** Adnam's Extra.

ENTERTAINMENT

1. Who plays DCI Ross Tanner in the television drama *Second Sight*?
2. On which island were the volunteers of television show *Castaway 2000* stranded?
3. Who plays security chief Dunne in the film *Snake Eyes*?
4. Who plays Greg Focker in the 2000 film *Meet the Parents*?
5. Who directed the 1948 film *Arch of Triumph*?
6. The 1955 film *The Beachcomber* is based on a story by which writer?
7. Who directed and starred in the 1996 musical film *Everone Says I Love You*?
8. In which U.S. state was film *The Evil Dead* shot?
9. Who played the villain Chandel in the 1960's *Batman* television series?
10. Who plays a Scottish hairdresser in the 2000 film *The Big Tease*?
11. What was the original title of Paul Thomas Anderson's film *Hard Eight*?
12. The 2000 film *Simpatico* is based on whose play?
13. In which year did the children's television show *Watch With Mother* come off the air?
14. What is Teri Hatcher's character name in the James Bond film *Tomorrow Never Dies*?
15. Who directed the 1999 film *Beloved* based on Toni Morrison's book?

ANSWERS **1.** Clive Owen **2.** Taransay **3.** Gary Sinise **4.** Ben Stiller **5.** Lewis Milestone **6.** W. Somerset Maugham **7.** Woody Allen **8.** Tennessee **9.** Liberace **10.** Craig Ferguson **11.** Sidney **12.** Sam Shepard **13.** 1980 **14.** Paris Carver **15.** Jonathan Demme.

SPORT

1. Who was the first Finn to win the World Formula 1 motor racing championship?
2. Who knocked Aston Villa out of the 1998/99 UEFA Cup?
3. Who ceased to be manager of Wolves in November 1998?
4. By what score did England beat the Netherlands in their Rugby World Cup qualifier in November 1998?
5. By what score did England beat the Czech Republic in a 1998 friendly at Wembley?
6. Who won the 1998/99 First Test in cricket between England and Australia?
7. Who knocked Liverpool out of the 1998/99 UEFA Cup?
8. Who did Jane Couch beat in the first official women's professional bout in the U.K.?
9. Who replaced Roy Hodgson as manager of Blackburn Rovers?
10. Which woman won the 1998 European Cross-Country Championships?
11. Who was named BBC Sports Personality of the Year in December 1998?
12. By how many runs did Australia defeat England in the Third Test in December, 1998?
13. Which horse won the 1998 King George VI Chase?
14. Which jockey won the 1953 and '54 Grand Nationals?
15. In which U.S. state was boxer Sonny Liston born?

ANSWERS **1.** Keke Rosberg **2.** Celta Vigo **3.** Mark McGhee **4.** 110-0 **5.** 2-0 **6.** It was a draw **7.** Celta Vigo **8.** Simona Lukic **9.** Brian Kidd **10.** Paula Radcliffe **11.** Michael Owen **12.** 205 **13.** Teeton Mill **14.** Bryan Marshall **15.** Arkansas.

POP

1. Who recorded the 1999 album *Rave Un2 the Joy Fantastic*?
2. Which duo made the 2000 album *The Skiffle Sessions - Live in Belfast*?
3. Which group recorded the albums *Aja* and *Gaucho*?
4. Who recorded the 1996 country album *Ten Thousand Angels*?
5. Which Australian group recorded the album *Redneck Wonderland*?
6. Which duo recorded the album *Brothers Gonna Work It Out*?
7. Which rock groups albums include *Be Here Now*?
8. What were the forenames of the Addrisi Brothers who had pop hits in the 1970s?
9. Who composed the songs *Kiss On My List* and *Private Eyes* for Hall and Oates?
10. Which former member of pop group Adam and the Ants and Bow Wow Wow joined the group Chiefs of Relief in 1988?

11. What were the singing group The Primettes nicknamed in the early 1960s?
12. Which member of the Cleveland band The Rockets co-founded the punk group The Dead Boys in 1977?
13. When was pop singer Dido born?
14. With which choir did the rock star Lenny Kravitz sing as an 11 year-old?
15. From which city in the south of England do the Rotator recording artists The Mystics hail?

ANSWERS 1. The Artist **2.** Van Morrison and Lonnie Donegan **3.** Steely Dan **4.** Mindy McCready **5.** Midnight Oil **6.** The Chemical Brothers **7.** Oasis **8.** Michael and Don **9.** Janna Allen **10.** Matthew Ashman **11.** The Supremes **12.** Stiv Bator **13.** Christmas Day, 1971 **14.** California Boys Choir **15.** Oxford.

SCIENCE

1. Chlorine was named after the Greek word for which colour?
2. During the Upper Cretaceous period the land mass of the Earth split into two super-continents. What was the northern one called?
3. What is the symbol of the element rubidium?
4. For what discovery was Harold Urey awarded the 1934 Nobel prize for chemistry?
5. What in mathematics do the initials HCF stand for?
6. In which year did the English mathematician Charles Babbage die?

7. What nationality was Ernst Beckmann, after whom a type of thermometer was named?
8. Which is the largest of the seven continents of the world?
9. Which fruit's scientific name is *Musa sapientum*?
10. How many tentacles does an octopus have?
11. What is a reg in a desert?
12. What is the tail fin of a fish also known as?
13. In which year was the Psi Particle discovered?
14. To which genus does the shrimp belong?
15. Which element's symbol is P?

ANSWERS 1. Green **2.** Laurasia **3.** Rb **4.** Heavy hydrogen **5.** Highest common factor **6.** 1871 **7.** German **8.** Asia **9.** Banana **10.** Eight **11.** A sandless area of gravel and rocks **12.** Caudal fin **13.** 1974 **14.** Crangon **15.** Phosphorus.

GENERAL KNOWLEDGE

1. How old was actor Oliver Reed when he died?
2. For which organization was Leila Khaled a terrorist in the 1970s?
3. Which European capital city was formerly known as Revel?
4. In which country is the skiing resort of Innsbruck?
5. Who in 2000 was the director-general of the prison service in Britain?
6. Which Liverpool footballer bought a group of houses in Hawarden, North Wales, for his family members?
7. Which comedian died in his sleep at the Chateau Marmont Hotel, West Hollywood, on March 5, 1982?
8. In which year was Anthony Blunt unmasked as a Soviet spy?
9. How much did the wedding cake of Michael Douglas and Catherine Zeta Jones cost?
10. Harvey and Hibby are characters in an advertising campaign for which British store?
11. What is the speed of the average avalanche?
12. Which car manufacturer makes the Xsara model?
13. Of which football team is comedian Stephen Fry a season ticket holder?
14. Which bird was Her Majesty the Queen photographed killing in November, 2000?
15. Who became FIDE world chess champion in 1999?

ANSWERS **1.** 61 **2.** PFLP (Popular Front for the Liberation of Palestine) **3.** Tallinn **4.** Austria **5.** Martin Narey **6.** Michael Owen **7.** John Belushi **8.** 1979 **9.** £70,000 **10.** Harvey Nichols **11.** 50 m.p.h. **12.** Citroen **13.** Norwich City **14.** Pheasant **15.** Alexander Khalifman.

ENTERTAINMENT

1. What is the heroine's surname in the 1980 film *Gloria*?
2. Who directed the 1982 film *Veronika Voss*?
3. Who plays *Patch Adams* in a the 1999 film?
4. Who directed the 1999 film *Waking Ned*?
5. Who played the title role in the 1998 film *Elizabeth*?
6. Which actor starred in, and co-produced, the 1999 film *Entrapment*?
7. What is Clint Eastwood's job in the 1956 film *Away All Boats*?
8. Who directed and starred in the 1996 film *August*?
9. Which *Boogie Nights* actor plays a rookie cop in the 1999 film *The Corruptor*?
10. Who plays Queen of Naboo in the film *The Phantom Menace*?
11. What job does Christina Ricci do in the film *Pecker*?
12. Which comedian stars in the 1998 film *My Giant*?
13. Who plays the male lead in the 1982 film comedy *Author! Author!*?
14. Who stars as a nun in the 1998 film *Madeline*?
15. What was the name of the ship of cartoon character *Captain Pugwash*?

ANSWERS 1. Swenson **2.** Rainer Werner Fassbinder **3.** Robin Williams **4.** Kirk Jones **5.** Cate Blanchett **6.** Sean Connery **7.** Medical orderly **8.** Anthony Hopkins **9.** Mark Wahlberg **10.** Natalie Portman **11.** She runs a launderette **12.** Billy Crystal **13.** Al Pacino **14.** Frances McDormand **15.** The Black Pig.

SPORT

1. Which was Richard Dunwoody's 1000th winner in Britain?
2. Who lost the 1994 Australian Open men's tennis final?
3. Who rode Shergar to victory in the 1981 Epsom Derby?
4. Who won the men's 5,000m and 10,000m at the 1956 Olympics?
5. What was the nickname of tennis player René Lacoste?
6. In which city was the footballer Denis Law born?
7. Who won the women's long jump at the 1966 Commonwealth Games?
8. Who won the 1998 Austrian Grand Prix in Formula 1?
9. Who won the 1998 German Grand Prix in Formula 1?
10. By what score did the U.S. beat Great Britain and Ireland in the 1998 Curtis Cup?
11. By what score did Arsenal defeat Manchester United in the 1998 Charity Shield?
12. Which team won Italy's 1998/99 Serie A title?
13. Who retained his WBC welterweight boxing title in May 1999 by beating Oba Carr?
14. Who scored the first goal in the 1999 F.A. Cup Final?
15. Who won the 1998/99 Scottish Premier League football title?

ANSWERS 1. Flakey Dove **2.** Todd Martin **3.** Walter Swinburn **4.** Vladimir Kuts **5.** The Crocodile **6.** Aberdeen **7.** Mary Rand **8.** Mika Hakkinen **9.** Mika Hakkinen **10.** 10-8 **11.** 3-0 **12.** A.C. Milan **13.** Oscar de la Hoya **14.** Teddy Sheringham **15.** Rangers.

POP

1. In which year was the musician and producer Brian Eno born?
2. What was the debut album by the group The Blue Nile?
3. Which group recorded the 1969 album *What We Did on Our Holidays*?
4. Which songwriter recorded the 1988 album *Worker's Playtime*?
5. On which record label did The Radha Krishna Temple chart in 1970 with *Govinda*?
6. Which band recorded the 1984 album *Ocean Rain*?
7. Which band recorded the 1990 album *Shake Your Money Maker*?
8. In which city were indie group The Blue Aeroplanes formed?
9. In which year did Radiohead have a Top Ten single with *Creep*?
10. In which year was the singer Gary 'US' Bonds born?
11. After what is the group Fatima Mansions named?
12. Sam Spoons and Vernon Dudley Bohey-Nowell were members of which 1960s group?
13. Who was the lead singer with the group Felt?
14. What was the debut album by the group Boston?
15. In which year did Queen first chart with *Another One Bites the Dust*?

ANSWERS **1.** 1948 **2.** A Walk Across the Rooftops **3.** Fairport Convention **4.** Billy Bragg **5.** Apple **6.** Echo and the Bunnymen **7.** The Black Crowes **8.** Bristol **9.** 1993 **10.** 1939 **11.** A Dublin housing estate **12.** Bonzo Dog Doo-Dah Band **13.** Laurence Hayward **14.** Boston **15.** 1980.

PEOPLE

1. *Smokin' Joe* is the 1996 autobiography of which boxer?
2. Which actor was a roommate of politician Al Gore at Harvard?
3. Who became Director General of the BBC in February, 2000?
4. Which political writer authored the satire *Primary Colors*?
5. In which year did Guccio Gucci open a leather goods shop in Florence?
6. Which firm was founded in 1859 by Moses Moses?
7. Mary Scurlock was the second wife of which man of letters?
8. Who was Lord Chancellor of England from 1529-32?
9. In which year was the fashion designer Bruce Oldfield born?
10. Which football team does the actor Phil Davis support?
11. Who is pictured on the back of a £50 note?
12. Who designed the Guggenheim Museum in Bilbao?
13. Which actress was spotted by Alfred Hitchcock when appearing in a diet drink commercial on television?
14. Which journalist became the Editorial Director of Aura magazine in May, 2000?
15. The nanny Ros Mark famously worked for which politician from 1994?

ANSWERS **1.** Joe Frazier **2.** Tommy Lee Jones **3.** Greg Dyke **4.** Joe Klein **5.** 1921 **6.** Moss Bros. **7.** Richard Steele **8.** Sir Thomas More **9.** 1950 **10.** West Ham United **11.** Sir John Houblon **12.** Frank Gehry **13.** Tippi Hedren **14.** Eve Pollard **15.** Tony Blair.

GENERAL KNOWLEDGE

1. Duroc is an American breed of which animal?
2. What does the abbreviation OPEC stand for?
3. Which artist won the 1991 Turner Prize?
4. Who wrote the novels *The Choir* and *The Rector's Wife*?
5. Which marital award did Kerry Doyland win in 1994?
6. What nutlike seed is produced by the tree *Prunus amygdalus*?
7. Who is Punch's wife in the traditional puppet show?
8. Which athlete was voted world champion budgie breeder in 1993?
9. What was awarded the accolade of 1993 Car of the Year by *What Car?* magazine?
10. What is the oil from the seed of the chaulmoogra tree used to treat?
11. Which TV award did Derek Johns win in 1993?
12. What in South Africa is a jukskei?
13. Which authoress won the 1990 Guardian Children's Fiction Award?
14. In which year did Tchaikovsky write the *1812 Overture*?
15. Which Nobel prize did Gary Becker win in 1992?

ANSWERS 1. Pig **2.** Organization of Petroleum Exporting Countries **3.** Anish Kapoor **4.** Joanna Trollope **5.** Clothes Show Bride of the Year **6.** Almond **7.** Judy **8.** Geoff Capes **9.** Ford Mondeo 1.8 GLX **10.** Leprosy **11.** Masterchef **12.** A game **13.** Anne Fine **14.** 1880 **15.** Economics.

ENTERTAINMENT

1. The store 'Al's Toy Barn' features in which the 2000 film?
2. In which year was the first television programme for children, *For the Children*, broadcast?
3. What was the subtitle of the 1981 film *Piranha Part Two*?
4. Who directed the 1999 film *Affliction*?
5. Who played the drug dealer Swanney in the film *Trainspotting*?
6. Who directed the 1998 film *Your Friends and Neighbors*?
7. Who directed the 1999 thriller film *In Dreams*?
8. Which cast member of film *The Full Monty* plays a musician in the film *Jack Frost*?
9. Who directed the 1999 film *8mm*?
10. Who played the villain Louie the Lilac in the 1960's *Batman* television series?
11. The true story of Brandon Teena is the basis of which film?
12. What job was Kelly Macdonald doing when she attended an open casting session for the film *Trainspotting*?
13. Which 2000 Oscar nominee grew up in York, England?
14. The 1960 film *Plein Soleil* and the 1977 film *The American Friend* were based on books by which author?
15. Who directed the 1999 film *You've Got Mail*?

ANSWERS **1.** Toy Story 2 **2.** 1946 **3.** The Spawning **4.** Paul Schrader **5.** Peter Mullan **6.** Neil LaBute **7.** Neil Jordan **8.** Mark Addy **9.** Joel Schumacher **10.** Milton Berle **11.** Boys Don't Cry **12.** Barmaid **13.** Janet McTeer **14.** Patricia Highsmith **15.** Nora Ephron.

SPORT

1. For which country does Jonty Rhodes play cricket?
2. Which team won the 1994 Winter Olympics men's ice hockey gold?
3. Who won the 1994 Andalucian Open in golf?
4. At what age did Judit Polgar become a chess grandmaster?
5. By how many runs did England beat South Africa in the Fifth Test in 1998?
6. Who scored the only goal in Chelsea's 1998 Super Cup victory over Real Madrid?
7. Who won the 1998 Belgian Grand Prix in Formula 1?
8. By what score did Sweden beat England in their European Championship qualifier in September 1998?
9. Where did Wales play their 'home' European Championship qualifier against Italy in September, 1998?
10. Who resigned as German football coach in 1998?
11. What nationality is tennis player Patrick Rafter?
12. Which teams competed in the 1994 Italian Cup Final in football?
13. Who won the men's Giant Slalom Alpine skiing title at the 1994 Olympics?
14. In which year was FIFA founded?
15. What nationality is golfer David Graham?

ANSWERS **1.** South Africa **2.** Sweden **3.** Carl Mason **4.** 15 **5.** 23 **6.** Gustavo Poyet **7.** Damon Hill **8.** 2-1 **9.** Anfield **10.** Bertie Vogts **11.** Australian **12.** Sampdoria and Ancona **13.** Markus Wasmeier **14.** 1904 **15.** Australian.

POP

1. With which song did Caroline Quentin and Leslie Ash chart in 1996?
2. In which year was the group Black Sabbath formed?
3. What was the title of Jesse Rae's only chart single in 1985?
4. John Plain and Jack Black were members of which London punk band?
5. In which year was Bryan Ferry born?
6. Which group recorded the 1994 album *Brother Sister*?
7. Which group recorded the 1984 album *The Works*?
8. What was the debut album of the group The Breeders?
9. Who recorded the 1986 album *Guitar Town*?
10. In which year did the Chocolate Watch Band form?
11. Who produced the 1995 album *The Bends* by Radiohead?
12. In which city did the group Clock DVA form?
13. What was the second album by The Ramones?
14. In which year did singer Eddie Cochran die?
15. In which city did Red Lorry Yellow Lorry form in 1982?

ANSWERS 1. Tell Him **2.** 1967 **3.** Over the Sea **4.** The Boys **5.** 1945 **6.** Brand New Heavies **7.** Queen **8.** Pod **9.** Steve Earle **10.** 1964 **11.** John Leckie **12.** Sheffield **13.** Leave Home **14.** 1960 **15.** Leeds.

ART AND LITERATURE

1. With which field of the arts is Hugo Häring associated?

2. In which Shakespeare play does the character Lucentio appear?

3. *Dream Catcher* is a memoir by which writer's daughter?

4. Which actress authored the 2000 novel *Snake*?

5. Who wrote the book *The Road to Nab End*?

6. Which artist produced the 1653 print *The Three Crosses*?

7. Which novelist won the Whitbread Prize in January 2001?

8. Who authored novel *The Women in His Life*?

9. Who painted the 1872 work *La Gare d'Argenteuil*?

10. Which writer stood for office in the 1990 Peruvian presidential election?

11. In which year was the Prado art gallery established?

12. In which year did Oscar Wilde die?

13. Who painted the 1877 work *Boats on the Seine*?

14. Who wrote the novel *One Fat Englishman*?

15. Who wrote the novel *The Crow Road*?

ANSWERS **1.** Architecture **2.** The Taming of the Shrew **3.** J.D. Salinger **4.** Mary Woronov **5.** William Woodruff **6.** Rembrandt **7.** Matthew Kneale **8.** Barbara Taylor Bradford **9.** Claude Monet **10.** Maria Vargas Llosa **11.** 1819 **12.** 1900 **13.** Alfred Sisley **14.** Kingsley Amis **15.** Iain Banks.

GENERAL KNOWLEDGE

1. Who played composer Richard Wagner in the 1956 film *Magic Fire*?
2. John Penrose is husband and manager of which television presenter?
3. Where was the 1999 FIDE world chess championship held?
4. What, in South Africa, is an opstoker?
5. Kuda Huraa is a part of which island group?
6. Who wrote the stage play *Naked Justice*?
7. What was the name of the woman schoolteacher killed in the Challenger space shuttle disaster?
8. Which actor was born Krishna Banji?
9. On what date was Britain's Holocaust Memorial Day celebrated in 2001?
10. 2001 film *The Claim* is based on which classic novel?
11. In which country is the skiing resort of Bonneval?
12. Which capital city was formerly known as Batavia?
13. What was the undercover name of FBI Special Agent Joe Pistone in 1976?
14. Approximately how many cups of coffee are drunk per day in the world?
15. What city was the capital of Egypt until 969 A.D.?

ANSWERS 1. Alan Badel **2.** Anne Robinson **3.** Las Vegas **4.** A trouble-maker **5.** The Maldives **6.** John Mortimer **7.** Christa McAuliffe **8.** Ben Kingsley **9.** 27 January **10.** The Mayor of Casterbridge by Thomas Hardy **11.** France **12.** Jakarta **13.** Donnie Brasco **14.** 2.5 billion **15.** Alexandria.

ENTERTAINMENT

1. Who composed the music for film *The Ghost and the Darkness*?
2. Who plays Colonel Tall in the 1999 film *The Thin Red Line*?
3. Which part did Laurence Olivier play in the film *Spartacus*?
4. Which character did Kate Winslet play in the film *Sense and Sensibility*?
5. Who directed the 1999 film *Gloria* which starred Sharon Stone?
6. *My Best Fiend* is a film by which director about which actor?
7. Which of Mickey Rooney's wives appeared with him in the 1954 film *The Atomic Kid*?
8. Who sings the song *Lydia the Tattooed Lady* in the 1939 film *At the Circus*?
9. Who directed the 1998 film *The Avengers*?
10. Which film director scripted the Warren Beatty film *Bugsy*?
11. Who directed the 1992 film *El Mariachi*?
12. Who plays television producer Earl Partridge in the film *Magnolia*?
13. Which actor played private eye McCready in the 2000 television drama *McCready And Daughter*?
14. Which British television network commissioned Jim Henson's company to make the show *The Hoobs*?
15. In which year did the children's show *Rainbow* first appear on television?

ANSWERS **1.** Jerry Goldsmith **2.** Nick Nolte **3.** Crassus **4.** Marianne Dashwood **5.** Sidney Lumet **6.** It is Werner Herzog's film about Klaus Kinski **7.** Elaine Davis **8.** Groucho Marx **9.** Jeremiah Chechik **10.** James Toback **11.** Robert Rodriguez **12.** Jason Robards Jr. **13.** Lorcan Cranitch **14.** Channel Four **15.** 1972.

SPORT

1. Who lost the final of the 1998 U.S. Open tennis ladies singles?
2. Who won the 1998 Italian Grand Prix in Formula 1?
3. Who lost the final of the 1998 U.S. Open tennis men's singles?
4. Who won the women's shot at the 1998 Commonwealth Games?
5. For which Italian football team did Des Walker play in 1992/3?
6. Who won the 1994 Thailand Open in snooker?
7. Who won the 1994 Tour of Murcia in cycling?
8. Who won the 1994 Portuguese Open in squash?
9. What nationality is golfer Nick Price?
10. Who won the 1994 women's British Indoor Bowls title?
11. Who won the 1994 Standard Register Ping golf tournament?
12. Who, in September 1998, broke the men's marathon record?
13. What age was Florence Griffith-Joyner when she died in 1998?
14. Who did Nick Faldo sack as his coach in 1998?
15. Who resigned as Swindon Town manager in September, 1998?

ANSWERS **1.** Martina Hingis **2.** Michael Schumacher **3.** Mark Philippoussis **4.** Judy Oakes **5.** Sampdoria **6.** James Wattana **7.** Melchor Mauri **8.** Jansher Khan **9.** Zimbabwean **10.** Julie Davies **11.** Laura Davies **12.** Ronaldo da Costa **13.** 38 **14.** David Leadbetter **15.** Steve McMahon.

POP

1. Which pop singer's albums include *Older*?
2. Which studio album by the group Suede features the songs *Trash* and *Beautiful Ones*?
3. Which Swedish group recorded the album *All Disco Dance Must End in Broken Bones*?
4. How did the songwriter Barbara Acklin die in 1998?
5. Which R & B singer got a residency at a Chicago club in the 1940s under the name 'Little Miss Sharecropper'?
6. Which songwriter's works include *(You're the) Devil in Disguise* for Elvis Presley?
7. How old was the singer Henry Rollins when he got his first tattoo?
8. Who recorded the country album *If I Don't Stay the Night*?
9. Which studio album by the group Fun Lovin' Criminals includes the songs *Korean Bodega* and *Love Unlimited*?
10. Which girl group's albums include *EV3*?
11. Under what name does the rapper Tiffany Lane record?
12. How did Berry Oakely of the Allman Brothers die?
13. Which pop group's albums include *Free Peace Sweet*?
14. Which group recorded the album *Electro-Shock Blues*?
15. Which pop singer's autobiography is entitled *Praying to the Aliens*?

ANSWERS **1.** George Michael **2.** Coming Up **3.** Whale **4.** Pneumonia **5.** La Vern Baker **6.** Bernie Baum **7.** 20 **8.** Mindy McCready **9.** 100% Colombian **10.** En Vogue **11.** Charli Baltimore **12.** In a motorcycle accident **13.** Dodgy **14.** Eels **15.** Gary Numan.

GEOGRAPHY

1. Salisbury is an industrial suburb of which Australian city?
2. In which sea is the island of Saba in the Netherlands Antilles?
3. Where in New Zealand is the city of Christchurch - North Island or South Island?
4. In which African country are the towns of Oran and Biskra?
5. What is the southernmost point of Nova Scotia, Canada?
6. In which South American country is the city of Pasto?
7. What is the capital of Surinam?
8. In which country is the World Heritage site of the Komodo National Park?
9. What is the capital of Pas-de-Calais department in France?
10. Passamaquoddy Bay in North America lies at the mouth of which river?
11. Which two countries are separated by the Strait of Gibraltar?
12. In which sea is the island of Pantelleria?
13. Vardo and Eckero are part of which Finnish island group?
14. Which is larger, the Gulf of Mexico or the Gulf of Guinea?
15. In which country is the volcano Laki?

ANSWERS 1. Adelaide **2.** Caribbean Sea **3.** South **4.** Algeria **5.** Cape Sable **6.** Colombia **7.** Paramaribo **8.** Indonesia **9.** Arras **10.** St. Croix River **11.** Spain and Morocco **12.** Mediterranean Sea **13.** Aland Islands **14.** Gulf of Mexico **15.** Iceland.

GENERAL KNOWLEDGE

1. What did the initials BOAC stand for in the world of transport?
2. In which year did HMS Lutine sink?
3. How many seats did the Liberal Party get in the 1966 election?
4. Under which party flag did Dick Taverne win a 1973 by-election in Lincoln?
5. Who was British Hairdresser of the Year in 1993?
6. Which London hotel won the Egon Ronay Hotel of the Year award in 1989?
7. Which was found to be the most popular hymn in a 1992 survey by the BBC's *Songs of Praise*?
8. What sort of creature is a cheese skipper?
9. Gralloch is the name given to the entrails of which animal?
10. What does the abbreviation IQ stand for?
11. What is the standard monetary unit of Thailand?
12. In which year was the Seventh Day Adventist Church founded?
13. Which three metals comprise the alloy alnico?
14. Which king of Poland converted Lithuania to Christianity?
15. What in India is the profession of a durzi?

ANSWERS 1. British Overseas Airways Corporation **2.** 1799 **3.** 12 **4.** Democratic Labour **5.** Andrew Collinge **6.** The Savoy **7.** Dear Lord and Father of Mankind **8.** A fly **9.** Deer **10.** Intelligence Quotient **11.** Baht **12.** 1863 **13.** Aluminium, nickel and cobalt **14.** Ladislaus II **15.** A tailor.

ENTERTAINMENT

1. Who took over from Nick Hancock as the presenter of television show *Room 101*?
2. Who directed the 1999 film documentary *Four Little Girls*?
3. Who plays tattoo artist Danny in the 1999 film comedy *This Year's Love*?
4. Who plays underworld boss Freddie Mays in the 2000 film *Gangster No. 1*?
5. Who played the female lead, Ella, in the 1975 film *Rollerball*?
6. Who played the character Ray Nicholet in the films *Jackie Brown* and *Out of Sight*?
7. The film *A Perfect Murder* starring Michael Douglas is a remake of which Alfred Hitchcock film?
8. Who plays motivational speaker Frank Mackey in the film *Magnolia*?
9. In which country is the film *Third World Cop* set?
10. Who plays Kevin Costner's father in the 1999 film *Message in a Bottle*?
11. Who played the villainess Marsha Queen of Diamonds in the 1960s *Batman* television series?
12. Who is the male lead in the 2000 film *Ordinary Decent Criminal*?
13. Who plays the tramp Mr. Summers in the 1999 film *All the Little Animals*?
14. In which year was children's television show *Play School* replaced by *Playdays*?
15. Which comedian starred in the 1999 film *Holy Man*?

ANSWERS 1. Paul Merton **2.** Spike Lee **3.** Douglas Henshall **4.** David Thewlis **5.** Maud Adams **6.** Michael Keaton **7.** Dial M For Murder **8.** Tom Cruise **9.** Jamaica **10.** Paul Newman **11.** Carolyn Jones **12.** Kevin Spacey **13.** John Hurt **14.** 1988 **15.** Eddie Murphy

SPORT

1. Which father and son won the Olympic hammer and javelin events respectively?
2. Who was African Footballer of the Year in 1976?
3. At which ground was David Gower's 100th Test match played?
4. Who in boxing was 'the Tylorstown Terror'?
5. At what weight was Pichit Sitbangprachan the IBF world champion from 1992-94?
6. Who won rugby league's 1994 Regal Trophy Final?
7. Who won the 1994 Moroccan Open in golf?
8. Which side knocked Liverpool out of the 1994 F.A. Cup?
9. Which pair won the 1964 Monte Carlo Rally?
10. Who was the arch-rival of skater Nancy Kerrigan?
11. In which country were the 1956 Winter Olympics held?
12. Who were the first team to win two World Cups in football?
13. What is the middle name of the footballer Jimmy Greaves?
14. When was the World Professional Billiards championship first held?
15. When was the first cricket Test series between India and England?

ANSWER **1.** Imre and Miklos Nemeth **2.** Roger Milla **3.** Headingley **4.** Jimmy Wilde **5.** Flyweight **6.** Castleford **7.** Anders Forbrand **8.** Bristol City **9.** Paddy Hopkirk and Henry Liddon **10.** Tonya Harding **11.** Italy **12.** Italy **13.** Peter **14.** 1870 **15.** 1932.

POP

1. In which year did Elvis Presley have a No. 1 U.K. single with *The Wonder of You*?
2. What was the debut L.P. of Dr. Feelgood?
3. Which U.S. singer's first solo chart single, in 1974, was *Just My Soul Responding*?
4. Who was the drummer in the group Dire Straits?
5. Which group had a Top 20 hit with *On a Rope* in 1996?
6. Who produced the album *Q: Are We Not Men? A: We Are Devo!*?
7. In which year did the Rolling Stones last have a UK No. 1 single?
8. Which group recorded 1981's *See the Whirl*?
9. Who duetted on the 1987 Top Ten single *Somewhere Out There*?
10. Which group's debut L.P. was called *Fresh Fruit for Rotting Vegetables*?
11. Which singer had a Top Ten single in 1992 with *One Shining Moment*?
12. Which group's second single was *Mattress of Wire*?
13. Which group's debut chart entry was 1996's *Take California*?
14. What was the debut album of Babes in Toyland?
15. Which group had a 1993 Top Ten single with *Almost Unreal*?

ANSWERS **1.** 1970 **2.** Down by the Jetty **3.** Smokey Robinson **4.** Pick Withers **5.** Rocket from the Crypt **6.** Brian Eno **7.** 1969 **8.** Delta 5 **9.** Linda Ronstadt and James Ingram **10.** The Dead Kennedys **11.** Diana Ross **12.** Aztec Camera **13.** Propellerheads **14.** Spanking Machine **15.** Roxette.

HISTORY

1. In which year did Napoleon Bonaparte die?

2. What was the Welsh dandy Beau Nash's forename?

3. Who was Emperor Nero's mother?

4. Which U.S. naval commander signed the Japanese surrender documents in 1945?

5. Which Irish political leader was known as 'the liberator'?

6. In which year was the Chelsea Flower Show first held?

7. Who became president of Argentina in 1988?

8. In which year was the Suez Canal opened?

9. In which year did Alcoholics Anonymous originate?

10. Who was king of France from 1610-43?

11. In which year did Baden-Powell form the Boy Scouts?

12. In which century did the scientist and philosopher Roger Bacon live?

13. Which soldier took Valencia in 1094?

14. In which year was President Clinton's Balanced Budget Act?

15. In which year was William Rufus killed in the New Forest?

ANSWERS 1. 1821 **2.** Richard **3.** Agrippina **4.** Nimitz **5.** Daniel O'Connell **6.** 1913 **7.** Carlos Menem **8.** 1869 **9.** 1935 **10.** Louis XIII **11.** 1908 **12.** 13th **13.** El Cid **14.** 1997 **15.** 1100.

GENERAL KNOWLEDGE

1. Who replaced politician Jörg Haider as leader of the FPO in Austria in February, 2000?
2. In which year did radio soap opera *The Archers* first go on the air?
3. What was the name of composer Ludwig van Beethoven's father?
4. In which country is the skiing resort of Garmisch Partenkirchen?
5. Which capital city was formerly known as Port Nicholson?
6. Who wrote the book *The Quantity Theory of Insanity*?
7. What was the surname at birth of Labour Party financial contributor Lord Hamlyn?
8. Who authored the stage play *Life x 3*?
9. In which year was the Earl's Court Great Wheel opened to the public?
10. In which year was soprano Barbara Bonney born?
11. In which African country is the beach resort of Hammamet?
12. The camel wrestling season in Turkey begins in January. In which month does it end?
13. Who played the composer Brahms in the 1947 film *Song of Love*?
14. Merlin Holland is the grandson of which writer?
15. Who wrote the novel *Paddy Clarke Ha Ha Ha*?

ANSWERS 1. Susanne Riess-Passer **2.** 1951 **3.** Johann **4.** Germany **5.** Wellington **6.** Will Self **7.** Hamburger **8.** Yasmina Reza **9.** 1895 **10.** 1956 **11.** Tunisia **12.** March **13.** Robert Walker **14.** Oscar Wilde **15.** Roddy Doyle.

ENTERTAINMENT

1. Who plays a former Nazi war criminal in the film *Apt Pupil*?
2. Who plays the central character Dedee Truitt in the film *The Opposite of Sex*?
3. Which 1998 film did *Seinfeld* co-creator Larry David direct and write?
4. 'A Soft Touch' and 'The Granton Star Cause' are stories in which 1998 film?
5. Which film won the 1979 Best Foreign Film Oscar?
6. Who plays Felicity Shagwell in the film *Austin Powers: The Spy Who Shagged Me*?
7. Who play Dogberry and Verges in the 1993 film *Much Ado About Nothing*?
8. Which leading actor plays a blind man in the 1998 film *At First Sight*?
9. What is Julia Roberts's character name in the film *Notting Hill*?
10. In which film does Jennifer Jason Leigh play games designer Allegra Geller?

11. Which two films, in 1967 & 1997, each won 11 Oscars?
12. Who directed and starred in the 1999 film *Guest House Paradiso*?
13. Who played composer Franz Schubert in the 1934 film *Blossom Time*?
14. Who directed the 1973 film *The Wicker Man*?
15. Who plays the character Sheldrake in Billy Wilder film *The Apartment*?

ANSWERS 1. Ian McKellen **2.** Christina Ricci **3.** Sour Grapes **4.** The Acid House **5.** The Tin Drum **6.** Heather Graham **7.** Michael Keaton and Ben Elton **8.** Val Kilmer **9.** Anna Scott **10.** eXistenZ **11.** Ben-Hur and Titanic **12.** Adrian Edmondson **13.** Richard Tauber **14.** Robin Hardy **15.** Fred MacMurray.

SPORT

1. Who won the 1990 Badminton horse trials?
2. When did Harry Vardon win the first of his British Open golf titles?
3. Who won the first Olympic men's hockey title?
4. Who was the first Formula 1 motor racing world champion?
5. Which year saw a dead heat in the university boat race?
6. In which year was volleyball introduced into the Olympic Games?
7. What nationality was the runner Kip Keino?
8. Who won the 1994 Regal Welsh Open snooker title?
9. Who scored all of England's points in their Calcutta Cup game in 1984?
10. In which year did Kapil Dev take his first Test wicket?
11. In which year did Graeme Souness take over as Liverpool boss?
12. In which year did golfer Henry Cotton die?
13. In which country was cricketer Colin Cowdrey born?
14. Which golfer won the 1994 Madeira Island Open?
15. Who won the 1994 Houston men's marathon?

ANSWERS 1. Nicola McIrvine **2.** 1896 **3.** England **4.** Nino Farina **5.** 1877 **6.** 1964 **7.** Kenyan **8.** Steve Davis **9.** Jonathan Callard **10.** 1978 **11.** 1991 **12.** 1987 **13.** India **14.** Mats Lanner **15.** Colin Moore.

POP

1. Which member of the group The 5th Dimension died in a fire in 1982?
2. What is pop singer Dido's surname?
3. Which groups albums include *In the Air* and *Through the Trees*?
4. *Fireworks City* is which group's second album?
5. Which group's debut album in 1998 was *Songs of Praise*?
6. Which group recorded the album *How to Operate with a Blown Mind*?
7. Which Nirvana album had the working titles 'Verse Chorus Verse' and 'Radio Friendly Unit Shifter'?
8. Which group recorded the 1998 album *Munki*?
9. Which group recorded the 1998 album *The Things We Make*?
10. Which singer was born Hugh Anthony Cregg III?
11. How was the northern soul singer Darrell Banks killed in 1970?
12. *Joya Magica* is which group's second album?
13. Which female singer recorded the album *Left of The Middle*?
14. With which musical form is the recording artist Sizzla associated?
15. Under what name does the singer Jim Heath perform?

ANSWERS 1. Daniel Beard **2.** Armstrong **3.** The Handsome Family **4.** Audioweb **5.** Bullyrag **6.** Lo-Fidelity Allstars **7.** In Utero **8.** The Jesus and Mary Chain **9.** Six By Seven **10.** Huey Lewis **11.** He was shot **12.** The 60ft Dolls **13.** Natalie Imbruglia **14.** Reggae **15.** Reverend Horton Heat.

ART AND LITERATURE

1. Who wrote the novel *The Heart Is A Lonely Hunter*?
2. Who wrote the novel *The Accidental Tourist*?
3. Whose paintings include the 18th Century work *Mrs.Oswald* which is in the National Gallery?
4. Who wrote the 1987 novel *Sarum*?
5. Who wrote the novel *The Maid of Buttermere*?
6. Which cartoonist's volumes include *The Impending Gleam*?
7. Who wrote the novel *A Son of the Circus*?
8. Who wrote the 1996 book *Worst Fears*?
9. Who wrote the novel *Talking It Over*?
10. Who wrote the novels *Sharpe's Tiger* and *Sharpe's Sword*?
11. In which Shakespeare play does the character Quince appear?
12. Who wrote the 1990 novel *Spider*?
13. Who wrote the 1994 novel *The Informers*?
14. Who wrote the novel *A Spell of Winter*?
15. Who wrote the novel *Gerald's Party*?

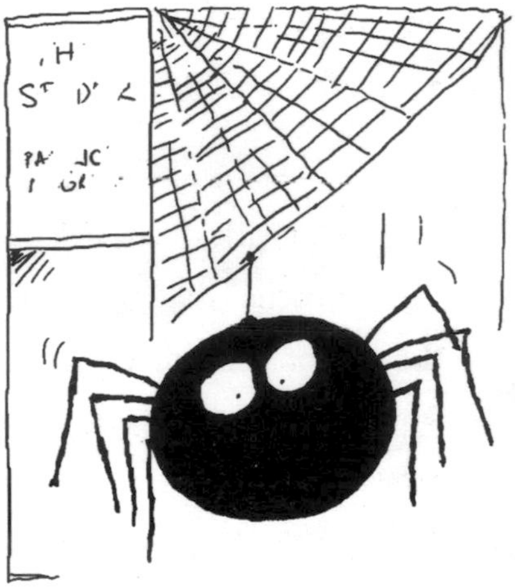

ANSWERS 1. Carson McCullers **2.** Anne Tyler **3.** Johann Zoffany **4.** Edward Rutherfurd **5.** Melvyn Bragg **6.** Glen Baxter **7.** John Irving **8.** Fay Weldon **9.** Julian Barnes **10.** Bernard Cornwell **11.** A Midsummer Night's Dream **12.** Patrick McGrath **13.** Bret Easton Ellis **14.** Helen Dunmore **15.** Robert Coover.

GENERAL KNOWLEDGE

1. Which movement grew from a Bible study group formed by Charles Taze Russell in 1872?
2. What synthetic plastic was created by Leo Baekeland in 1909?

3. What is the name of Bertie Wooster's club in stories by P.G. Wodehouse?
4. Which German Nazi was expelled from Bolivia in 1983 and convicted of crimes against humanity in France in 1987?
5. Which U.S. circus owner coined the phrase "There's a sucker born every minute"?
6. What does NAAFI stand for?
7. On what date was the Nagasaki bomb dropped?
8. Over what distance is The Oaks flat race run?
9. In which London street is the drama school RADA?
10. The Rag was the old nickname of which club in Pall Mall?
11. In which year did Georgia join the U.N.?
12. Which singer was born Vera Margaret Lewis?
13. What type of creature is a junco - a bird or a snake?
14. Which Russian leaders were known as B & K on their 1956 visit to Britain?
15. Who authored the novel *The Napoleon of Notting Hill*?

ANSWERS **1.** Jehovah's Witnesses **2.** Bakelite **3.** The Drones' Club **4.** Klaus Barbie **5.** P.T. Barnum **6.** Navy, Army and Air Force Institutes **7.** August 9, 1945 **8.** 1 and a half miles **9.** Gower Street **10.** Army and Navy Club **11.** 1992 **12.** Vera Lynn **13.** A bird **14.** Bulganin and Khruschev **15.** G.K. Chesterton.

ENTERTAINMENT

1. Who directed the 1998 film *Stepmom*?
2. Who stars as a heart-attack victim in the 1999 film *Heart*?
3. In which country was the film *The Matrix* shot?
4. Which English actor plays a travelling magician in the 1999 film *American Perfekt*?
5. Who directed the 1975 film *Coonskin*?
6. Who plays the title role in the 1959 film *The Mummy*?
7. Who plays the title role in the 1999 film *Captain Jack*?
8. Who plays booker Beverley in television comedy drama *Bob Martin*?
9. In which city is the 1999 film *Titanic Town* set?
10. Who plays Qui-Gon Jinn in the film *The Phantom Menace*?
11. Who plays pianist Cricket in the Bogart/Bacall film *To Have and Have Not*?
12. Who played the villain The Mad Hatter in the 1960s *Batman* television series?
13. The 1973 film *Executive Action* is about whose assassination?
14. Who played *The Elusive Pimpernel* in the 1950 film?
15. Who plays the title role in the 1996 film *Emma*?

ANSWERS 1. Chris Columbus **2.** Christopher Eccleston **3.** Australia **4.** David Thewlis **5.** Ralph Bakshi **6.** Christopher Lee **7.** Bob Hoskins **8.** Tracy-Ann Oberman **9.** Belfast **10.** Liam Neeson **11.** Hoagy Carmichael **12.** David Wayne **13.** John F. Kennedy **14.** David Niven **15.** Gwyneth Paltrow.

SPORT

1. Which athlete married the runner Ann Packer?
2. What is golfer Arnold Palmer's middle name?
3. Which rugby union prop played 55 times for France between 1975-83?
4. In what year was Desert Orchid born?
5. Who beat Tim Henman in the 1998 Wimbledon men's singles tennis semi-final?
6. By what score did Croatia beat Germany in the 1998 World Cup quarter-final?
7. What age was Joe Bugner when he won the WBF world heavyweight title in July, 1998?
8. What was the result of the Third Test between England and South Africa in 1998?
9. From which county cricket club did David Gower retire in 1993?
10. Which horse won the 1992 Grand National?
11. Who won the men's single luge gold at the 1994 Winter Olympics?
12. Which horse won the 1994 Hennessey Gold Cup?
13. By what score did France beat Croatia in their 1998 World Cup semi-final?
14. Which driver won the 1998 British Grand Prix?
15. Which runner took more than a second off the men's 1,500m record in July, 1998?

ANSWERS 1. Robbie Brightwell **2.** Daniel **3.** Robert Paparemborde **4.** 1979 **5.** Pete Sampras **6.** 3-0 **7.** 48 **8.** A draw **9.** Hampshire **10.** Party Politics **11.** Georg Hackl **12.** Jodami **13.** 2-1 **14.** Michael Schumacher **15.** Hicham El Guerrouj.

POP

1. From which African country does the singer Rozalla come?
2. Which former member of Badfinger committed suicide in 1983?
3. Which group had a Top 20 single in 1993 with *You're in a Bad Way*?
4. In which city were the group Balaam and the Angel from?
5. What are rappers Cheryl James & Sandra Denton better known as?
6. What was the debut album of the group Banco De Gaia?
7. Who duetted with Mike Sarne on the 1962 single *Will I What*?
8. Which group's debut L.P. was 1988's *Hope Against Hope*?
9. Which group had a 1997 Top Ten single with *Encore Une Fois*?
10. Who was the singer in the group Bauhaus?
11. Which group had a 1996 Top Ten single with *To Win Just One*?
12. On which studio album by The Beatles does *Norwegian Wood* appear?
13. Which comedian had a 1984 hit with *'Ullo John Got a New Motor*?
14. Which group's debut L.P. in 1990 was *Let Them Eat Bingo*?
15. Which rapper guested on the 1995 single *Hand of the Dead Body* by Scarface?

ANSWERS **1.** Zimbabwe **2.** Tom Evans **3.** St. Etienne **4.** Birmingham **5.** Salt-n-Pepa **6.** Maya **7.** Billie Davis **8.** The Band of Susans **9.** Sash **10.** Peter Murphy **11.** Saw Doctors **12.** Rubber Soul **13.** Alexei Sayle **14.** Beats International **15.** Ice Cube.

SCIENCE

1. In which city was Marie Curie born?
2. What in plant life is a lamina more commonly known as?
3. The Earth is a true sphere. True or false?
4. Who wrote the 1976 book *The Selfish Gene*?
5. Which element's symbol is F?
6. On which Greek island was the reddish-brown clayey earth *terra sigillata* found?
7. What is the SI unit of electrical capacitance?
8. How many chains in a furlong?
9. What in global warming does the abbreviation ODP stand for?
10. What nationality was 18th century scientist Daniel Bernoulli?
11. On the Beaufort scale what is the description of force 3?
12. Of what is cynophobia a fear?
13. During which era was the silurian period of geological time?
14. How many grams of fibre per 100 grams are there in figs?
15. What in acoustics does AM stand for?

ANSWERS 1. Warsaw **2.** The blade of a leaf **3.** False - it is an ellipsoid **4.** Richard Dawkins **5.** Fluorine **6.** Lemnos **7.** Farad **8.** 10 **9.** Ozone depletion potential **10.** Swiss **11.** Gentle breeze **12.** Dogs **13.** Palaeozoic **14.** 19 **15.** Amplitude modulation.

GENERAL KNOWLEDGE

1. In which country is the skiing resort of Gstaad?
2. How long was Brunel's ship the Great Eastern?

3. In which year was the drink Newcastle brown ale first brewed?
4. In November, 2000, how many busking musicians were licensed to play the Paris Metro Underground?
5. In which city is the largest covered square in Europe?
6. Which car manufacturer makes the V70 Cross Country?
7. In which year did the British get control of Florida in exchange for Havana?
8. In which year was the city of Alexandria, Egypt founded?
9. On which British island is Albany prison?
10. What was the name of composer Wolfgang Amadeus Mozart's father?
11. Who is the author of the play *Under the Blue Sky*?
12. Who wrote the novel *Cover Her Face*?
13. Randy Ober broke the world spitting record in 1981. With what distance?
14. How heavy was Robert Earl Hughes when he died in 1958?
15. Hikkaduwa is a beach centre on which island?

ANSWERS 1. Switzerland **2.** 692 feet **3.** 1927 **4.** 350 **5.** London **6.** Volvo **7.** 1763 **8.** 322 B.C. **9.** The Isle of Wight **10.** Leopold **11.** David Eldridge **12.** P.D. James **13.** 44 and a half feet **14.** 1069 lbs **15.** Sri Lanka.

ENTERTAINMENT

1. Who starred as *Elmer Gantry* in the 1960 film?
2. Who plays a lecturer on terrorism in the 1999 film *Arlington Road*?
3. Who directed the 1980 film *The Elephant Man*?
4. Who was a Best Supporting Actor Oscar nominee for the film *Primal Fear*?
5. What is Michael Caine's character name in the film *Little Voice*?
6. Who plays the title role in the 1974 film *Effi Briest*?
7. Who plays Marion Crane in the 1998 film *Psycho*?
8. Who played Jessica Drummond in the 1957 film *Forty Guns*?
9. Brad Dexter appeared in the film *The Magnificent Seven* thanks to the influence of which actor-singer?
10. *Death of a Gunfighter* was the first film directed by which fictitious person?
11. The 1972 film *The Carey Treatment* is based on a novel by which author?
12. Which comic actor wrote under the pseudonyms Jonathan Cobbold and Gerald Wiley?
13. In an unrealised film project who did Alfred Hitchcock cast as Hamlet in a version of Shakespeare's play?
14. In which city is the 1999 film *Venus Beauty* set?
15. The 1956 film *Attack* is a re-enactment of which battle?

ANSWERS 1. Burt Lancaster **2.** Jeff Bridges **3.** David Lynch **4.** Edward Norton **5.** Ray Say **6.** Hanna Schygulla **7.** Anne Heche **8.** Barbara Stanwyck **9.** Frank Sinatra **10.** Alan Smithee **11.** Michael Crichton **12.** Ronnie Barker **13.** Cary Grant **14.** Paris **15.** The Battle of the Bulge.

SPORT

1. Which football team won the 1996/7 European Cup-Winners' Cup?
2. Which team won the 1995/6 Scottish F.A. Cup?
3. "Schuss", a man on skis, was the unofficial mascot of which Winter Olympic Games?
4. Which team knocked Arsenal out of the F.A. Cup in January 1933?
5. In which year was the tennis player Björn Borg born?
6. Who was the French Open men's singles tennis champion in 1963?
7. Which team won the 1970 University Boat Race?
8. Which football team won the 1998/9 League Cup?
9. Who won the Olympic women's 200m in 1992?
10. Who was the 1999 British Open golf champion?
11. Who did West Ham United play in the quarter finals of the 2001 F.A. Cup?
12. Which non-league team knocked Sunderland out of the F.A. Cup in January 1949?
13. Which dog won the 1997 greyhound derby?
14. Which horse won the 1962 Epsom Derby?
15. Where was the boxer Muhammad Ali born?

ANSWERS 1. Barcelona **2.** Rangers **3.** 1968 Winter Olympics at Grenoble **4.** Walsall **5.** 1956 **6.** Roy Emerson **7.** Cambridge **8.** Tottenham Hotspur **9.** Gwen Torrence **10.** Paul Lawrie **11.** Tottenham Hotspur **12.** Yeovil **13.** Some Picture **14.** Larkspur **15.** Louisville, Kentucky.

POP

1. Which group had chart success in 1986 with *Rise* and *Home*?
2. How are Tanya Donelly and Kristin Hersh, formerly of Throwing Muses, related?
3. Which duo charted with 1995's *Independent Love Song*?
4. In which year was Chuck Berry born?
5. Who had a 1995 hit single with *Scatman's World*?
6. From which country do the band Bettie Serveert come?
7. Which group's debut chart single in 1997 was *Love is the Law*?
8. Whose 1986 album was *Atomizer*?
9. Which vocalist had a 1997 Top 20 hit with *Fly Like An Angel*?
10. How did Chris Bell, singer with the group Big Star, die?
11. Which group had a Top Ten single in 1997 with *Help the Aged*?
12. To what did the Australian group The Boys Next Door change their name in 1978?
13. In which year was singer Neil Sedaka born?
14. On which 1966 studio album by The Beatles did *Yellow Submarine* appear?
15. Which duo had a 1961 hit with *Bangers and Mash*?

ANSWERS 1. Public Image Limited **2.** Half-sisters **3.** Scarlet **4.** 1926 **5.** Scatman John **6.** Holland **7.** The Seahorses **8.** Big Black **9.** Seal **10.** In a car accident **11.** Pulp **12.** The Birthday Party **13.** 1939 **14.** Revolver **15.** Peter Sellers and Sophia Loren.

PEOPLE

1. Which famous castaway wrote the 2000 book *Faraway*?
2. Which actor penned the autobiography 'The Measure of the Man'?
3. Film producer Andrew MacDonald is a grandson of which famous producer-director?
4. Actress Jennifer Jason Leigh is the daughter of which actor?
5. In which year was Alfred Hitchcock knighted?
6. Actor Hilton McRae is married to which actress?
7. Nicoletta Braschi is the wife of which Italian actor-director?
8. What was the profession of actress Heather Graham's father?
9. In which year did Humphrey Bogart die?
10. From which university did actress Julianne Moore graduate in 1983?
11. With which avant garde jazz musician did the singer Juliette Greco have a relationship in the early 1950s?
12. Film director Martin Scorsese's editor Thelma Schoonmaker was married to which director?
13. Which rock star wrote the 1999 radio play *Lifehouse*?
14. In which country was actress Thandie Newton born?
15. Which actress is the mother of television show *Castaway 2000*'s Ben Fogle?

ANSWERS 1. Lucy Irvine **2.** Sidney Poitier **3.** Emeric Pressburger **4.** Vic Morrow **5.** 1980 **6.** Lindsay Duncan **7.** Roberto Benigni **8.** FBI agent **9.** 1957 **10.** Boston University **11.** Miles Davis **12.** Michael Powell **13.** Pete Townshend **14.** New Zealand **15.** Julia Foster.

GENERAL KNOWLEDGE

1. In which constellation is the star Bellatrix?
2. What was the country of Lesotho founded as in 1832?
3. Which explorer discovered the St. Lawrence River in Canada?
4. What is the dominant religion of Monaco?
5. Which World War II leader was supposed to have hoarded the 'Treasure of Dongo'?
6. Frederick Whitaker was prime minister of which country from 1882-83?
7. What sort of bird is a whimbrel?
8. Who was first president of independent Algeria?
9. What does the abbreviation ft-lb mean?
10. Mullingar is the county town of which Irish county?
11. What is the dominant religion of Nigeria?
12. In which century did Lady Godiva ride naked through the streets of Coventry?
13. What is the chief export of the island territory of Niue in the South Pacific?
14. Which two designers shared the Designer of the Year award in 1997 at the British Fashion Awards?
15. In which town is the University of Central Lancashire?

ANSWERS **1.** Orion **2.** Basutoland **3.** Jacques Cartier **4.** Roman Catholicism **5.** Mussolini **6.** New Zealand **7.** Curlew **8.** Ahmed Ben Bella **9.** foot-pound **10.** Westmeath **11.** Muslim **12.** 11th **13.** Coconut cream **14.** John Galliano and Alexander McQueen **15.** Preston.

ENTERTAINMENT

1. Who directed the 1996 film *Last Dance*?
2. Which talk-show hostess stars in the 1999 film *Beloved*?
3. Which comedy duo star in the 1950 film *At War With The Army*?
4. Who played *Ellery Queen, Master Detective* in a the 1940 film?
5. Who plays Dr. Evil in the *Austin Powers* film series?
6. Which Irish actor played a one-armed dishwasher in sitcom *Robin's Nest*?
7. Who directed and starred in the film *Schizopolis*?
8. Who directed the 1999 film *Pleasantville*?
9. What are the names of the four main characters in children's television show *The Tweenies*?
10. Who plays Merlin in the 2000 film *Merlin: The Return*?
11. In which year did the television show *Your Show of Shows* premiere in the U.S.?
12. Who are the male and female leads in the 2000 film *The Family Man*?
13. Who plays Jack Carter in the 1970 film *Get Carter*?
14. Which musician stars in the 1999 film *Parting Shots*?
15. Who plays a reporter who switches identities in Antonioni's film *The Passenger*?

ANSWERS 1. Bruce Beresford **2.** Oprah Winfrey **3.** Dean Martin & Jerry Lewis **4.** Ralph Bellamy **5.** Mike Myers **6.** David Kelly **7.** Steven Soderbergh **8.** Gary Ross **9.** Milo, Jake, Fizz, and Bella **10.** Rik Mayall **11.** 1950 **12.** Nicolas Cage and Téa Leoni **13.** Michael Caine **14.** Chris Rea **15.** Jack Nicholson.

SPORT

1. At which sport did Sadaharu Oh become famous?
2. Who was National Hunt champion jockey from 1949-52?
3. At which circuit was Niki Lauda badly burned in 1976?
4. For which Italian football team did Denis Law play?
5. In which county was England Test cricketer John Edrich born?

6. At what age did Duncan Edwards die following the Munich air disaster in 1958?
7. Who was president of the I.O.C. from 1946-52?
8. Who was the captain of the French rugby union side that toured South Africa in 1971?
9. Which U.S. Olympic 110m hurdles champion competed at the 1980 Winter Olympics in the bobsled event?
10. What nationality was world judo champion Brigitte Deydier?
11. Which Poland and Manchester City footballer died in a road accident in 1989?
12. At what age did Gareth Edwards win his first rugby union cap for Wales?
13. At which rugby league club did Joseph Egan become player-coach in 1950?
14. In which year did Joe DiMaggio marry Marilyn Monroe?
15. Who captained France's rugby union team on their 1984 tour of New Zealand?

ANSWERS **1.** Baseball **2.** Tim Molony **3.** Nürburgring **4.** Torino **5.** Norfolk **6.** 21 **7.** Sigfrid Edstrom **8.** Benoit Dauga **9.** Willie Davenport **10.** French **11.** Kazimierz Deyna **12.** 19 **13.** Leigh **14.** 1954 **15.** Philippe Dintrans.

POP

1. Which pop group comprised Andy Stephenson, Phil Rogers, Stephen Cousins and Motch Bondouche?
2. Which rock star's home in the 1960s was Cotchford Farm?
3. U-God and Ghostface Killah are members of which rap group?
4. In which year did the rock critic Lester Bangs die?
5. Which group's albums include *Sports* and *Fore!*?
6. Which member of the rock group Queen recorded the record album *Another World*?
7. Which group recorded the album *Tied and Tangled*?
8. Which song by the group the Jackson Five was covered by the group Cleopatra on the album *Comin' Atcha'*?
9. Which group recorded the album *My Obsession with Elizabeth Montgomery*?
10. Which group's albums include the 1998 collection *Kettle Whistle*?
11. Which alternative country group comprise husband and wife Brett and Rennie Sparks?
12. In which year did musician Bill Wyman leave the Rolling Stones?
13. Russel Jones is the real name of which rap star?
14. Which jazz musician won the 1996 Jazzpar prize?
15. Jean-Jacques Burnel is the bass player with which punk band?

ANSWERS **1.** Tribe of Toffs **2.** Brian Jones of the Rolling Stones **3.** Wu Tang Clan **4.** 1982 **5.** Huey Lewis and the News **6.** Brian May **7.** Glitterbox **8.** I Want You Back **9.** Daytona **10.** Jane's Addiction **11.** The Handsome Family **12.** 1993 **13.** Ol' Dirty Bastard **14.** Django Bates **15.** The Stranglers.

ART AND LITERATURE

1. Who wrote the novel *Whit*?
2. Who wrote the novel *Saint Maybe*?
3. In which Shakespeare play does the character Portia appear?
4. Michael Henchard and Donald Farfrae are characters in which novel?
5. Who wrote the novel *The House of Sleep*?
6. Who wrote the 1997 novel *Night Train*?
7. Who wrote the novel *The Wilt Alternative*?
8. Who draws the comic strip *Calvin and Hobbes*?
9. Who wrote the short story *The Langoliers*?
10. Who wrote the novel *Gumshoe*?
11. Who won the 1999 Turner Prize?
12. Which animal painter's works include *Euston* and *Whistlejacket*?
13. Who wrote the novel *The Bell Jar*?
14. Who wrote the novel *Cocaine Nights*?
15. Who wrote the novel *The Quiller Memorandum*?

ANSWERS 1. Iain Banks **2.** Anne Tyler **3.** The Merchant of Venice **4.** The Mayor of Casterbridge **5.** Jonathan Coe **6.** Martin Amis **7.** Tom Sharpe **8.** Bill Watterson **9.** Stephen King **10.** Neville Smith **11.** Steve McQueen **12.** George Stubbs **13.** Sylvia Plath **14.** J.G. Ballard **15.** Adam Hall

GENERAL KNOWLEDGE

1. Who wrote the novel *Earthly Powers*?
2. Which comedian directed and starred in the 1961 film *The Errand Boy*?
3. Which car manufacturer makes the RX300?
4. Actor Arnold Schwarzenegger holds dual nationality with which two countries?
5. Which publisher authored the book *Singular Encounters*, a collection of interviews with the famous?
6. On which island group was the beachwear section of the 2000 Miss World contest held?
7. In which country is the skiing resort of Sunshine?
8. Which capital city was formerly known as Bytown?
9. In which year did Garry Kasparov form the Professional Chess Association?
10. Who replaced Florence Ballard in the vocal group The Supremes?
11. In which year was the animator Joseph Barbera born?
12. Which Hollywood actor's childhood nickname was 'Bobby Milk'?
13. Which thriller writer authored the short stories *Finger Man* and *Pearls Are A Nuisance*?
14. Who plays Clint Eastwood's female partner in the 1976 film *The Enforcer*?
15. In which year did Sir Walter Raleigh die?

ANSWERS **1.** Anthony Burgess **2.** Jerry Lewis **3.** Lexus **4.** U.S.A. and Austria **5.** Naim Attallah **6.** The Maldives **7.** Canada **8.** Ottawa **9.** 1993 **10.** Cindy Birdsong **11.** 1911 **12.** Robert De Niro **13.** Raymond Chandler **14.** Tyne Daly **15.** 1618.

ENTERTAINMENT

1. Which operatic movie star was born Alfred Arnold Cocozza in 1921?
2. In which town was the actor Charles Laughton born?
3. Who played the wife of *Houdini* in the 1953 film?
4. December 10th, 1938, was the first day of shooting of which epic film?
5. Who directed the 1988 film *Rain Man*?
6. Who did Bob Hoskins play in the 1991 film *Hook*?
7. Who played *The Scarlet Pimpernel* in the 1934 film?
8. Who played the lead in the 1980 film *Sir Henry at Rawlinson End*?
9. Which actor was born Roy Harold Scherer Jr.?
10. In which city was Sophia Loren born?
11. During the making of which film did Bela Lugosi die?
12. What object does the camera follow in the title sequence of the film *Forrest Gump*?
13. Who played Mr. Pink in the film *Reservoir Dogs*?
14. What does Sidney Poitier build for a group of nuns in the film *Lilies of the Field*?
15. Who wrote the comedy drama *A Bit of a Do*?

ANSWERS **1.** Mario Lanza **2.** Scarborough **3.** Janet Leigh **4.** Gone With the Wind **5.** Barry Levinson **6.** Smee **7.** Leslie Howard **8.** Trevor Howard **9.** Rock Hudson **10.** Rome **11.** Plan 9 from Outer Space **12.** A feather **13.** Steve Buscemi **14.** A chapel **15.** David Nobbs.

SPORT

1. Which team knocked Arsenal out of the F.A. Cup in January 1992?
2. How many times have Third Lanark been Scottish League champions?
3. Who won the Olympic men's 100m in 1948?
4. Who won the Olympic women's 800m in 1984?
5. Who was the 1999 world men's indoor bowls champion?
6. Which animal was the official mascot of the 1976 Summer Olympics at Montreal?
7. Who did Manchester United beat in the quarter-finals of the 1998/9 F.A. Cup?
8. Which team knocked Burnley out of the F.A. Cup in February 1975?
9. Which team won the 1997 world series in baseball?
10. Which football team won the 1997/8 European Champions Cup?
11. Who was the 1990 rugby world player of the year?
12. Who was the French Open men's singles tennis champion in 1981?
13. Which horse won the 1950 Grand National?
14. Millie was one of the three official mascots of the 2000 Summer Olympics at Sydney. What type of animal was it?
15. Who played his 700th game for Arsenal on March 10th, 1992?

ANSWERS 1. Wrexham **2.** Once **3.** Harrison Dillard **4.** Doina Melinte **5.** Alex Marshall **6.** Amik the Beaver **7.** Chelsea **8.** Wimbledon **9.** Florida Marlins **10.** Real Madrid **11.** Brian Moore **12.** Björn Borg **13.** Freebooter **14.** Echidna **15.** David O'Leary.

POP

1. Which act had a 1995 Top Five hit with *The Bomb! (These Sounds Fall into My Mind)*?
2. Which band recorded the 1975 album *The Snow Goose*, based on a story by Paul Gallico?
3. Which group recorded the album *Straightaways*?
4. What was Part Four of *The Mole Trilogy* by the Residents?
5. Which band recorded the 1978 album *Candy-O*?
6. Which group had a 1995 No. 1 single with a re-mix of their 1994 hit *Dreamer*?
7. In which year did the New York Dolls release their debut L.P.?
8. Which guitarist recorded the 1989 album *Workbook*?
9. Which Australian singer wrote the novel *And the Ass Saw the Angel*?
10. Which group recorded the album *Electribal Memories*?
11. Tom Rowlands and Ed Simmons make up which electronic duo?
12. Which group's last Top Ten hit, in 1986, was *New Beginning (Mamba Seyra)*?
13. Henry Priestman was the only non-brother in which Liverpool-based 1980s group?
14. Which male singer had a 1997 Top Ten hit with *Phenomenon*?
15. Who recorded the album *Hymns to the Silence*?

ANSWERS **1.** Bucketheads **2.** Camel **3.** Son Volt **4.** The Big Bubble **5.** Cars **6.** Livin' Joy **7.** 1973 **8.** Bob Mould **9.** Nick Cave **10.** Electribe 101 **11.** The Chemical Brothers **12.** Bucks Fizz **13.** The Christians **14.** L.L. Cool J **15.** Van Morrison.

GEOGRAPHY

1. In which country is the World Heritage site of the Haghpat Monastery?
2. In which South American country is the port of Paysandu?
3. In which African country are the towns of Oyem and Franceville?
4. Lanzarote and Hierro are part of which Spanish island group?
5. Which is larger, the Baltic Sea or the Bering Sea?
6. In which country is the Wetterhorn mountain?
7. What is the approximate area in square miles of County Westmeath in the Republic of Ireland?
8. In which African country are the towns of Dese and Dire Dawa?
9. Bryher and Tresco are part of which U.K. island group?
10. In which country is the volcano Unzen?
11. In which country is the River Yesil Irmak?
12. Copenhagen is the chief town on which island?
13. How many minutes south of the equator is the Brazilian town of Uaupes?
14. What was the original name of the Indian hill town of Darjeeling?
15. In which country is the upland known as The Deccan?

ANSWERS **1.** Armenia **2.** Uruguay **3.** Gabon **4.** Canary Islands **5.** Bering Sea **6.** Switzerland **7.** 681 **8.** Ethiopia **9.** Scilly Isles **10.** Japan **11.** Turkey **12.** Zealand **13.** 8 **14.** Darling **15.** India.

GENERAL KNOWLEDGE

1. Which group of radicals were led by John Lilburne, John Wildman and William Walwyn?
2. What was the name of the German Republic that existed from 1919 to Hitler's accession in 1933?
3. What Soviet secret police agency replaced the former OGPU in 1934?
4. What sort of bird is a noddy?
5. In which poem by Edward Lear does the "great Gromboolian plain" appear?
6. Who was elected Conservative M.P. for Worthing West in 1997?
7. In which year did the cartoonist Michael Cummings die?
8. What did members of the South Pacific Commission agree to rename their organization in 1997?
9. Which actress was born Ruby Stevens?
10. How many strokes under par for a hole of golf is an albatross?
11. Which Scottish poet famously penned *The Tay Bridge Disaster*?
12. In which year was Sir Roger Casement executed for treason?
13. Which general's ghost haunts *Macbeth* in Shakespeare's play?
14. In which year was Siberian mystic Rasputin murdered?
15. What is former U.S. president Ronald Reagan's middle name?

ANSWERS 1. The Levellers **2.** Weimar Republic **3.** NKVD **4.** Tern **5.** The Dong with a Luminous Nose **6.** Peter Bottomley **7.** 1997 **8.** The Pacific Community **9.** Barbara Stanwyck **10.** Three **11.** William McGonagall **12.** 1916 **13.** Banquo **14.** 1916 **15.** Wilson.

ENTERTAINMENT

1. Who directed the 1999 film *Human Traffic*?
2. Who starred in the title role of the 1993 film *Son of the Pink Panther*?
3. Who plays a sports master in Ken Loach's film *Kes*?
4. Which actor made his debut as director with the 1998 film *Very Bad Things*?
5. Which actress in 1965 became the first woman to preside over the Cannes Film Fesival jury?
6. In which country is the 1954 film *Elephant Walk* set?
7. Which French actress played Cathy in the 1992 film *Wuthering Heights*?
8. Who directed Jane Horrocks in the original stage production of the play *Little Voice*?
9. Which theatre director's former wives include actress Leslie Caron and opera singer Maria Ewing?

10. Which playwright-actor plays a police sergeant in the film *A Clockwork Orange*?
11. What was the budget on the 1979 film *The Evil Dead*?
12. Which film won all five main Oscar awards in 1991?
13. *Camden Town Boy* was the original title of which comedy film?
14. Which actor won a Tony nomination in 2000 for his role as Salieri in a production of *Amadeus*?
15. Who plays Ray Winstone's wife in the film *The War Zone*?

ANSWERS 1. Justin Kerrigan **2.** Roberto Benigni **3.** Brian Glover **4.** Peter Berg **5.** Olivia de Havilland **6.** Ceylon **7.** Juliette Binoche **8.** Sam Mendes **9.** Peter Hall **10.** Steven Berkoff **11.** $350,000 **12.** The Silence of the Lambs **13.** The Tall Guy **14.** David Suchet **15.** Tilda Swinton.

SPORT

1. Which male athlete won the 1956 & '60 Olympic 400m hurdles title?
2. For which international side did New Zealand-born rugby union player Greg Davis play from 1963?
3. What nationality was Olympic swimming champion Victor Davis, who died in 1989?
4. Which Welsh rugby union player was appointed captain of the Lions tour of New Zealand in 1971?
5. Which world heavyweight boxing champion started his career as 'Kid Blackie'?
6. Which New Zealand batsman was Leicestershire cricket captain from 1936-8?
7. For which baseball team did Larry Doby play the majority of his career?
8. At what Olympic sport did tennis champion Lottie Dod win a medal in 1908?
9. What was the nickname of the French rugby union player Amedee Domenech?
10. Who won the 1947 World Snooker Championship?
11. Who did Roberto Duran defeat to take the world lightweight boxing title in 1972?
12. What was the nickname of Australian Rules football star Jack Dyer?
13. What nationality was the cyclist Oscar Egg?
14. At what sport was Ilona Elek an Olympic champion?
15. Which Australian rugby union player captained the side on the 1982 tour of New Zealand?

ANSWERS 1. Glenn Davis **2.** Australia **3.** Canadian **4.** John Dawes **5.** Jack Dempsey **6.** Stewart Dempster **7.** Cleveland Indians **8.** Archery **9.** The Duke **10.** Walter Donaldson **11.** Ken Buchanan **12.** Captain Blood **13.** Swiss **14.** Fencing **15.** Mark Ella.

POP

1. Which music group comprises Warren Ellis, Mick Turner and Jim White?
2. Which country singer's debut record album was *The Woman In Me*?
3. Which rapper recorded the 1998 album *My Way*?
4. On which studio album by the pop group Air are the tracks *Talisman* and *Kelly Watch the Stars*?
5. Which group's albums include *Decksanddrumsandrockandroll*?
6. Which pop group's debut album was called *Sixteen Stone*?
7. From which island are the pop group Bellatrix?
8. Which punk star offered to marry singer Chrissie Hynde when she encountered visa trouble in 1977?
9. In which year did the Elvis television special *Aloha From Hawaii* first air?
10. Which singer's No. 1 singles include *Life Is A Rollercoaster*?
11. Which vocal group's albums include 1999's *Fanmail*?
12. Which Irish singer won the 1970 Eurovision Song Contest?
13. Which San Francisco rock group's albums include *Countdown to Extinction* and *Youthanasia?*
14. Which album was awarded the initial Mercury Music Prize in 1992?
15. Who did Bill Wyman replace in the group the Rolling Stones?

ANSWERS 1. Dirty Three **2.** Shania Twain **3.** Usher **4.** Moon Safari **5.** Propellerheads **6.** Bush **7.** Iceland **8.** Sid Vicious **9.** 1973 **10.** Ronan Keating **11.** TLC **12.** Dana **13.** Megadeath **14.** *Screamadelica* by Primal Scream **15.** Dick Taylor.

HISTORY

1. The Evian Accords of the early 1960s resulted in independence for which country?
2. Who did vice-president Aaron Burr kill in a duel in 1804?
3. Who was American secretary of state from 1989-92?
4. In which year did Henry II invade Ireland and claim sovereignty?
5. In which year did Jane Seymour, Queen of England die?
6. Who became president of the Czech Republic in 1993?
7. In which city was Israeli statesman Abba Eban born?
8. Which king of Scotland died at the Battle of Flodden Field?
9. In which year was the Scottish hero William Wallace defeated by Edward I?
10. Who commanded the Russian force at the Battle of Balaclava?
11. In which year did the War of the Roses begin?
12. In which year did Elizabeth I die?
13. In which year did Richard I of England capture Cyprus?
14. Who was vice-president of the U.S. under Andrew Jackson from 1837-41?
15. The Abbé de Saint-Cyran was a founder of which reform movement in the Roman Catholic Church?

ANSWERS 1. Algeria **2.** Alexander Hamilton **3.** James Addison Baker III **4.** 1171 **5.** 1537 **6.** Vaclav Havel **7.** Cape Town **8.** James IV **9.** 1298 **10.** General Liprandi **11.** 1455 **12.** 1603 **13.** 1191 **14.** Martin van Buren **15.** Jansenism.

GENERAL KNOWLEDGE

1. In which African country are the towns of Mbeya and Tabora?
2. Who wrote the novel *Spanking the Maid*?
3. Who composed *Blooms of Dublin*, a musical version of James Joyce's book *Ulysses*?
4. What date features on Brunel's Royal Albert bridge at Saltash?
5. What price did the world's most expensive truffle fetch at auction in November, 2000?
6. Which actor directed and starred in 1978 film *The End*?
7. Who wrote the 2000 novel *Bookends*?
8. In which year did Murray Walker first commentate on motor sport?
9. According to the Prisons Handbook 2001, how many inmates has Birmingham prison?
10. Operation Sun Apple was the codename for the FBI's strike against which organization?
11. Which country won the 1970 Miss World contest?
12. What was the only state capital in the Confederacy not to be captured by Union troops in the U.S. Civil War?
13. In which year did the Reading Room in the British Museum originally open?
14. Which singer recorded the 1971 album *Tupelo Honey*?
15. In which European country are the towns of Sumy and Krivoy Rog?

ANSWERS **1.** Tanzania **2.** Robert Coover **3.** Anthony Burgess **4.** 1859 **5.** £4,635 **6.** Burt Reynolds **7.** Jane Green **8.** 1949 **9.** 1083 **10.** The Mafia **11.** Grenada **12.** Tallahassee **13.** 1857 **14.** Van Morrison **15.** Ukraine.

ENTERTAINMENT

1. Who played the author George Sand in the 1945 film *A Song to Remember*?
2. Who plays the private detective Argobast in the 1998 film *Psycho*?
3. Which Italian directed and starred in the films *Dear Diary* and *Aprile*?
4. Who plays the Lord of Summerisle in the 1973 film *The Wicker Man*?
5. Which actress starred in and helped produce the 1999 film *The Clandestine Marriage*?
6. What was the U.S. title of the 1946 film *A Matter of Life and Death*?
7. The 1968 film *Spirits of the Dead* is based on short stories by which author?
8. Who did Ringo Starr play in the 1975 film *Lisztomania*?
9. In which 1982 film did Madhur Jaffrey and Greta Scacchi appear?
10. What job does Christopher Eccleston do in the 1999 film *A Price Above Rubies*?
11. Who directed the 1977 film *The Chess Players*?
12. What is the name of the dog in the children's television show *The Tweenies*?
13. Who played the lead in the 1967 film *A Challenge For Robin Hood*?
14. Who played the villain The Minstrel in the 1960's *Batman* television series?
15. Who plays money lender Hugh Fennyman in the film *Shakespeare in Love*?

ANSWERS 1. Merle Oberon **2.** William H. Macy **3.** Nanni Moretti **4.** Christopher Lee **5.** Joan Collins **6.** Stairway to Heaven **7.** Edgar Allan Poe **8.** The Pope **9.** Heat and Dust **10.** A jeweller **11.** Satyajit Ray **12.** Doodles **13.** Barrie Ingham **14.** Van Johnson **15.** Tom Wilkinson.

SPORT

1. With which American football team did Carl Eller play his last two pro-seasons?
2. What time did Herb Elliott run in his 1960 Olympic 1500m win?
3. Paul Elvstrom won individual medals in the four Olympics from 1948-60. At what sport?
4. For which rugby league team did Keith Elwell play 239 consecutive games as hooker from 1977-82?
5. Who was Australian men's singles tennis champion from 1963-7?
6. Which decathlete did Olympic swimming champion Kornelia Ender marry following the collapse of her marriage to swimmer Roland Matthes?
7. Which sportswoman married Phil Christensen in 1990?
8. In what sport is the TEL machine used?
9. Who was the first black African to win an Olympic gold medal?
10. Who won the 1993 London men's marathon?
11. In which English county was Stanley Matthews born?
12. Where were the 1972 Winter Olympics held?
13. Which boxer was nicknamed 'the Manassa Mauler'?
14. Which team won the World Cup in snooker in 1979 & '80?
15. What was the nickname of boxer Willie Pep?

ANSWERS 1. Seattle Seahawks **2.** 3:35.6 **3.** Yachting **4.** Widnes **5.** Roy Emerson **6.** Steffen Grummt **7.** Jayne Torvill **8.** Tennis **9.** Abebe Bikila **10.** Eamonn Martin **11.** Staffordshire **12.** Sapporo, Japan **13.** Jack Dempsey **14.** Wales **15.** Will o' the Wisp.

POP

1. Baker, Clapton and Bruce - which band?
2. Which Sheffield gas fitter recorded the 1970 live album *Mad Dogs and Englishmen*?
3. With which 1970s pop band did Paul Avron Jeffreys, a victim of the Lockerbie air disaster, achieve fame?
4. Jennifer Warnes's 1987 album *Famous Blue Raincoat* was a collection of covers of which Canadian poet and songwriter's works?
5. Jimmy Somerville and Richard Coles - which duo?
6. Which soul singer was shot dead in Los Angeles in December 1964?
7. What is singer Alice Cooper's real name?
8. Who recorded the 1991 album *Peggy Suicide*?
9. Dolores O'Riordan is the lead singer with which band?
10. Which Missouri-born singer's albums include 1993's *Tuesday Night Music Club*?
11. Smith, Tolhurst, Dempset - which punk band?
12. Which band did Eddie Jobson leave when he joined Roxy Music?
13. Who is the 'King of the Surf Guitar'?
14. In which city was Terence Trent D'Arby born?
15. Who was the lead singer in the 1980s group Dead or Alive?

ANSWERS **1.** Cream **2.** Joe Cocker **3.** Cockney Rebel **4.** Leonard Cohen **5.** The Communards **6.** Sam Cooke **7.** Vincent Furnier **8.** Julian Cope **9.** The Cranberries **10.** Sheryl Crow **11.** The Cure **12.** Curved Air **13.** Dick Dale **14.** New York **15.** Peter Burns.

WORDS

1. What in New Zealand is a kumera?
2. Why might you cook using 'garam masala'?
3. What is the name of the mass of cartilage beneath the tongue in a dog?
4. What is a hornbeam - a bird or a tree?
5. What in printing does the abbreviation oct. mean?
6. The pub sign 'Goat and Compasses' is a corruption of what phrase?
7. What would you do with a 'lyra viol'?
8. Which saint is sometimes known as the Bishop of Hippo?
9. What is geoponics?
10. How many sides does an octagon have?
11. What sort of creature is a godwit?
12. What in the textile industry is a swatch?
13. What were fuggers?
14. What is the Latin word for vinegar?
15. What creature is known in Scottish dialect as clipshears?

ANSWERS 1. A sweet potato **2.** It is a mixture of spices **3.** Lytta **4.** A tree **5.** Octavo **6.** God en-compasses (us) **7.** Play it - it is a musical instrument **8.** St. Augustine **9.** The science of agriculture **10.** Eight **11.** A bird **12.** A sample of cloth, or book containing same **13.** German merchants **14.** Acetum **15.** Earwig.

GENERAL KNOWLEDGE

1. How old was the chess player Garry Kasparov when he became the world chess champion in 1985?
2. What was the surname at birth of film mogul Sam Goldwyn?
3. Who wrote the novel *Out of This World*?
4. Which actress directed, wrote, and starred in the 1991 film *The End of Innocence*?
5. In which European country are the towns of Oradea and Cluj-Napoca?
6. Which country did Irina Ovtchinnikova represent in the 2000 Miss World contest?
7. Who wrote the novel *Last Orders*?
8. Which of the Mitford sisters married Oswald Mosley in 1936?
9. Execution equipment manufacturer Fred A. Leuchter Jr. is known as, and was the subject of, which 1999 film?
10. Which film director wrote the 1991 novel *Los Gusanos*?
11. Where in New Zealand is the city of Whangarei - North Island or South Island?
12. In which year did the stunt man Evel Knievel attempt to jump over 13 double decker buses in England?
13. *Uppercuts and Dazes* is the autobiography of which television sports commentator?
14. Derry's Cross and the Barbican are locations in which Devon city?
15. In which year was the murderer John Wayne Gacy executed?

ANSWERS 1. 22 **2.** Goldfish **3.** Graham Swift **4.** Dyan Cannon **5.** Romania **6.** Estonia **7.** Graham Swift **8.** Diana **9.** Mr. Death **10.** John Sayles **11.** North Island **12.** 1975 **13.** Reg Gutteridge **14.** Plymouth **15.** 1994.

ENTERTAINMENT

1. The film *Heartburn* is about the break-up of which film director's marriage?
2. Which actor was originally offered the part of the photographer in the film *Blow-Up*?
3. What is the film actress Diane Keaton's real name?
4. What is the name of film director John Boorman's son who appears in the film *The Emerald Forest*?
5. What is Ripley's forename in the 1979 film *Alien*?
6. Who played the title role in the 1938 film *The Great Mr. Handel*?
7. Who plays Alvin Straight's brother Lyle in the 1999 film *The Straight Story*?
8. What is Kathleen Turner's character name in the 1981 film *Body Heat*?
9. What is John Cusack's character name in the film *Being John Malkovich*?
10. Which film won all five main Oscar awards in 1975?
11. On the set of which film did Kate Winslet meet husband Jim Threapleton?
12. Who scored Barry Levinson's 1990 film *Avalon*?
13. Who directed the black comedy film *The Exterminating Angel*?
14. Under what name is Joseph Saddler better known in the music business?
15. Which actress was known in the early 1970s as 'Hanoi Jane'?

ANSWERS 1. Nora Ephron **2.** Terence Stamp **3.** Diane Hall **4.** Charley **5.** Ellen **6.** Wilfred Lawson **7.** Harry Dean Stanton **8.** Matty Walker **9.** Craig Schwartz **10.** One Flew Over the Cuckoos Nest **11.** Hideous Kinky **12.** Randy Newman **13.** Luis Buñuel **14.** Grandmaster Flash **15.** Jane Fonda.

SPORT

1. For which country does Jonty Rhodes play cricket?
2. Which team won the 1994 Winter Olympics men's ice hockey gold?
3. Who won the 1994 Andalucian Open in golf?
4. At what age did Judit Polgar become a chess grandmaster?
5. By how many runs did England beat South Africa in the Fifth Test in 1998?
6. Who scored the only goal in Chelsea's 1998 Super Cup victory over Real Madrid?
7. Who won the 1998 Belgian Grand Prix in Formula 1?
8. By what score did Sweden beat England in their European Championship qualifier in September 1998?
9. Where did Wales play their 'home' European Championship qualifier against Italy in September, 1998?
10. Who resigned as the German football coach in 1998?
11. What nationality is tennis player Patrick Rafter?
12. Which teams competed in the 1994 Italian Cup Final in football?
13. Who won the men's Giant Slalom Alpine skiing title at the 1994 Olympics?
14. In which year was FIFA founded?
15. What nationality is the golfer David Graham?

ANSWERS **1.** South Africa **2.** Sweden **3.** Carl Mason **4.** 15 **5.** 23 **6.** Gustavo Poyet **7.** Damon Hill **8.** 2-1 **9.** Anfield **10.** Bertie Vogts **11.** Australian **12.** Sampdoria and Ancona **13.** Markus Wasmeier **14.** 1904 **15.** Australian.

POP

1. Evans, Simper, Lord, Blackmore and Paice - which band?
2. With which band does Rick Allen drum?
3. Fletcher, Gahan, Gore and Clarke - which 1980s band?
4. Which American punk band included the Casale and Mothersbaugh brothers?
5. Which blues artist's real name is Ellas McDaniel?
6. Which band's albums include *Love Over Gold* and *Communique*?
7. What name does Neil Hannon record under?
8. Which member of the group Dr. Feelgood died in 1994?
9. What is the singer Malcolm Rebennack better known as?
10. In which city was Thomas Dolby born?
11. Which Scottish singer's songs include *Mellow Yellow* and *Sunshine Superman*?
12. Jim Morrison was lead singer with which 1960s band?
13. *Thank You* was a 1995 covers album by which band?
14. Elston Gunn was an early stage name of which singer?
15. Bernie Leadon, Glenn Frey, Don Henley and Randy Meisner comprised which band?

ANSWERS **1.** Deep Purple **2.** Def Leppard **3.** Depeche Mode **4.** Devo **5.** Bo Diddley **6.** Dire Straits **7.** The Divine Comedy **8.** Lee Brilleaux **9.** Dr. John **10.** Cairo **11.** Donovan **12.** The Doors **13.** Duran Duran **14.** Bob Dylan **15.** The Eagles.

SCIENCE

1. What nationality was the physicist Giovanni Venturi?
2. How many vertices has a regular dodecahedron?
3. Why is it wrong to call a tsunami a tidal wave?
4. What do the initials CFC stand for with regard to greenhouse gases?
5. What is the name given to the branch of biology concerned with the classification of organisms?
6. Which is larger in area - the Mediterranean Sea or the Caribbean Sea?
7. What nationality was Jules Bordet, winner of the 1919 Nobel prize for medicine?
8. In which city was the 1992 UNCED conference held, that resulted in Agenda 21?
9. How many °C is 100°F?
10. What element composes approximately 28.5% of the Earth?
11. In which year did the inventor Alexander Graham Bell die?
12. Which English chemist wrote 1871's *Select Methods of Chemical Analysis*?
13. Which fruit's scientific name is *Ananas comosus*?
14. What type of rock is shale - igneous, metamorphic, or sedimentary?
15. Which country has the longest coastline?

ANSWERS 1. Italian **2.** 20 **3.** They aren't caused by tides but by subterranean earthquake, volcanic activity or subsidence **4.** Chlorofluorocarbon **5.** Taxonomy **6.** Caribbean **7.** Belgian **8.** Rio de Janeiro **9.** 38° **10.** Oxygen **11.** 1922 **12.** William Crookes **13.** Pineapple **14.** Sedimentary **15.** Canada.

GENERAL KNOWLEDGE

1. *When the Snow Melts* is the autobiography of which film producer?
2. In which country is the Karoo National Park?
3. Who wrote Nat King Cole's million seller *Nature Boy*?
4. Who wrote the 1985 short story collection *Black Venus*?
5. Who was the Miss England contestant in the 2000 Miss World contest?
6. Actor Jack Nicholson's contract stipluates that he won't work when his favourite basketball team is playing. Who are they?
7. Mob and troop are collective nouns for which Australian animal?
8. Who is to play Harry Potter in a 2001 film based on the works by J.K. Rowling?
9. In which African country are the towns of Kita and Mopti?
10. Which country won the 1999 Miss World contest?
11. In which year was the British artist Stephen Buckley born?
12. 1999 animated film The Iron Giant is based on a poem by which writer?
13. By what name did the artist Balthasar Klossowski de Rola become famous?
14. Which conductor married Elena Bashkirova in 1988?
15. Who played the male lead of a fashion photographer in the 1957 film *Funny Face*?

ANSWERS **1.** Cubby Broccoli **2.** South Africa **3.** Eden Ahbez **4.** Angela Carter **5.** Michelle Walker **6.** The L.A. Lakers **7.** Kangaroo **8.** Daniel Radcliffe **9.** Mali **10.** India **11.** 1944 **12.** Ted Hughes **13.** Balthus **14.** Daniel Barenboim **15.** Fred Astaire.

ENTERTAINMENT

1. Who plays D'Artagnan in the 1994 film *D'Artagnan's Daughter*?
2. In which opera is Marenka the central character?
3. Which mother and daughter were nominated for Tony Awards in 2000?
4. The 1999 film *Side Streets* is set in which city in the U.S.A.?
5. Who played composer Richard Wagner in the 1975 film *Lisztomania*?
6. How many times was Alfred Hitchcock nominated for an Oscar as Best Director?
7. Which author does Juliette Binoche play in the film *Les Enfants Du Siècle*?
8. Which recent Golden Globe winner read history at Harvard and speaks fluent Japanese?
9. What age was film director Rainer Werner Fassbinder when he died?
10. What was the first film seen by movie director Paul Schrader, at the age of 17?
11. In which country was actress Kathleen Robertson of the television show *Beverly Hills 90210* born?
12. What is the home town of film director Terrence Malick?
13. Derek Vinyard is the central character in which 1999 film?
14. How old was George Burns when he won his Best Supporting Actor Oscar for *The Sunshine Boys*?
15. Who played the villain The Archer in the 1960's *Batman* television series?

ANSWERS **1.** Philippe Noiret **2.** *The Bartered Bride* by Smetana **3.** Rosemary Harris and Jennifer Ehle **4.** New York **5.** Paul Nicholas **6.** Five **7.** George Sand **8.** Edward Norton **9.** 37 **10.** Anatomy of a Murder **11.** Canada **12.** Austin, Texas **13.** American History X **14.** 80 **15.** Art Carney.

SPORT

1. Who played in goal for Newcastle United in the 1999 F.A. Cup Final?
2. By how many runs did South Africa beat England in their 1999 World Cup Group A cricket match?
3. By how many wickets did Sri Lanka beat Zimbabwe in their 1999 World Cup Group A cricket match?
4. Who won the 1994 Tenerife Open golf title?
5. Who won the 1994 Benson and Hedges Masters snooker title?
6. In which city was golfer Fred Couples born?
7. Who won the men's long jump at the 1964 Olympics?
8. Who is the manager of Liverpool F.C.?
9. Against who, in 1998, was Chris Eubank stopped for the first time in his career?
10. Who lost in a play-off in the 1998 British Open golf tournament?
11. In what position did Justin Rose finish in the 1998 British Open golf tournament?
12. Which horse won the 1998 King George VI and Queen Elizabeth Stakes?
13. Which team bought Ruel Fox from Norwich City?
14. Who was the 1992 Olympic welterweight boxing title winner?
15. In which city was Monica Seles stabbed in 1993?

ANSWERS 1. Steve Harper **2.** 122 runs **3.** Four wickets **4.** David Gilford **5.** Alan McManus **6.** Seattle **7.** Lynn Davies **8.** Gerard Houllier **9.** Carl Thompson **10.** Brian Watts **11.** Equal fourth **12.** Swain **13.** Newcastle United **14.** Michael Carruth **15.** Hamburg.

POP

1. Which pop singer had No. 1 singles in 1996 with *Flava* and *I Feel You*?
2. Which rapper recorded the 1993 album *Black Reign*?
3. Which group released the live album *Paris Au Printemps* in 1980?
4. Which major label signed Prince in 1978?
5. Who was the original drummer in the indie group The Primitives?
6. Which pop group's first No. 1 single was 1997's *I Wanna Be The Only One*?
7. Which singer recorded the 2000 album *Sing When You're Winning*?
8. Which group pulled out of the infamous Bill Grundy-hosted show which made stars of the group the Sex Pistols?
9. What was the original full name of the group Pulp?
10. In which year did John Prine release his debut album *John Prine*?
11. From which city did the instrumental funk band The Meters hail?
12. Which group recorded the 2000 album *High Ball Me*?
13. Which rock group recorded the 2000 album *Dumbing Up*?
14. Who recorded the 1980 record album *Get Happy*?
15. Which U.S. group recorded the 1995 album *Tales from the Punchbowl*?

ANSWERS **1.** Peter Andre **2.** Queen Latifah **3.** Public Image Ltd. **4.** Warners **5.** Pete Tweedie **6.** Eternal **7.** Robbie Williams **8.** Queen **9.** Arabacus Pulp **10.** 1971 **11.** New Orleans **12.** Moose **13.** World Party **14.** Elvis Costello **15.** Primus.

PEOPLE

1. Which Tory M.P. referred to punk group Throbbing Gristle as the "wreckers of civilization"?
2. Which actress broke up with husband Jean-Michel Jarre in 1996?
3. What was the profession of film director Stanley Kubrick's father?
4. Which actor was born Warren Misell?
5. Who murdered Jesse James?
6. Which entertainer was born Danny Patrick Carroll in 1928?
7. Which comedian wrote the memoir *I Stole Freddie Mercury's Birthday Cake*?
8. Which Hollywood actor has twin daughters called Aquinnah and Schuyler?
9. Film studio producer Terry Melcher is son of which actress-singer?
10. In which year did Nicolas Cage and Patricia Arquette marry?
11. In which country was actress Isla Fisher, from the television soap *Home and Away,* born?
12. Which late Conservative M.P.'s first book was called *The Donkeys*?
13. What age was film director Jean Vigo when he died?
14. Which photographer and film director did the author Candace Bushnell live with when she moved to New York in 1978?
15. Which world chess champion was born Harry Weinstein?

ANSWERS 1. Nicholas Fairbairn **2.** Charlotte Rampling **3.** Doctor **4.** Warren Mitchell **5.** Robert Ford **6.** Danny La Rue **7.** Malcolm Hardee **8.** Michael J. Fox **9.** Doris Day **10.** 1995 **11.** Saudi Arabia **12.** Alan Clark **13.** 29 **14.** Gordon Parks **15.** Garry Kasparov

GENERAL KNOWLEDGE

1. In which constellation is the star Denebola?
2. In time keeping what do the initials GMT stand for?
3. In which city is De Montfort University?
4. In which month is the Up-Helly-Aa festival held in the town of Lerwick?
5. Of what is Michelangelo's sculpture *David* of 1501-4 made?
6. Which two liquids combine to make a 'Dog's Nose'?
7. Which is the only Great Lake of North America to be wholly within the USA?
8. What is the standard monetary unit of Japan?
9. Who in Greek mythology granted King Midas's wish that everything he touched be turned into gold?
10. Which German-born architect designed the Seagram Building in New York?
11. What is a yate?
12. Which Scottish philosopher wrote 1861's *Utilitarianism*?
13. Who wrote the play *A View from the Bridge*?
14. What is the 14th letter in the Greek alphabet?
15. In which year did bandleader Glenn Miller disappear over the English Channel?

ANSWERS **1.** Leo **2.** Greenwich Mean Time **3.** Leicester **4.** January **5.** Marble **6.** Gin and beer **7.** Lake Michigan **8.** Yen **9.** Dionysus **10.** Ludwig Mies van der Rohe **11.** A tree **12.** John Stuart Mill **13.** Arthur Miller **14.** Xi **15.** 1944.

ENTERTAINMENT

1. Which play by Samuel Beckett was originally written for the stage show *Oh! Calcutta!*?
2. In which year did Stephen Fry flee a production of Simon Gray's play *Cell Mates*?
3. Which unknown actress played Peggy in Rodgers and Hart's stage musical *I'd Rather be Right* in 1937?
4. Who plays Aramis in the 1994 film *D'Artagnan's Daughter*?
5. Which film director married the editor Alma Reville in the 1920s?
6. Who plays a Slovenian cleaning lady in the sitcom *Baddiel's Syndrome*?
7. Who played Duke the Dog-Faced Boy in the film *Big Top Pee-Wee*?
8. Which director made the student film *Joe's Bed-Stuy Barbershop: We Cut Heads*?
9. In which year did the play *Entertaining Mr. Sloane* premiere in the West End of London?
10. Who played the composer Liszt in the 1960 film *Song Without End*?

11. Who plays professor Denise Gaines in the 2000 film *Nutty Professor II: The Klumps*?
12. Who in 2000 hosted the television quiz show *The Weakest Link*?
13. What was the name of Alison Steadman's character in the television play *Abigail's Party*?
14. Who played the character Patrick in a 2000 television adaptation of Kingsley Amis's novel *Take A Girl Like You*?
15. Which actor was born Emmanuel Goldenberg?

ANSWERS 1. Breath **2.** 1995 **3.** Joy Hodges **4.** Sami Frey **5.** Alfred Hitchcock **6.** Morwenna Banks **7.** Benicio Del Toro **8.** Spike Lee **9.** 1964 **10.** Dirk Bogarde **11.** Janet Jackson **12.** Anne Robinson **13.** Beverley **14.** Rupert Graves **15.** Edward G. Robinson.

SPORT

1. In which city was the figure skater John Curry born?
2. Hurry On was the first Classic winner for which racehorse trainer?
3. In which year was Welsh rugby union star Gerald Davies born?
4. At which sport was New-York born John Davis an Olympic champion?
5. Which U.S. jockey won 8 out of 9 races at Arlington on August 13, 1989?
6. Which cyclist won the 1988 Tour de France?
7. Which U.S. jockey won the 1992 Eclipse Award after winning over $14m?
8. Which New Zealand women's squash player won the British Open from 1984-90?
9. At what sport did Klaus Dibiasi win three Olympic titles from 1968-76?
10. What was the nickname of Olympic hurdles champion Harrison Dillard?
11. For which three international teams did the footballer Alfredo Di Stefano play?
12. Which brothers won the Wimbledon men's doubles title from 1897-1905?
13. In which year was Olympic athlete Heike Drechsler born?
14. Which male high jumper won the 1956 Olympic title?
15. In which year was jockey Pat Eddery born?

ANSWERS **1.** Birmingham **2.** Fred Darling **3.** 1945 **4.** Weightlifting **5.** Pat Day **6.** Pedro Delgado **7.** Kent Desormeaux **8.** Susan Devoy **9.** Highboard diving **10.** Bones **11.** Spain, Colombia and Argentina **12.** Reggie and Laurie Doherty **13.** 1964 **14.** Charles Dumas **15.** 1952.

POP

1. Which TV comedy actors had a 1963 hit single with *At the Palace (Parts 1 & 2)*?
2. Who charted in 1996 with the single *Un-break My Heart*?
3. Which indie group had a minor hit in 1998 with *Candlefire*?
4. Which vocalist had a Top 20 hit in 1998 with *Sexy Cinderella*?
5. Which new country singer had a hit single in 1994 with *Standing Outside the Fire*?
6. Which Irish singer charted in 1995 with the single *The Snows of New York*?
7. Which former member of The Specials charted in 1997 with the single *Ballad of a Landlord*?
8. Which U.S. singer had a 1997 Top Ten single with *Bitch*?
9. Which group had a debut No. 1 single in 1997 with *Mmmbop*?
10. In which year was the singer Bobby Brown born?
11. Who was lead singer with the group A-Ha?
12. What is Boy George's real name?
13. In which town was Billy Bragg born?
14. Who was the guitarist in the early 1970s band Kippington Lodge?
15. What was Bronski Beat's debut hit single?

ANSWERS 1. Wilfrid Brambell & Harry H. Corbett **2.** Toni Braxton **3.** Dawn of the Replicants **4.** Lynden David Hall **5.** Garth Brooks **6.** Chris De Burgh **7.** Terry Hall **8.** Meredith Brooks **9.** Hanson **10.** 1969 **11.** Morten Harket **12.** George O'Dowd **13.** Barking **14.** Brinsley Schwarz **15.** Smalltown Boy.

ART AND LITERATURE

1. In which year did the artist Sonia Delaunay die?
2. Which Spanish artist painted the 1936 work *Autumnal Cannibalism*?
3. Which British artist painted the 1955 work *The Toilet*?
4. Which artist painted the 1952 work *A Man Who Suddenly Fell Over*?
5. Who wrote the novel *Searching for Caleb*?
6. Which British artist painted the 1914 work *The Mud Bath*?
7. Who wrote the novel *A Thousand Acres*?
8. Which Italian artist was killed by a fall from a horse in 1916?
9. In which year was the British artist Elizabeth Blackadder born?
10. Who wrote the novel *Complicity*?
11. Which sculptor produced the 1965 painted metal work *Orinoco*?
12. Who wrote the novel *The Hard Life*?
13. Which sculptor was born in Romania in 1876 and grew up as a shepherd boy?
14. Which French artist painted the 1906 work *The Pool of London*?
15. Who wrote the novel *Tintin in the New World*?

ANSWERS 1. 1979 **2.** Salvador Dali **3.** John Bratby **4.** Michael Andrews **5.** Anne Tyler **6.** David Bomberg **7.** Jane Smiley **8.** Umberto Boccioni **9.** 1931 **10.** Iain Banks **11.** David Annesley **12.** Flann O'Brien **13.** Constantin Brancusi **14.** André Derain **15.** Frederic Tuten.

GENERAL KNOWLEDGE

1. In which year did the TV presenter Jess Yates die?
2. In which country is the Ala Dag mountain range?
3. Which politician was the 1st Earl of Stockton?
4. Which murderer was released by Pilate in preference to Jesus?
5. What is the third largest state of the U.S. after Alaska and Texas?
6. What was the middle name of novelist Henry Miller?
7. Which poet wrote the 1637 masque *Comus*?
8. After which war did the Finns surrender the Karelian Isthmus to Russia?
9. In which year was the voluntary organization MIND founded?
10. Gannet Peak is the highest peak of which U.S. mountain range?
11. Which jazz composer's works include *The Black Saint and the Sinner Lady*?
12. Who wrote the novel *And The Ass Saw The Angel*?
13. In which year did the actor Robert Mitchum die?
14. What is the German name for Bavaria?
15. In which South American country is the port of Cartagena?

ANSWERS 1. 1993 **2.** Turkey **3.** Harold Macmillan **4.** Barabbas **5.** California **6.** Valentine **7.** John Milton **8.** The Winter War **9.** 1946 **10.** Wind River Range **11.** Charles Mingus **12.** Nick Cave **13.** 1997 **14.** Bayern **15.** Colombia.

ENTERTAINMENT

1. Who starred in the 1925 film *The Phantom of the Opera*?
2. Who played Fred Fenster in the film *The Usual Suspects*?
3. Which of the Three Musketeers does Jean-Luc Bideau play in the 1994 film *D'Artagnan's Daughter*?
4. Who played composer Paganini in the 1947 film *The Magic Bow*?
5. Who became the first million pound winner of television show *Who Wants To Be A Millionaire* in 2000?
6. Who plays Terry Donager in the 2000 film *Black and White*?
7. Which comedian presented the BBC2 television series *500 Bus Stops*?
8. Who directed the film *Beavis and Butt-Head Do America*?
9. Which actor played Dave Matthews in television soap *Family Affairs*?
10. Who writes the sitcom *Is It Legal*?
11. Who played Ethan Hawke's father in the film *Snow Falling On Cedars*?
12. *Puss Gets the Boot* was the first cartoon to feature which characters?
13. Who plays *D'Artagnan's Daughter* in a the 1994 film?
14. Who played Jenny in a 2000 television adaptation of Kingsley Amis's novel *Take A Girl Like You*?
15. In which year did jazzman Louis Armstrong die?

ANSWERS 1. Lon Chaney **2.** Benicio Del Toro **3.** Athos **4.** Stewart Granger **5.** Judith Keppel **6.** Robert Downey, Jr. **7.** John Shuttleworth **8.** Mike Judge **9.** Richard Hawley **10.** Simon Nye **11.** Sam Shepard **12.** Tom & Jerry **13.** Sophie Marceau **14.** Sienna Guillory **15.** 1971.

SPORT

1. Which female swimmer won the 1948 Olympic 400m title?
2. What nationality is Olympic swimming champion Tamas Darnyi?
3. Who was the 1970 Commonwealth Games men's long jump champion?
4. In which year was snooker player Steve Davis born?
5. In which year was skater Christopher Dean born?
6. At which field sport was Luis Delis a Pan-American champion?
7. At what age did US swimmer Donna de Varona compete in the 1960 Olympics?
8. In which city was England cricketer Ted Dexter born?
9. Which football player broke O.J. Simpson's record for rushing yards gained in a season in 1984?
10. Which baseball player was known as 'The Little Professor'?
11. Who coached the Chicago Bears from 1982-93?
12. In which country was cricketer Basil D'Oliveira born?
13. In 1950, Czech-born tennis player Jaroslav Drobny took out citizenship of which country?
14. Which jockey rode West Tip to victory in the 1986 Grand National?
15. In which year was jockey Paul Eddery born?

ANSWERS **1.** Ann Curtis **2.** Hungarian **3.** Lynn Davies **4.** 1957 **5.** 1958 **6.** Discus **7.** 13 **8.** Milan **9.** Eric Dickerson **10.** Dominic DiMaggio **11.** Mike Ditka **12.** South Africa **13.** Egypt **14.** Richard Dunwoody **15.** 1963.

POP

1. In which year did The Proclaimers release the album *Hit the Highway*?
2. Which U.S. singer-songwriter recorded the 2000 solo album *The Luxury of Time*?
3. Which group recorded the 1971 album *Pendulum*?
4. Which group recorded the 1985 album *Our Favourite Shop*?
5. Which pop singer's hit singles include ... *Baby One More Time*?
6. Which journalist did singer Claudia Brücken of the group Propaganda marry in the mid 1980s?
7. Which group recorded the album *Separations* in 1989?
8. Which group recorded the 1995 album *Looking in the Shadows*?
9. Which member of the group Red House Painters released the 2000 solo album *Rock 'n' Roll Singer*?
10. Who is the female singer in the hip-hop group Lucy Pearl?
11. Which singer recorded the 1972 album *Son of Schmilsson*?
12. Which singer released the 2000 album *Dancin' with Them that Brung Me*?
13. Which Tim Buckley song is covered by Dot Allison on the tribute album *Sing A Song To You*?
14. Which duo record under the name *Two Lone Swordsmen*?
15. Which group recorded the 1981 single *The Gospel Comes To New Guinea*?

ANSWERS 1. 1995 **2.** David Mead **3.** Creedence Clearwater Revival **4.** The Style Council **5.** Britney Spears **6.** Paul Morley **7.** Pulp **8.** The Raincoats **9.** Mark Kozelek **10.** Dawn Robinson **11.** Harry Nilsson **12.** Stacey Earle **13.** Sweet Surrender **14.** Andrew Weatherall and Keith Tenniswood **15.** 23 Skidoo.

GEOGRAPHY

1. What is Holy Island, off the coast of Northumberland, also called?
2. Which is the largest island of Japan?
3. Which country was renamed the Democratic Republic of Congo in 1997?
4. Yell is in which Scottish island group?
5. The Welland Ship Canal connects which two of the Great Lakes of North America?
6. Which is the larger island - North Uist or South Uist?
7. Which is the longest river in France?
8. The town of Sault Ste. Marie, Canada is connected by bridge to which town in Michigan?
9. What is the name of the Italian island in the Tyrrhenian Sea made famous in a novel by Dumas?
10. What are Nova Scotia, New Brunswick and Prince Edward Island collectively known as?
11. Which is the largest city in Alaska?
12. In which European country is the province of Albacete?
13. What is the capital of New York state?
14. On which river is the Belgian seaport of Antwerp?
15. On which river does the Devon tourist town of Barnstaple stand?

ANSWERS **1.** Lindisfarne **2.** Honshu **3.** Zaire **4.** Shetlands **5.** Erie and Ontario **6.** North Uist **7.** River Loire **8.** Sault Ste. Marie **9.** Monte Cristo **10.** The Maritime Provinces **11.** Anchorage **12.** Spain **13.** Albany **14.** River Scheldt **15.** River Taw.

GENERAL KNOWLEDGE

1. What are the two official languages of the island of Madagascar?
2. To which genus does the mint plant belong?
3. What nationality was the mathematician August Ferdinand Möbius?
4. What is the international car registration for Barbados?
5. What is the German name for Vienna?
6. In which year was the Mir space station put into earth orbit?
7. Whittret is a dialect word for which male animal?

8. Which Japanese writer's best known work is the four-volume *The Sea of Fertility*?
9. What is the collective noun for a flock of snipe?
10. Why is the wrybill plover so called?
11. Which European kingdom's islands include Falster and Bornholm?

12. What was the middle name of the U.S. poet Robert Frost?
13. In the world of finance, what do the letters GNP stand for?
14. In which year did actor Sir Donald Wolfit die?
15. In which year was the Wolfenden Report, which recommended the legalization of homosexual relations between consenting adults?

ANSWERS 1. French and Malagasy **2.** Mentha **3.** German **4.** BDS **5.** Wien **6.** 1986 **7.** Weasel **8.** Yukio Mishima **9.** Wisp **10.** It's bill is deflected to one side **11.** Denmark **12.** Lee **13.** Gross National Product **14.** 1968 **15.** 1957.

ENTERTAINMENT

1. Which punk rocker played 'Dick Slammer' in the film *Tapeheads*?
2. Which television presenter wrote the book *Downsize This! Random Threats From An Unarmed American*?
3. Of what secret organization is Homer made leader in the episode of The Simpsons entitled *Homer the Great*?
4. Who directed the 1997 film *Night Falls on Manhattan*?
5. Who directed the film *Crouching Tiger, Hidden Dragon*?
6. Who plays detective Pat Chappel in the television series *The Vice*?
7. What are the surnames of television comedy duo *Adam and Joe*?
8. Who played movie producer Peter Dragon in the television show *Action!*?
9. Who directed the 1998 film *Sliding Doors*?
10. In which film does Charlie Chaplin cook and eat a boot?
11. Who plays rabbi Jacob Schram in the film *Keeping the Faith*?
12. Which playwright scripted the 1990 film *Everybody Wins*?
13. Who directed the 1978 film *Eraserhead*?
14. What does Harrison Ford play in the 1966 film *Dead Heat On a Merry-Go-Round*?
15. Who plays a gang boss in the 1974 film *The Taking of Pelham One, Two, Three*?

ANSWERS 1. Stiv Bator **2.** Michael Moore **3.** Stonecutters **4.** Sidney Lumet **5.** Ang Lee **6.** Ken Stott **7.** Buxton & Cornish **8.** Jay Mohr **9.** Peter Howitt **10.** The Gold Rush **11.** Ben Stiller **12.** Arthur Miller **13.** David Lynch **14.** A bell hop **15.** Robert Shaw.

SPORT

1. What was "Magique", the official mascot of the 1992 Winter Olympics at Albertville?
2. Which non-league team knocked Birmingham out of the F.A. Cup in January 1986?
3. Who was the 1998 British Open golf champion?
4. Which team knocked Coventry out of the F.A. Cup in January 1989?
5. Which dog won the 1996 greyhound derby?
6. Which horse won the 1956 Epsom Derby?
7. Which football team won the 1999/00 League Cup?
8. Which football team won the 1995/6 European Champions Cup?
9. Which team won the 1996/7 Scottish F.A. Cup?
10. Who won the Olympic men's 200m in 1960?
11. Who were the 1996 cricket county champions?

12. Which animal was the official mascot of the 1984 Winter Olympics at Sarajevo?
13. In which country were the 1992 European Championships in football held?
14. Who won the Olympic women's 400m in 1972?
15. Which American Football team won Super Bowl XXXIII?

ANSWERS **1.** A snow imp **2.** Altrincham **3.** Mark O'Meara **4.** Sutton **5.** Shanless Slippy **6.** Lavandin **7.** Leicester City **8.** Juventus **9.** Kilmarnock **10.** Livio Berruti **11.** Leicestershire **12.** Vucko the Wolf **13.** Sweden **14.** Monika Zehrt **15.** Denver Broncos.

POP

1. Which Australian entertainer had a minor 1996 hit with *Bohemian Rhapsody*?
2. Which U.K. vocalist had a 1998 Top Five single with *My Star*?
3. Lorraine McIntosh was the angelic vocalist with which Scottish chart band?
4. Which female singer had Top 20 hits in 1998 with *You Think You Own Me* and *I Wanna Be Your Lady*?
5. Which comedian had a minor hit in 1996 with *Rockin' Good Christmas*?
6. What was singer Lola's only singles chart success, in 1987?
7. Which group recorded the album *Secret Watchers Built the World*?
8. From which European country did 1998 chart act Los Umberellos come?
9. Which male vocalist had a 1970 solo hit with *My Woman's Man*?
10. Which female vocal duo featured on Suggs's 1996 hit *Cecilia*?
11. What was singer Louise's first solo Top Ten hit single?
12. Who had a hit in 1980 with *Funkin' for Jamaica (N.Y.)*?
13. From which European country does the singer Hondy come?
14. Which vocal group had a 1997 Top 20 hit with *5 Miles to Empty*?
15. Which soul singer was born in Barnwell, South Carolina on May 3, 1933?

ANSWERS 1. Rolf Harris **2.** Ian Brown **3.** Deacon Blue **4.** Hinda Hicks **5.** Roy 'Chubby' Brown **6.** Wax the Van **7.** Mazey Fade **8.** Denmark **9.** Dave Dee **10.** Louchie Lou and Michie One **11.** Light of My Life **12.** Tom Browne **13.** Italy **14.** Brownstone **15.** James Brown.

HISTORY

1. Who became prime minister of Australia in 1932?
2. In which year did Columbus set sail on his third voyage to the New World?
3. Which historic house is known as the 'Palace of the Peak'?
4. In which year did a German air-raid destroy the 15c Coventry cathedral church?
5. In which century did the French philosopher Denis Diderot live?
6. As what was Charles Martel, leader of the Franks, known?
7. In which country was left-wing revolutionary Rosa Luxemburg born?
8. Who was prime minister of Canada from 1957-63?
9. Which U.S. soldier commanded the 42nd (Rainbow) Division in France in World War I?
10. At what age was Bernadette Devlin elected to the House of Commons?
11. In which ycar was the Battle of Dien Bien Phu?
12. Hearth-money was a 17c tax on which part of a house?
13. In which year was the Diet of Worms at which Martin Luther was asked to recant?
14. Who, in 1921, became Canada's first woman M.P.?
15. Bernardo O'Higgins was president of which country from 1818-23?

ANSWERS **1.** Joseph Lyons **2.** 1498 **3.** Chatsworth House **4.** 1940 **5.** 18th **6.** The Hammer **7.** Poland **8.** John George Diefenbaker **9.** Douglas MacArthur **10.** 21 **11.** 1954 **12.** Chimney **13.** 1521 **14.** Agnes Macphail **15.** Chile.

GENERAL KNOWLEDGE

1. Who wrote the novel *Mummy's Legs*?
2. Is San Francisco north or south of Los Angeles?
3. Where in England is the Bevere Vivis art gallery?
4. Who, or what, is Bartle Bogle Hegarty?
5. What was Pete Goss's yacht called in the 1997 Vendée Globe race?
6. In which county is the seaside resort of Frinton?
7. In which year in the early 20th century was the lady's slipper orchid declared extinct in Britain?
8. What destroyed the town of Shaturia in Bangladesh in 1989?
9. Which businessman built the 29 bedroom home 'Fair Field' in Long Island, New York?
10. Trina Gulliver is the women's No. 1 at which sport?
11. In which year was Eleanor of Aquitaine born?
12. *More Than a Hero* is a book about which boxer?
13. In which month of 1890 did Vincent van Gogh shoot himself in the chest and subsequently die?
14. In which African country is the plateau of sandstone called Fouta Djallon?
15. Which football team does the actress Emily Watson support?

ANSWERS 1. Kate Bingham **2.** North **3.** Worcester **4.** An advertising agency **5.** Aqua Quorum **6.** Essex **7.** 1917 **8.** A tornado **9.** Ira Rennet **10.** Darts **11.** 1122 **12.** Muhammad Ali **13.** July **14.** Guinea **15.** Arsenal.

ENTERTAINMENT

1. Who plays a sadistic railway conductor in the 1973 film *Emperor of the North*?
2. How much did Adam Sandler get for starring in the film *Little Nicky*?
3. Who directed the 2000 film *Flawless*?
4. What was the final film in the television series *Inspector Morse* called?
5. Who was the female lead in the 1995 film *The Englishman Who Went Up A Hill But Came Down A Mountain*?
6. Who plays a Canadian nurse in the 1996 film *The English Patient*?
7. Who plays Dr. Eve Simmons in the 1991 film *Eve of Destruction*?
8. Which former Doctor Who stars in the television drama *At Home With the Braithwaites*?
9. Who directed the 2000 film *Unbreakable*?
10. Who directed the 1949 film *Stray Dog*?
11. Who authored the stage play *Art*?
12. In which year did the animators William Hanna and Joseph Barbera produce the first *Tom & Jerry* cartoon?
13. Who directed the 1973 film *Enter the Dragon*?
14. Who plays the serviceman 'Dumbo' in the 1957 film *Escapade in Japan*?
15. Who plays Prince Salina in Visconti's film *The Leopard*?

ANSWERS **1.** Ernest Borgnine **2.** $25m **3.** Joel Schumacher **4.** The Remorseful Day **5.** Tara Fitzgerald **6.** Juliette Binoche **7.** Renée Soutendijk **8.** Peter Davison **9.** M. Night Shyamalan **10.** Akira Kurosawa **11.** Yasmina Reza **12.** 1940 **13.** Robert Clouse **14.** Clint Eastwood **15.** Burt Lancaster.

SPORT

1. For what fee did Kenny Dalglish join Liverpool from Celtic in 1977?
2. In which year was New Zealand rugby union star Andy Dalton born?
3. From which team did Dixie Dean join Everton in 1925?
4. Who was 1982 and '86 Commonwealth Games men's marathon champion?
5. For which football league team did Jimmy Dickinson play his entire career from 1943-65?
6. What was unusual about the first five horses in the 1983 Cheltenham Gold Cup?
7. Which Olympic swimmer in 1926 became the first woman to swim the English Channel?
8. Who was Middlesex cricket captain from 1953-57?
9. Who won the 1993 European Open in snooker?
10. Who was runner-up in the 1993 Johnnie Walker World Golf championship?
11. Which club signed David Rocastle from Leeds United?
12. When was Charlie Smirke's first Classic success as a jockey?
13. Who was the 1985 English flat race champion jockey?
14. Which country has hosted the Summer Olympics most times?
15. Was Australian cricketer Neil Harvey left-handed or right-handed?

ANSWERS 1. £440,000 **2.** 1951 **3.** Tranmere Rovers **4.** Rob de Castella **5.** Portsmouth **6.** They were all trained by Michael Dickinson **7.** Trudy Ederle **8.** Bill Edrich **9.** Stephen Hendry **10.** Fred Couples **11.** Manchester City **12.** 1934 **13.** Steve Cauthen **14.** U.S.A. **15.** Left-handed.

POP

1. *Hillbilly Shakespeare* was an album by Bap Kennedy of songs by which songwriter?
2. Which member of the Spice Girls released the solo single *Tell Me* in 2000?
3. Mark Gardener and Laurence Colbert of the group The Animalhouse were formerly in which indie group?
4. Who records under the name *Third Eye Foundation*?
5. Which group's second album was 1985's *Freaky Styley*?
6. In which year was the album *Graham Nash and David Crosby* originally released?
7. Which duo recorded the 2000 album *Death on Wild Onion Drive*?
8. Which female solo artist's hits of 2000 included the single *Something Deep Inside*?
9. What nationality are the group Tuesday Weld?
10. Which duo comprise Bill DeMain and Molly Felder?
11. Which pop group's first No. 1 single was 1997's *Never Ever*?
12. Who produced the debut album by The Pretenders in 1980?
13. In which year did the group Primal Scream release the album *Primal Scream*?
14. What was the name of Prince's first band, formed when he was in high school?
15. Which member of the group Gong recorded the 1977 album *Crystal Machine*?

ANSWERS 1. Hank Williams **2.** Melanie B. **3.** Ride **4.** Matt Elliott **5.** The Red Hot Chili Peppers **6.** 1972 **7.** Mucha Macho **8.** Billie Piper **9.** German **10.** Swan Dive **11.** All Saints **12.** Chris Thomas **13.** 1989 **14.** Grand Central **15.** Tim Blake.

ART AND LITERATURE

1. Which artist painted the 1954 work *Aberayron, Evening*?
2. Who wrote the novel *Birdy*?
3. Which French artist and lithographer died at Le Cannet in 1947?
4. Who wrote the short story collection *Sleep It Off Lady*?
5. Which artist produced the oil painting *Have a Nice Day, Mr. Hockney*?
6. Who wrote the novel *Last Orders*?
7. Which British artist painted the 1904 work *A Frosty March Morning*?
8. Who wrote the novel *The French Lieutenant's Woman*?
9. In which year did the artist Raoul Dufy die?
10. Who wrote the fantasy novel *The Drawing of the Dark*?
11. In which year was the British artist Alan Davie born?
12. Which Spanish artist made the 1936 sculpture *Lobster Telephone*?
13. Which artist painted the 1911 work *The Green Donkey*?
14. Which British artist's works include 1930's *The Snack Bar*?
15. Who wrote the novel *The African Queen*?

ANSWERS 1. John Aldridge **2.** William Wharton **3.** Pierre Bonnard **4.** Jean Rhys **5.** Peter Blake **6.** Graham Swift **7.** Sir George Clausen **8.** John Fowles **9.** 1953 **10.** Tim Powers **11.** 1920 **12.** Salvador Dali **13.** Marc Chagall **14.** Edward Burra **15.** C.S. Forester.

GENERAL KNOWLEDGE

1. In which year was the singer Madonna born?
2. What were the forenames of businessman F.W. Woolworth?
3. Which female Canadian singer recorded the album *Mingus*?
4. On which river is the German city of Worms?
5. What in the armed forces does the abbreviation WRNS stand for?
6. In which year was the siege of the Alamo?
7. On which sea is the port of Derbent, which was founded in the 6c?
8. What was the name of the month of fruit in the French Revolutionary calendar?
9. What is a gobo to a singer?
10. In which year was Swedish premier Olaf Palme shot?
11. What is the standard monetary unit of Nauru?
12. In which S. England city is the Pitt Rivers Museum?
13. Who wrote the novel *Across the River and into the Trees*?
14. Who created Doctor Dolittle?
15. Which city was capital of the British East Africa Protectorate from 1888 until 1907?

ANSWERS **1.** 1958 **2.** Frank Winfield **3.** Joni Mitchell **4.** Rhine **5.** Women's Royal Naval Service **6.** 1836 **7.** Caspian Sea **8.** Fructidor **9.** A shield put around a microphone to exclude unwanted sounds **10.** 1986 **11.** Australian dollar **12.** Oxford **13.** Ernest Hemingway **14.** Hugh Lofting **15.** Mombasa.

ENTERTAINMENT

1. Who won an Oscar for the music for Charlie Chaplin's film *Limelight*?
2. Who created the Miss World contest?
3. Who played the composer Berlioz in the 1947 film *La Symphonie Fantastique*?
4. Which of the Three Musketeers is played by Raoul Billerey in the 1994 film *D'Artagnan's Daughter*?
5. Who played Mark 'Chopper' Read in the 2000 film *Chopper*?
6. Who directed the 1994 film *Even Cowgirls Get the Blues*?
7. Who directed the 1979 film *The Europeans*, based on a novel by Henry James?
8. Who plays the king in the 1960 biblical film *Esther and the King*?
9. Which comedian plays the disciple Rufus in the 1999 film *Dogma*?
10. Who directed the 1999 film *81/2 Women*?
11. What is the first name of the founder of the town Springfield in television cartoon *The Simpsons*?
12. Which modern writer appeared as a child actor in the 1965 film *A High Wind in Jamaica?*
13. Who founded and led the Hollywood String Quartet?
14. Who directed the 1980 film *The Empire Strikes Back*?
15. Which British comedienne starred in the 1991 film *Enchanted April*?

ANSWERS **1.** Charlie Chaplin **2.** Eric Morley **3.** Jean-Louis Barrault **4.** Porthos **5.** Eric Bana **6.** Gus Van Sant **7.** James Ivory **8.** Richard Egan **9.** Chris Rock **10.** Peter Greenaway **11.** Jebediah **12.** Martin Amis **13.** Felix Slatkin **14.** Irvin Kershner **15.** Josie Lawrence.

SPORT

1. What are the names of the tennis-playing Williams sisters?
2. By what margin did New Zealand beat Australia in their 1999 Group B World Cup cricket match?
3. Which Huddersfield Town player broke Bradford City player Gordon Watson's leg, resulting in £900,000 damages in a 1999 court decision?
4. For which rugby union club side did Kyran Bracken and George Chuter play in 1999?
5. Who did Leeds rugby union club appoint as successor to coach Graham Murray in 1999?
6. What nationality is the cyclist Romans Vainsteins?
7. Who did Watford beat in the 1999 First Division play-off semi-finals?
8. What was tennis player Shirley Fry's first major singles title, in 1951?
9. For which Italian football club did Jimmy Greaves play in 1961?
10. With which team did basketball player Spencer Haywood finish his career?
11. In which city was Superbowl XXVIII played in 1994?
12. In which year did Sandy Lyle win the British Open title?
13. How many international rugby union caps did Willie John McBride get?
14. In which port was the runner Liz McColgan born?
15. Which horse was the only Epsom Derby winner of jockey Gordon Richards?

ANSWERS 1. Venus and Serena **2.** Five wickets **3.** Kevin Gray **4.** Saracens **5.** Dean Lance **6.** Latvian **7.** Birmingham **8.** French **9.** A.C. Milan **10.** Los Angeles Lakers **11.** Atlanta **12.** 1985 **13.** 80 **14.** Dundee **15.** Pinza.

POP

1. What was Dave Dee, Dozy, Beaky, Mick and Tich's only U.K. No. 1?
2. Which vocal group had a Top Ten single in 1998 with *Finally Found*?
3. What is the singer Michael Bolton's real name?
4. Which group had Top Ten success in 1997 with *You Showed Me*?
5. Which singer recorded the album *Highway 61 Revisited* in 1967?
6. Which duo had a 1993 Top 40 single with *Gloria*?
7. Which band recorded the 1997 album *Victory Parts*?
8. Which singer recorded the album *Come A Time* in 1978?
9. McGuinn, Clark, Clarke, Crosby & Hillman comprised which band in 1964?
10. Which group had a 1998 chart success with *A Nanny in Manhattan*?
11. Which country artist recorded the album of covers entitled *Step Inside This House*?
12. Which Dumbarton-born rock star is lead singer with the band Talking Heads?
13. Which group recorded the album *Possum Trot Plan*?
14. Which female singer had a 1994 Top 40 hit with *Skip to my Lu*?
15. Which singer featured on Malcolm McLaren's 1991 hit *Magic's Back (Theme from The Ghosts of Oxford Street)*?

ANSWERS **1.** Legend of Xanadu **2.** Honeyz **3.** Michael Bolotin **4.** Lightning Seeds **5.** Bob Dylan **6.** Van Morrison and John Lee Hooker **7.** A.C. Acoustics **8.** Neil Young **9.** The Byrds **10.** Lilys **11.** Lyle Lovett **12.** David Byrne **13.** Number One Cup **14.** Lisa Lisa **15.** Alison Limerick.

SCIENCE

1. What type of rock is slate - igneous, metamorphic or sedimentary?
2. Who wrote 1871's *The Descent of Man and Selection in Relation to Sex*?
3. What is the stalk of a leaf also known as?
4. In which year did Humphry Davy die?
5. What is the most common colour of the mineral garnet?
6. Which is larger in area - the Black Sea or the Red Sea?
7. Which French mathematician's last words were reputedly "so my soul, a time for parting"?
8. In which city was German physicist Max Planck born?
9. Which fruit's scientific name is *Citrus limon?*
10. What nationality was the physicist Christian Doppler?
11. Which element's symbol is O?
12. What is the chemical in plants that gives them their green colour?
13. Which 19c Swedish scientist pioneered the science of spectroscopy?
14. What nationality was the chemist Theodor Svedberg?
15. Which scientist's autobiography was *I Am a Mathematician - the Later Life of a Prodigy*?

ANSWERS 1. Metamorphic **2.** Charles Darwin **3.** The petiole **4.** 1829 **5.** Red **6.** Black Sea **7.** René Descartes **8.** Kiel **9.** Lemon **10.** Austrian **11.** Oxygen **12.** Chlorophyll **13.** Anders Angstrom **14.** Swedish **15.** Norbert Wiener.

GENERAL KNOWLEDGE

1. In which U.S. state were the presidents Thomas Jefferson and George Washington born?
2. What did the dairy firm Unigate rename themselves in 2000?
3. Which car manufacturer makes the Berlingo Multispace?
4. Who directed the 1974 film *Stardust*?
5. Who created the 1884 oil painting *Bobbin Winder*?
6. Which comedian authored the novel *Full Whack*?
7. Which businesswoman's 2000 autobiography is called *Business As Usual*?
8. What is the name of the eldest daughter of Al and Tipper Gore?
9. Electronic tagging, which is used for prisoners, is also called HDC. What does HDC stand for?
10. What disaster befell the Austrian village of Blons in 1954?
11. What organization did the aliens Toot and Ploot advertise in the 1970's?
12. For which financial institution did Howard Brown, star of a 2000 television advertising campaign, work?
13. In which Australian state is the coastal town of Cairns?
14. On whose novel was the 1953 film *The House of the Arrow* based?
15. In which country was the theatre director David Lan born?

ANSWERS **1.** Virginia **2.** Uniq **3.** Citroen **4.** Michael Apted **5.** Vincent Van Gogh **6.** Charles Higson **7.** Anita Roddick **8.** Karenna **9.** Home Detection Curfew **10.** Avalanche **11.** Butlin's Holiday Camps **12.** The Halifax **13.** Queensland **14.** A.E.W. Mason **15.** South Africa.

ENTERTAINMENT

1. Who was the female lead in the 1955 film *The End of the Affair*?
2. Which French pop singer stars in the 1980 film *Every Man for Himself*?
3. Which rock singer plays God in the 1999 film *Dogma*?
4. What is Brendan Fraser's character name in the film *Bedazzled*?
5. Charlie Chaplin's film *The Gold Rush* was made in 1925. When did it acquire a musical score?
6. Which actor started his showbiz career as wrestler Z-Gangsta?
7. How many people watched the 1968 Miss World contest on ITV?
8. With which field of the arts is Javier De Frutos associated?
9. Who plays Pandora Braithwaite in the 2001 television adaptation of book *Adrian Mole: The Cappuccino Years*?
10. The 1993 film *Demolition Man* is based on which book?
11. With which art form would you associate Merce Cunningham?
12. How did John Archer die in radio soap opera *The Archers*?
13. Who is the author of play *The Force of Change*?
14. Who won an Oscar for his score for the film *E.T. The Extra Terrestrial*?
15. In which US city is the 1971 film *Escape From the Planet of the Apes* set?

ANSWERS 1. Deborah Kerr **2.** Jacques Dutronc **3.** Alanis Morissette **4.** Elliott Richardson **5.** 1942 **6.** Tiny Lister **7.** 27.8m **8.** Dance, he's a choreographer **9.** Helen Baxendale **10.** Aldous Huxley's novel *Brave New World* **11.** Dance **12.** His tractor overturned **13.** Gary Mitchell **14.** John Williams **15.** Los Angeles.

SPORT

1. From which country did World Cup footballer Teofilio Cubillas hail?
2. At which field event did Ludvik Danek win Olympic gold in 1972?
3. On which horse did Bruce Davidson win the 1974 individual world three-day event championship?
4. Who is the only man to have held the world billiards and snooker titles at the same time?
5. Who was the captain of the 1959 British Lions rugby union tour of Australasia?
6. What nationality was the world singles badminton champion Flemming Delfs?
7. In which country was the motor racing driver Ralph De Palma born?
8. Which former rugby union star became South Africa's ambassador to London in 1979?
9. Which Indian hockey centre-forward won three Olympic golds from 1928-36?
10. Which Brazilian footballer managed the 1970 Peruvian World Cup team?
11. What were the forenames of the D'Inzeo brothers in equestrianism?
12. For which baseball team did Bobby Doerr play his entire career?
13. Was the New Zealand Test cricketer Martin Donnelly left-handed or right-handed?
14. On which island was West Indies cricketer Jeffrey Dujon born?
15. Which tennis player won the junior singles titles at all four Grand Slam tournaments in 1983?

ANSWERS **1.** Peru **2.** Discus **3.** Irish Cap **4.** Joe Davis **5.** Ronnie Dawson **6.** Danish **7.** Italy **8.** Dawie De Villiers **9.** Dhyan Chand **10.** Didi **11.** Raimondo and Piero **12.** Boston Red Sox **13.** Left-handed **14.** Jamaica **15.** Stefan Edberg.

POP

1. Which vocal group charted in 1997 with the song *4 Seasons of Loneliness*?
2. Which female vocalist's hits include the 1995 Top Five single *Not Over Yet*?
3. Which Israeli's debut chart single was 1998's *Diva*?
4. What was Boyzone's first No. 1 single?
5. Which U.S. singer charted in 1995 with a version of *Big Yellow Taxi*?
6. Which rock guitarist's real name is Saul Hudson?
7. What was the 1997 Top Ten single by the Brand New Heavies?
8. Which band had a 1998 hit with *Not If You Were The Last Junkie On Earth*?
9. Which female singer had a 1998 hit with the single *Have You Ever?*?
10. Which Spandau Ballet member had a 1992 solo hit with *Lost in Your Love*?
11. Which male singer had a minor hit in 1995 with the song *Vibrator*?
12. Tim Simenon is the brains behind which dance group?
13. Which Bon Jovi studio album included *You Give Love a Bad Name*?
14. In which city were the Boo Radleys formed?
15. What is the nickname of soul music bass player Donald Dunn?

ANSWERS 1. Boyz II Men **2.** Grace **3.** Dana International **4.** Words **5.** Amy Grant **6.** Slash **7.** You've Got a Friend **8.** The Dandy Warhols **9.** Brandy **10.** Tony Hadley **11.** Terence Trent D'Arby **12.** Bomb the Bass **13.** Slippery When Wet **14.** Liverpool **15.** Duck.

PEOPLE

1. Which television presenter had a car at the age of 18 with the registration number PAR 18?
2. Which country singer sold his house to finance the making of the film *South of Heaven, West of Hell*?
3. What was the middle name of comedian John Belushi?
4. In which year did the film producer and occultist Harry Smith die?
5. In which year was footballer Bruce Grobbelaar born?
6. At which high school was actress Kirsten Dunst a cheerleader?
7. Who married Cary Grant shortly after appearing with him in the film *Every Girl Should Be Married*?
8. Who wrote the monologue *Monster In A Box*?
9. In which year was the actor Benicio Del Toro born?
10. In which year was the stunt man Evel Knievel born?
11. Which songwriter and former husband of Liza Minnelli died in 1992?
12. Which pop star did model Melanie Sykes date for five years in the 1990s?
13. Which sportsman is the father of television presenter Kirsty Gallacher?
14. What age was the comedian Andy Kaufman when he died in 1984?
15. Debbie Mathers-Briggs is the mother of which rapper?

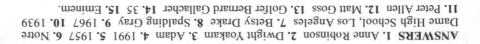

ANSWERS 1. Anne Robinson **2.** Dwight Yoakam **3.** Adam **4.** 1991 **5.** 1957 **6.** Notre Dame High School, Los Angeles **7.** Betsy Drake **8.** Spalding Gray **9.** 1967 **10.** 1939 **11.** Peter Allen **12.** Matt Goss **13.** Golfer Bernard Gallacher **14.** 35 **15.** Eminem.

GENERAL KNOWLEDGE

1. Who wrote the 1967 novel *The Fixer*?
2. In which James Bond film did Art Malik play an Afghan freedom fighter?
3. What is the value of the black ball in snooker?
4. From which team did Aston Villa buy the footballer Dion Dublin?
5. What is harmonica player Larry Adler's middle name?
6. What fruit is used to make the brandy framboise?
7. In which year did Patricia, wife of former president Nixon, die?
8. In which year was the first human heart transplant?
9. In which year was president Ford shot at by Sara Jane Moore?
10. The abbreviation gld stands for which unit of currency?
11. What is the standard monetary unit of Liechtenstein?
12. In which city is the Jewry Wall Museum?
13. What was Kinshasa formerly known as, until 1966?
14. Who was the faithful companion of Aeneas in the book *The Aeneid*?
15. Who was the Roman counterpart of the Greek goddess Demeter?

ANSWERS 1. Bernard Malamud **2.** The Living Daylights **3.** Seven points **4.** Coventry City **5.** Cecil **6.** Raspberry **7.** 1993 **8.** 1867 **9.** 1975 **10.** Guilder **11.** Swiss franc **12.** Leicester **13.** Léopoldville **14.** Achates **15.** Ceres.

ENTERTAINMENT

1. What is David Niven's profession in the 1939 film *Eternally Yours*?
2. What is Kurt Russell's character name in the 1996 film *Escape From L.A.?*
3. Who directed the 1998 film *Enemy of the State*?
4. Who plays Satan in the 1999 film *End of Days*?
5. In which year did songwriter Lionel Bart die?
6. In which television series was the central character called Lin Chung?
7. *Frog Baseball* was the title of the first episode of which television cartoon series?
8. The 1996 film *The Evening Star* is a sequel to which multi-Oscar winner?
9. Who played the lead in the 1989 film *Erik the Viking*?
10. In the film *The Cook, The Thief, His Wife & Her Lover*, who plays 'The Lover'?
11. Who directed the film *The Dream Life of Angels*?
12. Which comedy team starred in the 1946 film *A Night in Casablanca*?
13. About which sport is the 1977 film *Slap Shot*?
14. Who directed the film *Blue Velvet* which featured Dennis Hopper?
15. In which year was the film *A Matter of Life and Death* set?

ANSWERS 1. A magician **2.** Snake Plissken **3.** Tony Scott **4.** Gabriel Byrne **5.** 1999 **6.** The Water Margin **7.** Beavis and Butt-Head **8.** Terms of Endearment **9.** Tim Robbins **10.** Alan Howard **11.** Erick Zonca **12.** The Marx Brothers **13.** Ice hockey **14.** David Lynch **15.** 1945.

SPORT

1. What did football's Milk Cup become in 1987?
2. Who was the USPGA golf champion in 1996?
3. Which horse won the 1996 Epsom Derby?
4. For which London Premier League club does Joe Cole play?
5. Which cricketer, known as 'the Black Bradman' became the first black to captain the West Indies?
6. For which English speedway team did Ove Fundin spend most of his career competing?
7. Who scored twice for West Germany in the 1954 World Cup Final?
8. In which year did Everton win their first Division 1 football title?
9. Which ice hockey star is known as 'the Great One'?
10. Who became world welterweight boxing champion in 1898?
11. Who won the inaugural women's 5,000m title at the 1995 IAAF World Championships?
12. Who won the 1997 County Cricket championship?
13. Which country won the Federation Cup in tennis in 1998?
14. Which runner won the 1982 Commonwealth Games men's 1,500m title?
15. Which woman swimmer won the 1956 Olympic 400m freestyle title?

ANSWERS **1.** Littlewoods Cup **2.** Mark Brooks **3.** Shaamit **4.** West Ham United **5.** George Headley **6.** Norwich **7.** Helmut Rahn **8.** 1891 **9.** Wayne Gretzky **10.** Mysterious Billy Smith **11.** Sonia O'Sullivan **12.** Glamorgan **13.** Spain **14.** Steve Cram **15.** Lorraine Crapp.

POP

1. What is the surname of the recording artist A Guy Named Gerald?
2. What nationality are alternative country group Satellite Inn?
3. Which band sang Scotland's 1998 World Cup song *Don't Come Home Too Soon*?
4. Which artist's albums include *Spend a Night in the Box* and *Liquor in the Front*?
5. Which rock group's albums include 1995's *See You On The Other Side*?
6. Which pop group's first No. 1 single was 1982's *House of Fun*?
7. Which group had a 1964 Top 10 hit single with *Don't Bring Me Down*?
8. Who played drums on the album *Forever Now* by The Psychedelic Furs?
9. In which year did Professor Griff leave the rap group Public Enemy?
10. Which group recorded the 1991 album *Innuendo*?
11. Which studio album by Mansun includes the songs *Love* and *Sunshine*?
12. In which year did the Bay City Rollers have a No. 1 single with *Bye Bye Baby*?
13. Whose 2000 album debut was *Born To Do It*?
14. Which pop artist released the gold-selling album *Unleash the Dragon*?
15. On which studio album by John Prine does he cover the rock 'n' roll song *Ubangi Stomp*?

ANSWERS 1. Simpson **2.** Italian **3.** Del Amitri **4.** Reverend Horton Heat **5.** Mercury Rev **6.** Madness **7.** The Pretty Things **8.** Phil Calvert **9.** 1990 **10.** Queen **11.** Little Kix **12.** 1975 **13.** Craig David **14.** Sisqo **15.** Pink Cadillacs.

ART AND LITERATURE

1. Who wrote the novel *Celestial Navigation*?
2. Which British artist painted the 1967 work *Tocsin III*?
3. Who wrote the novel *Strandloper*?
4. In which year did the German artist Max Beckmann die?
5. What is the colour of the door in Peter Blake's 1962 mixed-media piece *The Toy Shop*?

6. Who wrote the novel *Walking on Glass*?
7. What fruit features in Giorgio de Chirico's 1913 painting *The Uncertainty of the Poet*?
8. Who wrote the novel *London Fields*?
9. Which artist painted the 1926 work *The First Communicants*?
10. In which year was the Italian artist Giacomo Balla born?
11. Who wrote the novel *The Naked and the Dead*?
12. Who wrote the novel *Kara's Game*?
13. Who wrote the novel *Dreams of Leaving*?
14. Which British artist painted the 1955 work *Man Carrying Pig*?
15. Which New York-born artist painted the 1958 work *Yellow Sky*?

ANSWERS **1.** Anne Tyler **2.** John Armstrong **3.** Alan Garner **4.** 1950 **5.** Green **6.** Iain Banks **7.** Bananas **8.** Martin Amis **9.** Balthus **10.** 1871 **11.** Norman Mailer **12.** Gordon Stevens **13.** Rupert Thompson **14.** Peter Coker **15.** Milton Avery.

GENERAL KNOWLEDGE

1. In which year did the television presenter Magnus Pyke die?
2. What did Thomas Carlyle refer to as 'The Dismal Science'?
3. Who wrote the novel *Rich Man, Poor Man*?
4. How old was the politician Barry Goldwater when he died in 1998?
5. Who was Foreign Secretary from 1919-24?
6. In which sport might you use the Conibear style?
7. Who wrote the 1867 poem *Dover Beach*?
8. In which U.S. state is Cape Cod?
9. Of which country was Süleyman Demirel prime minister from 1965-71?
10. What is the nationality of the author Janet Frame?
11. In which year did the baritone Tito Gobbi die?
12. In what sport do men compete for the Iroquois Cup?
13. Which actress was known as 'The Divine Sarah'?
14. In which year did the Albanian statesman Enver Hoxha die?
15. Which actress starred as Suzette in the 1986 film *Absolute Beginners*?

ANSWERS **1.** 1992 **2.** Economics **3.** Irwin Shaw **4.** 89 **5.** Lord Curzon **6.** Rowing **7.** Matthew Arnold **8.** Massachusetts **9.** Turkey **10.** New Zealander **11.** 1984 **12.** Lacrosse **13.** Sarah Bernhardt **14.** 1985 **15.** Patsy Kensit.

ENTERTAINMENT

1. Who directed the film *Swimming to Cambodia*?
2. Who directed the Will Hay comedy film *Ask A Policeman*?
3. Who wrote and directed the 1950 film *Orphée*?
4. The 1955 film *The Eternal Sea* is a biopic of which World War II admiral?
5. What is Ernest's full name in the 'Ernest' series of films starring Jim Varney?
6. Who starred as *The Entertainer* in the 1960 film?
7. Who did Colin Firth play in the film *Shakespeare in Love*?
8. Who played Dr. Helen Remington in the film *Crash*?
9. Who directed the 1990 film *Hardware*?
10. Who plays Jeanie Boulet in the television drama *E.R.*?
11. Who composed the score for the film *The Nightmare Before Christmas*?
12. Who directed the 1977 film *Equus*?
13. Who scored the 1998 film *The End of Violence* directed by Wim Wenders?
14. In which film by David Lynch do the characters Bobby Peru and Perdita feature?
15. Who plays the female lead in the 1970 film *Entertaining Mr. Sloane*?

ANSWERS **1.** Jonathan Demme **2.** Marcel Varnel **3.** Jean Cocteau **4.** John Hoskins **5.** Ernest P. Worrell **6.** Laurence Olivier **7.** Lord Wessex **8.** Holly Hunter **9.** Richard Stanley **10.** Gloria Reuben **11.** Danny Elfman **12.** Sidney Lumet **13.** Ry Cooder **14.** Wild At Heart **15.** Beryl Reid.

SPORT

1. What is cricketer Gordon Greenidge's first name?
2. In which county was UK water skier Mike Hazelwood born?
3. By what score did Brazil win on penalties in the 1994 World Cup Final?
4. Who won cycling's Giro d'Italia in 1997?
5. How many points did Preston North End accumulate in winning the inaugural Division 1 title in 1888/89?
6. Who won the 1994 men's hockey World Cup?
7. Which Leeds United player scored in the 1970 F.A. Cup Final and replay?
8. Who was world 500 c.c. motor cycling champion from 1994-98?
9. Which horse won the 1997 Grand National?
10. Who won the county championship in rugby union in 1957?
11. Which country won the 1978 Davis Cup?
12. Which world champion speedway rider died in 1963 at the age of 29?
13. Which country were the 1998 ice hockey world champions?
14. Who became world middleweight boxing champion in 1911?
15. Who won the 1991 IAAF World Championships women's 10,000m title?

ANSWERS 1. Cuthbert **2.** Lincolnshire **3.** 3-2 **4.** Ivan Gotti **5.** 40 **6.** Pakistan **7.** Mick Jones **8.** Michael Doohan **9.** Lord Gyllene **10.** Devon **11.** Sweden **12.** Peter Craven **13.** Sweden **14.** Cyclone Thompson **15.** Liz McColgan.

POP

1. Which male singer had a 1996 hit with *Devil's Haircut*?
2. Which Irish group's first chart single was *Runaway* in 1996?
3. Which group charted in 1996 with *Scooby Snacks*?
4. Which Jamaican singer had a 1998 Top Ten single with *Who Am I*?
5. On which record label do the group Belle and Sebastian record?
6. Which group had a 1997 Top 20 hit with *Fired Up!*?
7. Who had a 1996 chart entry with *My Unknown Love*?
8. Which group had a Top 40 hit in 1997 with the song *Mum's Gone to Iceland*?
9. Which group had a 1997 Top 20 hit with the song *We Have Explosive*?
10. What was Bentley Rhythm Aces's 1997 Top 20 single?
11. Whose debut L.P. in 1987 was entitled *Squirrel and G-Man Twenty Four Hour Party People Plastic Face Carnt Smile (White Out)*?
12. Who was lead singer with the group Van Der Graaf Generator?
13. *Back in the D.H.S.S.* was the debut L.P. of which group?
14. William Bailey is the real name of which rock singer?
15. Dave Ball and Richard Norris comprise which electronic duo?

ANSWERS **1.** Beck **2.** The Corrs **3.** Fun Lovin' Criminals **4.** Beenie Man **5.** Jeepster **6.** Funky Green Dogs **7.** Count Indigo **8.** Bennet **9.** Future Sound of London **10.** Bentley's Gonna Sort You Out **11.** Happy Mondays **12.** Peter Hammill **13.** Half Man Half Biscuit **14.** Axl Rose **15.** The Grid.

GEOGRAPHY

1. Is Airdrie east or west of Glasgow?
2. Which is larger - Alabama or Albania?
3. On which gulf is the Italian seaport of Amalfi?
4. In which South American country is the volcano Antisana?
5. Which strait connects the Mediterranean Sea to the Atlantic?
6. To which island republic does the Mediterranean island of Gozo belong?
7. What is the capital of Nova Scotia, Canada?
8. Which is larger - Lithuania or Latvia?
9. On which river does Leicester stand?
10. As what are the resorts of Paignton, Torquay and Brixham collectively known?
11. The town of Wagga Wagga is in which Australian state?
12. What is the name of the peninsula between Portsmouth and Bognor Regis?
13. What is the name of the group of chalk stacks in the English Channel off the west coast of the Isle of Wight?
14. What is the name of the town in S.E. France famous for nougat manufacture?
15. Which strait separates Sumatra from mainland Malaysia?

ANSWERS **1.** East **2.** Alabama **3.** Gulf of Salerno **4.** Ecuador **5.** Strait of Gibraltar **6.** Malta **7.** Halifax **8.** Latvia **9.** River Soar **10.** Torbay **11.** New South Wales **12.** Selsey Bill **13.** The Needles **14.** Montélimar **15.** Strait of Malacca.

GENERAL KNOWLEDGE

1. How long is the pitch in a game of boules?
2. In which month did the 2000 summer Olympics open?
3. In which African country are the towns of Thiès and Linguère?
4. Who was the Miss Northern Ireland contestant in the 2000 Miss World contest?
5. Robert Banks, author of the book *An Irrational Hatred of Luton* is a fan of which football team?
6. What is the nationality of darts player Raymond Barneveld?
7. What nationality is the film director Bille August?
8. Approximately how many people died when the Huang He River burst its banks in October, 1887?
9. In which year did Henry II of England die?
10. Which Nottinghamshire country singer recorded the album *Beautiful Day*?
11. Which famous building is also known as 'The Flavian Amphitheatre'?
12. In which year did the Playboy Club in London close?
13. What was the world's first jet airliner?
14. What was the nickname of the Tacoma Narrows bridge in Washington state?
15. In which U.S. state is the Denali National Park?

ANSWERS **1.** 15 metres **2.** September **3.** Senegal **4.** Julie Martin **5.** West Ham United **6.** Dutch **7.** Danish **8.** 900,000 **9.** 1189 **10.** Reg Cooper **11.** The Colosseum **12.** 1981 **13.** De Havilland Comet **14.** Gallopin' Gertie **15.** Alaska.

ENTERTAINMENT

1. Who played Dr. Banner in the TV drama *The Incredible Hulk*?
2. Who did Tony Robinson play in the TV comedy *Blackadder*?
3. In *Blake's 7* what was Blake's forename?
4. Who was the first host of the T.V. quiz *Blankety Blank*?
5. Which comic actor starred in the sitcom *Bless This House*?
6. In which 1935 film does Groucho Marx play Otis B. Driftwood?
7. Which gangster did Faye Dunaway play in a 1967 Arthur Penn film?
8. Who played 'a Girl' in the 1937 film *One Hundred Men and a Girl*?
9. Who played Tom Hagen in the film *The Godfather*?
10. Which cartoon character did Shelley Duvall play in a 1980 Robert Altman film?
11. Which actor is the boss of Malpaso Productions?
12. Who directed the 1961 film *Victim*?
13. Who directed the 1995 film *Steal Big, Steal Little*?
14. Who played Kevin McMaxford in the 1997 film *Spice World*?
15. Which 1951 film was based on the novel *Coup de Grace*?

ANSWERS 1. Bill Bixby **2.** Baldrick **3.** Roj **4.** Terry Wogan **5.** Sid James **6.** A Night at the Opera **7.** Bonnie Parker **8.** Deanna Durbin **9.** Robert Duvall **10.** Olive Oyl **11.** Clint Eastwood **12.** Basil Dearden **13.** Andrew Davis **14.** Barry Humphries **15.** Sirocco.

SPORT

1. In which city was snooker's 1993 European Open held?
2. With which sport is the Austrian Christian Mayer associated?
3. In what year did Danny Blanchflower join Tottenham Hotspur?
4. What length, in metres, did Mike Powell jump at the 1991 IAAF World Championships?
5. When did Red Rum land his last Grand National victory?
6. In which year did Ray Reardon last win the World Professional snooker title?
7. Who in boxing was 'the Bronx Bull'?
8. For which international side did footballer Socrates play?
9. Which event did Guy Drut win at the 1976 Olympics?
10. Who lost the 1991 U.S. Open men's singles tennis final?
11. What was the nickname of Canadian ice hockey star Yvan Cournoyer?
12. In which city was figure skater Robin Cousins born?
13. Which Italian won the 1984 Olympic men's 10,000m title?
14. Which cricketer captained Kent from 1957-71?
15. Why was US Olympic swimming champion Buster Crabbe not allowed to compete at water polo in the 1936 Olympics?

ANSWERS 1. Antwerp **2.** Skiing **3.** 1954 **4.** 8.95m **5.** 1977 **6.** 1978 **7.** Jake La Motta **8.** Brazil **9.** 110m hurdles **10** Jim Courier **11.** The roadrunner **12.** Bristol **13.** Alberto Cova **14.** Colin Cowdrey **15.** Because he had appeared in advertisements.

POP

1. In which year did Prince record the album *Prince*?
2. Which studio album by Public Image Ltd includes the tracks *Francis Massacre* and *Four Enclosed Walls*?
3. Who wrote Robbie Williams's hit *She's the One*?
4. Which group's albums include 1987's *The Uplift Mofo Party Plan*?
5. Which group's 1984 debut album was *Café Bleu*?
6. The album *Caroline Now!* is a tribute album released in 2000 dedicated to which songwriter and group?
7. Which rap group had a group of minders in their organization called Security of the First World?
8. Which pop group's first No. 1 single was 1993's *Pray*?
9. To which major label did the indie group The Primitives sign in 1987?
10. Which rock group released the album *Abandoned Shopping Trolley Hotline*?
11. Which group had a top five single in September, 2000 with the song *Natural*?
12. Which metal outfit released the album *Operation: Mindcrime*?
13. Which female singer recorded the 1991 Island album *Love and a Million Other Things*?
14. In which year were the group Radiohead formed?
15. Which comedian released the single *1,2,3,4 Get With The Wicked* in 2000?

ANSWERS 1. 1979 **2.** Flowers of Romance **3.** Karl Wallinger **4.** Red Hot Chili Peppers **5.** The Style Council **6.** Brian Wilson & the Beach Boys **7.** Public Enemy **8.** Take That **9.** RCA **10.** Gomez **11.** S Club 7 **12.** Queensrÿche **13.** Claudia Brücken **14.** 1988 **15.** Richard Blackwood.

HISTORY

1. In which year did the European Union replace the European Community?
2. In which year did Diana, Princess of Wales, die?
3. In which county is Chartwell, former home of Sir Winston Churchill?
4. Which princess was the only daughter of King George IV and Caroline of Brunswick?
5. In which year did Parliamentarians capture and sack Corfe Castle in Dorset?
6. What was Spanish soldier Rodrigo Diaz de Vivar better known as?
7. From which city did Sir Francis Chichester begin and end his solo circumnavigation of the world?
8. Which Chinese statesman wrote the book *Summing Up At Seventy* in 1957?

9. In which month of 1944 were the Germans expelled from Dieppe?
10. Who became Conservative M.P. for Oldham in 1900?
11. Which famous climber was the first to ascend the volcano Chimborazo in Ecuador in 1880?
12. In which city was David Lloyd George born in 1863?
13. In which year was the world's worst nuclear power accident, at Chernobyl?
14. Of which country was Porfirio Diaz president from 1884-1911?
15. In which year did the Ivory Coast officially become the Côte d'Ivoire?

ANSWERS **1.** 1993 **2.** 1997 **3.** Kent **4.** Charlotte **5.** 1645 **6.** El Cid Campeador **7.** Plymouth **8.** Chiang Kai-Shek **9.** September **10.** Winston Churchill **11.** Edward Whymper **12.** Manchester **13.** 1986 **14.** Mexico **15.** 1986.

GENERAL KNOWLEDGE

1. In which year did the National Coal Board take over the coal-mining industry?
2. Which Irish writer authored *At Swim-Two-Birds*?
3. What is the sweet Rahat Lakhoum better known as?
4. Which film director was born Allen Stewart Konigsberg?
5. Which U.S. president was known as 'Rail Splitter'?
6. What is the Middle Eastern dish of meat and rice known as dolmas wrapped in?
7. Who composed the opera *The Rake's Progress*?
8. What in Scotland is a kaleyard?
9. Who is the hero of the novel *Crime and Punishment*?
10. What was O'Connell Street, Dublin, previously known as?
11. Who composed the *Rasumovsky Quartets*?
12. Blepharitis is an inflammation of which part of the face?
13. What did *The Raven* quoth in the poem by Edgar Allan Poe?
14. On what subject are the Reckitt lectures given?
15. Approximately what area, in square miles, is the Portuguese territory of Macao?

ANSWERS 1. 1947 **2.** Flann O'Brien **3.** Turkish Delight **4.** Woody Allen **5.** Abraham Lincoln **6.** Vine leaves **7.** Stravinsky **8.** A vegetable garden **9.** Raskolnikov **10.** Sackville Street **11.** Beethoven **12.** Eyelids **13.** Nevermore **14.** Archaeology **15.** 6 square miles.

ENTERTAINMENT

1. Who played *Bachelor Father* in a 1970s sitcom?
2. In the film *The Cook, The Thief, His Wife & Her Lover*, who plays 'The Wife'?
3. Which comedy team starred in the 1935 film *A Night at the Opera*?
4. What is Hywel Bennett's profession in the 1972 film *Endless Night*?
5. What is the profession of Catherine Zeta Jones in the 1999 film *Entrapment*?
6. Who is the author of the play *Stones in His Pockets*?
7. Which Swedish supermodel plays the wife of Arnold Schwarzenegger in the film *Batman & Robin*?
8. Which film producer was born Vladimir Leventon in 1904?
9. Who plays Dr. Susan McAlester in the 1999 film *Deep Blue Sea*?
10. Which Oscar-winner is co-founder of Tri Be Ca Productions?
11. The proposed film *Thirty Three* was the last project of which film director?
12. Who directed the 2000 film *Rancid Aluminium*?
13. Who directed the 1999 film *Bowfinger*?
14. In which city was the conductor and pianist Daniel Barenboim born?
15. Who plays hairdresser Frankie in the 2000 film *Limbo*?

ANSWERS **1.** Ian Carmichael **2.** Helen Mirren **3.** The Marx Brothers **4.** Chauffeur **5.** An insurance investigator **6.** Marie Jones **7.** Vendela Thommessen **8.** Val Lewton **9.** Saffron Burrows **10.** Robert De Niro **11.** Donald Cammell **12.** Ed Thomas **13.** Frank Oz **14.** Buenos Aires **15.** Patricia Arquette.

SPORT

1. Which world welterweight boxing champion was born on St. Thomas in the U.S. Virgin Islands in 1938?
2. Who won cycling's Giro d'Italia in 1996?
3. Who won the 1995 and '97 IAAF World Championships women's 800m title?
4. Who won the 1994 women's hockey World Cup?
5. Which country were the 1997 ice hockey world champions?
6. Who was world 500cc motor cycling champion from 1990-92?
7. At what weight did Thomas Hearns win his first world boxing title in 1980?
8. Which U.S. runner won the women's 1500m & 3000m titles at the 1983 IAAF World Championships?
9. Who became world junior lightweight boxing champion in 1931?
10. Which jockey won the 1960 and '63 1,000 Guineas?
11. Who won rugby union's Swalec Cup in 1998?
12. Who was Welsh amateur snooker champion in 1975?
13. Which Australian bowler took 44 wickets in the 1935/36 Test series against South Africa?
14. Who became world lightweight boxing champion in 1942?
15. Which horse won the 1996 Grand National?

ANSWERS 1. Emile Griffith **2.** Pavel Tonkov **3.** Ana Quirot **4.** Australia **5.** Canada **6.** Wayne Rainey **7.** Welterweight **8.** Mary Decker **9.** Kid Chocolate **10.** Roger Poincelet **11.** Llanelli **12.** Terry Griffiths **13.** Clarrie Grimmett **14.** Beau Jack **15.** Rough Quest.

POP

1. Malcolm Owen died in 1980. With which band did he sing?
2. Sarah Cracknell is singer with which group?
3. Moore and Prater are the surnames of which soul duo?
4. Which Manchester group recorded the 1982 album *Sextet*?
5. Which group recorded the 1994 album *Ich Bin Ein Auslander*?
6. Which female singer formed All About Eve in 1985?
7. Which reggae star was born Max Elliott in 1960?
8. Which guitarist formed the Amboy Dukes in 1966?
9. In which year was guitarist Chris Rea born?
10. Which group recorded the 1991 album *I am the Greatest*?
11. Which group scored a 1997 top ten single with *All Mine*?
12. What was the debut single of group the Anti-Nowhere League?
13. What was the Real Thing's 1976 No. 1 single?
14. In which year did group A.R. Kane form?
15. Which group had a 1971 hit single with *Witch Queen of New Orleans*?

ANSWERS 1. The Ruts **2.** St. Etienne **3.** Sam and Dave **4.** A Certain Ratio **5.** Pop Will Eat Itself **6.** Julianne Regan **7.** Maxi Priest **8.** Ted Nugent **9.** 1951 **10.** A House **11.** Portishead **12.** Streets of London **13.** You To Me Are Everything **14.** 1986 **15.** Redbone.

WORDS

1. Who are 'the Slops'?
2. What in printing do the letters u.c. stand for?
3. What are the scopae of a bee?
4. Is gabbro a type of wood or rock?
5. What would you do with a zloty in Poland?
6. What bird is called a menura in Australia?
7. What type of fruit tree is a mazzard?
8. What type of creature is an emmet?
9. Who, or what, is 'small-back'?
10. What sort of creature is a scup?
11. What in medical terms is HRT?
12. What does the Latin phrase 'mea culpa' mean?
13. What is a ziff in Australian parlance?
14. What sort of creatures belong to the family *Gadidae*?
15. What is an 'enfant terrible'?

ANSWERS 1. The police **2.** Upper case **3.** The hairs used to collect pollen **4.** Rock **5.** Spend it **6.** Lyre-bird **7.** A cherry tree **8.** An ant **9.** Death **10.** A fish **11.** Hormone replacement therapy **12.** My fault **13.** A beard **14.** Fish **15.** A social or moral nuisance.

GENERAL KNOWLEDGE

1. Of which country was Sir John Grey Gorton prime minister from 1968 to 1971?
2. Which flag is known as the Red Duster?
3. What type of creature is a chacma?
4. Ragusa was the former Italian name of which port?
5. What type of creature is a kalong?
6. Which Labour M.P. for Jarrow was appointed Minister of Education in 1945?
7. Who wrote the novel *Conducting Bodies*?
8. How many paces to the minute is the double-time march in the U.S. army?
9. Who designed the 14-foot dinghy known as a Redwing?
10. In which year was the Reform Club in London founded?
11. Who authored the short story collection *Dubliners*?
12. Which two places did the bridge over the Rhine at Remagen link?
13. Who wrote the 1920 novel *The Rescue*?
14. Who authored the novel *The Tower of Trebizond*?
15. Which three countries formed the Triple Entente in World War One?

ANSWERS **1.** Australia **2.** Red Ensign **3.** Monkey **4.** Dubrovnik **5.** Bat **6.** Ellen Wilkinson **7.** Claude Simon **8.** 180 **9.** Uffa Fox **10.** 1832 **11.** James Joyce **12.** Cologne and Koblenz **13.** Joseph Conrad **14.** Rose Macaulay **15.** France, Britain and Russia.

ENTERTAINMENT

1. Who plays the title role in the 1951 film *Scrooge*?
2. What is Sophie Marceau's character name in the James Bond film *The World Is Not Enough*?
3. Who was the dancing partner of Fred Astaire in the 1955 film *Daddy Long Legs*?
4. Who played Estella in the 1946 film *Great Expectations*?
5. What is Ray Winstone's profession in the 1999 film *Fanny and Elvis*?
6. Who plays air-traffic controller Nick Calzone in the 1999 film *Pushing Tin*?
7. Which actress played Lulu in the classic 1928 silent film *Pandora's Box*?
8. Which actor recorded the record album *The Transformed Man* in the late 1960s?
9. Which comedy team starred in the 1937 film *A Day at the Races*?
10. In the film *The Cook, The Thief, His Wife & Her Lover*, who plays 'The Cook'?
11. In which 1990s sitcom did Su Pollard play Ivy Teasdale?
12. Which actress starred as pilot Carmen Ibanez in the film *Starship Troopers*?
13. Which comic actress plays talent booker Paula in sitcom *The Larry Sanders Show*?
14. Who plays Ichabod Crane in the 1999 film *Sleepy Hollow*?
15. What is Tim Roth's character name in the 1999 film *The Legend of 1900*?

ANSWERS 1. Alastair Sim **2.** Elektra King **3.** Leslie Caron **4.** Jean Simmons **5.** A car dealer **6.** John Cusack **7.** Louise Brooks **8.** William Shatner **9.** The Marx Brothers **10.** Richard Bohringer **11.** You Rang, M'Lord? **12.** Denise Richards **13.** Janeane Garofalo **14.** Johnny Depp **15.** 1900.

SPORT

1. What is Barcelona midfielder Fernando Macedo da Silva also known as?
2. In which Lancashire town was Australian rugby league player Bozo Fulton born?
3. Which Australian cricketer, who died in 1929, batted in every position in the order in his Test career?
4. Who trained 1956 Epsom Derby-winning horse Lavandin?
5. In which city was Superbowl XXIX played in 1995?
6. Who was world individual freshwater angling champion in 1980 and '83?
7. In which year did Newcastle United win their first Division One football title?
8. Which jockey's first win in the Prix de l'Arc de Triomphe was on Bot Mot III in 1966?
9. Which country did Hassiba Boulmerka, 1995 IAAF World Championship women's 1500m winner, represent?
10. Who won the 1997 Nat West Trophy in cricket?
11. Which Sussex cricketer is known as Baba Oily?
12. Which cricketer captained Sussex from 1973-7?
13. Which rider won the 1998 world individual three-day event championship?
14. Who scored the winning goal in West Ham United's 1980 FA Cup Final victory?
15. Who became world junior welterweight boxing champion in 1959?

ANSWERS **1.** Nano **2.** Warrington **3.** Syd Gregory **4.** Alec Head **5.** Miami **6.** Wolf-Rudiger Kremkus **7.** 1905 **8.** Freddy Head **9.** Algeria **10.** Essex **11.** Tony Cottey **12.** Tony Greig **13.** Blyth Tait **14.** Trevor Brooking **15.** Carlos Ortiz.

POP

1. Which singer charted in 1984 with the song *Theme From Cheers*?

2. What were the names of the two Allman Brothers?

3. Which blues singer had a minor hit in 1964 with *Shame Shame Shame*?

4. Which Birmingham band recorded the 1981 album *Playing With a Different Sex*?

5. Which duo had a Top 30 single in 1987 with *Soul Man*?

6. Which rap group recorded the 1991 album *The Low End Theory*?

7. Which group had a top ten single in 1997 with *Kowalski*?

8. Which group recorded the chart-topping song *Horse with No Name*?

9. Which duo charted in 1993 with the single *Resurrection*?

10. Which former member of The Alarm released the 1994 solo album *Breath*?

11. What was Jim Reeves' first U.K. chart single?

12. Which punk group released the flexi-disc *Love Lies Limp*?

13. Which group backed Vic Reeves on the 1991 hit *Born Free*?

14. What was the Angelic Upstarts' singer Thomas Mensforth also known as?

15. Which group had a 1988 Top 40 hit with *Minnie the Moocher*?

ANSWERS 1. Gary Portnoy **2.** Duane and Gregg **3.** Jimmy Reed **4.** Au Pairs **5.** Sam Moore and Lou Reed **6.** A Tribe Called Quest **7.** Primal Scream **8.** America **9.** Brian May & Cozy Powell **10.** Mike Peters **11.** He'll Have To Go **12.** Alternative T.V. **13.** The Roman Numerals **14.** Mensi **15.** Reggae Philharmonic Orchestra.

SCIENCE

1. What does BTU stand for in terms of heat?
2. What in meteorology is graupel?
3. How many gallons of beer are in an anker?
4. What type of cement did Joseph Aspdin patent in 1824?
5. What in computing does DPI stand for?
6. In which country does the hot wind khamsin blow in early summer?
7. How many hundredweights make up a ton?
8. What in computing does GIF stand for?
9. How many edges has a regular octahedron?
10. During which period of geological time did trilobites become extinct?
11. Of what is hypnophobia a fear?
12. Which German won the 1905 Nobel prize for medicine for his research on tuberculosis?
13. How many °F is 17°C?
14. Which French scientist founded the branch of physics that he named electrodynamics?
15. Who shared the 1903 Nobel prize for physics with the Curies?

ANSWERS **1.** British thermal unit **2.** Soft partially melted hail **3.** 10 **4.** Portland cement **5.** Dots per inch **6.** Egypt **7.** 20 **8.** Graphic image format **9.** 12 **10.** Permian **11.** Sleep **12.** Robert Koch **13.** 63° **14.** André Ampère **15.** Antoine Becquerel.

GENERAL KNOWLEDGE

1. In which century did English highwayman Dick Turpin live?
2. What was Anne Marie Grosholtz better known as?
3. What on a ship is a futtock?
4. In which year did senator Joe McCarthy die?
5. What type of creature is a karakul?
6. In which year was the Bank of England nationalized?
7. What is the name of Eliza's father in the play *Pygmalion*?
8. What is 25 x 25?
9. What type of fruit is a biffin?
10. Which South African clergyman received the 1984 Nobel peace prize?
11. In which island group is the U.S. naval base of Cavite?
12. Who was the leader of the Peasant's Revolt in 1381?
13. Who was elected Labour M.P. for Oldham West and Royton in 1997?
14. Which English translator of the Bible was burned as a heretic in Belgium in 1536?
15. In which year did French couturier Christian Dior die?

ANSWERS **1.** 18th **2.** Madame Tussaud **3.** A rib in the frame of a wooden vessel **4.** 1957 **5.** Sheep **6.** 1946 **7.** Alfred **8.** 625 **9.** Apple **10.** Desmond Tutu **11.** Philippines **12.** Wat Tyler **13.** Michael Meacher **14.** Wiliam Tyndale **15.** 1957.

ENTERTAINMENT

1. Who plays the king in the 1999 film *Anna and the King*?
2. Which director voices the part of a radio dispatcher in his 2000 film *Bringing Out the Dead*?
3. Jerry Lundegaard is the name of a car salesman in which 1990s film?
4. What is Edward G. Robinson's character name in the 1945 film *Scarlet Street*?
5. In which U.S. state is the film *The Blair Witch Project* set?
6. Who plays the title role in Luc Besson's film *Joan of Arc*?
7. Who stars as Australian woman Maddy in the 1999 film *Mad Cows*?
8. Which member of the Fiennes family directed brother Ralph in the 1999 film *Onegin*?
9. Which sitcom family comprised Ria, Ben, Adam, and Russell?
10. Which actor directed the television drama series *Real Women*?
11. Who plays the Dutch gardener Meneer Chrome in the 1997 film *The Serpent's Kiss*?
12. Who plays Angela in the 2000 film *Angela's Ashes*?
13. Who was the male star of the 1998 film *Among Giants*?
14. In which 2000 film does Denzel Washington play forensic officer Lincoln Rhyme?
15. *RKO 281* is a film about which film director?

ANSWERS 1. Chow Yun-Fat **2.** Martin Scorsese **3.** Fargo **4.** Chris Cross **5.** Maryland **6.** Milla Jovovich **7.** Anna Friel **8.** Martha **9.** The Parkinson family in Butterflies **10.** Phil Davis **11.** Ewan McGregor **12.** Emily Watson **13.** Pete Postlethwaite **14.** The Bone Collector **15.** Orson Welles.

SPORT

1. For which French club side did rugby union player Jean Gachassin become player/trainer in 1969?
2. Who in 1980 won all five men's Olympic speed skating titles?
3. In which city was Superbowl XXXI played in 1997?
4. Which country won the World Team Freshwater Angling title in 1996 and '97?
5. Geoff Hurst famously scored three goals in the 1966 World Cup final. How many players had scored twice in the final prior to that?
6. Who won the 1996 Nat West Trophy in cricket?
7. Who won the women's 200m title at the 1993 and '95 IAAF World Championships?
8. Which rider won the 1994 Badminton Horse Trials?
9. Which Essex cricketer is known as Dic Dic?
10. Who became world flyweight boxing champion in 1960?
11. Who were runners-up in football's Division One from 1891-93?
12. Who was the 1995 USPGA golf champion?
13. For which side did ice hockey player Bill Cook play his entire NHL career?
14. In which round did Henry Cooper floor Muhammad Ali in their 1963 fight?
15. Which Huddersfield rugby league player scored ten tries against Keighley in 1951?

ANSWERS 1. Stade de Bagnères **2.** Eric Heiden **3.** New Orleans **4.** Italy **5.** Five **6.** Lancashire **7.** Merlene Ottey **8.** Mark Todd **9.** Ashley Cowan **10.** Pone Kingpetch **11.** Preston North End **12.** Steve Elkington **13.** New York Rangers **14.** Fourth **15.** Lionel Cooper.

POP

1. Who produced Leonard Cohen's album *Death of a Ladies Man*?
2. Which legendary guitarist recorded the 2000 album *Hitomi*?
3. What nationality is the country music artist Kasey Chambers?
4. The albums *God*, *Murder* and *Love* released in 2000 were compilations of which singer's work?
5. Who recorded the 2000 solo album *My Music Loves You (Even If I Don't)*?
6. What was rock group King Crimson's second album called?
7. On the 2000 John Denver tribute album *Take Me Home*, which track is sung by Bonnie Prince Billy?
8. On which studio album by the group Queen does the track *Keep Yourself Alive* appear?
9. Which world leader was the uncle of Tom Morello of the group *Rage Against the Machine*?
10. Which studio album by the group Mott the Hoople includes the song *Marionette*?
11. What is the real name of recording artist Momus?
12. Which Welsh group recorded the album *Fixation with Long Journeys*?
13. Which pop group had a top ten single in 1988 with *The King of Rock'n' Roll*?
14. Which pop group had a 1981 No. 1 single with *Don't You Want Me*?
15. Cindy, Terry, Maxine and Dawn are the forenames of which 1990s girl group?

ANSWERS **1.** Phil Spector **2.** John Fahey **3.** Australian **4.** Johnny Cash **5.** Mike Randle **6.** In the Wake of Poseidon **7.** The Eagle and the Hawk **8.** Queen **9.** Jomo Kenyatta **10.** The Hoople **11.** Nick Currie **12.** Derrero **13.** Prefab Sprout **14.** Human League **15.** En Vogue.

PEOPLE

1. Which actor did actress Jean Simmons divorce in 1960?
2. In which year did the painter Edward Hopper die?
3. Anna Cornelia Carbentus was the mother of which artist?
4. How did the criminal Albert DeSalvo, also known as 'The Boston Strangler' die?
5. In which year was businesswoman Anita Roddick born?
6. Which art critic's middle names are Studley Forrest?
7. Who replaced Andrew Davis as chief conductor of the BBC Symphony Orchestra in 2000?
8. Which yachtsman was awarded the MBE and Legion d'Honneur for rescuing a fellow sailor in the 1997 Vendée Globe race?
9. Which scientist authored the book *Almost Like A Whale*?
10. What is George W. Bush's wife called?
11. To which British king was Eleanor of Aquitaine married?
12. Which French singer was the first wife of singer Andy Williams?
13. What is the full name of soul singer Ray Charles?
14. Which darts player is known as 'The Power'?
15. What are the forenames of the advertising executives the Saatchi Brothers?

ANSWERS 1. Stewart Granger **2.** 1967 **3.** Vincent Van Gogh **4.** He was stabbed to death in prison **5.** 1942 **6.** Robert Hughes **7.** Leonard Slatkin **8.** Peter Goss **9.** Steve Jones **10.** Laura **11.** Henry II **12.** Claudine Longet **13.** Ray Charles Robinson **14.** Phil Taylor **15.** Charles and Maurice.

GENERAL KNOWLEDGE

1. How high was the tsunami recorded in Litya Bay, Alaska in 1958?
2. Where in New Zealand is the city of Auckland - North Island or South Island?
3. In which year did the painter El Greco die?
4. In which year was the Herald of Free Enterprise ferry disaster?
5. In which year was the magazine Playboy first published?
6. What is unusual about the Blind Cow restaurant in Zurich?
7. Which play's 20,000th performance took place in December 2000?
8. Which car manufacturer makes the Arosa 16V Sport?
9. Who introduced the concept of a lottery to Paris in 1757?
10. Which car manufacturer makes the Octavia Estate?

11. What grade did Prince William get in A-Level Biology?
12. Which teams contested the 2000 European Champions League final in football?
13. Which German painter's works include *The Monk by the Sea*?
14. What did the management consultancy Andersen Consulting rename themselves in 2001?
15. What form of transport in the U.S. is a Winnebago?

ANSWERS 1. 1,720 feet **2.** North **3.** 1614 **4.** 1987 **5.** 1953 **6.** Customers eat in complete darkness **7.** The Mousetrap **8.** Seat **9.** Casanova **10.** Skoda **11.** C **12.** Valencia and Real Madrid **13.** Caspar David Friedrich **14.** Accenture **15.** A luxury motor home.

ENTERTAINMENT

1. Who plays a robot in the 2000 film *Bicentennial Man*?
2. Who wrote the 1981 film script *The Big Brass Ring* which remained unmade at the time of his death?
3. "Heads Will Roll" was the advertising slogan for which the 2000 film?
4. Who directed the 2000 film *The Darkest Light*?
5. Which 1970s sitcom was set in the accounts department of International Rentals?
6. Who did Colin Bean play in the sitcom *Dad's Army*?
7. In the film *The Cook, The Thief, His Wife & Her Lover*, who plays 'The Thief'?
8. Who directed the 2000 film *Angela's Ashes*?
9. Who plays a serial killer in Donald Cammell's film *White of the Eye*?
10. Who plays the television presenter Mike Wallace in the 1999 film *The Insider*?
11. Which British actress voices the character Jane in the 1999 Disney animated film *Tarzan*?
12. Who starred as Michael Flynn in Peter Mullan's film *Orphans*?
13. The 1999 film *Brokedown Palace* is about drug smuggling in which country?
14. The 1999 film *The Limey* starring Terence Stamp uses clips from which earlier film?
15. The singing group The Four Nightingales became which film comedy team?

ANSWERS 1. Robin Williams **2.** Orson Welles **3.** Sleepy Hollow **4.** Simon Beaufoy **5.** The Squirrels **6.** Private Sponge **7.** Michael Gambon **8.** Alan Parker **9.** David Keith **10.** Christopher Plummer **11.** Minnie Driver **12.** Douglas Henshall **13.** Thailand **14.** Poor Cow **15.** The Marx Brothers.

SPORT

1. Which husband and wife team won the 1986 Commonwealth Games small bore rifle pairs title?
2. Which Italian cyclist won the Giro d'Italia in 1953?
3. Who was the first man to win the world heavyweight boxing title under the Marquess of Queensbury Rules?
4. With what sport would you associate Joe Namath?
5. In which year was Pete Sampras born?
6. Which of the two equestrian Schockemöhle brothers is the elder?
7. What are Seattle's American football team called?
8. Which boxer was nicknamed 'the Fighting Marine'?
9. In which year was Alf Ramsey made England's football manager?
10. What was U.S. Olympic swimming champion Rowdy Gaines' real name?
11. Which female British swimmer won the 1956 Olympic 100m backstroke title?
12. Who was the 1960 Olympic women's figure skating champion?
13. Who scored Holland's consolation goal in the 1974 World Cup Final?
14. Who were runners-up in football's Division One from 1947-49?
15. Who won the women's 400m titles at the 1991 and '95 IAAF World Championships?

ANSWERS 1. Malcolm and Sarah Cooper **2.** Fausto Coppi **3.** Jim Corbett **4.** American football **5.** 1971 **6.** Alwin **7.** Seattle Seahawks **8.** Gene Tunney **9.** 1963 **10.** Ambrose Gaines IV **11.** Judy Grinham **12.** Carol Heiss **13.** Neeskens **14.** Manchester United **15.** Marie-José Pérec.

POP

1. What was Fat Les's 1998 Christmas hit?
2. Which group had a minor hit in 1992 with the single *Armchair Anarchist*?
3. From which country does singer Ricky Martin hail?
4. Which U.S. vocalist scored a 1997 hit with *Where Have All the Cowboys Gone*?
5. Who had a 1998 Top 10 single with *The Rockafeller Skank*?
6. From which country does singer Merril Bainbridge hail?
7. What was Kula Shaker's first Top 10 single?
8. Which was the first single by Rod Stewart to reach No. 1 in the U.K. and U.S.?
9. From which country does singer k.d. lang come?
10. Which group recorded the album *Made From Technetium*?
11. Which U.K. singer had a 1998 hit single with *Little Bit of Lovin'*?
12. Which duo charted in 1996 with the single *Better Watch Out*?
13. Which duo had a 1998 Top 30 single with *Most High*?
14. Which DJ recorded the 1994 album *One Step Ahead of the Spider*?
15. Which group charted in 1996 with the single *Release the Pressure*?

ANSWERS 1. Naughty Christmas (Goblin in the Office) **2.** Kingmaker **3.** Puerto Rico **4.** Paula Cole **5.** Fatboy Slim **6.** Australia **7.** Tattva **8.** Maggie May **9.** Canada **10.** Man or Astro-Man? **11.** Kele Le Roc **12.** Ant and Dec **13.** Page and Plant **14.** MC 900 FT Jesus **15.** Leftfield.

ART AND LITERATURE

1. Which artist painted the 1966 work *Portrait of Isabel Rawsthorne*?
2. Who wrote the short stories *The Lottery* and *My Life with R.H. Macy*?
3. Which artist painted the 1949 work *Questioning Children*?
4. Which German-born artist painted the 1982 oil *Adieu*?
5. Who wrote the novel *The Secret History*?
6. Which French artist painted the 1929 work *The Harvest*?
7. Who wrote the novel *My Idea of Fun*?
8. In which year did the artist Robert Delaunay die?
9. Which British artist painted the 1962 abstract work *Tribune*?
10. Which French artist painted the work *Le Jardinier Vallier*?
11. Who wrote the 1995 novel *Mister Sandman*?
12. Which French artist painted the 1915 work *Coffee*?
13. What nationality was the painter Jacques-Émile Blanche?
14. Which British sculptor's works include the 1977 steel object *Emma Dipper*?
15. Who wrote the 1992 novel *Poor Things*?

ANSWERS 1. Francis Bacon **2.** Shirley Jackson **3.** Karel Appel **4.** Georg Baselitz **5.** Donna Tartt **6.** Raoul Dufy **7.** Will Self **8.** 1941 **9.** Harold Cohen **10.** Paul Cézanne **11.** Barbara Gowdy **12.** Pierre Bonnard **13.** French **14.** Sir Anthony Caro **15.** Alisdair Gray.

GENERAL KNOWLEDGE

1. In which year was the British Legion founded?
2. What is the port of Smyrna now known as?
3. Between which two countries was the region of Livonia divided in 1918?
4. Which Agatha Christie detective features in *Evil Under the Sun*?
5. What is the Euxine Sea better known as?
6. In which year was Martin Luther King Jr. assassinated?
7. In which play by Henrik Ibsen is Mrs. Alving a character?
8. Which seaport is at the head of the Shannon estuary?
9. Which book of the Bible features the story of Noah's ark?
10. To what animal does the adjective corvine refer?
11. What line on a map connects places having an equal period of sunshine?
12. What is the major religion of Mali?
13. On which part of the body would you have worn a buskin in Ancient Greece?
14. How many ounces are there in a pound?
15. In what year did racing car designer Enzo Ferrari die?

ANSWERS 1. 1921 **2.** Izmir **3.** Latvia and Estonia **4.** Hercule Poirot **5.** Black Sea **6.** 1968 **7.** Ghosts **8.** Limerick **9.** Genesis **10.** Crow **11.** Isohel **12.** Muslim **13.** Foot **14.** 16 **15.** 1988.

ENTERTAINMENT

1. Which English comic actor plays a hotel manager in the 1999 film *The Out-of-Towners*?
2. What is Denise Richards' character name in the James Bond film *The World Is Not Enough*?
3. Which scriptwriter played WPC Kershaw in the soap *Albion Market*?
4. Who played the title role in the 1952 film *Angel Face*?
5. What is Gregory's surname in the 1999 film *Gregory's Two Girls*?
6. What are the forenames of the three students in the film *The Blair Witch Project*?
7. Who plays Balthus Van Tassel in the 2000 film *Sleepy Hollow*?
8. Which British actor plays Eddie Murphy's therapist in the film *Bowfinger*?
9. Which comedy actor played the novice spy Peter Chapman in 1990s sitcom *The Piglet Files*?
10. Which actress plays Sarah Beaumont in television soap *Neighbours*?
11. Which television cook plays the title role in the 1999 film *Cotton Mary*?

12. Who directed the 2000 film *Summer of Sam*?
13. Which 1999 film stars Sarah Michelle Gellar and a spell-casting crab?
14. What was Fred Astaire and Ginger Rogers' first film together?
15. Which comedy actor became landlord of *The Prince of Denmark* in the 1974 BBC sitcom of the same name?

ANSWERS **1.** John Cleese **2.** Dr. Christmas Jones **3.** Kay Mellor **4.** Jean Simmons **5.** Underwood **6.** Heather, Mike and Josh **7.** Michael Gambon **8.** Terence Stamp **9.** Nicholas Lyndhurst **10.** Nicola Charles **11.** Madhur Jaffrey **12.** Spike Lee **13.** Simply Irresistible **14.** Flying Down to Rio **15.** Ronnie Corbett.

SPORT

1. How many Test wickets did Fred Trueman take for England?
2. Who was the first sub 3 mins 50 secs miler?
3. Who won the 1980 World Professional Snooker championship?
4. How many players are in a rugby league side?
5. Who won her 25th golfing title at the 1993 Australian Ladies Masters?
6. Who in 1974 rode Cannonade to victory in the 100th Kentucky Derby?
7. In which year was England rugby union player Fran Cotton born?
8. Who won the 1948 British Open golf tournament?
9. Which golfer won the 1992 U.S. Masters golf tournament?
10. Who became world featherweight boxing champion in 1946?
11. Who won the 1996 County Cricket Championship?
12. Which jockey rode 1994 Epsom Derby winner Erhaab?
13. For which international rugby union side did John Gainsford play from 1960-67?
14. What was the nickname of swimmer Michael Gross?
15. What time did David Hemery run when he won the 1968 Olympic 400m hurdles?

ANSWERS **1.** 307 **2.** John Walker **3.** Cliff Thorburn **4.** 13 **5.** Laura Davies **6.** Angel Cordero **7.** 1947 **8.** Henry Cotton **9.** Fred Couples **10.** Willie Pep **11.** Leicestershire **12.** Willie Carson **13.** South Africa **14.** The albatross **15.** 48.12 secs.

POP

1. Which vocalist had a minor 1996 hit with *The Mill Hill Self Hate Club*?
2. Who sang the theme song to the James Bond film *Licence to Kill*?
3. Who duetted with Fish on the 1995 single *Just Good Friends*?
4. What was Collapsed Lung's 1998 hit single?
5. Gene Simmons and Paul Stanley formed which band in 1972?
6. Which female singer recorded the album *Deadline on My Memories*?
7. Which vocalist featured on Pato Banton's 1995 hit *Bubbling Hot*?
8. Which group had a minor chart hit in 1994 with *Big Gay Heart*?
9. Which blues guitarist's guitar is named Lucille?
10. Which female vocalist had single success in 1992 with *Walking on Broken Glass*?
11. Which heavy metal band did Rob Halford join in 1971?
12. Which group's debut Top 10 single was 1997's *Nancy Boy*?
13. Which group recorded the 1987 album *Crooked Mile*?
14. What was Gary Barlow's second solo No. 1 single?
15. Which was the only single by The Supremes to reach No. 1 in the U.K. and the U.S.?

ANSWERS **1.** Edward Ball **2.** Gladys Knight **3.** Sam Brown **4.** Eat My Goal **5.** Kiss **6.** Billie Ray Martin **7.** Ranking Roger **8.** Lemonheads **9.** B.B. King **10.** Annie Lennox **11.** Judas Priest **12.** Placebo **13.** Microdisney **14.** Love Won't Wait **15.** Baby Love.

GEOGRAPHY

1. What are the three Medway towns?
2. On which river is Davenport, Iowa?
3. In which European country are the Dauphiné Alps?
4. What is the approximate area, in square miles, of the U.S. state of Vermont?
5. The rivers Tapajos and Xingu are tributaries of which river?
6. Lake Titicaca straddles which two South American countries?
7. How many minutes north of the equator is the Brazilian city of Macapa?
8. In which country is the volcano Coseguina?
9. In which year did the town of West Hartlepool become part of Hartlepool?
10. Bruges is the capital of which province of Belgium?
11. What is the state capital of West Virginia?
12. In which African country is the town of Welkom?
13. In which English county is the village of Delabole?
14. What Australian river is the largest tributary of the Murray?
15. Which is larger: Lake Titicaca or Lake Ontario?

ANSWERS 1. Chatham, Gillingham and Rochester **2.** Mississippi **3.** France **4.** 9609 sq.m. **5.** Amazon **6.** Peru and Bolivia **7.** Five **8.** Nicaragua **9.** 1967 **10.** West Flanders **11.** Charleston **12.** South Africa **13.** Cornwall **14.** Darling **15.** Lake Ontario.

GENERAL KNOWLEDGE

1. In which year did jazz player Louis Armstrong die?

2. Who wrote *The Last of the Mohicans*?

3. In which English county is Farnborough?

4. What is an 'eye dog'?

5. Which U.S. film actress was born Harlean Carpentier?

6. What is the gestation period in months of a llama?

7. Which publishing firm did Carmen Calill found in 1973?

8. Who composed the opera *Artaxerxes* which was first performed in 1762?

9. Which organization was formerly known as the Spastics Association?

10. What breed of dog is also called a Persian greyhound?

11. Who directed the 1978 film *Pretty Baby*?

12. Who was president of the U.S. from 1881-85?

13. Which French dish translates as 'cock with wine'?

14. On which river is the town of Evesham?

15. Why is a heart cherry so called?

ANSWERS 1. 1971 **2.** James Fenimore Cooper **3.** Hampshire **4.** One trained to control sheep by staring at them **5.** Jean Harlow **6.** Eleven **7.** Virago **8.** Thomas Arne **9.** Scope **10.** Saluki **11.** Louis Malle **12.** Chester A. Arthur **13.** Coq au vin **14.** Avon **15.** Because of its shape.

ENTERTAINMENT

1. Who directed the 2000 film *A Room for Romeo Brass*?
2. Who played the female lead of a Paris fashion model in the 1957 film *Funny Face*?
3. The 1999 film *Detroit Rock City* centres on which real heavy metal group?
4. Who plays Ed in the 1999 film *Edtv*?
5. What in 1999 became the highest-grossing German film in the United States since *Das Boot*?
6. Which 1970s British sitcom derived from the long-running U.S. show *Good Times*?
7. What was the profession of James Bolam's character Figgis in the sitcom *Only When I Laugh*?
8. What were the name of Fletcher's son and daughter in *Going Straight*, the follow-up to the sitcom *Porridge*?
9. Who wrote the book on which the 1996 film *Sleepers* is based?
10. On whose novel is the film *Walkabout*, starring Jenny Agutter, based?
11. Who plays the female lead in the 1999 film *Anna and the King*?
12. Who directed the film *Alien3*?
13. Which *Trainspotting* actor stars in the film *julien donkey-boy*?
14. In which year did animators William Hanna and Joseph Barbera first meet?
15. What was the U.S. version of Channel 5 game show *Touching the Truck* called?

ANSWERS 1. Shane Meadows **2.** Audrey Hepburn **3.** Kiss **4.** Matthew McConaughey **5.** Run Lola Run **6.** The Fosters **7.** Lorry driver **8.** Ingrid and Raymond **9.** Lorenzo Carcaterra **10.** James Vance Marshall **11.** Jodie Foster **12.** David Fincher **13.** Ewen Bremner **14.** 1937 **15.** Hands on a Hardbody.

SPORT

1. With which team did American football star Forrest Gregg finish his playing career in 1971?
2. Who in the 1947/48 series against Australia became the first Indian cricketer to hit centuries in each innings of a Test?
3. Who scored twice for France in their 1998 World Cup Final victory?
4. Which football team won four out of five Football League titles between 1895 and 1900?
5. Who scored Liverpool's consolation goal in the 1971 FA Cup Final?
6. Which rugby league club did Andy Gregory join in 1979?
7. Who became world light heavyweight boxing champion in 1916?
8. What was the nationality of 1933 Wimbledon men's singles tennis champion Jack Crawford?
9. In which city was U.S. golfer Ben Crenshaw born?
10. Which Australian rugby league centre was nicknamed 'The Crow'?
11. Who took over the captaincy of the New Zealand Test cricket team in 1990?
12. Who captained Holland in the 1974 football World Cup final?
13. What was the nickname of American baseball star Sam Crawford?
14. What nationality was Olympic athlete Joaquim Cruz?
15. In billiards, what is Whitechapel?

ANSWERS **1.** Dallas Cowboys **2.** Vijay Hazare **3.** Zidane **4.** Aston Villa **5.** Steve Heighway **6.** Widnes **7.** Battling Levinsky **8.** Australian **9.** Austin, Texas **10.** Michael Cronin **11.** Martin Crowe **12.** Johan Cruyff **13.** Wahoo Sam **14.** Brazilian **15.** The act of potting one's opponent's white ball.

POP

1. Which former member of the group Echo and the Bunnymen released the 2000 album *Performance* under the name Glide?
2. In which year did the pop group Five Star reach No. 2 in the singles chart with *Rain or Shine*?
3. Which group recorded the albums *Bayou Country* and *Green River*?
4. In which year did The Carpenters have a No. 2 single with *Yesterday Once More*?
5. Who replaced Palmolive in the punk group The Raincoats?
6. In which year did Elvis Presley have a U.K. hit with the single *An American Trilogy*?
7. Which legendary reggae producer is nicknamed 'Scratch'?
8. Which duo had Top 10 single hits in 1981 with *Under Your Thumb* and *Wedding Bells*?
9. Which former member of the group Genesis recorded the 2000 album *Sketches of Satie* with his brother John?
10. Which group recorded the 1980 album *What's the Matter Boy?*?
11. Which former member of the group The Boo Radleys released a mini album in 2000 under the guise *Brave Captain*?
12. Which pop group recorded the 2000 single *Who the Hell Are You?*
13. Which female singer recorded the 2000 single *Boy Next Door*?
14. From which European country do the group Kent hail?
15. Which two former members of the group Public Image Ltd comprise half of the group The Damage Manual?

ANSWERS 1. Will Sergeant **2.** 1986 **3.** Creedence Clearwater Revival **4.** 1973 **5.** Ingrid Weiss **6.** 1972 **7.** Lee Perry **8.** Godley and Creme **9.** Steve Hackett **10.** Vic Godard & the Subway Sect **11.** Martin Carr **12.** Madison Avenue **13.** Jamelia **14.** Sweden **15.** Jah Wobble and Martin Atkins.

HISTORY

1. Who was king of Castile from 1035-65?
2. Leaders of which plot to kill Queen Elizabeth were executed in 1586?
3. In which year was Sir Thomas Wentworth, 1st Earl of Stafford, beheaded following a charge of high treason?
4. Who succeeded to the U.S. presidency on the death of Zachary Taylor?
5. In which year of World War II did Donald Bailey invent the Bailey Bridge?
6. In which year was Robespierre executed?
7. Which composer famously visited Staffa in 1829?
8. Anastasio Bustamante was president of which country from 1837-41?
9. Who was prime minister of the Bulgarian People's Republic from 1946-49?
10. In which year did the Folies-Bergère Theatre open in Paris?
11. In which year of World War II was the battleship Admiral Graf Spee scuttled?
12. Which future president of the U.S. served as governor of Massachusetts from 1919-20?
13. In which year did William III land at Torbay?
14. Where in 1854 was there a rebellion of Australian miners?
15. In which year did Gerald Ford become president of the U.S.?

ANSWERS 1. Ferdinand I **2.** Babington's Plot **3.** 1641 **4.** Millard Fillmore **5.** 1941 **6.** 1794 **7.** Mendelssohn **8.** Mexico **9.** Georgi Dimitrov **10.** 1869 **11.** 1939 **12.** John Calvin Coolidge **13.** 1688 **14.** Eureka Stockade, Ballarat **15.** 1974.

GENERAL KNOWLEDGE

1. How high is the world's tallest building, Petronas Towers?
2. In which African country are the towns of Kano and Lafia?
3. How many people were killed following a hurricane in Galveston, Texas in 1900?
4. In which year did musician Bill Wyman audition for the Rolling Stones?
5. Which car manufacturer makes the Astra and Agila models?
6. In which German city is the famous kabarett club called The Thistle?
7. What was the journey taken by the world's first jet airliner in 1952?
8. Why did Sunderland fruit and veg seller Steve Thoburn appear in court in January 2001?
9. Which movie star plays in the rock band 30-odd Foot of Grunts?
10. How many members of the Academy of Motion Picture Arts and Sciences were eligible to vote for the 2001 Oscar Awards?
11. In which year did Vincent Van Gogh first move to London to work for Goupil & Cie art dealers?
12. In the U.S., is Dallas north-east or north-west of New Orleans?
13. In which city is the proposed 2000 feet tall building at 7 South Dearborn to be built?
14. Where in England is the Arnolfini gallery?
15. Who played Sergeant Trotter in the stage play The Mousetrap from 1953-5 in the West End?

ANSWERS **1.** 1,483 feet **2.** Nigeria **3.** 6,000 **4.** 1962 **5.** Vauxhall **6.** Berlin **7.** Heathrow to Johannesburg **8.** For using an imperial rather than metric set of scales **9.** Russell Crowe **10.** 5,722 **11.** 1873 **12.** North-west **13.** Chicago **14.** Bristol **15.** Richard Attenborough.

ENTERTAINMENT

1. What is the screen name of actress Camille Javal?
2. Which actress is the elder sister of Warren Beatty?
3. Who delivered Alan Bennett's 1988 television monologue *A Cream Cracker Under the Settee*?
4. Who directed the 1989 film *Driving Miss Daisy*?
5. Who played *Joan of Arc* in the 1948 film?
6. Which dramatist wrote *The Odd Couple*?
7. In which city was the French workers' co-operative group Théâtre du Soleil formed?
8. Which Nigerian playwright and Nobel prize winner studied English at Leeds University?
9. Which character did John Bentley play in the original *Crossroads*?
10. Which ventriloquist's dolls include Lord Charles and Ali Cat?
11. In which soap opera did The Waterman's Arms feature?
12. Who did Terence Alexander play in TV's *Bergerac*?
13. Who played Siegfried Farnon in the TV show *All Creatures Great and Small*?
14. Which U.S. comedy series was based on *Till Death Us Do Part*?
15. The French town of Nouvion was the setting of which sitcom?

ANSWERS **1.** Brigitte Bardot **2.** Shirley MacLaine **3.** Thora Hird **4.** Bruce Beresford **5.** Ingrid Bergman **6.** Neil Simon **7.** Paris **8.** Wole Soyinka **9.** Hugh Mortimer **10.** Ray Alan **11.** Albion Market **12.** Charlie Hungerford **13.** Robert Hardy **14.** All in the Family **15.** 'Allo 'Allo!

SPORT

1. Which football team won the 1994/5 FA Cup?
2. Who did Arsenal play in the quarter finals of the 2001 FA Cup?
3. Syd was one of the three official mascots of the 2000 Summer Olympics in Sydney. What type of animal was it?
4. Which horse won the 1962 Grand National?
5. In which year was footballer Frank Beckenbauer born?
6. Who was the French Open men's singles tennis champion in 1988?
7. In which country were the 1986 football World Cup finals held?
8. Who won the Olympic men's 200m in 1988?
9. Which team won the 1996 world series in baseball?
10. Who was the 1994 British Open golf champion?
11. Which team knocked Newcastle out of the FA Cup in February 1972?
12. What was unusual about boxer Darrin Morris' rise in the WBO rankings from seventh to fifth in March 2001?
13. Which football team won the 1995/6 European Cup-Winners' Cup?
14. Which non-league team knocked Liverpool out of the FA Cup in January 1959?
15. Who were the 1997 cricket county champions?

ANSWERS **1.** Everton **2.** Blackburn Rovers **3.** Platypus **4.** Kilmore **5.** 1945 **6.** Mats Wilander **7.** Mexico **8.** Joe DeLoach **9.** New York Yankees **10.** Nick Price **11.** Hereford **12.** He died in 2000 **13.** Paris St. Germain **14.** Worcester **15.** Glamorganshire.

POP

1. Which singer guested on the 1995 single *Just the One* by the Levellers?
2. In which year did singer Janis Joplin die?
3. Which Scottish singer had a 1995 hit with *A Girl Like You*?
4. Which woman singer released the mini-LP *Girl at Her Volcano*?
5. Which singer's albums include 1993's *Too Long in Exile*?
6. Who left Jethro Tull in 1969 to form Blodwyn Pig?
7. Which vocal group's chart debut was 1997's *Slam Dunk (Da Funk)*?
8. Which singer had a 1995 hit with *R to the A*?
9. Which group recorded the album *In Utero*?
10. Which singer had a 1996 Top 10 hit with *Dance into the Light*?
11. Which group charted in 1995 with the single *Downtown Venus*?
12. Which easy-listening combo got to No. 2 in December 1995 with a cover of *Wonderwall* by Oasis?
13. Who was lead singer with the group Jesus Jones?
14. Which duo from *Coronation Street* had a minor hit in 1995 with *Something Stupid*?
15. How are Steve Jansen and David Sylvian of the group Japan related?

ANSWERS **1.** Joe Strummer **2.** 1970 **3.** Edwyn Collins **4.** Rickie Lee Jones **5.** Van Morrison **6.** Mick Abrahams **7.** 5IVE **8.** C.J. Lewis **9.** Nirvana **10.** Phil Collins **11.** P.M. Dawn **12.** Mike Flowers Pops **13.** Mike Edwards **14.** Amanda Barrie & Johnny Briggs **15.** They are brothers.

ART AND LITERATURE

1. Who wrote the 2001 novel *Declare?*
2. In which city did artist Marcel Duchamp live from 1915-23?
3. Who wrote the novel *The Water-Method Man*?
4. Which painter did the artist Sonia Terk marry in 1910?
5. Which artist painted the 1937 portrait *Winifred Burger*?
6. Who wrote the short story collection *Myths of the Near Future*?
7. In which year did the British artist Martin Bloch die?
8. Which British artist created the 1961 painted work *Tuesday*?
9. Who wrote the novel *The Sweet-Shop Owner*?
10. Which British artist painted the 1938 work *Dover Front* which is housed in the Tate Gallery?
11. In which year did the British artist and critic Michael Ayrton die?
12. Who wrote the 1995 novel *Splitting*?
13. In which year was British sculptor and painter Geoffrey Clarke born?
14. Which British sculptor's works include the 1955 bronze *Ophelia*?
15. Who wrote the novel *The Unbearable Lightness of Being*?

ANSWERS **1.** Tim Powers **2.** New York **3.** John Irving **4.** Robert Delaunay **5.** Sir William Coldstream **6.** J.G. Ballard **7.** 1954 **8.** Peter Blake **9.** Graham Swift **10.** Graham Bell **11.** 1975 **12.** Fay Weldon **13.** 1924 **14.** Reg Butler **15.** Milan Kundera.

GENERAL KNOWLEDGE

1. Which Canadian humorist wrote *Sunshine Sketches of a Little Town*?
2. Which creature did Fafnir become in Norse mythology?
3. On which river is the Austrian city of Linz?
4. LPG is an alternative to petrol. For what do the initials stand?
5. What was the name given to the 1623 massacre by the Dutch of English merchants in the Spice Islands?
6. Which Scottish river reaches the North Sea at Berwick?
7. Who wrote the play *Top Girls*?
8. Who directed the 1980 film *Kagemusha*?
9. What is the international car registration for Bahrain?
10. What type of creature is a gayal?
11. Who wrote the 1516 work *Utopia*?
12. What is the capital of Chad?
13. What is the musical instrument an English horn better known as?
14. Who wrote the novel *The Dark Arena*?
15. The island Corregidor lies at the entrance to which bay?

ANSWERS **1.** Stephen Leacock **2.** Dragon **3.** Danube **4.** Liquid petroleum gas **5.** Amboina massacre **6.** Tweed **7.** Caryl Churchill **8.** Akira Kurosawa **9.** BRN **10.** Ox **11.** Sir Thomas More **12.** Ndjamena **13.** Cor anglais **14.** Mario Puzo **15.** Manila Bay.

ENTERTAINMENT

1. Which writer does Geoffrey Rush play in the film *Quills*?
2. Which former Coronation Street star hosts the Channel 5 game show *The Mole*?
3. Who played *Judge John Deed* in a 2001 BBC television drama?
4. Who directed the 1991 film *Shadows and Fog*?
5. Who directed the 1976 film *Logan's Run*?
6. Who starred as *Joe* in the 1970 film?
7. Who directed the 1985 film *Lust in the Dust*?
8. In which television soap opera does the character Nick Cotton appear?
9. What is the name of John Godber's theatre company in Hull?
10. Who directed the 1956 film *Stranger at My Door*?
11. What is the profession of Ben Harper, played by Robert Lindsay, in the sitcom *My Family*?
12. Which actor is the founder of theatre company Northern Broadsides?
13. Who plays 'Professor Xavier' in the film *X-Men*?
14. In which 2000 film does the character 'Boris the Blade' appear?
15. What nationality is the classical violinist Gidon Kremer?

ANSWERS 1. Marquis de Sade **2.** Glenn Hugill **3.** Martin Shaw **4.** Woody Allen **5.** Michael Anderson **6.** Peter Boyle **7.** Paul Bartel **8.** EastEnders **9.** Hull Truck **10.** William Witney **11.** Dentist **12.** Barrie Rutter **13.** Patrick Stewart **14.** Snatch **15.** Latvian.

SPORT

1. Which British Open golf champion was born in Goldsboro, North Carolina?
2. Briton Chloe Cowan is a light-heavyweight at which sport?
3. Scottish rugby union player James McLaren plays for which French club?
4. Which U.S. boxer was nicknamed 'The Human Windmill'?
5. Which Durham cricketer is known as 'Dr. Chaplaw'?
6. Who was the world individual freshwater angling champion from 1996-98?
7. Janina Kurkowska was world individual champion at which sport from 1931-4?
8. Out of 129 javelin competitions between 1970-80 how many did Ruth Fuchs win?
9. Which Italian footballer scored a consolation goal in their 1970 World Cup final defeat?
10. What did the Football League Cup become in 1982?
11. Who became undisputed world cruiserweight boxing champion in 1988?
12. Who won the 1998 Nat West Trophy in cricket?
13. Which cricketer was the second man, after W.G. Grace, to score 100 hundreds?
14. On which horse did Vaughan Jeffries win the 1994 world individual three-day event championship?
15. Who was the 1997 USPGA golf champion?

ANSWERS 1. Mark O'Meara **2.** Judo **3.** Bourgoin **4.** Harry Greb **5.** Steven Chapman **6.** Alan Scotthorne **7.** Archery **8.** 113 **9.** Boninsegna **10.** The Milk Cup **11.** Evander Holyfield **12.** Essex **13.** Tom Hayward **14.** Bounce **15.** Davis Love III.

POP

1. What was Billie's second No. 1 hit single?
2. Which act had a 1998 summer Top Five hit with the song *Carnaval de Paris*?
3. From which European country do the chart act Course come?
4. Which group had a 1996 hit with *The Secret Vampire Soundtrack* EP?
5. Which Icelandic singer had a 1996 Top Ten hit with *Hyperballad*?
6. Which U.S. singer's only U.K. hit was *It's Better To Have (and Don't Need)*?
7. Which group had a minor 1997 hit with *Native New Yorker*?
8. Who got to No. 1 in 1996 with *Ooh Aah...Just a Little Bit*?
9. Which soul singer's album *Call Me* ended with the track *Jesus is Waiting*?
10. In which year did The Grateful Dead member Pigpen die?
11. Which group had a 1973 hit single with *Radar Love*?
12. Which group released the 1977 live album *Playing the Fool*?
13. Which group formed at Charterhouse public school in 1975?
14. Who was the frontman of the group The Boomtown Rats?
15. Who released the 1971 album *What's Going On*?

ANSWERS 1. Girlfriend **2.** Dario G **3.** Holland **4.** Bis **5.** Björk **6.** Don Covay **7.** Black Box **8.** Gina G **9.** Al Green **10.** 1973 **11.** Golden Earring **12.** Gentle Giant **13.** Genesis **14.** Bob Geldof **15.** Marvin Gaye.

SCIENCE

1. How many faces has a regular tetrahedron?
2. What is the radius of the Earth's inner core in kilometres?
3. What unit of length is equal to 0.9144 of a metre?
4. At which Cambridge college did Isaac Newton study?
5. Which scientist delivered the 1953 Reith Lectures?
6. Who became professor of chemistry at the Sorbonne in 1867?
7. How many seconds are there in a solar day?
8. Which element composes approximately 36% of the Earth?
9. In which year was English molecular biologist Francis Crick born?
10. Which element is directly below silver in the Periodic table?
11. What is the name given to a DNA molecule that is able to replicate in a cell?
12. What is the word 'smog' a corruption of?
13. What nationality was the doctor and alchemist Paracelsus?
14. How many minutes are there in a degree of an angle?
15. Which Italian mathematician born in 1858 promoted the universal language interlingua?

ANSWERS 1. Four **2.** 1,222km **3.** A yard **4.** Trinity College **5.** J. Robert Oppenheimer **6.** Louis Pasteur **7.** 86,400 **8.** Iron **9.** 1916 **10.** Gold **11.** Replicon **12.** Smoke-fog **13.** Swiss **14.** 60 **15.** Giuseppe Peano.

GENERAL KNOWLEDGE

1. On which London Underground line is the station of Fulham Broadway?
2. In which of his films does Alfred Hitchcock appear outside a courthouse holding a camera?
3. What type of animal is a Rambouillet?
4. Which car manufacturer makes the Corsa?
5. What grade did Princess Anne get in A-Level History?
6. In which valley is the French wine Sancerre produced?
7. Between which post-war years was Shropshire officially called Salop?
8. What was the interim capital of Pakistan from 1959-67?
9. How tall is the world's former tallest building, the Sears Tower?
10. In which African country are the towns of Kandi and Abomey?
11. PAs are a type of boot worn by mountaineers. After whom are they named?
12. What is the name in Norse mythology for the ultimate destruction of the gods in a battle with evil?
13. In which year was the airline Qantas founded?
14. Of which country was Nicola Pasic prime minister from 1912-18?
15. What type of tree is a sallow?

ANSWERS 1. District **2.** Young and Innocent **3.** Sheep **4.** Vauxhall **5.** D **6.** Loire valley **7.** 1974-80 **8.** Rawalpindi **9.** 1,450 feet **10.** Benin **11.** Pierre Allain **12.** Ragnarök **13.** 1920 **14.** Serbia **15.** A willow tree.

ENTERTAINMENT

1. Which comedian's characters include 'the Frank Pharmacist'?
2. In which film does the number plate KAZ 2AY feature?
3. Who wrote the music and lyrics for the stage show *Merrily We Roll Along*?
4. Who plays the title role in the 2000 film *Cecil B. Demented*?
5. Who directed the films *Hot Shots!* and *Hot Shots! Part Deux*?
6. Who directed the 1974 film *California Split*?
7. Which actor and actress starred in the 1945 film *The Wicked Lady*?
8. Who played Lucinda in the 1997 film *Oscar and Lucinda*?
9. Who directed the 1984 film *The Karate Kid*?
10. About which famous comedian is the play *Frankie and Tommy* by Garry Lyons?
11. In which television soap opera did the character Jez Quigley appear?
12. Who directed the 1949 film *The Golden Stallion* which starred Roy Rogers?
13. Who played the lead in the 1984 film *Bert Rigby, You're A Fool*?
14. Who plays 'Rogue' in the film *X-Men*?
15. Who is the overweight star of Percy Adlon's films *Bagdad Café* and *Rosalie Goes Shopping*?

ANSWERS **1.** Harry Enfield **2.** Cast Away **3.** Stephen Sondheim **4.** Stephen Dorff **5.** Jim Abrahams **6.** Robert Altman **7.** James Mason and Margaret Lockwood **8.** Cate Blanchett **9.** John G. Avildsen **10.** Tommy Cooper **11.** Coronation Street **12.** William Witney **13.** Robert Lindsay **14.** Anna Paquin **15.** Marianne Sägebrecht.

SPORT

1. What was the nickname of American football star Joe Greene?
2. Which England footballer's international career was ended by a car crash in 1962?
3. Who won the 1998 County Cricket championship?
4. Who won the 1998 women's hockey World Cup?
5. Which horse won the 1997 Epsom Derby?
6. Who won cycling's Giro d'Italia in 1998?
7. Who became world heavyweight boxing champion in 1905?
8. Which two Italian teams contested the 1998 UEFA Cup final?
9. On which island was Viv Richards born?
10. In which year was Hana Mandlikova born?
11. Who won the women's javelin silver at the 1988 Olympics?
12. With what sport would you associate Alberto Tomba?
13. Who did Roberto Duran defeat in his 100th professional fight?
14. Who won the 1993 Johnnie Walker World Championship in golf?
15. Which three teams were in the Republic of Ireland's group in the 1994 World Cup?

ANSWERS 1. Mean Joe **2.** Johnny Haynes **3.** Leicestershire **4.** Australia **5.** Benny the Dip **6.** Marco Pantani **7.** Marvin Hart **8.** Internazionale and Lazio **9.** Antigua **10.** 1962 **11.** Fatima Whitbread **12.** Skiing **13.** Tony Menefee **14.** Larry Mize **15.** Mexico, Norway and Italy.

POP

1. In which year did the group The Presidents of the United States of America form?
2. Which Italian DJ had a No. 1 single in 2000 with *Groovejet (If This Ain't Love)*?
3. Who played drums on the single *Stop Your Sobbing* by The Pretenders?
4. Which two members of the group Queen were originally in the band Smile?
5. Which English session pianist replaced Gary Duncan in the band Quicksilver Messenger Service?
6. Which former member of the group Technotronic records under the name Me One?
7. Who is the lead singer with the group Angelou?
8. Which studio album by Prince includes the song *I Feel For You*?
9. Which rapper released the solo album *Pawns in the Game*?
10. Which group had a 1973 hit single with *Stuck in the Middle with You*?
11. Which male solo artist won three awards at the 2000 MOBO ceremony?
12. In which year did the pop group Mud have a No. 1 single with *Tiger Feet*?
13. Who recorded the 2000 solo album *Isotopes*?
14. Rob Mazurek and Chad Taylor comprise which group?
15. Which rap group recorded the 2000 album *Art Official Intelligence (Mosaic Thump)*?

ANSWERS 1. 1993 **2.** Spiller **3.** Gary Mackleduff **4.** Brian May and Roger Taylor **5.** Nicky Hopkins **6.** Eric Martin **7.** Holly Lerski **8.** Prince **9.** Professor Griff **10.** Stealers Wheel **11.** Craig David **12.** 1974 **13.** Rusty Squeezebox **14.** Chicago Underground Duo **15.** De La Soul.

PEOPLE

1. Which actress was Miss Malaysia in 1983?
2. Which writer created the Italian policeman Aurelia Zen?
3. How old was comedian Chris Farley when he died in 1998?
4. What is the name of the wife of jazz singer George Melly?
5. Who was the first centrefold in Playboy magazine?
6. Which football club does the poet Ian McMillan famously support?
7. In which year did Theodor Geisel, also known as Dr. Seuss, die?
8. Which former member of the Rolling Stones once took a hat-trick at the Oval in a charity cricket match?
9. What is the name of actor Mel Gibson's father?
10. What is the first name of celebrity O.J. Simpson?
11. What grade did Prince Edward get in A-Level English?
12. Which actress turned up unannounced and disoriented at a stranger's house in Cantua Creek, California in August, 2000?
13. Who was Home Secretary in 1967?
14. Which politician is the father of Baroness Jay?
15. Which U.S. politician's wife once played drums in a band called the Wild Cats?

ANSWERS 1. Michelle Yeoh **2.** Michael Dibdin **3.** 33 **4.** Diana **5.** Marilyn Monroe **6.** Barnsley **7.** 1991 **8.** Bill Wyman **9.** Hutton **10.** Orenthal **11.** C **12.** Anne Heche **13.** Roy Jenkins **14.** James Callaghan **15.** Al Gore's wife Tipper.

GENERAL KNOWLEDGE

1. In which year did Paris become the capital of France?
2. On which London Underground line is the station of Leyton?
3. What grade did Prince William get in A-Level History of Art?
4. Who finished second in the Vendée Globe yacht race which finished in 2001?
5. What in Germany is a Ratskeller?
6. What, historically, was pavage?
7. What is the melting point of radium?
8. In which U.S. state is the 309ft high Rainbow Bridge?
9. What type of creature is a painted lady?
10. What in Roman mythology were the Parcae?
11. What is the currency of Qatar?
12. What might a woman have done with a partlet in the 16th century - worn it or baked with it?
13. Which river is known as the Isis at Oxford?
14. What type of bird is a saker?
15. In which city is the world's tallest building, Petronas Towers?

ANSWERS 1. 987 **2.** Central **3.** B **4.** Ellen MacArthur **5.** The cellar of a town hall **6.** A tax towards paving streets **7.** 700° C **8.** Utah **9.** A butterfly **10.** The goddesses of Fate **11.** Riyal **12.** Worn it - it was a garment covering the neck and shoulders **13.** The Thames **14.** A falcon **15.** Kuala Lumpur.

ENTERTAINMENT

1. Who voices the character Bart in cartoon series *The Simpsons*?
2. Who played Kimberly in the sitcom *Diff'rent Strokes*?
3. Who plays the jewel thief Nyah Nordoff-Hall in the film *Mission: Impossible 2*?
4. Who directed the 1993 film *Cold Heaven*?
5. In which year did the presenter Mark Curry leave the television show *Blue Peter*?

6. What is the name of Melanie Griffths' character in the 2000 film *Cecil B. Demented*?
7. Who directed the 1955 film *The Big Knife*?
8. Which film director began working as a clerk in a telephone company in Madrid?
9. Who directed the 1954 film *Creature From the Black Lagoon*?
10. Who directed the 1987 film *Ironweed*?
11. Who directed the 1981 television series *The Flame Trees of Thika*?
12. Who directed the 1958 film *The Bonnie Parker Story*?
13. Who plays 'Wolverine' in the film *X-Men*?
14. Who plays the outlaw Roy O'Bannon in the film *Shanghai Noon*?
15. Who plays Rose in the 2000 film *Timecode*?

ANSWERS 1. Nancy Cartwright **2.** Dana Plato **3.** Thandie Newton **4.** Nicolas Roeg **5.** 1989 **6.** Honey Whitlock **7.** Robert Aldrich **8.** Pedro Almovodar **9.** Jack Arnold **10.** Hector Babenco **11.** Roy Ward Baker **12.** William Witney **13.** Hugh Jackman **14.** Owen Wilson **15.** Salma Hayek.

SPORT

1. What nationality is Olympic gymnast Yukio Endo?
2. At what diving discipline did Ingrid Engel retain her Olympic title in 1964?
3. Which South African rugby union winger won 33 caps from 1960-69?
4. At which sport did Phil and Tony Esposito excel?
5. How many goals did Eusebio score in his 64 internationals for Portugal?
6. From which state does U.S. Olympic swimmer Janet Evans hail?
7. Who ran 61.5 yards in 10 seconds before scoring for Manchester United against Arsenal in April 1999?
8. In Superbowls XI, XIV, XVII and XXI the attendance topped 100,000. What was the venue on all four occasions?
9. Where were the 1983 IAAF World Championships held?
10. Which country did Martin Fiz represent in winning the marathon at the 1995 IAAF World Championships?
11. Which two Italian teams contested the 1995 UEFA Cup final?
12. Who was men's singles World badminton champion in 1987 and '89?
13. Who scored the only goal in the 1996 FA Cup final?
14. Who won the 1968 Olympic men's 400m title?
15. Which Olympic skier did tennis player Chris Evert marry in 1988?

ANSWERS 1. Japanese **2.** Springboard diving **3.** Jan Engelbrecht **4.** Ice hockey **5.** 41 **6.** California **7.** Ryan Giggs **8.** Pasadena **9.** Helsinki **10.** Spain **11.** Parma and Juventus **12.** Yang Yang **13.** Eric Cantona **14.** Lee Evans **15.** Andy Mill.

POP

1. Which single by The Monkees reached No. 1 in the U.K. and U.S.?
2. Which U.S. vocal group had a 1997 hit with *Don't Let Go (Love)*?
3. Which record in 1998 gave Linda McCartney her only singles chart success?
4. Which Scottish poet recorded the album *Dandruff*?
5. In which West Midlands town were Ned's Atomic Dustbin formed?
6. In which town was Bill Nelson of Be Bop Deluxe born?
7. Which duo had a 1992 hit with the single *Runaway Train*?
8. Who was the featured singer on the 1997 hit *I Wanna Be the Only One* by Eternal?
9. How many solo No. 1 singles has Paul McCartney had?
10. Who scored a 1995 Top 10 single with *Here Comes the Hotstepper*?
11. Which group had a minor hit in 1993 with the song *Lenny Valentino*?
12. What was Dee-Lite's 1990 hit album called?
13. From which country does vocalist Mory Kante come?
14. In which year did the Eurythmics have a No. 1 hit with *There Must Be An Angel (Playing With My Heart)*?
15. Which group had a 1989 hit album with *3 Feet High and Rising*?

ANSWERS **1.** I'm a Believer **2.** En Vogue **3.** Wide Prairie **4.** Ivor Cutler **5.** Stourbridge **6.** Wakefield **7.** Elton John and Eric Clapton **8.** BeBe Winans **9.** One - Pipes Of Peace **10.** Ini Kamoze **11.** The Auteurs **12.** World Clique **13.** Guinea **14.** 1985 **15.** De La Soul.

ART AND LITERATURE

1. Who wrote the novel *Milton in America*?

2. In which year did the artist Balthus die?

3. Which singer features on the front cover of a magazine in Peter Blake's 1961 work *Self-Portrait with Badges*?

4. Who wrote the short story collection *Delta of Venus*?

5. Who wrote the novel *The End of the Road*?

6. Which Spanish artist painted the 1937 work *Metamorphosis of Narcissus*?

7. Whose sculptures include the 1911 work *Maiastra*?

8. Who wrote the novel *The Woman Who Walked Into Doors*?

9. Which British artist painted the 1940 watercolour *Gallabat: Guns Firing on Metemma*?

10. Which British sculptor's works include the 1965 steel object *Yellow Swing*?

11. Who wrote the novel *Pnin*?

12. What everyday object was turned into the 1915 work of art *In Advance of the Broken Arm* by Marcel Duchamp?

13. Who wrote the 1999 novel *Chocolat*?

14. Which British artist produced the 1977 screenprint *Bananas and Leaves*?

15. In which year did the British artist David Bomberg die?

ANSWERS 1. Peter Ackroyd **2.** 2001 **3.** Elvis Presley **4.** Anaïs Nin **5.** John Barth **6.** Salvador Dali **7.** Constantin Brancusi **8.** Roddy Doyle **9.** Edward Bawden **10.** Sir Anthony Caro **11.** Vladimir Nabokov **12.** A snow shovel **13.** Joanne Harris **14.** Patrick Caulfield **15.** 1957.

GENERAL KNOWLEDGE

1. What would you do with an Aldis lamp?
2. In which century did philosopher Saint Thomas Aquinas live?
3. In old Irish law, what was an eric?
4. In which year was actor Marlon Brando born?
5. What is the largest country of South America?
6. What was entertainer Sir Harry Lauder's real first name?
7. Who directed the 1994 film *Shallow Grave*?
8. At which school would a Harrovian have been educated?
9. What does the Latin word *'conubium'* mean?
10. Who was the ninth president of the U.S.?
11. What was the annual boarding fee in 1997 at Winchester College?
12. Who composed the song *St. Louis Blues*?
13. On which Loch is the Scottish village of Ullapool?
14. Who composed the opera *Le Grand Macabre*?
15. On which river is the city of Lincoln?

ANSWERS **1.** Transmit morse code **2.** 13th **3.** A fine paid by a murderer to the family of his victim **4.** 1924 **5.** Brazil **6.** Hugh **7.** Danny Boyle **8.** Harrow **9.** Marriage **10.** William Henry Harrison **11.** £15,345 **12.** W.C. Handy **13.** Loch Broom **14.** Gyorgy Ligeti **15.** River Witham.

ENTERTAINMENT

1. Michael Hutchence, Richard O'Brien and Jason Donovan were reportedly the original trio of lead actors proposed for which film?
2. Who is the female lead in the film *Mad City* which stars Dustin Hoffman?
3. Who directed the 1982 film *Blue Thunder*?
4. Who directed the 1969 film *Oh! What a Lovely War*?
5. Which 1992 film starring Whoopi Goldberg was directed by Emile Ardolino?
6. Who directed the 1953 film history of the ocean *The Sea Around Us*?
7. Who is the female star of the 2000 film *The Cell*?
8. Which actress starred in the films *Jerry Maguire* and *Me, Myself & Irene*?
9. Who does Rebecca Romijn-Stamos play in the film *X-Men*?
10. Who plays psychology professor Alex in the film *Bad Timing*?
11. Which actor on the television show *Suddenly Susan* committed suicide in 1999?
12. What is the profession of Charlotte Uhlenbroek, who appeared in the 2000 television documentary series *Cousins*?
13. What was the first name of film director Orson Welles?
14. What is Benicio Del Toro's character name in the film *Snatch*?
15. Who directed the 1996 film *Up Close & Personal*?

ANSWERS **1.** Priscilla, Queen of the Desert **2.** Mia Kershner **3.** John Badham **4.** Richard Attenborough **5.** Sister Act **6.** Irwin Allen **7.** Jennifer Lopez **8.** Renée Zellweger **9.** Mystique **10.** Art Garfunkel **11.** David Strickland **12.** Zoologist **13.** George **14.** Frankie Four-Fingers **15.** Jon Avnet.

SPORT

1. Whose first of six St. Leger winners as a trainer was 1962's Hethersett?
2. Which was the first country to stage football's European Championship finals twice?
3. Which cyclist won the 1994 Giro d'Italia?
4. Which country did 1998 Olympic 5,000m speed skating champion Tomas Gustafson represent?
5. Which team won the men's 4x100m relay at the 1995 and '97 IAAF World Championships?
6. Which horse won the 1998 1,000 Guineas?
7. Who won rugby union's Pilkington Cup in 1998?
8. Who was Olympic 1000m sprint cycling champion in 1984 & '88?
9. How many internationals did footballer Giacinto Facchetti play for Italy between 1962-77?
10. What is Nick Faldo's middle name?
11. What was world Formula 1 motor racing champion Juan Fangio's middle name?
12. Who took 6-52 and 6-46 for Pakistan in 1954 against England at the Oval?
13. What was the nickname of baseball star Bob Feller?
14. At what event was Adhemar Ferreira da Silva an Olympic champion in 1952 and '56?
15. Which individual fencing gold did Anja Fichtel take at the 1988 Olympics?

ANSWERS **1.** Dick Hern **2.** Italy **3.** Evgeny Berzin **4.** Sweden **5.** Canada **6.** Cape Verdi **7.** Saracens **8.** Lutz Hesslich **9.** 94 **10.** Alexander **11.** Manuel **12.** Fazal Mahmoud **13.** Rapid Robert **14.** Triple Jump **15.** Women's foil.

POP

1. What was Katrina and the Waves's 1997 Top 10 single?
2. Which single by Roy Orbison reached No. 1 in the U.K. and the U.S.?
3. Which singer's first singles success was 1996's *Crazy Chance*?
4. Which male singer had a minor hit in 1992 with the single *Lover Lover Lover*?
5. Who is the female member of the group New Order?
6. Which group had a 1997 Top 10 single with *Hard To Say I'm Sorry*?
7. Which group did Dave Grohl form after Nirvana split?
8. Which duo had a Top 30 hit in 1995 with *'Haunted'*?
9. Who was the original drummer in the group Oasis?
10. Which U.S. artist recorded the album *Tit...an opera*?
11. In which year did Janet Key first chart with *Silly Games*?
12. Which female singer recorded the album *I Do Not Want What I Haven't Got*?
13. Which female singer had a Top 20 hit in 1998 with the song *Adia*?
14. Which traditional song did Don McLean record on the album *American Pie*?
15. Which group recorded the album *Pioneer Soundtracks*?

ANSWERS **1.** Love Shine a Light **2.** Oh Pretty Woman **3.** Kavana **4.** Ian McCulloch **5.** Gillian Gilbert **6.** Az Yet **7.** Foo Fighters **8.** Shane MacGowan and Sinead O'Connor **9.** Tony McCarroll **10.** Dogbowl **11.** 1979 **12.** Sinead O'Connor **13.** Sarah McLachlan **14.** Babylon **15.** Jack.

GEOGRAPHY

1. Aberdeen lies between the mouths of which two rivers?
2. In which American state are the Everglades, an extensive marshy region?
3. On what Mediterranean island is the seaport of Famagusta?
4. Which skiing city is capital of Isère department in France?
5. Which county is known as the 'Garden of England'?
6. Mombasa is the chief seaport of which country?
7. On which river is the Portuguese city of Lisbon?
8. In which Italian hill town is the Palio horse race festival held?
9. What is the highest mountain on the Isle of Man?
10. The Segovia River forms the boundary between which two Central American countries?
11. The city of Nome, centre of a gold rush in 1900, is in which U.S. state?
12. Which river separates Victoria and New South Wales, Australia?
13. The Plains of Abraham are near which Canadian city?
14. In which African country is the seaport of Agadir?
15. In which European country is the town of Altdorf?

ANSWERS **1.** Don and Dee **2.** Florida **3.** Cyprus **4.** Grenoble **5.** Kent **6.** Kenya **7.** Tagus **8.** Siena **9.** Snaefell **10.** Nicaragua and Honduras **11.** Alaska **12.** Murray River **13.** Quebec **14.** Morocco **15.** Switzerland.

GENERAL KNOWLEDGE

1. On whose book is the 1998 film *The Gingerbread Man* based?

2. On which London Underground line is the station of Wimbledon Park?

3. What is the U.S. equivalent of lightning chess?

4. Of which country was Antonio de Oliveira Salazar dictator from 1932-68?

5. What is a paterfamilias?

6. Of which state of Brazil is Curitiba the capital?

7. Which car manufacturer makes the PT Cruiser?

8. In which year did production of the foodstuff Spam start in the U.S.?

9. In which year did the Rose of Tralee festival begin?

10. How much did a 500g tin of Almas Diamond caviar cost in August 2000?

11. What item of clothing is Ellery Chun credited with inventing?

12. How many combinations are there if you roll two dice?

13. In poker, when dealt the initial five cards, what are the odds of having a royal flush?

14. Which actress' house at 100 Sunset Boulevard was nicknamed 'the Pink Palace'?

15. To what would you attach a paravane?

ANSWERS 1. John Grisham **2.** District **3.** Rapid transit chess **4.** Portugal **5.** The male head of a household **6.** Parana **7.** Chrysler **8.** 1937 **9.** 1959 **10.** £7,352 **11.** The Hawaiian shirt **12.** 36 **13.** 500,000-1 **14.** Jayne Mansfield **15.** The bow of a vessel.

ENTERTAINMENT

1. Whose first feature film as a director was 1995's *Bad Boys*?
2. Who directed the 1951 film *The Browning Version*?
3. Who played Arnold in the sitcom *Diff'rent Strokes*?
4. Who voices the character Principal Skinner in cartoon series *The Simpsons*?
5. Which 2000 film used the largest ever water tank in film history?
6. In which year did the presenter Diane Louise Jordan join television show *Blue Peter*?
7. Which actor won a Tony for his role in the show *Me and My Girl*?
8. *8 Million Ways To Die* was which director's last film?
9. Which actor and actress starred in the 1943 film *The Man in Grey*?
10. Who directed the 1996 film *Grace of my Heart*?
11. Who directed the film *Nurse Betty*?
12. What is George Clooney's character name in the film *O Brother, Where Art Thou*?
13. Who voices the character Ginger in the animated film *Chicken Run*?
14. Who directed the 1998 film *Hope Floats*?
15. Who directed Scottish Opera's 2000 production of *Das Rheingold*?

ANSWERS **1.** Michael Bay **2.** Anthony Asquith **3.** Gary Coleman **4.** Harry Shearer **5.** The Perfect Storm **6.** 1990 **7.** Robert Lindsay **8.** Hal Ashby **9.** James Mason and Margaret Lockwood **10.** Allison Anders **11.** Neil LaBute **12.** Everett Ulysses McGill **13.** Julia Sawalha **14.** Forest Whitaker **15.** Tim Albery.

SPORT

1. What nationality is Olympic skiing champion Michela Figini?
2. By how many seconds did Greg LeMond beat Laurent Fignon to win the 1989 Tour de France?
3. In which English county was world heavyweight boxing champion Bob Fitzsimmons born?
4. At what field event was John Flanagan Olympic champion from 1900-1908?
5. Which country did 1964 Olympic skiing champion Christl Haas represent?
6. Which Australian pair won the 1962 Wimbledon men's doubles tennis championship?
7. Who was manager of Watford F.C. during the 1998/9 season?
8. At what weight did boxer Kaosai Galaxy win a 1984 world title?
9. In which city was Superbowl XXXII played in 1998?
10. What nationality was figure skater Sonja Henie?
11. Which country won the World Team Freshwater Angling title in 1987 & '88?
12. Who was 1976 & '80 Olympic men's marathon winner?
13. Which world Formula 1 motor racing champion was the son of a Scottish sheep farmer?
14. For which ice hockey team did Bobby Clarke play from 1969-84?
15. In which city is the headquarters of the English Basketball Association?

ANSWERS **1.** Swiss **2.** Eight **3.** Cornwall **4.** Hammer **5.** Austria **6.** Fred Stolle & Bob Hewitt **7.** Graham Taylor **8.** Bantamweight **9.** San Diego **10.** Norwegian **11.** England **12.** Waldemar Cierpinski **13.** Jim Clark **14.** Philadelphia Flyers **15.** Leeds.

POP

1. Who plays bass on Bap Kennedy's album *Love Street*?
2. Which group recorded the 2000 album *Warning*?
3. In which city were the rock band Queensrÿche formed?
4. Which group released the 1973 album *Grand Hotel*?
5. Who released the 1980 album *Dirty Mind*?
6. Which U.S. vocal group had No. 1 singles in 1995 with *Boom Boom Boom* and *Don't Stop (Wiggle Wiggle)*?
7. What was Elvis Presley's last single on Sun Records?
8. Which studio album by Radiohead features the song *Anyone Can Play Guitar*?
9. Which group released the 1987 album *Midnight to Midnight*?
10. Which Canadian group recorded the 2000 album *Between the Bridges*?
11. Which member of Oasis was previously in the group Ride?
12. Which pop group recorded the 1991 album *Stars*?
13. Which 1985 single by Madonna was her first U.K. No. 1 hit?
14. Which guitarist in Spooky Tooth joined the group Mott the Hoople and assumed the name Ariel Bender?
15. Which singer-songwriter recorded the 2000 album *Shylingo*?

ANSWERS 1. Herbie Flowers **2.** Green Day **3.** Seattle **4.** Procol Harum **5.** Prince **6.** Outhere Brothers **7.** I Forgot To Remember To Forget **8.** Pablo Honey **9.** The Psychedelic Furs **10.** Sloan **11.** Andy Bell **12.** Simply Red **13.** Into the Groove **14.** Luther Grosvenor **15.** Tim Gibbons.

HISTORY

1. Which Scottish castle did Prince Albert purchase in 1852?
2. In which year did Peter the Great of Russia die?
3. In which year was the Tiananmen Square uprising in Beijing?
4. In which French port did Beau Brummel die in 1840?
5. Which French general became professor of strategy at the École Supérieure de Guerre in 1894?
6. In which year did Richard Byrd become the first person to fly over the South Pole?
7. In which century was badminton invented at Badminton House?
8. In which country was al-Fatah, the militant Palestinian organization, founded in 1962?
9. In which year was journalist and M.P. John Wilkes expelled from the House of Commons?
10. In which year was the European Court of Justice established?
11. Which future president of the U.S. served as governor general of the Philippines in 1901?
12. Which politician published the best-selling book *Greater Britain* in 1868?
13. Who was responsible for the Education Act of 1944?
14. Who was appointed commander of the New Model Army in 1645?
15. In which year was the American Declaration of Independence?

ANSWERS 1. Balmoral **2.** 1725 **3.** 1989 **4.** Caen **5.** Ferdinand Foch **6.** 1929 **7.** 19th **8.** Kuwait **9.** 1764 **10.** 1957 **11.** William Howard Taft **12.** Sir Charles Wentworth Dilke **13.** R.A. Butler **14.** Thomas Fairfax **15.** 1776.

GENERAL KNOWLEDGE

1. Which of the four wings of the National Gallery in London houses paintings from 1700-1900?
2. What grade did Princess Anne get in A-Level Geography?
3. On which London Underground line is the station of Knightsbridge?
4. In which African country are the towns of Waw and Bor?
5. Approximately how long in miles is the River Saar of France and Germany?
6. In which ocean is the island of Saipan?
7. In which year was the Salvation Army founded?
8. A Salmanazar is a wine bottle holding the equivalent of how many bottles?
9. Who was the Greek goddess of peace?
10. From which country does the boardgame pachisi originate?
11. What in the game of poker is Broadway?
12. In which year did the Royal Navy dockyard at Chatham close?
13. Of which football club is television executive Michael Grade a director?
14. What is the name of the preservative numbered E290?
15. What fruit is also known as the key fruit?

ANSWERS 1. East Wing **2.** E **3.** Piccadilly **4.** Sudan **5.** 153 miles **6.** Pacific Ocean **7.** 1865 **8.** 12 **9.** Irene **10.** India **11.** A high straight hand **12.** 1984 **13.** Charlton Athletic **14.** Carbon dioxide **15.** Samara.

ENTERTAINMENT

1. Which comedian's real name is Robert Harper?
2. Which U.S. actor starred in the 1985 comedy film *Macaroni*?
3. Which Jane Austen novel inspired the 1995 film *Clueless*?
4. Who played Tara King in *The Avengers*?
5. Who directed the 1998 film *Pleasantville*?
6. In which city was choreographer George Balanchine born?
7. Who directed the 1998 film comedy *Waking Ned*?
8. Who played Trotsky in the 1972 film *The Assassination of Trotsky*?
9. Who played Michael Faraday in the 1998 film *Arlington Road*?
10. Which comedian's characters include Portuguese singer Tony Ferrino?
11. Who directed the 1998 film *A Simple Plan*?
12. Who played Garth Algar in the 1992 film *Wayne's World*?
13. Who played Harry in the film *When Harry Met Sally*?
14. What are the forenames of the comedy duo French and Saunders?
15. Who did Bob Hoskins play in the film *Who Framed Roger Rabbit?*?

ANSWERS **1.** Bobby Ball **2.** Jack Lemmon **3.** Emma **4.** Linda Thorson **5.** Gary Ross **6.** St. Petersburg **7.** Kirk Jones **8.** Richard Burton **9.** Jeff Bridges **10.** Steve Coogan **11.** Sam Raimi **12.** Dana Carvey **13.** Billy Crystal **14.** Dawn and Jennifer **15.** Eddie Valiant.

SPORT

1. What were the names of the four Snow Owls that were the official mascots of the 1998 Winter Olympics at Nagano?
2. Which dog won the 1994 greyhound derby?
3. Which football team won the 1994/5 UEFA. Cup?
4. Who was the French Open men's singles tennis champion in 1971?
5. Which team knocked Leeds out of the FA Cup in February 1971?
6. For which Spanish football team did Abel Resino set a goalkeeping record for clean sheets in March 1991?
7. Who won the Olympic women's 800m in 1988?
8. Which team won the 1998/9 Scottish FA Cup?
9. In which country were the 1996 European Championships in football held?
10. Who was the 1995 rugby world player of the year?
11. In which year was swimmer Matt Biondi born?
12. Which football team won the 1996/7 League Cup?
13. How many times have Kilmarnock been Scottish League champions?
14. Which team won the 1960 University Boat Race?
15. Which horse won the 1947 Epsom Derby?

ANSWERS 1. Sukki, Nokki, Lekki and Tsukki **2.** Moral Standards **3.** Parma **4.** Jan Kodes **5.** Colchester **6.** Atletico Madrid **7.** Sigrun Wodars **8.** Rangers **9.** England **10.** Gavin Hastings **11.** 1965 **12.** Leicester City **13.** Once **14.** Oxford **15.** Airborne.

POP

1. From which South American country did instrumental group Azymuth come?
2. Which male vocalist had a 1997 Top 10 hit with the song *Gotham City*?
3. Which duo from the group U2 had a 1996 hit with *Theme from Mission: Impossible*?
4. Which album was the first release on Virgin Records?
5. Which group's first singles chart hit was *Punka* in 1996?
6. Which band, formed in 1978, consisted of the duo Paul Humphries and Andy McCluskey?
7. Which single by the Pet Shop Boys reached No. 1 in both the UK and the US?
8. In which town was singer John Otway born?
9. Which U.S. singer had a 1998 No. 3 single with *Stranded*?
10. Which group recorded the 1988 album *Nothing's Shocking*?
11. Which female vocal group had a 1998 hit with *Life Ain't Easy*?
12. Which Irish group had a minor chart hit in 1997 with *Mexican Wave*?
13. Who was the featured vocalist on the 1997 No. 1 *I'll Be Missing You* by Puff Daddy?
14. What was singer Sean Maguire's first singles chart entry in 1994?
15. On which record label did Madonna record the 1998 single *Ray of Light*?

ANSWERS **1.** Brazil **2.** R. Kelly **3.** Adam Clayton and Larry Mullen **4.** Tubular Bells **5.** Kenickie **6.** Orchestral Manoeuvres in the Dark **7.** West End Girls **8.** Aylesbury **9.** Lutricia McNeal **10.** Jane's Addiction **11.** Cleopatra **12.** Kerbdog **13.** Faith Evans **14.** Someone to Love **15.** Maverick.

WORDS

1. What is the name of the syrup made from pomegranate juice used in various drinks?
2. What is the name for a small group of whales or seals?
3. What sort of food is sapsago?
4. What sort of animal is a saki?
5. What sort of bird is a culver?
6. What does the theatrical expression 'to get the big bird' mean?
7. Monetarily speaking, how much was a bender?
8. Why wouldn't 'blue beans' do you any good?
9. What is a 'cat-o'-nine-tails'?
10. Which country is known as the 'cockpit of Europe'?
11. What is botanomancy?
12. On which part of the body would you wear a bendigo?
13. What is the name given to a large stone resting on two others like a table?
14. From what is the Japanese drink sake made?
15. What is a Salvo in Australian slang?

ANSWERS **1.** Grenadine **2.** Pod **3.** Cheese **4.** Monkey **5.** Pigeon **6.** To be hissed on stage **7.** Sixpence **8.** They're bullets **9.** A nine-lash whip **10.** Belgium **11.** Divination by leaves **12.** The head - it is a hat **13.** A cromlech **14.** Rice **15.** A member of the Salvation Army.

GENERAL KNOWLEDGE

1. Which bird is *Gallinago gallinago*?
2. In which year was the Paris landmark the Arc de Triomphe completed?
3. On which shore of Lake Geneva is the town of Lausanne?
4. What nationality was naval surgeon James Lind?
5. In which year did Arthur Scargill become president of the NUM?
6. Who wrote the play *Riders to the Sea*?
7. Which building on Muswell Hill was known as 'Ally Pally'?
8. Who was the second wife of Henry VIII?
9. Which artist designed the cover for the Beatles' LP *Sergeant Pepper's Lonely Hearts Club Band*?
10. In which city is the novel *The Aspern Papers* set?
11. Which city on the Rio Grande lies opposite Ciudad Juarez?
12. Who was England Test cricket captain 1966-67?
13. On which survey ship did Charles Darwin sail from 1831-36?
14. What nationality was the novelist Knut Hamsun?
15. Which forest features in Shakespeare's play *As You Like It*?

ANSWERS 1. Snipe **2.** 1836 **3.** North **4.** Scottish **5.** 1981 **6.** J.M. Synge **7.** Alexandra Palace **8.** Anne Boleyn **9.** Peter Blake **10.** Venice **11.** El Paso **12.** Brian Close **13.** H.M.S. Beagle **14.** Norwegian **15.** Forest of Arden.

ENTERTAINMENT

1. Which British actor plays villain Raymond Calitri in the film *Gone in 60 Seconds*?
2. Who directed the 2000 film *Almost Famous*?
3. Who directed the 2000 film *Goya in Bordeaux*?
4. Who was the female star of the film *Last Tango in Paris*?
5. In the 2001 television show *When Louis Met Paul and Debbie* who were the three participants?
6. Who directed the 1978 film *My Brilliant Career*?
7. Whose first cinema film as director was 1989's *Queen of Hearts*?
8. Which film was named *Those Daring Young Men in their Jaunty Jalopies* in the United States?
9. Who played Willis in the sitcom *Diff'rent Strokes*?
10. Who voices the character Marge in cartoon series *The Simpsons*?
11. Who plays Austrian detective Netusil in the film *Bad Timing*?
12. What is the surname of the star of television comedy show *Norm*?
13. Who directed the 1998 film *The Negotiator*?
14. What is Jeffrey Tambor's character name in television's *The Larry Sanders Show*?
15. In which year did Janet Ellis join television show *Blue Peter* as a presenter?

ANSWERS **1.** Christopher Eccleston **2.** Cameron Crowe **3.** Carlos Saura **4.** Maria Schneider **5.** Louis Theroux, Paul Daniels and Debbie McGee **6.** Gillian Armstrong **7.** Jon Amiel **8.** Monte Carlo Or Bust! **9.** Todd Bridges **10.** Julie Kavner **11.** Harvey Keitel **12.** Macdonald **13.** F. Gary Gray **14.** Hank Kingsley **15.** 1983.

SPORT

1. Who scored 163 points on the 1957 All Blacks rugby union tour of Australia?
2. In which year was the first European Championship in football?
3. Who was the 1992 Olympic women's high jump champion?
4. Who won the 1995 Nat West Trophy in cricket?
5. Who were runners up in football's Division One from 1970-72?
6. Which Essex cricketer is known as Jimmy Widges?
7. Which rider won the 1995 Badminton Horse Trials?
8. Which Scotland international footballer killed himself in June 1957 by throwing himself in front of a train?
9. Which team won the men's 4 x 400m relay title at the 1993, '95 and '97 IAAF World Championships?
10. Which country did 1984 Olympic gymnastics gold medal winner Koji Gushiken represent?
11. Who was the 1994 USPGA golf champion?
12. In which year was Australian distance runner Ron Clarke born?
13. At what team sport did Leslie Claudius win three Olympic golds?
14. For which baseball team did Roberto Clemente play his entire career from 1955-72?
15. Who in 1949 became England's youngest ever Test cricketer?

ANSWERS **1.** Don Clarke **2.** 1960 **3.** Heike Henkel **4.** Warwickshire **5.** Leeds United **6.** Tim Hodgson **7.** Bruce Davidson **8.** Hughie Gallacher **9.** USA **10.** Japan **11.** Nick Price **12.** 1937 **13.** Hockey **14.** Pittsburgh Pirates **15.** Brian Close.

POP

1. What was Arsenal F.C.'s 1998 Top 10 hit single?
2. Which duo charted in 1987 with *Another Step (Closer To You)*?
3. Which female vocalist had a No. 1 in 1998 with *Believe*?
4. Which was the first single by Madonna to reach No. 1 in both the UK and US?
5. Who had a No. 1 in 1995 with *Cotton Eye Joe*?
6. Which group's debut hit single in 1989 was called *Getting Away With It*?
7. Which vocal group had a 1992 Top 10 hit with *I'm Doing Fine Now*?
8. Which vocal duo had a 1957 hit with *Gonna Get Along Without Ya Now*?
9. Which group had a minor hit in 1998 with the song *Madagasga*?
10. What was Pearl Jam's only U.K. Top Ten single, in 1994?
11. Which singer featured on the 1992 single *I Like It* by Overweight Pooch?
12. Which rapper had a 1998 Top 20 single with *Beep Me*?
13. Which group charted in 1998 with *Keep on Dancin' (Let's Go)*?
14. Which group recorded the album *Freaky Trigger*?
15. Which group had a 1998 hit single with *Come Back to What You Know*?

ANSWERS 1. Hot Stuff **2.** Kim Wilde and Junior **3.** Cher **4.** Papa Don't Preach **5.** Rednex **6.** Electronic **7.** The Pasadenas **8.** Patience and Prudence **9.** Art of Trance **10.** Spin the Black Circle **11.** Ce Ce Peniston **12.** Missy 'Misdemeanour' Elliot **13.** Perpetual Motion **14.** Win **15.** Embrace.

SCIENCE

1. Which Scottish mathematician devised logarithms?
2. Is the element selenium radioactive?
3. What is the name given to the areas of ocean between 40° and 50° latitude in the southern hemisphere?
4. In the abbreviation cDNA what does c stand for?
5. What is the name given to an experiment carried out on a living body?
6. In pressure how many pascals equal 1 millibar?
7. Which element's symbol is Y?
8. What is the name given to a change of wind direction in an anticlockwise manner?
9. What is the equation of the Perfect Gas Law?
10. Which Scottish scientist's nickname at school was 'Dafty'?
11. Which English scientist constructed the first practical electromagnet?
12. Which element is directly below tin in the Periodic Table?
13. Of what is flaschenblitz a form?
14. What was inventor Thomas Edison's middle name?
15. In which year did Foucault construct the gyroscope?

ANSWERS **1.** John Napier **2.** No **3.** Roaring Forties **4.** Complementary **5.** In vivo **6.** 100 **7.** Yttrium **8.** Backing **9.** pV=nRT **10.** James Clerk Maxwell **11.** William Sturgeon **12.** Lead **13.** Lightning **14.** Alva **15.** 1852.

GENERAL KNOWLEDGE

1. In which of his films does Alfred Hitchcock appear leaving a pet shop with two terriers?
2. Which British sculptor's works include the 1952 bronze *Bird*?
3. In which 1962 film did Peter Sellers play the character Clare Quilty?
4. Which comedienne wrote the story collection *Camberwell Beauty*?
5. What does the London firm of GJ Cleverley specialise in making?
6. What in Spain is the dish 'pa amb oli'?
7. What weight was Dylan, the baby of Michael Douglas and Catherine Zeta Jones, at birth?
8. In which year did lawyer George Carman become a QC?
9. Which two England players were at the crease when David Gower flew over a Queensland v England cricket match?
10. In poker, when dealt the initial five cards, what are the odds of having a straight flush?
11. What was the name given to the twelve legendary peers of Charlemagne's court?
12. In which year did the arctic explorer Sir W.E. Parry attempt to reach the North Pole?
13. On which line is the London Underground station Marble Arch?
14. In which African country are the towns of Tibati and Garoua?
15. In which year did U.S. vice president Dan Quayle famously misspell the word potato?

ANSWERS **1.** The Birds **2.** Dame Elisabeth Frink **3.** Lolita **4.** Jenny Eclair **5.** Shoes **6.** Bread drizzled with olive oil **7.** 7 lb 7 oz **8.** 1971 **9.** Allan Lamb and Robin Smith **10.** 83,333-1 **11.** Paladins **12.** 1827 **13.** Central **14.** Cameroon **15.** 1982.

ENTERTAINMENT

1. In which month was the Isle of Wight festival in 1970?
2. Who played Andy Warhol in the 1997 film *Basquiat*?
3. Who was the male star in the film *Last Tango in Paris*?
4. Which comedian stars in the 2001 film *Down to Earth*?
5. Who directed the 1969 film *Zabriskie Point*?
6. Who voices the character Lisa in cartoon series *The Simpsons*?
7. Who authored the play *Solemn Mass for a Full Moon in Summer*?
8. Who voices the character Rocky Rhodes in the film *Chicken Run*?
9. What is Nicolas Cage's character name in the film *Gone in 60 Seconds*?
10. Who played Van Gogh in the 1956 film *Lust For Life*?
11. Who are the male and female leads in the 2001 film *Sweet November*?
12. In which year did film director Lindsay Anderson die?
13. What nationality is the film director Dario Argento?
14. Who directed the 1973 film *The Harrad Experiment*?
15. What is Ray Winstone's character name in the film *Sexy Beast*?

ANSWERS 1. August **2.** David Bowie **3.** Marlon Brando **4.** Chris Rock **5.** Michelangelo Antonioni **6.** Yeardley Smith **7.** Michael Tremblay **8.** Mel Gibson **9.** Memphis Raines **10.** Kirk Douglas **11.** Keanu Reeves and Charlize Theron **12.** 1994 **13.** Italian **14.** Ted Post **15.** Gary Dove.

SPORT

1. Who was top scorer for Australia in their 1999 cricket World Cup Group B game against New Zealand?
2. Which footballer was the 1990 BBC Sports Personality of the Year?
3. How many wickets did Joel Garner take in the 1984 Test series against Australia?
4. What nationality is Anders Gärdebud, winner of the 1976 Olympic 3,000m steeplechase title?
5. In which year was cricketer Rachel Heyhoe-Flint born?
6. In which year was cricketer Mike Gatting born?
7. Which Denver player was MVP in the XXXII Superbowl in 1998?
8. Which Estonia-born wrestler was known as 'the Russian Lion'?
9. Who was world individual fly fishing champion in 1994 and '97?
10. Which footballer scored a consolation goal for the Czech Republic in the 1996 European Championship final?
11. In which year was footballer John Charles born?
12. How many international caps did Bobby Charlton win for England?
13. Which Somerset cricketer is known as Skirlog?
14. Who won the 1994 Nat West Trophy in cricket?
15. Which rider won the 1997 Badminton Horse Trials?

ANSWERS 1. Darren Lehmann **2.** Paul Gascoigne **3.** 31 **4.** Swedish **5.** 1939 **6.** 1957 **7.** Terrell Davis **8.** George Hackenschmidt **9.** Pascal Cognard **10.** Berger **11.** 1931 **12.** 106 **13.** Adrian Pierson **14.** Worcestershire **15.** David O'Connor.

POP

1. Which rap group had hits in 1998 with *Jayou* and *Concrete Schoolyard*?
2. Which group released the 1999 live album *Mad for Sadness*?
3. On which record label was Keith Emerson's *Honky Tonk Train Blues* a hit?
4. Which group had a 1997 hit with *A Life Less Ordinary*?
5. Which was the only single by Meat Loaf to reach No. 1 in the U.K. and the U.S.?
6. Which male vocalist had a 1989 Top 10 single with *Americanos*?
7. Which male singer had Top 10 singles in 1998 with *Save Tonight* and *Falling in Love Again*?
8. Who had a 1991 chart hit with *It's Grim Up North*?
9. Which duo had a 1994 Top 40 hit with *True Love Ways*?
10. Which group won a Mercury Music Prize for the album *Elegant Slumming*?
11. What was the title of Ellis, Beggs and Howard's only singles chart entry?
12. Which female singer recorded the 1989 album *Strange Angels*?
13. In which year was singer Howard Jones born?
14. From which European country does singer Leila K come?
15. Which group recorded the 1995 album *The Honeymoon Suite*?

ANSWERS 1. Jurassic 5 **2.** Arab Strap **3.** Manticore **4.** Ash **5.** I'd Do Anything For Love (But I Won't Do That) **6.** Holly Johnson **7.** Eagle-Eye Cherry **8.** Justified Ancients of Mu Mu **9.** David Essex and Catherine Zeta Jones **10.** M People **11.** Big Bubbles, No Troubles **12.** Laurie Anderson **13.** 1955 **14.** Sweden **15.** Butterfly Child.

PEOPLE

1. Which London boutique owner is sister of the Marquess of Bristol?
2. Which rock star's Sussex country house, Redlands, was raided by the police in 1967?
3. In which year did the jazz musician Gil Evans die?
4. Who is the famous mother of actress Kate Hudson?
5. In which year did the economist J.M. Keynes die?
6. Who won the Vendée Globe yacht race which finished in 2001?
7. Who painted the 1759 work *Sigismunda*?
8. With which field of the arts is Mexican Luis Barragan associated?
9. Which singer has fronted the groups Slippery Elm, Clover, and the News?
10. Who became Scotland's first minister in 2000, following the death of Donald Dewar?
11. Which darts player is known as 'the Viking'?
12. In which year did the composer Sergei Rachmaninov die?
13. Who won the 1945 Nobel prize for physics?
14. Who was the father of Salome in the New Testament?
15. In which year was the German statesman Walter Rathenau assassinated?

ANSWERS **1.** Lady Victoria Hervey **2.** Keith Richards **3.** 1988 **4.** Goldie Hawn **5.** 1946 **6.** Michel Desjoyeaux **7.** William Hogarth **8.** Architecture **9.** Huey Lewis **10.** Henry McLeish **11.** Andy Fordham **12.** 1943 **13.** Wolfgang Pauli **14.** Herodias **15.** 1922.

GENERAL KNOWLEDGE

1. Which U.S. state is known as the 'Badger State'?
2. Who wrote the novel *Not To Disturb*?
3. What is a mangosteen - a piece of armour or a tree?
4. From which club did Manchester United sign Andy Cole?
5. Which drink consists of pineapple juice, rum and coconut?
6. Who did Roger Moore play in TV drama *The Persuaders*?
7. What do Australians refer to as the Apple Isle?
8. What was the Roman counterpart of the Greek goddess Eos?

9. Who wrote the 1968 play *Plaza Suite*?
10. What was the birthplace of writer Dr. Johnson?
11. What is the peepul tree also known as?
12. What is the name of the black-and-yellow beetle which is a serious pest of potatoes?
13. What is the name of Princess Anne's daughter?
14. Who composed the opera *The Cunning Little Vixen*?
15. What sort of creature is a habu?

ANSWERS 1. Wisconsin **2.** Muriel Spark **3.** Tree **4.** Newcastle United **5.** Piña Colada **6.** Brett Sinclair **7.** Tasmania **8.** Aurora **9.** Neil Simon **10.** Lichfield **11.** The bo tree **12.** Colorado beetle **13.** Zara **14.** Leos Janacek **15.** Snake.

ENTERTAINMENT

1. Who voices the character Apu in cartoon series *The Simpsons*?
2. Who is the male lead in the 1954 film *PHFFFT*?
3. At which film studios did Alfred Hitchcock make his 1926 film *The Lodger*?
4. In which year did the first kabarett theatre open in Germany?
5. What are the name of television's three *Butt-Ugly Martians*?
6. Who voices the character Pacha in the Disney film *The Emperor's New Groove*?
7. Who played Picasso in the 1952 film *Surviving Picasso*?
8. Who plays Sam Ryan in the television series *Silent Witness?*
9. Who plays Bosley in the 2000 film *Charlie's Angels*?
10. In which city did the stage play The Mousetrap open in October 1952?
11. Who directed the 1998 film *The Gingerbread Man*?
12. What in 2001 became the U.K.'s highest grossing foreign-language film of all time?
13. Which duo scripted the film *Honest* starring the pop group All Saints?
14. Which comic actor authored the novel *Getting Rid of Mr. Kitchen*?
15. Which film director was married to the actress Rhonda Fleming from 1966-71?

ANSWERS 1. Hank Azaria **2.** Jack Lemmon **3.** Gainsborough Studios **4.** 1901 **5.** B Bop-A-Luna, 2-T-Fru-T and Do-Wah Diddy **6.** John Goodman **7.** Anthony Hopkins **8.** Amanda Burton **9.** Bill Murray **10.** Nottingham **11.** Robert Altman **12.** Crouching Tiger, Hidden Dragon **13.** Dick Clement and Ian La Frenais **14.** Charles Higson **15.** Hall Bartlett.

SPORT

1. What was the nickname of American football star George Halas?
2. Who was the 1997 World Matchplay golf champion?
3. Which country won the 1997 Davis Cup?
4. Who was runner-up to Daley Thompson in the 1984 Olympic decathlon?
5. Who was 1995 and '96 125cc motor cycling world champion?
6. Who won an Olympic Nordic skiing gold medal in 1960 at the age of 35 years and 52 days?
7. Who won the 1993 County Cricket Championship?
8. Who was the 1960 Olympic men's 5,000m champion?
9. Which Australian rugby union player was capped 36 times from 1968-82?
10. Which jockey won the 1980 Epsom Derby on Henbit?
11. In which city was tennis player Rosemary Casals born?
12. Which male tennis player won the 1982 Junior singles title at Wimbledon?
13. Which golfer won the 1970 U.S. Masters tournament?
14. Which race horse trainer's first Classic winner was Bolonski in 1975?
15. What nationality is motor cycling champion Alberto 'Johnny' Cecotto?

ANSWERS 1. Papa Bear **2.** Vijay Singh **3.** Sweden **4.** Jürgen Hingsen **5.** Haruchika Aoki **6.** Veikko Hakulinen **7.** Middlesex **8.** Murray Halberg **9.** John Hipwell **10.** Willie Carson **11.** San Francisco **12.** Pat Cash **13.** Billy Casper **14.** Henry Cecil **15.** Venezuelan.

POP

1. Which male singer had a Top 40 hit in 1995 with *Wonderful*?
2. Which male vocal group had Top 20 hits in 1997 with *Let Me In* and *All Out Of Love*?
3. In which year did Tom Jones have a hit single with *The Young New Mexican Puppeteer*?
4. What was the debut album from Bristol-based group Straw?
5. Who had a 1995 No. 1 single with *Boombastic*?
6. Whose only chart hit was 1959's *A Pub with No Beer*?
7. Which group recorded the album *OK Computer*?
8. Which group had a 1997 chart hit with *Hey Child*?
9. Which single by Marvin Gaye was a No. 1 hit in the U.K. and U.S.?
10. Which group had a No. 4 single in 1998 with *Lost in Space*?
11. Which group had a No. 6 single in 1998 with *Lost in Space*?
12. Which group had a minor 1997 hit with *Chemical # 1*?
13. Which group recorded the album *The Royal Scam*?
14. Which of Jive Bunny's three No. 1 singles went straight into the chart at that position?
15. In which year did Joy Division first chart with the single *Love Will Tear Us Apart*?

ANSWERS **1.** Adam Ant **2.** OTT **3.** 1972 **4.** Shoplifting **5.** Shaggy **6.** Slim Dusty **7.** Radiohead **8.** East 17 **9.** I Heard it Through the Grapevine **10.** Apollo Four Forty **11.** The Lighthouse Family **12.** Jesus Jones **13.** Steely Dan **14.** Let's Party **15.** 1980.

ART AND LITERATURE

1. Which British artist's works include the 1954 print *Skull and Pomegranate*?
2. Which French artist's sculptures include the work *Dancer Putting on her Stocking*?
3. Who wrote the novel *A Passage To India*?
4. Which British artist painted the 1966 work *Star of Bethlehem*?
5. Which artist produced the 1961 painted work *The First Real Target*?
6. Who wrote the novel *A Patchwork Planet*?
7. Whose volumes of stories include *If the River was Whiskey*?

8. Who wrote the 1983 novel *Coming From Behind*?
9. Which artist painted the 1909 work *A Favourite Custom*?
10. In which Italian city was artist Giacomo Balla born?
11. Who wrote the novel *Nothing Like the Sun*?
12. Who wrote the novel *Nexus*?
13. Which British artist's works include the 1934 gouache *Dancing Skeletons*?
14. Which British artist's works include the painting *Lucrecia Borgia Reigns in the Vatican in the Absence of Pope Alexander VI*?
15. Who wrote the novel *This Sporting Life*?

ANSWERS 1. Prunella Clough **2.** Edgar Degas **3.** E.M. Forster **4.** John Bellany **5.** Peter Blake **6.** Anne Tyler **7.** T.C. Boyle **8.** Howard Jacobson **9.** Sir Lawrence Alma-Tadema **10.** Turin **11.** Anthony Burgess **12.** Henry Miller **13.** Edward Burra **14.** Frank Cadogan Cowper **15.** David Storey.

GENERAL KNOWLEDGE

1. Who was Roman emperor from 14-37 A.D.?
2. Of which European country is Arad a county?
3. In which country is the Zoo bridge?
4. Which saint's feast day is December 7th?
5. Of which country is the letter J the international car index mark?
6. In which European country is the port of Cherbourg?
7. Which major city does Barajas airport serve?
8. The element barium derives its name from the Greek word for what?
9. What is the official language of Bangladesh?
10. What does the forename Paul mean?
11. Which president of the United States served just 31 days?
12. Who wrote the opera *La Traviata*?
13. Which biblical character's mistress was Delilah?
14. In which year was the initial Live Aid concert?
15. How large in square miles is the republic of San Marino?

ANSWERS 1. Tiberius **2.** Romania **3.** Germany **4.** Ambrose **5.** Japan **6.** France **7.** Madrid **8.** Heavy **9.** Bengali **10.** Small **11.** William Harrison **12.** Verdi **13.** Samson **14.** 1985 **15.** 24 sq. miles.

ENTERTAINMENT

1. What is Michael Douglas' character name in the film *Wonder Boys*?
2. Who played Eddie Scrooge in the 2000 television drama *A Christmas Carol*?
3. What was the original name of the character Kuzco in the Disney film *The Emperor's New Groove*?
4. In which children's television show do Dr. Damage and Emperor Bog appear?
5. Who plays 'J.D.' in the film *Thelma And Louise*?
6. Who is the female lead in the 1954 film *PHFFFT*?
7. Who directed the 2000 film *The Grinch*?
8. What was the surname of 'Nasty Nick' in British television's first *Big Brother* series?
9. Who plays memory loss victim Leonard Shelby in the film *Memento*?
10. Which stage play began life as a half-hour radio play called *Three Blind Mice* in 1947?
11. Who played Michelangelo in the 1965 film *The Agony and the Ecstasy*?
12. Who voices the character Homer in the cartoon series *The Simpsons*?
13. Who is the director of the 2001 film *The Gangs of New York*?
14. Who directed the 1933 film *The Testament of Dr. Mabuse*?
15. Which blues legend is the basis for the play *I Just Stopped to See the Man* by Stephen Jeffreys?

ANSWERS **1.** Grady Tripp **2.** Ross Kemp **3.** Manco **4.** Butt-Ugly Martians **5.** Brad Pitt **6.** Judy Holliday **7.** Ron Howard **8.** Bateman **9.** Guy Pearce **10.** The Mousetrap **11.** Charlton Heston **12.** Dan Castellaneta **13.** Martin Scorsese **14.** Fritz Lang **15.** Robert Johnson.

SPORT

1. At what age did Alex Higgins win the 1972 World Professional Snooker championships?
2. Who was the USPGA golf champion from 1924-7?
3. Who was men's javelin champion at the 1993 and '95 IAAF World Championships?
4. Who was 1994 and '95 men's World Indoor Bowls champion?
5. Which cyclist won the 1994 Vuelta A España?
6. Who was world 250cc motor cycling champion in 1988 and '89?
7. Who won rugby union's Pilkington Cup from 1984-7?
8. Who in 1961 became the first American to win the world Formula 1 motor racing title?
9. For which international rugby union side did Michel Celaya play?
10. Who did Marcel Cerdan knock out in 1948 to take the world middleweight boxing title?
11. What was Indian bowler Bhagwant Chandrasekhar's highest batting score in Tests?
12. In which city was footballer Herbert Chapman born in 1875?
13. Who succeeded Ian Chappell as Australian Test cricket captain?
14. What are jockey Willie Carson's middle names?
15. At what sport does Austrian Tomas Stangassinger compete?

ANSWERS 1. 23 **2.** Walter Hagen **3.** Jan Zelezny **4.** Andy Thomson **5.** Tony Rominger **6.** Sito Pons **7.** Bath **8.** Phil Hill **9.** France **10.** Tony Zale **11.** 22 **12.** Sheffield **13.** Greg Chappell **14.** Hunter Fisher **15.** Skiing.

POP

1. In which U.S. city are the group The Apples In Stereo based?
2. Which pop group's hit singles include 2000's release *In Demand*?
3. Which pop group's first No. 1 single in 1999 was *Heartbeat/Tragedy*?
4. Which member of the pop group Blur plays piano on the track *I Go To Sleep* from the 1995 album *Isle of View* by The Pretenders?
5. Which pop group appeared in the 1969 Norman Wisdom film *What's Good for the Goose?*
6. Which blues artist recorded the 2000 album *Making Love is Good For You*?
7. Which singer-songwriter released the 1996 album *Sell, Sell, Sell*?
8. Under what name did Bristol-based Debbie Parsons release the 2000 album *Hidden Cinema Soundtrack*?
9. Who was the lead guitarist on the 1972 album *Malo* by Malo?
10. Which group's first U.K. single was 1984's *Dr. Mabuse*?
11. Which Swedish DJ records under the name 'Riley and Clay'?
12. Which member of Roxy Music recorded the 1982 album *Primitive Guitars*?
13. Which group recorded the 1988 album *Confessions of a Pop Group*?
14. Which singer had a 1994 No. 1 single with *Without You*?
15. Which Irish rock group released the 2000 single *Beautiful Day*?

ANSWERS **1.** Denver **2.** Texas **3.** Steps **4.** Damon Albarn **5.** The Pretty Things **6.** B.B. King **7.** David Gray **8.** Foehn **9.** Jorge Santana **10.** Propaganda **11.** Richard Johansson **12.** Phil Manzanera **13.** The Style Council **14.** Mariah Carey **15.** U2.

GEOGRAPHY

1. In which town in Kent would you find the promenade The Pantiles?
2. The Shatt-al-Arab river is formed by the union of which two rivers?
3. Riga is the capital of which European country?
4. Naxos is the largest of which group of Greek islands?
5. On which German river is the porcelain town of Meissen?
6. Which six countries border the Black Sea?
7. On which river does Berlin stand?
8. Mount Marcy is the highest peak of which North American mountain range?
9. In which bay is the former prison island of Alcatraz?
10. What did the country of Upper Volta become in 1984?
11. The commercial centre of which city in Illinois is called 'The Loop'?
12. What crop accounts for 75% of Cuba's exports?
13. To which South American country do the Galapagos Islands belong?
14. Which is longer - the River Forth or the River Tees?
15. The Atlantic coastal resort of Hollywood is in which U.S. state?

ANSWERS **1.** (Royal) Tunbridge Wells **2.** Tigris & Euphrates **3.** Latvia **4.** Cyclades **5.** River Elbe **6.** Bulgaria, Georgia, Romania, Russia, Turkey & Ukraine **7.** River Spree **8.** Adirondack Mountains **9.** San Francisco **10.** Burkina Faso **11.** Chicago **12.** Sugar **13.** Ecuador **14.** Forth **15.** Florida.

GENERAL KNOWLEDGE

1. In which year was Longchamps horse racecourse created?
2. Which artist and writer founded the Kelmscott Press?
3. Baldy Mountain is the highest point of which Canadian province?
4. Who wrote the novel *Empire of the Sun*?
5. What would you do with a brisling - eat it or wear it?
6. Which of the Seven Wonders of the World was destroyed by an earthquake in 225 B.C.?
7. In music, what is four-four time also known as?
8. In which century did Nell Gwyn live?
9. Who wrote *The Silmarillion*?
10. Which English county's administrative centre is Dorchester?
11. On what part of the body would you wear a jandal?
12. Which former Jamaican prime minister died in 1997?
13. Which two actors starred in the 1974 film *Freebie and the Bean*?
14. What is the name of the female reproductive part of a flower?
15. Who was president of the Central African Republic from 1972-76?

ANSWERS 1. 1857 **2.** William Morris **3.** Manitoba **4.** J.G. Ballard **5.** Eat it - it's a fish **6.** Colossus of Rhodes **7.** Common time **8.** 17th **9.** J.R.R. Tolkien **10.** Dorset **11.** On the foot **12.** Michael Manley **13.** James Caan and Alan Arkin **14.** Pistil **15.** Jean Bokassa.

ENTERTAINMENT

1. In which of his films does Alfred Hitchcock appear being pushed in a wheelchair in an airport?
2. In which city was the film director Fritz Lang born?
3. Who plays Leonardo DiCaprio's father in the 2001 film *The Gangs of New York*?
4. Who plays Sara Gaskell in the film *Wonder Boys*?
5. What is the name of the dog in the children's television show *Butt-Ugly Martians*?
6. Who wrote the 1737 opera *Castor et Pollux*?
7. Who played Mao Zedong in the 1987 premiere of John Adams's opera *Nixon in China*?
8. Who wrote the music for the 2000 stage show *In the Penal Colony*?
9. Who played Toulouse-Lautrec in the 1952 film *Moulin Rouge*?
10. Who were the male and female leads in the 1968 film *Sweet November*?
11. What is Woody Allen's character name in the film *Small Time Crooks*?
12. Which film director's works premiere at the Senator Theatre, Baltimore?
13. Who directed the 1979 kung fu movie *Drunken Master*?
14. Who does Sue Johnston play in television comedy show *The Royle Family*?
15. What was the stage name of French tragic actress Elisa Félix?

ANSWERS 1. Topaz **2.** Vienna **3.** Liam Neeson **4.** Frances McDormand **5.** Dog **6.** Jean Philippe Rameau **7.** John Duykers **8.** Philip Glass **9.** José Ferrer **10.** Anthony Newley and Sandy Dennis **11.** Ray Winkler **12.** John Waters **13.** Yuen Wo Ping **14.** Barbara Royle **15.** Rachel.

SPORT

1. Who won the world middleweight boxing title in 1980 by defeating Alan Minter?
2. Who was world Formula 1 motor racing championship runner-up from 1963-5?
3. Which American won the decathlon title at the 1991, '93 and '95 IAAF World Championships?
4. Which member of the Chappell family played only three Tests for Australia, in 1981?
5. Who did Bob Charles beat in a play-off to win the 1963 British Open golf tournament?
6. In which city was world heavyweight boxing champion Ezzard Charles born?
7. By what score did Ronnie O'Sullivan win the 1993 U.K. snooker final?
8. Which greyhound's life story was told in the 1935 film *Wild Boy*?
9. Which trainer was associated with the horse Red Rum?
10. Which Brazilian scored in every game of the 1970 World Cup Finals?
11. Who won the 1993 RAC Rally?
12. Which country won both men and women's team archery golds at the 1988 Olympics?
13. Which country won the 1976 European championships in football?
14. Who was men's world cross country champion from 1986-9?
15. Who were the first cricket county champions in 1864?

ANSWERS **1.** Marvin Hagler **2.** Graham Hill **3.** Dan O'Brien **4.** Trevor **5.** Phil Rodgers **6.** Chicago **7.** 10-6 **8.** Mick the Miller **9.** Ginger McCain **10.** Jairzinho **11.** Juha Kankkunen **12.** South Korea **13.** Czechoslovakia **14.** John Ngugi **15.** Surrey.

POP

1. What was Aqua's third No. 1 single?
2. Which female vocalist had a 1994 Top 20 single with *Reach*?
3. What was the title of Blur's 1995 No. 1 single?
4. Which group released the 1999 single *Get the Keys and Go*?
5. Which single by Gloria Gaynor was a No. 1 hit in the U.K. and U.S.?
6. Which group had hit singles in 1980 with *United* and *Breaking the Law*?
7. Which group revisited the charts after a six year absence with 1997's *Nothing Lasts Forever*?
8. Which group recorded the album *I Should Coco*?
9. From which country does singer Tina Arena come?
10. Which ex-member of Take That had solo success in 1996 with *Child*?
11. What was Patti Page's only singles chart hit, in 1953?
12. Which female singer featured on the 1997 hit *All My Time* by Paid and Live?
13. Which group charted in 1983 with *Scatterlings of Africa*?
14. Which indie group had a Top 20 hit in 1995 with *Great Things*?
15. Which U.S. vocal group had a 1995 hit with *Freek 'N You*?

ANSWERS **1.** Turn Back Time **2.** Judy Cheeks **3.** Country House **4.** Llama Farmers **5.** I Will Survive **6.** Judas Priest **7.** Echo and the Bunnymen **8.** Supergrass **9.** Australia **10.** Mark Owen **11.** (How Much is) That Doggie in the Window **12.** Lauryn Hill **13.** Juluka **14.** Echobelly **15.** Jodeci.

HISTORY

1. In which year did J. Edgar Hoover become Director of the F.B.I.?
2. In which year was the Festival of Britain?
3. Which king was the intended victim of Fieschi's Plot in 1835?
4. The International Monetary Fund was established by the Bretton Woods Agreement of which year?
5. Which international criminal police organization was established in 1923 in Vienna?
6. In which year was the island of Iwo Jima returned to Japan by the U.S.?
7. In which year was the mountain K-2 first climbed?
8. What was the year of the Louisiana Purchase?
9. In which century was the Taj Mahal built?
10. Who opened the 'Bloody Assize' in Taunton in 1685?
11. Which famous rail bridge disaster happened on December 28th, 1879?
12. The Anti-Saloon League of America was succeeded in 1948 by which organization?
13. In which year did the Pilgrim Fathers establish Thanksgiving Day?
14. In which year of the 18c was Lisbon devastated by an earthquake?
15. Gudrun Esslin was a founder member of which German terrorist group?

ANSWERS 1. 1924 **2.** 1951 **3.** Louis Philippe of France **4.** 1944 **5.** Interpol **6.** 1968 **7.** 1954 **8.** 1803 **9.** 17th **10.** Judge Jeffreys **11.** Tay Bridge disaster **12.** Temperance League of America **13.** 1621 **14.** 1755 **15.** Baader-Meinhof Gang.

GENERAL KNOWLEDGE

1. What are the two robots called in the film *Star Wars*?
2. What is the capacity of Sydney's Olympic Stadium?
3. Whose volumes of poetry include *Glad to Wear Glasses*?
4. What country did the states of Uri, Unterwalden and Schwyz become in 1291?
5. Which car manufacturer makes the V70 XC?
6. In which U.S. city did the actor Mark Wahlberg grow up?
7. Who played Adolf Hitler in the film *Soft Beds, Hard Battles*?
8. Which car manufacturer makes the Insight model?
9. Who became chairwoman of the English National Ballet in 2000?
10. In poker, when dealt the initial five cards, what are the odds of having two pairs?
11. What in South America is a pareira?
12. On which London Underground lines is the station Shepherd's Bush?
13. Where in New Zealand is the city of Wellington - North Island or South Island?
14. Which famous book's authorship is credited to an Indian sage called Vatsayana?
15. Of what is musophobia the fear?

ANSWERS 1. R2D2 and C-3PO **2.** 110,000 **3.** John Hegley **4.** Switzerland **5.** Volvo **6.** Boston **7.** Peter Sellers **8.** Honda **9.** Angela Rippon **10.** 21-1 **11.** A climbing plant **12.** Hammersmith & City and Cenral **13.** North **14.** The Kama Sutra **15.** Mice.

ENTERTAINMENT

1. Which actor was Oscar-nominated for the 1997 film *The Apostle*?

2. What was the surname of the Major in the sitcom *Fawlty Towers*?

3. Who played *Mary of Scotland* in the 1936 film?

4. What was thc subtitle of the 1994 film *City Slickers II*?

5. Ernest Bloch's only opera was a version of which Shakespeare play?

6. Who played Skeletor in the 1987 film *Masters of the Universe*?

7. Which 1896 Puccini opera is set in the Latin Quarter of Paris?

8. Who directed the 1998 film *The Faculty*?

9. In which year did comedian Marty Feldman die?

10. Which English bass created the role of Swallow in the opcra *Peter Grimes*?

11. Who directed the 1959 film *Porgy and Bess*?

12. What dance does Salome perform in the opera *Salome* by Strauss?

13. "I don't think we're in Kansas anymore" - which 1939 film?

14. Who is Prince Ramiro's valet in the Rossini opera *La Cenerentola*?

15. In which city was composer Frederick Delius born?

ANSWERS 1. Robert Duvall **2.** Gowen **3.** Katharine Hepburn **4.** The Legend of Curly's Gold **5.** Macbeth **6.** Frank Langella **7.** La Bohème **8.** Robert Rodriguez **9.** 1982 **10.** Owen Brannigan **11.** Otto Preminger **12.** The Dance of the Seven Veils **13.** The Wizard of Oz **14.** Dandini **15.** Bradford.

SPORT

1. Who was the French Open men's singles tennis champion in 1968?

2. Which football team won the 1997/8 European Cup-Winners' Cup?

3. Ollie was one of the three official mascots of the 2000 Summer Olympics at Sydney. What type of animal was it?

4. Who was the 1998 world men's indoor bowls champion?

5. Which football team won the 1995/6 UEFA Cup?

6. Which dog won the 1995 greyhound derby?

7. In which country were the 1990 football World Cup finals held?

8. Who was the 1992 rugby world player of the year?

9. Which football team won the 1996/7 European Champions Cup?

10. Who won the Olympic men's 200m in 1964?

11. How many times have Dundee United been Scottish League champions?

12. Which football team won the 1998/9 FA Cup?

13. Which team won the 1998 world series in baseball?

14. Which football team won the 1995/6 League Cup?

15. Which team won the 1950 University Boat Race?

ANSWERS 1. Ken Rosewall **2.** Chelsea **3.** Kookaburra **4.** Paul Foster **5.** Bayern Munich **6.** Moaning Lad **7.** Italy **8.** Will Carling **9.** Borussia Dortmund **10.** Henry Carr **11.** Once **12.** Manchester United **13.** New York Yankees **14.** Aston Villa **15.** Cambridge.

POP

1. Who charted in 1998 with the single *Because I Got It Like That*?
2. Which duo released the album *Fear of Fours* in 1999?
3. What was the only solo single by John Lennon to reach No. 1 in the U.K. and U.S. charts?
4. In which year was singer Billy Joel born?
5. From which country does DJ and producer Armin hail?
6. Who had a No. 1 single in 1995 with *Boom Boom Boom*?
7. Which duo had a 1996 hit with *Live Like Horses*?
8. Which singer recorded the album *Frank's Wild Years*?
9. Under which name did Isaac Hayes have a 1998 Christmas hit single?
10. What was the title of Jennifer Paige's 1998 hit single?
11. Which group recorded the 1997 hit *Novocaine for the Soul*?
12. Which singer had a minor hit single in 1994 with *Girl U Want*?
13. In which year did Louise Nurding leave the group Eternal?
14. Which pop group helped out Nottingham Forest F.C. on the single *We've Got the Whole World in Our Hands*?
15. Which group recorded the 1995 album *Bite It*?

ANSWERS **1.** The Jungle Brothers **2.** Lamb **3.** (Just Like) Starting Over **4.** 1949 **5.** Holland **6.** Outhere Brothers **7.** Elton John & Luciano Pavarotti **8.** Tom Waits **9.** Chef **10.** Crush **11.** The Eels **12.** Robert Palmer **13.** 1995 **14.** Paper Lace **15.** Whiteout.

ART AND LITERATURE

1. Which U.S. printmaker made the 1973 lithograph *Big Red Wrench in a Landscape*?
2. Who wrote the short story volume *I Sing the Body Electric!*?
3. Which Spanish artist painted the 1936 work *Forgotten Horizon*?
4. Who wrote the novel *Myra Breckinridge*?
5. Which artist painted the 1913 work *Abstract Speed - The Car has Passed*?
6. Which Cubist artist painted the work *Clarinet and Bottle of Rum on a Mantelpiece*?
7. Who wrote the 1988 novel *Wyrd Sisters*?
8. Who wrote the book *The Long Dark Tea-Time of the Soul*?
9. Which British artist painted the 1956 work *Image of the Fish God*?
10. In which year did the British artist Sir Max Beerbohm die?
11. Which British artist painted the 1962 work *The Identi-Kit Man*?
12. Who wrote the novel *Perfume*?
13. Who wrote the novel *Taking Apart the Poco Poco*?
14. Which British artist painted the 1912 work *Horse Sale at the Barbican*?
15. Which sculptor produced the 1969 work *Bluebeard's Wife*?

ANSWERS 1. Jim Dine **2.** Ray Bradbury **3.** Salvador Dali **4.** Gore Vidal **5.** Giacomo Balla **6.** Georges Braque **7.** Terry Pratchett **8.** Douglas Adams **9.** Alan Davie **10.** 1956 **11.** Derek Boshier **12.** Patrick Süskind **13.** Richard Francis **14.** Robert Bevan **15.** Arman.

GENERAL KNOWLEDGE

1. Which member of the pumpkin family might you find in a bathroom?
2. Which order of insects includes the beetles?
3. What is the name of the French national theatre opened in Paris in 1680?
4. In which year did the British submarine Thetis sink in Liverpool Bay?
5. What is the standard monetary unit of Mexico?
6. On which island was cricketer Brian Lara born?
7. On which river is the town of Limerick?
8. What is the most famous novel of Erich Maria Remarque?
9. Which BBC soap opera was set in the village of Los Barcos?
10. Who directed the 1993 film *The Piano*?
11. Which philosopher wrote *The Rights of Man*?
12. Which horse won the 1995 Grand National?
13. Who is the detective in the novel *The Moonstone*?
14. Which bird is also known as an apteryx?
15. Of which country was Sir John Hall prime minister from 1879-82?

ANSWERS **1.** Loofah **2.** Coleoptera **3.** Comédie Française **4.** 1939 **5.** Peso **6.** Trinidad **7.** Shannon **8.** All Quiet on the Western Front **9.** Eldorado **10.** Jane Campion **11.** Thomas Paine **12.** Royal Athlete **13.** Sergeant Cuff **14.** Kiwi **15.** New Zealand.

ENTERTAINMENT

1. Who did actor Ricky Tomlinson play in the soap opera *Brookside*?
2. Who directed the 1956 film *Beyond a Reasonable Doubt*?
3. In which of his films does Alfred Hitchcock appear sitting in a hotel lobby with a baby?
4. In which year did actress Letitia Dean leave the cast of *EastEnders*?

5. Who played Samantha Failsworth in the soap *Coronation Street*?
6. Who stars as Caroline in the sitcom *Caroline in the City*?
7. Which soap opera provided Kylie Minogue with her first acting job?
8. Who played the title role in the 1936 film *Rembrandt*?
9. Who is the male star of the 1997 film *Box of Moonlight*?
10. Who played Kelly Taylor in the television drama series *Beverly Hills 90210*?
11. Who played Bruce Willis's girlfriend in the film *Pulp Fiction*?
12. Who played Tina Seabrook in the television drama series *Casualty*?
13. In which year was the episode of sitcom *Fawlty Towers* entitled *The Germans* first shown on television?
14. Who voices the part of the cat Smokey in the film *Stuart Little*?
15. Who plays television's *Burnside*?

ANSWERS **1.** Bobby Grant **2.** Fritz Lang **3.** Torn Curtain **4.** 1995 **5.** Tina Hobley **6.** Lea Thompson **7.** The Sullivans **8.** Charles Laughton **9.** John Turturro **10.** Jennie Garth **11.** Maria de Medeiros **12.** Claire Goose **13.** 1975 **14.** Chazz Palminteri **15.** Chris Ellison.

SPORT

1. Who lost the 1975 World Snooker championship to Ray Reardon, 31-30?
2. Who in 1987 became the first Australian to win the world 500cc motorcycling title?
3. Which horse won the 1997 1,000 Guineas?
4. What was Brazilian footballer Manoel Francisco dos Santos better known as?
5. Which Olympic athlete became an ITV newscaster in September 1955?
6. Which Mexican boxer was WBC super-featherweight champion from 1984-87?
7. In which country was footballer Eusebio born?
8. In which American state was tennis player Chris Evert born?
9. Which two events did Jackie Joyner-Kersee win at the 1988 Olympics?
10. Which All Black scored three tries against Scotland on his debut in 1993?
11. With what Olympic event is Dwight Stones associated?
12. Which Dane won the 1971 World Individual speedway title?
13. Who finished third in the 1974 football World Cup?
14. In which year did Jack Charlton win his first England cap?
15. When did John McEnroe win his first Wimbledon men's singles tennis title?

ANSWERS **1.** Eddie Charlton **2.** Wayne Gardner **3.** Sleepytime **4.** Garrincha **5.** Chris Chataway **6.** Julio Cesar Chavez **7.** Mozambique **8.** Florida **9.** Long jump and heptathlon **10.** Jeff Wilson **11.** High jump **12.** Ole Olsen **13.** Poland **14.** 1965 **15.** 1981.

POP

1. Which girl group recorded the 2000 album *Masterpiece Theatre*?
2. Which group recorded the 2000 album *The Construkction of Light*?
3. For which tennis player was the song *Don't Get Me Wrong* by The Pretenders reputedly written?
4. Who had a Top 10 single in September 2000 with *Most Girls*?
5. Which group had a 1983 No. 1 single with *Too Shy*?
6. Which studio album by Prince contains the song *Alphabet St.*?
7. On which studio album by Queen does the song *Crazy Little Thing Called Love* appear?
8. Which Tim Buckley song do Shelleyan Orphan cover on the tribute album *Sing A Song To You*?
9. Who sang the song *I Believe* which was the theme tune to the film *Billy Elliot*?
10. Which guitarist joined the Rolling Stones in 1975?
11. In which year did the pop group The Alarm have a Top 20 single with the song *68 Guns*?
12. Which country artist released the album *The Captain* in 2000?
13. For which group did Mick Ralphs leave Mott the Hoople in 1973?
14. Which group recorded the 2000 album *Exclusively Talentmaker!*?
15. Who composed the album *Fire At Keaton's Bar and Grill* which featured Debbie Harry and Elvis Costello?

ANSWERS 1. En Vogue **2.** King Crimson **3.** John McEnroe **4.** Pink **5.** Kajagoogoo **6.** Lovesexy **7.** The Game **8.** Buzzin' Fly **9.** Stephen Gately **10.** Ron Wood **11.** 1983 **12.** Kasey Chambers **13.** Bad Company **14.** Optiganally Yours **15.** Roy Nathanson.

SCIENCE

1. How many vertices does a cube have?
2. What nationality was the scientist Copernicus?
3. How many kilogrammes are there in a quintal?
4. What sort of creature was the prehistoric mammal a procoptodon?
5. What nationality was scientist Johann Lambert?
6. Which four main blood groups did Karl Landsteiner identify in 1901?
7. How many gallons are in a peck?
8. In which year was Charon, satellite of Pluto, discovered?
9. What is the term for air that has a temperature of 0ºC or less?
10. Which U.S. physicist constructed the first working laser?
11. How many centilitres are there in one decilitre?
12. In which Italian city was Marconi born?
13. Which 19c Austrian monk discovered the basic principles of heredity?
14. Which element is directly above antimony in the Periodic Table?
15. In which continent is the Brickfielder a very hot N.E. wind?

ANSWERS 1. Eight **2.** Polish **3.** 100 **4.** Kangaroo **5.** German **6.** A,O,B, and AB **7.** 2 **8.** 1978 **9.** Air frost **10.** Theodore Maiman **11.** 10 **12.** Bologna **13.** Gregor Mendel **14.** Arsenic **15.** Australia.

GENERAL KNOWLEDGE

1. In which year did the former Labour M.P. Leo Abse leave the House of Commons?
2. What did Brent Pollard buy for £3,000 plus V.A.T. in February 2001?
3. In which South American country is the inland port of San Fernando?
4. How much, not including buyers' premium and VAT, did the brain from the Body Zone go for at the Millennium Dome sale in February 2001?
5. Whose fictional creation is investigative reporter Jack Parlabane?
6. What grade did Prince William get in A-Level Geography?
7. On which London Underground line is the station of Highgate?
8. In which European country is the village of Sadowa?
9. Which vegetable's New Latin name is *Pastinaca sativa*?
10. Which university did Sara Paretsky's detective creation V.I. Warshawski attend?
11. Which hand in the game of poker is known as the boat?
12. Who wrote the 2000 novel *Horse Heaven*?
13. In which year did lawyer George Carman defend Jeremy Thorpe on charges of conspiracy to kill?
14. Which port houses the University of Puerto Rico?
15. With which field of scientific activity would you associate Alan Rex Sandage?

ANSWERS 1. 1987 **2.** The Millennium Dome giant hamster (and cheese) **3.** Venezuela **4.** £700 **5.** Christopher Brookmyre **6.** A **7.** Northern **8.** Czech Republic **9.** Parsnip **10.** University of Chicago **11.** Full House **12.** Jane Smiley **13.** 1979 **14.** San Juan **15.** Astrology.

ENTERTAINMENT

1. In which of his films does Alfred Hitchcock appear in silhouette through the door of a Registrar of Births and Deaths?
2. Who played Anaïs Nin in the film *Henry and June*?
3. Which architect introduced the 2000 television series *The Shock of the Old*?
4. In which 1938 film did Cary Grant play the character Dr. David Huxley?
5. In which five films did the actors Humphrey Bogart and Edward G. Robinson appear together?
6. Who voices the part of the cat Snowbell in the film *Stuart Little*?
7. Who directed and wrote the film *Up 'n' Under* which starred Neil Morrissey?
8. In which year was J.R. shot in the television show *Dallas*?
9. Who plays the wife of Keanu Reeves in the film *The Devil's Advocate*?
10. Who plays the 'Big Brother' figure Christof in the film *The Truman Show*?
11. Which five television presenters launched TV-am in 1983?
12. Who played Hamlet in an August 2000 stage production at the National Theatre in London?
13. In which 2000 television series did Sada Walkington appear?
14. In which 1990 film did Julia Roberts play the character Vivian Ward?
15. Who played Adolf Hitler in the 1966 film *What Did You Do in the War, Daddy?*?

ANSWERS 1. Family Plot **2.** Maria de Medeiros **3.** Piers Gough **4.** Bringing Up Baby **5.** Key Largo, Brother Orchid, Bullets or Ballots, Kid Galahad, The Amazing Dr. Clitterhouse **6.** Nathan Lane **7.** John Godber **8.** 1980 **9.** Charlize Theron **10.** Ed Harris **11.** Robert Kee, Michael Parkinson, Anna Ford, David Frost and Angela Rippon **12.** Simon Russell Beale **13.** Big Brother **14.** Pretty Woman **15.** Carl Ekberg.

SPORT

1. What is the nationality of golfer Roberto De Vicenzo?
2. In which year was racing driver Jackie Stewart born?
3. Over what distance in metres is the Prix de L'Arc de Triomphe run?
4. Who won the Tour de France from 1969-72?
5. Which cycling Luxembourger was nicknamed 'the Angel of the Mountains'?
6. Who rode the 1973 Epsom Derby winner Morston?
7. In which year was Sir Richard Hadlee born?
8. Which three Germans have each scored twice in football's European Championship final?
9. Which club were runners-up in Football's Premier League in 1996 & '97?
10. Who was the 1998 World matchplay golf champion?
11. Who won the 1994 County Cricket Championship?
12. In which institution did jockey Sam Chifney die in 1807?
13. At what sport did Eddy Choong, 'the Pocket Prodigy from Penang' excel?

14. For which international football team did Hector Chumpitaz play?
15. What was the nickname of Australian rugby league star Clive Churchill?

ANSWERS 1. Argentinian **2.** 1939 **3.** 2,400m **4.** Eddie Merckx **5.** Charly Gaul **6.** Edward Hide **7.** 1951 **8.** Müller (1972), Hrubesch (1980) and Bierhoff (1996) **9.** Newcastle United **10.** Mark O'Meara **11.** Warwickshire **12.** Fleet Prison in London **13.** Badminton **14.** Peru **15.** The Little Master.

POP

1. Which group had a 1998 Christmas hit with *I Am in Love With the World*?
2. Whose only singles chart hit was 1965's *Bye Bye Blues*?
3. Which group recorded the 1969 album *Younger Than Yesterday*?
4. Which group's minor hits in 1998 included *Buzzin'* and *Black White*?
5. In which year did The Clash release their debut album?
6. Which female vocalist's only chart entry was 1966's *Witches' Brew*?
7. Which duo had a U.K. and U.S. No. 1 single with *I Knew You Were Waiting (For Me)*?
8. Which boxer featured on the 1996 hit *Walk Like a Champion* by Kaleef?
9. Under what name did Colin Blunstone record the 1969 hit *She's Not There*?
10. Which D.J. released the 1996 album *Archive One*?
11. Which group had a 1997 No. 2 single with *Tubthumping*?
12. Which U.S. group recorded the 1971 album *Nantucket Sleighride*?
13. Who is lead singer with the Manchester band M People?
14. Which duo had a 1958 No. 1 single with the song *When*?
15. From which European country does instrumentalist and producer Atgoc come?

ANSWERS **1.** Chicken Shed Theatre **2.** Bert Kaempfert **3.** The Byrds **4.** Asian Dub Foundation **5.** 1977 **6.** Janie Jones **7.** George Michael & Aretha Franklin **8.** Prince Naseem **9.** Neil MacArthur **10.** Dave Clarke **11.** Chumbawamba **12.** Mountain **13.** Heather Small **14.** Kalin Twins **15.** Italy.

PEOPLE

1. Which Scot won the 1904 Nobel prize for chemistry?
2. What is the name of politician Jack Straw's Oxford undergraduate son?
3. How did blues legend Robert Johnson die?
4. Of which country was Adam Rapacki foreign minister from 1956-68?
5. Which French writer authored the 1959 novel *Aimez-vous Brahms?*?
6. Which pope's original name was Giovanni Battista Montini?
7. In which year did U.S. general George Patton die?
8. What was the nickname of Australian poet Andrew Barton Paterson?
9. Which physicist won the 1975 Nobel peace prize?
10. Who was tsar of Russia from 1796-1801?
11. Who in Greek mythology killed Patroclus?
12. Which architect designed the U.S. embassy in London?
13. In which year was Chung Hee Park, the president of the Republic of Korea, assassinated?
14. Which actor owns a statue of himself called 'the Age of Steel'?
15. Which member of the royal family dressed up as the script of a Shakespearean sonnet for Lord Montagu of Beaulieu's 70th birthday party?

ANSWERS 1. Sir William Ramsay **2.** William **3.** He was poisoned **4.** Poland **5.** Françoise Sagan **6.** Paul VI **7.** 1945 **8.** Banjo **9.** Andrei Sakharov **10.** Paul I **11.** Hector **12.** Eero Saarinen **13.** 1979 **14.** Sylvester Stallone **15.** Prince Edward.

GENERAL KNOWLEDGE

1. What in Devon is a grockle?
2. What was Toy of the Year in 1980?
3. Which Austrian-born film director made the thriller *The Testament of Dr. Mabuse*?
4. Who authored the children's book *The Ghost of Thomas Kempe*?
5. Of which country was Joseph Coates prime minister from 1925-28?
6. What is the name of the female demon in Jewish folklore who attempts to kill new-born children?
7. What was the nickname of Richard de Clare, Earl of Pembroke?
8. In which country was artist George Grosz born?
9. What does the title of the children's book of verse *Struwwelpeter* translate as?
10. EX is the abbreviation for which postcode area?
11. Which operetta by Sigmund Romberg features *The Drinking Song*?
12. Which D.J.'s show won Melody Maker Radio Show of the Year award 1984-93?
13. What name was given to Holy Roman Emperor Frederick II?
14. In which city is George Eliot's novel *Romola* set?
15. What was the pen-name of Sir Arthur Quiller-Couch?

ANSWERS **1.** A tourist **2.** Rubik's Cube **3.** Fritz Lang **4.** Penelope Lively **5.** New Zealand **6.** Lilith **7.** Strongbow **8.** Germany **9.** Shock-headed Peter **10.** Exeter **11.** The Student Prince **12.** John Peel **13.** Stupor Mundi **14.** Florence **15.** Q.

ENTERTAINMENT

1. Who did John Thaw play in the 1992 biopic *Chaplin*?

2. In which 1963 film did Peter Sellers play the character Reverend John Smallwood?

3. In which 1995 film did actress Madonna play a singing telegram girl?

4. In which of his films does Alfred Hitchcock appear leaving a train carrying a cello?

5. Who did the actress Sue Johnston play in soap opera *Brookside*?

6. In which television cartoon series has the character 'Sexual Harassment Panda' appeared?

7. Who directed the 1997 film *The Winner* which starred Michael Madsen?

8. Who were the two male stars of the 1991 film *Harley Davidson And the Marlboro Man*?

9. In which 1939 film did Cary Grant play the character Archibald Cutter?

10. In which 1938 film did Humphrey Bogart play the character James Frazier?

11. Who played the title role in the 1962 film *Hitler*?

12. In which year was the original West End production of Alan Bennett's play *Forty Years On*?

13. Who plays the character Steamer in the 1988 film *Mystic Pizza*?

14. Who voices the title character in the film *Stuart Little*?

15. Under what collective name are comedians Bernie Mac, DL Hughley, Steve Harvey and Cedric the Entertainer known?

ANSWERS 1. Fred Karno **2.** Heavens Above! **3.** Blue in the Face **4.** The Paradine Case **5.** Sheila Grant **6.** South Park **7.** Alex Cox **8.** Don Johnson and Mickey Rourke **9.** Gunga Din **10.** Angels With Dirty Faces **11.** Richard Basehart **12.** 1970 **13.** Matt Damon **14.** Michael J. Fox **15.** The Kings of Comedy.

SPORT

1. In which sport did Haydn Bunton and Haydn Bunton, Jr. win the Sandover Medal?
2. In which city was cyclist Beryl Burton born?
3. Which baseball player died in 1941 of the disease amyotrophic lateral schlerosis, which was later named after him in the U.S.?
4. Which Dallas player was MVP in Superbowl XXX in 1996?
5. At which individual sport was Hans Deutgen world champion from 1947-50?
6. Which football team were runners-up in the 1966 European Champions Cup?
7. Who won the 1992 Nat West Trophy in cricket?
8. Which tennis player won the 1956 U.S. singles title, denying Lew Hoad the Grand Slam in the final?
9. Who, in fencing, was 1998 world sabre champion?
10. Which team did Sheffield United defeat to win the 1925 FA Cup final?
11. Which horse won the 1993 Breeders Cup Classic?
12. In which year was the first women's cricket Test match?
13. Who was the founder of the modern Olympic Games?
14. Who was Olympic heavyweight boxing champion in 1968?
15. In what year was the Modern Pentathlon introduced into the Olympics?

ANSWERS **1.** Australian Rules Football **2.** Leeds **3.** Lou Gehrig **4.** Larry Brown **5.** Archery **6.** Partizan Belgrade **7.** Northants **8.** Ken Rosewall **9.** Luigi Tarantino **10.** Cardiff City **11.** Arcangues **12.** 1934 **13.** Baron de Coubertin **14.** George Foreman **15.** 1912.

POP

1. Which female singer had a 1996 Top 10 single with *Escaping*?
2. Which single by Phil Collins reached No.1 both in the U.K. and U.S.?
3. Which duo's debut chart hit was 1996's *I Am I Feel*?
4. Which singing duo had a 1995 hit with *Had To Be*?
5. On which label did Dinosaur Jr. chart in 1994 with the song *Feel the Pain*?
6. What was the title of Oasis's only No.1 single in 1997?
7. Who is the singer with the group *Nine Inch Nails*?
8. Which group's debut L.P. in 1975 was *Late Night Movies, All Night Brainstorms*?
9. Which indie group recorded the album *When Animals Attack*?
10. What was the first No.1 single for the group All Saints?
11. Which U.K. vocal group's first U.K. Top 10 single was 1996's *Don't Make Me Wait*?
12. Which male singer had a 1998 Top 10 with *Crazy Little Party Girl*?
13. Which male singer featured on the 1998 hit *True to your Heart* by 98 Degrees?
14. Who recorded the album *Gorgeous George*?
15. Which group recorded the 1997 Top 20 hit *Spiderwebs*?

ANSWERS **1.** Dina Carroll **2.** A Groovy Kind of Love **3.** Alisha's Attic **4.** Cliff Richard & Olivia Newton-John **5.** Blanco Y Negro **6.** D'You Know what I Mean? **7.** Trent Reznor **8.** The Doctors of Madness **9.** Cable **10.** Never Ever **11.** 911 **12.** Aaron Carter **13.** Stevie Wonder **14.** Edwyn Collins **15.** No Doubt.

ART AND LITERATURE

1. Who wrote the novel *Young Adolf*?
2. British painter Vanessa Bell was the sister of which famous author?
3. Who wrote the 2000 novel *Blackberry Wine*?
4. In which year did the British artist Sir William Coldstream die?
5. Which poet authored the volume *Beyond Our Kennel*?
6. Which British artist painted the 1961 work *Break-off*?
7. Who wrote the novels *Mother Night* and *Breakfast of Champions*?
8. In Frank Auerbach's painting *Small Head of E.O.W.*, who is E.O.W.?
9. Who wrote the novel *Hawksmoor*?
10. Which British sculptor's works include 1962's *Twister I*?
11. Who wrote the novel *The Great Gatsby*?
12. In which year did the British artist Sir Muirhead Bone die?
13. Who wrote the 1997 novel *Enduring Love*?
14. Which artist made the 1931 print *Snake in the Grass, Alas*?
15. Who wrote the novel *Of Human Bondage*?

ANSWERS 1. Beryl Bainbridge **2.** Virginia Woolf **3.** Joanne Harris **4.** 1987 **5.** John Hegley **6.** Gillian Ayres **7.** Kurt Vonnegut **8.** Stella West **9.** Peter Ackroyd **10.** Lynn Chadwick **11.** F. Scott Fitzgerald **12.** 1953 **13.** Ian McEwan **14.** John Banting **15.** W. Somerset Maugham.

GENERAL KNOWLEDGE

1. Which sea creature was found in the River Thames in 2000 - the first example of its species found there since 1976
2. How many gold medals did Britain win at the 2000 Summer Olympics?
3. Beating Pakistan in December 2000 gave England's cricket team their third Test series victory in a row. Against which two countries were the first two series' victories?
4. Who wrote the children's book *The Sheep-Pig*?
5. Who is the French star of the 1959 film *Babette Goes to War*?
6. In poker, when dealt the initial five cards, what are the odds of having three of a kind?
7. Which was the first product on U.S. television to have its own advertising jingle?
8. On which London Underground line is the station of Hyde Park Corner?
9. What grade did Prince Edward get in A-Level History and Politics?
10. In which Asian country is the port of Saida?
11. Who wrote the 2000 novel *Eclipse*?
12. Who in Judaism is a sandek?
13. How much, not including buyers' premium and VAT, did a heart from the Body Zone sell for at the Millennium Dome sale in February 2001?
14. What type of creature is a pademelon?
15. What breed of dog is a papillon?

ANSWERS 1. Sea horse **2.** 11 **3.** Zimbabwe and West Indies **4.** Dick King-Smith **5.** Brigitte Bardot **6.** 47-1 **7.** Spam **8.** Piccadilly **9.** D **10.** Lebanon **11.** John Banville **12.** A man who holds a baby being circumcized **13.** £1,500 **14.** Wallaby **15.** Spaniel.

ENTERTAINMENT

1. Who played Mr. Blond in the film *Reservoir Dogs*?
2. Which song did Angela Rippon famously sing on a *Morecambe and Wise Christmas Show*?
3. Who plays Miss B. Haven in the film *Batman & Robin*?
4. Who played Number 6 in the 1960s television drama series *The Prisoner*?
5. Who played Private Reese in Steven Spielberg's comedy film *1941*?
6. Who played Len Fairclough in the soap opera *Coronation Street*?
7. In which 1940 film did Cary Grant play the character Walter Burns?
8. In which 1938 film did Humphrey Bogart play the character 'Rocks' Valentine?
9. Who did Dan Aykroyd play in the 1992 biopic *Chaplin*?
10. In which 1976 film did Peter Sellers play the character Sidney Wang?
11. Which 1956 film featured the debuts of Rip Torn and Eli Wallach?
12. What, in 2000, was the proposed name change for the pub the Rovers' Return in soap *Coronation Street*?
13. Who plays 'Storm' in the film *X-Men*?
14. Who plays Tamara in the 1999 film *Titus*?
15. What is Stacy Keach's character name in the film *Fat City*?

ANSWERS **1.** Michael Madsen **2.** Let's Face the Music and Dance **3.** Vivica Fox **4.** Patrick McGoohan **5.** Mickey Rourke **6.** Peter Adamson **7.** His Girl Friday **8.** The Amazing Dr. Clitterhouse **9.** Mack Sennett **10.** Murder By Death **11.** Baby Doll **12.** The Boozy Newt **13.** Halle Berry **14.** Jessica Lange **15.** Billy Tully.

SPORT

1. Which footballer took over the captaincy of Real Madrid in 1964 following the departure of Di Stefano?
2. Which jockey won the 1997 and '98 2,000 Guineas?
3. Who was men's shot champion at the 1987, '91 and '93 IAAF World Championships?
4. Who was 1998 French Open tennis women's singles champion?
5. What was the nickname of Canadian ice hockey player Bernard Geoffrion?
6. Which U.S. Olympic swimming champion was known as 'Mr. Machine'?
7. How many Scottish international caps did Sir Matt Busby win?
8. Which Spanish footballer scored four against Denmark in their 1986 World Cup Finals game?
9. What was the nickname of Canadian ice hockey player Glenn Hall?
10. Which batsman was the first to reach 4,000 runs and 5,000 runs in Test cricket?

11. Who in 1960 became the first man to win gold medals at six successive Olympic Games?
12. For which international side did footballer Germano de Figuereido play?
13. Who was 1996 world matchplay golf champion?
14. Who won the 1993 Paris Indoor tennis title?
15. Who won the 1993 Australian Grand Prix in Formula 1?

ANSWERS **1.** Francisco Gento **2.** Mick Kinane **3.** Werner Günthör **4.** Arantxa Sanchez Vicario **5.** Boom-Boom **6.** Mike Burton **7.** One **8.** Emilio Butragueno **9.** Mr. Goalie **10.** Jack Hobbs **11.** Aladar Gerevich **12.** Portugal **13.** Ernie Els **14.** Goran Ivanisevic **15.** Ayrton Senna.

POP

1. Who produced the album *Pod* by The Breeders?
2. Which Pink Floyd studio album includes the track *Shine On You Crazy Diamond*?
3. Who was the vocalist in the 1960s band The Deviants?
4. Who produced Bap Kennedy's debut album *Domestic Blues*?
5. Which pop act had a Top 10 single in 2000 with the song *Body Groove*?
6. Which former member of the punk group The Damned features on the album *Invisible Movies* by Slipper?
7. Which member of Roxy Music recorded the 1976 album *Listen Now*?
8. Prince's album *Parade* was the soundtrack to which of his films?
9. In which year was the singer P.J. Harvey born?
10. In which city did the rock group The Pixies form?
11. Which female singer recorded the 1999 album *Kaleidoscope*?
12. Which group recorded the 2000 album *Painting It Red*?
13. Which pop group had a 1998 No. 1 single with song *Doctor Jones*?
14. James Dean Bradfield is the lead singer in which rock group?
15. Which group had a 2000 hit single with the song *Overload*?

ANSWERS 1. Steve Albini **2.** Wish You Were Here **3.** Mick Farren **4.** Steve Earle **5.** Architechs featuring Nana **6.** Rat Scabies **7.** Phil Manzanera **8.** Under the Cherry Moon **9.** 1970 **10.** Boston **11.** Kelis **12.** The Beautiful South **13.** Aqua **14.** Manic Street Preachers **15.** Sugababes.

GEOGRAPHY

1. In which state is the Australian seaport of Bunbury?
2. Which dance is the state capital of West Virginia?
3. The Crimea Peninsula is part of which European country?
4. East London is a seaport and holiday resort in which African country?
5. Which insect is the largest river of Papua New Guinea?
6. On which island is the volcano of Hekla?
7. In which Canadian province is the Jasper National Park?
8. Which peninsula of China lies opposite Hong Kong Island?
9. In which eastern European country is the university city of Lublin?
10. In which American country is the Mesa del Norte plateau?
11. The Painted Desert lies in which U.S. state?
12. On which Mediterranean island is the seaport of Palermo?
13. In which English county is the market town of Rugby?
14. On which river is the Russian city of Tomsk?
15. What town is the capital of the Seychelles?

ANSWERS **1.** Western Australia **2.** Charleston **3.** Ukraine **4.** South Africa **5.** Fly River **6.** Iceland **7.** Alberta **8.** Kowloon Peninsula **9.** Poland **10.** Mexico **11.** Arizona **12.** Sicily **13.** Warwickshire **14.** River Tom **15.** Victoria.

GENERAL KNOWLEDGE

1. Where would you write an apostil?
2. Which French novelist wrote *Gigi*?
3. In Arthurian legend who was the faithful wife of Geraint?
4. Which British actor starred as an Interpol agent in the 1972 film *Kill! Kill! Kill!*?
5. At approximately what altitude in feet is the city of La Paz - 10,000, 20,000 or 30,000?
6. What was once drunk in the British navy to prevent scurvy?
7. Who was Best Actor winner at the 1991 Laurence Olivier awards?
8. What was Melody Maker TV Show of the Year in their 1993 polls?
9. Which shipping forecast area is due south of Viking?
10. On which island does the aye-aye live?
11. What fish is *Anguilla anguilla*?
12. Who composed the opera *Pimpinone*?
13. What is the surname of *Lucky Jim* in the novel by Amis?
14. Of which country was Guzman Blanco president from 1873 to 1877?
15. Which ocean liner was brought to Long Beach, California in 1967?

ANSWERS 1. In a margin (it is a marginal note) **2.** Colette **3.** Enid **4.** James Mason **5.** 10,000 **6.** Lime juice **7.** Nigel Hawthorne **8.** Red Dwarf **9.** Forties **10.** Madagascar **11.** Eel **12.** Georg Telemann **13.** Dixon **14.** Venezuela **15.** Queen Mary.

ENTERTAINMENT

1. Who directed the 1999 film *Titus* which starred Anthony Hopkins?
2. Who is the female lead in the 1987 film *Baby Boom*?
3. In which of his films does Alfred Hitchcock appear carrying a violin case and smoking a cigarette?
4. Who directed the 1968 film *The Blood of Fu Manchu*?
5. Which female cast member of the film *Stuart Little* speaks fluent Swedish?
6. What was the name of the character played by Cary Grant in *The Philadelphia Story*?
7. In which 1948 film did Humphrey Bogart play the character Frank McCloud?
8. In which 1991 film did Julia Roberts play the character Tinkerbell?
9. In which 1960 film did Peter Sellers play the character Dodger Lane?
10. Who starred in a recreation of the 1964 film *Fail Safe* on live television in the U.S. in April 2000?
11. Who plays Dr. Eudora Fletcher in the 1983 film *Zelig*?
12. Who directed the 1939 film *Babes in Arms*?
13. Who is the male star of the 1973 film *Badlands*?
14. Who is the female star of the 1933 film *Baby Face*?
15. Who is the main presenter of the long-running Channel 4 television show *Eurotrash*?

ANSWERS **1.** Julie Taymor **2.** Diane Keaton **3.** Spellbound **4.** Jesus Franco **5.** Geena Davis **6.** C.K. Dexter Haven **7.** Key Largo **8.** Hook **9.** Two Way Stretch **10.** George Clooney **11.** Mia Farrow **12.** Busby Berkeley **13.** Martin Sheen **14.** Barbara Stanwyck **15.** Antoine De Caunes.

SPORT

1. Who was 1952 and '56 Olympic Modern Pentathlon champion?
2. Who was 1998 Australian Open men's singles tennis champion?
3. Which golfer won the 1950 U.S. Open, a year after a serious car accident?
4. In what year did Sonny Liston die?
5. Who won the 1993 World Rally Drivers championship?
6. Which cricket team finished bottom in the 1992 and '93 county championship?
7. Which England rugby union centre won 28 consecutive caps between 1953 and 1959?
8. Who trained the 1936 Epsom Derby winner Mahmoud?
9. At what field event did Tamara Bykova set three world records in 1983-4?
10. What was the nickname of American Football star Elroy Hirsch?
11. Who won the men's discus title at the IAAF World Championships from 1991 to 1997?
12. Who was 1994 World Professional Billiards champion?
13. Who was 1996 World Outdoor Bowls men's champion?
14. Which cyclist won the Vuelta A España in 1995?
15. Which American was 1956 and '60 Olympic men's 110m hurdles champion?

ANSWERS 1. Lars Hall **2.** Petr Korda **3.** Ben Hogan **4.** 1970 **5.** Juha Kankkunen **6.** Durham **7.** Jeff Butterfield **8.** Frank Butters **9.** High jump **10.** Crazy Legs **11.** Lars Riedel **12.** Peter Gilchrist **13.** Tony Allcock **14.** Laurent Jalabert **15.** Lee Calhoun.

POP

1. Which female vocalist had a 1994 hit with *Cornflake Girl*?
2. Which male singer had a minor chart hit in 1992 with *Machine + Soul*?
3. In which city was Celine Dion born?
4. What was Oasis's first No.1 single?
5. Which singer had a minor hit in 1993 with *London's Brilliant*?
6. Which group's 1996 Top 10 singles included *Walkaway* and *Sandstorm*?
7. Which member of Stump recorded the solo album. *Stolen Jewels*?
8. Who had a No.1 single in 1997 with *Don't Speak*?
9. Which Italian artist had a 1996 hit with *X-Files*?
10. What was Ocean Colour Scene's first Top 10 single?
11. Which single by Culture Club reached No.1 in the U.K. and U.S.?
12. Which U.K. group had a 1996 Top 10 hit with *Good Enough*?
13. Which group recorded the album *Retreat From Memphis*?
14. Which female singer had a 1998 hit with *Maybe I'm Amazed*?
15. Which act had a minor hit in July 1998 with *Nagasaki Badger*?

ANSWERS **1.** Tori Amos **2.** Gary Numan **3.** Quebec **4.** Some Might Say **5.** Wendy James **6.** Cast **7.** Kev Hopper **8.** No Doubt **9.** D.J. Dado **10.** You've Got it Bad **11.** Karma Chameleon **12.** Dodgy **13.** The Mekons **14.** Carleen Anderson **15.** Disco Citizens.

HISTORY

1. Which king of Mercia killed King Oswald of Northumbria in 642?
2. Which Jewish sect seized the fortress of Masada in 66 A.D.?
3. Who was elected president of France in June 1969?
4. Which English children's author married Trotsky's secretary Evgenia Shelepin?
5. Which American was president of the Screen Actors' Guild from 1947-52?
6. At which castle was the investiture of the Prince of Wales in 1969?
7. Which king founded Trinity College, Cambridge?
8. In which year did Canberra officially become capital of Australia?
9. Who was the first Archbishop of Canterbury?
10. Who formed the Cato Street Conspiracy of 1820?
11. In which year of World War I was nurse Edith Cavell executed by the Germans?
12. In which year was the First Factory Act passed?
13. In which year did the Spanish Civil War end?
14. In which year was the Falklands War?
15. At the end of which year did the farthing cease to be legal tender?

ANSWERS **1.** Penda **2.** Zealots **3.** Georges Pompidou **4.** Arthur Ransome **5.** Ronald Reagan **6.** Caernarvon **7.** Henry VIII **8.** 1910 **9.** Augustine **10.** Arthur Thistlewood **11.** 1915 **12.** 1802 **13.** 1939 **14.** 1982 **15.** 1960.

GENERAL KNOWLEDGE

1. On which island was actress Lillie Langtry born?
2. On what river is the city of Lima, Peru?
3. What was Toy of the Year in 1986?
4. Who were the legendary founders of Rome?
5. What is the site of the French Foreign Office in Paris?
6. What type of animal is a Border Leicester?
7. Which Italian actress received an honorary Academy Award in 1991?
8. Which fictional detective was aided by the Baker Street Irregulars?
9. For what is *cocky's joy* Australian slang?
10. Adam's Bridge links the island of Mannar to which country?
11. Who was Best Actress winner at the 1987 Laurence Olivier Awards?
12. What does the Latin phrase *cogito, ergo sum* translate as?
13. Who was the second son of Noah in the Old Testament?
14. Who was British prime minister 1763-65?
15. In which year did Qatar join the U.N.?

ANSWERS **1.** Jersey **2.** Rimac **3.** Transformers **4.** Romulus and Remus **5.** Quai d'Orsay **6.** A sheep **7.** Sophia Loren **8.** Sherlock Holmes **9.** Golden syrup **10.** India **11.** Judi Dench **12.** I think, therefore I am **13.** Japheth **14.** George Grenville **15.** 1971.

ENTERTAINMENT

1. Which U.S. rock group appear in the film *Back to the Future III*?
2. Who plays a one-armed man in the 1955 film *Bad Day At Black Rock*?
3. Who plays Turner in the 1989 film *Turner and Hooch*?
4. Who provided all the voices for the 1990 television cartoon series *Billy the Fish*?
5. Who played Juror No. 12 in the 1957 film *12 Angry Men*?
6. Which musician directed, produced, and starred in the 1979 film *Baby Snakes*?
7. Which comedian stars in the 1986 film *Back to School*?
8. Who played Dean Selwyn Makepeace in the 1986 sitcom *Hell's Bells*?
9. Who plays Captain Nemo in the 1978 film *The Amazing Captain Nemo*?
10. Who play *Twins* in the 1988 film of that name?
11. In which 1984 film does Robert Redford play the character Roy Hobbs?
12. Who plays Anita in the 1961 film *West Side Story*?
13. Who play Heathcliff and Cathy in the 1970 film version of *Wuthering Heights*?
14. Who wrote the 1984 sitcom *The Hello Goodbye Man*?
15. In which 1936 film did Humphrey Bogart play the character Duke Mantee?

ANSWERS 1. Z.Z. Top **2.** Spencer Tracy **3.** Tom Hanks **4.** Harry Enfield **5.** Robert Webber **6.** Frank Zappa **7.** Rodney Dangerfield **8.** Derek Nimmo **9.** José Ferrer **10.** Danny De Vito and Arnold Schwarzenegger **11.** The Natural **12.** Rita Moreno **13.** Timothy Dalton and Anna Calder-Marshall **14.** David Nobbs **15.** The Petrified Forest.

SPORT

1. Which football team won the 1994/5 European Cup-Winners' Cup?
2. What was the name of the official mascot of the 1996 Summer Olympics at Atlanta?
3. Who was the 1997 British Open golf champion?
4. Which team won the 1997/8 Scottish FA Cup?
5. Who won the Olympic women's 100m in 1976?
6. Who won the Olympic men's 400m in 1952?
7. Which football team won the 1997/8 UEFA Cup?
8. Who was the French Open men's singles tennis champion in 1956?
9. In which year was long jumper Bob Beamon born?
10. Which football team won the 1997/8 FA Cup?
11. Which horse won the 1955 Grand National?
12. Who were the 1998 cricket county champions?
13. Which animal was the official mascot of the 1980 Winter Olympics at Lace Placid?
14. Which team won the 1980 University Boat Race?
15. Which American Football team won Super Bowl XXXI?

ANSWERS 1. Real Zaragoza **2.** Izzy **3.** Justin Leonard **4.** Hearts **5.** Annegret Richter **6.** George Rhoden **7.** Internazionale **8.** Lew Hoad **9.** 1946 **10.** Arsenal **11.** Quare Times **12.** Leicestershire **13.** Roni the Raccoon **14.** Oxford **15.** Green Bay Packers.

POP

1. With which group did Celine Dion record the 1998 hit *Immortality*?
2. Which female vocalist had a Top 10 hit in 1997 with the song *You Might Need Somebody*?
3. Which duo had a 1985 No.1 single with *Dancing in the Street*?
4. Which group recorded the 1999 album *The Unauthorised Biography of Reinhold Messner*?
5. Which Australian group had a 1991 hit with *I Touch Myself*?
6. Which was the only single by Ray Charles to reach No.1 in both the U.S. and U.K. charts?
7. Which singer had a 1998 No.1 single with *Deeper Underground*?
8. Who had a 1997 No.1 single with *You're Not Alone*?
9. Which U.S. group had a minor hit in 1993 with *Johnny Mathis' Feet*?
10. Which Oasis copyists charted in 1996 with *I'd Like to Teach the World to Sing*?
11. Which singer recorded the album *Brutal Youth*?
12. Whose debut album is 1999's *Avant Hard*?
13. Which group had a 1997 Top 10 with *I'm a Man not a Boy*?
14. Which song gave James a Top 10 single in 1997?
15. What was the real name of rapper Notorious B.I.G.?

ANSWERS **1.** The Bee Gees **2.** Shola Ama **3.** David Bowie and Mick Jagger **4.** Ben Folds Five **5.** Divinyls **6.** I Can't Stop Loving You **7.** Jamiroquai **8.** Olive **9.** American Music Club **10.** No Way Sis **11.** Elvis Costello **12.** Add N to X **13.** North and South **14.** She's a Star **15.** Christopher Wallace.

WORDS

1. What word meaning 'belonging to a village' has come to mean a heathen?
2. 'The black ox has never trod upon his foot' refers to a man who is not what?
3. What in Australia is a wagga - a bed covering or a poisonous berry?
4. For what do North American Indians use a watap - smoking or sewing?
5. What would you do with kummel - soak clothes in it or drink it?
6. What article of clothing is named after the German for 'leather trousers'?
7. From what phrase does the 'loran' navigation system derive its name?
8. What in Spain is a zapateado?
9. Yite is the Scottish word for which bird?
10. Which German phrase meaning 'wonder child' is given to a child prodigy?
11. What does VDU stand for in computer terminology?
12. What sort of creature is a wentletrap - a dog or a mollusc?
13. Is wowser Australian slang for a - drunkard or a teetotaller?
14. What is belly-timber?
15. What is a Blindman's Lantern?

ANSWERS **1.** Pagan **2.** Married **3.** Bed covering **4.** Sewing - it is a thread **5.** Drink it **6.** Lederhosen **7.** Long Range Navigation **8.** A dance **9.** Yellowhammer **10.** Wunderkind **11.** Visual Display Unit **12.** A mollusc **13.** A teetotaller **14.** Food **15.** A walking stick.

GENERAL KNOWLEDGE

1. Which card in the game of poker is nicknamed a bullet?
2. How long in km is the Persian unit of distance the parasang?
3. Who wrote the 2000 novel *How the Dead Live*?
4. In which year did sculptor Sir Jacob Epstein die?
5. On which London Underground line is the station of Goldhawk Road?
6. Where did the dance called a passepied originate?
7. Britain's gold medal tally at the 2000 Summer Olympics was the highest since which year?
8. What nationality is the visual artist Rodney Graham?
9. In which African country are the towns of Bouar and Bossangoa?
10. On what day of the week was Christmas Day 1863?
11. Which city houses the University of Utah?
12. Who wrote the novel *Talking to Addison*?
13. Who plays Horace Hardwick in the 1935 film *Top Hat*?
14. Truk and Kusac are part of which American island group?
15. In which year was the U.S. satellite Galileo launched?

ANSWERS 1. Ace **2.** 5.5 km **3.** Will Self **4.** 1959 **5.** Hammersmith & City **6.** Breton **7.** 1920 **8.** Canadian **9.** Central African Republic **10.** Friday **11.** Salt Lake City **12.** Jenny Colgan **13.** Edward Everett Horton **14.** Caroline Islands **15.** 1989.

ENTERTAINMENT

1. Who directed the 1983 film *Christine*?
2. Which Australian operatic soprano made her debut in Brussels in 1887?
3. Which comedian was born Charles Springall in 1925?
4. Which Benjamin Britten opera was premiered at Aldeburgh in June 1960?
5. In which year did actor Peter Cushing die?
6. In which opera does the aria *Nessun Dorma* appear?
7. What nationality was baritone Titta Ruffo?
8. Ffynnon Garw Hill is central to the plot of which 1995 film?
9. Which writing duo created the sitcom *Drop the Dead Donkey*?

10. Which folk singer was born in Okemah, Oklahoma?
11. Which member of the Monty Python team scripted the 1983 film *The Missionary*?
12. Which actress played 'Annie Oakley' in a 1935 film?
13. Who played Tom Joad in the film *The Grapes of Wrath*?
14. Which actor was born Bernard Schwarz?
15. Who is the lead singer/songwriter with the group Wilco?

ANSWERS **1.** John Carpenter **2.** Dame Nellie Melba **3.** Charlie Drake **4.** A Midsummer Night's Dream **5.** 1994 **6.** Turandot **7.** Italian **8.** The Englishman Who Went Up a Hill but Came Down a Mountain **9.** Andy Hamilton & Guy Jenkin **10.** Woody Guthrie **11.** Michael Palin **12.** Barbara Stanwyck **13.** Henry Fonda **14.** Tony Curtis **15.** Jeff Tweedy.

SPORT

1. Which French rugby union player scored 30 points against Zimbabwe in the 1987 World Cup?
2. Why did motor racer Malcolm Campbell call his cars *Bluebird*?
3. Which Ireland rugby union player scored 21 points against Scotland in 1982?
4. In which year was Australian rugby union star David Campese born?
5. Which cricketer in 1906 scored 2,385 runs and took 208 wickets in a first class season?
6. Who won the men's hammer event at the 1983 and '87 IAAF World Championships?
7. Who was 1996 World Outdoor Bowls women's champion?
8. Who were All-Ireland League rugby union champions in the 1997/98 season?
9. Who was 1997 and '98 men's individual world modern pentathlon champion?
10. Who was 1998 Australian Open women's singles tennis champion?
11. At what Olympic sport did Mexican Ernesto Campo win gold in 1984?
12. At what Olympic sport did Mexican Joaquin Capilla win gold in 1956?
13. For what country did Antonio Carbajal play in the football World Cup finals five times from 1950-66?
14. Who won the 1993 Volvo Masters golf championship?
15. For which country did Hasely Crawford win the 1976 Olympic 100m?

ANSWERS 1. Didier Cambérabéro **2.** After a play by Maeterlinck **3.** Ollie Campbell **4.** 1962 **5.** George Hirst **6.** Sergey Litvinov **7.** Carmelita Anderson **8.** Shannon **9.** Sebastien Deleigne **10.** Martina Hingis **11.** Walking **12.** Diving **13.** Mexico **14.** Colin Montgomerie **15.** Trinidad & Tobago.

POP

1. On which studio album by the group The Police does the song *Message in a Bottle* feature?
2. Which group's debut album was called *Box Frenzy*?
3. Which pop group recorded the 2000 single *Music Is My Radar*?
4. Which 1980s pop group's 'Best of' album is entitled *Gold*?
5. Which group recorded the 1972 album *What a Bunch of Sweeties*?
6. With which group did Andy Irvine play in prior to Planxty?
7. Which group released the 1995 album *Jesus Wept*?
8. Which group did Huw Williams form in late 1987?
9. Which rapper records under the name Canibus?
10. Which 1980s band returned with the mainly acoustic album *Strip* in 2000?
11. In which city are the group Movietone based?
12. On which label was Monaco's album *Monaco* recorded?
13. Which group recorded the 1968 album *Mass in F Minor*?
14. Which group recorded the 2000 album *Rated R*?
15. What nationality is singer Iggy Pop's father?

ANSWERS 1. Regatta De Blanc **2.** Pop Will Eat Itself **3.** Blur **4.** Spandau Ballet **5.** The Pink Fairies **6.** Sweeney's Men **7.** PM Dawn **8.** The Pooh Sticks **9.** Germaine Williams **10.** The Chameleons **11.** Bristol **12.** Papillon **13.** The Electric Prunes **14.** Queens of the Stone Age **15.** British.

SCIENCE

1. What is the name of the outermost layer in the earth's mantle?
2. What in physical geography is a drumlin?
3. How many square metres are there in an are?
4. Which Englishman won the 1935 Nobel prize for physics for confirming the existence of the neutron?
5. Why is tungsten so called?
6. In which year was Uranus discovered?
7. Which acid constitutes the preservative E210?
8. Which two scientists won the 1951 Nobel prize for physics?
9. Which Russian physicist led the team that exploded the first soviet atomic bomb?
10. From what phrase did the dinosaur triceratops derive its name?
11. Who discovered the planet Pluto in 1930?
12. Which scientist constructed the first cyclotron?
13. What nationality was biologist Anton von Leeuwenhoek?
14. On the Mohs scale of hardness what is No. 2?
15. What is lignite also known as?

ANSWERS **1.** Lithosphere **2.** A small hill formed by the action of a glacier **3.** 100 **4.** Sir James Chadwick **5.** After the Swedish phrase 'heavy stone' **6.** 1781 **7.** Benzoic acid **8.** Ernest Walton and John Cockcroft **9.** Igor Kurchatov **10.** Three-horned **11.** Clyde Tombaugh **12.** Ernest Lawrence **13.** Dutch **14.** Gypsum **15.** Brown coal.

GENERAL KNOWLEDGE

1. In which country is the Shajin Telescope?
2. Which is larger - Lake Winnipeg or Lake Erie?
3. In which year did Hurricane Fifi hit the Honduras?
4. On which London Underground line is the station of Bethnal Green?
5. Where might you wear a pampootie?
6. In poker, when dealt the initial five cards, what are the odds of having a flush?
7. In which African country are the towns of Misratah and Banghazi?
8. What was the duration of the manned space mission Gemini III of 1965?
9. What material is No. 7 on the Mohs' hardness scale?
10. On what day of the week was Christmas Day 1804?
11. In Verdi's opera *Aida*, whose daughter is the title character?
12. Who directed the 1957 film *12 Angry Men*?

13. How much, not including buyers' premium and VAT, did an eye from the Body Zone sell for at the Millennium Dome sale in February, 2001?
14. What type of creature is a panchax?
15. In which country is the World Heritage site of the Tongariro National Park?

ANSWERS **1.** Ukraine **2.** Lake Erie **3.** 1974 **4.** Central **5.** On the foot - it's a slipper **6.** 508-1 **7.** Libya **8.** 4 hr 53 min **9.** Quartz **10.** Tuesday **11.** Amonasro, the King of Ethiopia **12.** Sidney Lumet **13.** £500 **14.** A fish **15.** New Zealand.

ENTERTAINMENT

1. In which 1941 film did Cary Grant play the character Johnnie Aysgarth?

2. In which of his films does Alfred Hitchcock appear on a train to Santa Rosa playing cards?

3. Who provided the musical accompaniment on the television sketch show *Hello Cheeky*?

4. In which 1989 film does Kevin Costner play the character Ray Kinsella?

5. In which 1989 film does Danny De Vito play the character Gavin D'Amato?

6. Who directed the film *The Milagro Beanfield War*?

7. The 1956 film musical *The Opposite Sex* is a 1956 remake of which 1939 film?

8. Who played Angel Clare in the 1979 film *Tess*?

9. Who plays Aramis in the 1993 film *The Three Musketeers*?

10. In which 1962 film does Paul Newman play Chance Wayne?

11. Who plays Goose in the 1986 film *Top Gun*?

12. Who played Dr. Rex Regis in the 1990s sitcom *Health and Efficiency*?

13. Who starred in the title role of the 1957 film *Baby Face Nelson*?

14. Who directed the 2000 film *The Cell*?

15. In which 1950 film did Marilyn Monroe play the character Claudia Casswell?

ANSWERS 1. Suspicion **2.** Shadow of a Doubt **3.** Denis King **4.** Field of Dreams **5.**
The War of the Roses **6.** Robert Redford **7.** The Women **8.** Peter Firth **9.** Charlie Sheen
10. Sweet Bird of Youth **11.** Anthony Edwards **12.** Roger Lloyd Pack **13.** Mickey Rooney
14. Tarsem Singh **15.** All About Eve.

SPORT

1. At which sport did American Tommy Hitchcock excel in the 1920s and '30s?
2. At what sport was Vicki Cardwell British Open champion in 1983?
3. Which Irish footballer captained the Rest of Europe against Great Britain in Glasgow in 1947?
4. Who was 1988 and '97 World Indoor Bowls men's champion?
5. In which year was former England rugby union captain Will Carling born?
6. How were Indian opening batsmen Gundappa Viswanath and Sunil Gavaskar related?
7. Which Green Bay player was MVP in Superbowl XXXI?
8. Who in 1961 became the youngest ever world champion 250cc motor cyclist?
9. Who was world individual fly fishing champion in 1992 and '96?
10. Which French cyclist was nicknamed 'the Badger'?
11. Which football team were runners-up in the 1960 European Champions Cup?
12. In which country were the first modern Winter Olympics held?
13. What sport do you associate with Drew Henry?
14. In how many Tests did David Gower captain England?
15. Which country won the 1993 Heineken World Cup in golf?

ANSWERS 1. Polo **2.** Squash **3.** Johnny Carey **4.** Hugh Duff **5.** 1965 **6.** Brothers-in-law **7.** Desmond Howard **8.** Mike Hailwood **9.** Pierluigi Cocito **10.** Bernard Hinault **11.** Eintracht Frankfurt **12.** France **13.** Snooker **14.** 32 **15.** U.S.A.

POP

1. On which label did Catatonia chart with the 1998 hit *Mulder and Scully*?
2. Which group released the 1999 album *The Soft Bulletin*?
3. From which European country did instrumental group Don Pablo's Animals come?
4. Which single by Dexy's Midnight Runners reached No.1 in the U.K. and U.S.?
5. What was the title of White Town's 1997 No.1 single?
6. What was Peter Andre's first No.1 hit single?
7. Which song gave Duran Duran a No.1 hit in the U.K. and U.S.?
8. Which U.S. vocal group had a 1998 Top 10 hit with *How Deep is your Love*?
9. With which song did Prodigy have a November 1996 No.1 hit?
10. Which pop musician was born Keigo Oyamada?
11. Which duo had a 1995 Top 30 hit with *Secret Love*?
12. Who had a 1998 Top 10 hit with *Hard Knock Life (Ghetto Anthem)*?
13. Which group released the 1984 album *Learning to Crawl*?
14. Which guitarist had a minor 1994 hit with *Hibernaculum*?
15. Who had a Top 10 single in 1998 with *Gone Till November*?

ANSWERS **1.** Blanco Y Negro **2.** Flaming Lips **3.** Italy **4.** Come on Eileen **5.** Your Woman **6.** Flava **7.** The Reflex **8.** Dru Hill **9.** Breathe **10.** Cornelius **11.** Daniel O'Donnell and Mary Duff **12.** Jay-Z **13.** The Pretenders **14.** Mike Oldfield **15.** Wyclef Jean.

PEOPLE

1. Who was Archbishop of Canterbury from 1559-75?
2. Which drama school did the actress Sue Johnston attend?
3. Which rock star has installed a pub in his house called the Barracuda Inn?
4. Which publisher authored the autobiography *An Unseemly Man*?
5. Which actor campaigned with Martin Bell in the Tatton constituency in the 1997 general election?
6. Which football team does actress Tina Hobley support?
7. In which year did the French composer Maurice Ravel die?
8. In which year did Angela Rippon read her last BBC news bulletin?
9. What nationality is the model Rebecca Romijn's father?
10. In which year did the philosopher Friedrich Nietzsche die?
11. Who did television presenter Anthea Turner marry in August 2000?
12. Which footballer authored the 2000 autobiography *Psycho*?
13. In which year was Ken Dodd acquitted of tax-dodging charges?
14. In which city did the artist Max Ernst die?
15. Where did Paul and Sheryl Gascoigne get married in 1996?

ANSWERS **1.** Matthew Parker **2.** Webber Douglas **3.** John Entwistle of the Who **4.** Larry Flynt **5.** David Soul **6.** Arsenal **7.** 1937 **8.** 1982 **9.** Dutch **10.** 1900 **11.** Grant Bovey **12.** Stuart Pearce **13.** 1989 **14.** Paris **15.** Hanbury House.

GENERAL KNOWLEDGE

1. What type of creature is a green leek?
2. Which cartoonist created the character Colonel Blimp?
3. Which political group killed USAF captain John Birch in 1945?
4. What is the name given to a tooth having one point?
5. To whom did the Crime Writers' Association award the Diamond Dagger in 1988?
6. What mollusc is also called a sea-ear?
7. Who played *Superman* in a 1978 film?
8. Who won Pipe Smoker of the Year award in 1987?
9. Approximately how large in area is Andorra in square miles - 80, 180 or 280?
10. What is the French equivalent of the English surname Wood?
11. What is the standard monetary unit of Samoa?
12. Which shipping forecast area is due north of German Bight?
13. What is the Religious Society of Friends also called?
14. Which essayist wrote *Essays of Elia*?
15. In which country was athlete Eric Liddell born?

ANSWERS 1. A parrot **2.** David Low **3.** Chinese communists **4.** Cuspid **5.** John Le Carré **6.** Ormer **7.** Christopher Reeve **8.** Barry Norman **9.** 180 **10.** Dubois **11.** Tala **12.** Fisher **13.** The Quakers **14.** Charles Lamb **15.** China.

ENTERTAINMENT

1. Who directed the 1983 film *Baby It's You*?
2. Who plays a hitman in the 1989 film *Catchfire* which is also known as *Backtrack*?
3. In which of his films does Alfred Hitchcock appear in a newspaper advertisement for Reduco Obesity Slayer?
4. Who plays Barry in the 2000 film *High Fidelity*?
5. In which the 1940 film did Humphrey Bogart play the character Jack Buck?
6. Who did Kevin Kline play in the 1992 biopic *Chaplin*?
7. Who plays Saturninus in the 1999 film *Titus*?
8. Who is the male lead in the 1982 film *The Year of Living Dangerously*?
9. What was Jim Davidson's character name in the sitcom *Home James!*?
10. Who played Juror No. 2 in the 1957 film *12 Angry Men*?
11. In which 1991 film does Kevin Costner play the character Jim Garrison?
12. Who starred as Bottom in a 1964 ITV production of the play *A Midsummer Night's Dream*?
13. What is Lee Marvin's character name in the 1953 film *The Wild One*?
14. Who directed the 1988 film *Working Girl*?
15. What was the title of the 1941 sequel to the 1934 film *The Thin Man*?

ANSWERS **1.** John Sayles **2.** Dennis Hopper **3.** Lifeboat **4.** Jack Black **5.** Brother Orchid **6.** Douglas Fairbanks **7.** Alan Cumming **8.** Mel Gibson **9.** Jim London **10.** John Fiedler **11.** JFK **12.** Benny Hill **13.** Chino **14.** Mike Nichols **15.** Shadow of the Thin Man.

SPORT

1. Who was Champion National Hunt jockey in 1966/7 and '67/8?
2. Which basketball player was leading scorer in the NBA from 1974-76?
3. What was baseball star James A. Hunter also known as?
4. Which team won the 1998 Benson & Hedges Cup in cricket?
5. With which British speedway team did Barry Briggs end his career?
6. For what country did rugby union player Colin Meads play?
7. In which year was the 'Suffragettes' Derby when Emily Davison died?
8. Which football club was originally called Singers F.C.?
9. Who was the first black boxer to win the world heavyweight title?
10. Which country finished third in the 1954 World Cup in football?
11. Which Briton was 1993 world men's individual modern pentathlon champion?
12. With which team did ice hockey star Tim Horton end his career?
13. What is the middle name of cricketer Merv Hughes?
14. In which city was rugby player Ellery Hanley born?
15. How many caps did John Pullin win for England at rugby union?

ANSWERS **1.** Josh Gifford **2.** Bob McAdoo **3.** Catfish **4.** Lancashire **5.** Hull **6.** New Zealand **7.** 1913 **8.** Coventry City **9.** Jack Johnson **10.** Austria **11.** Richard Phelps **12.** Buffalo Sabres **13.** Gregory **14.** Leeds. **15.** 42.

POP

1. Which U.K. group charted in 1997 with *Swallowed* and *Bone Driven*?
2. Which was Spacedust's 1998 No. 1 single?
3. Which Jamaican act had a minor 1996 hit with *Every kinda people*?
4. Which group recorded the album *If You're Feeling Sinister*?
5. Which U.S. rock act had a 1997 hit with *Falling in Love (Is Hard on the Knees)*?
6. Which group had a 1997 Top 20 single with *Step into my World*?
7. Which group released the 1998 album *Flying Low*?
8. Which late singer recorded the 1994 album *Grace*?
9. Which group recorded the 1996 album *Murder Ballads*?
10. Which group released the album *Looking for a Day in the Night*?
11. Which country songwriter recorded the album *Old No. 1*?
12. Which group's albums include *Abacab*?
13. Which group recorded the album *Look Mom No Head!*?
14. Which group's only singles chart hit was 1970's *Vehicle*?
15. From which European country do instrumental duo Age of Love hail?

ANSWERS **1.** Bush **2.** Gym and Tonic **3.** Chaka Demus and Pliers **4.** Belle and Sebastian **5.** Aerosmith **6.** Hurricane # 1 **7.** Willard Grant Conspiracy **8.** Jeff Buckley **9.** Nick Cave and the Bad Seeds **10.** The Lilac Time **11.** Guy Clark **12.** Genesis **13.** The Cramps **14.** Ides of March **15.** Italy.

ART AND LITERATURE

1. Who wrote the novel *Harriet Said...*?
2. In which year did British artist Lady Edna Clarke Hall die?
3. Who wrote the novel *Dad*?
4. Which British artist painted the 1963 work *Still Life with Dagger*?
5. Who wrote the novel *The Terrible Threes*?
6. In which year did the Kiev-born sculptor Alexander Archipenko become an American citizen?
7. In Peter Blake's painting *On the Balcony* the cover of which magazine is obscuring the face of one of the seated figures?
8. Who wrote the novel *Oscar and Lucinda*?
9. Who wrote the novel *The Color Purple*?
10. Which British artist painted the 1935 work *Commotion in the Cattle Ring*?
11. Who wrote the 1996 novel *The Insult*?
12. In which year was the British artist Edward Burra born?
13. Who wrote *The Screwtape Letters*?
14. Who wrote the novel *Wide Sargasso Sea*?
15. Who wrote the novel *A History of the World in 101/2 Chapters*?

ANSWERS **1.** Beryl Bainbridge **2.** 1979 **3.** William Wharton **4.** Patrick Caulfield **5.** Ishmael Reed **6.** 1928 **7.** Life **8.** Peter Carey **9.** Alice Walker **10.** James Bateman **11.** Rupert Thompson **12.** 1905 **13.** C.S. Lewis **14.** Jean Rhys **15.** Julian Barnes.

GENERAL KNOWLEDGE

1. What is the English name of the constellation whose Latin name is *Dorado*?
2. In which year was the Seki-Lines comet first seen?
3. On what day of the week was Christmas Day 1968?
4. In the USA, what is the state flower of Ohio?
5. In the United States of America, CT is the zip code of which state?
6. On which London Underground line is the station of Tufnell Park?
7. What in the game of poker is a kicker?
8. What does the London firm of Lobb's specialise in making?
9. In which year did the French painter Henri Fantin-Latour die?
10. In which year was the space mission Sputnik 2 launched?
11. Formigar and Pico are part of which Portuguese island group?
12. In which year did Typhoon Vera hit Japan?
13. In which African country is the World Heritage site of the Simien National Park?
14. Approximately how many stars are visible to the naked eye?
15. What might you do in Italy with a panettone?

ANSWERS 1. Swordish **2.** 1962 **3.** Wednesday **4.** Scarlet carnation **5.** Connecticut **6.** Northern **7.** The highest unpaired card in a hand **8.** Shoes **9.** 1904 **10.** 1957 **11.** Azores **12.** 1959 **13.** Ethiopia **14.** 6,000 **15.** Eat it - it's a spiced loaf.

ENTERTAINMENT

1. In which 1983 film did Jack Nicholson play the character Garrett Breedlove?
2. Who plays Shadwell in the 1954 film *Three Coins in the Fountain*?
3. The 1958 film *The Badlanders* is a western remake of which earlier film?
4. In which 1964 film does Alec Guinness play Marcus Aurelius?
5. In which 1966 film does Michael Caine play the character Michael Finsbury?
6. Who plays Aramis in the 1973 film *The Three Musketeers*?
7. Who plays the blind man in the 1974 film comedy *Young Frankenstein*?
8. Who played *The Babe* in the 1992 film?
9. Which two comedians co-starred in the London stage revue *Paris By Night* in 1955-6?
10. In which year was the comedian Lenny Henry born?
11. In which 1944 film did Cary Grant play the character Mortimer Brewster?
12. Which 1972 film set in the American Civil War was the directing debut of Robert Benton?
13. Who directed the *Back to the Future* series of movies?
14. Who played the character Trillian in the 1981 sitcom *The Hitch-Hiker's Guide To The Galaxy*?
15. Which of the acting McGann brothers starred in the 1986 sitcom *Help!* as the character Tex?

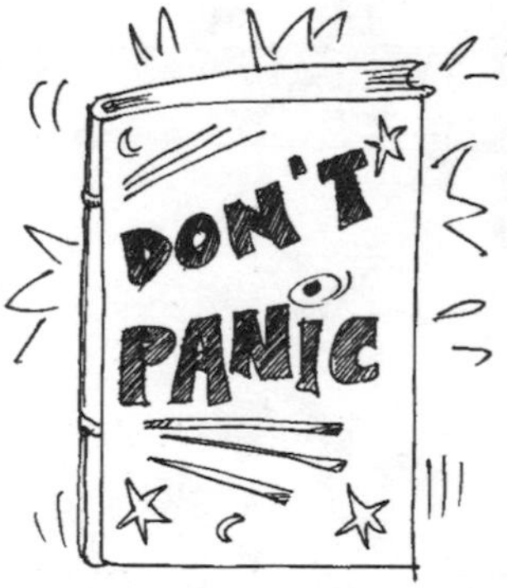

ANSWERS **1.** Terms of Endearment **2.** Clifton Webb **3.** The Asphalt Jungle **4.** The Fall of the Roman Empire **5.** The Wrong Box **6.** Richard Chamberlain **7.** Gene Hackman **8.** John Goodman **9.** Tommy Cooper and Benny Hill **10.** 1958 **11.** Arsenic and Old Lace **12.** Bad Company **13.** Robert Zemeckis **14.** Sandra Dickinson **15.** Stephen McGann.

SPORT

1. When did Haile Gebrselassie win the first of his 10,000m titles at the IAAF World Championships?
2. In the 12 years from 1987-98, how many times did Michael Jordan finish top scorer in the NBA?
3. At which club was Roger Uttley when he won 23 rugby union caps for England from 1973-80?
4. In which city was judo star Karen Briggs born?
5. In which athletics field event might you see a 'Brill bend'?
6. What was the nickname of Boston Bruins ice hockey star Frankie Brimsek?
7. Which Pakistan cricketer in 1952 became the world's youngest Test wicket-keeper?
8. Who were Welsh League champions in rugby union in 1997/98?
9. In which year was Canadian ice hockey star Gordie Howe born?
10. Who won the 3,000m steeplechase at the IAAF World Championships three times between 1991 and '95?
11. Which Canadian rower was nicknamed 'the Boy in Blue'?
12. Which cyclist won the Vuelta A España in 1998?
13. Which Canadian ice hockey star was nicknamed 'the Golden Jet'?
14. Which brothers were world double sculls rowing champions in 1978 and '79?
15. Which world Formula 1 motor racing champion died in 1992 of a heart attack?

ANSWERS 1. 1993 **2.** Ten **3.** Gosforth **4.** Hull **5.** High jump **6.** Mister Zero **7.** Hanif Mohammad **8.** Swansea **9.** 1928 **10.** Moses Kiptanui **11.** Ned Hanlan **12.** Abraham Olano **13.** Bobby Hull **14.** Alf and Frank Hansen **15.** Denny Hulme.

POP

1. Which duo had a 1995 Top 10 hit with *Yes*?
2. Which model had a minor hit in 1994 with *Love and Tears*?
3. Which duo had a 1998 Christmas hit with *Especially For You*?
4. With which single did The Animals have a No. 1 both in the UK and US?
5. Which eccentric pop artist wrote the comic opera *Stinkfoot*?
6. Whose 1999 album is called *Viva El Amor*?
7. With which song did Robbie Williams have a September 1998 No. 1 single?
8. What name do duo Benoit Dunkel and Nicolas Godin record under?
9. Which solo artist recorded the album *Here Come the Warm Jets*?
10. Sharleen Spiteri is lead singer with which group?
11. Which female vocal group had a 1998 Top 20 single with *Telefunkin*?
12. Which singer/songwriter released the 1999 album *Thanksgiving*?
13. With which John Lennon song did Jimmy Nail have a 1995 Top 40 hit?
14. What was Billy Idol's first solo chart single in 1982?
15. What was the name of Jewel Aken's only Top 30 single, in 1965?

ANSWERS 1. McAlmont and Butler **2.** Naomi Campbell **3.** Denise and Johnny **4.** House of the Rising Sun **5.** Vivian Stanshall **6.** The Pretenders **7.** Millennium **8.** Air **9.** Brian Eno **10.** Texas **11.** N-Tyce **12.** Boo Hewerdine **13.** Love **14.** Hot in the City **15.** The Birds and the Bees.

GEOGRAPHY

1. Rhodes and Tilos are part of which Greek island group?
2. In which Australian state is the town of Dandenong?
3. The Vestmann Islands are situated off of which European country?
4. In which English county is the town of Wellingborough?
5. Of which state of India is Calcutta the capital?
6. Which formerEnglish county's administrative centre was Kendal?
7. In which country is the World Heritage site of the Messil Pit fossil site?
8. In which African country is the town of Debra Markos?
9. At the junction of which three countries is Mount Roraima in South America?
10. Dawly in Shropshire is part of which new town?
11. What is the capital of Tenerife?
12. In which European country is the cathedral town of Teruel?
13. In which country are the ruins known as Tell el Amerna found?
14. On which river is the capital of Honduras, Tegucigalpa?
15. Lampedusa and Linosa are part of which Italian island group?

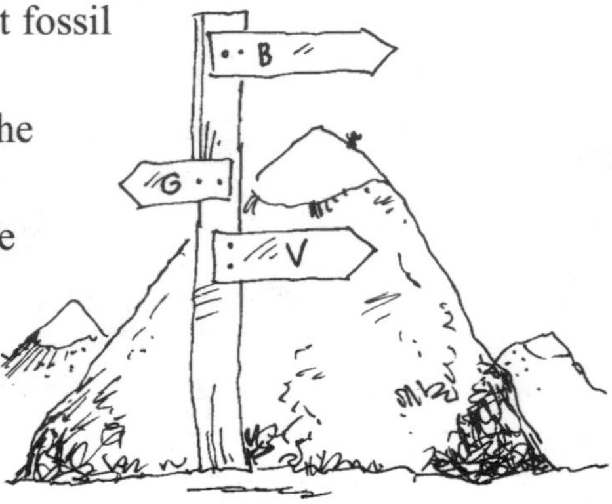

ANSWERS **1.** Dodecanese **2.** Victoria **3.** Iceland **4.** Northamptonshire **5.** West Bengal **6.** Westmorland **7.** Germany **8.** Ethiopia **9.** Brazil, Guyana and Venezuela **10.** Telford **11.** Santa Cruz **12.** Spain **13.** Egypt **14.** Choluteca River **15.** Pelagian Islands.

GENERAL KNOWLEDGE

1. What does the Latin phrase *bona fide* mean?
2. In which year was Charles I of England executed?
3. Who wrote the play *All God's Chillun Got Wings*?
4. In which country is the ancient city of Ecbatana?
5. Who won the title of World's Strongest Man in 1993?
6. To whom did the Crime Writers' Association award the Diamond Dagger in 1987?
7. Which model at Madame Tussauds was voted Hero of Entertainment in 1986?
8. In which year did saxophone player Sidney Bechet die?
9. In which year did Hurricane Hugo claim 504 lives?
10. Who authored *The World is Full of Married Men*?
11. In which country are the Lammermuir Hills?
12. Who created the strip cartoon *Blondie*?
13. In what field of entertainment might you win the Maskelyne award?
14. Who wrote the novel *Rosemary's Baby*?
15. Who designed the Volkswagen motor car?

ANSWERS **1.** Good faith **2.** 1649 **3.** Eugene O'Neill **4.** Iran **5.** Gary Taylor **6.** P.D. James **7.** Benny Hill **8.** 1959 **9.** 1989 **10.** Jackie Collins **11.** Scotland **12.** Chic Young **13.** Magic **14.** Ira Levin **15.** Ferdinand Porsche.

ENTERTAINMENT

1. How many episodes of the sitcom *The Dickie Henderson Show* were made from 1960-68?
2. Which 1934 film was Shirley Temple's first starring vehicle?
3. In which of his films does Alfred Hitchcock appear through an office window wearing a cowboy hat?
4. In which 2000 film does the shop 'Championship Vinyl' feature?
5. In which 1954 film did Humphrey Bogart play the character Linus Larrabee?
6. In which 1990 film did actress Madonna play Breathless Mahoney?
7. Who are the two male leads in the 1990 film *Bad Influence*?
8. Who directed the 1948 film *The Treasure of the Sierra Madre*?
9. What is the middle name of George Logan's comedy character Dr. Evadne Hinge?
10. Who plays Captain Nemo in the 1961 film *Mysterious Island*?
11. In which 1973 film does Robert Redford play the character Johnny Hooker?
12. Who plays the character Midge in the 1958 film *Vertigo*?
13. What is Harry's surname in the film *When Harry Met Sally...*?
14. Which husband and wife team have starring roles in the 1957 film *Witness for the Prosecution*?
15. Who played the male and female leads in the 1978 film version of *The 39 Steps*?

ANSWERS 1. 115 **2.** Baby Takes A Bow **3.** Psycho **4.** High Fidelity **5.** Sabrina **6.** Dick Tracy **7.** Rob Lowe and James Spader **8.** John Huston **9.** Mona **10.** Herbert Lom **11.** The Sting **12.** Barbara Bel Geddes **13.** Burns **14.** Charles Laughton and Elsa Lanchester **15.** Robert Powell & Karen Dotrice.

SPORT

1. Which 1980 Olympic swimming champion was nicknamed 'Bones'?
2. Which Dallas player was MVP in Superbowl XXVIII in 1994?
3. Which football team won the European Champions Cup in 1971?
4. Who was 1998 World Professional Billiards Champion?
5. Who scored Arsenal's winner in the 1936 FA Cup final against Sheffield United?
6. Which horse won the 1997 2,000 Guineas?
7. Who won the 1978 WBC world heavyweight boxing title by beating Ken Norton?
8. Who was world professional darts champion from 1984-86?
9. Which men's doubles tennis partnership won the Australian title from 1946-50?
10. In which city was equestrian star David Broome born?
11. Which tennis player won all three ladies titles at the US championships from 1912-14?
12. Who won the women's 100m and 200m at the 1972 Olympics?
13. In which sport might you see a Double Lutz?
14. How many points does red score in archery?
15. How high off the ground in feet is a basketball hoop?

ANSWERS 1. Ute Geweniger **2.** Emmitt Smith **3.** Ajax **4.** Geet Sethi **5.** Ted Drake **6.** Entrepreneur **7.** Larry Holmes **8.** Eric Bristow **9.** Adrian Quist & John Bromwich **10.** Cardiff **11.** Mary Browne **12.** Renate Stecher **13.** Ice dancing **14.** Eight **15.** 10 feet.

POP

1. Which vocalist featured on the 1995 hit *Fee Fi Fo Fum* by Candy Girls?
2. Which female artist had a 1997 Top 20 single with *Waterloo Sunset*?
3. What was the title of the 1998 No.1 single by Manic Street Preachers?
4. Which female vocalist had a hit in May 1998 with *Where are you*?
5. Which group recorded the album *The Light user Syndrome*?
6. From which European country do duo Nalin & Kane hail?
7. Which group's albums include *Voyage to the Bottom of the Road*?
8. Which U.S. rapper had a 1996 Top 20 with *If I Ruled the World*?
9. Which group had a Top 40 hit in 1998 with *Ain't goin' to Goa*?
10. In which year did Scottish singer Karl Denver die?
11. What was Natalie Imbruglia's first Top Ten single?
12. From which European country does the act Natural Born Grooves come?
13. Which group released 1999 album *The Hush*?
14. Who recorded the album *Wolf Songs for Lambs*?
15. Which song by Rick Astley was a No.1 in both the UK and US?

ANSWERS 1. Sweet Pussy Pauline **2.** Cathy Dennis **3.** If You Tolerate This Your Children Will Be Next **4.** Imaani **5.** The Fall **6.** Germany **7.** Half Man Half Biscuit **8.** Nas **9.** Alabama 3 **10.** 1998 **11.** Torn **12.** Belgium **13.** Texas **14.** Jonathan Fire*Eater **15.** Never Gonna Give You Up.

HISTORY

1. In which year was Pompeii buried by the eruption of Mount Vesuvius?
2. In which year did the SALT 1 talks begin?
3. Mary of Teck was the wife of which British king?
4. Who captured Babylon in 539 B.C. and incorporated it into the Persian Empire?
5. In which year did British Columbia join the Dominion of Canada?
6. Which African politician authored the 1962 book *Zambia Shall Be Free*?
7. Thomas of Woodstock was the youngest son of which king?
8. Who commanded the troops at Fort Sumter that fired the first shots by the North in the U.S. Civil War?
9. In which year was the Battle of Lepanto?
10. Which Palestinian guerrilla group seized 11 Israelis at the 1972 Munich Olympics?
11. In which year did gangster John Dillinger die?
12. In which year was Abraham Lincoln assassinated?
13. Who was king of Spain from 1759-88?
14. Which king of Greece died in 1964?
15. In which year was the cruise ship the Achille Lauro hijacked by the P.L.O.?

ANSWERS 1. 79 A.D. **2.** 1969 **3.** George V **4.** Cyrus the Great **5.** 1871 **6.** Kenneth Kaunda **7.** Edward III **8.** Abner Doubleday **9.** 1571 **10.** Black September **11.** 1934 **12.** 1865 **13.** Charles III **14.** Paul I **15.** 1985.

GENERAL KNOWLEDGE

1. Who created the 1888 oil painting *Portrait of a One-Eyed Man*?
2. On what day of the week was Christmas Day 1995?
3. In which African country is the World Heritage site of the archaeological site of Volubilis?
4. In which year was the Amoco Cadiz oil disaster?
5. In poker, when dealt the initial five cards, what are the odds of having a straight?
6. Paitrick is a Scottish word for which bird?
7. On which London Underground line is the station of Harlesden?
8. In which European language is the actress Sandra Bullock fluent?
9. Who or what is the Polisario Front?
10. What type of creature is a wentletrap?
11. What is a Very light?
12. What is the state bird of Alaska, U.S.A.?
13. What is the capital of Northern Territory, Australia?
14. Who was the last king of Judah?
15. In which year did the yeomanry merge into the Territorial Army?

ANSWERS 1. Vincent Van Gogh **2.** Monday **3.** Morocco **4.** 1978 **5.** 283-1 **6.** Partridge **7.** Bakerloo **8.** German **9.** An African organization whose aim is the independence of the Sahara **10.** Mollusc **11.** A coloured flare **12.** Willow ptarmigan **13.** Darwin **14.** Zedekiah **15.** 1907.

ENTERTAINMENT

1. Who plays Porthos in the 1998 film *The Man in the Iron Mask*?
2. In which 1990 film does Arnold Schwarzenegger play Detective John Kimble?
3. Who wrote and starred in the 1972 sitcom *His Lordship Entertains*?
4. In which 1992 film does Kevin Costner play the character Frank Farmer?
5. Which comedian stars in the 1961 film *Bachelor in Paradise*?
6. Who did Diane Lane play in the 1992 biopic *Chaplin*?
7. In which 1966 film did Cary Grant play the character Sir William Rutland?
8. Who played the character Albert in the 1970s children's show *Here Come the Double Deckers*?
9. Which Oscar-winner starred in the 1984 film *Bachelor Party*?
10. In which 1957 film does Alec Guinness play Colonel Nicholson?
11. Who voices the character Roger Rabbit in the 1988 film *Who Framed Roger Rabbit*?
12. Who plays an ex-convict in the 1965 film *Baby the Rain Must Fall*?
13. What was Siobhan Redmond's character name in the sitcom *The High Life*?
14. Which 1968 sitcom featured the characters Pongo Little and Grizzly Bear Ryan?
15. Who played Edwin Flagg in the 1962 film *What Ever Happened to Baby Jane?*?

ANSWERS 1. Gérard Depardieu **2.** Kindergarten Cop **3.** Ronnie Barker **4.** The Bodyguard **5.** Bob Hope **6.** Paulette Goddard **7.** Walk, Don't Run **8.** Melvyn Hayes **9.** Tom Hanks **10.** The Bridge on the River Kwai **11.** Charles Fleischer **12.** Steve McQueen **13.** Shona Spurtle **14.** Her Majesty's Pleasure **15.** Victor Buono.

SPORT

1. Which West Indies bowler took 26 wickets in the 1973 Test series against Australia?
2. Who was 1998 French Open men's singles tennis champion?
3. Who in 1987 became the first woman to win two singles titles at the World Badminton championships?
4. How many players are in a volleyball team?
5. With which sport would you associate John Naber and Peter Rocca?
6. Which Olympic sportswoman married athlete Valery Borzov?
7. Who was 1989 world amateur snooker champion?
8. In which year did Jan Kodes win the men's singles at Wimbledon?
9. With which team did Rogers 'Rajah' Hornsby begin his baseball career?
10. Which year saw the first replay in the European Champions Cup in football?
11. What did football's Littlewoods Cup become in 1991?
12. Which American won the men's 110m hurdles title at the IAAF World Championships in 1983, '87, and '91?
13. By what score did Europe win the 1997 Ryder Cup?
14. What was the nickname of Jacques Brugnon, doubles ace of the 'Four Musketeers' tennis group?
15. Who was president of the International Olympic Committee from 1952-72?

ANSWERS 1. Lance Gibbs **2.** Carlos Moya **3.** Han Aiping **4.** Six **5.** Swimming **6.** Lyudmila Tourischeva **7.** Ken Doherty **8.** 1973 **9.** St. Louis Cardinals **10.** 1974 **11.** Rumbelows League Cup **12.** Greg Foster **13.** 14 and a half - 13 and a half **14.** Toto **15.** Avery Brundage.

POP

1. From which African country does singer Alberta hail?
2. Which group had a 1997 No.2 single with *Lovefool*?
3. Which group had a 1997 hit with *Barrel of a Gun*?
4. Which group had a 1998 No.1 with *Bootie Call*?
5. Which U.S. duo had a 1983 hit with *Last Night a DJ Saved My Life*?
6. Which singer's albums include *Tupelo Honey*?
7. Which group's debut album is *Songs for a Barbed Wire Fence*?
8. Which was the only single by the Beach Boys to hit No. 1 in both the U.K. and U.S.?
9. Which duo sang the minor 1994 hit *The Day I Fall in Love*?
10. Which female singer featured on the 1996 hit *One and One* by Robert Miles?
11. Which group's albums include *Huevos* and *Up on the Sun*?
12. Which group recorded the album *Baby's Got a Gun*?
13. In which year did singer Ricky Nelson die?
14. With which song did Madonna have a 1998 No. 1 single?
15. From which European country does the singer Alda come?

ANSWERS 1. Sierra Leone **2.** The Cardigans **3.** Depeche Mode **4.** All Saints **5.** Indeep **6.** Van Morrison **7.** Dakota Suite **8.** Good Vibrations **9.** Dolly Parton & James Ingram **10.** Maria Nayler **11.** Meat Puppets **12.** The Only Ones **13.** 1985 **14.** Frozen **15.** Iceland.

ART AND LITERATURE

1. Who wrote the novel *Interview with the Vampire*?
2. Which British artist painted the 1920 work *Chrysanthemums*?
3. Who wrote the 1994 book *Burning Bright*?
4. In which year was the British sculptor Kenneth Armitage born?
5. Who wrote the novella *Chronicle of a Death Foretold*?
6. Who wrote the novel *The Dalkey Archives*?
7. Who wrote the novel *The Girl With Green Eyes*?
8. Who wrote the novel *The Butcher Boy*?
9. In which year did the London-born artist John Banting die?
10. Who wrote the short stories *Two Blue Birds* and *The Woman Who Rode Away*?
11. Who wrote the novel *Last Exit to Brooklyn*?
12. Who wrote the novel *Sexing the Cherry*?
13. Who wrote the novel *Burmese Days*?
14. Who wrote the novel *Setting Free the Bears*?
15. Who authored the novels *Disturbance* and *Kilbrack*?

ANSWERS 1. Anne Rice **2.** Vanessa Bell **3.** Helen Dunmore **4.** 1916 **5.** Gabriel Garcia Marquez **6.** Flann O'Brien **7.** Edna O'Brien **8.** Patrick McCabe **9.** 1971 **10.** D.H. Lawrence **11.** Hubert Selby Jr. **12.** Jeanette Winterson **13.** George Orwell **14.** John Irving **15.** Jamie O'Neill.

GENERAL KNOWLEDGE

1. What was Toy of the Year in 1966?
2. What are the Carmelites also known as?
3. Which Italian football club did Diego Maradona join in 1984?
4. *The Monocled Mutineer* is the story of which person?
5. What is the name of the nine-headed monster in Greek mythology?
6. In which year did French engineer A.G. Eiffel die?
7. As what is the Book of Changes more commonly known?
8. What is the middle name of film director D.W. Griffith?
9. Who was the 1972 U.S. Open men's singles tennis champion?
10. Which mime artist is associated with the character 'Bip'?
11. Who starred as *Gregory's Girl* in 1982?
12. Who won Pipe Smoker of the Year award in 1984?
13. What bird is also called a titlark?
14. Who wrote the novel *The Top of the Hill*?
15. Who wrote the play *Entertaining Mr. Sloane*?

ANSWERS **1.** Action Man **2.** White Friars **3.** Napoli **4.** Percy Toplis **5.** Hydra **6.** 1923 **7.** I Ching **8.** Wark **9.** Ilie Nastase **10.** Marcel Marceau **11.** Dee Hepburn **12.** Henry Cooper **13.** Pipit **14.** Irwin Shaw **15.** Joe Orton.

ENTERTAINMENT

1. The 1993 film *Backbeat* is a biopic about which pop group?
2. In which film does Alec Guinness play Jamesir Bensonmum?
3. Who directed the 1972 film *What's Up Doc*?
4. Who directed the 1991 film *Backdraft*?
5. In which 1973 film does Paul Newman play the character Henry Gondorff?
6. In which 1985 film does Arnold Schwarzenegger play the character Kalidor?
7. What is the name of James Finlayson's character in the 1937 Laurel and Hardy film *Way Out West*?
8. Which pair wrote and appeared in the 1964 comedy series *How To Be An Alien*?
9. What disaster is central to the plot of the 1956 film *Back From Eternity*?
10. Who plays Lola in the 1956 film *Trapeze*?
11. Who plays Ice in the 1986 film *Top Gun*?
12. Who plays Cardinal Richelieu in the 1948 film *The Three Musketeers*?
13. In which 1975 film does Michael Caine play the character Peachy Carnehan?
14. In which 1963 film does Jack Nicholson play Rexford Bedlo?
15. In which 1990s sitcom did the character Ambrose Stebbings appear?

ANSWERS **1.** The Beatles **2.** Murder By Death **3.** Peter Bogdanovich **4.** Ron Howard **5.** The Sting **6.** Red Sonja **7.** Mickey Finn **8.** Frank Muir and Denis Norden **9.** An air crash **10.** Gina Lollobrigida **11.** Val Kilmer **12.** Vincent Price **13.** The Man Who Would Be King **14.** The Raven **15.** The House of Windsor.

SPORT

1. Who won the 1957 Wimbledon women's singles tennis championship?
2. Which team did American Football star Paul Hornung play for after leaving Notre Dame in 1956?
3. Who scored both goals for Newcastle United in the 1951 F.A. Cup final?
4. Who in fencing was 1997 and '98 world foil champion?
5. How high in feet and inches is the net in volleyball?
6. Which Yorkshire-born bowls player was awarded the CBE in 1980?
7. At which fencing discipline did Georges Buchard win three individual world titles between 1927 and 1933?
8. Whose record of 27 English classic winners did Lester Piggott surpass in 1984?
9. Who, on 20th July, 1984, became the first man to throw over 100m with a javelin?
10. Which cyclist won the 1996 and '97 Vuelta A España?
11. In which year did Mike Teague win his 27th and final rugby union cap for England?
12. Who took 30 wickets in his debut Test series for the West Indies against India in 1958/9?
13. Who won the men's high jump at the 1993 and '97 IAAF World Championships?
14. In which country did England Test cricketer Walter Hammond settle after his retirement?
15. At what was Dmitri Svatkovsky men's individual world champion in 1994 and '95?

ANSWERS 1. Althea Gibson **2.** Green Bay Packers **3.** Jackie Milburn **4.** Serey Golubitsky **5.** Seven feet one inch **6.** David Bryant **7.** Épée **8.** Frank Buckle **9.** Uwe Hohn **10.** Alex Zülle **11.** 1993 **12.** Wes Hall **13.** Javier Sotomayor **14.** South Africa **15.** Modern Pentathlon.

POP

1. Which female vocalist had a 1998 Top 10 single with *My All*?
2. Which U.S. rap duo charted in 1998 with *Halls of Illusion*?
3. Which female vocalist had a 1998 chart hit with *What's Your Sign*?
4. How many singles by the Beatles got to No.1 in both the U.S. and U.K.?
5. Which country singer recorded the album *Grievous Angel*?
6. Which songwriter recorded the 1971 album *Magnetic South*?
7. From which European country does singer Neja hail?
8. Which group had a 1995 No. 2 hit with the song *Don't give me your life*?
9. Which U.K. singer had a 1995 Top 30 with *Rough with the Smooth*?
10. Who had a No.1 single in 1998 with *You Make Me Wanna*?
11. Which group's albums include *Trompe Le Monde*?
12. Which vocal group had a 1998 Top Five single with *No, no, no*?
13. In which year did singer Michael Hutchence die?
14. Which was David Bowie's only single to reach No.1 in the U.S. and U.K.?
15. With which song did The Verve have a No.1 single in 1997?

ANSWERS **1.** Mariah Carey **2.** Insane Clown Posse **3.** Des'Ree **4.** 12 **5.** Gram Parsons **6.** Michael Nesmith **7.** Italy **8.** Alex Party **9.** Shara Nelson **10.** Usher **11.** The Pixies **12.** Destiny's Child **13.** 1997 **14.** Let's Dance **15.** The Drugs Won't Work.

SCIENCE

1. What in physical geography is a nunatak?
2. Which German astronomer's Third Law states that 'the square of a planet's periodic time is proportional to the cube of its mean distance from the sun'?

3. What is the symbol for the element thulium?
4. What is the colouring agent E102 also called?
5. What sort of creature was the prehistoric smilodon?
6. What is the name given to a straight line that joins two points on the circumference of a circle?
7. How many grams of fat per 100 grams are there in a Mars bar?
8. Approximately what percentage of a chocolate biscuit is sugar?
9. In which year was Cordelia, a satellite of Uranus, discovered?
10. Which element is to the immediate left of antimony in the Periodic Table?
11. In which century did English physicist James Joule live?
12. Is the element polonium radioactive?
13. What is the name of the larger of the two bones in the lower section of the arm?
14. What is the atomic number of silver?
15. What is the name given to the highest point of a triangle?

ANSWERS 1. An isolated mountain peak projecting through the surface of surrounding glacial ice **2.** Johann Kepler **3.** Tm **4.** Tartrazine **5.** A sabre-toothed cat **6.** Chord **7.** 19 **8.** 33% **9.** 1986 **10.** Tin **11.** 19th **12.** Yes **13.** Ulna **14.** 47 **15.** Apex.

GENERAL KNOWLEDGE

1. What is the English name of the constellation whose Latin name is *Vulpecula*?
2. On which group of islands is the Isaac Newton Telescope?
3. In the United States of America, TX is the zip code of which state?
4. On what day of the week was Christmas Day 1952?
5. In which year did Hurricane Hugo hit South Carolina?
6. What material is No. 4 on the Mohs' hardness scale?
7. Which is larger - the North Sea or the Black Sea?
8. Who wrote the 2000 short story collection *Piranha to Scurfy*?
9. In the U.S.A., where is the nene the state bird?
10. In which country is the World Heritage site of the Tikal National Park?
11. In which year did cricketer David Gower famously fly over a Queensland v .England match?
12. In which year did Lowell George of the rock group Little Feat die?
13. Which British artist's works include the 1918 painting *The Tea Pot*?
14. How much, not including buyers' premium and V.A.T., did the England soccer shirt-wearing mannequin sell for at the Millennium Dome sale in February 2001?
15. What, in parts of Africa, is sango?

ANSWERS **1.** Fox **2.** Canary Islands **3.** Texas **4.** Thursday **5.** 1989 **6.** Fluorite **7.** North Sea **8.** Ruth Rendell **9.** Hawaii **10.** Guatemala **11.** 1991 **12.** 1979 **13.** Mark Gertler **14.** £900 **15.** A language.

ENTERTAINMENT

1. Who played the gardener, Dithers, in the 1969 sitcom *Hark At Barker*?
2. Who is the male star of the 1943 World War II film *Background to Danger*?
3. In which 2000 film does Arnold Schwarzenegger play the character Adam Gibson?
4. In which 1958 film does Jack Nicholson play the character Jimmy Wallace?
5. In which 1980 film does John Travolta play the character Bud?
6. Who composed the 1836 opera *The Ban on Love*?
7. Who did Harvey Lembeck play in *The Phil Silvers Show*?
8. In which year was the comedian Mike Harding born?
9. Who is the male star of the 1945 World War II film *Back to Bataan*?
10. Who plays Athos in the 1998 film *The Man in the Iron Mask*?
11. In which 1992 film do the characters English Bob and William Munny appear?

12. In which year did the television show *The Twilight Zone* begin in the U.S.?
13. Which comedienne played five different roles in the 1985 television series *Happy Families*?
14. In which 1953 film did Marilyn Monroe play the character Rose Loomis?
15. In which 1957 film did Peter Sellers play the character Sonny MacGregor?

ANSWERS **1.** David Jason **2.** George Raft **3.** The 6th Day **4.** The Cry Baby Killer **5.** Urban Cowboy **6.** Richard Wagner **7.** Corporal Barbella **8.** 1944 **9.** John Wayne **10.** John Malkovich **11.** Unforgiven **12.** 1959 **13.** Jennifer Saunders **14.** Niagara **15.** The Naked Truth.

SPORT

1. Who were Scottish League champions in rugby union in the 1997/8 season?

2. Which skier won the 1984 Olympic 5km, 10km and 20km cross-country golds?

3. Who was 1996 World Professional Billiards champion?

4. Which U.S. cyclist won the 1988 Giro d'Italia?

5. Who took 28 wickets for the West Indies on the 1976 England tour?

6. Who was men's pole vault champion in the IAAF World Championships from 1983-97?

7. For which Italian club side did Swedish footballer Kurt Hamrin sign in 1956?

8. Which controversial athlete married Mike Pieterse in 1989?

9. Who won all three men's tennis titles at Wimbledon in 1937?

10. At what Olympic sport did Romanian Olga Bularda win medals?

11. Who did Craig Brown replace as Scotland football manager?

12. With which sport is Cedric Pioline associated?

13. What nationality is golfer Joakim Haeggman?

14. From which club did Manchester United sign goalkeeper Mark Bosnich in 1999?

15. With which sport is Desmond Douglas associated?

ANSWERS **1.** Watsonians **2.** Marja-Liisa Hämäläinen **3.** Mike Russell **4.** Andy Hampsten **5.** Michael Holding **6.** Sergey Bubka **7.** Juventus **8.** Zola Budd **9.** Don Budge **10.** Rowing **11.** Andy Roxburgh **12.** Tennis **13.** Swedish **14.** Aston Villa **15.** Table tennis.

POP

1. Which female vocalist hit the charts in 1998 with the song *Uh la la la*?
2. Which female singer had a 1996 Top 10 with *In Too Deep*?
3. In which year was Janet Jackson born?
4. Which vocal group had a 1995 Top 10 single with *I Need You*?
5. What was the title of Run-DMC vs Jason Nevin's 1998 No. 1 single?
6. Which group recorded the 1971 album *There's a Riot Goin' On*?
7. On which label did Moby release the 1999 album *Play*?
8. In which year did New Edition chart with the single *Hit me off*?
9. Which female singer duetted with Big Dee Irwin on the 1963 hit *Swinging on a Star*?
10. Which group recorded the live album *Severe Tire Damage*?
11. Which group recorded the 1994 album *San Francisco*?
12. With which song did Tatyana Ali have a hit in November 1998?
13. Which group's last chart hit single was 1967's *Green Street Green*?
14. With what song did Michael Jackson score a 1997 No.1 single?
15. Which singer recorded the album *The Cult of Ray*?

ANSWERS **1.** Alexia **2.** Belinda Carlisle **3.** 1966 **4.** Deuce **5.** It's Like That **6.** Sly & the Family Stone **7.** Mute **8.** 1996 **9.** Little Eva **10.** They Might Be Giants **11.** American Music Club **12.** Daydreamin' **13.** New Vaudeville Band **14.** Blood on the Dancefloor **15.** Frank Black.

PEOPLE

1. In which city was the sculptor Sir Jacob Epstein born?
2. Who starred in a controversial poster campaign for the perfume Opium in 2000 which was the most complained about ad of the year?
3. Which visual artist wrote the novel *The System of Landor's Cottage*?
4. On which island was actress Tia Carrere born?
5. Who was named Personality of the Year in the Daily Mail National Television Awards for 1955-6?
6. Who won the Emmy award for Outstanding Lead Actress in a Comedy Series for 1991-2?
7. Which Roman emperor began the building of the colosseum?
8. Which architect designed the Victoria Memorial in 1911?
9. In which year did the actor Johnny Weissmuller die?
10. Which author wrote the 2000 memoir *Experience*?
11. Which British artist's works include the 1965 series of lithographs entitled *Spinning Man*?
12. In which year was the actress Tia Carrere born?
13. Which university did the comedian Harry Enfield attend?
14. At which university did the actress Meryl Streep study?
15. Which actress was born Demetria Gene Guynes?

ANSWERS **1.** New York **2.** Sophie Dahl **3.** Rodney Graham **4.** Hawaii **5.** Benny Hill **6.** Candice Bergen **7.** Vespasian **8.** Aston Webb **9.** 1984 **10.** Martin Amis **11.** Dame Elisabeth Frink **12.** 1967 **13.** York **14.** Yale **15.** Demi Moore.

GENERAL KNOWLEDGE

1. Who wrote the thriller *The Ice House*?
2. Which space mission was launched first - Gemini 6 or Gemini 7?
3. Mikonos and Kithnos are part of which Greek island group?
4. In the United States of America, of which state is AZ the zip code?
5. In which year was Jupiter's moon Metis discovered?
6. What was the approximate population in thousands of the Italian city of Verona in 1992?
7. In poker, when dealt the initial five cards, what are the odds of having four of a kind?
8. In which country is the Gros Morne National Park World Heritage?
9. Which U.S. rap singer's albums include 1999's *The Slim Shady L.P.*?
10. In which year was the Kharg 5 oil disaster?
11. What is the state bird of Delaware, U.S.A.?
12. What was the Latin name of St. Albans?
13. What in South Africa are padkos?
14. On which London Underground line is the station of Kilburn Park?
15. If you have committed parricide, what crime have you performed?

ANSWERS **1.** Minette Walters **2.** Gemini 7 **3.** Cyclades **4.** Arizona **5.** 1979 **6.** 255 thousand **7.** 4,166-1 **8.** Canada **9.** Eminem **10.** 1989 **11.** Blue Hen Chicken **12.** Verulamium **13.** Snacks and provisions used for a journey **14.** Bakerloo **15.** Killed one or both of your parents.

ENTERTAINMENT

1. In which 1986 film did actress Madonna play the character Gloria Tatlock?
2. Who played Albert Tatlock in soap *Coronation Street*?
3. Who directed the 1998 film *Babe: Pig in the City*?
4. Who plays William H. Bonney in the 1988 film *Young Guns*?
5. In which 1997 film does Jack Nicholson play the character Melvin Udall?
6. Who plays D'Artagnan in the 1993 film *The Three Musketeers*?
7. Who plays the female lead of a hooker in the 1981 film *Back Roads*?
8. Who starred in the title role of the 1948 film *The Babe Ruth Story*?
9. Who played Juror No. 4 in the 1957 film *12 Angry Men*?
10. In which year did the show *Gilligan's Island* premiere on U.S. television?
11. In which 1994 film does Arnold Schwarzenegger play the character Harry Tasker?
12. In which 1983 film does Michael Caine play the character Dr. Frank Bryant?
13. What is Eddie Murphy's character name in the 1983 film *Trading Places*?
14. Who directed the 1941 film *Babes on Broadway*?
15. Who does Harry Shearer play in the 1984 film *This Is Spinal Tap*?

ANSWERS 1. Shanghai Surprise **2.** Jack Howarth **3.** George Miller **4.** Emilio Estevez **5.** As Good As It Gets **6.** Chris O'Donnell **7.** Sally Field **8.** William Bendix **9.** E.G. Marshall **10.** 1964 **11.** True Lies **12.** Educating Rita **13.** Billy Ray Valentine **14.** Busby Berkeley **15.** Derek Smalls.

SPORT

1. In which Welsh city was rugby league star Billy Boston born?
2. Who was 1960 Olympic men's long jump champion?
3. For which county cricket team did Ian Botham play from 1987-91?
4. In which year did Geoffrey Boycott make his Yorkshire debut?
5. Of the eleven women's New York Marathons between 1978 and '88, how many did Grete Waitz win?
6. Who was basketball's leading scorer in the NBA from 1953-55?
7. In which year did Sir Len Hutton make his Test debut?
8. What is rugby union player William Henry Hare also known as?
9. Who was women's world middleweight judo champion from 1982-86?
10. Which team won the 1996 Benson & Hedges Cup in cricket?
11. Which female U.S. Olympic volleyball player died in 1986 of Marfan's Syndrome?
12. In which year did cyclist Reg Harris die?
13. Which former Olympic women's 200m silver winner was disqualified in a 1976 semi-final for two false starts?
14. Who defeated Max Baer to win the world heavyweight title in 1935?
15. Who was captain of South Australia's cricket team from 1935-48?

ANSWERS **1.** Cardiff **2.** Ralph Boston **3.** Worcestershire **4.** 1962 **5.** Nine **6.** Neil Johnston **7.** 1937 **8.** Dusty **9.** Brigitte Deydier **10.** Lancashire **11.** Flo Hyman **12.** 1992 **13.** Raelene Boyle **14.** James Braddock **15.** Donald Bradman.

POP

1. From which country did duo Mouth and MacNeal hail?
2. Who had Top 10 singles with *We Are Glass* and *She's Got Claws*?
3. Mike Barson was keyboard player with which band from 1978-83?
4. Which Welsh rock band's albums include 1976's *The Welsh Connection*?
5. What is singer Derek Dick better known as?
6. Which singer/songwriter recorded the 1973 album *Solid Air*?
7. Which city do Massive Attack come from?
8. In which year was John Mayall born?
9. In which city was Curtis Mayfield born?
10. In which city was Meat Loaf born?
11. In what year did producer Joe Meek commit suicide?
12. Which 'Goth' band released the albums *Carved in Sand* and *Grains of Sand*?
13. Which Canadian singer was born Roberta Joan Anderson?
14. In which city was Alanis Morissette born?
15. What is rock musician Ian Kilminster better known as?

ANSWERS **1.** The Netherlands **2.** Gary Numan **3.** Madness **4.** Man **5.** Fish **6.** John Martyn **7.** Bristol **8.** 1933 **9.** Chicago **10.** Dallas **11.** 1967 **12.** The Mission **13.** Joni Mitchell **14.** Ottawa **15.** Lemmy.

ART AND LITERATURE

1. Who wrote the novel *All Quiet on the Western Front*?
2. Where in North Devon is the Burton art gallery?
3. Who wrote the stage play *Port Authority*?
4. Who painted *The Arnolfini Marriage*?
5. Whose book *Bad Blood* won the 2001 Whitbread biography prize?
6. In which year did the painter Rosso Fiorentino die?
7. Who painted the mid-15th century work *The Battle of San Romano*?
8. Who wrote the 1991 novel *The Wimbledon Poisoner*?
9. Where in England is the Atkinson art gallery?
10. What was the middle name of dramatist R.B. Sheridan?
11. *Cocky Patriot* is a 1980 artwork by which duo?
12. Which thriller writer authored the novel *Icon*?
13. Who wrote the 1991 novel *Dirty Tricks*?
14. In which century did the artist Francesco Guardi live?
15. Who created the 1888 oil painting *The Pink Peach Tree*?

ANSWERS 1. Erich Maria Remarque **2.** Bideford **3.** Conor McPherson **4.** Van Eyck **5.** Lorna Sage **6.** 1540 **7.** Paolo Uccello **8.** Nigel Williams **9.** Southport **10.** Brinsley **11.** Gilbert and George **12.** Frederick Forsyth **13.** Michael Dibdin **14.** 18th century **15.** Vincent Van Gogh.

GENERAL KNOWLEDGE

1. Who won Member to Watch award at the 1987 Parliamentarian of the Year luncheon?
2. Lyons is the capital of which French department?
3. In which German-occupied country were the EAM the leftist resistance in World War II?
4. In Israel, what monetary unit is one-hundredth of a shekel?
5. What in Hindu mythology is amrita?
6. Which Scottish psychiatrist wrote the book *The Divided Self*?
7. Who was Melody Maker's Top Male Jazz Singer 1955-68?
8. What is the official language of Libya?
9. Who authored the novel *A Laodicean*?
10. Otalgia is the technical name for what illness?
11. What is the chief port of Tanzania?
12. Which musical instrument is also called a sweet potato?
13. Which London hotel won the Egon Ronay Hotel of the Year award in 1978?
14. What is the name of the secret intelligence agency of Israel?
15. To whom did the Crime Writers' Association award the Diamond Dagger in 1991?

ANSWERS **1.** Gordon Brown **2.** Rhône **3.** Greece **4.** Agora **5.** Food of the gods which bestows immortality **6.** R.D. Laing **7.** Frank Sinatra **8.** Arabic **9.** Thomas Hardy **10.** Earache **11.** Dar es Salaam **12.** Ocarina **13.** The Ritz **14.** Mossad **15.** Ruth Rendell.

ENTERTAINMENT

1. What was the 1936 sequel to the 1934 film *The Thin Man*?
2. Who play Heathcliff and Cathy in the 1992 film version of *Wuthering Heights*?
3. Who plays Peggy Macroon in the 1948 film *Whisky Galore*?
4. In which year was the entertainer Dickie Henderson born?
5. Who played Hannah Miller in the US sitcom *Anything But Love*?
6. Who directed the 1952 film *The Bad and the Beautiful*?
7. What profession do Adam Baldwin and Mike Jolly take up in the 1986 film *Bad Guys* after being ousted from the police force?
8. Who plays Athos in the 1993 film *The Three Musketeers*?
9. Which comedy actress played Mrs. Briggs in the 1987 sitcom *High & Dry*?
10. In which 1968 film does Michael Caine play the character Nicholas Urfe?
11. In which 1958 film does Paul Newman play the character Ben Quick?
12. Which legendary film actor's son, John, makes his film debut in the 1990 film *Bad Jim*?
13. Who played the male and female leads in the 1935 film version of *The 39 Steps*?
14. What was unusual about Elizabeth Bennett's roles in the sitcoms *Home To Roost* and *You Again?*?
15. Which U.S. comedian and actor was nicknamed 'The Great One'?

ANSWERS **1.** After the Thin Man **2.** Ralph Fiennes and Juliette Binoche **3.** Joan Greenwood **4.** 1922 **5.** Jamie Lee Curtis **6.** Vincente Minnelli **7.** Wrestlers **8.** Kiefer Sutherland **9.** Diana Coupland **10.** The Magus **11.** The Long, Hot Summer **12.** Clark Gable **13.** Robert Donat & Madeleine Carroll **14.** She played the same role in both, the latter being the U.S. version of the former, English, original **15.** Jackie Gleason.

SPORT

1. How many caps did rugby union player Mike Gibson win for Ireland from 1964-79?
2. In which year was badminton player Gillian Gilks born?
3. Which former holder of the men's 400m and 800m world record was killed whilst fighting in World War II in March 1944?
4. Which team won the World Bowl in American Football in 1995?
5. Which year saw Feyenoord's only European Champions Cup win?
6. Which basketball player was leading scorer in the NBA in 1956 and '59?
7. By what score did Eric Bristow beat Dave Whitcombe in the 1986 World Professional Darts Championship?
8. At which course was the 1998 British Open golf championship held?
9. How many caps did W.J.A. 'Dave' Davies win for England at rugby union?
10. By what score did Europe win the 1995 Ryder Cup?
11. Who scored a hat-trick for Blackpool in their 1953 FA Cup final win?
12. What was the score in the England v Sweden 1999 European Championship qualifier in football?
13. Which horse won the 1996 2,000 Guineas?
14. Who was men's British Open squash champion 1976-81?
15. Which team won the 1997 Benson & Hedges Cup in cricket?

ANSWERS **1.** 69 **2.** 1950 **3.** Rudolf Harbig **4.** Frankfurt Galaxy **5.** 1970 **6.** Bob Pettit **7.** 6-0 **8.** Royal Birkdale **9.** 22 **10.** 14 and a half - 13 and a half **11.** Stan Mortensen **12.** 0-0 **13.** Mark of Esteem **14.** Geoff Hunt **15.** Surrey.

POP

1. Which female vocalist had a hit in August 1997 with *4 Page Letter*?
2. Which group released the 1999 album *The Days of our Nights*?
3. Which duo had a 1998 hit with *Long Time Coming*?
4. Which folk singer recorded the 1999 album *Ravenchild*?
5. Which member of the group Dave Dee, Dozy, Beaky, Mick and Tich was John Dymond?
6. Which U.S. group released the album *Echo* in 1999?
7. Who had a 1996 No. 1 with *Breakfast at Tiffany's*?
8. Who co-wrote the 1970s track *Abdulmajid* with David Bowie?
9. Which French duo had a 1994 hit single with *Sweet Lullaby*?
10. On which studio album does Bob Dylan's *One More Cup of Coffee* appear?
11. Which 1970s group released the album *Something for the Weekend* in 1999?
12. Which group recorded the album *Crooked Rain, Crooked Rain*?
13. On which studio album by Neil Young and Crazy Horse does the song *Piece of Crap* appear?
14. In which year was Human League singer Phil Oakey born?
15. Which Australia-based rock group had a minor hit in 1996 with *Hail Caesar*?

ANSWERS 1. Aaliyah **2.** Luna **3.** Bump & Flex **4.** Maddy Prior **5.** Beaky **6.** Tom Petty and the Heartbreakers **7.** Deep Blue Something **8.** Brian Eno **9.** Deep Forest **10.** Desire **11.** Stackridge **12.** Pavement **13.** Sleeps with Angels **14.** 1955 **15.** AC/DC.

GEOGRAPHY

1. Lake Titicaca is on the border of which two South American countries?
2. Which island of the Inner Hebrides houses Fingal's Cave?
3. In which U.S. state is the Sequoia National Park?
4. The seaport of Port Gentil is in which African country?
5. Paphos is an ancient city on which Mediterranean island?
6. In which ocean is the island republic of Nauru?
7. In which English county is the holiday resort of Minehead?
8. Horney Peak is the highest point of which U.S. mountain range?
9. In which African country is the state of Tigré?
10. Split is a seaport on which European sea?
11. What is the name of the peninsula at the head of the Red Sea?
12. In which county of northern England is the market town of Shap?
13. The Ile de Ré is off the coast of which French seaport?
14. On which British island is the seaport of Ramsey?
15. In which European country is the region of Transylvania?

ANSWERS **1.** Peru and Bolivia **2.** Staffa **3.** California **4.** Gabon **5.** Cyprus **6.** Pacific Ocean **7.** Somerset **8.** Black Hills **9.** Ethiopia **10.** Adriatic Sea **11.** Sinai Peninsula **12.** Cumbria **13.** La Rochelle **14.** Isle of Man **15.** Romania.

GENERAL KNOWLEDGE

1. Who wrote the 2000 novel *My Canapé Hell*?
2. In which year was the space mission Sputnik 1 launched?
3. Salina and Lipari are part of which Italian island group?
4. What material is 9 on the Mohs' hardness scale?
5. In which country is the volcano Helgafell?
6. On what day of the week was Christmas Day 1961?
7. In the U.S.A., where is the cactus wren the state bird?
8. What is the English name of the constellation whose Latin name is *Cetus*?
9. What is the approximate area in square miles of County Wexford, Republic of Ireland?
10. Which Cheshire village is the birthplace of writer Lewis Carroll?
11. Which architect designed the Victoria and Albert Museum in 1909?
12. What type of creature is a Weimaraner?
13. What in France is a papeterie?
14. In which year was the Flixborough disaster which killed 28 people?
15. Which former member of the Spice Girls had a 1999 No. 1 hit single with the song *Lift Me Up*?

ANSWERS **1.** Imogen Edwards-Jones **2.** 1957 **3.** Aeolian Islands **4.** Corundum **5.** Iceland **6.** Monday **7.** Arizona **8.** Whale **9.** 908 sq.m. **10.** Daresbury **11.** Aston Webb **12.** Dog **13.** A box for papers and writing materials **14.** 1974 **15.** Geri Halliwell.

ENTERTAINMENT

1. In which year did the comic actor Bonar Colleano die?
2. Who play the two male leads in the 1995 comedy drama *Bad Boys*?
3. Who plays the lead in the 1951 British film *The Bad Lord Byron*?
4. What was the 1944 sequel to the 1934 film *The Thin Man*?
5. Who wrote the 1997 Channel 5 comedy show *Hospital!*?
6. Who play the leading couple in 1993 Britflick *Bad Behaviour*?
7. In which 1946 film did Cary Grant play the character T.R. Devlin?
8. In which 1953 film did Marilyn Monroe play the character Lorelei Lee?
9. In which 1996 film did Julia Roberts play the character Kitty Kiernan?
10. Who does James Cagney play in the 1942 film biopic *Yankee Doodle Dandy*?
11. Who directed the 1988 film *Women on the Verge of a Nervous Breakdown*?
12. Which 1845 opera by Verdi is set in Peru?
13. What profession does Charlton Heston have in the 1953 film *Bad For Each Other*?
14. Which actor's previous incarnations include that of folk singer 'The Covered Man'?
15. In which 1944 film did Humphrey Bogart play the character Harry Morgan?

ANSWERS 1. 1934 **2.** Will Smith and Martin Lawrence **3.** Dennis Price **4.** The Thin Man Goes Home **5.** Laurie Rowley **6.** Stephen Rea and Sinead Cusack **7.** Notorious **8.** Gentlemen Prefer Blondes **9.** Michael Collins **10.** George M. Cohan **11.** Pedro Almodovar **12.** Alzira **13.** A doctor **14.** David Soul **15.** To Have And Have Not.

SPORT

1. Which U.S. tennis player won the 1960 French women's singles title?
2. Who was the 1998 U.S. Open women's singles tennis champion?
3. Which cricketing all-rounder was known as the 'W.G. Grace of Australia'?
4. For which four Italian teams did footballer Liam Brady play?
5. Who scored from the penalty spot for Tottenham in their 1962 F.A. Cup final win?
6. Of his 31 matches as England Test captain, how many did Mike Brearley lose?
7. Who won the 1993 and '95 men's 5,000m title at the IAAF World Championships?
8. Baseball player Harry Breechen was nicknamed after which animal?
9. In which year did motor racing champion James Hunt die?
10. Who was women's world bantamweight judo champion from 1993-97?
11. Who scored the only goal in the 1990 football World Cup final?
12. Who scored for West Germany in both the 1974 and '82 World Cup finals?
13. Who in boxing was 'the Boston Gob'?
14. In which American state was jockey Steve Cauthen born?
15. What nationality was motor racing driver Bruce McLaren?

ANSWERS **1.** Darlene Hard **2.** Lindsay Davenport **3.** George Giffin **4.** Juventus, Internazionale, Sampdoria and Ascoli **5.** Danny Blanchflower **6.** 4 **7.** Ismael Kirui **8.** The Cat **9.** 1993 **10.** Ryoko Tamura **11.** Andreas Brehme **12.** Paul Breitner **13.** Jack Sharkey **14.** Kentucky **15.** New Zealander.

POP

1. What was the first Top 10 album in the U.K. for the group Heart?
2. Which singer recorded the 2000 album *Vanguard*?
3. Which Brazilian artist recorded the 1971 album *Olha Quem Chega*?
4. Who was the lead singer of the 1990s group Helium?
5. Which group recorded the 2000 album *Felt Mountain*?
6. Which group's first album was 1979's *Y*?
7. In which year did the group The Poison Girls disband?
8. Who originally played accordion in the group The Pogues?
9. Which group headlined at the '14 Hour Technicolour Dream' all-nighter at Alexandra Palace on April 29th 1967?
10. Which singer with the group The Pink Fairies was born John Alder?
11. Which pop group had a 1997 No. 1 single with *Barbie Girl*?
12. In which year did The Jimi Hendrix Experience have a No. 3 single with *Purple Haze*?
13. Which duo recorded the 1982 Top 10 album *Private Eyes*?
14. Which singer recorded the 1982 Top 10 album *Killer on the Rampage*?
15. Who did Andy Summers replace in the group The Police?

ANSWERS **1.** Bad Animals **2.** Finlay Quaye **3.** Tania Maria **4.** Mary Timony **5.** Goldfrapp **6.** The Pop Group **7.** 1989 **8.** Jimmy Fearnley **9.** Pink Floyd **10.** Twink **11.** Aqua **12.** 1967 **13.** Hall and Oates **14.** Eddy Grant **15.** Henry Padovani.

HISTORY

1. In which year did Blondin first walk across the Niagara Falls on a tightrope?
2. In which year did Peter Abelard become tutor to Héloïse?
3. Who succeeded Antoninus Pius as Roman emperor in 161 A.D.?
4. Who was regent of the Netherlands from 1559-67?
5. In which year did Karl Marx die?
6. In which year did the Korean War end?
7. King John, who died in 1216, was the youngest son of which king?
8. In which year did Richard the Lionheart set forth on the Third Crusade?
9. Which U.S. president was born in Stonewall, Texas, in 1908?
10. Who was British prime minister from 1852-55?
11. Who was Conservative secretary of state for social services from 1970-74?
12. Which U.S. abolitionist published the newspaper 'The Liberator' in 1831?
13. Who was the mother of Mary, Queen of Scots?
14. Who was U.S. secretary of state from 1949-53?
15. In which year was Bacon's rebellion, a protest of farmers against the governor of Virginia?

ANSWERS 1. 1859 **2.** 1117 **3.** Marcus Aurelius **4.** Margaret of Parma **5.** 1883 **6.** 1953 **7.** Henry II **8.** 1189 **9.** Lyndon B. Johnson **10.** Earl of Aberdeen **11.** Keith Joseph **12.** William Lloyd Garrison **13.** Mary of Guise **14.** Dean Acheson **15.** 1676.

GENERAL KNOWLEDGE

1. Who scored the winning goal for Wimbledon in the 1988 F.A. Cup Final?
2. Who wrote the 2000 novel *Fred And Edie*?
3. In which year was the space mission Surveyor 1 launched?
4. Which is larger, the Mediterranean Sea or the Arabian Sea?
5. Which five states of the USA have the western meadowlark as their state bird?
6. In which year was Saturn's moon Pan discovered?
7. What is the English name of the constellation whose Latin name is *Draco*?
8. In which island group is the Keck Telescope situated?
9. What was the forename of Mr. Fargo, who co-founded the Wells, Fargo & Company express mail service?
10. On which London Underground line is the station of Wood Green?
11. Which British cyclist won gold at the 2000 Olympics in the 1km time trial?
12. What was the name of the wartime code-breaking machine stolen from Bletchley Park Museum in April 2000?
13. Which chesspiece moves in an L-shaped direction?
14. In which year was the Ekofisk oil disaster?
15. Which card in the game of poker is nicknamed a cowboy?

ANSWERS 1. Lawrie Sanchez **2.** Jill Dawson **3.** 1966 **4.** Arabian Sea **5.** Oregon, North Dakota, Nebraska, Montana and Kansas **6.** 1990 **7.** Dragon **8.** Hawaii **9.** William **10.** Piccadilly **11.** Jason Queally **12.** Enigma **13.** Knight **14.** 1977 **15.** King.

ENTERTAINMENT

1. Who played Ma Larkin in the TV drama series *The Darling Buds of May*?
2. Who directed the 1950 film *In A Lonely Place*?
3. Which actor played Dixie Dean in the T.V. drama *Boys from the Blackstuff*?
4. Who played Lord Rustless in the 1972 sitcom *His Lordship Entertains*?
5. Who played Commander George Gideon in the police drama series *Gideon's Way*?
6. What was Eddie Munster's middle name in the T.V. comedy *The Munsters*?
7. Who directed the 1968 film *The Charge of the Light Brigade*?
8. What was Starsky's forename in *Starsky and Hutch*?
9. In which city was comic Les Dawson born?
10. What was John Wayne's character name in the 1956 film *The Searchers*?
11. Which actor played Hauptmann Reinicke in World War II TV drama *Enemy at the Door*?
12. What was Ryan O'Neal's character name in the 1970 film *Love Story*?
13. In which city did composer Gustav Mahler die?
14. Who directed the 1997 film *In And Out*?
15. Who directed the 1990 film *An Angel At My Table*?

ANSWERS 1. Pam Ferris **2.** Nicholas Ray **3.** Tom Georgeson **4.** Ronnie Barker **5.** John Gregson **6.** Wolfgang **7.** Tony Richardson **8.** Dave **9.** Manchester **10.** Ethan Edwards **11.** Simon Cadell **12.** Oliver Barrett IV **13.** Vienna **14.** Frank Oz **15.** Jane Campion.

SPORT

1. Which horse won the 1956 Grand National?
2. Who was the French Open men's singles tennis champion in 1986?
3. Which American Football team won Super Bowl XXXII?
4. In which country were the 1998 football World Cup finals held?
5. Which football team won the 1996/7 UEFA Cup?
6. Who won the Olympic men's 200m in 1948?
7. Who won the Olympic women's 200m in 1964?
8. "Schneemann", a red-hatted snowman, was the official mascot of which Winter Olympic Games?
9. Which team won ice hockey's Stanley Cup in 1971/2?
10. Which horse won the 1972 2000 Guineas?
11. Which golfer was the runner-up in the 1996 world matchplay championship?
12. Which player was runner-up in the 1980 world professional darts championship?
13. Which county won cricket's Nat West Trophy in 1998?
14. Who was the world professional billiards champion in 1984?
15. Which team were NBA champions in basketball in 1989?

ANSWERS 1. ESB **2.** Ivan Lendl **3.** Denver Broncos **4.** France **5.** Schalke **6.** Melvin Patton **7.** Edith Maguire **8.** 1976 Winter Olympics at Innsbruck **9.** Boston Bruins **10.** High Top **11.** Vijay Singh **12.** Bobby George **13.** Essex **14.** Mark Wildman **15.** Detroit Pistons.

POP

1. Which group had a 1998 hit with *Kung Fu Fighting*, featuring Carl Douglas?
2. Which Canadian singer/songwriter released the 1999 album *Whereabouts*?
3. Which singer released the albums *Imperial Bedroom* and *Trust*?
4. Which Swedish group had a Top 10 single in 1998 with *Life is a Flower*?
5. In which country was singer Engelbert Humperdinck born?
6. With which single did Abba have a No. 1 in both the UK and the US?
7. Which Scottish group recorded the 1998 Scotland World Cup song *Don't Come Home Too Soon*?
8. Which single by the Spice Girls entered at No. 1 in the singles chart in December 1998?
9. Which female singer had a hit single in 1969 with *Walk on Gilded Splinters*?
10. Which group recorded the albums *Wild Honey* and *Smiley Smile*?
11. Who recorded the album *Oedipus Schmoedipus*?
12. Who recorded the album *Odelay!*?
13. From which country does singer Youssou N'Dour come?
14. Which act had a 1998 hit with the single *Paradise City*?
15. From which European country do duo A.D.A.M. featuring Amy come?

ANSWERS **1.** Bus Stop **2.** Ron Sexsmith **3.** Elvis Costello **4.** Ace of Base **5.** India **6.** Dancing Queen **7.** Del Amitri **8.** Goodbye **9.** Marsha Hunt **10.** The Beach Boys **11.** Barry Adamson **12.** Beck **13.** Senegal **14.** N-Trance **15.** France.

WORDS

1. What type of animal is a kob?
2. What does LCD stand for in electrical equipment?
3. What is the part of the body called the lumbus also known as?
4. When in Russia would you eat zakuski - before or after the main dish?
5. What sort of creature is a whippoorwill?
6. What would you do with orts - wear them or eat them?
7. What sort of animal is a kulan?
8. What number does the letter L represent in Roman numerals?
9. What in cricket is a long-hop?
10. What, in Australia and New Zealand, is a zambuck?
11. What would you do with waragi - fry it or drink it?
12. 'An old parrot does not mind the stick' is the Latin equivalent of which proverb?
13. What is the name given to a piece of music opening a concert?
14. What in the theatre is an 'oyster part'?
15. What sort of creature is a leghorn?

ANSWERS **1.** An antelope **2.** Liquid Crystal Display **3.** Loin **4.** Before - they are hors d'oeuvres **5.** A bird **6.** Eat them - they're scraps **7.** Wild ass **8.** 50 **9.** An easily hit short-pitched ball **10.** A St. John ambulance attendant **11.** Drink it - it is an alcoholic drink **12.** You can't teach an old dog new tricks **13.** Overture **14.** An actor who appears or speaks only once **15.** A domestic fowl.

GENERAL KNOWLEDGE

1. In which European country is the region of Graubünden?
2. Who won Member to Watch award at the 1991 Parliamentarian of the Year luncheon?
3. Who won Pipe Smoker of the Year award in 1988?
4. What is the island of Fernando Po now called?
5. What sort of creature is a cisco - a bird or a fish?
6. In which year was a controversial glass pyramid erected in the forecourt of the Louvre art gallery?
7. Who is the hero of the novel *Kidnapped* by R.L. Stevenson?
8. Which saint was the first English martyr?
9. The Chianti mountain range is in which mountain group?
10. Ameslan is a communications system. Of what is the word a corruption?
11. What nationality was orchestral conductor Eugen Jochum?
12. Who was Muse of History in Greek mythology?
13. Which model at Madame Tussauds was voted Hero of Entertainment in 1984?
14. To whom did the Crime Writers' Association award the Diamond Dagger in 1989?
15. What is the approximate area of Easter Island in square miles - 32, 64 or 128?

ANSWERS 1. Switzerland **2.** David Mellor **3.** Ian Botham **4.** Bioko **5.** Fish **6.** 1989 **7.** David Balfour **8.** St. Alban **9.** Apennines **10.** American sign language **11.** German **12.** Clio **13.** Boy George **14.** Dick Francis **15.** 64.

ENTERTAINMENT

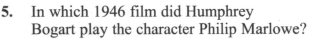

1. In which 1993 film did Julia Roberts play the character Darby Shaw?

2. What is Arnold Schwarzenegger's character name in the film *Total Recall*?

3. Who directed the 1987 Britflick *Wish You Were Here*?

4. In which of his films does Alfred Hitchcock appear in a class reunion photo?

5. In which 1946 film did Humphrey Bogart play the character Philip Marlowe?

6. Who plays Momma in the 1987 film comedy *Throw Momma from the Train*?

7. Who plays Athos in the 1973 film *The Three Musketeers*?

8. In which 1998 film does Robert Redford play the character Tom Booker?

9. In which year did the television show *thirtysomething* begin in the US?

10. Who played telephone operator Chris Cross in the television drama *The Hello Girls*?

11. In which country was the actress Charlize Theron born?

12. In which 1959 film did Marilyn Monroe play the character Sugar Kane?

13. Who directed the 1987 film *Three Men and a Baby*?

14. In which 1969 film does Michael Caine play the character Charlie Croker?

15. Who plays Eric, a viking, in the 1958 film *The Vikings*?

ANSWERS 1. The Pelican Brief **2.** Doug Quaid **3.** David Leland **4.** Dial M For Murder **5.** The Big Sleep **6.** Anne Ramsey **7.** Oliver Reed **8.** The Horse Whisperer **9.** 1987 **10.** Letitia Dean **11.** South Africa **12.** Some Like It Hot **13.** Leonard Nimoy **14.** The Italian Job **15.** Tony Curtis.

SPORT

1. In which year did footballer Brian Clough win his two caps for England?
2. On which Scottish loch was motor racing driver John Cobb killed in 1952?
3. What was unusual about Henri Cochet's 1927 Wimbledon men's singles title win?
4. From which university did Sebastian Coe get a degree in economics?
5. Which Chinese diver became the first woman to score over 600 points in a springboard competition in 1988?
6. When was the only European Championship final in football to result in a replay?
7. Which New York Yankees baseball star was known as 'Old Reliable'?
8. In which year did Watford finish runners-up to Liverpool in Division One?
9. Who won the 1967 Belgian motor racing Grand Prix?
10. Who finished first in the women's 200m final at the 1995 IAAF World Championships but was later disqualified?
11. Who won the 1995 County Cricket Championship?
12. At what age did figure skater Cecilia Colledge appear in the 1932 Winter Olympics?
13. Which British speedway rider won the 1976 World Individual championship?
14. What age was gymnast Nadia Comaneci when she competed at the 1976 Montreal Olympics?
15. With which baseball team did Earle Combs play his entire career, from 1924-35?

ANSWERS **1.** 1959 **2.** Loch Ness **3.** He came back from two sets down in the quarter finals, semis and final **4.** Loughborough **5.** Gao Min **6.** 1968 **7.** Tommy Henrich **8.** 1983 **9.** Dan Gurney **10.** Gwen Torrence **11.** Warwickshire **12.** 11 **13.** Peter Collins **14.** 14 **15.** New York Yankees.

POP

1. What was Dave Angel's minor hit single in 1997?
2. Which single reached No.1 in the U.S. and U.K. for Foreigner?
3. Who recorded the album *Hard Nose the Highway*?
4. Which actor had a 1962 Top 20 single with *Love Me Tender*?
5. Which singer had a 1969 Top 10 single with *Good Morning Starshine*?
6. Which U.S. group had a 1991 Top 40 hit with *The King is Half Undressed*?
7. Which male singer had a 1997 Top 40 single with *Golden Brown*?
8. Which group had a minor hit in 1995 with the single *I Hate Rock 'N' Roll*?
9. Which act had a 1998 Top 10 hit with the song *Kung Fu*?
10. Which rapper had a 1997 Top 40 single with *You Can't Stop the Reign*?
11. What was Italian vocalist Drupi's first UK hit single?
12. Which group had a 1997 hit with *Toxygene*?
13. Which group had a 1996 hit with *Walking on the Milky Way*?
14. What was the title of Mark Morrison's 1996 No.1 single?
15. Which group had 1997 Top 10 singles with *Satan* and *The Saint*?

ANSWERS **1.** Tokyo Stealth Fighter **2.** I Want to Know What Love is **3.** Van Morrison **4.** Richard Chamberlain **5.** Oliver **6.** Jellyfish **7.** Omar **8.** Jesus and Mary Chain **9.** 187 Lockdown **10.** Shaquille O'Neal **11.** Vado Via **12.** The Orb **13.** Orchestral Manoeuvres in the Dark **14.** Return of the Mack **15.** Orbital.

SCIENCE

1. Whose work in synthesizing DDT won him the 1948 Nobel prize for medicine?
2. In the Mohs scale of hardness what is No. 7?
3. Who authored 1988's *A Brief History of Time?*
4. What is the name given to a rock fragment between 0.2 and 2.3 inches in diameter?
5. Which element has the atomic number 50?
6. In which year did astronomer Edmund Halley die?

7. What is the melting point of plutonium in °C?
8. Who discovered carbolic acid in 1834?
9. A hyper arid area is one which experiences no rainfall in a 12 month period. Approximately what percentage of the world's land area is hyper arid?
10. What in chemistry does HPLC stand for?
11. Which element's symbol is Ho?
12. In which century did Dutch mathematician Christiaan Huygens live?
13. What is the name given to the point on the Earth's surface directly above the focus of an earthquake?
14. Which English physician discovered vaccination?
15. Which dinosaur's name derived from the phrase 'earthquake lizard'?

ANSWERS **1.** Paul Muller **2.** Quartz **3.** Stephen Hawking **4.** A pebble **5.** Tin **6.** 1742 **7.** 640° **8.** Friedlieb Runge **9.** 6% **10.** High performance liquid chromatography **11.** Holmium **12.** 17th **13.** Epicentre **14.** Edward Jenner **15.** Seismosaurus.

GENERAL KNOWLEDGE

1. On which London Underground line is the station of Maida Vale?
2. In poker, when dealt the initial five cards, what are the odds of having a full house?
3. In which year was the space mission Early Bird launched?
4. Which King of Norway began the conversion of the country to Christianity?
5. What is the English name of the constellation whose Latin name is *Circinus*?
6. Which unit of distance in navigation is equal to one tenth of a sea mile?
7. Who wrote the 2000 novel *Cardiff Dead*?
8. In which year did Hurricane Joan hit the Caribbean?
9. What is the state flower of Utah, U.S.A.?
10. Who was the 1978 Commonwealth men's 10,000m champion?
11. What do the initials VHS stand for?
12. Which Scottish burgh is the birthplace of scientist Sir Alexander Fleming?
13. Who is the heroine of Shakespeare's play *As You Like It*?
14. Which cyclist won the 1987 Giro d'Italia?
15. In which continent would you encounter the wind known as a pampero?

ANSWERS 1. Bakerloo **2.** 694-1 **3.** 1965 **4.** Olaf I **5.** Compasses **6.** A cable **7.** John Williams **8.** 1988 **9.** Sego lily **10.** Brendan Foster **11.** Video home system **12.** Darvel **13.** Rosalind **14.** Stephen Roche **15.** South America.

ENTERTAINMENT

1. What is Grace Jones' character name in the 1985 film *A View To A Kill*?
2. Who plays Al Capone in the 1987 film *The Untouchables*?
3. In which mid-1960s television series was the phrase 'Open Channel D' often heard?
4. In which of his films does Alfred Hitchcock appear boarding a train with a double bass?
5. In which 1955 film did Humphrey Bogart play the character Glenn Griffin?
6. In which 1987 film did Madonna play the character Nikki Finn?
7. In which 1962 film did Peter Sellers play the character Pearly Gates?
8. In which 1951 film does Alec Guinness play the character Sidney Stratton?
9. Who plays Captain Nemo in the 1954 film *20,000 Leagues Under the Sea*?
10. Who won the Emmy award for Outstanding Lead Actress in a Comedy Series for 1988-9?
11. In which of his films does Alfred Hitchcock appear sitting on a bus next to Cary Grant?
12. What is Clint Eastwood's actress daughter, who featured in the 1984 movie *Tightrope*, called?
13. Who plays 'Cyclops' in the film *X-Men*?
14. Who directed the 1992 film *Bad Lieutenant*?
15. Who directed the 1983 film *Yentl*?

ANSWERS 1. May Day **2.** Robert De Niro **3.** The Man from U.N.C.L.E. **4.** Strangers on a Train **5.** The Desperate Hours **6.** Who's That Girl? **7.** The Wrong Arm of the Law **8.** The Man in the White Suit **9.** James Mason **10.** Candice Bergen **11.** To Catch A Thief **12.** Alison **13.** James Marsden **14.** Abel Ferrera **15.** Barbra Streisand.

SPORT

1. Which swimmer won the 1984 Olympic men's 100m and 200m backstroke?
2. Who scored San Marino's goal in their 1993 football World Cup qualifier against England?
3. How many African teams were at the 1994 football World Cup finals?
4. Who won the 1st Test in the 1993 cricket series between Australia and New Zealand?
5. In which year was Billie-Jean King born?
6. Which motor racing driver's sister, Pat, did rally star Erik Carlsson marry in 1964?
7. In which year did heavyweight boxing champion Primo Carnera die?
8. At what weight was Georges Carpentier world champion from 1920 to 1922?
9. Who was 1964 Olympic men's 200m champion?
10. Which team did Sheffield United beat 3-0 to win the 1915 FA Cup final?
11. Who won the 1993 Nat West Trophy in cricket?
12. Which rider won the 1998 Badminton horse trials?
13. Which Middlesex cricketer is known as 'Bloodaxe'?
14. Which horse won the 1996 1,000 Guineas?
15. How many times did Wigan rugby league player Kenneth Gee play for England?

ANSWERS **1.** Rick Carey **2.** Davide Gualtieri **3.** Three **4.** It was a draw **5.** 1943 **6.** Stirling Moss **7.** 1967 **8.** Light-heavyweight **9.** Henry Carr **10.** Chelsea **11.** Warwickshire **12.** Chris Bartle **13.** Mark Ramprakash **14.** Bosra Sham **15.** 33.

POP

1. Which female vocalist featured on Paul Anka's 1974 hit *(You're) Having My Baby*?
2. Which group had a 1998 No.1 single with *Freak Me*?
3. Which group had a 1997 hit with *North Country Boy*?
4. Which U.K. group had chart success in 1996 with *Not So Manic Now*?
5. Which group had a minor hit in 1998 with *Iloverocknroll*?
6. Which single by the Four Tops reached No.1 in the U.K. and U.S.?
7. Which group had a 1976 hit single with *Sunshine Day*?
8. Who had a 1996 No.1 single with *Jesus to a Child*?
9. In which year was Donny Osmond born?
10. Which duo had a 1992 No.1 hit with *Would I Lie To You*?
11. With which song did Simply Red have a No.1 single in 1995?
12. Which group scored a chart hit in 1995 with a cover of the song *White Lines (Don't Do It)*?
13. In which year was singer Gilbert O'Sullivan born?
14. What was Rickie Lee Jones' only hit single?
15. Which group recorded the 1993 album *There is No-one What Will Take Care of You*?

ANSWERS 1. Odia Coates **2.** Another Level **3.** The Charlatans **4.** Dubstar **5.** The Jesus and Mary Chain **6.** Reach Out I'll Be There **7.** Osibisa **8.** George Michael **9.** 1957 **10.** Charles and Eddie **11.** Fairground **12.** Duran Duran **13.** 1946 **14.** Chuck E's in Love **15.** The Palace Brothers.

PEOPLE

1. Who became manager of Celtic FC in 2000?
2. In which year was singer-actress Kylie Minogue born?
3. Which actress married the film director Louis Malle in 1980?
4. Whose debut novel was entitled *The Last Samurai*?
5. Dinah Manoff is the actress daughter of which actress?
6. Who became president of Russia in 1991?
7. Which French philosopher's works include 1951's *Waiting for God*?
8. What was the forename of Mr. Wells, who co-founded the Wells, Fargo & Company express mail service?
9. Which actress married rock star Freddy Moore at the age of 18?
10. What was the profession of actress Sandra Bullock's mother Helga?
11. Who was the leader of the Liberal Democrat party in Britain from 1988-99?
12. Who was the German designer of the Volkswagen car?
13. Who was the 1980 world matchplay golf champion?
14. Who was Canadian prime minister from 1980-84?
15. In which year was supermodel Kate Moss born?

ANSWERS 1. Martin O'Neill **2.** 1968 **3.** Candice Bergen **4.** Helen DeWitt **5.** Lee Grant **6.** Boris Yeltsin **7.** Simone Weil **8.** Henry **9.** Demi Moore **10.** Opera singer **11.** Paddy Ashdown **12.** Ferdinand Porsche **13.** Greg Norman **14.** Pierre Trudeau **15.** 1974.

GENERAL KNOWLEDGE

1. What is the melting point of terbium?
2. What is the state flower of South Carolina, U.S.A.?
3. On which London Underground line is the station of Pimlico?
4. Which card in the game of poker is nicknamed a fishhook?
5. In which year was the Torrey Canyon oil disaster?
6. What is a Notre-Dame Pick-Me-Up?
7. Who directed the 1946 film *Brief Encounter*?
8. In which year was the Australian space mission WRESAT launched?
9. What was the duration of the manned space mission Gemini VII in 1965?
10. On what day of the week was Christmas Day 1996?
11. HI is the zip code of which state in the USA?
12. What is the English name of the constellation whose Latin name is *Columba*?
13. Who rules in a pantisocracy?
14. Who was a British gold medal winner at the 2000 Olympics in the men's double trap shooting event?
15. Who won the Best Director Oscar for his debut film at the helm with *Dances With Wolves*?

ANSWERS 1. 1356ºC **2.** Yellow jessamina **3.** Victoria **4.** Jack **5.** 1967 **6.** A cocktail **7.** David Lean **8.** 1967 **9.** 330 hr 35 min **10.** Wednesday **11.** Hawaii **12.** Dove **13.** Everyone **14.** Richard Faulds **15.** Kevin Costner.

ENTERTAINMENT

1. Who is the male lead in the 1946 film *The Yearling*?
2. Which singer plays LaBoeuf in the 1969 film *True Grit*?
3. In which 1958 film did Paul Newman play Brick Pollitt?
4. Who played Juror No. 6 in the 1957 film *12 Angry Men*?
5. Who played Jackie Conner Harris in the sitcom *Roseanne*?
6. In which of his films did Alfred Hitchcock appear mailing a letter at a village postbox?
7. In which 1974 film did Peter Sellers play Queen Victoria?
8. In which 1987 film did Arnold Schwarzenegger play the character Ben Richards?
9. Which two regular voice artists on the cartoon show *The Simpsons* appeared in the 1990s sitcom *Herman's Head*?
10. Who did Danny Most play in the sitcom *Happy Days*?
11. In which film did Michael Caine play the character Lt. Gonville Bromhead?
12. Who played D'Artagnan in the 1979 film *The Fifth Musketeer*?
13. In which Benjamin Britten opera does the aria *Tickling a Trout, Poaching a Hare* feature?
14. *My Favourite Orkan* was a 1978 episode of which sitcom?
15. Who played Heathcliff and Cathy in the 1939 film version of *Wuthering Heights*?

ANSWERS 1. Gregory Peck **2.** Glen Campbell **3.** Cat on a Hot Tin Roof **4.** Ed Binns **5.** Laurie Metcalf **6.** Suspicion **7.** The Great McGonagall **8.** The Running Man **9.** Hank Azaria and Yeardley Smith **10.** Ralph Malph **11.** Zulu **12.** Cornel Wilde **13.** Albert Herring **14.** Happy Days **15.** Laurence Olivier and Merle Oberon.

SPORT

1. In which US state is the Preakness Stakes horse race run?
2. Which Australian state side did cricketer Richie Benaud captain from 1955-64?
3. Stellan Bengtsson won the 1971 world singles table tennis title. Which country did he represent?
4. In which city was former world light-welterweight champion boxer Wilfred Benitez born?
5. Which Italian boxer won the 1960 Olympic welterweight title?
6. How many caps did England rugby union player William Wavell-Wakefield win for his country?
7. Which English football team lost in the 1966 European Cup Winners' Cup final?
8. Irene de Kok was women's light-heavyweight judo champion in 1986 and '87. Which country did she represent?
9. Which Mexican man won the 1994 and '95 New York Marathon?
10. What did Nick Faldo score in the first round of the 1999 US Masters golf tournament?
11. Which horse won the Oaks in 1997?
12. Who was 1998 Wimbledon women's singles tennis champion?
13. Who won rugby union's European Cup in the 1997/98 season?
14. Which British women's basketball team were league champions from 1996-98?
15. Who led Pakistan to victory in the 1992 cricket World Cup?

ANSWERS 1. Maryland **2.** New South Wales **3.** Sweden **4.** New York **5.** Nino Benvenuti **6.** 31 **7.** Liverpool **8.** Netherlands **9.** German Silva **10.** 80 **11.** Reams of Verse **12.** Jana Novotna **13.** Bath **14.** Sheffield Hatters **15.** Imran Khan.

POP

1. What was Stevie Wonder's only 1973 Top 10 single?
2. Who recorded the 1998 album *Voice of an Angel?*
3. Nina Persson is lead singer with which group?
4. Which child star had a 1974 hit with *Ma, He's Making Eyes at Me?*
5. Who had a 1975 hit single with *Sending out an S.O.S.?*
6. The video for whose single, *Temper Temper*, was banned in 1998 by the BBC?
7. Which Radio One disc jockey was awarded the OBE in June 1998?
8. Whose debut solo album was *Unfinished Monkey Business?*
9. Which group backed Dave Edmunds on the 1981 single *The Race is On?*
10. From which European country do Technotronic originate?
11. What was the only U.K. hit, in 1964, of Helmut Zacharias?
12. Which Australian vocalist had a Top 10 hit in 1978 with *Love is in the Air?*
13. Who recorded the 1998 album *What Another Man Spills?*
14. Which U.S. singer drowned in the Mississippi River in June 1997?
15. What was Womack and Womack's 1988 Top 10 single?

ANSWERS 1. You are the Sunshine of my Life **2.** Charlotte Church **3.** The Cardigans **4.** Lena Zavaroni **5.** Retta Young **6.** Goldie **7.** John Peel **8.** Ian Brown **9.** Stray Cats **10.** Belgium **11.** Tokyo Melody **12.** John Paul Young **13.** Lambchop **14.** Jeff Buckley **15.** Teardrops.

ART AND LITERATURE

1. In which year did the artist Giovanni Paolo Panini die?
2. Which of the four wings of the National Gallery in London houses paintings from 1600-1700?
3. Which artist's works include the 1898 painting *Faa Iheihe*?
4. Which Cuban author wrote the 2000 book *Outcast*?
5. Who is the writer mother of author Carlo Gébler?
6. At which London art gallery did the *Ant Noises 2* exhibition open in 2000?
7. In which year did the painter Jean-Honoré Fragonard die?
8. Who painted the 1875 work *Mr. and Mrs. Edwin Edwards*?
9. On which floor of the Louvre in Paris is the Watteau Room, first or second?
10. Where in England is the Admiral Blake Museum?
11. At which London art establishment was the 2000 exhibition called *Apocalypse*?
12. Whose art works include 1995's *Horror At Home* which is in the form of a giant ashtray?
13. In which century did the painter Thomas Gainsborough live?
14. In which year did the Van Gogh Museum in Amsterdam open?
15. Which 17th century artist's works include *A Winter Scene with Skaters near a Castle*?

ANSWERS **1.** 1765 **2.** North Wing **3.** Paul Gauguin **4.** José Latour **5.** Edna O'Brien **6.** Saatchi gallery **7.** 1806 **8.** Fantin-Latour **9.** Second **10.** Bridgwater **11.** Royal Academy **12.** Damien Hirst **13.** 18th century **14.** 1973 **15.** Hendrick Avercamp.

GENERAL KNOWLEDGE

1. What colour are the trunk and branches of the ghost gum tree?
2. What does the abbreviation IFF mean in military parlance?
3. What shape is a converging meniscus lens?
4. In which year did France last recapture Calais from England?
5. In which year was the horse Shergar stolen?
6. Which actress became Greek minister of culture in 1985?
7. Which French chef was known as 'The King of Cooks'?
8. What is the international car registration for Cyprus?
9. In which county is the town of Gillingham?
10. In what year was the storming of the Bastille?
11. Hg is the symbol of which element?
12. Which military leader was known as the 'Corsican ogre'?
13. In what year was the St. Valentine's Day massacre?
14. Who was born first - John Lennon or Yoko Ono?
15. What type of clothing was an acton in medieval Europe?

ANSWERS 1. White **2.** Identification, Friend or Foe? **3.** Crescent-shaped **4.** 1558 **5.** 1983 **6.** Melina Mercouri **7.** Escoffier **8.** CY **9.** Kent **10.** 1789 **11.** Mercury **12.** Napoleon **13.** 1929 **14.** Yoko Ono **15.** A jacket or jerkin.

ENTERTAINMENT

1. What was the 1947 sequel to the 1934 film *The Thin Man*?
2. Who plays Doug Roberts in the 1974 film *The Towering Inferno*?
3. What is Dorothy's surname in the film *The Wizard of Oz*?
4. Who did the actor Paul Ford play in television's *The Phil Silvers Show*?
5. In which 1988 film does Michael Caine play the character Lawrence Jamieson?
6. In which 1960 film does Jack Nicholson play Wilbur Force?
7. What is Tia Carrere's character name in the 1992 film *Wayne's World*?
8. Who play Gudrun and Ursula Brangwen in the 1969 film *Women in Love*?
9. The comedians Hope and Keen are sons of which comedians?
10. Who played the children's entertainer Uncle Sammy in the sitcom *Hi-de-Hi!*?
11. In which 1971 film does Jack Nicholson play Jonathan Fuerst?
12. In which 1946 film does Alec Guinness play Herbert Pocket?
13. What is Dan Aykroyd's character name in the 1983 film *Trading Places*?
14. In which Verdi opera do the characters Foresto, Odabella and Ezio appear?
15. Who played Juror No. 9 in the 1957 film *12 Angry Men*?

ANSWERS 1. Song of the Thin Man **2.** Paul Newman **3.** Gale **4.** Colonel Hall **5.** Dirty Rotten Scoundrels **6.** The Little Shop of Horrors **7.** Cassandra **8.** Glenda Jackson and Jennie Linden **9.** Syd and Max Harrison **10.** Kenneth Connor **11.** Carnal Knowledge **12.** Great Expectations **13.** Louis Winthorpe III **14.** Attila **15.** Joseph Sweeney.

SPORT

1. Who in 1992 won both the Tour de France and the Giro d'Italia?
2. Who did Chelsea defeat in the 1971 European Cup Winners' Cup final?
3. Who won the men's 800m at the 1987 and '91 IAAF World Championships?
4. What was the nickname of England rugby union player C.H. Pillman?
5. Which team won the 1994 Benson & Hedges Cup in cricket?
6. In which year did French rugby union player Pierre Berbizier make his international debut?
7. For which motor racing team did Gerhard Berger drive from 1990-92?
8. For which team did baseball player Yogi Berra play in 14 World Series?
9. In which year was footballer George Best born?
10. Which female tennis player won the 1946 Wimbledon & US singles tennis titles?
11. In which year was the Davis Cup first competed for?
12. In which American state was golfer Ben Hogan born?
13. With what sport would you associate Pat Pocock?
14. What distinction did boxer Henry Armstrong achieve in 1938?
15. What is the nationality of snooker player Kirk Stevens?

ANSWERS 1. Miguel Indurain **2.** Real Madrid **3.** Billy Konchellah **4.** Cherry **5.** Warwickshire **6.** 1981 **7.** McLaren **8.** New York Yankees **9.** 1946 **10.** Pauline Betz **11.** 1900 **12.** Texas **13.** Cricket **14.** He was the first man to hold three world titles at different weights at the same time **15.** Canadian.

POP

1. Which male duo had a novelty hit in 1975 with their spoof of the song *If?*
2. On which record label do B*Witched record?
3. Rob Pilatus died in 1998. With which group did he achieve notoriety?
4. What was Barbra Streisand's first UK Top 20 single?
5. Only one of the Top 10 singles by The Wombles refrained from using the words 'Womble' or 'Wombling'. What was it?
6. Which US dance group featured on Teenage Fan Club's 1994 single *Fallin?*
7. Which female vocalist recorded the 1969 album *Postcard?*
8. Who recorded the 1998 album *Moon Safari?*
9. Of which group is Ben Ottewell a member?
10. What was country star Faron Young's only Top 10 UK single?
11. Which female singer featured on 1987 single *The Rhythm Divine* by Yello?
12. Who is the female vocalist with the group Catatonia?
13. Who recorded the 1998 album *This is Hardcore?*
14. Which group recorded the 1975 Top 20 single *Why Did You Do It?*
15. Which female singer recorded the 1998 album *Is This Desire?*

ANSWERS 1. Yin and Yan **2.** Epic **3.** Milli Vanilli **4.** Second Hand Rose **5.** Banana Rock **6.** De La Soul **7.** Mary Hopkin **8.** Air **9.** Gomez **10.** It's Four in the Morning' **11.** Shirley Bassey **12.** Cerys Matthews **13.** Pulp **14.** Stretch **15.** P.J. Harvey.

GEOGRAPHY

1. In which country is the rice-growing town of Budge-Budge?
2. Lanzarote and Tenerife belong to which island group?
3. In which English county is the picturesque village of Clovelly?
4. In which European country is the village of Blenheim, scene of a 1704 battle?
5. Monta Rosa, the highest mountain in the Pennine Alps, is on the border between which two countries?
6. In which country is the seaport of Aden?
7. In which county of the Republic of Ireland is Arklow?
8. On which of North America's Great Lakes does the city of Buffalo stand?
9. Carson City is the capital of which US state?
10. Which strait connects the Sea of Marmara with the Aegean Sea?
11. Bridgeport is the largest city in which U.S. state?
12. Buganda is a province of which African country?
13. Castries is the capital of which West Indies island?
14. Vienna and Belgrade lie on the banks of which river?
15. On which Scottish island are the Cuillin Hills?

ANSWERS 1. India **2.** The Canary Islands **3.** Devon **4.** Germany **5.** Switzerland and Italy **6.** Yemen **7.** Wicklow **8.** Lake Erie **9.** Nevada **10.** Dardanelles **11.** Connecticut **12.** Uganda **13.** St. Lucia **14.** River Danube **15.** Skye.

GENERAL KNOWLEDGE

1. Which U.S. financier and diplomat won the 1925 Nobel peace prize?
2. Who was the Roman goddess of fortune?
3. In which year was the Penny Post introduced?
4. From which country did the US buy Florida?
5. On which island would you find the animal called an indris?
6. What does RADAR stand for?
7. Of what number is 30 the square root?
8. What monarch is found on a Penny Black stamp?
9. In what year was Harrods founded?
10. In what year was the Jarrow hunger march?
11. Camoodi is a Caribbean name for which snake?
12. What is the name of the woollen fabric which covers a billiard table?
13. What was the name of the half man/half fish god worshipped by the Philistines in the Bible?
14. Who played the third television *Doctor Who?*
15. Who is James Bond's service chief?

ANSWERS 1. Charles Dawes **2.** Fortuna **3.** 1840 **4.** Spain **5.** Madagascar **6.** Radio detection and ranging **7.** 900 **8.** Queen Victoria **9.** 1849 **10.** 1936 **11.** Anaconda **12.** Baize **13.** Dagon **14.** Jon Pertwee **15.** M.

ENTERTAINMENT

1. What was the 1984 sequel to the 1968 film *2001: A Space Odyssey*?
2. Who is the female lead in the 1956 film *War and Peace*?
3. Which British actress played Ann Anderson in the U.S. sitcom *House Calls*?
4. What are the surnames of *The Two Jakes* in the 1990 film of that name?
5. Which trio of actresses play *The Witches of Eastwick* in the 1987 film?
6. In which 1976 film does Robert Redford play the character Bob Woodward?
7. Who composed the opera *Ascanio in Alba*?
8. In which year did the television show *The Honeymooners* first air in the U.S.?
9. Who plays Aramis in the 1998 film *The Man in the Iron Mask*?
10. Which character sings the *Toreador Song* in Bizet's opera *Carmen*?
11. Who wrote the 1983 sitcom *The Happy Apple* which starred Leslie Ash?
12. In which 1960 film does Alec Guinness play Lt. Col. Jock Sinclair?
13. In which 2000 film does Michael Caine play the character Dr. Royer-Collard?
14. Who played John Connor in the 1991 film *Terminator 2: Judgment Day*?
15. In which 1983 film does Robert Duvall play Mac Sledge?

ANSWERS **1.** 2010 **2.** Audrey Hepburn **3.** Lynn Redgrave **4.** Gittes and Berman **5.** Cher, Susan Sarandon and Michelle Pfeiffer **6.** All the President's Men **7.** Mozart **8.** 1955 **9.** Jeremy Irons **10.** Escamillo **11.** Keith Waterhouse **12.** Tunes of Glory **13.** Quills **14.** Edward Furlong **15.** Tender Mercies.

SPORT

1. Which team won the 1974 European Cup Winners' Cup?
2. How many caps did Peter Jackson win for England at rugby union from 1956-63?
3. Which U.S. basketball team won the NBA title from 1952-54?
4. What nationality was cyclist Felice Gimondi?
5. By what score did John Lowe defeat Leighton Rees in the 1979 World Professional Darts championship?
6. Who was runner-up in the 1969 and '70 World Formula 1 motor racing championships?
7. Who won the 1996 British Open Golf Championship?
8. Which team won the World Bowl in American Football in 1996?
9. At which course was the 1997 British Open golf championship held?
10. Who did rugby league star Brian Bevan play for after his 16 years at Warrington?
11. At what field event did Udo Beyer win gold at the 1976 Olympics?
12. Which jockey won the 1967 Cheltenham Gold Cup on Woodland Venture?
13. What was unusual about the shoes Abebe Bikila wore to win the 1960 Olympic marathon?
14. In which US state was Olympic swimming champion Matt Biondi born?
15. Who was captain of the U.S. basketball 'Dream Team' at the 1992 Olympics?

ANSWERS **1.** Magdeburg **2.** 20 **3.** Minneapolis Lakers **4.** Italian **5.** 5-0 **6.** Jacky Ickx **7.** Tom Lehman **8.** Scottish Claymores **9.** Royal Troon **10.** Blackpool Borough **11.** Shot put **12.** Terry Biddlecombe **13.** Their absence - he ran barefoot **14.** California **15.** Larry Bird.

POP

1. Which studio album by Madonna features the tracks *Nobody's Perfect* and *Don't Tell Me*?
2. Who recorded the 1978 live album *TV Eye*?
3. What nationality is the rapper Peaches?
4. What album by Prefab Sprout was renamed Two Wheels Good in the US?
5. Which country artist recorded the 2000 instrumental album *Night and Day*?
6. Under what name does rapper Lawrence Parker record?
7. Which Planxty studio album includes the song *P stands for Paddy*?
8. From which U.S. state do the group The Kingsbury Manx hail?
9. In which year did the group The Chameleons form?
10. Who recorded the 1982 Top 10 album *Midnight Love*?
11. Who recorded the 1980 Top 10 album *Defector*?
12. What was the group Pink Floyd's debut single?
13. Which studio album by P.J. Harvey includes the song *C'mon Billy*?
14. Which group's first single was 1978's *Piano Lessons*?
15. Which studio album by Cinerama includes the tracks *Superman* and *Lollobrigida*?

ANSWERS **1.** Music **2.** Iggy Pop **3.** Canadian **4.** Steve McQueen **5.** Willie Nelson **6.** KRS-ONE **7.** Cold Blow and the Rainy Night **8.** North Carolina **9.** 1981 **10.** Marvin Gaye **11.** Steve Hackett **12.** Arnold Layne **13.** To Bring You My Love **14.** The Poison Girls **15.** Disco Volante.

HISTORY

1. In which year did the Klondike gold rush begin?
2. In which year was Sydney Harbour Bridge officially opened?
3. What annual event started in Islington in 1886 before moving to Olympia and Earl's Court?
4. In which year was Mary, Queen of Scots executed?
5. In which century was the Supreme Court of the U.S.A. established?
6. In which year did Friends of the Earth form?
7. In which year did work begin on the Suez Canal?
8. In which year did George II of England die?
9. In which county is Tolpuddle, home of the Tolpuddle Martyrs?
10. In which year did Prince Albert die?
11. In which year did the Korean War begin?
12. In which city was the United Nations charter signed in June 1945?
13. Paragraph 31 of the Magna Carta concerns the taking of what, without consent?
14. What was the name of the merchant who first signed the American Declaration of Independence?
15. Who became Empress of Russia in 1762?

ANSWERS 1. 1896 **2.** 1932 **3.** Crufts **4.** 1587 **5.** 18th **6.** 1971 **7.** 1859 **8.** 1760 **9.** Dorset **10.** 1861 **11.** 1950 **12.** San Francisco **13.** Wood **14.** John Hancock **15.** Catherine II.

GENERAL KNOWLEDGE

1. Who wrote the book *The Scold's Bridle*?
2. What is the state bird of Vermont in the US?
3. On which London Underground line is the station of Regent's Park?
4. In which South American country is the World Heritage site of the mining town of Potosi?
5. Which jazz musician provided the music for the film *Saturday Night and Sunday Morning*?
6. Which English royal house ruled from 1485 to 1603?
7. What is the full name of the Territorial Army?
8. Which nonmetallic element has the atomic number 52?
9. In the US, what type of vehicle is a weasel?
10. In cooking, what is the main ingredient of borsch?
11. Which was the last comedy film to win Best Picture Oscar?
12. On which novel by Roy Horniman was the film *Kind Hearts and Coronets* based?
13. In which year was the Chinese space mission Long March launched?
14. In which year did Hurricane Beulah hit Texas?
15. On what day of the week was Christmas Day 1856?

ANSWERS 1. Minette Walters **2.** Hermit thrush **3.** Bakerloo **4.** Bolivia **5.** Johnny Dankworth **6.** Tudor **7.** The Territorial and Volunteer Reserve **8.** Tellurium **9.** One with caterpillar tracks for use in the snow **10.** Beetroot **11.** Annie Hall **12.** Israel Rank **13.** 1970 **14.** 1967 **15.** Thursday.

ENTERTAINMENT

1. Who plays Porthos in the 1993 film *The Three Musketeers*?
2. Who plays the character Sam in the 1979 film *10*?
3. In which 1958 film does Alec Guinness play Gulley Jimson?
4. Which British dramatist authored the 1988 play *Shoeshine*?
5. Who composed the 1821 opera *Der Freischütz*?
6. Who played Darlene Conner in the sitcom *Roseanne*?
7. In which opera by Mussorgsky does the aria *Song of the Parrot* appear?
8. What is the middle name of Patrick Fyffe's comedy character Dame Hilda Bracket?
9. Who played Juror No. 8 in the 1957 film *12 Angry Men*?
10. In which 1980s sitcom did the newspaper *The Daily Crucible* appear?
11. In which 1993 film does Robert Redford play the character John Gage?
12. Who directed the 1987 film *The Untouchables*?
13. In which 1969 film does William Holden play the character Pike Bishop?
14. In which 1992 film does Michael Caine play the character Ebenezer Scrooge?
15. Who won the Emmy award for Outstanding Lead Actor in a Comedy Series for 1991-2?

ANSWERS **1.** Oliver Platt **2.** Julie Andrews **3.** The Horse's Mouth **4.** Arnold Wesker **5.** Carl von Weber **6.** Sara Gilbert **7.** Boris Godunov **8.** Nemone **9.** Henry Fonda **10.** Hot Metal **11.** Indecent Proposal **12.** Brian De Palma **13.** The Wild Bunch **14.** The Muppet Christmas Carol **15.** Craig T. Nelson.

SPORT

1. Who in American Football was 'the Gipper'?
2. Who won the 1998 men's hockey world cup?
3. In which year did Marc Girardelli make his Olympic debut?
4. Which French team lost the 1976 European Champions Cup final to Bayern Munich?
5. What did manager Joe McCarthy call baseball star Gabby Hartnett?
6. Which English team lost the 1976 European Cup Winners' Cup final to Anderlecht?
7. Which country are football team Deportivo La Coruna from?
8. At what sport does Mary Joe Fernandez compete?
9. Who refereed the 1993 Holland v England World Cup qualifier?
10. Who won the 16th game in the 1993 PCA World Chess championship?
11. In what sport is the Lugano Cup competed for?
12. In which year did Helsinki stage the Summer Olympic Games?
13. What nationality was tennis champion Jean Borotra?
14. Who in boxing was known as 'the Black Cloud'?
15. Who were 1988 Superbowl champions in American Football?

ANSWERS 1. George Gipp **2.** Netherlands **3.** 1988 **4.** St. Etienne **5.** The Perfect Catcher **6.** West Ham United **7.** Spain **8.** Tennis **9.** Karl-Josef Assenmacher **10.** Nigel Short **11.** Walking **12.** 1952 **13.** French **14.** Larry Holmes **15.** Washington Redskins.

POP

1. Which record provided Thin Lizzy with their highest singles chart placing?
2. Which group recorded the album *Emotional Rescue?*
3. Dennis Greaves was singer/guitarist with which early 1980s blues band?
4. Who was lead singer in the group Dead or Alive?
5. Who was bass player in The Clash?
6. How many No.1 singles did Yazoo have?
7. Which record provided punk band X-Ray Spex with their highest singles chart placing?
8. Which member of the Rolling Stones had a solo hit single with *(si si) Je suis un rock star?*
9. Which group recorded the *Shortsharpshock* EP in 1993?
10. What was the first record bought by Siouxsie Sioux, according to an interview with magazine *The Face* in 1980?
11. Which actor had a hit single in 1971 with *The Way You Look Tonight?*
12. Which song by The Jam was inspired by a poem entitled *Entertainment?*
13. How many solo No.1 singles has Stevie Wonder had?
14. Which 1973 Christmas hit featured vocal backing by, among others, the Stockland Green Bilateral School First Year Choir?
15. Who recorded 1981 album *Don't Follow Me, I'm Lost Too?*

ANSWERS **1.** Whiskey in the Jar **2.** The Rolling Stones **3.** Nine Below Zero **4.** Pete Burns **5.** Paul Simonon **6.** None **7.** Germ Free Adolescents **8.** Bill Wyman **9.** Therapy? **10.** 'ABC' by The Jackson Five **11.** Edward Woodward **12.** That's Entertainment **13.** One **14.** 'I Wish It Could Be Christmas Everyday' by Wizzard **15.** Pearl Harbour.

ART AND LITERATURE

1. Where in England is the Beecroft art gallery?
2. Which of the four wings of the National Gallery in London houses paintings from 1260-1510?
3. Who created the 1888 oil painting *Emperor Moth*?
4. In which century did the painter Eugène Fromentin live?
5. Who authored the book *Sitting Among the Eskimos*?
6. Which comedian authored the novel *Happy Now*?
7. With which field of the arts is Nicholas Grimshaw associated?
8. Which Australian is the senior art critic for *Time* magazine?
9. In which play does the character Captain Bluntschli appear?
10. Who painted the 1867/8 work *The Execution of Maximilian*?
11. In which year did the artist Guido Reni die?
12. By what name is the painter Giovanni Battista Rosso known?
13. Which artist's works include 1917's *Portrait of a Redskin*?
14. Who authored the 2000 novel *The Biographer's Tale*?
15. On which floor of the Louvre in Paris is the Boucher Room - first or second?

ANSWERS 1. Southend-on-Sea **2.** Sainsbury Wing **3.** Vincent Van Gogh **4.** 19th century **5.** Maggie Graham **6.** Charles Higson **7.** Architecture **8.** Robert Hughes **9.** Arms and the Man by George Bernard Shaw **10.** Edouard Manet **11.** 1642 **12.** Rosso Fiorentino **13.** Paul Klee **14.** A.S. Byatt **15.** Second.

GENERAL KNOWLEDGE

1. In which year did Winston Churchill die?
2. On which island was singer Freddie Mercury born?
3. What is the name of the decorated dart thrust into a bull's neck or shoulder in bullfighting?
4. What is the Jewish holiday Yom Kippur also known as?
5. What type of creature is a gilthead - a snake or a fish?
6. What is the Latin name for Switzerland?
7. What is the name of the Grand Canal in Venice?
8. How long, approximately, is Route 66?
9. In mythology, how many heads did the giant Geryon have?
10. What was the name of King Arthur's magic sword?
11. Who are the feuding families in the play *Romeo and Juliet?*
12. What was the name of the league of ten cities including Damascus established in 63 BC by Pompey?
13. What in US history was a forty-niner?
14. What is the standard monetary unit of Lesotho?
15. In which year was Imelda Marcos stabbed in Pasay City, Philippines?

ANSWERS **1.** 1965 **2.** Zanzibar **3.** Banderilla **4.** Day of Atonement **5.** Fish **6.** Helvetia **7.** Grand Canal **8.** 2,200 miles **9.** Three **10.** Excalibur **11.** Montagues and Capulets **12.** Decapolis **13.** A prospector in the 1849 California gold rush **14.** Loti **15.** 1972.

ENTERTAINMENT

1. Who played Lieutenant Barbara Duran in the US show *Operation Petticoat* from 1977-8?
2. In which year did the television show *The Man from U.N.C.L.E.* begin in the U.S.?
3. What is Sally's surname in the film *When Harry Met Sally...*?
4. What was the 1939 sequel to 1934 film *The Thin Man*?
5. In which 1987 film does Arnold Schwarzenegger play Major Alan 'Dutch' Schaefer?
6. Which actor portrays himself in the 1955 film *To Hell And Back*?
7. Which singer plays Barbara Pegg in the 1967 film *To Sir With Love*?
8. In Leonard Bernstein's opera *Candide,* is the part of the Governor of Buenos Aires sung by a bass or tenor?
9. In which 1981 sitcom did the character Zaphod Beeblebrox appear?
10. In which television show did the characters David Addison and Maddie Hayes appear?
11. How many episodes, including the pilot, were there of the sitcom *Happy Days*?
12. Who plays Athos in the 1979 film *The Fifth Musketeer*?
13. Who played Jingo Asakuma in the 1993 film *Rising Sun*?
14. In which 1955 film does Alec Guinness play Professor Marcus?
15. In which 1978 film does Jack Nicholson play the character Henry Moon?

ANSWERS 1. Jamie Lee Curtis **2.** 1964 **3.** Albright **4.** Another Thin Man **5.** Predator **6.** Audie Murphy **7.** Lulu **8.** Tenor **9.** The Hitch-Hiker's Guide To The Galaxy **10.** Moonlighting **11.** 256 **12.** José Ferrer **13.** Tia Carrere **14.** The Ladykillers **15.** Goin' South.

SPORT

1. Which country were 1980 Olympic men's basketball champions?
2. In which year was the World Professional Darts championship first held?
3. Of which country was David Houghton a Test cricket captain?
4. Who scored Leeds United's consolation goal in the 1965 FA Cup final?
5. Which team won the 1995 Benson & Hedges Cup in cricket?
6. Who won the men's 1500m title at the IAAF World Championships in 1991, '93 and '95?
7. Which Kenyan won the 1997 and '98 men's New York Marathon?
8. Which U.S. basketball team won the NBA title eight years in a row from 1958-66?
9. Who beat Rudy Hartono to win the 1975 All-England badminton championships?
10. In which year did Ray Illingworth take over as England Test cricket captain from Colin Cowdrey?
11. Which year saw the first replay in a European Cup Winners' Cup final in football?
12. Who captained Spurs to their Cup and League double of 1961?
13. In which country was French rugby union star Serge Blanco born?
14. Dutch triple jumper Jan Blankers was coach, and later husband, to which athlete?
15. Which footballer made 109 appearances for the USSR from his debut in 1972?

ANSWERS **1.** Yugoslavia **2.** 1978 **3.** Zimbabwe **4.** Billy Bremner **5.** Lancashire **6.** Noureddine Morceli **7.** John Kagwe **8.** Boston Celtics **9.** Svend Pri **10.** 1969 **11.** 1962 **12.** Danny Blanchflower **13.** Venezuela **14.** Fanny Koen **15.** Oleg Blokhin.

POP

1. Which duo had a 1990 hit with *Birdhouse in Your Soul*?
2. Which duo penned Chris Farlowe's hit *Out Of Time*?
3. Which rock singer remarked that 'the largest flying land mammal is the absent mind'?
4. Whose albums include 1979's *Squeezing Out Sparks*?
5. Which group recorded the 1980 album *Freedom Of Choice*?
6. Who was bass player in The Beatles?
7. Which actor had a No.2 single in 1987 with *Under the Boardwalk*?
8. Which guitar instrumental provided Mason Williams with a 1968 hit single?
9. Whose only U.K. hit single was 1984's *Break My Stride*?
10. How many No.1 singles has Kim Wilde had?
11. Which duo charted in 1986 with *The Skye Boat Song*?
12. Which group recorded the 1980 album *Ska'N'B*?
13. Which vocalist had a 1984 single hit with *High Energy*?
14. Which group's early singles included *Jumping Someone Else's Train*?
15. Which member of The Who recorded the solo album *Empty Glass*?

ANSWERS 1. They Might Be Giants **2.** Mick Jagger and Keith Richard **3.** Captain Beefheart **4.** Graham Parker and the Rumour **5.** Devo **6.** Paul McCartney **7.** Bruce Willis **8.** Classical Gas **9.** Matthew Wilder **10.** None **11.** Roger Whittaker and Des O'Connor **12.** Bad Manners **13.** Evelyn Thomas **14.** The Cure **15.** Pete Townshend.

SCIENCE

1. What nationality was mathematician Leonhard Euler?
2. Which scientist became an assistant to Humphry Davy in 1813?
3. Which Italian-born physicist helped test the first atomic bomb in 1943?
4. After whom is the element nobelium named?
5. Which element has the atomic number 99?
6. What is the blue variety of the mineral corundum?
7. What is the symbol for the element platinum?
8. In which century did the scientist Robert Boyle live?
9. In which year did astronomer Galileo die?
10. What nationality was astronomer Anders Celsius?
11. In which century did German physicist Hermann von Helmholtz live?

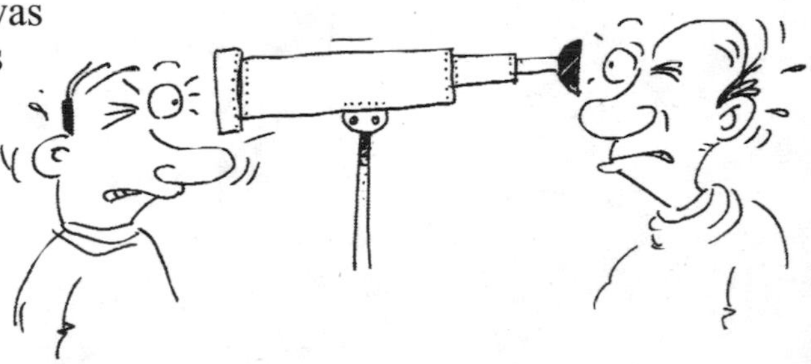

12. Which 17c French lawyer is regarded as the creator of the modern theory of numbers?
13. Which English physicist, born in 1635, formulated the law of elasticity?
14. Which 18c Scottish chemist evolved the theory of latent heat?
15. What is the Moho discontinuity?

ANSWERS 1. Swiss **2.** Michael Faraday **3.** Enrico Fermi **4.** Alfred Nobel **5.** Einsteinium **6.** Sapphire **7.** Pt **8.** 17th **9.** 1642 **10.** Swedish **11.** 19th **12.** Pierre de Fermat **13.** Robert Hooke **14.** Joseph Black **15.** The boundary between the crust and the mantle of the Earth.

GENERAL KNOWLEDGE

1. In which year did Hurricane Bob hit the north east of the USA?
2. What is the state flower of Mississippi, USA?
3. Which England bowler took 5-14 against West Indies in their second innings at Headingley in the 2000 4th Test?
4. What are the three ingredients of the cocktail called a vodka sunrise?
5. What is a téléphérique?
6. How many are there in a ternion?
7. In which year did Tel Aviv incorporate the city of Jaffa?
8. What is stretched on a frame called a tenter?
9. In the US, of which state is AK the zip code?
10. In which year was Saturn's moon Hyperion discovered?
11. What is the English name of the constellation whose Latin name is *Lacerta*?
12. WG is the international car registration for which island?
13. In which US state is Daytona Beach?
14. On which London Underground line is the station of Arsenal?
15. In which year was the Exxon Valdez oil disaster?

ANSWERS 1. 1991 **2.** Magnolia **3.** Andy Caddick **4.** Vodka, orange juice and grenadine **5.** A mountain cable car **6.** Three **7.** 1950 **8.** Cloth **9.** Alaska **10.** 1848 **11.** Lizard **12.** Grenada **13.** Florida **14.** Piccadilly **15.** 1989.

ENTERTAINMENT

1. What is Adolfo Celi's character name in the film *Thunderball*?
2. Who plays King Agamemnon in the 1980 film *Time Bandits*?
3. In which 1999 film does Kevin Costner play the character Garret Blake?
4. Who played Juror No. 7 in the 1957 film *12 Angry Men*?
5. In which 1942 film do Spencer Tracy and Katharine Hepburn play Sam Craig and Tess Harding?
6. Who plays the character Jenny in the 1979 film *10*?
7. Who composed the 1735 opera *Alcina*?
8. In which 1992 film does Jack Nicholson play Col. Nathan R. Jessup?
9. In which 1994 film does Arnold Schwarzenegger play Dr. Alex Hesse?
10. Who played the male and female leads in the 1959 film version of *The 39 Steps*?
11. In which year did the television show *Northern Exposure* begin in the US?
12. What was the name of the family dog in the sitcom *Empty Nest*?
13. Who plays Captain Nemo in the 1969 film *Captain Nemo and the Underwater City*?
14. Who are the two male leads in the 1954 film *White Christmas*?
15. In which 1966 film did Peter Sellers play the character Doctor Pratt?

ANSWERS 1. Emilio Largo **2.** Sean Connery **3.** Message in a Bottle **4.** Jack Warden **5.** Woman of the Year **6.** Bo Derek **7.** Handel **8.** A Few Good Men **9.** Junior **10.** Kenneth More & Taina Elg **11.** 1990 **12.** Dreyfuss **13.** Robert Ryan **14.** Bing Crosby and Danny Kaye **15.** The Wrong Box.

SPORT

1. Who was world rallying champion in 1984?
2. By what score did Valencia beat Arsenal on penalties in the 1980 European Cup Winners' Cup final?
3. Which US basketball team won the NBA title from 1996-98?
4. Who retained her US Open tennis singles title in 1955?
5. Which horse won the Oaks in 1998?
6. Who was Wimbledon women's singles tennis champion in 1997?
7. In which year did Geoff Hurst sign as a professional for West Ham United?
8. Which cyclist won the Tour de France three times in a row from 1953-5?
9. In which US state was Olympic figure skating champion Brian Boitano born?
10. Which golfer won the British Amateur title three times in a row, 1968-70?
11. On which island was Australian Test cricketer David Boon born?
12. Which horse won the 1993 Melbourne Cup?
13. Which game was patented in the year 1874 under the name of Sphairistike?
14. Who won the 1993 Skoda Snooker Grand Prix?
15. Who won the 1993 Madrid Open in golf?

ANSWERS 1. Stig Blomqvist **2.** 5-4 **3.** Chicago Bulls **4.** Doris Hart **5.** Shahtoush **6.** Martina Hingis **7.** 1959 **8.** Louis Bobet **9.** California **10.** Michael Bonallack **11.** Tasmania **12.** Vintage Crop **13.** Lawn tennis **14.** Peter Ebdon **15.** Des Smyth.

POP

1. Who recorded the 1986 album *Deep in the Heart of Nowhere*?
2. Which US vocalist's albums include *Breakaway* and *Water Mark*?
3. Which US vocalist recorded the albums *I Want You* and *Let's Get It On*?
4. Which group recorded the 1965 album *Ferry Cross the Mersey*?
5. Which member of the Gibb family recorded the 1984 solo album *Now Voyager*?
6. Who recorded the 1980 album *Never Forever*?
7. Which group recorded the 1979 single *Where's Captain Kirk?*?
8. Which group were Kevin Rowland and Al Archer in prior to Dexy's Midnight Runners?
9. What was Wham's first No.1 single?
10. Who had a 1987 Top 40 single with *Ba-Na-Na-Bam-Boo*?
11. Which guitarist reached the Top 10 singles chart in 1959 with *Guitar Boogie Shuffle*?
12. Which group had a Top 30 single in 1984 with *The Lion's Mouth*?
13. Which solo male singer hit the charts in 1964 with *Boys Cry*?
14. Which comic actor had a 1953 Top 10 hit with *Wonderful Copenhagen*?
15. Who recorded 1959 No.1 single *Here Comes Summer*?

ANSWERS 1. Bob Geldof **2.** Art Garfunkel **3.** Marvin Gaye **4.** Gerry and the Pacemakers **5.** Barry **6.** Kate Bush **7.** Spizz Energi **8.** The Killjoys **9.** Wake Me Up Before You Go Go **10.** Westworld **11.** Bert Weedon **12.** Kajagoogoo **13.** Eden Kane **14.** Danny Kaye **15.** Jerry Keller.

PEOPLE

1. Which television cook married Juliette Norton in June 2000?
2. How old was comedian Kenneth Horne when he died in 1969?
3. Which French general was commander in chief of the Allied armies in France in 1940?
4. Who in the New Testament was the father of the apostles James and John?
5. Which German meteorologist is regarded as the originator of the theory of continental drift?

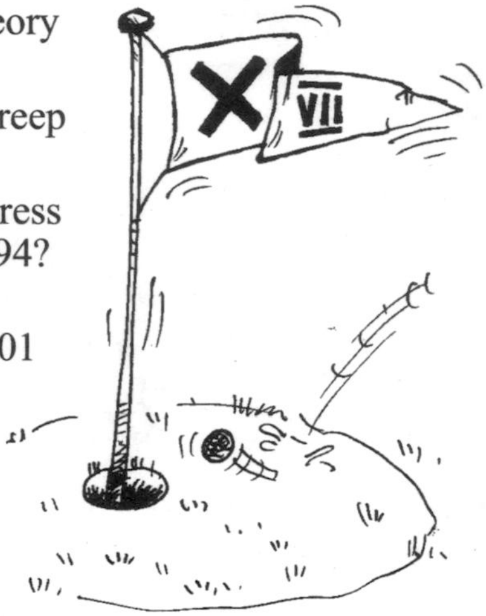

6. In which year was actress Meryl Streep born?
7. At which unusual venue did the actress Gillian Anderson get married in 1994?
8. Which actress's $3m Beverly Hills mansion caught fire in February 2001 with her and fiance Tom Green inside?
9. What is the name of the son of singer Madonna and film director Guy Ritchie?
10. What did actor Michael Madsen's father do for a living?
11. Who was chancellor of West Germany from 1982-90?
12. In which year was the singer Elvis Presley drafted into the army?
13. Who was 1980 and 1984 Olympic men's 1500m champion?
14. Which stand-up comedian's real name is Royston Vasey?
15. Who has written the books *An Evil Cradling* and *Turlough*?

ANSWERS **1.** Jamie Oliver **2.** 61 **3.** Maxime Weygand **4.** Zebedee **5.** Alfred Wegener **6.** 1949 **7.** The 17th hole of a golf course in Hawaii **8.** Drew Barrymore **9.** Rocco **10.** He was a firefighter **11.** Helmut Kohl **12.** 1958 **13.** Sebastian Coe **14.** Roy 'Chubby' Brown **15.** Brian Keenan.

GENERAL KNOWLEDGE

1. What type of food is badderlocks?
2. What is the name given to the nest or hollow where a hare lives?
3. In which year did Louis Bleriot first cross the English Channel by aeroplane?
4. What is Ido?
5. How many U.S. presidents have had George as their first name?
6. Who was the chief character in Johnny Speight's *Till Death Us Do Part?*
7. In which year was Julius Caesar assassinated?
8. Which king authored 1604's *A Counterblast to Tobacco?*
9. Where is the Sea of Rains?
10. Which U.S. journalist authored 1919 book *The American Language?*
11. Which island was once called Van Diemen's Land?
12. Which element's symbol is Md?
13. Which cartoonist created the strip *Peanuts?*
14. Which religious figure is carried on the gestatorial chair?
15. What would you do with a callop - eat it or ride in it?

ANSWERS 1. Seaweed **2.** A form **3.** 1909 **4.** An artificial language **5.** Two **6.** Alf Garnett **7.** 44 B.C. **8.** James I **9.** The moon **10.** H.L. Mencken **11.** Tasmania **12.** Mendelevium **13.** Charles Schulz **14.** The pope **15.** Eat it - it's an edible fish.

ENTERTAINMENT

1. In which the 1994 film did Kim Basinger play the character Carol McCoy?
2. What was the name of the character played by Harrison Ford in the 1992 film *Patriot Games*?
3. What was the name of the character played by Steve McQueen in the 1960 film *The Magnificent Seven*?
4. How many episodes of the television show *Gilligan's Island* were made for television?
5. Who plays Maverick in the 1986 film *Top Gun*?
6. In which the 1960 film does Alec Guinness play the character Jim Wormold?
7. In which year did the television show *Get Smart* premiere on U.S. television?
8. Who played Lily Bart in the 2000 film *The House of Mirth*?
9. Who played Christine Keeler in the 1989 film *Scandal*?
10. In which the 1973 film does Robert Redford play the character Hubbell Gardner?
11. Who composed the opera *Andrea Chénier*?
12. Who played Juno Skinner in the 1994 film *True Lies*?
13. Who plays D'Artagnan in the 1973 film *The Three Musketeers*?
14. In which the 1985 film does Arnold Schwarzenegger play the character Col. John Matrix?
15. In which the 1957 film did Peter Sellers play the character Percy Quill?

ANSWERS 1. The Getaway **2.** Jack Ryan **3.** Vin **4.** 98 **5.** Tom Cruise **6.** Our Man In Havana **7.** 1965 **8.** Gillian Anderson **9.** Joanne Whalley-Kilmer **10.** The Way We Were **11.** Umberto Giordano **12.** Tia Carrere **13.** Michael York **14.** Commando **15.** The Smallest Show on Earth.

SPORT

1. In which town was Tony Jacklin born?
2. With which sport do you associate Jack Kramer?
3. For which modern Olympics was the flame first carried from Greece?
4. Whose first winner as an amateur jockey in 1986 was Gulfland?
5. In which year was the first British motor racing Grand Prix held?
6. For which Cup did 'Magic' compete with 'Cambria' in 1870?
7. Who beat Romania 51-0 in their first rugby union game of 1993/4?
8. Who was women's world Open judo champion from 1980-86?
9. Who won rugby league's Challenge Cup in 1998?
10. Which man won the New York Marathon from 1980-82?
11. Who were runners-up from 1986-88 in the British men's basketball league?
12. How many times did Bill Beaumont captain England rugby union side?
13. Which German football league club did Franz Beckenbauer play for from 1980-2?
14. Who was the first German winner of the Wimbledon men's singles tennis championship?
15. In which city was 1970's distance runner David Bedford born?

ANSWERS **1.** Scunthorpe **2.** Tennis **3.** 1936 **4.** Princess Anne **5.** 1926 **6.** The America's Cup **7.** France **8.** Ingrid Berghmans **9.** Sheffield Eagles **10.** Alberto Salazar **11.** Kingston **12.** 21 **13.** Hamburg **14.** Boris Becker **15.** London.

POP

1. What was R & J Stone's 1976 hit single?
2. Rebecca Storm's 1985 single *The Show* was the theme tune of which T.V. series?
3. Of which group is Bobby Gillespie a member?
4. Which group's hit singles include 1980's *Bear Cage* and *Who wants the world?*
5. Which instrumental group charted in 1963 with *Wipe Out?*
6. Which duo had a hit in 1963 with the song *Deep Purple?*
7. Which group had Top Ten hits with *The Dean and I* and *Wall Street Shuffle?*
8. What was the title of Justin Hayward and John Lodge's 1975 hit L.P.?
9. What was the alliterative 1975 No.1 single of the Bay City Rollers?
10. Which group had a 1990 No. 1 single with *Dub be good to me?*
11. Bedrocks charted in 1968 with which song by the Beatles?
12. Who is the lead singer of the band Garbage?
13. Who recorded the 1998 album *Mezzanine?*
14. *16 Bars* was the last Top Ten single, in 1976, for which vocal group?
15. After their 1967 No.1 *Massachusetts*, the Bee Gees charted with similarly titled songs. What were they called?

ANSWERS 1. We do it **2.** Connie **3.** Primal Scream **4.** The Stranglers **5.** The Surfaris **6.** Nino Tempo and April Stevens **7.** 10 c.c. **8.** Blue Jays **9.** Bye Bye Baby **10.** Beats International **11.** Ob-la-di, Ob-la-da **12.** Shirley Manson **13.** Massive Attack **14.** The Stylistics **15.** 'World', and 'Words'.

ART AND LITERATURE

1. Which comedian authored the novel *King of the Ants*?
2. In which museum and art gallery is Francisco Guardi's *The Doge on the Bucentaur at the Venice Lido on Ascension day* housed?
3. Where in England is the Abbot Hall art gallery?
4. Which artist had a professorship at Düsseldorf Academy in 1933?
5. Who authored the 1797 novel *The Italian*?
6. Who authored the 1815 play *Paul Pry*?
7. About what is the poem *O the Chimneys* by Nelly Sachs?
8. Who authored the children's book *Shadow of the Minotaur*?
9. In which year did writer Ian McEwan first attend the University of East Anglia?
10. Which German painter's works include *The Abbey in the Oak Wood*?
11. In which year did the artist Goya die?
12. Which religious leader is floored by a meteor in Maurizio Cattelan's sculpture *La Nona Ora*?
13. In which century did the English poet Coventry Patmore live?
14. Who wrote the novels *Tara Road* and *Circle of Friends*?
15. Which comedienne has authored the novel *Whistling for the Elephants*?

ANSWERS **1.** Charles Higson **2.** The Louvre **3.** Kendal, Cumbria **4.** Paul Klee **5.** Ann Radcliffe **6.** John Poole **7.** Nazi extermination camps **8.** Alan Gibbons **9.** 1970 **10.** Caspar David Friedrich **11.** 1828 **12.** The Pope **13.** 19th century **14.** Maeve Binchy **15.** Sandi Toksvig.

GENERAL KNOWLEDGE

1. Who was the 2000 U.S. Open men's singles tennis champion?
2. Who were the winners of the 2000 County Championship in cricket?
3. In which country is the Effelsberg Radio Telescope?
4. In which year was the Lexell comet first seen?
5. In the U.S.A., what is the state flower of Vermont?
6. Who was the Roman god of boundaries?
7. Edward Sapir is an anthropologist noted for his studies of which group of people?
8. In which year did the former Conservative Party politician Enoch Powell die?
9. Who was the 1980 Olympic men's 100m champion?
10. How many legs does a teapoy have?
11. What does a tensimeter measure?
12. Of which state of the U.S.A. is GA the zip code?
13. On what day of the week was Christmas Day, 1978?
14. Who won Best Director Oscar for their debut film at the helm with *Ordinary People*?
15. Who was the twin brother of Jacob in the Old Testament?

ANSWERS 1. Marat Safin **2.** Surrey **3.** Germany **4.** 1770 **5.** Red clover **6.** Terminus **7.** North American Indians **8.** 1998 **9.** Allan Wells **10.** Three **11.** Differences in vapour pressure **12.** Georgia **13.** Monday **14.** Robert Redford **15.** Esau.

ENTERTAINMENT

1. In which the 1950 film did Marilyn Monroe play the character Angela Phinlay?
2. Who plays D'Artagnan in the 1948 film *The Three Musketeers*?
3. Which child actress made her big screen debut as Margaret Jessup in the 1980 film *Altered States*?
4. Which musical instrument did Meryl Streep learn to play for her role in the 1999 film *Music of the Heart*?
5. In which the 1969 film does Jack Nicholson play George Hanson?
6. In which the 1951 film does Alec Guinness play the character Holland?
7. In which the 1984 film did Kim Basinger play the character Memo Paris?
8. Who play Josef and Maria Tura in the 1942 film *To Be Or Not To Be*?
9. In which the 1996 film does Kevin Costner play the character Roy McAvoy?
10. Who played Juror No. 1 in the 1957 film *12 Angry Men*?
11. What was the name of the character played by Harrison Ford in the 1973 film *American Graffiti*?
12. What salary did Demi Moore earn for the film *G.I. Jane*?
13. In which year did the television show *The Brady Bunch* premiere on U.S. television?
14. Who played Lord Rustless in the 1969 sitcom *Hark At Barker*?
15. In which Berlioz opera does the character Fieramosca appear?

ANSWERS 1. The Asphalt Jungle **2.** Gene Kelly **3.** Drew Barrymore **4.** Violin **5.** Easy Rider **6.** The Lavender Hill Mob **7.** The Natural **8.** Jack Benny and Carole Lombard **9.** Tin Cup **10.** Martin Balsam **11.** Bob Falfa **12.** $11m **13.** 1969 **14.** Ronnie Barker **15.** Benvenuto Cellini.

SPORT

1. Which male won the badminton singles at the 1972 Olympics when it was a demonstration sport?
2. How many caps did David Duckham win for England at rugby union?
3. Who was men's British Open squash champion 1958-61?
4. With which club side did French footballer Alain Giresse end his career?
5. By what score did Dennis Priestley beat Eric Bristow in the 1991 World Professional Darts Championship?
6. Which club won the world bowl in American Football in 1997?
7. Who was the 1998 U.S. Open golf champion?
8. Which club lost the 1981 European Cup Winners' Cup Final?
9. Which woman was 1979 World Student 100m champion?
10. How many runs did cricketer Neil Harvey score in his 79 Tests for Australia from 1948-63?
11. Who won the men's 800m event at the 1995 & '97 IAAF World Championships?
12. Who was the first Indian bowler to take 200 Test wickets?
13. What was cricketer Alec Bedser's twin brother called?
14. Who was 1986 European Footballer of the Year?
15. Which New Zealander won the 1984 World Outdoor Singles title at bowls?

ANSWERS **1.** Rudy Hartono **2.** 36 **3.** Azam Khan **4.** Marseille **5.** 6-0 **6.** Barcelona Dragons **7.** Lee Janzen **8.** Carl Zeiss Jena **9.** Marlies Göhr **10.** 6149 **11.** Wilson Kipketer **12.** Bishen Bedi **13.** Eric **14.** Igor Belanov **15.** Peter Belliss.

POP

1. Which group recorded the album *Good Morning Spider?*
2. On which record label did The *Sugarcubes* record 1992 hit *Hit?*
3. What was the title of Five Star's 1986 No.1 album?
4. On which record label was Fleetwood Mac's 1968 album *Fleetwood Mac* released?
5. Who recorded the 1984 album *How Men Are?*
6. Which group recorded 1986 album *London 0 Hull 4?*
7. Which singer recorded 1980 L.P. *The Up Escalator?*
8. Frantz, Weymouth, Harrison, Byrne - which group?
9. Which group recorded the 1980 album *Sandinista?*
10. What was Freddie Bell and the Bellboys' only U.K. single hit?
11. What was trumpet player Eddie Calvert's second No.1 single?
12. Who had a 1986 Top Ten single with *Word Up?*
13. In which year was *Happy Talk* a No.1 single for Captain Sensible?
14. Whose Top Ten singles include 1988's *Circle in the Sand* and *I Get Weak?*
15. Which group recorded the 1998 album *Celebrity Skin?*

ANSWERS 1. Sparklehorse **2.** One Little Indian **3.** Silk and Steel **4.** Blue Horizon **5.** Heaven 17 **6.** The Housemartins **7.** Graham Parker **8.** Talking Heads **9.** The Clash **10.** Giddy-up-a-ding-dong **11.** Cherry Pink and Apple Blossom White **12.** Cameo **13.** 1982 **14.** Belinda Carlisle **15.** Hole.

GEOGRAPHY

1. Umnak and Unimak are part of which American island group?
2. Tehran, the capital of Iran, is at the foot of which group of mountains?
3. Which river separates the Isle of Thanet from the English mainland?
4. In which country is the Teutoburger Wald mountain range?
5. In which European country is the port of Velsen?
6. In which South American country is the city of Temuco?
7. Which African river joins the Bomu River to form the Ubangi?
8. Which U.S. river is formed by the confluence of the Seneca and Tugaloo Rivers in South Carolina?
9. Of which province of the Netherlands is Middelburg the capital?
10. The Teton Range of mountains lies mainly in which state of the U.S.?
11. What was capital of Spanish Morocco from 1912-56?
12. Bozcaada is the modern Turkish name for which Aegean island?
13. Which county of the Republic of Ireland lies between Longford and Monaghan?
14. Which island is the largest in the Alexander Archipelago in S.E. Alaska?
15. Which U.S. state's capital is Bismarck?

ANSWERS **1.** Aleutian Islands **2.** The Elburz Mountains **3.** Stour **4.** Germany **5.** The Netherlands **6.** Chile **7.** Uele **8.** Savannah **9.** Zeeland **10.** Wyoming **11.** Tetuan **12.** Tenedos **13.** County Cavan **14.** Prince of Wales Island **15.** North Dakota.

GENERAL KNOWLEDGE

1. In which year was Jean-Paul Marat assassinated?
2. Who did William Shakespeare marry in 1582?
3. Who was born first - Laurel or Hardy?
4. In which year did inventor John Logie Baird die?
5. In radio terminology what does the abbreviation CW stand for?
6. In which U.S. state is Fort Lauderdale?
7. What is ghee?
8. LS is the abbreviation for which postcode area?
9. On November 27, 1970, Pope Paul VI was nearly attacked by a knifeman in which airport?
10. What is the standard monetary unit of Laos?
11. Where in Hampshire is the National Motor Museum?
12. Who invented the Kenwood Chef electric food mixer?
13. Who wrote the novel *Absalom, Absalom!?*
14. What is the name of the scientific study of sound and sound waves?
15. Which poet authored *The Cotter's Saturday Night?*

ANSWERS 1. 1793 **2.** Anne Hathaway **3.** Laurel **4.** 1946 **5.** Continuous waves **6.** Florida **7.** Clarified butter used in Indian cookery **8.** Leeds **9.** Manila **10.** Kip **11.** Beaulieu **12.** Ken Wood **13.** William Faulkner **14.** Acoustics **15.** Robert Burns.

ENTERTAINMENT

1. In which year did the television show *Twin Peaks* begin in the U.S.?
2. In which opera by Leonard Bernstein is the aria *I Will Be Assimilated*?
3. Who plays Porthos in the 1973 film *The Three Musketeers*?
4. In which the 1996 film does Robert Redford play the character Warren Justice?
5. Who composed the 1709 opera *Agrippina*?
6. In which year did the television show *Mission: Impossible* begin in the U.S.?
7. What was the name of the character played by Steve McQueen in the 1971 film *Le Mans*?
8. In which film did Meryl Streep play the character Kate Mundy?
9. In which the 1969 film did Peter Sellers play the character Sir Guy Grand?
10. In which the 1955 film did Cary Grant play the character John Robie?
11. In which the 1996 film does Arnold Schwarzenegger play U.S. Marshal John Kruger?
12. What were the forenames of the stand-up comedians Hope and Keen?
13. Which character sings the aria *Lieben, Hassen, Hoffen, Zagen* in Richard Strauss's opera *Ariadne auf Naxos*?
14. Who won the Emmy award for Outstanding Lead Actress in a Comedy Series for 1989-90?
15. In which the 1993 film did Drew Barrymore play the character Bjergen Kjergen?

ANSWERS 1. 1990 **2.** Candide **3.** Frank Finlay **4.** Up Close & Personal **5.** Handel **6.** 1966 **7.** Michael Delaney **8.** Dancing at Lughnasa **9.** The Magic Christian **10.** To Catch A Thief **11.** Eraser **12.** Mike and Albie **13.** Harlequin **14.** Candice Bergen **15.** Wayne's World 2.

SPORT

1. Which United States threesome won the 1993 Dunhill Cup in golf?
2. Which teams competed in the 1993 baseball World Series?
3. In which year was athlete Carl Lewis born?
4. Which horse won the 1984 Irish Derby?
5. At what weight was Chris Finnegan Olympic boxing champion in 1968?
6. Who was 1960 Olympic men's 100m champion?
7. Which man won the 1984 and '85 New York Marathon?
8. What did the Rumbelows League Cup in football become in 1993?
9. Which team won the 1993 Benson & Hedges Cup in cricket?
10. Which British women's basketball team were runners-up in the league in 1997 & '98?
11. What was New Zealand rugby union player Sid Going's middle name?
12. Who rode 1998 Epsom Derby-winning horse High-Rise?
13. Who was 1996 Wimbldeon men's singles tennis champion?
14. Who won the Five Nations championship in rugby union in 1998?
15. Who knocked out Yum Dong-Kyun in 1977 to win the WBC super-bantamweight boxing title?

ANSWERS **1.** Payne Stewart, John Daly & Fred Couples **2.** Toronto Blue Jays and Philadelphia Phillies **3.** 1961 **4.** El Gran Senor **5.** Middleweight **6.** Armin Hary **7.** Orlando Pizolato **8.** Coca-Cola Cup **9.** Derbyshire **10.** Thames Valley Ladies **11.** Milton **12.** Olivier Peslier **13.** Richard Krajicek **14.** France **15.** Wilfredo Gomez.

POP

1. Which group recorded the 2000 album *Relationship of Command*?
2. Which single by The Police namechecks the writer Nabokov?
3. Which group, led by John McLaughlin, recorded the 1972 album *Birds of Fire*?
4. Which group recorded the 2000 album *Museum of Imaginary Animals*?
5. Who recorded the 1980 album *Soldier*?
6. Which group recorded the album *The Good, the Bad and the Funky*?
7. In which year did Don McLean have a No. 1 single with the song *Crying*?
8. Who recorded the 1989 Top Ten album *Electric Youth*?
9. What was the first Top Ten album in the U.K. for the group Fairport Convention?
10. Which duo recorded the 2000 album *Maroon*?
11. Which country artist recorded the 2000 album *Red Dirt Girl*?
12. Which group backed Jimmy Page on the album *Live At The Greek*?
13. Who produced the 1991 album *Seamonsters* by The Wedding Present?
14. Which singer-songwriter had a 1987 Top Five single with *(Something Inside) So Strong*?
15. Which group recorded the 1981 Top Ten album *Hit 'n' Run*?

ANSWERS 1. At the Drive-In **2.** Don't Stand So Close To Me **3.** The Mahavishnu Orchestra **4.** Pram **5.** Iggy Pop **6.** Tom Tom Club **7.** 1980 **8.** Debbie Gibson **9.** Angel Delight **10.** The Webb Brothers **11.** Emmylou Harris **12.** The Black Crowes **13.** Steve Albini **14.** Labi Siffre **15.** Girlschool.

HISTORY

1. In which century did Samuel de Champlain discover and name Lake Champlain, U.S.A.?
2. In which year did publishing company Simon and Schuster print the first book of crossword puzzles?
3. In which year did Oliver Cromwell become Lord Protector?
4. In which year was the Boston Tea Party?
5. Which king of France initiated the War of the Devolution in 1667?
6. In which year did the Crimean War end?
7. In which year was the South Sea Bubble financial crisis?
8. In which year was Queen Victoria proclaimed Empress of India?
9. In which year was Robert Devereux, 2nd Earl of Essex, beheaded?
10. Which French politician formed the National Front in 1972?
11. In which year was the 'Popish Plot'?
12. In which U.S. state was Abraham Lincoln born?

13. Which U.S. zoologist, author of *Gorillas in the Mist*, was found murdered in 1985?
14. Which queen of Henry VIII was imprisoned in the Tower of London in May 1536?
15. In which year did the War of the Spanish Succession begin?

ANSWERS **1.** 17th **2.** 1924 **3.** 1653 **4.** 1773 **5.** Louis XIV **6.** 1856 **7.** 1720 **8.** 1877 **9.** 1601 **10.** Jean-Marie Le Pen **11.** 1678 **12.** Kentucky **13.** Dian Fossey **14.** Anne Boleyn **15.** 1701.

GENERAL KNOWLEDGE

1. In which town is Keele University?
2. Who assassinated prime minister Spencer Perceval in 1812?
3. On which part of the body would you wear a ghillie?
4. Where in Dorset is there a museum housing 300 tanks?
5. In which year was the Battle of Marengo?
6. How old was Buddy Holly when he died?
7. Which U.S. president was present at the Yalta Conference?
8. Calpe was the ancient name for which limestone promontory?
9. How old was Frank Sinatra when he died?
10. In which year was Indian film producer Ismail Merchant born?
11. Costa Smeralda is a resort area of which Mediterranean island?
12. Of which country is 'Waitangi Day' the national day?
13. Who wrote the letter *De Profundis* to Lord Alfred Douglas?
14. Which imaginary country features in *The Prisoner of Zenda?*
15. Which U.S. state is nicknamed the 'Diamond State'?

ANSWERS 1. Newcastle under Lyme **2.** John Bellingham **3.** On the foot - it is a shoe **4.** Bovington Camp **5.** 1800 **6.** 22 **7.** Franklin D. Roosevelt **8.** Rock of Gibraltar **9.** 82 **10.** 1936 **11.** Sardinia **12.** New Zealand **13.** Oscar Wilde **14.** Ruritania **15.** Delaware.

ENTERTAINMENT

1. Who composed 1830 comic opera *Fra Diavolo?*
2. Which Australian comedian scripted and starred in 1990 film *Almost an Angel?*
3. What is the real name of comic Harry Hill?
4. Who did Laurence Naismith play in T.V. show *The Persuaders!?*
5. What was voted Best Film at the 1971 Cannes Film Festival?
6. Who played Simon Harrap in 1980's sitcom *Me & My Girl?*
7. Who directed 1974 film *The Cars That Ate Paris?*
8. What was Gail's maiden name in *Coronation Street?*
9. What nationality is composer Keith Humble?
10. Who played Jo Grant in T.V. show *Doctor Who?*
11. Which comedian was born Bob Davies in Birmingham in 1945?
12. Who directed 1940 film *The Philadelphia Story?*
13. Who directed 1990 film *The Grifters?*
14. Who plays *Expresso Bongo* in a 1959 film?
15. Which actor played Tom Chance in sitcom *Chance in a Million?*

ANSWERS **1.** Daniel Auber **2.** Paul Hogan **3.** Matthew Hall **4.** Judge Fulton **5.** The Go-Between **6.** Richard O'Sullivan **7.** Peter Weir **8.** Potter **9.** Australian **10.** Katy Manning **11.** Jasper Carrott **12.** George Cukor **13.** Stephen Frears **14.** Cliff Richard **15.** Simon Callow.

SPORT

1. Which horse won the 1955 Epsom Derby?
2. Who was the French Open men's singles tennis champion in 1969?
3. In which country were the 1984 European Championships in football held?
4. Which football team won the 1998/9 European Cup-Winners' Cup?
5. Who won the Olympic men's 400m in 1948?
6. What were the names of the polar bears who were the official mascots of the 1988 Winter Olympics at Calgary?
7. Who won the Olympic women's 400m in 1980?
8. Which team won Super Bowl XVIII in American Football in 1984?
9. Who was the 1976 world freshwater fishing champion?
10. What nationality was the 1959 world archery champion Stig Thysell?
11. Who scored two goals in the 1978 football World Cup Final?
12. Who did Nottingham Forest beat in the 1979 European Cup Final?
13. Who were English Football League champions in 1929 and 1930?
14. What nationality is boxer Antonio Diaz?
15. Which country won the 1992 Thomas Cup in badminton?

ANSWERS 1. Phil Drake **2.** Rod Laver **3.** France **4.** Lazio **5.** Arthur Wint **6.** Hidy and Howdy **7.** Marita Koch **8.** Los Angeles Raiders **9.** Dino Bassi **10.** Swedish **11.** Mario Kempes **12.** Malmo **13.** Sheffield Wednesday **14.** Mexican **15.** Malaysia.

POP

1. Who recorded the 1998 album *There's Something Going On?*
2. From which country did band Sutlans of Ping F.C. hail?
3. Which group recorded 1980 album *Strange Boutique?*
4. Who produced the album *End of the Century* by the Ramones?
5. Which group recorded 1980 album *Sound Affects?*
6. What was the name of Madonna's 1998 album?
7. Who duetted on 1979 hit single *No More Tears (Enough is Enough)?*
8. Which artist recorded 1981 hit single *Bette Davis Eyes?*
9. How many U.K. No.1 singles did The Carpenters have?
10. Who scored a 1978 Top ten single with *Do it do it again?*
11. David Cassidy's 1973 No. 1 *Daydreamer* was a double A-side with which song?
12. Who recorded the 1983 album *North of a Miracle?*
13. Which entertainer had a hit with *Little White Berry* in 1960?
14. Which entertainer had a hit with *Little White Bull* in 1959'?
15. Who recorded the song collection *10 Bloody Marys and 10 How's Your Fathers?*

ANSWERS 1. Babybird **2.** Ireland **3.** The Monochrome Set **4.** Phil Spector **5.** The Jam **6.** Ray of Light **7.** Donna Summer and Barbra Streisand **8.** Kim Carnes **9.** None **10.** Raffaella Carra **11.** The Puppy Song **12.** Nick Heyward **13.** Roy Castle **14.** Tommy Steele **15.** Elvis Costello.

WORDS

1. What in Russia is a kibitka?
2. Lactic refers to which liquid?
3. What ancient Roman unit of weight corresponded to a pound?
4. Which board game derives its name from the Latin 'I play'?
5. What sort of creature is a wobbegong - a shark or a bird of prey?
6. What is the Greek word for finger-nail?
7. What is a kier?
8. What would you do with laksa in Malaysia - eat it or drink it?
9. What sort of creature is a limpkin?
10. What is the sixth letter in the Greek alphabet?
11. What is the wildebeest also known as?
12. What nickname was given to Sir Robert Peel when Chief Secretary for Ireland between 1812-1818?
13. What, in Islam, is the word for the will of Allah?
14. What would you do with langoustine - paint with it or eat it?
15. Which type of pasta is named after the Italian phrase 'small tongues'?

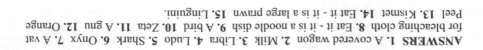

ANSWERS **1.** A covered wagon **2.** Milk **3.** Libra **4.** Ludo **5.** Shark **6.** Onyx **7.** A vat for bleaching cloth **8.** Eat it - it is a noodle dish **9.** A bird **10.** Zeta **11.** A gnu **12.** Orange Peel **13.** Kismet **14.** Eat it - it is a large prawn **15.** Linguini.

GENERAL KNOWLEDGE

1. Who was the 1981 & 1982 Australian Open men's singles tennis champion?

2. In which century were the Texas Rangers originally formed?

3. When was V-E Day?

4. What sort of bird is a verdin?

5. Of which of the United States of America is WY the zip code?

6. In which year was Pluto's moon Charon discovered?

7. Where might you wear a terai?

8. In which year was the space mission Explorer 1 launched?

9. Elephant and Deception are part of which island group?

10. On what day of the week was Christmas Day, 1940?

11. In which year was the Battle of Marengo, at which Napoleon defeated the Austrians?

12. In which century was the dome of Florence cathedral built?

13. What is the 1783 Treaty of Paris also known as?

14. In which country is the Arecibo Telescope?

15. In which year was the Donati comet first seen?

ANSWERS 1. Johan Kriek **2.** 19th century **3.** May 8, 1945 **4.** A tit **5.** Wyoming **6.** 1978 **7.** On your head - it's a felt hat **8.** 1958 **9.** South Shetland Islands **10.** Wednesday **11.** 1800 **12.** 15th century **13.** The Treaty of Versailles **14.** Puerto Rico **15.** 1858.

ENTERTAINMENT

1. In which the 1992 film did Kim Basinger play the character Holly Would?
2. In which the 1981 film does Jack Nicholson play the character Frank Chambers?
3. Who plays Aramis in the 1952 film *At Sword's Point*?
4. Who played Juror No. 5 in the 1957 film *12 Angry Men*?
5. In which Benjamin Britten opera does the aria *I Am Your Spaniel* feature?
6. Which actress did Joel Schumacher briefly fire from the set of the film *St. Elmo's Fire* because of drug problems?
7. Who plays the title role in the 1967 film *Thoroughly Modern Millie*?
8. In which year did the television show *Star Trek* begin in the U.S.?
9. In which Mozart opera do the characters Despina and Dorabella feature?
10. What was Drew Barrymore's character name in the 2000 film *Charlie's Angels*?
11. What was the name of the character played by Michael Douglas in the 1997 film *The Game*?
12. What was the name of the character played by Steve McQueen in the 1972 film *The Getaway*?
13. Which television show won an Emmy in 1987-8 for Outstanding Comedy Series?
14. What is Bastienne's profession in Mozart's opera *Bastien und Bastienne*?
15. Which husband and wife star in the 1966 film *Who's Afraid of Virginia Woolf*?

ANSWERS **1.** Cool World **2.** The Postman Always Rings Twice **3.** Dan O'Herlihy **4.** Jack Klugman **5.** A Midsummer Night's Dream **6.** Demi Moore **7.** Julie Andrews **8.** 1966 **9.** Cosi fan tutte **10.** Dylan Sanders **11.** Nicholas Van Orton **12.** Carter 'Doc' McCoy **13.** The Wonder Years **14.** Shepherdess **15.** Richard Burton and Elizabeth Taylor.

SPORT

1. Who retained the WBA featherweight boxing title in September 1993?
2. Where were the 1995 IAAF World Championships held?
3. Which team won the 1997 world series in baseball?
4. Which team won the 1993 AXA Life League in cricket?
5. Who was the men's light-heavyweight judo champion in 1995 & '97?
6. In which year did racehorse trainer Gordon Richards die?
7. Which England Test cricket captain played for Southampton in the 1902 F.A. Cup Final?
8. Which horse won the 1997 St. Leger?
9. Who was the losing finalist in the world professional snooker championship from 1952-54?

10. Celtic were runners-up to Rangers in the Scottish Premier League in the 1995/96 season. In which season had they last finished in the top two?
11. Who won the Boston women's marathon from 1994-96?
12. Which country were men's world champions at coxless four rowing in 1997 & '98?
13. Who won the 1984 Olympic men's 5000m title?
14. What nationality was baseball player Luis Aparicio?
15. What fruit gave Swedish table-tennis star Mikael Appelgren his nickname?

ANSWERS **1.** Park Yung-kyun **2.** Gothenburg **3.** Florida Marlins **4.** Glamorgan **5.** Pawel Nastula **6.** 1998 **7.** C.B. Fry **8.** Silver Patriarch **9.** Walter Donaldson **10.** 1987/88 **11.** Uta Pippig **12.** Great Britain **13.** Said Aouita **14.** Venezuelan **15.** The Apple.

POP

1. Which member of the Gibb family recorded the 1978 album *Shadow Dancing*?
2. Who was lead singer with the group Sham 69?
3. Derwood and Mark Laff were members of which punk group?
4. Which group recorded 1980 album *Hypnotised*?
5. Which U.S. vocalist had a 1962 hit with *Send Me the Pillow That You Dream On*?
6. What was singer Tiny Tim's only U.K. hit single?
7. On which label did The Timelords record their No.1 *Doctorin' the Tardis*?
8. Who charted in 1987 with *The Future's So Bright I Gotta Wear Shades*?
9. Who had a hit in 1982 with *The Lion Sleeps Tonight*?
10. Which comic actor had a 1983 Christmas hit with *Christmas Countdown*?
11. Under what name did Jonathan King record 1972 hit *Loop di Love*?
12. What was the last No.1 single, in 1966, for The Kinks?
13. Which comedian had a 1968 Top Forty hit with *On Mother Kelly's Doorstep*?
14. Which fictional character did Landscape sing of in a 1981 hit?
15. Which group's 1980 hit singles included *Dance Yourself Dizzy* and *Substitute*?

ANSWERS 1. Andy **2.** Jimmy Pursey **3.** Generation X **4.** The Undertones **5.** Johnny Tillotson **6.** Great Balls of Fire **7.** KLF Communications **8.** Timbuk 3 **9.** Tight Fit **10.** Frank Kelly **11.** Shag **12.** Sunny Afternoon **13.** Danny La Rue **14.** Norman Bates **15.** Liquid Gold.

SCIENCE

1. Which is the thinnest of the earth's three crustal types - transitional, oceanic or continental?
2. During which era was the Jurassic period of geological time?
3. What is an aquifer?
4. On the Mohs scale of hardness what is No. 8?
5. What do the letters AC stand for in electrical appliances?
6. Which Hungarian-born Nobel prize winner is credited with the invention of holography?
7. What in physical geography is an erg?
8. What is the melting point in °C of carbon?
9. What is the symbol for the element actinium?
10. What is the name given to an angle of less than 90° in mathematics?

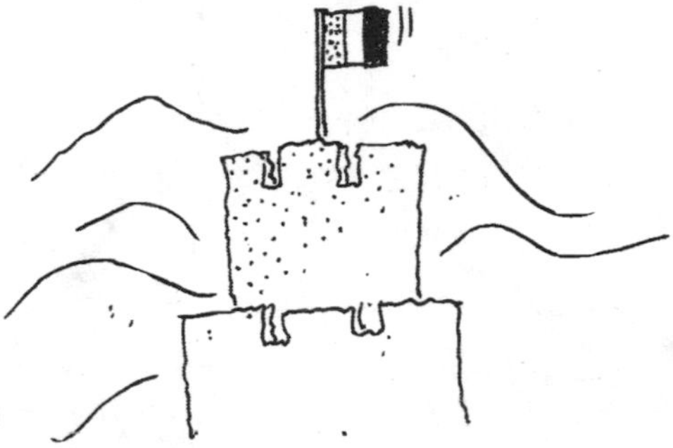

11. What in geological terms is creep?
12. Who discovered the element thorium?
13. In which year did English chemist Henry Cavendish die?
14. What is the mass of partially decomposed organic matter in soil called?
15. Which German bacteriologist, born in 1854, pioneered the science of chemotherapy?

ANSWERS **1.** Oceanic **2.** Mesozoic **3.** A stratum of rock containing water **4.** Topaz **5.** Alternating current **6.** Dennis Gabor **7.** An area of shifting sand dunes in a desert **8.** 3530 **9.** Ac **10.** Acute angle **11.** The gradual deformation of a rock by stress **12.** J.J. Berzelius **13.** 1810 **14.** Humus **15.** Paul Ehrlich.

GENERAL KNOWLEDGE

1. What is the fifth book of the New Testament?
2. In which city is the University of Essex?
3. Who authored 1977 novel *Unknown Man No. 89*?
4. On which island of Asia is the village of Bantam?
5. Who wrote the ballad *The Absent-minded Beggar*?
6. In mythology, who was the mother of Arcas?
7. Who was British prime minister 1905-8?
8. The Corbillon Cup is competed for by women at which sport?
9. Approximately how many million people in the world spoke Tamil in 1993?
10. At which castle was Mary Queen of Scots executed in 1587?
11. In which year did *Coronation Street* begin on ITV?

12. What was county town of the former county of Merioneth?
13. To which island is the bird called a mesite confined?
14. Who composed the song-cycle *Dichterliebe*?
15. What is a Sam Browne?

ANSWERS 1. Acts of the Apostles **2.** Colchester **3.** Elmore Leonard **4.** Java **5.** Rudyard Kipling **6.** Callisto **7.** Henry Campbell-Bannerman **8.** Table tennis **9.** 68 **10.** Fotheringay Castle **11.** 1960 **12.** Dolgellau **13.** Madagascar **14.** Schumann **15.** A military belt.

ENTERTAINMENT

1. In which 2000 comedy film do Renée Zellweger and Greg Kinnear star?
2. Which character is played by Julie Hesmondhalgh in the television drama *Coronation Street*?
3. In which the 1983 film did Kim Basinger play the character Domino?
4. In which the 1997 film did Julia Roberts play the character Alice Sutton?
5. Who plays D'Artagnan in the 1998 film *The Man in the Iron Mask*?
6. Who was the broadcaster husband of Esther Rantzen who died in September, 2000?
7. Who is the director of the 1997 film *The Ice Storm*?
8. In which year did the television show *The Monkees* begin in the U.S.?
9. What salary did Demi Moore earn for the film *Striptease*?
10. Who are the three main stars of television comedy sketch show *Smack the Pony*?
11. Who played Juror No. 10 in the 1957 film *12 Angry Men*?
12. In which opera by Mascagni do the characters Lola and Turiddu feature?
13. In which year did the television show *L.A. Law* premiere on U.S. television?
14. In which film did Meryl Streep play the character Francesca Johnson?
15. In which the 1994 film did Drew Barrymore play the character Lilly Laronette?

ANSWERS **1.** Nurse Betty **2.** Hayley **3.** Never Say Never Again **4.** Conspiracy Theory **5.** Gabriel Byrne **6.** Desmond Wilcox **7.** Ang Lee **8.** 1966 **9.** $12.5m **10.** Fiona Allen, Doon Mackichan and Sally Phillips **11.** Ed Begley **12.** Cavalleria Rusticana **13.** 1986 **14.** The Bridges of Madison County **15.** Bad Girls.

SPORT

1. With which sport is coach Don Shula associated?
2. Where were the 1928 Summer Olympics held?
3. In what sport is the MacRobertson Shield competed for?
4. Which sport do the San Diego Padres compete in?
5. Who captained the Australia cricket side in their 1987 World Cup win?
6. How many sets did Bjorn Borg lose in his 1976 Wimbledon singles title win?
7. How old was golfer Julius Boros when he won the 1968 USPGA?
8. Which French tennis player was known as the 'Bouncing Basque'?
9. Which England rugby union player died on May 5, 1915, killed by a sniper's bullet?
10. Who won the 1987 men's 5,000m title at the IAAF World Championships?
11. Which Briton won the 1991 women's New York Marathon?
12. Billy Hardin competed at the 1964 Olympics in the 400m hurdles. At which Olympics did his father win the same event?
13. Who were English league champions in rugby union in the 1997/98 season?
14. Who retained her U.S. Open tennis singles title in 1961?
15. What was the nickname of Canadian ice hockey star Michael Bossy?

ANSWERS 1. American Football **2.** Amsterdam **3.** Croquet **4.** Baseball **5.** Allan Border **6.** None **7.** 48 **8.** Jean Borotra **9.** Ronnie Poulton-Palmer **10.** Said Aouita **11.** Liz McColgan **12.** 1936 **13.** Newcastle **14.** Darlene Hard **15.** The Goal Machine.

POP

1. What was Lord Rockingham's XI's 1958 No. 1 single?
2. Who had a Top Twenty single in 1986 with *Amityville (The House on the Hill)*?
3. What was Paul McCartney's first solo U.K. Top Ten single?
4. Which actor and actress had a 1990 Top Five single with *Kinky Boots*?
5. In which year did Madonna have a No.1 single with *Vogue*?
6. Who recorded 1992 single *Motorcycle Emptiness*?
7. What was Pigmeat Markham's only U.K. hit single, in 1968?
8. What was the B-Side of Lee Marvin's No.1 single *Wand'rin' Star*?
9. Whose first chart single was 1984's *Get Out Of Your Lazy Bed*?
10. What was Matthews' Southern Comfort's only No.1 single?
11. Which vocal duo had a 1987 No.1 single with *Respectable*?
12. Which punk band had hit singles with *Offshore Banking Business* and *The Sound of the Suburbs*?
13. With whom did Freddie Mercury duet on 1987 single *Barcelona*?
14. Which biblical pair scored a 1972 Top 30 hit for Middle of the Road?
15. How many No.1 hit singles did The Monkees have?

ANSWERS **1.** Hoots Mon **2.** Lovebug Starski **3.** Another Day **4.** Patrick MacNee and Honor Blackman **5.** 1990 **6.** Manic Street Preachers **7.** Here Comes the Judge **8.** 'I Talk To the Trees' by Clint Eastwood **9.** Matt Bianco **10.** Woodstock **11.** Mel and Kim **12.** The Members **13.** Montserrat Caballé **14.** Samson and Delilah **15.** One.

PEOPLE

1. In which year did the painter Velasquez die?
2. In which year was the civil engineer Thomas Telford born?
3. What was the profession of painter Canaletto's father?
4. Which British women's cyclist won a bronze medal at the 2000 Olympics in the 3000m individual pursuit event?
5. Who was King of England from 1037-40?
6. Which artist won the 2000 Mercury Music Prize?
7. What is the name of the French prime minister elected in 1997?
8. Which Italian became the new coach of Chelsea F.C. in 2000?
9. In which year did the logician John Venn die?
10. In which century did the English diplomat Sir William Temple live?
11. In which year did the mountaineer Tenzing Norgay die?
12. Who was the 1988 U.S. Open men's singles tennis champion?
13. Whose wife in the New Testament was Sapphira?
14. With which field of the arts is John Quinlan Terry associated?
15. Which economist authored the 1899 work *The Theory of the Leisure Class*?

ANSWERS 1. 1660 **2.** 1757 **3.** A theatrical scene painter **4.** Yvonne McGregor **5.** Harold I **6.** Badly Drawn Boy **7.** Lionel Jospin **8.** Claudio Ranieri **9.** 1932 **10.** 17th century **11.** 1986 **12.** Mats Wilander **13.** Ananias **14.** Architecture **15.** Thorstein Veblen.

GENERAL KNOWLEDGE

1. What was English novelist Elizabeth Cleghorn Stevenson better known as?
2. What sort of crop is burley, which is grown especially in Kentucky?
3. In which year was the Battle of the Boyne?
4. What stone is associated with a 45th wedding anniversary?
5. In what year was Walt Disney born?
6. Which country's international car registration is RCH?
7. In which year did playwright Ben Travers die?
8. Which vegetable has the varieties Nevada and Canberra?
9. What line is coloured green on a London underground map?
10. Which politician was Chancellor of the Exchequer from 1947-50?
11. On what date is Flag Day in the U.S.?
12. In which country was the Auschwitz concentration camp?
13. On which river is the Indian city of Gauhati?
14. For what does the abbreviation HMSO stand?
15. Who became archbishop of Canterbury in 1945?

ANSWERS 1. Mrs. Gaskell **2.** Tobacco **3.** 1690 **4.** Sapphire **5.** 1901 **6.** Chile **7.** 1980 **8.** Cauliflower **9.** District **10.** Stafford Cripps **11.** June 14 **12.** Poland **13.** Brahmaputra **14.** His/Her Majesty's Stationery Office **15.** Geoffrey Fisher.

ENTERTAINMENT

1. Who is the assistant of Mr. Burns in the television cartoon show *The Simpsons*?
2. In which year did the television show *My Three Sons* begin in the US?
3. Which actress plays Pauline Fowler in the soap *EastEnders*?
4. Which English actor was a Best Supporting Actor Oscar nominee for the film *Rob Roy*?
5. Which actress's television roles include Ling Woo in *Ally McBeal*?
6. In which episode of the television show *The Man from U.N.C.L.E.* did William Shatner and Leonard Nimoy appear as guest stars?
7. What was the name of the character played by Michael Douglas in the 2000 film *Traffic*?
8. What was the name of the character played by Harrison Ford in the 1986 film *The Mosquito Coast*?
9. What was Drew Barrymore's character name in the 1995 film *Batman Forever*?
10. Which Hollywood actress played Jackie Templeton from 1982-3 on US soap opera *General Hospital*?
11. Who directed the 1995 film *Clueless*?
12. Who was the director of the 1974 film *Death Wish*?
13. Who were the male and female stars of the 2000 film *The Luzhin Defence*?
14. Which actress played Margaret Meldrew in the sitcom *One Foot in the Grave*?
15. Which actor played Norm in the sitcom *Cheers*?

ANSWERS 1. Smithers **2.** 1960 **3.** Wendy Richard **4.** Tim Roth **5.** Lucy Liu **6.** The Project Strigas Affair **7.** Robert Wakefield **8.** Allie Fox **9.** Sugar **10.** Demi Moore **11.** Amy Heckerling **12.** Michael Winner **13.** John Turturro and Emily Watson **14.** Annette Crosbie **15.** George Wendt.

SPORT

1. What age was Wentworth Gore when he won the 1908 Wimbledon singles title?
2. In which year did the UEFA Cup replace the Inter-Cities Fairs Cup?
3. Who was British Open men's squash champion from 1950-55?
4. Who was MVP in Superbowl XIII and XIV in American Football?
5. Who was the 1995 US Open golf champion?
6. Who was the 1998 world professional snooker champion?
7. What was baseball star Leon Allen Goslin also known as?
8. Who was All-England women's badminton champion from 1961-64?
9. Who beat Bastia 3-0 on aggregate in the 1978 UEFA Cup final?
10. Which Olympic swimming champion announced her retirement in 1973 at the age of 16 years, 9 months?
11. What was the nickname of US jockey Eddie Arcano?
12. Which Argentinian was appointed manager of Swindon Town in 1989?
13. Who was manager of Leeds United when they reached the 1975 European Cup final?
14. Who won the Lancome Trophy in golf in 1993?
15. Which boxer retained his WBO Middleweight title in September 1993?

ANSWERS **1.** 40 **2.** 1972 **3.** Hashim Khan **4.** Terry Bradshaw **5.** Corey Pavin **6.** John Higgins **7.** Goose **8.** Judy Hashman **9.** PSV Eindhoven **10.** Shane Gould **11.** Banana Nose **12.** Ossie Ardiles **13.** Jimmy Armfield **14.** Ian Woosnam **15.** Chris Pyatt.

POP

1. On which label was the single *When Will I See You Again* by the Three Degrees?
2. Which group recorded the 1980 album *Mad About the Wrong Boy*?
3. Which 2-Tone group's first single was *Away*?
4. Which group recorded the 1980 album *Do A Runner*?
5. Who recorded the 1983 LP *Duck Rock*?
6. Which member of Roxy Music recorded the album *Diamond Head*?
7. Which member of the Pixies recorded the solo album *Teenager of the Year*?
8. Which reggae band recorded the songs *Plastic Smile* and *Shine Eye Gal*?
9. What was Rufus Thomas' only Top 20 hit single?
10. Who recorded the 1999 album *Post Orgasmic Chill*?
11. Which group recorded the 1980 album *Kilimanjaro*?
12. Who was the female singer with the punk group Penetration?
13. Which group had a 1961 hit with *The Lion Sleeps Tonight*?
14. Who recorded the 1980 album *Signing Off*?
15. In which country was ska singer Laurel Aitken born?

ANSWERS 1. Philadelphia International **2.** The Attractions **3.** Swinging Cats **4.** Athletico Spizz 80 **5.** Malcolm McLaren **6.** Phil Manzanera **7.** Frank Black **8.** Black Uhuru **9.** Do the Funky Chicken **10.** Skunk Anansie **11.** The Teardrop Explodes **12.** Pauline Murray **13.** The Tokens **14.** UB40 **15.** Cuba.

ART AND LITERATURE

1. Who wrote the novel *The Burglar Who Thought He Was Bogart*?
2. Which of the four wings of the National Gallery in London houses paintings from 1510-1600?
3. Who wrote the 2000 novel *Boiling a Frog*?
4. On which floor of the Louvre in Paris is the Rembrandt Room - first or second?
5. Who wrote the 1999 novel *Something Stupid*?
6. Who wrote the book *Emerald Germs of Ireland*?
7. Which German painter's works include *The Chasseur in the Woods*?
8. Who wrote the 2000 novel *Bettany's Book*?
9. Who wrote the Whitbread-winning novel *Leading the Cheers*?
10. Which British artist's works include the 1941 painting *Hartland Point from Boscastle*?
11. Who wrote the 2000 novel *In the Shape of a Boar*?
12. Which British artist's works include the 1902 painting *The Return from the Ride*?
13. Who wrote the 2000 novel *How It Ended*?
14. Which British artist's works include the 1966 screenprint *Acrobats*?
15. Who wrote the novel *Turning Thirty*?

ANSWERS **1.** Lawrence Block **2.** West Wing **3.** Christopher Brookmyre **4.** Second **5.** Victoria Corby **6.** Patrick McCabe **7.** Caspar David Friedrich **8.** Thomas Keneally **9.** Justin Cartwright **10.** Charles Ginner **11.** Lawrence Norfolk **12.** Charles Wellington Furse **13.** Jay McInerney **14.** Ian Hamilton Finlay **15.** Mike Gayle.

GENERAL KNOWLEDGE

1. In which year was photographer David Bailey born?
2. What is the standard monetary unit of Botswana?
3. Which was founded first - Balliol College, Oxford or Magdalen College, Oxford?
4. What in Australia is a bundy?
5. Who was chief photographer of the magazine *Rolling Stone* from 1973-83?
6. Whose painting, *Woman Nude Before Garden*, was damaged in May 1999 by a Utrecht psychiatric patient?
7. What is the approximate population in millions of Cape Town - 2, 3 or 4?
8. What is Tintin's dog Snowy called in the original stories?
9. In which year was the Aberfan disaster?
10. Who wrote the absurdist play *The Cresta Run*?
11. What is the name given to the lowest temperature theoretically attainable?
12. In which county is the fishing port of Fleetwood?
13. What is the middle name of actor Dustin Hoffman?
14. In which novel by Charles Dickens does Miss Rosa Dartle appear?
15. In which year was the Battle of Flodden?

ANSWERS **1.** 1938 **2.** Pula **3.** Balliol **4.** A time clock at one's workplace **5.** Annie Liebovitz **6.** Picasso **7.** 2 million **8.** Milou **9.** 1966 **10.** N.F. Simpson **11.** Absolute zero **12.** Lancashire **13.** Lee **14.** David Copperfield **15.** 1513.

ENTERTAINMENT

1. Which serial killer film released in 2000 starred Brittany Murphy and Jay Mohr?
2. Who played Juror No. 3 in the 1957 film *12 Angry Men*?
3. Who played D'Artagnan in the 1952 film *At Sword's Point*?
4. What was the name of the character played by Harrison Ford in the 1993 film *The Fugitive*?
5. Who did Kim Basinger replace in the role of Vicki Vale in the film *Batman*?
6. Which stand-up comics were the team captains on the 2000 television debating game *Head On Comedy*?
7. Which 1999 animated film featured Miranda Richardson as the voice of Anna Leonowens?
8. Who played the title role in US sitcom *Coach*?
9. What did the alien *ALF* reveal his true name to be in the US sitcom of the same name?
10. What was the name of the character played by Michael Douglas in the 1987 film *Wall Street*?
11. In which film did Meryl Streep play the character Suzanne Vale?
12. Where is the soap opera *Coronation Street* set?
13. Which actors play television policemen *Dalziel and Pascoe* on the BBC?
14. What animal did Sandra Bullock discover she was allergic to whilst working on the film *Two if by Sea*?
15. Which actor plays the character Magneto in the 2000 film *X-Men*?

ANSWERS 1. Cherry Falls **2.** Lee J. Cobb **3.** Cornel Wilde **4.** Dr. Richard David Kimble **5.** Sean Young **6.** Bill Bailey and Ed Byrne **7.** The King And I **8.** Craig T. Nelson **9.** Gordon Shumway **10.** Gordon Gekko **11.** Postcards from the Edge **12.** Weatherfield **13.** Warren Clarke and Colin Buchanan **14.** Horses **15.** Sir Ian McKellen.

SPORT

1. Which unfashionable team lost the 1935 Scottish FA Cup final?
2. Who did John Spencer defeat in the 1969 World Professional Snooker Championship final?
3. Which country were women's quad sculls rowing world champions from 1994-98?
4. Which boxer published the autobiography *Gloves, Glory and God*?
5. At what sport was Frenchwoman Catherine Arnaud a world and European champion?
6. Which motor racing driver was killed testing a Ferrari at Monza in May 1955?
7. Which team won the 1994 AXA Life League in cricket?
8. What is former cricketer David Gower's middle name?
9. Who did Ipswich Town defeat in the 1981 UEFA Cup final?
10. What field event is Kate Staples associated with?
11. Who won the men's 200m at the 1976 Olympics?
12. The Jets and Giants represent which city in American Football?
13. In which sport did Kate Allenby win a bronze medal at the 2000 Olympics in Sydney?
14. Which England Test cricketer once shared the world record for the long jump?
15. Which horse won the 1967 Aintree Grand National?

ANSWERS 1. Hamilton Academicals **2.** Gary Owen **3.** Germany **4.** Henry Armstrong **5.** Judo **6.** Alberto Ascari **7.** Warwickshire **8.** Ivon **9.** AZ 67 Alkmaar **10.** Pole vault **11.** Don Quarrie **12.** New York **13.** Modern Pentathlon **14.** C.B. Fry **15.** Foinavon.

POP

1. Which group recorded the 1988 album *Birth School Work Death*?
2. Jackie Hamilton, Gary McAndless, Austin Barnett - which Irish pop group?
3. Which mod revival band recorded the 1980 album *Behind Closed Doors*?
4. Webb, Baillie, Jobson, Adamson - which Scottish group?
5. Which artist recorded the 1980 album *Scary Monsters and Super Creeps*?
6. Dave Barbarossa and Leigh Gorman were members of which 1980s pop group?
7. Which group recorded the albums *Glory Road* and *Future Shock*?
8. Which group recorded the 1980 LP *Black Sea*?
9. Which member of Roxy Music recorded the 1973 album *These Foolish Things*?
10. Which punk band comprised the members Vanian, Scabies, James and Sensible?
11. Who was the lead singer of the group Magazine?
12. Who recorded the LP *Too-Rye-Ay*?
13. Which group recorded the 1980 LP *Get Happy*?
14. On which studio album does Van Morrison perform *Crazy Love*?
15. On which LP did the Mekons record the song *Charlie Cake Park*?

ANSWERS **1.** The Godfathers **2.** The Moondogs **3.** Secret Affair **4.** The Skids **5.** David Bowie **6.** Bow Wow Wow **7.** Gillan **8.** X.T.C. **9.** Bryan Ferry **10.** The Damned **11.** Howard Devoto **12.** Dexy's Midnight Runners **13.** Elvis Costello and the Attractions **14.** Moondance **15.** Honky Tonkin'.

GEOGRAPHY

1. Antananarivo is the capital of which island?
2. Which mountain is also known as Monte Cervino and Mont Corvin?
3. Which is larger - Morocco or Mozambique?
4. In which country is Lake Nipissing?
5. In which European country is the copper-producing town of Rio Tinto?
6. In which ocean is the Rockall Deep submarine trench?
7. Which is the largest island of the Inner Hebrides in Scotland?
8. In which country is the ancient city of Tarsus?
9. Which African country is sandwiched between Benin and Ghana?
10. In which South American country is the port of Valparaiso?
11. In which U.S. state are the volcanoes Mauna Loa and Mauna Kea?
12. What is the capital of Mauritius?
13. Auckland is on North Island, New Zealand. True or false?
14. What is the name of the former island penal colony at the entrance of Table Bay, South Africa?
15. Which is larger - Poland or Sri Lanka?

ANSWERS 1. Madagascar **2.** Matterhorn **3.** Mozambique **4.** Canada **5.** Spain **6.** Atlantic Ocean **7.** Skye **8.** Turkey **9.** Togo **10.** Chile **11.** Hawaii **12.** Port Louis **13.** True **14.** Robben Island **15.** Poland.

GENERAL KNOWLEDGE

1. From which African country do the Temne people come?
2. In which year was the space mission Luna 1 launched?
3. In which year was Neptune's moon Proteus discovered?
4. What flavour does the liqueur amaretto have?
5. Which music hall comedian played Falstaff in the 1944 film *Henry V*?
6. Which cricketer replaced Brian Lara as the West Indies Test cricket captain in 2000?
7. What is the state capital of Louisiana?
8. What is the melting point of technetium?
9. What type of creature is the teledu of S.E. Asia?
10. What does the latex of the sapodilla tree yield?
11. What is the state flower of Indiana, U.S.A.?
12. On what day of the week was Christmas Day 1984?
13. Who was the god of sleep in Greek mythology?
14. Venice is the capital of which region of Italy?
15. What type of creature is a Texel?

ANSWERS 1. Sierra Leone **2.** 1959 **3.** 1989 **4.** Almonds **5.** George Robey **6.** Jimmy Adams **7.** Baton Rouge **8.** 2204°C **9.** Badger **10.** Chicle **11.** Peony **12.** Tuesday **13.** Hypnos **14.** Veneto **15.** Sheep.

ENTERTAINMENT

1. Who devised the 2000 television series *Attachments*?
2. Who played D'Artagnan in the 1939 film *The Three Musketeers*?
3. In which film did Meryl Streep play the character Susan Traherne?
4. What was Mike Farrell's character name in the television sitcom *M*A*S*H* ?
5. What is the name of the villainess played by Glenn Close in the 1996 film *101 Dalmatians*?
6. Which act won the first Perrier Comedy Award at the 1981 Edinburgh Fringe Festival?
7. Who played Juror No. 11 in the 1957 film *12 Angry Men*?
8. What was the name of the character played by Michael Douglas in the 1987 film *Fatal Attraction*?
9. For how much did Tom Parker sign Elvis Presley to RCA records?
10. Which actor's television roles included Capt. Mainwaring in *Dad's Army*?
11. Which television presenter hosted the first series of Channel 4's *Big Brother*?
12. What was to have been the original title of Stephen Daldry's the 2000 film *Billy Elliot*?
13. Who wrote the 2000 film *Elephant Juice* which starred Daniela Nardini?
14. Who does Helen Baxendale play in the ITV drama series *Cold Feet*?
15. Who starred in and co-wrote the Channel 4 sitcom *Black Books*?

ANSWERS 1. Tony Garnett **2.** Don Ameche **3.** Plenty **4.** Capt. B.J. Hunnicut **5.** Cruella De Vil **6.** Cambridge Footlights **7.** George Voskovec **8.** Dan Gallagher **9.** $35,000 **10.** Arthur Lowe **11.** Davina McCall **12.** Dancer **13.** Amy Jenkins **14.** Rachel Bradley **15.** Dylan Moran.

SPORT

1. By what score did Aberdeen defeat Celtic on penalties in the 1990 Scottish FA Cup Final?
2. Where were the 1997 IAAF World Championships held?
3. Which team won the 1998 world series in baseball?
4. Which horse won the 1998 St. Leger?
5. Who was men's world middleweight judo champion in 1987 and '89?
6. In tennis, who won the 1993 Romanian Open?
7. Who were 1988 men's Olympic basketball champions?
8. Which sportsman was ousted in 1997 as MP for Falmouth and Camborne?
9. Where were the 20th Summer Olympics held?
10. Who in snooker is known as 'the Grinder'?
11. Which Austrian motor racing driver was 1970 Formula 1 world champion?
12. What nationality was tennis player Maria Bueno?
13. In which year did tennis player Arthur Ashe die?
14. Who won the 1984 Olympic women's 100m title?
15. Which rugby league player was player-coach at Wigan from 1963-9?

ANSWERS 1. 9-8 **2.** Athens **3.** New York Yankees **4.** Nedawi **5.** Fabien Canu **6.** Goran Ivanisevic **7.** USSR **8.** Sebastian Coe **9.** Munich **10.** Cliff Thorburn **11.** Jochen Rindt **12.** Brazilian **13.** 1993 **14.** Evelyn Ashford **15.** Eric Ashton.

POP

1. What was the first Top 10 album in the UK for the group Family?
2. Which duo recorded the 1976 Top 10 album *Breakaway*?
3. Which solo singer recorded the 2000 album *Fear of Flying*?
4. Which studio album by The Police includes the track *Every Breath You Take*?
5. Who originally played whistle in the group The Pogues?
6. Which group recorded the 1969 film soundtrack *More*?
7. Which group recorded the 1972 Top 10 album *Moving Waves*?
8. What was the first Top 10 album in the UK for the group Cockney Rebel?
9. Who recorded the 1979 album *New Values*?
10. Which country artist recorded the 1985 album *The Ballad of Sally Rose*?
11. Which duo recorded the 2000 album *Balls*?
12. Which group recorded the album *The Blossom Filled Streets*?
13. Which legend plays harmonica on the Prefab Sprout track *Nightingales*?
14. At which university did rock musician Frank Black study anthropology?
15. Which Bob Dylan song features on the album *Words and Music* by Planxty?

ANSWERS **1.** Family Entertainment **2.** Gallagher and Lyle **3.** Mya **4.** Synchronicity **5.** Spider Stacy **6.** Pink Floyd **7.** Focus **8.** The Psychomodo **9.** Iggy Pop **10.** Emmylou Harris **11.** Sparks **12.** Movietone **13.** Stevie Wonder **14.** University of Massachusetts **15.** Pity the Poor Immigrant.

HISTORY

1. In which year was the Battle of Marston Moor?
2. Who was defeated by Franklin D. Roosevelt in the 1944 U.S. presidential election?
3. What was American philanthropist James Buchanan Brady known as?
4. In which year did William III become sole sovereign?
5. In which century did French mathematician Pierre de Fermat live?
6. Which Portuguese navigator was killed by chieftain Lapu-Lapu in 1521?
7. John Hopkins University was formed in which Maryland city in 1876?
8. In which year did Charles II of England sell Dunkirk to Louis XIV of France?
9. In which year was the Great Fire of London?
10. In which year did Ramsay MacDonald die?
11. In which year did Henry VIII marry Catherine of Aragon?
12. What did Edward I erect in 1291 in memory of his wife Elaine?
13. Which king of Scotland was killed at Alnwick in 1093?
14. In which year was Nelson Mandela released from prison at the age of 71?
15. In which year was the Chappaquidick incident in which Mary Jo Kopechne drowned?

ANSWERS **1.** 1644 **2.** Thomas E. Dewey **3.** Diamond Jim **4.** 1694 **5.** 17th **6.** Ferdinand Magellan **7.** Baltimore **8.** 1662 **9.** 1666 **10.** 1937 **11.** 1509 **12.** Charing Cross **13.** Malcolm III **14.** 1990 **15.** 1969.

GENERAL KNOWLEDGE

1. In which year was Prince Charles born?
2. Which actress was born Vivian Mary Hartley?
3. Who in May 1999 became the first Asian minister in the government?
4. Where is the World War II destroyer HMS Cavalier now housed?
5. Which Secretary of State for Northern Ireland resigned in 1992 after singing on television?
6. Of what whole number is 5.4772255 the square root?
7. What is the name given to the holder of the chair of French at Oxford?
8. In which year was the Battle of Midway?
9. What is the name of the former slum area of Washington which is the site of the headquarters of the CIA?
10. In which year did comedian Willie Rushton die?
11. Who wrote the children's story *The Midnight Folk*?
12. In which year did scientist Alexander Fleming die?
13. What is the name of the dog in the film *The Wizard of Oz*?
14. Which is the 'Beaver State' of the U.S.?
15. In which year did author Stella Gibbons die?

ANSWERS 1. 1948 **2.** Vivien Leigh **3.** Keith Vaz **4.** Chatham dockyard **5.** Peter Brooke **6.** 30 **7.** Foch professor **8.** 1942 **9.** Foggy bottom **10.** 1996 **11.** John Masefield **12.** 1955 **13.** Toto **14.** Oregon **15.** 1989.

ENTERTAINMENT

1. How many foreign language films have been nominated for Best Picture Oscar?
2. Who won Best Director Oscar for their debut film at the helm, *American Beauty*?
3. Who scored the 1981 film *Chariots of Fire*?
4. What is Paul McGann's character name in the film *Withnail & I*?
5. Who plays the character Flash Harry in the 1954 film *The Belles of St. Trinian's*?
6. For which two films did Billy Wilder win Best Director Oscar?
7. Who plays Porthos in the 1979 film *The Fifth Musketeer*?
8. Which cinematographer shot the film *The Third Man*?
9. Which singer played the character Khadijah James in the U.S. sitcom *Living Single*?
10. Who scripted the 1994 film *Four Weddings and a Funeral*?
11. Which music hall comedian was known as 'The Prime Minister of Mirth'?
12. How many Oscar nominations did the film *The Full Monty* receive?
13. What was the name of the character played by Michael Douglas in the 1984 film *Romancing the Stone*?
14. Which late *Coronation Street* actor has a prominent role in the film *Get Carter*?
15. For which two films did Michael Caine win Best Supporting Actor Oscar awards?

ANSWERS 1. Six **2.** Sam Mendes **3.** Vangelis **4.** Marwood **5.** George Cole **6.** The Apartment and The Lost Weekend **7.** Alan Hale Jr. **8.** Robert Krasker **9.** Queen Latifah **10.** Richard Curtis **11.** George Robey **12.** Four **13.** Jack Colton **14.** Bryan Mosley **15.** Hannah and Her Sisters & The Cider House Rules.

SPORT

1. For which country did Asif Iqbal play Test cricket from 1964-80?
2. To what did US jockey Brian Asmussen legally change his name?
3. With what sport might you associate Reading-born Nigel Aspinall?
4. Which basketball team did Red Auerbach coach to eight consecutive NBA titles in the 1950s and '60s?
5. Who was men's world middleweight judo champion in 1995 and '97?
6. Who were rugby league world cup winners 1975-95?
7. Who was the 1998 men's world open squash champion?
8. What colour ball is worth two points in snooker?
9. Who were Olympic men's volleyball champions in 1984 and '88?
10. Who won the U.S. Open men's singles tennis championship from 1979-81?
11. Who won the 1988 Olympic men's 100m breaststroke swimming title?
12. In which country was orienteering invented?
13. Who was captain of the 1993 European Ryder Cup team?
14. In which city was Martina Navratilova born?
15. Which famous footballing brothers were born in Ashington, Northumberland?

ANSWERS 1. Pakistan **2.** Cash **3.** Croquet **4.** Boston Celtics **5.** Jeon Ki-Young **6.** Australia **7.** Jonathan Power **8.** Yellow **9.** United States **10.** John McEnroe **11.** Adrian Moorhouse **12.** Sweden **13.** Bernard Gallacher **14.** Prague **15.** Bobby and Jack Charlton.

POP

1. How many Top 10 singles did the Thompson Twins have in the UK?
2. What is singer Buster Bloodvessel's real name?
3. Who recorded the 1999 album *Twisted Tenderness*?
4. In which year did trombone player Don Drummond die?
5. Which female vocalist had a 1988 No. 1 with *I Think We're Alone Now*?
6. Who was the original bass player in the group Killing Joke?
7. Who was the lead singer of Scottish group The Associates?
8. Which reggae group recorded the album *Live and Direct* at the 1983 Notting Hill Carnival?
9. Which band recorded the songs *Warlord of the Royal Crocodiles* and *Salamanda Palaganda*?
10. Which group recorded the album *See jungle! See jungle! Go join your gang yeah, city all over! Go ape crazy!*?
11. On which studio LP did David Bowie record *Sound and Vision*?
12. Fripp, Wetton and Bruford comprised which band in 1974?
13. Who recorded the LP *Fresh Fruit in Foreign Places*?
14. On which label did Joy Division's *Unknown Pleasures* LP appear?
15. Which Sting song appears on Grace Jones's album *Nightclubbing*?

ANSWERS 1. Five **2.** Doug Trendle **3.** Electronic **4.** 1969 **5.** Tiffany **6.** Youth **7.** Billy Mackenzie **8.** Aswad **9.** Tyrannosaurus Rex **10.** Bow Wow Wow **11.** Low **12.** King Crimson **13.** Kid Creole and the Coconuts **14.** Factory Records **15.** Demolition Man.

ART AND LITERATURE

1. Who wrote the children's book *The Big Bazoohley*?
2. In which year did the artist Henri Gaudier-Brzeska die?
3. Who wrote the novel *Quite Ugly One Morning*?
4. In which year was the British artist Tracey Emin born?
5. Who wrote the novel *Knowledge of Angels*?
6. Who wrote the 2000 novel *To the Hermitage*?
7. Which British artist's works include the 1950 painting *Esperston*?
8. Who wrote the novel *Prodigal Summer*?
9. Which French artist's works include 1861's *A Plate of Apples*?
10. Who writes books about pathologist Kay Scarpetta?
11. Which pair of artists' works include the 1972 video installation *In the Bush*?
12. Who wrote the novel *The Book of Evidence*?
13. Which British artist's works include 1916 painting *The Tea Party*?
14. Who wrote the 2000 short story collection *The Hill Bachelors*?
15. Who wrote the 2000 novel *Pagan Babies*?

ANSWERS **1.** Peter Carey **2.** 1915 **3.** Christopher Brookmyre **4.** 1963 **5.** Jill Paton Walsh **6.** Malcolm Bradbury **7.** Sir William Gillies **8.** Barbara Kingsolver **9.** Henri Fantin-Latour **10.** Patricia Cornwell **11.** Gilbert and George **12.** John Banville **13.** Hilda Fearon **14.** William Trevor **15.** Elmore Leonard.

GENERAL KNOWLEDGE

1. In which year was the Test Act repealed in England?
2. On which part of the body might you wear a veldskoen?
3. What is the English name of the constellation whose Latin name is *Lepus*?
4. Who wrote the 2000 novel *Immaculate Conceit*?
5. In which year was the communications satellite ECHO 1 launched?
6. In which year did Hurricane Opal hit Florida?
7. What is the state flower of New Hampshire, U.S.A.?
8. In which year was the Swift-Tuttle comet first seen?
9. Who or what is a wharfinger?
10. On which river is Dayton, Ohio?
11. Which film was nominated for 9 Oscars in 1941 but won none?
12. Which son of Odysseus and Circe in Greek mythology killed his father and then married his father's widow?
13. What is the fifteenth letter in the Greek alphabet?
14. To which mammal does the adjective *porcine* refer?
15. Of which of the United States of America is MO the zip code?

ANSWERS 1. 1828 **2.** The foot, it's a boot **3.** Hare **4.** Stella Duffy **5.** 1960 **6.** 1995 **7.** Purple lilac **8.** 1862 **9.** The owner of manager of a wharf **10.** (Great) Miami River **11.** The Little Foxes **12.** Telegonus **13.** Omicron **14.** Pig **15.** Missouri.

ENTERTAINMENT

1. Who does Helena Bonham Carter play in the film *A Room With A View*?
2. The film Titanic won 11 Oscars. For how many Oscars was it nominated?
3. Which three Best Picture Oscar winners last over three and a half hours long?
4. Which actor's performance as Tony Soprano in the television show *The Sopranos* won him an Emmy in 2000?
5. Who directed the 1943 documentary *Fires Were Started*?
6. Who directed the 1998 film *Elizabeth*?
7. Who starred as Robert of Huntingdon in the 1980s television series *Robin of Sherwood*?
8. For which two films did Melvyn Douglas win Best Supporting Actor Oscar awards?
9. How many Best Actress Oscar nominations has Meryl Streep received?
10. Which character was played by Lisa Riley in the soap *Emmerdale*?
11. Who plays Aramis in the 1979 film *The Fifth Musketeer*?
12. Which rap duo starred in the 1990 film *House Party*?
13. Which film won more Oscars - *Lawrence of Arabia* or *Amadeus*?
14. Who directed the 1996 film *Trainspotting*?
15. In which 1979 comedy film does the song *Always Look On the Bright Side Of Life* feature?

ANSWERS 1. Miss Honeychurch **2.** 14 **3.** Ben-Hur, Gone With the Wind and Lawrence of Arabia **4.** James Gandolfini **5.** Humphrey Jennings **6.** Shekhar Kapur **7.** Jason Connery **8.** Hud & Being There **9.** 10 **10.** Mandy Dingle **11.** Lloyd Bridges **12.** Kid 'N' Play **13.** Amadeus **14.** Danny Boyle **15.** Monty Python's Life of Brian.

SPORT

1. Which team won the 1995 AXA Life League in cricket?
2. By what score did Rangers beat Hearts in the 1996 Scottish FA Cup Final?
3. Who was men's world light-middleweight judo champion in 1981?
4. What nationality is Nordic skier Berit Aunli?
5. What was the nickname of tennis player Henry Wilfred Austin?
6. In which year was US tennis player Tracy Austin born?
7. Hashim Khan and Azam Khan contested the British Open squash final three times between 1953 and '59. How were they related?
8. Which horse won the 1989 Irish Derby?
9. At which sport do the Pittsburgh Penguins compete?
10. For which motor-racing team did Damon Hill drive in 1996?
11. With which sport do you associate Bob Pettit?
12. Which India cricketer made centuries in each of his first three Tests, beginning in 1984?
13. At what sport did Shirley Babashoff win eight Olympic medals?
14. Which Commonwealth Games javelin winner was born in Sidcup, Kent, in 1969?
15. Which heavyweight boxer was known as 'the Livermore Larruper'?

ANSWERS 1. Kent **2.** 5-1 **3.** Neil Adams **4.** Norwegian **5.** Bunny **6.** 1962 **7.** Brothers **8.** Old Vic **9.** Ice hockey **10.** Williams-Renault **11.** Basketball **12.** Mohammad Azharuddin **13.** Swimming **14.** Steve Backley **15.** Max Baer.

POP

1. Who backed Yazz on her 1988 No. 1 single *The Only Way Is Up*?
2. On which record label did X.T.C. record their 1979 single *Making Plans for Nigel*?
3. Who recorded the 1998 album *Psyence Fiction*?
4. The composer of *Blue Suede Shoes* died in 1998. Who was he?
5. At which famous New York venue was Portishead's live album *PNYC* recorded?
6. In which year did the Sweet chart with the song *Love is like Oxygen*?
7. Which duo had the 1979 hit single *With You I'm Born Again*?
8. What was the only UK Top 10 single registered by Talking Heads?
9. Which group's only album chart entry was 1974's *Spyglass Guest*?
10. In which year did Haircut 100's *Pelican West* album chart?
11. Who was the proprietor of Glasgow's Postcard Records?
12. Which singer fronted the group The 13th Floor Elevators?
13. Which punk group recorded the album *Fulham Fallout*?
14. Which member of Roxy Music recorded the solo album *In Search of Eddie Riff*?
15. Who recorded the 1998 album *Philophobia*?

ANSWERS **1.** The Plastic Population **2.** Virgin **3.** Unkle **4.** Carl Perkins **5.** Roseland Ballroom **6.** 1978 **7.** Billy Preston and Syreeta **8.** Road to Nowhere **9.** Greenslade **10.** 1982 **11.** Alan Horne **12.** Roky Erickson **13.** The Lurkers **14.** Andy Mackay **15.** Arab Strap.

SCIENCE

1. Of what is diamond a crystalline form?
2. In which German city was Albert Einstein born?
3. In an equilateral triangle, what does each of the angles measure in degrees?
4. What is the name given to a 12-sided polygon?
5. What is a collection of gas above an oil deposit called?
6. What in mechanics does the abbreviation KE stand for?
7. What is a collarbone also called?
8. How many grams of fat per 100 grams are there in butter?
9. For what did Donald Glaser win the 1960 Nobel prize for physics?
10. What is the boiling point in °C of aluminium?
11. What is one half of a sphere called?
12. In which century did the inventor Henry Bessemer live?
13. Which mineral is the main source of mercury?
14. What was the nationality of Jagadis Bose, known for his studies of electric waves?
15. What bone in the inner ear is also called the incus?

ANSWERS 1. Carbon **2.** Ulm **3.** 60° **4.** Dodecagon **5.** Gas cap **6.** Kinetic energy **7.** Clavicle **8.** 82 **9.** Development of the bubble chamber **10.** 251° **11.** A hemisphere **12.** 19th **13.** Cinnabar **14.** Indian **15.** Anvil.

GENERAL KNOWLEDGE

1. What is the name given to a small hammer used by an auctioneer?
2. In which year did Constantine II of Greece abdicate?
3. What is the US term for a pedestrian crossing?
4. What is the name given to the broad flat limb of seals and penguins?
5. On what date was Easter Sunday in 1990?
6. What is the standard monetary unit of Ecuador?
7. What in ecology is the name given to the area in which an animal normally ranges?
8. In which province is the Irish county of Leitrim?
9. What is the approximate population of Buenos Aires in millions - 7, 10 or 13?
10. What do the initials of the organization ACAS stand for?
11. Who wrote the collection of essays *Abinger Harvest*?
12. In which year did broadcaster Brian Redhead die?
13. What is the home of Fulham F.C.?
14. Of what whole number is 9.9498743 the square root?
15. What is the more common name of the butterfly bush?

ANSWERS 1. Gavel **2.** 1974 **3.** Crosswalk **4.** Flipper **5.** April 15 **6.** Sucre **7.** Home range **8.** Connaught **9.** 10 million **10.** Advisory Conciliation and Arbitration Service **11.** E.M. Forster **12.** 1994 **13.** Craven Cottage **14.** 99 **15.** Buddleia.

ENTERTAINMENT

1. Who directed the 1999 film *Deep Blue Sea*?
2. Who played the title role of *Dr. No* in the 1962 film?
3. Who plays Colonel Brandon in the 1995 film *Sense and Sensibility*?
4. Which star of the 1964 film *Zulu* also co-produced the film?
5. Which character is played by Adam Woodyatt in the television soap *EastEnders*?
6. Who plays Porthos in the 1952 film *At Sword's Point*?
7. Which 1975 Norman Jewison film starring James Caan is set in the year 2018?
8. The film Ben Hur won 11 Oscars in 1959. For how many Oscars was it nominated?
9. Which black actor was chosen to play *Henry VI* by the Royal Shakespeare Company at Stratford in November 2000?
10. Who directed the 1960 film *Peeping Tom*?
11. Who played Julie Christie's three suitors in the 1967 film *Far From the Madding Crowd*?
12. The phrase "Fear can hold you prisoner. Hope can set you free" features on the poster for which 1994 film?
13. Which theatre director's first film as director was *The Madness of King George*?
14. How many Best Actor Oscar nominations has Jack Lemmon received?
15. Which two films were each nominated for 11 Oscars but won none?

ANSWERS 1. Renny Harlin **2.** Joseph Wiseman **3.** Alan Rickman **4.** Stanley Baker **5.** Ian Beale **6.** Alan Hale Jr. **7.** Rollerball **8.** 12 **9.** David Oyewolo **10.** Michael Powell **11.** Alan Bates, Peter Finch and Terence Stamp **12.** The Shawshank Redemption **13.** Nicholas Hytner **14.** Seven **15.** The Turning Point & The Color Purple.

SPORT

1. Which snooker player beat Ronnie O'Sullivan in the Irish Open in December 1998?
2. What did Ian Woosnam score in the first round of the 1999 U.S. Masters?
3. Who was MVP in Superbowl I and II in American Football?
4. For which rugby league side did Andy Goodway sign in July 1985?
5. By what score did Everton beat Rapid Vienna in the 1985 European Cup Winners' Cup Final?
6. Who won the 1993 men's 100m title at the IAAF World Championships?
7. Against which international side did Gary McAllister play for Scotland in April 1999 - his first such game for 16 months?
8. Who won the 1996 U.S. Open golf championship?
9. Which tennis player married Roger Cawley in 1975?
10. Who was 1998 British Open men's squash champion?
11. Which was the only horse to beat Brigadier Gerard in the 1972 Benson & Hedges Gold Cup at York?
12. What was the nickname of Spanish cyclist Federico Bahamontes?
13. Which England Test cricketer captained Essex from 1961-66?
14. In which year did Virginia Wade win the Wimbledon singles title?
15. Where were the Summer Olympic Games held in 1900?

ANSWERS 1. Jimmy Michie **2.** 71 **3.** Bart Starr **4.** Wigan **5.** 3-1 **6.** Linford Christie **7.** Czech Republic **8.** Steve Jones **9.** Evonne Goolangong **10.** Peter Nicol **11.** Roberto **12.** Eagle of Toledo **13.** Trevor Bailey **14.** 1977 **15.** Paris.

POP

1. With which standard did Mari Wilson have a Top 30 single in 1983?
2. In which year did Jackie Wilson first chart in the U.K. with *Reet Petite*?
3. Who recorded the 1998 album *Fin de Siècle*?
4. Which former drummer with Black Sabbath and Rainbow died in 1998?
5. What was the debut album of the group Delakota?
6. Who recorded the 1998 album *Kingsize*?
7. On which record label did Sweet Sensation record their No. 1 single *Sad Sweet Dreamer*?
8. In which year did Taffy chart with *I Love My Radio (My Dee Jay's Radio)*?
9. Which guitarist's albums include 1975's *Voyage of the Acolyte*?
10. Hadley, Norman, Keeble, Kemp and Kemp - which group?
11. Which U.S. electronic band comprises Alan Vega and Martin Rev?
12. Which poet recorded the 1979 mini-album *Walking Back to Happiness*?
13. What was Take That's first No. 1 single?
14. Which group recorded the 1998 album *Nu-clear Sounds*?
15. On which record label did Yazoo score five Top 20 singles between 1982 and '90?

ANSWERS **1.** Cry Me a River **2.** 1957 **3.** The Divine Comedy **4.** Cozy Powell **5.** One Love **6.** The Boo Radleys **7.** Pye **8.** 1987 **9.** Steve Hackett **10.** Spandau Ballet **11.** Suicide **12.** John Cooper Clarke **13.** Pray **14.** Ash **15.** Mute.

PEOPLE

1. Which Labour M.P. was appointed Secretary of State for International Development in 1997?

2. Which former Speaker of the House of Commons died in 1997?

3. Which U.S. television magnate founded Cable News Network in 1980?

4. In which year was the composer Giuseppe Verdi born?

5. Who is the actress-model wife of the pop star David Bowie?

6. In which year did the painter Luca Carlevaris die?

7. Which British athlete was the 2000 Olympic heptathlon champion?

8. Which rapper was born Dana Owens?

9. Who was the Holy Roman Emperor from 1378-1400?

10. Who was the British governor general of Bengal from 1797-1805?

11. In which city was the fashion designer Karl Lagerfeld born in 1938?

12. What was the nickname given during the 2000 Olympics to swimmer Eric Moussambani of Equatorial Guinea?

13. What was the nickname of the aviator Manfred von Richthofen?

14. In which year did the British naval commander Horatio Nelson die?

15. In which year did the actor-singer Anthony Newley die?

ANSWERS 1. Clare Short **2.** George Thomas **3.** Ted Turner **4.** 1813 **5.** Iman **6.** 1731 **7.** Denise Lewis **8.** Queen Latifah **9.** Wenceslaus I **10.** Richard Wellesley **11.** Hamburg **12.** The Eel **13.** The Red Baron **14.** 1805 **15.** 1999.

GENERAL KNOWLEDGE

1. What is the English name of the constellation whose Latin name is *Musca*?
2. Which three film westerns have won Best Picture Oscar?
3. In which year was the weather satellite Tiros 1 launched?
4. In which year was Mars' moon Phobos discovered?
5. On which London Underground line is the station of White City?
6. In which country was the 1968 film *Carry On Up the Khyber* filmed?
7. Which king's head was on the English silver coin called a teston?
8. What type of bird is a veery?
9. In which country is Tepic the capital of Nayarit state?
10. What is the ninth letter of the Hebrew alphabet?
11. Which actor has won three Best Supporting Actor Oscar awards?
12. In which country is the World Heritage site of Butrinti?
13. What was the duration of the manned space mission Apollo XIII of 1970?
14. On what day of the week was Christmas Day 1884?
15. In the US, what is the state bird of Louisiana?

ANSWERS **1.** Fly **2.** Dances With Wolves, Unforgiven and Cimarron **3.** 1960 **4.** 1877 **5.** Central **6.** Wales **7.** Henry VIII **8.** Thrush **9.** Mexico **10.** Teth **11.** Walter Brennan **12.** Albania **13.** 142 hr 54 min **14.** Thursday **15.** Eastern brown pelican.

ENTERTAINMENT

1. Who are the four male stars of the 2000 film *Space Cowboys*?
2. Which 1998 Walt Disney animated film is based on a Chinese legend?
3. Who scripted the 1952 film *The Cruel Sea*?
4. For which two films did Shelley Winters win Best Supporting Actress Oscar awards?
5. Which two films won the Best Picture Oscar without their directors being nominated as Best Director?
6. Who plays Sherif Ali in the 1962 film *Lawrence of Arabia*?
7. Who are the male and female leads in the 1973 film *Don't Look Now*?
8. Who choreographed the 1948 film *The Red Shoes*?
9. Which Oscar-winning actress has a small role as Chiquita in the film *The Lavender Hill Mob*?
10. Who wrote the 1968 film *If...*?
11. Who are the male and female stars of the 2000 film *Hollow Man*?
12. For which three films did William Wyler win Best Director Oscar?
13. Who played the lead role in Alan Bennett's *A Woman of No Importance* on television?
14. Which actor played the crime boss Marsellus in the 1994 film *Pulp Fiction*?
15. Before the 2001 Academy Award nominations were announced, which seven actors had won the Best Actor Award twice?

ANSWERS 1. Clint Eastwood, Tommy Lee Jones, James Garner and Donald Sutherland **2.** Mulan **3.** Eric Ambler **4.** The Diary of Anne Frank & A Patch of Blue **5.** Grand Hotel and Driving Miss Daisy **6.** Omar Sharif **7.** Donald Sutherland and Julie Christie **8.** Robert Helpmann **9.** Audrey Hepburn **10.** David Sherwin **11.** Kevin Bacon and Elisabeth Shue **12.** Ben-Hur, Mrs. Miniver and The Best Years of Our Lives **13.** Patricia Routledge **14.** Ving Rhames **15.** Tom Hanks, Spencer Tracy, Fredric March, Dustin Hoffman, Jack Nicholson, Gary Cooper and Marlon Brando.

SPORT

1. Who won the women's marathon title at the 1983 IAAF World Championships?
2. Who became the first president of the French Professional Footballers' Union in 1963?
3. Who was the 1993 world women's singles badminton champion?
4. Which cyclist won the 1998 Tour de France?
5. Who was the 1998 USPGA golf champion?
6. Which men's team won the European Club Champions Cup in hockey from 1988-95?
7. Which horse won the 1998 Grand National?
8. Who was men's open judo champion 1987-91?
9. Which country won the Thomas Cup in badminton in 1986, '88 and '90?
10. Which politician is the life president of the Raith Rovers Supporters Club?
11. Who was the 1988 Superbikes world champion in motor cycling?
12. Of which country was Imre Földi the greatest weightlifter?
13. In which year did Hank Aaron hit his 715th home run, breaking Babe Ruth's record of 714?
14. To what did basketball player Lew Alcindor change his name after embracing the Muslim faith?
15. In which year did leg-spin bowler Abdul Qadir make his Test debut for Pakistan?

ANSWERS 1. Grete Waitz **2.** Just Fontaine **3.** Susi Susanti **4.** Marco Pantani **5.** Vijay Singh **6.** Uhlenhorst Mülheim **7.** Earth Summit **8.** Naoya Ogawa **9.** China **10.** Gordon Brown **11.** Carl Fogarty **12.** Hungary **13.** 1973 **14.** Kareem Abdul-Jabbar **15.** 1977.

POP

1. Who had a hit single with *Wordy Rappinghood*?
2. Which instrumental group charted with *The Ice Cream Man* in 1963?
3. Who recorded the 1999 album *Rides*?
4. What was the title of Echo and the Bunnymen's early 1999 album release?
5. What nationality was 1980s pop artist Nash the Slash?
6. Which Jamaican vocalist had a 1969 hit single with *Red Red Wine*?
7. On which label did Tracie chart in 1983 with *The House That Jack Built*?
8. Who produced the ABC album *The Lexicon of Love*?
9. Which US glam band recorded the album *Too Much Too Soon*?
10. On which 1982 studio album did Van Morrison record *Cleaning Windows*?
11. What was Morrissey's first solo album called?
12. Which author is quoted on the back of Mott the Hoople's album *Mott*?
13. What was T'Pau's follow-up single to the No. 1 *China in your Hand*?
14. Which T.Rex song did Bauhaus release as a single in late 1980?
15. Which group charted with *John Kettley (is a Weatherman)*?

ANSWERS 1. Tom Tom Club **2.** The Tornados **3.** Reef **4.** What Are You Going To Do With Your Life **5.** Canadian **6.** Tony Tribe **7.** Respond **8.** Trevor Horn **9.** New York Dolls **10.** Beautiful Vision **11.** Viva Hate **12.** D.H. Lawrence **13.** Valentine **14.** Telegram Sam **15.** Tribe of Toffs.

ART AND LITERATURE

1. Whose volumes of poetry include *Dog*?
2. Who wrote the 2000 novel *The Best A Man Can Get*?
3. Which British artist's works include the 1923 painting *The Servant Girl*?
4. Which artist's works include the 1927 painting *Forest and Dove*?
5. Who wrote the novel *Seven-Week Itch*?
6. Who wrote the 2000 novel *Le Mariage*?
7. Which British artist's works include the 1970 lithograph *Small Horse and Rider*?
8. Who wrote the 2000 novel *In the Fall*?
9. Which British artist's works include the 1951 painting *Music*?
10. Who wrote the short story collection *Hit Man*?
11. Whose sculptures include the 1926 bronze *The Visitation*?
12. Whose debut novel in 2000 was *Iron Shoes*?
13. Who painted the 1753 work *Psyche showing her Sisters her Gifts From Cupid*?
14. Who wrote the novel *Mr. Commitment*?
15. Who wrote the 2001 novel *Half in Love*?

ANSWERS 1. John Hegley **2.** John O'Farrell **3.** Mark Gertler **4.** Max Ernst **5.** Victoria Corby **6.** Diane Johnson **7.** Dame Elisabeth Frink **8.** Jeffrey Lent **9.** Barnett Freedman **10.** Lawrence Block **11.** Sir Jacob Epstein **12.** Molly Giles **13.** Jean-Honoré Fragonard **14.** Mike Gayle **15.** Justin Cartwright.

GENERAL KNOWLEDGE

1. Josip Broz was the original name of which world leader?
2. What are the two main ingredients of the West Indian dish cou-cou?
3. A farrow is a litter of which farmyard animals?
4. Where on the body would you wear a heitiki?
5. Approximately how many million people visited Edinburgh Castle in 1990 - 1, 2 or 3?
6. Approximately how many million people spoke the Hungarian language in 1993?
7. What type of bird is a gadwall - a duck or a swan?
8. What is the German equivalent of the English surname Taylor?
9. There were 127 centres for the Samaritans in the U.K. in 1971. How many were there in 1981?
10. What is the young of a goose called?
11. What is the French name of the German city Aachen?
12. Which Russian word meaning 'restructuring' became popular in the 1980s?
13. In which year was Oliver Cromwell born?
14. What is the standard monctary unit of Bangladesh?
15. What was the most popular breed of pedigree cats registered in 1992?

ANSWERS 1. Marshal Tito **2.** Corn meal and okra **3.** Piglets **4.** Around the neck **5.** 1 million **6.** 14 million **7.** Duck **8.** Schneider **9.** 180 **10.** A gosling **11.** Aix-la-Chapelle **12.** Perestroika **13.** 1599 **14.** Taka **15.** Persian long hair.

ENTERTAINMENT

1. Who composed the 1986 opera *Mask of Orpheus*?
2. Who did Richard Todd portray in the 1955 film *The Dam Busters*?
3. Who plays Nancy in the 1948 film *Oliver Twist*?
4. Which film won more Oscars - *The Sting* or *Cabaret*?
5. The film West Side Story won 10 Oscars in 1961. For how many Oscars was it nominated?
6. Who composed the opera *The Knot Garden*?
7. Which three films won the Best Picture Oscar but won no other awards?
8. Which actress played Rita Tushingham's mother in the 1961 film *A Taste of Honey*?
9. Who directed the 1965 film *The Ipcress File*?

10. Who directed the 1986 film *Caravaggio*?
11. Which animated children's television programme featured the character Idris the dragon?
12. Which 2000 sci-fi film starred John Travolta and Forest Whitaker?
13. Who choreographed the 1978 work *Not Necessarily Recognizable Objectives*?
14. Who won Best Director Oscar for their debut film at the helm with *West Side Story*?
15. What is Julie Christie's character name in the 1970 film *The Go-Between*?

ANSWERS 1. Harrison Birtwistle **2.** Guy Gibson **3.** Kay Walsh **4.** Cabaret **5.** 11 **6.** Michael Tippett **7.** Broadway Melody, Grand Hotel & Mutiny on the Bounty **8.** Dora Bryan **9.** Sidney J. Furie **10.** Derek Jarman **11.** Ivor the Engine **12.** Battlefield Earth **13.** David Gordon **14.** Jerome Robbins **15.** Marian Maudsley.

SPORT

1. Who was runner-up in the 1994 Formula 1 motor racing world championship?
2. Which team were Scottish football league champions from 1905-1910?
3. Who is the only Yorkshire wicket-keeper to have made 1000 runs in a season three times?
4. Which boxer lost to Tommy Morrison in a WBO world heavyweight title fight in June 1993?
5. Who won the women's marathon at the 1987 IAAF World Championships?
6. How many times was Arsenal player Ray Bowden capped for England?
7. Who did Manchester United defeat in the semi-final of the 1998/9 European Champions League?
8. What height in metres did Dick Fosbury jump to win the 1968 Olympic gold?
9. Where were the 1987 IAAF World Championships held?
10. Which country won the Uber Cup in badminton five times between 1984 and '92?
11. At what sport did Canadian Sid Abel excel?
12. Who was the 1924 Olympic men's 100m champion?
13. Rosemarie Ackermann won a 1976 Olympic gold at which field event?
14. What is the name of Philadelphia's American Football team?
15. Which Division One football league team were once known as St. Judes?

ANSWERS **1.** Damon Hill **2.** Celtic **3.** David Bairstow **4.** George Foreman **5.** Rosa Mota **6.** Six **7.** Juventus **8.** 2.24m **9.** Rome **10.** China **11.** Ice hockey **12.** Harold Abrahams **13.** High jump **14.** Philadelphia Eagles **15.** Q.P.R.

POP

1. Which female singer's surname is Gudmundsdottir?
2. Which female singer recorded the 1982 hit *Ieya*?
3. Who is lead singer with the group *Gay Dad*?
4. Under what name do Paul and Phil Hartnoll usually record?
5. What name did Frank Tovey record under in the 1980s?
6. 'Two fat persons, click, click, click...' - which Ian Dury song?
7. Which German group had a hit in 1982 with *Da da da*?
8. Who recorded the album *Quit Dreaming And Get On The Beam*?
9. Which group had hit singles in 1973 with *Crazy*, *Hypnosis* and *Dynamite*?
10. Who played lead guitar on *Champagne Supernova* by Oasis?
11. Which U.S. group recorded the 1978 album *The Modern Dance*?
12. What was Toto's highest placed U.K. single?
13. On which label did Ultrasound record their album *Everything Picture*?
14. Which group recorded the album *Gentlemen Take Polaroids*?
15. Who recorded the 1999 album *The Marshall Suite*?

ANSWERS **1.** Björk **2.** Toyah **3.** Cliff Jones **4.** Orbital **5.** Fad Gadget **6.** Hit me with your rhythm stick **7.** Trio **8.** Bill Nelson **9.** Mud **10.** Paul Weller **11.** Pere Ubu **12.** Africa **13.** Nude **14.** Japan **15.** The Fall

GEOGRAPHY

1. In which European country is the cathedral city of Breda?
2. Caen is the capital of which French department?
3. In which English county are the Clee Hills?
4. In which European country is the village of Fatima, a centre of Roman Catholic pilgrimage?
5. Drammen is a seaport in which European country?
6. Which village in West Yorkshire was the home of the Brontë sisters?
7. Des Moines is the capital of which U.S. state?
8. Mount Kosciusko is the highest peak in which continent?
9. In which ocean is the volcanic Lord Howe Island?
10. Off which English county do the Manacle Rocks, a dangerous reef, lie?
11. The Mosquito Coast is an area of which Central American country?
12. What is the capital of the Czech Republic?
13. On which bay is the Spanish seaside resort of Santander?
14. Which is larger - the Sudan or Chile?
15. Ujpest is an industrial suburb of which eastern European country?

ANSWERS 1. The Netherlands **2.** Calvados **3.** Shropshire **4.** Portugal **5.** Norway **6.** Haworth **7.** Iowa **8.** Australia **9.** Pacific Ocean **10.** Cornwall **11.** Nicaragua **12.** Prague **13.** Bay of Biscay **14.** Sudan **15.** Hungary.

GENERAL KNOWLEDGE

1. On what day of the week was Christmas Day 1981?
2. In the US, what is the state bird of Colorado?
3. What is the English name of the constellation whose Latin name is *Aquila*?
4. In which country is the ESO New Technology Telescope?
5. How many minutes south of the equator is the volcano Cotopaxi?
6. In which South American country is the World Heritage site of Los Katios National Park?
7. In which year was Midori melon liqueur launched in the United States?
8. Who was the male lead in the 1946 film *A Matter of Life and Death*?
9. In which year was the French satellite A-1 Asterix launched?
10. Which member of Britain's silver medal-winning three-day event team at the 2000 Olympics rode the mount Shear H20?
11. To which country was the former child actress Shirley Temple US ambassador from 1989-92?
12. In which game do you commence play by teeing off?
13. How much of a country does a tetrarchy rule?
14. Which jockey rode Sinndar to victory in the 2000 Epsom Derby?
15. What was the name of the system of training to music originally taught by Émile Jacques-Dalcroze?

ANSWERS **1.** Friday **2.** Lark bunting **3.** Eagle **4.** Chile **5.** 40 **6.** Colombia **7.** 1978 **8.** David Niven **9.** 1965 **10.** Leslie Law **11.** Czechoslovakia **12.** Golf **13.** A fourth **14.** Johnny Murtagh **15.** Eurhythmics.

ENTERTAINMENT

1. What is Jonathan Pryce's character name in the film *Brazil*?
2. Which character is played by Lisa Kudrow in the sitcom *Friends*?
3. Which actor's film roles include Mark Renton in the 1996 film *Trainspotting*?
4. What is Thelma's surname in the film *Thelma & Louise*?
5. In which year was the Kirov Ballet company formed?
6. Who directed the 2000 film *The Million Dollar Hotel*?
7. John Ford was nominated five times for Best Director Oscar and won four times. For which picture did he fail to pick up the award?
8. Who directed the 1986 film *Mona Lisa*?
9. Who directed the 1996 film *The Long Kiss Goodnight*?
10. Who composed the opera *The Rape of Lucretia*?
11. How many Best Actor Oscar nominations did Laurence Olivier receive?
12. To which actress is Robert Donat handcuffed in the film *The 39 Steps*?
13. Which music hall comedian played Tony Weller in the 1952 film *The Pickwick Papers*?
14. Who directed the 1947 film *Brighton Rock*?
15. Which 2000 film starred Paul Newman and Linda Fiorentino?

ANSWERS 1. Sam Lowry **2.** Phoebe **3.** Ewan McGregor **4.** Dickinson **5.** 1935 **6.** Wim Wenders **7.** Stagecoach **8.** Neil Jordan **9.** Renny Harlin **10.** Benjamin Britten **11.** 9 **12.** Madeleine Carroll **13.** George Robey **14.** John Boulting **15.** Where the Money Is.

SPORT

1. For which rugby league club did Neil Fox make his debut in 1956?
2. Who trained Aldaniti to win the 1981 Grand National?
3. Which team won Superbowl XV in 1981, beating Philadelphia 27-10?
4. Which two Italian teams contested the 1991 UEFA Cup final?
5. Who was European men's singles badminton champion from 1992-96?
6. Which cyclist won the 1997 Tour de France?
7. Which football team does Alastair Campbell, chief press secretary to Tony Blair, support?
8. What job did bowls player Janet Ackland do prior to turning professional in 1980?
9. In which city was tennis player Andre Agassi born?
10. What nationality was motor cyclist Giacomo Agostini?
11. Who was Spencer Oliver fighting in 1998 when a punch left him brain-damaged?
12. Who was Pakistan's top scorer in their 1999 cricket World Cup Group B game against Scotland?
13. Who won the women's 100m hurdles at the 1993 and '95 IAAF World Championships?
14. Wigan rugby league player Wes Davies is the grandson of which rugby league star?
15. Which football team were Scottish League runners-up from 1923-26?

ANSWERS **1.** Wakefield Trinity **2.** Josh Gifford **3.** Oakland Raiders **4.** A.S. Roma and Internazionale **5.** Paul-Erik Høyer-Larsen **6.** Jan Ullrich **7.** Burnley **8.** Art teacher **9.** Las Vegas **10.** Italian **11.** Sergei Devakov **12.** Yousuf Youhana **13.** Gail Devers **14.** Billy Boston **15.** Airdrieonians.

POP

1. Which male singer recorded the 1982 album *Killer on the Rampage*?
2. Which Manchester group recorded the early 1980s album *Pindrop*?
3. What was Gilbert O'Sullivan's debut LP called?
4. What was Roy Orbison's middle name?
5. Peter Perrett was singer/songwriter for which late 1970s punk band?
6. Which make of guitar is Wreckless Eric holding on the cover of his debut LP?
7. Whose 1979 live album was called *Live Rust*?
8. Which group recorded the song *There's No Lights on the Christmas Tree, Mother, They're Burning Big Louie Tonight* on the album *Framed*?
9. Which punk band recorded the 1978 album *The Scream*?
10. What was Slade's first No. 1 single?
11. Ron and Russell Mael form the basis of which group?
12. Which duo comprised the group Soft Cell?
13. Which actor features on the cover of *The Queen is Dead* by The Smiths?
14. Which member of the Velvet Underground produced Patti Smith's album *Horses*?
15. Which songwriting duo wrote the song *Itchycoo Park*?

ANSWERS **1.** Eddy Grant **2.** The Passage **3.** Himself **4.** Kelton **5.** The Only Ones **6.** Rickenbacker **7.** Neil Young & Crazy Horse **8.** The Sensational Alex Harvey Band **9.** Siouxsie & the Banshees **10.** Cos I Luv You **11.** Sparks **12.** Marc Almond and David Ball **13.** Alain Delon **14.** John Cale **15.** Steve Marriott and Ronnie Lane.

HISTORY

1. Who was Israeli prime minister from 1948-53?
2. In which year was Malta awarded the George Cross?
3. In which year did Martin Luther nail his 95 Theses to the Wittenberg Church door?
4. In which year was the Croix de Guerre instituted in France?
5. Which London institution moved from Throgmorton St. to Old Broad St. in 1972?
6. In which year was Desmond Tutu made archbishop of Cape Town?
7. What was the official residence of the N. Ireland prime minister until 1972?
8. Who succeeded Indira Gandhi in 1977 as prime minister of India?
9. In which year was Joan of Arc burnt at the stake?
10. Which famous diamond was presented to Edward VII in 1907?
11. Who succeeded François Mitterand as French president in 1995?
12. In which year was Sir Thomas More executed?
13. In which year did the Shakespeare Memorial Theatre at Stratford-on-Avon burn down?
14. Where in Pennsylvania was there a major nuclear accident in 1979?
15. In which year did Ivan the Terrible become Tsar of Russia?

ANSWERS **1.** David Ben Gurion **2.** 1942 **3.** 1517 **4.** 1915 **5.** London Stock Exchange **6.** 1986 **7.** Stormont **8.** Morarji Desai **9.** 1431 **10.** Cullinan diamond **11.** Jacques Chirac **12.** 1535 **13.** 1926 **14.** Three Mile Island **15.** 1547.

GENERAL KNOWLEDGE

1. Which book did Miles Coverdale famously translate into English in 1535?
2. Which playing card is known as the Curse of Scotland?
3. Who wrote the 1901 play *Dance of Death*?
4. In which year did comedian Lenny Bruce die?
5. In Norse mythology, from what type of tree was the first man created?
6. In Greek mythology, how many fates were there?
7. What nationality was the comic film actor Fernandel?
8. What would you do with a helicon - play it or dance it?
9. For what would you use Benesh notation?
10. Who was commander-in-chief of British forces at Bunker Hill in 1775?
11. In which year was the Chinese Cultural Revolution?
12. Which Jules Verne character is associated with the submarine *Nautilus*?
13. Where are the resort beaches of Meadfoot, Oddicombe, and Redgate?
14. Who was the beaten Wimbledon men's singles tennis finalist in 1974?
15. Which gulf separates the Red Sea from the Arabian Sea?

ANSWERS 1. The Bible **2.** Nine of Diamonds **3.** August Strindberg **4.** 1966 **5.** Ash **6.** Three **7.** French **8.** Play it - it's a musical instrument **9.** Recording the movements of a ballet **10.** Thomas Gage **11.** 1966 **12.** Captain Nemo **13.** Torquay **14.** Ken Rosewall **15.** Gulf of Aden.

ENTERTAINMENT

1. Which 2000 television drama by Kay Mellor featured Alison Steadman and Gaynor Faye?
2. Which teen movie of 2000 starred the actors Breckin Meyer and Seann William Scott?
3. Who composed the 1850 opera *Lohengrin*?
4. For which three films did Frank Capra win Best Director Oscar?
5. Which film won more Oscars - *Patton* or *Gandhi*?
6. Which character does Francis L. Sullivan play in the 1946 film *Great Expectations*?
7. Who plays Captain Buncher in the 1949 film *Whisky Galore!*?
8. Who directed the 1969 film *The Italian Job*?
9. Who choreographed the 1892 ballet *The Nutcracker*?
10. What is James Nesbitt's character name in the television drama *Cold Feet*?
11. Who directed the 1971 film *Sunday, Bloody Sunday*?
12. For which two films did Anthony Quinn win Best Supporting Actor Oscar awards?
13. For which film did Emma Thompson win a Best Actress Oscar?
14. Which actor played Ricky Butcher in the soap opera *EastEnders*?
15. Who directed the 1949 film *Passport to Pimlico*?

ANSWERS **1.** Fat Friends **2.** Road Trip **3.** Richard Wagner **4.** It Happened One Night, Mr. Deeds Goes to Town and You Can't Take It With You **5.** Gandhi **6.** Jaggers **7.** Compton Mackenzie **8.** Peter Collinson **9.** Lev Ivanov **10.** Adam Williams **11.** John Schlesinger **12.** Viva Zapata! and Lust For Life **13.** Howards End **14.** Sid Owen **15.** Henry Cornelius.

SPORT

1. Which golfer won the Algarve Open in April 1999?
2. Who was the first man to win the Indianapolis 500 race four times?
3. Who was European women's singles badminton champion in 1990 and '92?
4. Who scored the only goal in the 1995 FA Cup final?
5. Who won the women's 400m hurdles at the 1993 IAAF World Championships?
6. Who won the women's long jump in 1987 and '91 at the IAAF World Championships?
7. Who was the 1996 US Masters golf champion?
8. Which Toulouse Olympique rugby league player captained the French national side from 1969-70?
9. Which Ugandan won the 1972 Olympic men's 400m hurdles title?
10. Which Hungarian was 1967 European Footballer of the Year?
11. In which sport is the Henry Leaf Cup played for?
12. Where were the 1984 Summer Olympics held?
13. Which sport are Tian Bingye and Li Yongbo linked with?
14. At what racecourse are the 1,000 Guineas and 2,000 Guineas held?
15. At which golf course were the 1985 and '89 Ryder Cups held?

ANSWERS 1. Vanslow Phillips **2.** A.J. Foyt **3.** Pernille Nedergaard **4.** Paul Rideout **5.** Sally Gunnell **6.** Jackie Joyner-Kersee **7.** Nick Faldo **8.** Georges Aillères **9.** John Akii-Bua **10.** Florian Albert **11.** Real Tennis **12.** Los Angeles **13.** Badminton **14.** Newmarket **15.** The Belfry.

POP

1. Which US group recorded the 1985 album *No Free Lunch*?
2. Who produced Gary Glitter's 1972 LP *Glitter*?
3. Who was the lead singer of the US group *The Gun Club*?
4. Who is the lead singer with the group James?
5. On which 1979 studio album did The Jam's song *The Eton Rifles* appear?
6. Joanne Catherall and Susanne Sulley are singers with which group?
7. What is the name of Courtney Love's group?
8. Which group's debut album featured the song *Lemon Firebrigade*?
9. Who recorded the 1989 album *New York*?
10. Which blues artist wrote the song *Take Out Some Insurance*?
11. Which US punk group had a hit with *Sheena is a Punk Rocker*?
12. Keith Reid and Gary Brooker were the songwriting force behind which group?
13. Charlie Reid and Craig Reid comprise which singing duo?
14. Who wrote the song *Simon Smith and the Amazing Dancing Bear*?
15. Which singer worked for the Crown Electric Company in 1953 as a truck driver?

ANSWERS **1.** Green on Red **2.** Mike Leander **3.** Jeffrey Lee Pierce **4.** Tim Booth **5.** Setting Sons **6.** The Human League **7.** Hole **8.** Haircut One Hundred **9.** Lou Reed **10.** Jimmy Reed **11.** The Ramones **12.** Procol Harum **13.** The Proclaimers **14.** Randy Newman **15.** Elvis Presley.

WORDS

1. Which foodstuff is named after the French word for 'crescent'?
2. What is the name given to one of the 10 black-belt grades of proficiency in judo?
3. In anatomy, what is the dorsum better known as?
4. If something were falcate, what would it be shaped like?
5. What in heraldry is a 'fesse point'?
6. What method of transport in the U.S. is a jitney?
7. What is the card dealer at a gaming table called?
8. Which plant is named after the French phrase 'tooth of a lion'?
9. What is the name for a male duck?
10. What is the U.S. term for autumn?
11. What is a 'hug-me-tight'?
12. What animal is known in West Africa as a jocko?
13. The Curragh is an Irish racecourse. What is a curragh?
14. For what title is D.B.E. an abbreviation?
15. What is the name given to light rain whose droplets are less than 0.5mm in diameter?

ANSWERS **1.** Croissant **2.** Dan **3.** The back **4.** A sickle **5.** The midpoint of a shield **6.** A small passenger-carrying bus **7.** Croupier **8.** Dandelion **9.** Drake **10.** Fall **11.** A woman's knitted jacket **12.** Chimpanzee **13.** Coracle **14.** Dame Commander of the Order of the British Empire **15.** Drizzle.

GENERAL KNOWLEDGE

1. In which year was Jupiter's moon Leda discovered?
2. In which year was the biographical dictionary *Who's Who* first published?
3. Which of the quarter days in England falls on March 25?
4. Which supernatural being in Arthurian legend is identified with the enchantress Vivien?
5. On what day of the week was Christmas Day 1914?
6. In which year did Hurricane Gordon hit Florida and Alabama?
7. In which year did the dancer and choreographer Martha Graham die?
8. In which year was the Kohoutek comet first seen?
9. Which village in South Vietnam was the site of a massacre by U.S. troops of over 400 civilians in 1968?
10. Which village in Berkshire is the site of the Atomic Weapons Research Establishment?
11. In the United States of America, what is the state flower of New Jersey?
12. What is the English name of the constellation whose Latin name is *Lupus*?
13. What might you do in the U.S. with a pandowdy?
14. In which country is the World Heritage site of Kaziranga National Park?
15. In which year was the space mission Voyager 1 launched?

ANSWERS 1. 1974 **2.** 1849 **3.** Lady Day **4.** The Lady of the Lake **5.** Friday **6.** 1994 **7.** 1991 **8.** 1973 **9.** My Lai **10.** Aldermaston **11.** Purple violet **12.** Wolf **13.** Eat it - it's a fruit pie **14.** India **15.** 1977.

ENTERTAINMENT

1. Which Hollywood actor narrated the 1981 series *Big Jim and the Figaro Club*?
2. In which year was the singer Placido Domingo born?
3. Which film was voted 1948 Best Motion Picture in the New York Film Critics Awards?
4. In which year was *Abba - the Movie* released?
5. Which writing duo penned the 1982 sitcom *The Further Adventures of Lucky Jim*?
6. Who played Tommy Devon in the 1974 series *The Zoo Gang*?
7. Who played Clark Gable in the 1976 film *Gable and Lombard*?
8. Who composed the music for the ballet *The Wooden Prince*?
9. Which duo from *Whose Line is it Anyway* starred in the 1992 sitcom *The Big One*?
10. In which year was comedian Jimmy Jewel born?
11. Who choreographed the 1951 ballet *Pineapple Poll*?
12. Who directed the 1997 film *The Game*?
13. Who was television's *The Gaffer*?
14. Who played Heinrich Himmler in the film *The Eagle Has Landed*?
15. Who did Liza Minnelli play in the 1972 film *Cabaret*?

ANSWERS **1.** Bob Hoskins **2.** 1941 **3.** The Treasure of the Sierra Madre **4.** 1977 **5.** Dick Clement & Ian La Frenais **6.** John Mills **7.** James Brolin **8.** Bela Bartok **9.** Sandi Toksvig & Mike McShane **10.** 1909 **11.** John Cranko **12.** David Fincher **13.** Bill Maynard **14.** Donald Pleasence **15.** Sally Bowles.

SPORT

1. Who scored for Sunderland in their 1998/99 league fixture at Bradford City?
2. In which year was athlete Brendan Foster born?
3. Which former batsman coached the 1999 Bangladesh World Cup cricket side?
4. Which country did Astrid Kumbernuss represent in winning women's shot at the 1995 and '97 IAAF World Championships?
5. Which horse won the 1995 St. Leger?
6. Who was men's heavyweight judo champion 1979-83?
7. Which former world professional snooker champion was born in Wishaw?
8. In which year did rally driver Roger Clark die?
9. Which cricketer scored the earliest century in the history of the county championship on April 15 1999?
10. Which former Sheffield United player managed Benfica, winning them three Portuguese league titles?
11. What was the nickname of baseball star Jimmy Foxx?
12. Where were the 1991 IAAF World Championships held?
13. Who scored the fourth goal for Brazil in the 1970 World Cup final?
14. Which millionaire woman golfer won the US Girls' Junior Amateur title in 1973?
15. Which Australian bowler exceeded 40 wickets twice in a series against England, in 1981 and '89?

ANSWERS **1.** Niall Quinn **2.** 1948 **3.** Gordon Greenidge **4.** Germany **5.** Classic Cliche **6.** Yasuhiro Yamashita **7.** John Higgins **8.** 1998 **9.** Dougie Brown **10.** Jimmy Hagan **11.** Double X **12.** Tokyo **13.** Carlos Alberto **14.** Amy Alcott **15.** Terry Alderman.

POP

1. Which pop group released the 2000 album *Howdy!*?
2. Which female singer released the 2000 album *Light Years*?
3. Which Frenchman wrote six tracks on Madonna's album *Music*?
4. Under what name do pop duo Jacqui Askew and Carri Blake record?
5. What is the home town of French dance act Phunky Data?
6. From which town do the group Speedvark hail?
7. Who recorded the 1981 album *Party*?
8. What was the first Top 10 album in the UK for the group The Faces?
9. Which group recorded the 1970 Top 10 album *Thank Christ for the Bomb*?
10. Which boy band released the 2000 single *My Love*?
11. In which year was the song *Modern Love* a No. 2 single for David Bowie?
12. Which girl group recorded the 2000 album *Forever*?
13. In which year did The Police release their first live album?
14. From which country do the group Sigur Ros hail?
15. Which Australian group recorded the album *The Friends of Rachel Worth*?

ANSWERS **1.** Teenage Fanclub **2.** Kylie Minogue **3.** Mirwais **4.** Shampoo **5.** Grenoble **6.** Hemel Hempstead **7.** Iggy Pop **8.** A Nod's As Good As A Wink...To A Blind Horse **9.** Groundhogs **10.** Westlife **11.** 1983 **12.** Spice Girls **13.** 1995 **14.** Iceland **15.** The Go-Betweens.

ENTERTAINMENT

1. Who did Dan Blocker play in the TV show *Bonanza*?
2. *Barnacle Bill* is the theme music of which children's show?
3. Who played *Andy Capp* in the TV version of the comic strip?
4. Who played Rocky Holeczek in the 1995 film *Roommates*?
5. Who played the title role in the 1975 film *Rooster Cogburn*?
6. Who directed the film *Rosencrantz and Guildenstern are Dead* from his own play?
7. Who directed the 1965 film comedy *Rotten to the Core*?
8. Who directed the 1989 film *She-Devil*?
9. Which actor is conned into becoming *The Sheriff of Fractured Jaw* in the 1958 film?
10. Who directed and starred in the 1924 film *Sherlock, Jr.*?
11. Who directed the 1997 film *Scream 2*?
12. Which 1955 film tells the tale of the ship *Ergenstrasse*?
13. Who played Peter Loew in the 1988 film *Vampire's Kiss*?
14. Who directed the 1996 film *The Van*?
15. Who did Jonathan Rhys Meyers play in the 1998 film *Velvet Goldmine*?

ANSWERS **1.** Hoss Cartwright **2.** Blue Peter **3.** James Bolam **4.** Peter Falk **5.** John Wayne **6.** Tom Stoppard **7.** John Boulting **8.** Susan Seidelman **9.** Kenneth More **10.** Buster Keaton **11.** Wes Craven **12.** The Sea Chase **13.** Nicolas Cage **14.** Stephen Frears **15.** Brian Slade.

GENERAL KNOWLEDGE

1. Bucephalus was the favourite horse of which historical figure?
2. Approximately how many people visited Shakespeare's birthplace in Stratford in 1991 - 300,000, 500,000 or 700,000?
3. In which city is the University of Strathclyde?
4. In which year did author Laurie Lee die?
5. Who in May 1999 became professor of poetry at Oxford?
6. What is the art of cutting hedges into ornamental shapes?
7. What was the middle name of Dame Ngaio Marsh?
8. Who was the biblical sister of Mary and Lazarus?
9. In which year was the Battle of the Falaise Gap in World War II?
10. Who wrote the 1925 play *Fallen Angels*?
11. What is the name given to the opening move in chess in which a chessman is sacrificed to secure an advantageous position?
12. What is the name of the fat knight in the play *Henry IV*?
13. What colour is the liqueur crème de menthe?
14. What is the Finnish name for Finland?
15. On which ship did Napoleon formally surrender after defeat at Waterloo?

ANSWERS 1. Alexander the Great **2.** 500,000 **3.** Glasgow **4.** 1997 **5.** Paul Muldoon **6.** Topiary **7.** Edith **8.** Martha **9.** 1944 **10.** Noël Coward **11.** Gambit **12.** Sir John Falstaff **13.** Green **14.** Suomi **15.** HMS Bellerophon.

ENTERTAINMENT

1. Who played the young Christy Brown in the film *My Left Foot*?
2. How many Best Actor Oscar nominations has Peter O'Toole received?
3. In and around which South Yorkshire town was the film *Kes* shot?
4. Who directed the 1939 film *Goodbye, Mr. Chips*?
5. Which character was played by Adrian Edmondson in the sitcom *The Young Ones*?
6. Who composed the 1842 opera *Nabucco*?
7. Other than four-times winner Katharine Hepburn, which ten actresses have each won Best Actress Oscar Award twice?
8. Near which London railway station is the villains' hideout in the 1955 film *The Ladykillers*?
9. Who plays Uncle Monty in the film *Withnail & I*?
10. Who directed the 1966 film *A Man For All Seasons*?
11. Who directed the 1962 film *The Loneliness of the Long Distance Runner*?
12. Who was the director of the 1988 film *Colors*?
13. Which 1999 feature film was actor Tim Roth's directorial debut?
14. What was Carrie Fisher's character name in the film *Star Wars*?
15. What was the name of Lady Penelope's chauffeur in the television puppet series *Thunderbirds*?

ANSWERS 1. Hugh O'Connor **2.** 7 **3.** Barnsley **4.** Sam Wood **5.** Vyvyan **6.** Verdi **7.** Luise Rainer, Jodie Foster, Elizabeth Taylor, Sally Field, Jane Fonda, Olivia De Havilland, Ingrid Bergman, Bette Davis, Vivien Leigh and Glenda Jackson **8.** St. Pancras **9.** Richard Griffiths **10.** Fred Zinnemann **11.** Tony Richardson **12.** Dennis Hopper **13.** The War Zone **14.** Princess Leia Organa **15.** Parker.

SPORT

1. Who was European women's singles badminton champion in 1996 and '98?
2. Which Premier League football team does Chief Secretary to the Treasury Alan Milburn support?
3. At which sport does Graham Garden play for Great Britain?
4. In which year did Adi Dassler make his first pair of running shoes?
5. Who rode Midnight Court to win the Cheltenham Gold Cup in 1978?
6. Which Scottish football team were League Champions from 1928-31?
7. Who was runner-up in the 1995 world Formula 1 motor racing championship?
8. Which woman won the 1980 Boston marathon but was later discovered to have run only the last two miles of it?
9. In which year did Grant Fox make his All Black debut in rugby union?
10. Which team won the 1995 world series in baseball?
11. Which Finn won the 1000 Lakes Rally from 1978-80?
12. In which year did Mohammed Ali regain the world heavyweight title from George Foreman?
13. At what sport did American Elizabeth Allan-Shetter excel?
14. Who finished third in the 1993 Belgian Grand Prix?
15. Who was the Australian Open men's singles title winner in 1989 and '90?

ANSWERS 1. Camilla Martin **2.** Newcastle United **3.** Ice hockey **4.** 1920 **5.** John Francombe **6.** Rangers **7.** Damon Hill **8.** Rosie Ruiz **9.** 1985 **10.** Atlanta Braves **11.** Markku Alen **12.** 1974 **13.** Water skiing **14.** Alain Prost **15.** Ivan Lendl.

POP

1. Who had a No. 2 single in 1977 with *Ain't Gonna Bump No More (With No Big Fat Woman)*?
2. Which artist recorded the albums *Rebel Yell* and *Whiplash Smile*?
3. Who was lead singer with the group Amen Corner?
4. Which songwriting duo penned *Sittin' on a Fence* for 1960s act Twice As Much?
5. Which group recorded the album *Thirty Thousand Feet Over China*?
6. Which singer formed the group Doll By Doll in 1977?
7. Brian Eno's song *King's Lead Hat* was intentionally an anagram of which group?

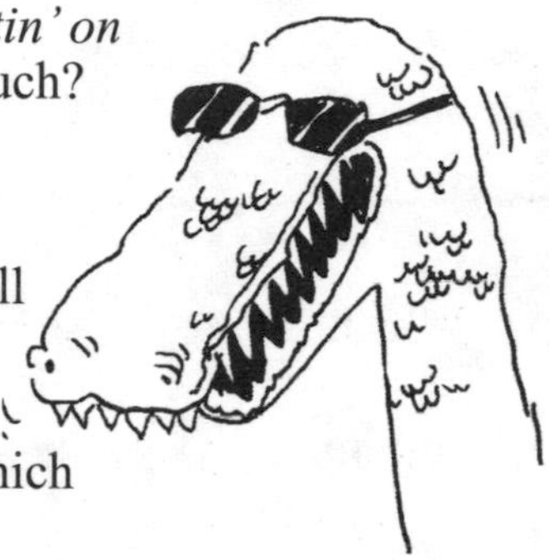

8. Whose hit singles included *Metal Guru* and *Truck On (Tyke)*?
9. Which vocal group's hits included *Psychedelic Shack* and *My Girl*?
10. Which US band had a 1977 hit album with *Marquee Moon*?
11. Who was lead singer with The Undertones?
12. Which 1960s icon recorded the 1983 album *Climate of Hunter*?
13. John Foxx was the lead singer with which latterly successful punk band?
14. Who recorded the 1981 album *The Flowers of Romance*?
15. On which label did Them record the 1965 hit *Here Comes the Night*?

ANSWERS **1.** Joe Tex **2.** Billy Idol **3.** Andy Fairweather Low **4.** Mick Jagger and Keith Richard **5.** The Passions **6.** Jackie Leven **7.** Talking Heads **8.** T.Rex **9.** Temptations **10.** Television **11.** Feargal Sharkey **12.** Scott Walker **13.** Ultravox **14.** Public Image Ltd **15.** Decca.

PEOPLE

1. In which year was the Japanese fashion designer Issey Miyake born?
2. Which famous dress designer fashioned rock group Queen's outfits in the early 1970s?
3. Which member of Britain's silver medal-winning three-day event team at the 2000 Olympics rode the mount Jaybee?
4. Which painter married Hortense Fiquet in 1886?
5. Which American Indian leader was defeated at Tippecanoe in 1811?
6. Eleutherios Venizelos was prime minister of which country from 1928-32?
7. Who was the 2000 Olympic men's 100m champion?
8. In which year did the German aircraft designer Ernst Heinkel die?
9. Which racing-car designer was born in Modena, Italy in 1898?
10. Who was the President of the European Commission from 1985-94?
11. What is actress Gillian Anderson's middle name?
12. Which Montreal-born male tennis player switched to play for Great Britain in May 1995?
13. Which football and showbiz agent authored the 1998 biography *Monster!*?
14. What was the Italian painter Alberto Burri's original profession?
15. In which year was the singer Sam Cooke shot and killed?

ANSWERS 1. 1938 **2.** Zandra Rhodes **3.** Ian Stark **4.** Paul Cézanne **5.** Tecumseh **6.** Greece **7.** Maurice Greene **8.** 1958 **9.** Enzo Ferrari **10.** Jacques Delors **11.** Leigh **12.** Greg Rusedski **13.** Eric Hall **14.** Doctor **15.** 1965.

GENERAL KNOWLEDGE

1. In which year was the US satellite Clementine launched?
2. In the United States of America, what is the state flower of Illinois?
3. On what day of the week was Christmas Day 1928?
4. In which year did the opera singer Kathleen Ferrier die?
5. In which year was Jupiter's moon Sinope discovered?
6. Which port in Canada is the capital of Newfoundland?
7. In Greek mythology, what bird was Tereus turned into for raping his sister-in-law?
8. What type of creature in Australia is a vedalia?
9. LA is the zip code of which state in the USA?
10. A panatella is a thin long cigar. What does panatella mean in Italian?
11. Who directed the 1980 film *Gregory's Girl*?
12. In which airport does Alexander Calder's 14 metre-wide mobile *Red, Black, and Blue* hang?
13. The work teriyaki in Japanese cookery is made up of the words 'teri' and 'yaki'. What do these translate as?
14. Where on a dog might you find a terret?
15. How far away in light years is the star Vega?

ANSWERS 1. 1994 **2.** Butterfly violet **3.** Tuesday **4.** 1953 **5.** 1914 **6.** St. John's **7.** Hoopoe **8.** Ladybird **9.** Louisiana **10.** Small loaf **11.** Bill Forsyth **12.** Dallas **13.** Glaze and boil **14.** Its collar - it's the name of the ring to which a lead is attached **15.** 26.

ENTERTAINMENT

1. The film *Gigi* won 9 Oscars in 1958. For how many Oscars was it nominated?
2. For which two films did Peter Ustinov win Best Supporting Actor Oscar awards?
3. Who plays Lara in the 1965 film *Doctor Zhivago*?
4. Who directed the 1958 film *Room at the Top*?
5. Who composed the 1968 opera *Punch and Judy*?
6. Who choreographed the 1975 ballet *The Four Seasons*?
7. Which British actor had a starring role in the romantic comedy film *The Truth About Cats & Dogs*?
8. What is Gwyneth Paltrow's character name in the film *Shakespeare in Love*?
9. Who scored the 1983 film *Local Hero*?
10. How many Oscars did the film *The Bridge on the River Kwai* win?
11. Who choreographed the 1958 ballet *Ondine*?
12. Who authored the play *Mojo* which was filmed in 1998?
13. Who directed the 1964 film *Goldfinger*?
14. Who played King George in the film *The Madness of King George*?
15. Which film won more Oscars - *On the Waterfront* or *Out of Africa*?

ANSWERS **1.** 9 **2.** Spartacus and Topkapi **3.** Julie Christie **4.** Jack Clayton **5.** Harrison Birtwistle **6.** Kenneth Macmillan **7.** Ben Chaplin **8.** Viola De Lesseps **9.** Mark Knopfler **10.** Seven **11.** Frederick Ashton **12.** Jez Butterworth **13.** Guy Hamilton **14.** Nigel Hawthorne **15.** On the Waterfront.

SPORT

1. Who defeated Chelsea in the semi-final of the 1998/9 European Cup Winners' Cup?
2. Which boxer won a gold medal as a heavyweight at the 1964 Olympics?
3. What was the middle name of cricketer W.G. Grace?
4. Which swimmer was named Australian of the Year in 1967?
5. Who was 1964 Olympic men's 100m champion?
6. For which county side did cricketer Tom Graveney play from 1948-60?
7. Which team won Superbowl V in 1971 in American Football?
8. With which side did basketball star Walt Frazier end his playing career?
9. Who won the women's shot at the 1991 and '93 IAAF World Championships?
10. What was the winning boat in the 1995 America's Cup?
11. Which English Test cricketer was chairman of the Test selectors from 1955-61?
12. Who won the inaugural world men's triathlon championship in 1989?
13. Which team did Phog Allen coach in winning the 1952 Olympic basketball title?
14. What is the nationality of snooker player Doug Mountjoy?
15. In cycling, who won the 1993 World Road Race?

ANSWERS 1. Real Mallorca **2.** Joe Frazier **3.** Gilbert **4.** Dawn Fraser **5.** Bob Hayes **6.** Gloucestershire **7.** Baltimore Colts **8.** Cleveland Cavaliers **9.** Zhihong Huang **10.** Black Magic 1 **11.** Gubby Allen **12.** Mark Allen **13.** The U.S. **14.** Welsh **15.** Lance Armstrong.

POP

1. Which U.K. group's only Top Ten single was 1970s *Love Like a Man*?
2. On which label did Terrorvision record their hits *Oblivion* and *My House*?
3. Which singer recorded the hit albums *The Last Waltz* and *A Man without Love*?
4. Which group recorded the album *Autoamerican*?
5. Which group recorded the album *Kings of the Wild Frontier*?
6. From which city did group Young Marble Giants hail?
7. On which studio album by Siouxsie and the Banshees did the single *Christine* appear?
8. What was Echo and the Bunnymen's debut single?
9. On what date did John Lennon die?
10. Which US group featured the talents of Black Francis and Mrs. John Murphy?
11. What is the girl's name in Pulp's song *Disco 2000*?
12. The 1981 album *Talk Talk Talk* was recorded by the group Talk Talk - true or false?
13. What is unusual about the cover of the 1979 LP *The Return of the Durutti Column*?
14. Who recorded the album *New Boots and Panties*?
15. Who is the driving force behind the group *The The*?

ANSWERS 1. Ten Years After **2.** Total Vegas **3.** Engelbert Humperdinck **4.** Blondie **5.** Adam and the Ants **6.** Cardiff **7.** Kaleidoscope **8.** Pictures on My Wall **9.** December 8, 1980 **10.** The Pixies **11.** Deborah **12.** False, it was by the Psychedelic Furs **13.** It is covered in sandpaper **14.** Ian Dury **15.** Matt Johnson.

ART AND LITERATURE

1. Who wrote the novel *Model Behaviour*?
2. Which British artist's works include the 1960 painting *Dance, Blue and Yellow*?
3. Who wrote the novel *A Desert in Bohemia*?
4. Which British artist's works include the 1967 painting *Haystack in a Field*?
5. Who wrote the 2000 novel *When We Were Orphans*?
6. Which artist's works include the 1930 sculpture *Construction in a Niche*?
7. Who wrote the novel *Gaglow*?
8. Who wrote the 2001 novel *True History of the Kelly Gang*?
9. Which British artist's works include the 1967 wood and mixed media piece *Starlit Waters*?
10. Who wrote the 2000 novel *The Last Precinct*?
11. Which British artist's works include the 1928 portrait *Marguerite Kelsey*?
12. Which US writer's works include the 1946 novel *Delta Wedding*?
13. Which German dramatist authored the 1891 play *The Awakening of Spring*?
14. Who wrote the 2000 short story collection *Diamond Dust*?
15. Who wrote the 2000 novel *The River King*?

ANSWERS **1.** Jay McInerney **2.** Anthony Frost **3.** Jill Paton Walsh **4.** Sheila Fell **5.** Kazuo Ishiguro **6.** Naum Gabo **7.** Esther Freud **8.** Peter Carey **9.** Ian Hamilton Finlay **10.** Patricia Cornwell **11.** Meredith Frampton **12.** Eudora Welty **13.** Frank Wedekind **14.** Anita Desai **15.** Alice Hoffman.

GENERAL KNOWLEDGE

1. In which country was architect Le Corbusier born?
2. Who replaced John Reid as transport minister in May 1999?
3. What does A&R stand for in the music industry?
4. Which poet is associated with Dove Cottage in Grasmere?
5. Abbotsford was the home of which Scottish author?
6. What are usually kept in an earthenware pot called a gallipot?
7. In what card game might you use the Culbertson system?
8. Who wrote the 1932 play *Dangerous Corner*?
9. What type of art form is Hans Henze's *The Tedious Way to the Place of Natasha Ungeheuer*?
10. Who wrote the novel *Caravan to Vaccares*?
11. Who was the Roman god of wine?
12. On what island is the volcano Askja?
13. In which year was Queen Elizabeth II born?
14. What was the original name of entertainer Tommy Steele?
15. In which ocean are the Marquesas Islands?

ANSWERS **1.** Switzerland **2.** Helen Liddell **3.** Artists and Repertoire **4.** William Wordsworth **5.** Sir Walter Scott **6.** Ointments **7.** Bridge **8.** J.B. Priestley **9.** An opera **10.** Alistair Maclean **11.** Bacchus **12.** Iceland **13.** 1926 **14.** Thomas Hicks **15.** Pacific Ocean.

ENTERTAINMENT

1. Who played Major Langton in the television drama series *The Shillingbury Tales*?
2. How many Best Actor Oscar nominations did Richard Burton receive?
3. Who plays '1st Irishman' in the 1981 film *The Long Good Friday*?
4. In which year did the Winter Garden theatre in New York open?
5. Which Scottish composer's first opera was 1967's *The Decision*?
6. Who choreographed the 1950 ballet *Don Quixote*?
7. Which television drama series features the animal Diefenbaker?
8. What is Andrew Strong's character name in the film *The Commitments*?
9. Who directed the 1973 film *The Day of the Jackal*?
10. Who plays playwright Christopher Marlowe in the film *Shakespeare in Love*?
11. Who authored the 1980 play *The Dresser*?
12. Who was the creator of the television puppet Basil Brush?
13. Who starred as *Tank Girl* in the 1995 film?
14. Who did Cathy, the daughter of comedian Phil Silvers, play in the sitcom *Happy Days*?
15. Who did Michael Crawford play in the television series *Sir Francis Drake*?

ANSWERS 1. Lionel Jeffries **2.** 6 **3.** Pierce Brosnan **4.** 1911 **5.** Thea Musgrave **6.** Ninette de Valois **7.** Due South **8.** Decco Cuffe **9.** Fred Zinnemann **10.** Rupert Everett **11.** Ronald Harwood **12.** Ivan Owen **13.** Lori Petty **14.** Jenny Piccalo **15.** John Drake.

SPORT

1. What nationality is synchronized swimming champion Sylvie Fréchette?
2. Who was the 1997 US Masters golf champion?
3. What age was Steffi Graf when she won her first Grand Slam title in 1987?
4. In which make of car did Jones, Reuter and Wurtz win the 1996 Le Mans race?
5. How many century opening partnerships did Gordon Greenidge and Desmond Haynes record for the West Indies?
6. Following Liverpool's 2-1 defeat in the 1971 FA Cup final, which was the next defeated team to register a goal in the final?
7. Which Scottish football team were runners-up in the League in 1933 and '34?
8. Which two Italian teams met in the 1990 UEFA Cup final?
9. Which American Football star was known as 'the Galloping Ghost'?
10. Which boxer was born Thomas Rocca Barbella?
11. Who won the women's javelin title at the 1987 IAAF World Championships?
12. Who scored the only goal in the 1985 FA Cup final?
13. Jose Altafini played for Brazil in football's 1958 World Cup. Which country did he play for in the 1962 World Cup?
14. Which Briton won the 1952 Olympic women's figure skating title?
15. Which Texas-born American Football star of the 1960s was known as 'Bambi'?

ANSWERS **1.** Canadian **2.** Tiger Woods **3.** 17 **4.** Porsche **5.** 16 **6.** Liverpool, in 1977 **7.** Motherwell **8.** Juventus and Fiorentina **9.** Red Grange **10.** Rocky Graziano **11.** Fatima Whitbread **12.** Norman Whiteside **13.** Italy **14.** Jeanette Altwegg **15.** Lance Alworth.

POP

1. On which label did Frankie Goes to Hollywood record their 1984 LP *Welcome to the Pleasuredome*?
2. How did Peter Gabriel's 1986 studio album *So* differ from its four predecessors?
3. Which group's albums include *Heartbreaker* and *Fire and Water*?
4. Which Irish guitarist's albums included *Deuce* and *Tattoo*?
5. Who recorded 1978's *Well, Well, Said the Rocking Chair* LP?
6. Which groups albums included 1979's *The Adventures of the Hersham Boys*?
7. Which group had a No. 1 single with *Ebeneezer Goode*?
8. Which group had a No. 1 single in Thailand with the song *Ocean Pie*?
9. What is Texas-born singer Karen Johnson better known as?
10. Which duo recorded the 1966 album *Parsley, Sage, Rosemary and Thyme*?
11. Which group's debut album in 1979 was *Life in a Day*?
12. What was the first single of the band Simply Red?
13. Which US singer's first single, in 1961, was *Cufflinks and a Tie Clip*?
14. Sahm, Kagan, Perez, Meyer and Morin - which 1960s band?
15. Which group were formed in Leeds in 1980 by Andrew Eldritch and Gary Marx?

ANSWERS **1.** ZTT **2.** It wasn't called 'Peter Gabriel' **3.** Free **4.** Rory Gallagher **5.** Dean Friedman **6.** Sham 69 **7.** The Shamen **8.** Shed Seven **9.** Michelle Shocked **10.** Simon & Garfunkel **11.** Simple Minds **12.** Money's Too Tight (to mention) **13.** Nancy Sinatra **14.** Sir Douglas Quintet **15.** Sisters of Mercy.

GEOGRAPHY

1. What is the capital of Uzbekistan?
2. In which country of the Americas is the state of Tabasco?

3. In which European country is the town of Schiedam, which is associated with the gin industry?
4. In which African country is Ujiji, meeting place of Stanley and Livingstone?
5. In which European country is the resort town of Spa?
6. Sandbach is a market town in which English county?
7. In which U.S. state is the tourist town of Redondo Beach?
8. On which river is the motor car manufacturing town of Pontiac?
9. Which Italian city lies at the foot of Mount Vesuvius opposite ancient Pompeii?
10. In which South American country is the oil refining town of Moron?
11. Which is larger - Massachusetts or Maine?
12. Which strait separates Chile and Tierra del Fuego?
13. On which river is Louisville, Kentucky?
14. In which English county is the holiday resort of Looe?
15. In which island group is Ibiza?

ANSWERS 1. Tashkent **2.** Mexico **3.** The Netherlands **4.** Tanzania **5.** Belgium **6.** Cheshire **7.** California **8.** Clinton River **9.** Naples **10.** Venezuela **11.** Maine **12.** Magellan Strait **13.** Ohio River **14.** Cornwall **15.** The Balearic Islands.

GENERAL KNOWLEDGE

1. What was the first month of the French Revolutionary calendar?
2. How many masts does a schooner called a tern have?
3. In which year was the dancer Ruth St. Denis born?
4. Who is Scarlett O'Hara's third husband in the novel *Gone with the Wind*?
5. Which principality in S.W. Europe includes the port La Condamine?
6. Which town in Surrey houses Charterhouse School?
7. Which town in central Italy was the birthplace of St. Francis?
8. What is Venus's looking glass?
9. What was the approximate population in millions of the state of Texas in 1996?
10. What was the name of the sea that lay between the two supercontinents of Laurasia and Gondwanaland?
11. In which year was the space mission Viking 1 launched?
12. In which African country is the World Heritage site of Ichkeul National Park?
13. WI is the zip code of which state in the U.S.A.?
14. In the United States of America, what is the state flower of Georgia?
15. In which sport might you employ a veronica?

ANSWERS **1.** Vendémiaire **2.** Three **3.** 1879 **4.** Rhett Butler **5.** Monaco **6.** Godalming **7.** Assisi **8.** A purple-flowered plant **9.** 19m **10.** Tethys **11.** 1975 **12.** Tunisia **13.** Wisconsin **14.** Cherokee rose **15.** Bullfighting.

ENTERTAINMENT

1. Which two actors played Dr. Rudy Wells in the 1970s series *The Six Million Dollar Man*?
2. The film *The Last Emperor* won 9 Oscars in 1987. For how many Oscars was it nominated?
3. Who won Best Director Oscar for their debut film at the helm, *Terms of Endearment*?
4. Who wrote the screenplay for the 1992 film *The Crying Game*?
5. Who directed the 1967 film *This Sporting Life*?
6. Who directed the 1993 film *The Remains of the Day*?
7. Which character is played by Chris Barrie in the sitcom *Red Dwarf*?
8. Who plays *Xena - Warrior Princess* on television?
9. Who is the male lead in the 2000 film *What Lies Beneath*?
10. For which 1990 film did Whoopi Goldberg win a Best Supporting Actress Oscar?
11. Who are the male and female stars of the 1968 film *The Thomas Crown Affair*?
12. Which theatrical dame played Lady Bracknell in oscar Wilde's *The Importance of Being Earnest* at the National Theatre in 1982?
13. Which veteran comedian played Shifty Shafer in the television series *The Beverly Hillbillies*?
14. Which comedian played the postal worker Frank Draper in soap *Coronation Street*?
15. For which two films did Jason Robards win Best Supporting Actor Oscar awards?

ANSWERS 1. Alan Oppenheimer and Martin E. Brooks **2.** 9 **3.** James L. Brooks **4.** Neil Jordan **5.** Lindsay Anderson **6.** James Ivory **7.** Arnold J. Rimmer **8.** Lucy Lawless **9.** Harrison Ford **10.** Ghost **11.** Steve McQueen and Faye Dunaway **12.** Judi Dench **13.** Phil Silvers **14.** Paul Shane **15.** All the President's Men and Julia.

SPORT

1. In which year did Curtly Ambrose make his Test debut for the West Indies?
2. Which England Test wicket-keeper was manager and secretary of Kent from 1960-74?
3. French football defender Manuel Amoros won a record 82 international caps. How many goals did he score in those games?
4. Who, in 1999, became the second German to play in an FA Cup final?
5. Which team won the 1996 world series in baseball?
6. Which cyclist won the 1996 Tour de France?
7. Which footballer scored for both sides in the 1981 FA Cup final?
8. Which footballer scored for both sides in the 1987 FA Cup final?
9. Who was world rally champion 1996-8?
10. Who was Wimbledon men's singles tennis champion in 1960?
11. Who was English flat racing champion in 1961, '62 and '63?
12. In which US state was swimmer Mark Spitz born?
13. Which yacht deprived the USA of the America's Cup in 1983?
14. Which golfer won the 1993 Canon European Masters?
15. Which team were Scottish football league champions in 1951 and '52?

ANSWERS 1. 1988 **2.** Leslie Ames **3.** One **4.** Dietmar Hamann **5.** New York Yankees **6.** Bjarne Riis **7.** Tommy Hutchison **8.** Gary Mabbutt **9.** Tommi Makinen **10.** Neale Fraser **11.** Scobie Breasley **12.** California **13.** Australia II **14.** Barry Lane **15.** Hibernian.

POP

1. Which group recorded the albums *Surf's Up* and *Sunflower*?
2. Which guitarist's albums include *Jack Orion*?
3. In which year was Prince's album *1999* released?
4. Which group's early songs included *Interstellar Overdrive* and *Astronomy Domine*?
5. In which year was the first gig in the UK by the band The Pixies?
6. In which year Roy Orbison have a No. 1 single with *Oh Pretty Woman*?
7. In which year did the Electric Light Orchestra have a Top 20 with *Showdown*?
8. In which year did the Beatles have a No. 1 single with *Can't Buy Me Love*?
9. Which group recorded the album *Skull & Bones*?
10. Which punk singer began in the group Queen Elizabeth?
11. Which film director was in singer Bryan Ferry's first band?
12. Who recorded the 1997 solo album *Still Burning*?
13. Which group recorded the 1980 Top 10 album *Glory Road*?
14. Who recorded the 1973 Top 10 album *These Foolish Things*?
15. What was the first Top 10 album in the UK for the group Everything But the Girl?

ANSWERS 1. The Beach Boys **2.** Bert Jansch **3.** 1982 **4.** Pink Floyd **5.** 1988 **6.** 1964 **7.** 1973 **8.** 1964 **9.** Cypress Hill **10.** Wayne County **11.** Mike Figgis **12.** Mike Scott **13.** Gillan **14.** Bryan Ferry **15.** Love Not Money.

PEOPLE

1. What was French murderer Henri Desire Landru better known as?
2. What was the maiden name of event rider Lucinda Green?
3. What were the forenames of the Kray Brothers?
4. Who first drew the strip cartoon *Jane* in 1932?
5. What was the stage name of actress Gertrude Klasen?
6. Who did Michelle Gayle play in *EastEnders*?
7. What was the middle name of painter L.S. Lowry?
8. Which cartoonist created the syndicated comic strip *Archie*?
9. Which TV cook is associated with Norwich City F.C.?
10. Which cartoonist created the comic book hero *Captain America*?
11. What was the name of the wife of radio quiz show host Wilfred Pickles?
12. What was the middle name of author J.B. Priestley?
13. Keith Cooper was the unlikely star of which TV documentary series?
14. Which feminist wrote the book *The Whole Woman*?
15. Who was the male star of the film *You've Got Mail*?

ANSWERS **1.** Bluebeard **2.** Lucinda Prior-Palmer **3.** Ronnie and Reggie **4.** Norman Pett **5.** Gertrude Lawrence **6.** Hattie Tavernier **7.** Stephen **8.** Bob Montana **9.** Delia Smith **10.** Jack Kirby **11.** Mabel **12.** Boynton **13.** The House **14.** Germaine Greer **15.** Tom Hanks.

GENERAL KNOWLEDGE

1. What is the English name of the constellation whose Latin name is *Cancer*?
2. RI is the zip code of which state of the USA?
3. What is the state bird of Georgia in the USA?
4. In which year did the jazz musician John Coltrane die?
5. In which year was the Hale-Bopp comet first seen?
6. What is the administrative centre of North Yorkshire?
7. What is the name of the house in the novel *Rebecca*?
8. What is the state flower of Connecticut, U.S.A.?
9. In which century did the Danish-born painter Asmus Jacob Carstens live?
10. Who authored the 1859 novel *A Tale of Two Cities*?
11. Which African river forms the border between Zambia and Zimbabwe?
12. In which year was Neptune's moon Triton discovered?
13. Who was the director of the 1931 film *Frankenstein*?
14. In music, which note has the time value of half a semibreve?
15. Who was the 2000 Olympic women's singles tennis champion?

ANSWERS 1. Crab **2.** Rhode Island **3.** Brown Thrasher **4.** 1967 **5.** 1995 **6.** Northallerton **7.** Manderley **8.** Mountain laurel **9.** 18th century **10.** Charles Dickens **11.** Zambezi **12.** 1846 **13.** James Whale **14.** Minim **15.** Venus Williams.

ENTERTAINMENT

1. For which two films did Dianne Wiest win Best Supporting Actress Oscar awards?
2. Who plays the missing Miss Froy in the 1938 film *The Lady Vanishes*?
3. Who starred in the title role of the 1985 biblical film *King David*?
4. Who choreographed the 1928 ballet *Apollo*?
5. Who composed the opera *The Fair Maid of Perth*?
6. Who played Lou Lewis in the television drama series *Shine On Harvey Moon*?
7. Who played Jane Seymour in the 1970 television drama series *The Six Wives of Henry VIII*?
8. Which actress plays Peggy Mitchell in the soap opera *EastEnders*?
9. Who was voted Most Popular Comedy Performer winner at the 2000 National TV Awards?
10. Who wrote the screenplay for the 1982 film *Gandhi*?
11. Which film won more Oscars - *Shakespeare in Love* or *One Flew Over the Cuckoo's Nest*?
12. Who wrote the screenplay for the 1963 film *The Servant*?
13. Who composed the 1962 opera *King Priam*?
14. Who choreographed the 1981 ballet *Isadora*?
15. How many Best Actress Oscar nominations has Anne Bancroft received?

ANSWERS 1. Hannah and Her Sisters and Bullets Over Broadway **2.** Dame May Whitty **3.** Richard Gere **4.** George Balanchine **5.** Georges Bizet **6.** Nigel Planer **7.** Anne Stallybrass **8.** Barbara Windsor **9.** Michael Barrymore **10.** John Briley **11.** Shakespeare in Love **12.** Harold Pinter **13.** Michael Tippett **14.** Kenneth Macmillan **15.** 5.

SPORT

1. Where were the 1993 IAAF World Championships held?
2. Which 1970 England football World Cup squad member died in June 1998?
3. Who did Lazio defeat in the semi-final of the 1998/9 European Cup Winners' Cup?
4. Which country did Trine Hattestad, winner of the 1993 and '97 women's javelin title at the IAAF World Championships, represent?
5. Which horse won the 1996 St. Leger?
6. Which Scottish football team were championship runners-up four times out of five from 1960-64?
7. Who was men's heavyweight judo champion 1993-97?
8. Who partnered John Lowe to win the first World Pairs title at darts in 1986?
9. Which successful baseball team of the 1970s were known as 'The Big Red Machine'?
10. Which boxing weight division is between Heavyweight and Light-heavyweight?
11. Where were the equestrian events for the Melbourne Olympics held?
12. In which year was Lester Piggott born?
13. Who was Olympic men's 5,000m and 10,000m champion in 1972 and '76?
14. What is a luge?
15. How many times in succession did Bjorn Borg win Wimbledon?

ANSWERS 1. Stuttgart **2.** Keith Newton **3.** Lokomotiv Moscow **4.** Norway **5.** Shantou **6.** Kilmarnock **7.** David Douillet **8.** Bob Anderson **9.** Cincinnati Reds **10.** Cruiserweight **11.** Stockholm **12.** 1935 **13.** Lasse Viren **14.** A light one-man toboggan **15.** Five.

POP

1. What was the identity of Miss X, who had a hit single in 1963 with *Christine*?
2. Which girl singer recorded the 1998 album *Honey to the B*?
3. Who recorded the 1998 album *Decksandrumsandrockandroll*?
4. What was the title of Ringo Starr's 1998 solo album?
5. Which female singer recorded the 1999 album *Central Reservation*?
6. Which trio recorded the 1994 hit single *All For Love*?
7. Who had a 1981 hit single with *Swords of a Thousand Men*?
8. What was the title of Whitney Houston's 1987 No. 1 album?
9. Perrin, Wright, Finney, Nicholls, Sidebottom - which 1980s Manchester group?
10. Which member of the Police recorded under the name of Klark Kent?
11. Which group's albums included *Fickle Heart* and *The Game's Up*?
12. Who was lead guitarist with the band Roxy Music?
13. What was the name of The Beat's elderly Jamaican saxophone player?
14. Which punk group recorded the album *Kiss Me Deadly*?
15. Who produced the 1979 debut LP by The Specials?

ANSWERS 1. Joyce Blair **2.** Billie **3.** Propellerheads **4.** Vertical Man **5.** Beth Orton **6.** Sting, Rod Stewart and Bryan Adams **7.** Ten Pole Tudor **8.** Whitney **9.** The Distractions **10.** Stewart Copeland **11.** Sniff 'n' the Tears **12.** Phil Manzanera **13.** Saxa **14.** Gen X **15.** Elvis Costello.

ART AND LITERATURE

1. Who wrote the 2000 novel *Emotionally Weird*?
2. Which Irish writer was awarded the 1923 Nobel prize for literature?
3. What is the name of the wolf-boy in Rudyard Kipling's *The Jungle Book*?
4. Who wrote the 2000 book *Bad Timing*?
5. Who wrote the Manhattan-based novel *Story of My Life*?
6. What was the full name of the painter James Whistler?
7. Which author's non-fiction works include 1920's *The Outline of History*?
8. Who wrote the novel *Elvis Has Left the Building*?
9. Who wrote the Scottish thriller *Country of the Blind*?
10. Which British artist's works include the 1952 lithograph *Blue Moon*?
11. Which artist's works include the 1908 painting *Gardening*?
12. Who wrote the 2000 book *Hit List*?
13. Which pair of artists' works include the 1972 video installation *Gordon's Makes Us Drunk*?
14. Who wrote the short story collection *Ship Fever*?
15. Whose sculptures include the 1908 bronze *Euphemia Lamb*?

ANSWERS 1. Kate Atkinson **2.** W.B. Yeats **3.** Mowgli **4.** Kate Le Vann **5.** Jay McInerney **6.** James Abbott McNeill Whistler **7.** H.G. Wells **8.** Tania Kindersley **9.** Christopher Brookmyre **10.** Terry Frost **11.** Natalya Goncharova **12.** Lawrence Block **13.** Gilbert and George **14.** Andrea Barrett **15.** Sir Jacob Epstein.

GENERAL KNOWLEDGE

1. Which size of paper is larger - A4 or A5?
2. The king, queen and jack in a pack of cards are known as court cards. What are they known as in the U.S.?
3. In sport, what is fartlek also called?
4. What is the approximate population of Algiers in millions - 1.2, 1.7 or 2.2?
5. Who preceded Claudius I as Roman emperor?
6. In which city is the University of Surrey?
7. Who succeeded Binyamin Netanyahu as Israeli prime minister in 1999?
8. In which year did cosmonaut Yuri Gagarin die?
9. Which Labour cabinet minister died suddenly in May 1999?
10. What does the French phrase 'raison d'être' mean?
11. Which birthstone is associated with the month of January?
12. In which year was athlete Harold Abrahams born?
13. In house purchasing what does MIRAS stand for?
14. In World War II what did the German phrase 'Drang nach Osten' mean?
15. Which famous fictional character's mother was Aase?

ANSWERS **1.** A4 **2.** Face cards **3.** Interval training **4.** 1.7 million **5.** Caligula (Gaius Caesar) **6.** Guildford **7.** Ehud Barak **8.** 1968 **9.** Derek Fatchett **10.** Reason for being **11.** Garnet **12.** 1899 **13.** Mortgage interest relief at source **14.** Drive to the East **15.** Peer Gynt.

ENTERTAINMENT

1. Which character was played by Keenan Wynn in the television series *Dallas* from 1978-80?
2. In which 1967 film does Marlon Brando play the character Ogden Mears?
3. Who played the character Marilyn Gates in the original television series *Crossroads*?
4. Which *Coronation Street* actress was born Cathryn Helen Wigglesworth?
5. How many Best Actor Oscar nominations has Paul Newman received?
6. Who choreographed the 1937 ballet *Checkmate*?
7. In which 1994 film does Jim Carrey play the character Lloyd Christmas?
8. Which actor played the lead in the 1999 film *The Straight Story*?
9. In which year did the Windmill Theatre open in London?
10. Which character was played by Barbara Stanwyck in the soap *Dynasty* from 1985-6?
11. In which 1971 film does Woody Allen play the character Fielding Mellish?
12. Which television drama series features the character Constable Benton Fraser?
13. Who composed the opera *Die Fledermaus*?
14. In which 1996 film does Sean Connery play the character John Patrick Mason?
15. Which film won more Oscars - *From Here To Eternity* or *Dances With Wolves*?

ANSWERS **1.** Digger Barnes **2.** A Countess from Hong Kong **3.** Sue Nicholls **4.** Helen Worth **5.** Eight **6.** Ninette de Valois **7.** Dumb & Dumber **8.** Richard Farnsworth **9.** 1931 **10.** Constance Colby **11.** Bananas **12.** Due South **13.** Johann Strauss **14.** The Rock **15.** From Here To Eternity.

SPORT

1. Which golfer won the U.S. Open from 1903-5 after having emigrated from Scotland?
2. French rugby union player and Olympic athlete Georges André was nicknamed after which animal?
3. Who was the 1978 World Formula 1 motor racing champion?
4. For which French rugby union side did Rob Andrew play from 1991-2?
5. Who scored 27 points for Scotland against Romania in a 1987 rugby union match?
6. Who was MVP in Superbowl XVI and XIX in American Football?
7. What nationality is six-times Olympic canoeing gold medal winner Gert Fredriksson?
8. Which Scottish team did IFK Gothenburg beat in the 1987 UEFA Cup final?
9. Who became president of FIFA in 1974?
10. Which cyclist won the 1995 Tour de France?
11. Which baseball star was known as 'the Fordham Flash'?
12. In which city was US basketball star Connie Hawkins born?
13. Which horse won the 1978 Grand National?
14. Which golfer won the British Open from 1954-56?
15. From which country were speedway stars Ivan Mauger and Barry Briggs?

ANSWERS **1.** Willie Anderson **2.** The Bison **3.** Mario Andretti **4.** Toulouse **5.** Gavin Hastings **6.** Joe Montana **7.** Swedish **8.** Dundee United **9.** João Havelange **10.** Miguel Indurain **11.** Frank Frisch **12.** New York **13.** Lucius **14.** Peter Thomson **15.** New Zealand.

POP

1. What was the name of the country music album by Elvis Costello and the Attractions?
2. Which group recorded the 1983 album *Strive to Survive Causing Least Suffering Possible*?
3. What was the title of the Human League's 1980 No. 1 album?
4. What was the debut album from Midlands group *The Beat*?
5. Which female singer's albums include 1980's *The Blue Meaning*?
6. Who was lead singer with the US band Dead Kennedys?
7. What was the debut album of Echo and the Bunnymen?
8. Which studio album by Orchestral Manoeuvres in the Dark featured *Enola Gay*?
9. Which country singer wrote the song *Funny How Time Slips Away*?
10. What were the forenames of the Walker Brothers?
11. On which 1966 LP did the Supremes record *You Can't Hurry Love*?
12. Ralf Hütter and Florian Schneider are members of which group?
13. Which group recorded the LP *Zenyatta Mondatta*?
14. Who was the lead singer with The Teardrop Explodes?
15. Which vocal group recorded the 1967 album *Reach Out*?

ANSWERS **1.** Almost Blue **2.** A Flux of Pink Indians **3.** Dare **4.** I Just Can't Stop It **5.** Toyah **6.** Jello Biafra **7.** Crocodiles **8.** Organisation **9.** Willie Nelson **10.** Scott, John and Gary **11.** A' Go Go **12.** Kraftwerk **13.** The Police **14.** Julian Cope **15.** The Four Tops.

ART AND LITERATURE

1. Whose sculptures include 1913's *Unique Forms of Continuity in Space*?
2. Which artist painted 1910's *Piano and Lute*?
3. Who wrote the novel *Mary Anne*?
4. Which artist painted 1913's *Violin and Guitar*?
5. Who painted 1912's *Simultaneous Windows*?
6. Whose books include *The Talented Mr. Ripley*?
7. What was the original name of painter Robert Indiana?
8. Who wrote the novel *Carmen* on which Bizet's opera was based?
9. What nationality is the writer Sara Lidman?
10. Who wrote *The Friends of Eddie Coyle*?
11. Whose crime novels include *The Seven Dials Mystery*?
12. In which novel does the character Squire Allworthy appear?
13. Who wrote the children's tale *The Little Prince*?
14. Which 1922 novel by D.H. Lawrence features a flautist as the central character?
15. In which 1742 novel by Henry Fielding do Squire Booby and Mrs. Slipshod feature?

ANSWERS **1.** Umberto Boccioni **2.** Georges Braque **3.** Daphne du Maurier **4.** Picasso **5.** Robert Delaunay **6.** Patricia Highsmith **7.** Robert Clarke **8.** Prosper Mérimée **9.** Swedish **10.** George V. Higgins **11.** Agatha Christie **12.** The History of Tom Jones **13.** Antoine de Saint-Exupéry **14.** Aaron's Rod **15.** The Adventures of Joseph Andrews.

GENERAL KNOWLEDGE

1. What is the marsh plant water hemlock also called?
2. In Russia what is a feldsher?
3. Which horse won the 1977 Grand National?
4. What creature is also called an ant bear?
5. Who wrote the novel *Smiley's People*?
6. Who was the companion of Don Quixote?
7. Which actor played the Joker in the television show *Batman*?
8. What is the name of the private eye in the novel *The Maltese Falcon*?
9. Which racecourse hosts the Irish Derby?
10. Who wrote the novels *Clarissa* and *Pamela*?
11. In Australia, what sort of animal is a brumby?
12. Which treaty ended the War of Spanish Succession?
13. Which prison was demolished following the death of Rudolf Hess?
14. Who became Secretary of State for War in 1960?
15. In which year did the collection of monies to fund the BBC first begin?

ANSWERS 1. Cowbane **2.** A medical doctor's assistant **3.** Red Rum **4.** Aardvark **5.** John Le Carré **6.** Sancho Panza **7.** Cesar Romero **8.** Sam Spade **9.** The Curragh **10.** Samuel Richardson **11.** A wild horse **12.** Treaty of Utrecht **13.** Spandau **14.** John Profumo **15.** 1922.

ENTERTAINMENT

1. How many Best Actress Oscar nominations has Deborah Kerr received?
2. Who plays the farmer Ted Burgess in the 1970 film *The Go-Between*?
3. Which character does Catherine Cusack play in the television series *Ballykissangel*?
4. Who played the character Clifford Leyton in the original television series *Crossroads* which ended in 1988?
5. In which 1980s sitcom starring Ralph Bates did the 1-2-1 Club encounter group feature?
6. In which 1964 film does Warren Beatty play the character Vincent Bruce?
7. Which character was played by Priscilla Presley in television's *Dallas* from 1983-88?
8. In which year was the Bolshoi Ballet company formed?
9. Which theatrical dame played Lady Plyant in Congreve's *The Double Dealer* at the Old Vic in 1959?
10. Who played the character Minnie Caldwell in the television series *Coronation Street*?
11. In which 1989 film does Marlon Brando play the character Ian McKenzie?
12. Who commissioned Mozart's opera *Idomeneo*?
13. In which 1997 film does Jim Carrey play the character Fletcher Reede?
14. Which character was played by Helmut Berger in the television series *Dynasty* from 1983-4?
15. Who won Best Director Oscar for their debut film at the helm, *Marty*?

ANSWERS 1. 6 **2.** Alan Bates **3.** Frankie Sullivan **4.** Johnny Briggs **5.** Dear John **6.** Lilith **7.** Jenna Wade **8.** 1776 **9.** Maggie Smith **10.** Margot Bryant **11.** A Dry White Season **12.** The Elector of Bavaria **13.** Liar Liar **14.** Peter De Vilbis **15.** Delbert Mann.

SPORT

1. By how many points did Mike Hawthorn beat Stirling Moss to win the 1958 World Formula 1 motor racing title?
2. Who was the 1998 U.S. Masters golf champion?
3. Which Danish badminton player lost in the final of the 1987 men's world championship?
4. Lily Gower beat R.C.J. Beaton in 1905 to win the Croquet Open Championships. What did they do together later that year?
5. Which Scottish football team were league champions from 1966-74?
6. Who won the Boston men's marathon from 1993-95?
7. Which country were men's world champions at quad sculls rowing from 1994-98?
8. Who skippered the America's Cup-winning boat *Stars and Stripes* in 1987 and '88?
9. What, in the Tour de France, is the 'maillot jaune'?
10. For prowess at which sport was American Earl Anthony known as 'The Doomsday Stroking Machine'?
11. Which golfer won the 1978 world matchplay championship?
12. Who in football was 'the Galloping Major'?
13. When was the last British Grand Prix in motor racing held at Aintree?
14. Who were the 1987 rugby union world cup winners?
15. With which sport do you associate Norbert Koof and Hartwig Steenken?

ANSWERS **1.** One **2.** Mark O'Meara **3.** Morten Frost **4.** Marry each other **5.** Celtic **6.** Cosmas N'Deti **7.** Italy **8.** Dennis Conner **9.** Yellow jersey **10.** Bowling **11.** Isao Aoki **12.** Ferenc Puskas **13.** 1962 **14.** New Zealand **15.** Showjumping.

POP

1. Which female singer recorded the 1989 album *Electric Youth*?

2. Which male vocalist recorded the 1973 album *Touch Me*?

3. Which group recorded the 1980 album *Trance and Dance*?

4. Which wacky US group recorded the single *Rock Lobster*?

5. What was the title of the second LP by The Specials?

6. What is reggae singer Winston Rodney better known as?

7. Who was Stevie Wonder's writing partner on the song *Do Yourself a Favour*?

8. Which American cult band's LPs include *The Tunes of Two Cities*?

9. Who was the lead singer of Dexy's Midnight Runners?

10. Which album proclaimed itself 'The Fourth Roxy Music album'?

11. Mark E. Smith is the lead singer with which Manchester group?

12. Which trio recorded the 1983 album *Waiting*?

13. Which reggae group recorded the album *Two Sevens Clash*?

14. Martin L. Gore is the keyboard player with which group?

15. Which duo recorded the albums *L* and *Ismism*?

ANSWERS 1. Debbie Gibson **2.** Gary Glitter **3.** Martha and the Muffins **4.** The B-52's **5.** More Specials **6.** Burning Spear **7.** Syreeta Wright **8.** The Residents **9.** Kevin Rowland **10.** Country Life **11.** The Fall **12.** Fun Boy Three **13.** Culture **14.** Depeche Mode **15.** Godley and Creme.

PEOPLE

1. Who, in his guise as Otis Lee Crenshaw, was the winner of the Perrier Comedy Award at the 2000 Edinburgh Fringe Festival?
2. Which former child actor starred in the London stage production in 2000 of the show *Madame Melville*?
3. What is the actress Sandra Bullock's middle name?
4. Who was a silver medal-winner at the 2000 Olympics for Britain in the women's middleweight judo event?
5. In which century did the Dutch painter Gerard Terborch live?
6. Who was men's triple jump champion at the 2000 Olympics?
7. Which Palestinian leader shared the 1994 Nobel peace prize?
8. Who was the 1996 world Formula 1 motor racing champion?
9. Which Scottish cyclist won the Kellogg's Tour of Britain in 1989?
10. Who was the late husband of former model Anna Nicole Smith?
11. Who was the U.S. vice president from 1977-81?
12. Which actor-singer was born Stuart Goddard in 1954?
13. Which maiden in Greek mythology agreed to marry any man who could defeat her in a running race?
14. Who was the 1996 Australian Open men's singles tennis champion?
15. Which rower carried the British flag at the 2000 Olympics opening ceremony?

ANSWERS **1.** Rich Hall **2.** Macaulay Culkin **3.** Annette **4.** Kate Howey **5.** 17th century **6.** Jonathan Edwards **7.** Yasser Arafat **8.** Damon Hill **9.** Robert Millar **10.** J. Howard Marshall II **11.** Walter Mondale **12.** Adam Ant **13.** Atalanta **14.** Boris Becker **15.** Matthew Pinsent.

GENERAL KNOWLEDGE

1. In which year did the English poet George Gordon Byron die?

2. Who was the Greek virgin goddess of wisdom and prudent warfare?

3. What is the English name of the constellation whose Latin name is *Monoceros*?

4. In which year was the U.K. satellite Prospero launched?

5. What type of insect is a velvet ant?

6. In which year was Uranus' moon Oberon discovered?

7. Who authored the 1948 novel *The Ides of March*?

8. Which Shakespeare play features the characters Celia and Frederick?

9. Which Eurasian plant is also called a bluebottle?

10. What was the name of the car driven by Andy Green which broke the sound barrier on land in October 1997?

11. Who was the poet laureate from 1968-72?

12. Who is the author of the 1978 play *Plenty*?

13. Which is the largest island of the Inner Hebrides in Scotland?

14. What is the official language of Venezuela?

15. ME is the zip code of which state in the U.S.A.?

ANSWERS 1. 1824 **2.** Athena **3.** Unicorn **4.** 1971 **5.** Wasp **6.** 1787 **7.** Thornton Wilder **8.** As You Like It **9.** Cornflower **10.** Thrust SSC **11.** Cecil Day-Lewis **12.** David Hare **13.** Skye **14.** Spanish **15.** Maine.

ENTERTAINMENT

1. Which actor starred as Ernest Springer in the 1982 sitcom *Dead Ernest*?
2. Who directed the 1991 film *The Indian Runner*?
3. Who directed the 1979 film *Mad Max*?
4. In which year was composer Henry Mancini born?
5. Who played Fitz in the 1980 sitcom *Holding the Fort*?
6. Who played Everton Bennett in the 1970's drama *Empire Day*?
7. Who played Augusto Odone in the 1992 film *Lorenzo's Oil*?
8. Which comedienne played nurse Elaine Dobbs in the 1993 TV drama *Tender Loving Care*?
9. Who plays Albert Finney's secretary in the 1968 film *Charlie Bubbles*?
10. Who played Joe Sugden in *Emmerdale Farm*?
11. Who played TV's *Murphy Brown*?
12. Who composed the 4-Act opera *Manon Lescaut*?
13. Who co-wrote and starred in the sitcom *Dear Mother...Love Albert*?
14. Who directed the 1937 film *Lost Horizon*?
15. Who directed the 1987 film *Angel Heart*?

ANSWERS 1. Andrew Sachs **2.** Sean Penn **3.** George Miller **4.** 1924 **5.** Matthew Kelly **6.** Norman Beaton **7.** Nick Nolte **8.** Dawn French **9.** Liza Minnelli **10.** Frazer Hines **11.** Candice Bergen **12.** Puccini **13.** Rodney Bewes **14.** Frank Capra **15.** Alan Parker.

SPORT

1. What was the name of the official mascot of the 1992 Summer Olympics at Barcelona?
2. Who won the Olympic women's 400m in 1968?
3. In which country were the 1988 European Championships in football held?
4. Who was the French Open men's singles tennis champion in 1973?
5. Which baseball team won the 1930 World Series?
6. Which team were NBA champions in basketball in 1970?
7. Which country won the 1995 Cricket World Cup?
8. Which player was runner-up in the 1979 world professional darts championship?
9. Which horse won the 1998 1000 Guineas?
10. Which team won ice hockey's Stanley Cup in 1998/9?
11. Which golfer was the runner-up in the 1997 world matchplay championship?
12. Which woman won the 1996 New York marathon?
13. Which English football teams met in the 1972 U.E.F.A. Cup Final?
14. Which team lost the 1985 Milk Cup Final in football to Norwich City?
15. Which country won the 1982 Thomas Cup in badminton?

ANSWERS 1. Cobi **2.** Colette Besson **3.** West Germany **4.** Ilie Nastase **5.** Philadelphia Athletics **6.** New York Knicks **7.** Sri Lanka **8.** Leighton Rees **9.** Cape Verdi **10.** Dallas Stars **11.** Ernie Els **12.** Anuta Catuna **13.** Spurs and Wolves **14.** Sunderland **15.** China.

POP

1. Which US vocalist had a 1976 hit with *I Recall a Gypsy Woman*?
2. Who recorded the 1998 album *Songs from Ally McBeal*?
3. Which group recorded the album *Gran Turismo*?
4. Which singer recorded the 1979 album *The Pleasure Principle*?
5. Which group recorded the concept album *The Lamb Lies Down on Broadway*?
6. Which French songwriter recorded the 1971 album *Histoire De Melody Nelson*?
7. Which group recorded the 1999 album *Bury the Hatchet*?
8. Which member of the group Yes recorded the 1975 L.P. *Beginnings*?
9. Which reggae group recorded the album *Handsworth Revolution*?
10. Who recorded the album *Doc at the Radar Station*?
11. *Another Music in a Different Kitchen* was the debut album of which band?
12. Which songwriting team's hits include *Alfie* and *I Say a Little Prayer*?
13. Milton Reame-James was the keyboard player in which 1970s band?
14. Who recorded the 1998 album *A Thousand Leaves*?
15. Which rap duo had a 1982 hit single with *Magic's Wand*?

ANSWERS 1. Don Williams **2.** Vonda Shepard **3.** The Cardigans **4.** Gary Numan **5.** Genesis **6.** Serge Gainsbourg **7.** The Cranberries **8.** Steve Howe **9.** Steel Pulse **10.** Captain Beefheart and the Magic Band **11.** Buzzcocks **12.** Bacharach & David **13.** Cockney Rebel **14.** Sonic Youth **15.** Whodini.

ART AND LITERATURE

1. Which crime writer's books include *Final Curtain* and *Opening Night*?
2. Who wrote the short story collection *Some Rain Must Fall*?
3. Who wrote the 2000 novel *A Good House*?
4. Which British artist's works include the 1975 screenprint *Tree Shells*?
5. Who wrote the 1999 novel *Jumping the Green*?
6. Which British artist's works include the 1968 watercolour *Still Life with Blue Gloves*?
7. Who authored the 1990 novel *Longshot*?
8. Who wrote the 2000 novel *Martha Peake*?
9. Whose sculptures include the 1915 bronze *Portrait of Iris Beerbohm Tree*?
10. Who wrote the novel *The Middle Kingdom*?
11. Which British artist's works include the 1914 plaster sculpture *Garden Ornament*?
12. Who authored the 1941 novel *The Song of Bernadette*?
13. Which architect designed the Admiralty Arch in 1911?
14. Who wrote the novel *Eating Cake*?
15. Which visual artist recorded the music album *Getting It Together In The Country*?

ANSWERS 1. Ngaio Marsh **2.** Michael Faber **3.** Bonnie Burnard **4.** Ian Hamilton Finlay **5.** Leslie Schwartz **6.** Sir William Gillies **7.** Dick Francis **8.** Patrick McGrath **9.** Sir Jacob Epstein **10.** Andrea Barrett **11.** Henri Gaudier-Brzeska **12.** Franz Werfel **13.** Aston Webb **14.** Stella Duffy **15.** Rodney Graham.

GENERAL KNOWLEDGE

1. After which king of France was Louisville, Kentucky named?
2. What is the standard monetary unit of Romania?
3. In which year was the Free Church of Scotland formed?

4. Why might you not welcome a visit from a boomslang?
5. Which shipping forecast area is N.W. of the Faeroes?
6. Clichy is an industrial suburb of which French city?
7. What is the approximate mileage from Land's End to John O'Groats by road?
8. Which pair of British aviators made the first non-stop transatlantic flight in 1919?
9. What was the Toy of the Year in 1969?
10. The Marie Celeste left New York before being found abandoned. Which was its port of destination?
11. On what Mediterranean island is Syracuse?
12. Who won the Pipe Smoker of the Year award in 1983?
13. In which year did Anne of Cleves marry Henry VIII?
14. What is the approximate area in square miles of the island of Elba - 86, 186 or 286?
15. Who keeps *The Diary of a Nobody*?

ANSWERS 1. Louis XVI **2.** Leu **3.** 1843 **4.** It's a poisonous snake **5.** South-East Iceland **6.** Paris **7.** 876 miles **8.** Alcock and Brown **9.** Hot Wheels **10.** Genoa **11.** Sicily **12.** Patrick Moore **13.** 1540 **14.** 86 **15.** Charles Pooter.

ENTERTAINMENT

1. Which actress played Jan Howard in the television drama series *Howard's Way*?
2. Which actor played Burt Campbell in the sitcom *Soap*?
3. Which actor starred as Len in the 2000 television drama series The Sins?
4. What is the subtitle of the 2000 film *Blair Witch 2*?
5. Who choreographed the 1965 ballet *Romeo and Juliet*?
6. Which theatrical dame played Célimène in Molière's *The Misanthrope* at the National Theatre in 1973?
7. In which 1974 film does Warren Beatty play the character Joseph Frady?
8. Which character was played by Ian McShane in *Dallas*?
9. In which 1989 film does Jim Carrey play the character Wiploc?
10. For which 1954 film was James Mason a Best Actor Oscar nominee?
11. Who played the character Jackie Dobbs in the television series *Coronation Street*?
12. In which 1979 film does Woody Allen play the character Isaac Davis?
13. Which actor won an Emmy for Outstanding Lead Actor in a Comedy Series in 2000?
14. Which actor played David St. Hubbins in the film spoof *This Is Spinal Tap*?
15. Which character was played by Bernard Hill in the 1982 television drama series *Boys from the Blackstuff*?

ANSWERS **1.** Jan Harvey **2.** Richard Mulligan **3.** Pete Postlethwaite **4.** Book of Shadows **5.** Kenneth Macmillan **6.** Diana Rigg **7.** The Parallax View **8.** Don Lockwood **9.** Earth Girls Are Easy **10.** A Star is Born **11.** Margi Clarke **12.** Manhattan **13.** Michael J. Fox **14.** Michael McKean **15.** Yosser Hughes.

SPORT

1. What was the name of Denis Compton's elder brother who kept wicket for Middlesex?
2. What was the nickname of ice hockey player Lionel Conacher?
3. Which French rugby union club side did Jean Condom move to in 1986?
4. In which city was US triple jumper Mike Conley born?
5. Which boxer was world light-heavyweight champion from 1939-41?
6. What was the profession of American yachtsman Dennis Conner's father?
7. Who scored a consolation goal for Holland in their 1978 World Cup Final defeat?
8. Which Australian wicket-keeper played in 51 Tests from 1957-66?
9. Who was the last player to score for the losing team in a football World Cup Final?
10. Who was the 1972 Olympic men's 200m breaststroke swimming champion?
11. Which cyclist won the 1995 Giro d'Italia?
12. Who was world 250cc motor cycling champion from 1994-97?
13. Which Swedish tennis player designed the Stockholm stadium for the 1912 Olympics?
14. Which team won rugby union's Swalec Cup from 1991-3?
15. Which country were the 1996 world ice hockey champions?

ANSWERS 1. Leslie **2.** Big Train **3.** Biarritz **4.** Chicago **5.** Billy Conn **6.** Tuna fisherman **7.** Nanninga **8.** Wally Grout **9.** Rudi Völler, in 1986 **10.** John Hencken **11.** Tony Rominger **12.** Massimiliano Biaggi **13.** Torben Grut **14.** Llanelli **15.** Czech Republic.

POP

1. Which singer duetted with Elvis Costello on the song *The Only Flame in Town*?
2. What was the title of Fleetwood Mac's 1987 No. 1 album?
3. Which duo recorded the 1987 album *Seduced and Abandoned*?
4. Who recorded the 1980 album *Without Radar*?
5. What was the debut single from the group Magazine?
6. In which year did Joy Division singer Ian Curtis kill himself?
7. Which production company did Ian Marsh and Martyn Ware form after quitting The Human League?
8. Which group recorded the 1981 single *Is Vic there?*?
9. Who was the original manager of the group Spandau Ballet?
10. Which girl group recorded the 1980 album *The Story So Far*?
11. Which poet recorded the album *Snap, Crackle (&) Bop*?
12. Which poet recorded the album *Bass Culture*?
13. What was the title of Foreigner's 1984 No. 1 album?
14. Who recorded the 1994 album *Let Love In*?
15. Who wrote the 1972 hit *Sea Side Shuffle*?

ANSWERS **1.** Daryl Hall **2.** Tango in the Night **3.** Hue and Cry **4.** The Yachts **5.** Shot by Both Sides **6.** 1980 **7.** The British Electric Foundation **8.** Department S **9.** Steve Dagger **10.** The Modettes **11.** John Cooper Clarke **12.** Linton Kwesi Johnson **13.** Agent Provocateur **14.** Nick Cave and the Bad Seeds **15.** Jona Lewie.

GEOGRAPHY

1. In which African country is the seaport of Dar-es-Salaam?
2. On which river is Ilkley, West Yorkshire?
3. In which ocean is the former penal settlement of Devil's Island?
4. In which Central American republic is the volcano Irazu?
5. On which river is the German port of Dresden?
6. Irian Jaya forms the western part of which island?
7. In which European country are the forested highlands of Hunsrück?
8. Carantuohil is the highest peak of which mountain group?
9. In which country is the airport town of Dum-Dum?
10. On which West Indies island would you find the ports of Kingston and Montego Bay?
11. Which strait lies between the Persian Gulf and the Gulf of Oman?
12. In which English county is the River Lyn, scene of severe flooding in 1952?
13. On which U.S. river is the Hoover Dam?
14. Which is larger - Luxembourg or Liechtenstein?
15. Lusaka is the capital of which African country?

ANSWERS **1.** Tanzania **2.** River Wharfe **3.** Atlantic Ocean **4.** Costa Rica **5.** River Elbe **6.** New Guinea **7.** Germany **8.** Macgillicuddy's Reeks **9.** India **10.** Jamaica **11.** Strait of Hormuz **12.** Devon **13.** Colorado **14.** Luxembourg **15.** Zambia.

GENERAL KNOWLEDGE

1. What is the state flower of Wyoming, USA?
2. Who wrote the 1955 novel *Marjorie Morningstar*?
3. What is the English name of the constellation whose Latin name is Corvus?
4. In which year was the Japanese space mission Oshumi launched?
5. In which decade of the 18th century were the Wars of the Vendée in France?
6. What was the approximate population in millions of Venezuela in 1993?
7. Which month of the French Revolutionary calendar was the windy month?
8. In which year was Uranus's moon Puck discovered?
9. Which river forms most of the border between Cornwall and Devon?
10. Which British philosopher authored the book *Principles of Mathematics*?
11. Which island of the Scilly Isles houses Abbey Gardens?
12. Which important post is held by Michael Martin, M.P.?
13. Which property on a standard Monopoly board is immediately before the 'Go To Jail' square?
14. Who became the new world chess champion in 2000?
15. Under what name was the 1968 novel *Colonel Sun* written by Kingsley Amis?

ANSWERS 1. Indian paintbrush **2.** Herman Wouk **3.** Crow **4.** 1970 **5.** 1790's **6.** 20m **7.** The sixth month, Ventôse **8.** 1986 **9.** Tamar **10.** Bertrand Russell **11.** Tresco **12.** Speaker of the House of Commons **13.** Piccadilly **14.** Vladimir Kramnik **15.** Robert Markham.

ENTERTAINMENT

1. Who was voted Best Actress (In a Musical/Comedy) at the 1973 Golden Globes?
2. What is actor the David Soul's real name?
3. Gimme Shelter was a 1970 documentary film about which pop group?
4. Who directed the 1955 film *The Ladykillers*?
5. Who played Angie in the sitcom *Lame Ducks*?
6. Which comic duo wrote and starred in TV's *Bottom*?
7. Who composed the 1982 opera *The Photographer*?
8. Who did Diana Ross portray in the 1972 film *Lady Sings the Blues*?
9. Which comic actor played Mr. Kent in the 1982 sitcom *Goodbye Mr. Kent*?
10. Which comedian starred in the 1990 film *The Adventures of Ford Fairlane*?
11. On a story by whom was the 1998 film *The Gingerbread Man* based?
12. Who directed the film *Edward Scissorhands*?
13. In which year was the International Folk Music Council formed?
14. Who produced and directed the 1969 film *Can Hieronymus Merkin Ever Forget Mercy Humppe and Find True Happiness*?
15. Which movie won the Best Film accolade at the 1957 British Academy Awards?

ANSWERS **1.** Glenda Jackson **2.** David Solberg **3.** Rolling Stones **4.** Alexander Mackendrick **5.** Lorraine Chase **6.** Rik Mayall & Adrian Edmondson **7.** Philip Glass **8.** Billie Holiday **9.** Richard Briers **10.** Andrew Dice Clay **11.** John Grisham **12.** Tim Burton **13.** 1947 **14.** Anthony Newley **15.** The Bridge on the River Kwai.

SPORT

1. For which Italian football club did Ruud Gullit sign in July 1993?
2. Which cricketer scored over 3000 first-class runs three times, in 1923, ‘28 and ‘33?
3. Which was the first country to host football’s World Cup finals twice?
4. What nationality is former world speed skating champion Erik Gundersen?
5. In which year did Stephen Hendry win his first World Professional snooker title?
6. Who won the 1956 Olympic men’s hammer competition?
7. Who was Wimbledon ladies singles champion 1952-54?
8. Which American male tennis star retired in 1992 after winning 109 singles titles?
9. At which field event did Italian Adolfo Consolini win Olympic gold in 1948?
10. For which Lancashire League cricket side did Sir Learie Constantine play for ten years?
11. Which horse won the 1993 Grand National at Aintree?
12. Which team won the 1988 F.A. Cup Final?
13. At which sport were Tom Morris Snr. and Tom Morris Jnr. successful?
14. When was the last all-British women’s singles final at Wimbledon?
15. In which U.S. state was Ed Moses born?

ANSWERS 1. Sampdoria **2.** Patsy Hendren **3.** Mexico **4.** Danish **5.** 1990 **6.** Hal Connolly **7.** Maureen Connolly **8.** Jimmy Connors **9.** Discus **10.** Nelson **11.** None did - it was abandoned **12.** Wimbledon **13.** Golf **14.** 1961 **15.** Ohio.

POP

1. Which group recorded the 1970 Top Ten album *Fire and Water*?
2. Who is the mainstay of recording artists Mekon?
3. Which Pink Floyd song started out as *Games For May*?
4. Which Spandau Ballet song did PM Dawn's *Set Adrift on Memory Bliss* sample heavily?

5. Which pop group's albums include 2000's *Fragments of Freedom*?
6. Which post-punk group's albums include *Real Life* and *The Correct Use of Soap*?
7. Which comic songwriter played congas on Pink Military's record album *Do Animals Believe In God?*?
8. Which group did Johnyy Moynihan form after leaving the group Planxty?
9. Who is the guitar-playing brother of Prefab Sprout's Paddy MacAloon?
10. What was the first Top Ten album in the U.K. for the group Heaven 17?
11. Which brothers front the group Grand Drive?
12. Which solo artist recorded the 1975 Top Ten album *Breakaway*?
13. Which group recorded the 1982 Top Ten album *Fabrique*?
14. On which studio album by The Pogues do the tracks *White City* and *Down All the Days* appear?
15. Which group recorded the 2000 album *A Rock in the Weary Land*?

ANSWERS 1. Free **2.** John Gosling **3.** See Emily Play **4.** True **5.** Morcheeba **6.** Magazine **7.** Neil Innes **8.** De Dannan **9.** Martin MacAloon **10.** The Luxury Gap **11.** Danny and Julian Wilson **12.** Art Garfunkel **13.** Fashion **14.** Peace and Love **15.** The Waterboys.

ENTERTAINMENT

1. Which comedy scriptwriting team wrote *Brush Strokes*?
2. What kind of creature was Captain Morgan in the 1950s TV series *The Buccaneers*?
3. In which early 1970s drama series did the character Laughing Spam Fritter appear?
4. What was the central character in the ITV drama *Public Eye* called?
5. What was Walt Disney's middle name?
6. In which city was actor Robert Donat born?
7. Which actor was born Issur Danielovich Demsky?
8. Which gangster did Richard Dreyfuss play in the 1973 film *Dillinger*?
9. Which Scottish singer achieved fame after appearing in the BBC show *The Big Time*?
10. Which Hollywood actress played Victoria Barkley in the 1960s western drama series *The Big Valley*?
11. Who played Tosh Lines in *The Bill*?
12. What was the name of the dog in the series *The Bionic Woman*?
13. Which actress was born Hedwig Eva Maria Kiesler in 1913?
14. In which film did Burt Lancaster play H.H. Hunsecker?
15. Which actress starred in the 1976 remake of *King Kong*?

ANSWERS 1. John Esmonde and Bob Larbey **2.** Monkey **3.** Budgie **4.** Frank Marker **5.** Elias **6.** Manchester **7.** Kirk Douglas **8.** Baby Face Nelson **9.** Sheena Easton **10.** Barbara Stanwyck **11.** Kevin Lloyd **12.** Max **13.** Hedy Lamarr **14.** Sweet Smell of Success **15.** Jessica Lange.

GENERAL KNOWLEDGE

1. Of which country was Bülent Ecevit the prime minister from 1978-79?

2. Gregory's powder is a laxative. From what plant is it made?

3. In which year did the actor Burt Lancaster die?

4. In what county of the Republic of Ireland is Lifford?

5. What unit in meteorology is used to measure cloud cover?

6. To whom did the Crime Writers' Association award the Diamond Dagger in 1986?

7. Who composed *The Sorcerer's Apprentice*?

8. Who became Home Secretary in 1997?

9. Who won the Pipe Smoker of the Year award in 1985?

10. Who wrote the play *Man and Superman*?

11. Who composed the television opera *Tobias and the Angel*?

12. Which pop group had a 1974 hit with *Costafine Town*?

13. Which Scottish film director coined the word 'documentary'?

14. In which county is Loughborough?

15. In which year was the Battle of Balaclava?

ANSWERS 1. Turkey **2.** Rhubarb **3.** 1994 **4.** Donegal **5.** Okta **6.** Eric Ambler **7.** Paul Dukas **8.** Jack Straw **9.** Jimmy Greaves **10.** George Bernard Shaw **11.** Sir Arthur Bliss **12.** Splinter **13.** John Grierson **14.** Leicestershire **15.** 1854.

ENTERTAINMENT

1. Which 2000 film starred Liz Hurley as Lucifer?
2. Who composed the 1843 opera *The Flying Dutchman*?
3. On which short story by Phillip K. Dick is the 1990 film *Total Recall* based?
4. The film *The English Patient* won 9 Oscars in 1996. For how many Oscars was it nominated?
5. Who wrote the screenplay for the 1963 film *Tom Jones*?
6. Who choreographed the 1957 ballet *The Prince of the Pagodas*?
7. Which woman was the runner up in the 2000 *Big Brother* television competition?
8. In which 1975 film does Warren Beatty play the character George Roundy?
9. In which 1989 film does Sean Connery play the character Professor Henry Jones Sr.?
10. Which character was played by Howard Keel in the soap *Dallas* from 1981-91?
11. Who played the character Carmel Finnan in the television series *Coronation Street*?
12. Who composed the 1827 opera *The Illustrious Stranger*?
13. Who did Patrick McGoohan play in the television series *Danger Man*?
14. Who plays the character Drew Decker in the film *Scary Movie*?
15. Who stars as Dr. Malcolm Crowe in the 1999 film *The Sixth Sense*?

ANSWERS 1. Bedazzled **2.** Richard Wagner **3.** We Can Remember It For You Wholesale **4.** 12 **5.** John Osborne **6.** John Cranko **7.** Anna Nolan **8.** Shampoo **9.** Indiana Jones and the Last Crusade **10.** Clayton Farlow **11.** Catherine Cusack **12.** Isaac Nathan **13.** John Drake **14.** Carmen Electra **15.** Bruce Willis.

PEOPLE

1. With which TV presenter was Sophie Rhys-Jones shown to be frolicking in 1988 in a 1999 newspaper story?
2. Who is the Labour leader of the House of Lords?
3. Which circus trainer was convicted of cruelty to a chimpanzee in January 1999?
4. To which D.J. is radio presenter Zoë Ball married?
5. Which celebrity chef was reputedly the first person in Britain to have worn disposable nappies?
6. Which actress, star of the film *Hideous Kinky*, was called 'Blubber' at school?
7. Who wrote the novel *Tara Road*?
8. Which newspaperwoman wrote the novel *Married Alive*?
9. Who played Bianca in *EastEnders*?
10. Who was sacked as England's football coach in February 1999?
11. Which former Conservative MEP was caught bringing drugs and pornography into the UK in February 1999?
12. Which comedian wrote the novel *Blast from the Past*?
13. The film *Hilary and Jackie* told the story of which cellist?
14. Jane McDonald was the unlikely star of which TV documentary series?
15. Who starred as Alice in a 1998 TV version of *Alice Through the Looking-Glass*?

ANSWERS **1.** Chris Tarrant **2.** Baroness Jay **3.** Mary Chipperfield **4.** Norman Cook **5.** Antony Worrall Thompson **6.** Kate Winslet **7.** Maeve Binchy **8.** Julie Birchill **9.** Patsy Palmer **10.** Glenn Hoddle **11.** Tom Spencer **12.** Ben Elton **13.** Jacqueline du Pré **14.** The Cruise **15.** Kate Beckinsale.

POP

1. Which was Lionel Richie's only single to hit No. 1 in the U.K. and U.S.?
2. Which vocalist featured on Babyface's 1997 hit *How Come, How Long*?
3. Which D.J. recorded the 1991 album *Words Escape Me*?
4. Which Dutch duo are also known as Itty Bitty Boozy Woozy?
5. Which group had a 1996 Top 40 hit with *Tishbite*?
6. Which act had a Top Five hit in 1992 with *Iron Lion Zion*?
7. Which group had a 1997 Top Ten single with *Choose Life*?
8. Who was the drummer of the group Led Zeppelin?
9. Who had a 1996 Top Ten single with *Blurred*?
10. Which guitarist had a minor chart hit in 1996 with the single *Cannibals*?
11. Whose first solo album was entitled *She's So Unusual*?
12. Which group scored a Top 30 single hit in 1997 with *Debaser*?
13. Which act charted in 1996 with *The Boy with the X-Ray Eyes*?
14. What are the forenames of k.d. lang?
15. Under which name did Jonathan King record the 1976 hit *It Only Takes a Minute*?

ANSWERS 1. Hello **2.** Stevie Wonder **3.** M.C. Buzz B **4.** Klubbheads **5.** The Cocteau Twins **6.** Bob Marley and the Wailers **7.** PF Project **8.** John Bonham **9.** Pianoman **10.** Mark Knopfler **11.** Cyndi Lauper **12.** The Pixies **13.** Babylon Zoo **14.** Kathy Dawn **15.** One Hundred Tons and a Feather.

WORDS

1. What in Russia is a kazachok?
2. What creatures live in an apiary?
3. What does the musical term 'da capo' mean?
4. What does the German word dachshund mean?
5. What, in the Caribbean, is a duppy?
6. What type of food is a fairing?
7. What, in Portugal, is a fado?
8. In printing, what is the narrowest rule in paper production?
9. What in law is a 'felo de se'?
10. Kaph is the 11th letter in which alphabet?
11. What would you do with a kanzu - fly it or wear it?
12. What type of garment is a 'Jacky Howe'?
13. What is an ICBM?
14. What sort of creature is a 'fer-de-lance'?
15. What, in Asia, is dacoity?

ANSWERS **1.** A dance **2.** Bees **3.** To be repeated from the beginning **4.** Badger dog **5.** A spirit or ghost **6.** Sweet circular biscuit made with butter **7.** A melancholy folk song **8.** Feint **9.** Suicide **10.** Hebrew **11.** Wear it - it's a long-sleeved garment **12.** A sleeveless shirt **13.** An intercontinental ballistic missile **14.** A snake **15.** Robbery by an armed gang.

GENERAL KNOWLEDGE

1. What is the name of the preservative numbered E239?
2. In the U.S.A., what is the zip code of Iowa?
3. At which university is Prince William studying?
4. Conservative deputy chairman David Prior is the son of which former Conservative cabinet minister?
5. Which river in England flows to the North Sea at South Shields?
6. What is the English name of the constellation whose Latin name is Pavo?
7. What is the state flower of Texas, U.S.A.?
8. Of what is ornithophobia the fear?
9. In which year was the Indian satellite Rohini launched?
10. Where in Paris is there an 18ft high statue of Charles De Gaulle?
11. What part of the body did a piece of armour called a ventail cover?
12. In which book by Charles Dickens does the wine merchant Edward Murdstone appear?
13. Which city in the Netherlands was the residence of Charles II of England during his exile?
14. What is another name for a quarter-note in music?
15. What nationality is the conductor Edouard van Remoortel?

ANSWERS 1. Hexamine **2.** IA **3.** University of St. Andrews **4.** Jim Prior **5.** River Tyne **6.** Peacock **7.** Bluebonnet **8.** Birds **9.** 1980 **10.** Champs Elysses **11.** The lower part of the face **12.** David Copperfield **13.** Breda **14.** Crotchet **15.** Belgian.

ENTERTAINMENT

1. Which music hall comedian was known as 'The Cheeky Chappie'?
2. Which film director has a production company called Bad Hat Harry Productions?
3. Which film won more Oscars - *My Fair Lady* or *Schindler's List*?
4. On which U.S. soap did Sarah Michelle Gellar appear from 1993-5 as Kendall Lang?
5. What is the character name of Alan Bates in the 1964 film *Zorba the Greek*?
6. Who directed the 1932 film *Boudu Saved From Drowning*?
7. Who choreographed the 1978 solo dance work *Water Motor*?
8. In which 1973 film does Woody Allen play the character Miles Monroe?
9. In which 1976 film does Marlon Brando play the character Robert E. Lee Clayton?
10. Which character was played by Gayle Hunnicutt in the television show *Dallas* from 1989-91?
11. Which comedian played the character Wally Soper in the television series *Crossroads* which ended in 1988?
12. Who played the character Ravi Desai in the television series *Coronation Street*?
13. Which actor was born Walter Matuchanskayasky in 1920?
14. What was James Bolam's character name in the 1984 television series *The Beiderbecke Affair*?
15. In which 1964 television series did John Thaw play Sgt. John Mann?

ANSWERS **1.** Max Miller **2.** Bryan Singer **3.** My Fair Lady **4.** All My Children **5.** Basil **6.** Jean Renoir **7.** Trisha Brown **8.** Sleeper **9.** The Missouri Breaks **10.** Vanessa Beaumont **11.** Max Wall **12.** Saeed Jaffrey **13.** Walter Matthau **14.** Trevor Chaplin **15.** Redcap.

ART AND LITERATURE

1. "It is a truth universally acknowledged that a single man in possession of a good fortune, must be in want of a wife". The opening lines of which novel?
2. Whose sculptures include 1946's *Pelagos*?
3. Whose sculptures include 1944's *The Table is Set*?
4. Who wrote *One Hundred Years of Solitude*?
5. Which artist said "Art is only a substitute while the beauty of life is still deficient"?
6. Who wrote *The Levanter*?
7. Who painted 1905's *Women in front of Fireplace*?
8. Who wrote *To Kill a Mockingbird*?
9. Who painted 1920's *Family Picture*?
10. Who wrote *The House of Mirth*?
11. Whose sculptures included 1929's *Reclining Woman*?
12. Who wrote the story *Cannery Row*?
13. Who wrote *The Tenant of Wildfell Hall*?
14. Of what art movement is Gino Severini's painting *Dancer-Helix-Sea* an example?
15. Whose plays include *Ivanov* and *The Seagull*?

ANSWERS **1.** Pride and Prejudice, by Jane Austen **2.** Barbara Hepworth **3.** Max Ernst **4.** Gabriel Garcia Marquez **5.** Piet Mondrian **6.** Eric Ambler **7.** André Derain **8.** Harper Lee **9.** Max Beckmann **10.** Edith Wharton **11.** Alberto Giacometti **12.** John Steinbeck **13.** Anne Brontë **14.** Futurism **15.** Anton Chekhov.

POP

1. Which male vocal group had a 1997 Top 30 hit with *Can We Talk...*?
2. Which group had hits in 1993 with *Why Are People Grudgeful* and *Behind the Counter*?
3. Which U.S. group recorded the album *Kick Out the Jams*?
4. Which U.S. group had a 1997 hit single with *A.D.I.D.A.S.*?
5. Which male vocal group first charted in 1995 with the single *We've Got It Goin' On*?
6. Which was the first single by The Rolling Stones to reach No. 1 in the U.S. and U.K.?
7. Which group's debut chart hit in 1983 was *Destination Zululand*?
8. Which actor/singer's first chart hit was 1998's *The Heart's Lone Desire*?
9. Which male singer had a 1995 Top 30 single with *Like Lovers Do*?
10. From which city were the group The La's?
11. Which male singer had a 1995 hit single with *Rock and Roll is Dead*?
12. Which female vocalist featured on the 1998 single *One* by Busta Rhymes?
13. Which Japanese group charted in 1997 with the single *Mon Amour Tokyo*?
14. What is funk bass player Robert Bell's nickname?
15. Which U.S rapper featured on Goldie's 1997 hit *Digital*?

ANSWERS **1.** Code Red **2.** The Fall **3.** MC5 **4.** Korn **5.** Backstreet Boys **6.** (I can't get no) Satisfaction **7.** King Kurt **8.** Matthew Marsden **9.** Lloyd Cole **10.** Liverpool **11.** Lenny Kravitz **12.** Erykah Badu **13.** Pizzicato Five **14.** Kool **15.** KRS One.

ENTERTAINMENT

1. In which European city was the film director Mike Nichols born?
2. In which year did Southern Television come into being?
3. Who was *Mr. John Jorrocks* in the 1960s BBC TV serial?
4. Who played Len Tollit in the 1994 sitcom *Once Upon A Time In The North*?
5. Who directed the 1995 film *Money Train*?
6. Who starred as a parole officer in the 1949 film *Shockproof*?
7. Who directed the 1970 film *Drive, He Said*?
8. Who wrote the 1999 spoof football TV documentary *Bostock's Cup*?
9. Who directed the 1965 film *Never Too Late*?
10. Who plays Mrs. Warboys in the comedy series *One Foot in the Grave*?
11. Who played Lt. Buntz in *Hill Street Blues*?
12. Which detective's housekeeper was Mrs. Bardell in a 1960s TV series?
13. Who played Josie Packard in the TV drama *Twin Peaks*?
14. Who played Nero in the BBC historical drama *I, Claudius*?
15. Who played Sandy Richardson in the TV soap *Crossroads*?

ANSWERS **1.** Berlin **2.** 1958 **3.** Jimmy Edwards **4.** Bernard Hill **5.** Joseph Ruben **6.** Cornel Wilde **7.** Jack Nicholson **8.** Chris England **9.** Bud Yorkin **10.** Doreen Mantle **11.** Dennis Franz **12.** Sexton Blake **13.** Joan Chen **14.** Christopher Biggins **15.** Roger Tonge.

GENERAL KNOWLEDGE

1. Which U.S. president was known as JFK?
2. In which year was Princess Anne born?
3. Who was king of France from 1498-1515?
4. Who was the mother of Richard II, who was also known as the Fair Maid of Kent?
5. Which D.J. was host of Melody Maker's Radio Show of the Year awards, 1974-78?
6. What is Job's-tears - a type of grass or a type of wine?
7. Which comedian won the 1981 Laurence Olivier Best Comedy Performance of the Year award?
8. In which year was cult leader Charles Manson born?
9. What does the New Zealand expression 'up the boohai' mean?
10. To whom did the Guild of Professional Toastmasters award the accolade of Best After-Dinner Speaker of the Year in 1989?
11. Who won the 1977 *Mastermind* title?
12. What was U.S. president Grover Cleveland's first name?
13. In which year did King Edward VIII die?
14. Which town was awarded the Resort of the Year title in 1992 by the English Tourist Board?
15. In which year did Mao Tse-tung die?

ANSWERS **1.** John Fitzgerald Kennedy **2.** 1950 **3.** Louis XII **4.** Joan **5.** Alan Freeman **6.** Grass **7.** Rowan Atkinson **8.** 1934 **9.** Completely lost **10.** Margaret Thatcher **11.** Sir David Hunt **12.** Stephen **13.** 1972 **14.** Bournemouth **15.** 1976.

ENTERTAINMENT

1. Who played Chief Superintendent Strange in the television series *Inspector Morse*?
2. Who was the French composer of the symphonic sketches entitled *La Mer*?
3. In which 2000 film did Lewis McKenzie and Robert Carlyle star?
4. Which martial arts expert is the star of the 2000 film *Romeo Must Die*?
5. The 2000 film *Purely Belter* centred around a quest for season tickets for which football team?
6. Who played the 1970s television detective *Barnaby Jones*?
7. Who was the chief cartoon adversary of the character *Road Runner*?
8. Which US comedian was known as 'The Thief of Bad Gags'?
9. How many Best Actress Oscar nominations has Susan Hayward received?
10. Who plays Itzhak Stern in the film *Schindler's List*?
11. In which 1996 film does Jim Carrey play the character Chip Douglas?
12. In which 1998 film does Sean Connery play the character Sir August de Wynter?
13. Which character was played by Joel Fabiani in the television series *Dynasty* from 1985-6?
14. Who plays the character Duggie Ferguson in the television series *Coronation Street*?
15. Who played the character Reg Lamont in the original run of the television series *Crossroads*?

ANSWERS 1. James Grout **2.** Claude Debussy **3.** There's Only One Jimmy Grimble **4.** Jet Li **5.** Newcastle United **6.** Buddy Ebsen **7.** Wile E. Coyote **8.** Milton Berle **9.** 5 **10.** Ben Kingsley **11.** The Cable Guy **12.** The Avengers **13.** King Galen of Moldavia **14.** John Bowe **15.** Reginald Marsh.

PEOPLE

1. Which former MP wrote the novel *Venice Midnight*?
2. Who played television's *Jonathan Creek*?
3. In which city did spy Kim Philby die in 1988?
4. Who played *Father Ted* on television?
5. Which Korean is head of the Unification Church?
6. Who was manager of The Beatles in the 1960s?
7. Who did Ramon Mercader assassinate in 1940?
8. Who directed the 1968 cult erotic film *Vixen*?
9. Tonya Flynt Vega is the daughter of which US pornographer?
10. Who is Liberal Democrat MP for Yeovil?
11. Which IRA defector, killed in 1999, wrote the book *Killing Rage*?
12. Jeremy Spake was the unlikely star of which TV documentary series?
13. Who wrote the play *The Four Alice Bakers*?
14. Who quit in January 1999 as Gordon Brown's press secretary?
15. What is the name of the England rugby union captain embroiled in a 1999 drug scandal?

ANSWERS 1. Gyles Brandreth **2.** Alan Davies **3.** Moscow **4.** Dermot Morgan **5.** Sung Myung Moon **6.** Brian Epstein **7.** Trotsky **8.** Russ Meyer **9.** Larry Flynt **10.** Paddy Ashdown **11.** Eamon Collins **12.** Airport **13.** Fay Weldon **14.** Charlie Whelan **15.** Lawrence Dallaglio.

POP

1. Which group's albums include 1993's *Why Do They Call Me Mr. Happy?*?
2. Which group recorded the 1970 album *Home*?
3. Which pop group's debut album was *Yo! Bum Rush the Show*?
4. What was the first singles chart entry for The Pogues?
5. Who is better known as Jamiroquai?
6. Who recorded the albums *Bad* and *Thriller*?
7. Who in 1989 recorded the album *Heart-Shaped World*?
8. Which rap artist recorded the album *Nature of a Sista*?
9. Which female vocalist featured on the song *History Repeating* by The Propellerheads?
10. Which group recorded the album *Pablo Honey*?
11. Which group had a Top 30 entry in 1997 with the song *Battle of Who Could Care Less*?
12. Who replaced Paul Di'anno as the vocalist of Iron Maiden?
13. Whose second album was *In-a-gadda-da-vida*?
14. Which group's hit singles included *Saturn 5* and *This Is How It Feels*?
15. What is singer William Broad better known as?

ANSWERS **1.** Nomeansno **2.** Procol Harum **3.** Public Enemy **4.** A Pair of Brown Eyes **5.** Jason Kay **6.** Michael Jackson **7.** Chris Isaak **8.** Queen Latifah **9.** Shirley Bassey **10.** Radiohead **11.** Ben Folds Five **12.** Bruce Dickinson **13.** Iron Butterfly **14.** Inspiral Carpets **15.** Billy Idol.

PEOPLE

1. In which year did the ballet dancer Ruth Page die?
2. In which year was the choreographer Antony Tudor born?
3. Who authored the 1892 play *Lady Windermere's Fan*?
4. Which Portuguese navigator discovered the sea route from Portugal to India around the Cape of Good Hope?
5. Which West Indies bowler took 26 wickets in the 1987/8 Test series against India?
6. Which lyricist's songs include the standards *Moon River* and *Blues in the Night*?
7. Which golfer won the 1997 Canon European Masters tournament?
8. Who was the 1979 winner of the Nobel peace prize?
9. Which was the elder of the Carracci brothers who painted in the late 16th century?
10. In which year did the painter Ford Madox Brown die?
11. In which year did the opera singer Dame Clara Butt die?
12. Which soul singer was born in Prattsville, Alabama, on March 18, 1941?
13. In which year was the choreographer Mark Morris born?
14. Who was a silver medal winner for Britain in the men's kayak slalom singles event at the 2000 Olympics?
15. Which poet's autobiography was entitled *World Within World*?

ANSWERS 1. 1991 **2.** 1908 **3.** Oscar Wilde **4.** Vasco Da Gama **5.** Courtney Walsh **6.** Johnny Mercer **7.** Constantino Rocca **8.** Mother Teresa **9.** Agostino Carracci **10.** 1893 **11.** 1936 **12.** Wilson Pickett **13.** 1956 **14.** Paul Ratcliffe **15.** Stephen Spender.

GENERAL KNOWLEDGE

1. In which Spanish city was the composer Manuel de Falla born?
2. Of what is parthenophobia the fear?
3. At which fence on the Grand National course did the horses Ashley House and Carl's Wager unseat their riders in 1984?
4. A musette is a French variation of which instrument?
5. Which constellation contains the stars Rigel and Betelgeuse?
6. What is the name of the preservative numbered E270?
7. What is the state flower of Alaska, U.S.A.?
8. In which year was the Arend-Roland comet first seen?
9. Which three actors played Mr. Freeze in the 1960s *Batman* television series?
10. What is the property immediately after 'Go To Jail' on a standard Monopoly board?
11. Which Arsenal footballer was sent off in his first two Premier League games in the 2000/01 season?
12. On which island was the composer Peter Sculthorpe born?
13. Which team ball game was won at the 2000 Olympics by the Netherlands in the men's event and Australia in the women's event?
14. Of which country is the letter I the international car index mark?
15. Who plays Annelle Dupuy Desoto in the 1989 film *Steel Magnolias*?

ANSWERS **1.** Cadiz **2.** Girls **3.** The Chair **4.** Bagpipe **5.** Orion **6.** Lactic acid **7.** Forget-me-not **8.** 1957 **9.** Eli Wallach, George Sanders and Otto Preminger **10.** Regent Street **11.** Patrick Vieira **12.** Tasmania **13.** Hockey **14.** Italy **15.** Daryl Hannah.

ENTERTAINMENT

1. In which 1987 film does Warren Beatty play the character Lyle Rogers?
2. Who does Marlon Brando play in the 1978 film *Superman*?
3. In which 1985 television series did John Thaw play the character Henry Willows?
4. Who played Karl Stromberg in the film *The Spy Who Loved Me*?
5. Who plays Senator Morton in the 1951 film *Strangers on a Train*?
6. Who plays Clairee Belcher in the 1989 film *Steel Magnolias*?
7. Who played the character Anne-Marie Wade in the television series *Crossroads* which ended in 1988?
8. Who does Mitzi Gaynor play in the film *South Pacific*?
9. Who plays Petruchio in the 1967 film *The Taming of the Shrew*?
10. In which 1993 film does Sean Connery play the character John Connor?
11. Who plays Iris Steensman in the film *Taxi Driver*?
12. Who played the villainess Minerva in the 1960s *Batman* television series?
13. Who played the character Derek Wilton in the television series *Coronation Street*?
14. Who wrote, directed, and starred in the 2000 film *Sidewalks of New York*?
15. Who composed the opera *Sir John in Love*?

ANSWERS **1.** Ishtar **2.** Jor-El **3.** Home to Roost **4.** Curt Jurgens **5.** Leo G. Carroll **6.** Olympia Dukakis **7.** Dee Hepburn **8.** Nellie Forbush **9.** Richard Burton **10.** Rising Sun **11.** Jodie Foster **12.** Zsa Zsa Gabor **13.** Peter Baldwin **14.** Edward Burns **15.** Ralph Vaughan Williams.

GENERAL KNOWLEDGE

1. Which pop star wrote the *Liverpool Oratorio* in 1991?
2. In which county is the resort town of Aldeburgh?
3. Which South African prime minister was assassinated in 1966?
4. Of what is the southern African garment a kaross made?
5. Which Austrian politician was secretary-general of the UN from 1972-81?
6. Which US adventurer was briefly president of Nicaragua from 1856-57?
7. A Russian word meaning 'fast' is used to denote a small restaurant. What is it?
8. Who compiled a dictionary entitled *A Table Alphabeticall* in 1604?
9. Who authored the fishing text *The Compleat Angler*?
10. In which year was Kevin Keegan born?
11. Which chief justice of the U.S. supreme court headed the commission that investigated the assassination of President Kennedy?
12. Who wrote the 1954 work *The Doors of Perception*?
13. Who was Ronald Reagan's defense secretary from 1981-87?
14. What type of creature is a keitloa?
15. Which Christian denomination did Thomas and Alexander Campbell found in 1809?

ANSWERS 1. Paul McCartney **2.** Suffolk **3.** Hendrik Verwoerd **4.** Skins **5.** Kurt Waldheim **6.** William Walker **7.** Bistro **8.** Robert Cawdrey **9.** Izaak Walton **10.** 1951 **11.** Earl Warren **12.** Aldous Huxley **13.** Caspar Weinberger **14.** Rhinoceros **15.** The Disciples of Christ.

POP

1. Which U.S. group had a minor hit in 1995 with *Free, Gay and Happy*?
2. Which group recorded the album *Odyshape*?
3. Which group had a 1997 Top Five single with *Flash*?
4. Which singer recorded the 1983 album *Legendary Hearts*?
5. Which group recorded the 1990 album *Goo*?
6. Which rap singer appeared in the film *Tank Girl* as a kangaroo?
7. Which city were the band The Human League from?
8. What was the blues singer Chester Arthur Burnett better known as?
9. Which U.S. group had a 1995 hit single with *'74-'75*?
10. Which group's debut chart single was *This is a Call* in 1995?
11. What was the 1998 Top Five hit for The Beastie Boys?
12. Who had a U.K. and U.S. No. 1 single in 1995 with *Gangsta's Paradise*?
13. Which group promoted themselves as 'The Fourth Best Band in Hull'?
14. *Shine On* was the debut single, in 1987, of which band?
15. Which group's debut album was *The Right to be Italian*?

ANSWERS 1. Coming Out Crew **2.** The Raincoats **3.** BBE **4.** Lou Reed **5.** Sonic Youth **6.** Ice-T **7.** Sheffield **8.** Howlin' Wolf **9.** The Connells **10.** Foo Fighters **11.** Intergalactic **12.** Coolio **13.** The Housemartins **14.** House of Love **15.** Holly and the Italians.

ART AND LITERATURE

1. Who wrote the 2000 novel *The Shape of Snakes*?

2. Who wrote the novel *The Voyage of the Narwhal*?

3. Which British artist's works include the 1919 painting *Nude With Flying Swans*?

4. Who wrote the 2000 novel *The.PowerBook*?

5. What nationality is the artist Pol Bury?

6. Who is the author of the 1980 novel *Princess Daisy*?

7. Who wrote the detective novel *Calendar Girl*?

8. In which century did the English painter Charles Brooking live?

9. Who wrote the 2000 novel *From Caucasia, With Love*?

10. Which English painter's works include *Chaucer at the Court of Edward III*?

11. Which art dealer commissioned illustrations for the book *Dead Souls* from the artist Marc Chagall?

12. Who authored the 2000 novel *Marrow*?

13. Who authored the book *Harry's Mad*?

14. In which year was the U.S. artist Paul Cadmus born?

15. Who wrote the 1867 verse play *Peer Gynt*?

ANSWERS 1. Minette Walters **2.** Andrea Barrett **3.** Meredith Frampton **4.** Jeanette Winterson **5.** Belgian **6.** Judith Krantz **7.** Stella Duffy **8.** 18th century **9.** Danzy Senna **10.** Ford Madox Brown **11.** Ambroise Vollard **12.** Tiffanie Drake **13.** Dick King-Smith **14.** 1904 **15.** Henrik Ibsen.

GENERAL KNOWLEDGE

1. What colour are the stripes on a barber's pole?
2. How many golfers take part in a four-ball?
3. In law, what is the name given to the essential point of an action?
4. In which city is Cartwright Hall Art Gallery?
5. On what does a leopard snake mostly feed?
6. Which of the wives of Henry VIII was executed in 1542?
7. Which two types of dog appear in Landseer's painting *Dignity and Impudence*?
8. Which German battleship sank HMS Hood?
9. What is the professional organisation of British magicians called?
10. The Discobolus is a 5c BC sculpture by Myron of what type of athlete?
11. Who authored the novel *Mrs. de Winter*?
12. In which present day country does the ancient region of Mesopotamia lie?
13. In which city was the artist Pierre Auguste Renoir born?
14. Who was the 38th president of the U.S.?
15. What is the international car registration for Iraq?

ANSWERS 1. Red and white **2.** Four **3.** The gist **4.** Bradford **5.** Rodents **6.** Catherine Howard **7.** A bloodhound and a Scotch terrier **8.** Bismarck **9.** The Magic Circle **10.** Discus thrower **11.** Susan Elizabeth Hill **12.** Iraq **13.** Limoges **14.** Gerald Ford **15.** IRQ.

ENTERTAINMENT

1. Who composed the operas *King Roger* and *Hagith*?

2. Who plays the character Major Koenig in the 2001 film *Enemy at the Gates*?

3. Who played the villain King Tut in the 1960's *Batman* television series?

4. Who directed and starred in the 2000 film *Brother*?

5. Who plays Richard Gere's daughter Dee Dee in the film *Dr. T and the Women*?

6. Who composed the 1850 symphonic poem *Prometheus*?

7. Who hosted the ill-fated U.S. game show *You're In the Picture*, of which only one episode was aired?

8. In which 1977 film does Woody Allen play the character Alvy Singer?

9. In which 1955 film does Marlon Brando play the character Sky Masterson?

10. Who plays Patsy Cline in the 1985 biopic *Sweet Dreams*?

11. Who composed the music for the ballet *Grohg*?

12. What was the Minneapolis Symphony Orchestra renamed in 1968?

13. Which real life politician does Bruce Greenwood portray in the 2000 film *Thirteen Days*?

14. Which Oscar-winner stars as "Billy" Sunday in the 2000 film *Men of Honor*?

15. Who stars as Laine Hanson in the 2000 film *The Contender*?

ANSWERS 1. Karol Szymanowski **2.** Ed Harris **3.** Victor Buono **4.** Takeshi Kitano **5.** Kate Hudson **6.** Liszt **7.** Jackie Gleason **8.** Annie Hall **9.** Guys and Dolls **10.** Jessica Lange **11.** Aaron Copland **12.** Minnesota Orchestra **13.** John F. Kennedy **14.** Robert De Niro **15.** Joan Allen.

PEOPLE

1. What was nun Agnes Gonxha Bojaxhiu better known as?
2. Which comedian formed the band Poor White Trash and the Little Big Horns after performing at Ben Elton's wedding?
3. What wasthe criminal Robert Franklin Stroud also known as?
4. Who played Theodore Roosevelt in the 1962 film *The Longest Day*?
5. Which US criminal was famously killed by Lana Turner's daughter in 1958?
6. Who plays Josh Griffiths in the TV drama *Casualty*?
7. Which US murderer killed eight student nurses in Chicago in July 1966?
8. Which 1997 film starred the same four principal actors as *A Fish Called Wanda*?
9. Which male wrote the book *Monica's Story*?
10. Who starred as *Trojan Eddie* in the 1996 film?
11. What was the name of the husband and killer of actress/model Dorothy Stratten?
12. Bad Bob, Wendy and Vince are all animated companions of which character?
13. Which US criminal ordered the killing of rival 'Legs' Diamond?
14. What were Clarissa Dickson and Jennifer Paterson better known as?
15. Maureen Rees was the unlikely star of which TV documentary series?

ANSWERS 1. Mother Teresa **2.** Lenny Henry **3.** The Birdman of Alcatraz **4.** Henry Fonda **5.** Johnny Stompanato **6.** Ian Bleasdale **7.** Richard Franklin Speck **8.** Fierce Creatures **9.** Andrew Morton **10.** Stephen Rea **11.** Paul Snider **12.** Rex the Runt **13.** Dutch Schultz **14.** Two Fat Ladies **15.** Driving School.

POP

1. Which Irish group had hits in 1994 with *Zombie* and *Linger*?
2. Which group had a 1996 Top Ten single with *Fat Neck*?
3. On which Bob Dylan studio album does the song *Idiot Wind* appear?
4. Which songwriter's works include *Amsterdam*, *Jojo* and *Orly*?
5. Which singer had a 1997 hit with *Midnight in Chelsea*?
6. Hudson, Manuel, Helm, Danko and Robcrtson comprised which band?
7. Who recorded the 1985 album *Hounds of Love*?
8. Which vocalist featured on the 1996 hit *No Diggity* by Blackstreet?
9. Donald Fagen and Walter Becker were the songwriting team in which group?
10. Andersson, Faltskog, Lyngstad and Ulvaeus comprised which group?
11. Which male rapper had a 1997 No. 2 single with *I Shot the Sheriff*?
12. Who is lead singer with the group ABC?
13. In which year did Bon Scott of AC/DC die following a drinking binge?
14. Which group had a minor hit in 1993 with *Stresss*?
15. *Dirk Wears White Sox* was the first album from which group?

ANSWERS **1.** The Cranberries **2.** Black Grape **3.** Blood on the Tracks **4.** Jacques Brel **5.** Jon Bon Jovi **6.** The Band **7.** Kate Bush **8.** Dr. Dre **9.** Steely Dan **10.** Abba **11.** Warren G **12.** Martin Fry **13.** 1980 **14.** Blaggers I.T.A. **15.** Adam and the Ants.

GEOGRAPHY

1. Whose population is larger - Danville, Virginia or Danville, Illinois?
2. Which Spanish province is larger in area - Alicante or Cadiz?
3. Spain's Bishop of Urgel is co-governor of which principality?
4. In which year did Antigua and Barbuda become independent from the UK?
5. Which river forms the western border between Switzerland and Liechtenstein?
6. Which river forms the NE border of Bolivia with Brazil?
7. Which strait separates Alaska from Asia?
8. In which ocean are the Bonin Islands?
9. Which country lies to the east of Yemen?
10. In which European country is the village of Fatima, a place of Roman Catholic pilgrimage?
11. Of which French department is Évreux the capital?
12. Wilmington is the chief seaport of which U.S. state?
13. Which major river feeds the Caspian Sea?
14. Marseilles is the capital of which department of France?
15. Which US state lies north of Wyoming?

ANSWERS **1.** Danville, Virginia **2.** Cadiz **3.** Andorra **4.** 1981 **5.** Rhine **6.** Guapore **7.** Bering Strait **8.** Pacific Ocean **9.** Oman **10.** Portugal **11.** Eure **12.** Delaware **13.** Volga **14.** Bouches-du-Rhône **15.** Montana.

GENERAL KNOWLEDGE

1. What is the state bird of New Hampshire in the United States of America?
2. What is the name of the food colouring numbered E100?
3. Of what is amathophobia the fear?
4. In which country did the Scottish composer Erik Chisholm die?
5. What is another name for a half-note in music?
6. In which city was the composer Dmitri Kabalevsky born?
7. What nationality is the baritone Tom Krause?
8. How many shillings were in a guinea?
9. The skeleton of the legendary horse Eclipse is kept in a museum in which town?
10. According to a 2000 survey by Datamonitor, how long does an average worker spend on a midday mealbreak?
11. In which year was Sir Thomas More beheaded?
12. Since when has the science fiction writer Arthur C. Clarke lived in Sri Lanka?
13. Where was the 2000 Labour Party conference held?
14. Who was Al Gore's running mate in the 2000 presidential election?
15. Of which country is the letter E the international car index mark?

ANSWERS **1.** Purple finch **2.** Curcumin **3.** Dust **4.** South Africa **5.** Minim **6.** St. Petersburg **7.** Finnish **8.** 21 **9.** Newmarket **10.** 38mins **11.** 1535 **12.** 1956 **13.** Brighton **14.** Joseph Lieberman **15.** Spain.

ENTERTAINMENT

1. Who composed the 1746 oratorio *Judas Maccabaeus?*
2. Who won the Best Actress award at the 1979 Cannes Film Festival?
3. Who directed the 1965 film *Alphaville?*
4. How were the actors Bill and Jon Pertwee related?
5. What was Milo O'Shea's character name in the comedy show *Me Mammy?*
6. What are the comedians Paul and Barry Elliot better known as?
7. Who directed the 1996 film *Crash?*
8. Who directed the 1942 film *Casablanca?*
9. Who played Phyllis Pearce in *Coronation Street?*
10. What nationality was the composer Engelbert Humperdinck?
11. What job did Ian Lavender do in sitcom *Have I Got You...Where You Want Me?*
12. Who directed the 1998 film *Rounders?*
13. Which comedian stars in the 1963 sketch *Same Procedure As Last Year* which is shown annually in Scandinavia at New Year?
14. Which comic actor plays Mr. Grocer in the 1997 film *Grosse Pointe Blank?*
15. Who stars as a fashion photographer in the film *Eyes of Laura Mars?*

ANSWERS **1.** Handel **2.** Sally Field **3.** Jean-Luc Godard **4.** They were cousins **5.** Bunjy Kennefick **6.** The Chuckle Brothers **7.** David Cronenberg **8.** Michael Curtiz **9.** Jill Summers **10.** German **11.** Dentist **12.** John Dahl **13.** Freddie Frinton **14.** Dan Aykroyd **15.** Faye Dunaway.

SPORT

1. Which animal was the official mascot of the 1980 Summer Olympics at Moscow?

2. Who won the Olympic men's 800m in 1972?

3. In which country were the 1980 European Championships in football held?

4. Who was the French Open men's singles tennis champion in 1965?

5. Who did Nottingham Forest beat in the 1980 European Cup Final?

6. Who was women's marathon champion at the 1997 World Championships?

7. Which country won the 1981 Uber Cup in badminton?

8. Which baseball team won the 1935 World Series?

9. Which team were NBA champions in basketball in 1975?

10. Which county won cricket's Natwest Trophy in 1999?

11. Which player was runner-up in the 1978 world professional darts championship?

12. Which golfer was the the runner-up in the 1999 world matchplay championship?

13. What nationality is boxer Stefano Zoff?

14. Who scored Arsenal's winner in the 1936 F.A. Cup Final?

15. Who scored Chelsea's consolation goal in the 1967 F.A. Cup Final?

ANSWERS 1. Misha the Bear **2.** David Wottle **3.** Italy **4.** Fred Stolle **5.** Hamburg **6.** Hiromi Suzuki **7.** Japan **8.** Detroit Tigers **9.** Golden State Warriors **10.** Gloucester **11.** John Lowe **12.** Mark O'Meara **13.** Italian **14.** Ted Drake **15.** Bobby Tambling.

POP

1. Which female vocalist had a 1997 Top 10 single with *Everything*?
2. Which group had a minor hit in 1990 with *The Sex of It*?
3. From which European country does the singer Gala come?
4. Which group's Top 10 singles include *Stupid Girl* and *Push It*?
5. Which punk group recorded the song *Gary Gilmore's Eyes*?
6. Which rock singer was born Steven Talarico?
7. Who had a 1992 single with *The Days of Pearly Spencer*?
8. Which female singer recorded the 1996 album *Boys for Pele*?
9. Who was bass player in the group The Animals?
10. On which island was singer Joan Armatrading born?
11. Whose solo albums include 1970's *The Madcap Laughs*?
12. What did Paul McCartney announce on April 10 1970?
13. Which group's second album was called *Choke*?
14. Who had a hit single in 1967 with *Hi-Ho Silver Lining*?
15. Wilson, Wilson, Pierson, Strickland and Schneider made up which band?

ANSWERS **1.** Mary J. Blige **2.** Kid Creole and the Coconuts **3.** Italy **4.** Garbage **5.** The Adverts **6.** Steve Tyler **7.** Marc Almond **8.** Tori Amos **9.** Chas Chandler **10.** St. Kitts **11.** Syd Barrett **12.** The break-up of the Beatles **13.** The Beautiful South **14.** Jeff Beck **15.** The B-52's.

ENTERTAINMENT

1. In which year did *Multi-Coloured Swap Shop* end on BBC1?
2. In which country was the actor Anthony Quinn born?
3. In which year did *Jim'll Fix It* begin on BBC1?
4. What was Herbert Lom's character name in the medical drama series *The Human Jungle*?
5. Which *Coronation Street* actress played Tracy Glazebrook in the comedy show *Joking Apart*?
6. Who played Betty Smith in the ITV police drama *Hunter's Walk*?
7. In which year did Carlton Television take to the air?
8. Who played hippy Robert Croft in *Coronation Street*?
9. In which country was the actress Carmen Miranda born?
10. Who succeeded Johnny Carson as host on NBC's *Tonight Show*?
11. In which city was the actor Vincent Price born?
12. What was Chan Kwan better known as in the puppet series *Captain Scarlet and The Mysterons*?
13. Who played Messalina in the BBC historical drama *I, Claudius*?
14. Who played Sam Cade in the TV police drama *Cade's County*?
15. Who played Morgana in the 1981 film *Excalibur*?

ANSWERS 1. 1982 **2.** Mexico **3.** 1975 **4.** Dr. Roger Corder **5.** Tracie Bennett **6.** Ruth Madoc **7.** 1993 **8.** Martin Shaw **9.** Portugal **10.** Jay Leno **11.** St. Louis **12.** Harmony Angel **13.** Sheila White **14.** Glenn Ford **15.** Helen Mirren.

GENERAL KNOWLEDGE

1. What type of creature is a grassquit - a crab or a bird?
2. What does the abbreviation RUC stand for in the world of Irish politics?
3. In which year did Hurricane Allen result in 272 deaths?
4. What is the standard monetary unit of Spain?
5. Which shipping forecast area is due east of Sole?
6. In which year was the Salvation Army founded?
7. What is the colour of the traffic light used as a warning between red and green?
8. On which gulf is the Nigerian port of Lagos?
9. Who was the minstrel in Robin Hood's band of merry men?
10. Who was Melody Maker's British Female Jazz Vocalist of the Year 1964-70?
11. Which London hotel won the Egon Ronay Hotel of the Year title in 1970?
12. Who won the 1960 Queen's Gold Medal for Poetry?
13. What is bohea?
14. Who won 1980's *Mastermind* title?
15. Corinium was the Latin name of which English market town?

ANSWERS **1.** A bird **2.** Royal Ulster Constabulary **3.** 1980 **4.** Peseta **5.** Plymouth **6.** 1865 **7.** Amber **8.** Gulf of Guinea **9.** Allan-a-Dale **10.** Cleo Laine **11.** The Inn on the Park **12.** John Betjeman **13.** A black Chinese tea **14.** Fred Housego **15.** Cirencester.

ENTERTAINMENT

1. What historical event is the setting for the 2001 film *Enemy at the Gates*?
2. Who composed the 1817 song *Death and the Maiden*?
3. Who directed the 2000 film *Dr. T and the Women*?
4. Who composed the 1968 musical work *Stimmung*?
5. Who played the villainess The Siren in the 1960's *Batman* television series?
6. Which character was played by Ali McGraw in *Dynasty* in 1985?
7. What is the full name of Shirley MacLaine's character in the film *Sweet Charity*?
8. Who plays Shelby Eatenton Latcherie in the 1989 film *Steel Magnolias*?
9. Which Austrian composer's works include the song cycle *Kindertotenlieder*?
10. Which actress played Cpl. Nancy Thorpe in the television drama *Soldier, Soldier*?
11. Which character was played by John Saxon in the television soap *Dynasty* from 1982-4?
12. What is Burt Lancaster's character name in the 1957 film *Sweet Smell of Success*?
13. Who plays Stella Kowalski in the 1951 film *A Streetcar Named Desire*?
14. Who stars as Scott Hastings in the 1992 film *Strictly Ballroom*?
15. Who composed the music theatre piece *Blind Man's Buff*?

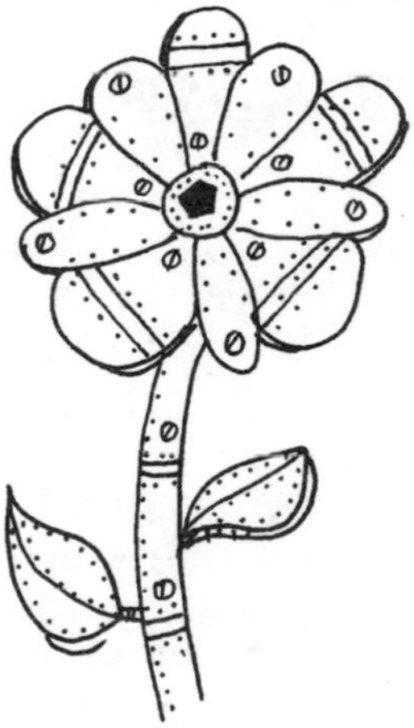

ANSWERS **1.** The siege of Stalingrad **2.** Schubert **3.** Robert Altman **4.** Karlheinz Stockhausen **5.** Joan Collins **6.** Lady Ashley Mitchell **7.** Charity Hope Valentine **8.** Julia Roberts **9.** Gustav Mahler **10.** Holly Aird **11.** Rashid Ahmed **12.** J.J. Hunsucker **13.** Kim Hunter **14.** Paul Mercurio **15.** Peter Maxwell Davies.

GENERAL KNOWLEDGE

1. What was the first name of Nazi leader Joseph Goebbels?
2. Which Italian composer and musical rival of Mozart taught Liszt and Schubert?
3. Which German admiral was the commander of the High Sea Fleet at the Battle of Jutland in 1916?
4. Who was the chancellor of West Germany 1974-83?
5. A Dick test is used to determine a person's immunity to what disease?
6. Which architect supervised the rebuilding of the House of Commons after World War II?
7. What was the middle name of US Union general William Sherman?
8. The inlet of the Bosporus called the Golden Horn forms the harbour of which city?
9. Which Ukraine-born U.S. engineer built the first successful helicopter?
10. Which English field marshal was governor general of Australia from 1953-60?
11. Who was prime minister of Rhodesia from 1964-79?
12. Who was prime minister of Portugal from 1976-78?
13. Who wrote the 1971 novel *Bear Island*?
14. What sort of creature is a hoopoe?
15. What is the standard monetary unit of Paraguay?

ANSWERS **1.** Paul **2.** Antonio Salieri **3.** Reinhard Scheer **4.** Helmut Schmidt **5.** Scarlet fever **6.** Giles Gilbert Scott **7.** Tecumseh **8.** Istanbul **9.** Igor Sikorsky **10.** William Joseph Slim **11.** Ian Smith **12.** Mario Soares **13.** Alistair Maclean **14.** Bird **15.** Guarani.

POP

1. Siobhan Fahey and Marcella Detroit comprised which duo?
2. Which group's albums included *The Impossible Dream* and *Tomorrow Belongs to Me*?
3. Singer Henry Samuel is better known as what?
4. In which year was Smokey Robinson born?
5. Glen Matlock, Midge Ure, Rusty Egan and Steve New - which group?
6. Who is the lead singer of R.E.M.?
7. In which year did Otis Redding die?
8. Ricardo Wayne Penniman is better known as whom?
9. Lowell George, Bill Payne, Roy Estrada and Rick Hayward formed which band?
10. In which seaside town were the rock band Little Angels formed?
11. Which singer recorded 1970's *Tumbleweed Connection* album?
12. In which year did Buddy Holly die?
13. The Human Beanz became which band in 1967?
14. Who released the 1976 album *Teenage Depression*?
15. In which city did Echo and the Bunnymen form?

ANSWERS **1.** Shakespears Sister **2.** The Sensational Alex Harvey Band **3.** Seal **4.** 1940 **5.** The Rich Kids **6.** Michael Stipe **7.** 1967 **8.** Little Richard **9.** Little Feat **10.** Scarborough **11.** Elton John **12.** 1959 **13.** Love Sculpture **14.** Eddie and the Hot Rods **15.** Liverpool.

ART AND LITERATURE

1. Who wrote the 1911 novel *The Innocence of Father Brown*?
2. Which Italian sculptor's works include *Theseus and the Minotaur*?
3. Which sculptor created the large bronze *Nymph of Fontainebleu*?
4. Who wrote the 2000 novel *Maya*?
5. Who wrote the novel *A Chance Child*?
6. Who was the poet laureate from 1850-92?
7. In which century did the Flemish painter David Teniers the Younger live?
8. Who wrote the 2000 novel *Golden Deeds*?
9. Which Russian-born artist authored the 1931 autobiography *Ma Vie*?
10. Who wrote the novel *Persuading Annie*?
11. In which year did the Canadian abstract artist Jack Bush die?
12. What was Lisa Jewell's best-selling follow-up to the novel *Ralph's Party*?
13. What is the term applied to painters who imitated the style of Caravaggio in the early 17th century?
14. Who wrote the 2000 novel *The Wild*?
15. What was painter Jan Brueghel known as?

ANSWERS 1. G.K. Chesterton **2.** Antonio Canova **3.** Benvenuto Cellini **4.** Jostein Gaarder **5.** Jill Paton Walsh **6.** Alfred Tennyson **7.** 17th century **8.** Catherine Chidgey **9.** Marc Chagall **10.** Melissa Nathan **11.** 1977 **12.** Thirty-Nothing **13.** Caravaggisti **14.** Esther Freud **15.** 'Velvet' Brueghel.

GENERAL KNOWLEDGE

1. Who wrote the 1699 poem *The Dispensary*?
2. In which year did Kenya join the United Nations?
3. In which year did the painter Francis Bacon die?
4. Who was president of the Philippines from 1965-86?
5. Who wrote the play *A Doll's House*?
6. In which county is the port of Watchet?
7. As what is the plant *Amaranthus caudatus* better known?
8. In which year was Grand Duchess Anastasia of Russia believed to have been executed?
9. What is the more familiar name of the fish called the bummalo?
10. Which pop singer of the 1970's was formerly known as Shane Fenton?
11. What is a Joey Hooker - a snake or a plant?
12. What is the capital of Moldova?
13. Who was Melody Maker Top Female Jazz Singer from 1957-70?
14. Who wrote the novel *Castle Rackrent*?
15. In which Welsh village was the TV series *The Prisoner* filmed?

ANSWERS **1.** Sir Samuel Garth **2.** 1963 **3.** 1992 **4.** Ferdinand Marcos **5.** Henrik Ibsen **6.** Somerset **7.** Love-lies-bleeding **8.** 1918 **9.** Bombay Duck **10.** Alvin Stardust **11.** A plant **12.** Kishinev **13.** Ella Fitzgerald **14.** Maria Edgeworth **15.** Portmeirion.

ENTERTAINMENT

1. Who composed the 1907 'English Rhapsody' for orchestra *Brigg Fair*?
2. Which actress played the character Jo in the film *Fever Pitch*?
3. Who played the villainess Dr. Cassandra in the 1960s *Batman* television series?
4. What is Marlon Brando's character name in the film *The Teahouse of the August Moon*?
5. Who plays Truvy Jones in the 1989 film *Steel Magnolias*?
6. Boieldieu's opera *The White Lady* is based on works by which author?
7. Who wrote the hymn *Hark, the Herald Angels Sing*?
8. To which composer is the song cycle *Let us Garlands Bring* by Gerald Finzi dedicated?
9. Which 2000 film stars Adam Sandler as a son of the devil?
10. Which real life politician does Steven Culp portray in the 2000 film *Thirteen Days*?
11. Who plays the character Vassily Zaitsev in the 2001 film *Enemy at the Gates*?
12. Who plays Richard Gere's secretary Carolyn in the film *Dr. T and the Women*?
13. Who composed the 1904 tone poem *In the South*?
14. Who directed and stars in the 2000 film *Best in Show*?
15. Which Oscar-winner stars as Carl Brashear in the 2000 film *Men of Honor*?

ANSWERS 1. Frederick Delius **2.** Holly Aird **3.** Ida Lupino **4.** Sakini **5.** Dolly Parton **6.** Walter Scott **7.** Charles Wesley **8.** Ralph Vaughan Williams **9.** Little Nicky **10.** Bobby Kennedy **11.** Jude Law **12.** Shelley Long **13.** Edward Elgar **14.** Christopher Guest **15.** Cuba Gooding Jr.

GEOGRAPHY

1. On which island of Asia is the resort of Kandy?
2. On which river is the Yugoslavian town of Leskovac?
3. On which sea is the Italian seaport of Leghorn?
4. In which African country is the seaport of Sfax?
5. On which Mediterranean island is the resort town of Sliema?
6. Trim is the county town of which county of the Republic of Ireland?
7. Which river meets the sea at Bideford in Devon?
8. On which island of Asia is the seaport of Surabaya?
9. Which city is the capital of Costa Rica?
10. Which U.S. state houses the towns of Toledo, Akron, and Dayton?
11. Which is larger - Norway or Finland?
12. In which country is the seaport of Murmansk?
13. In which country of S.W. Asia is the seaport of Abadan?
14. On which river is the Indian city of Agra?
15. What is the capital of Turkey?

ANSWERS **1.** Sri Lanka **2.** River Morava **3.** Ligurian Sea **4.** Tunisia **5.** Malta **6.** Meath **7.** Torridge **8.** Java **9.** San José **10.** Ohio **11.** Finland **12.** Russia **13.** Iran **14.** Jumna **15.** Ankara.

POP

1. Which group's last Top Ten single in the 1990s was *Friday I'm In Love*?
2. Which vocalist featured on the 1994 hit by Bono *In the Name of the Father*?
3. Which U.S. rapper charted in 1997 with *All That I Got Is You*?
4. Which group charted in 1996 with the single *C'mon Kids*?
5. Which indie group had a 1998 Top 40 hit with *Whippin' Piccadilly*?
6. Which group had a Top Ten hit in 1995 with *Shoot Me With Your Love*?
7. Which group had a minor hit in 1964 with *Get Your Feet Out Of My Shoes*?
8. Which indie group had minor hits with *Sweet Johnny* and *Patio Song*?
9. Which male singer had a hit in 1996 with *Hallo Spaceboy*?
10. From which country does the rapper Da Hool hail?
11. Which French group had a 1997 hit single with *Around the World*?
12. Which male vocal group had Top Ten hits in 1997 with *Love Guaranteed* and *Wonderful Tonight*?
13. What was the third album by the group Blood, Sweat and Tears?
14. Which band's 1975 live album was called *On Your Feet Or On Your Knees*?
15. What did the band Seymour change their name to for their first single *She's So High*?

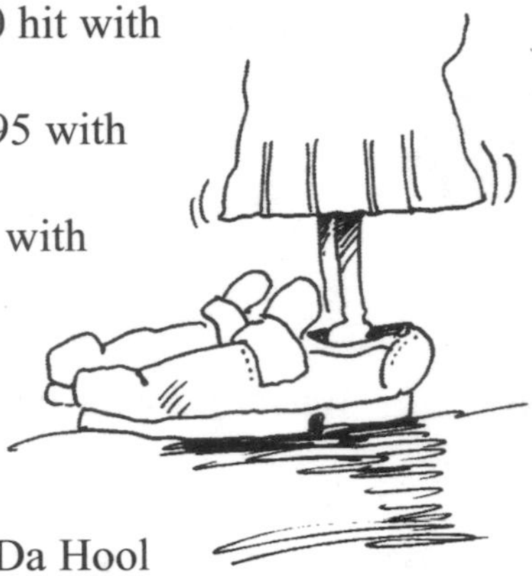

ANSWERS 1. The Cure **2.** Gavin Friday **3.** Ghostface Killah **4.** The Boo Radleys **5.** Gomez **6.** D:Ream **7.** The Boothill Foot-Tappers **8.** Gorky's Zygotic Mynci **9.** David Bowie **10.** Germany **11.** Daft Punk **12.** Damage **13.** Blood, Sweat and Tears 3 **14.** Blue Oyster Cult **15.** Blur.

WORDS

1. What is eisell?
2. In which sport might you use a suplex?
3. What would you do with a parfait - eat it or drive it?
4. What is a 'slug-abed'?
5. What would you do with a lur - cook with it or play it?
6. What in ancient Greece was a scyphus?
7. Of what is a 'nunny bag' made?
8. Why might a lewis be useful in the building trade?
9. Where on your body is the nape?
10. What, in defence, does MIDAS stand for?
11. In which sport might you play a 'long jenny'?
12. What is the male equivalent of a mermaid?
13. What is the name of the enclosed space in a law court where the accused sits?
14. What might you do with a burley - play it or smoke it?
15. By what name is the creature a cachalot also called?

ANSWERS **1.** Wormwood wine **2.** Wrestling - it is a hold **3.** Eat it - it is a dessert **4.** A late riser **5.** Play it - it is a Danish musical instrument **6.** A drinking vessel **7.** Sealskin **8.** It is a device for lifting heavy stones **9.** The back of the neck **10.** Missile Defence Alarm System **11.** Billiards **12.** Merman **13.** Dock **14.** Smoke it - it is tobacco **15.** A sperm whale.

GENERAL KNOWLEDGE

1. Of what is cynophobia the fear?
2. What is the name of the preservative numbered E200?
3. In the United States of America, what is the state flower of Oklahoma?
4. Which boxer carried the Irish flag in the opening ceremony of the 1996 Olympic Games?
5. How old was Rosanna Della Corta when she gave birth in 1994?
6. In which year was the murderer Ian Brady given two life sentences?
7. For which league football club did Southampton's Kevin Davies make his league debut?
8. Film director Nora Ephron is named after a character in which play?
9. In which country is the skiing resort of Arc 2000?
10. At which airport did the actor Gérard Depardieu survive an air crash in 1996?
11. Of which country is the letter D the international car index mark?
12. Which major city does Blagnac airport serve?
13. Which saint's feast day is June 20th?
14. What is another name for an eighth-note in music?
15. In 1999, how many people were caught trying to cross from Mexico into the U.S.A.?

ANSWERS **1.** Dogs **2.** Sorbic acid **3.** Mistletoe **4.** Francis Barrett **5.** 63 **6.** 1966 **7.** Chesterfield **8.** Nora in Ibsen's play *A Doll's House* **9.** France **10.** Madrid **11.** Germany **12.** Toulouse **13.** Alban **14.** Quaver **15.** 1,579,010.

ENTERTAINMENT

1. On whose play was the 1955 film *The Seven Year Itch* starring Marilyn Monroe based?
2. Who plays Richard Gere's sister-in-law Peggy in the film *Dr. T and the Women*?
3. Which actor directed the 2000 film *All the Pretty Horses*?
4. Who played the villain False Face in the 1960s *Batman* television series?
5. What, musically, is the EFDSS?
6. With which instrument is the musician Watson Forbes associated?
7. What, musically, is a Hochzeitsmarsch?
8. Who directed the 2000 film *Tigerland*?
9. Who plays the character Danilov in the 2001 film *Enemy at the Gates*?
10. With which instrument is Dame Moura Lympany associated?
11. Gellenflöte is the German term for which musical instrument?
12. Who composed the 1909 symphonic poem *In the Faery Hills*?
13. What was Holly Hunter's character name in the film *The Piano*?
14. For which 1977 film was Peter Firth a Best Supporting Actor Oscar nominee?
15. What nationality was the composer Vincent D'Indy?

ANSWERS **1.** George Axelrod **2.** Laura Dern **3.** Billy Bob Thornton **4.** Malachi Throne **5.** English Folk Dance and Song Society **6.** Viola **7.** Wedding march **8.** Joel Schumacher **9.** Joseph Fiennes **10.** Piano **11.** Clarinet **12.** Arnold Bax **13.** Ada McGrath **14.** Equus **15.** French.

GENERAL KNKOWLEDGE

1. What was the name of the U.S. architect and engineer born in 1895 who developed the geodesic dome?
2. What would you do with a bergère?
3. What was the informal name given to the British 7th Armoured Division who fought in N. Africa from 1941-42?
4. Which Italian politician was murdered in 1978 by the Red Brigades?
5. Approximately how long in miles is the Khyber Pass?
6. What was the profession of the Boston nationalist Paul Revere who made a famous ride in 1775?
7. In which year did the politician Cecil Rhodes die?
8. What is a kiekie?
9. Which German aviator commanded the 11th Chasing Squadron in World War I?
10. Which U.S. millionaire founded the Standard Oil Company in 1870?
11. Who succeeded McKinley as U.S. president following his assassination?
12. What was the nickname of German field marshal Erwin Rommel?
13. Who was the archbishop of Canterbury from 1980-91?
14. In which year was Mount McKinley in Alaska first climbed?
15. How many generals fought in the Wars of the Diodochi for control of the empire of Alexander the Great after his death?

ANSWERS 1. R. Buckminster Fuller **2.** Sit in it - it's a type of chair **3.** The Desert Rats **4.** Aldo Moro **5.** 33 miles **6.** Silversmith **7.** 1902 **8.** A climbing plant **9.** Baron von Richthofen **10.** John D. Rockefeller **11.** Theodore Roosevelt **12.** The Desert Fox **13.** Robert Runcie **14.** 1913 **15.** Six.

POP

1. Which U.S. singer had a 1997 hit with *A Change Would Do You Good*?
2. Which group had a minor hit in 1996 with *Do Wah Diddy Diddy*?
3. Which food gave Laurent Garnier a minor hit in 1997?
4. Which group's hits include 1998's *Solomon Bites the Worm*?
5. Which group's hits include the 1994 single *Pineapple Head*?
6. Which group had a 1997 No. 1 hit with *Beetlebum*?

7. Which female singer had a 1997 Top Ten hit with the song *Do You Know*?
8. Which male singer had a 1995 hit with *Can I Touch You...There*?
9. Which reformed group had a 1998 hit with *I Just Wanna Be Loved*?
10. Which group had a 1995 hit with *Something for the Pain*?
11. What was Elbow Bones and the Racketeers' 1984 hit single?
12. Which group's highest singles chart entry was the 1996 song *For the Dead*?
13. Which member of the Clash formed Big Audio Dynamite?
14. Which member of the Skids formed Big Country?
15. John Disco, Manda Rin and Sci-Fi Steve comprise which band?

ANSWERS **1.** Sheryl Crow **2.** Blue Melons **3.** Crispy Bacon **4.** The Bluetones **5.** Crowded House **6.** Blur **7.** Michelle Gayle **8.** Michael Bolton **9.** Culture Club **10.** Bon Jovi **11.** A Night in New York **12.** Gene **13.** Mick Jones **14.** Stuart Adamson **15.** Bis.

PEOPLE

1. In which country was the comedy actress Carmen Silvera born?

2. In which year was the actor William Shatner born?

3. In which year was the television presenter Valerie Singleton born?

4. In which year did the jazz bass player Jaco Pastorius die?

5. In which year did the German conductor Carl Muck die?

6. Who became prime minister of the Republic of Ireland in 1997?

7. Which *Coronation Street* actor was born William Cleworth Piddington?

8. Who became prime minister of Israel in 1996?

9. In which year did the Apache Indian chief Cochise die?

10. What is the real name of the Eco-warrior ‘Swampy’?

11. Which pop singer’s full name is Florian Cloud De Bounevialle Armstrong?

12. Which actress did Kevin Bacon marry in 1988?

13. Which British author was born Mary Aline Mynors Farmar?

14. What is the actress Téa Leoni’s full name?

15. Who is the director of the Royal Botanic Gardens at Kew?

ANSWERS 1. Canada **2.** 1931 **3.** 1937 **4.** 1987 **5.** 1940 **6.** Bertie Ahern **7.** Bill Tarmey **8.** Benjamin Netanyahu **9.** 1874 **10.** Daniel Hooper **11.** Dido **12.** Kyra Sedgwick **13.** Mary Wesley **14.** Elizabeth Téa Pantaleoni **15.** Peter Crane.

GENERAL KNOWLEDGE

1. What is the Greek name for the city of Nicosia?
2. What was the subtitle of the film *Star Wars Episode 1*?
3. In which year was the Haigh murder case trial?
4. In which county of the southwest is Dartington Hall?
5. What is a facsimile transmission system more commonly known as?
6. In which year did the Crimean War end?
7. In which city did the Belgrade Theatre open in 1958?
8. In which year did the First Fleet of convict ships arrive in Port Jackson, Australia?
9. Which cartoon cat famously 'kept on walking'?
10. Of what whole number is 7.74596 the square root?
11. In which novel by Charles Dickens does Vincent Crummles appear?
12. What was the first national anthem of the U.S.?
13. Which caddish character in *Tom Brown's Schooldays* reappeared in stories by George MacDonald Fraser?
14. John Nyren was the son of the founder of which cricket club?
15. What is bully beef?

ANSWERS **1.** Lefkosia **2.** The Phantom Menace **3.** 1949 **4.** Devon **5.** Fax **6.** 1856 **7.** Coventry **8.** 1788 **9.** Felix the Cat **10.** 60 **11.** Nicholas Nickleby **12.** Hail Columbia! **13.** Flashman **14.** Hambledon Club **15.** Tinned corned beef.

ENTERTAINMENT

1. For which 1965 film was Frank Finlay a Best Supporting Actor Oscar nominee?
2. What nationality is the composer Giacinto Scelsi?
3. Which was the first company in Britain to market L.P.s?
4. Who plays Richard Gere's wife Kate in the film *Dr. T and the Women*?
5. Who played the villain The Sandman in the 1960s *Batman* television series?
6. Who directed the 1999 film remake of *The Haunting*?
7. In which city is the 1999 film *Orphans* set?
8. Who played Godber in the sitcom *Porridge*?
9. Who starred as a legless gangster in the 1920 film *The Penalty*?
10. Who played Fidel Castro in the 1969 film *Che!*?
11. Which film won all five main Oscar awards in 1934?
12. At the Cannes Film Festival, what was the Grand Prix International renamed in 1955?
13. Which singer was born Frank Abelson?
14. Which orchestra is based in the town of Rishon Le-Zion in Israel?
15. Who directed the 1995 film *Tom and Huck*?

ANSWERS 1. Othello **2.** Italian **3.** Decca **4.** Farrah Fawcett **5.** Michael Rennie **6.** Jan De Bont **7.** Glasgow **8.** Richard Beckinsale **9.** Lon Chaney **10.** Jack Palance **11.** It Happened One Night **12.** Palme d'Or **13.** Frankie Vaughan **14.** Israel Symphony Orchestra **15.** Peter Hewitt.

PEOPLE

1. What is the name of Robin Cook's ex-wife, author of *A Slight and Delicate Creature*?
2. How much, in dollars, did Bill Clinton pay to Paula Jones to settle the sexual harassment case against him?
3. Who played *Little Voice* in the 1999 film?
4. Which politician wrote the novel *The Eleventh Commandment*?
5. Which actor starred in, and directed, the film *Bulworth*?
6. Who is the Governor of the Bank of England?
7. Which U.S. chat show host starred in the 1999 film *Beloved*?
8. Melanie Blatt is a singer with which vocal group?
9. Which *Coronation Street* actor died in February 1999 in Shipley?
10. The king of Jordan died in Febraury 1999. What was his name?
11. Who wrote the 1999 novel *Glamorama*?
12. Which comedian is the brains behind the Radio 1 show *Blue Jam*?
13. Which singer won the Best Single and Best Video awards at the 1999 Brits?
14. What were the forenames of the three outlaw Younger Brothers?
15. What was the US traitor Iva Toguri d'Aquino better known as?

ANSWERS **1.** Margaret **2.** $850,000 **3.** Jane Horrocks **4.** Jeffrey Archer **5.** Warren Beatty **6.** Eddie George **7.** Oprah Winfrey **8.** All Saints **9.** Bryan Mosley **10.** King Hussein **11.** Bret Easton Ellis **12.** Chris Morris **13.** Robbie Williams **14.** Bob, Jim, Cole **15.** Tokyo Rose.

POP

1. Who was the lead singer with the group American Music Club?
2. Which group recorded the 1980 album *Back in Black*?
3. Which singer's albums include *Reg Strikes Back* and *A Simple Man*?
4. Which female vocal duo had a 1978 hit with *Boogie Oogie Oogie*?
5. Who recorded the song *All I Want For Christmas Is A Dukla Prague Away Kit*?
6. From which country did 1970s keyboard maestro Bo Hannson hail?
7. What was John Lennon's 1975 album of cover versions called?
8. Who wrote Jerry Lee Lewis's hit *Breathless*?
9. David Hidalgo and Louie Perez are the main songwriters in which group?
10. Which songwriter recorded the 1991 album *West of Rome*?
11. Who recorded the 1998 album *The Sky is Too High*?
12. Which children's choir had a 1981 hit with *My Mum is One in a Million*?
13. How many Top Ten U.K. singles did Tavares have?
14. What was the Teardrop Explodes' only Top Ten single?
15. What was the title of Cockney Rebel's 1974 chart album?

ANSWERS 1. Mark Eitzel **2.** AC/DC **3.** Elton John **4.** A Taste of Honey **5.** Half Man Half Biscuit **6.** Sweden **7.** Rock 'n' Roll **8.** Otis Blackwell **9.** Los Lobos **10.** Vic Chesnutt **11.** Graham Coxon **12.** The Children of Tansley School **13.** Four **14.** Reward **15.** The Psychomodo.

ART AND LITERATURE

1. Who wrote the 2000 novel *Thanksgiving*?
2. Who wrote the 2000 novel *The Flight of the Maidens*?
3. Under which artist did Caravaggio train in Milan?
4. As what was the painter Michelangelo Cerquozzi known?
5. Who wrote the novel *The Unconsoled*?
6. In which year did the Canadian artist Emily Carr die?
7. In which year was the painter Paul Cézanne first given a one-man show by Ambroise Vollard?
8. What was the name of the second 'Bridget Jones' book penned by Helen Fielding?
9. On which book was the 1959 film *I'm All Right Jack* based?
10. Who wrote the thriller *The Echo*?
11. In which century did the painter Pieter Breugel the Elder live?
12. What was the middle name of the painter Edward Burne-Jones?
13. What nationality was the poet Émile Verhaeren?
14. To which city did the American painter Charles Burchfield move in 1921?
15. Who wrote the 2000 short story collection *The Means of Escape*?

ANSWERS **1.** Michael Dibdin **2.** Jane Gardam **3.** Simone Peterzano **4.** Michelangelo of the Battles **5.** Kazuo Ishiguro **6.** 1945 **7.** 1895 **8.** The Edge of Reason **9.** *Private Life* by Alan Hackney **10.** Minette Walters **11.** 16th century **12.** Coley **13.** Belgian **14.** Buffalo **15.** Penelope Fitzgerald.

GENERAL KNOWLEDGE

1. In which European country is the port of Bergen?
2. Of which country is the letter N the international car index mark?
3. In which European country is La Stampa a national newspaper?
4. In which year was the award the Croix de Guerre established in France?
5. Which saint's feast day is December 31st?
6. In which country is the Poti dam?
7. In which year was the cookery writer Sophie Grigson born?
8. Who was the king of Spain from 1759-88?
9. What was the middle name of the former Canadian prime minister Pierre Trudeau?
10. What is the official language of Uruguay?
11. What is the FAO within the United Nations?
12. The element chlorine derives its name from the Greek word for what?
13. In which country is the Angostura bridge?
14. In Norse mythology, of what is Tyr the god?
15. Fyn and Bornholm are counties of which European country?

ANSWERS 1. Norway **2.** Norway **3.** Italy **4.** 1915 **5.** Sylvester **6.** Argentina **7.** 1959 **8.** Charles III **9.** Elliott **10.** Spanish **11.** Food and Agricultural Organization **12.** Green **13.** Venezuela **14.** Battle **15.** Denmark.

ENTERTAINMENT

1. Which movie won Best Film at the 1959 British Academy Awards?
2. Who directed the 1953 film *Glen or Glenda*?
3. What, musically, is a 'tampon double'?
4. Who composed the opera *Ruslan and Lyudmila*?
5. Under what name did Sam Spiegel produce the 1951 film *The African Queen*?
6. Who directed the remake in 1979 of Hitchcock's *The Lady Vanishes*?
7. Who played Foggy Dewhurst in the TV comedy *Last of the Summer Wine*?
8. Which ex-*Coronation Street* actor played George Fairchild in the 1980's comedy series *Brass*?
9. Who played King Arthur in the 1963 film *Lancelot and Guinevere*?
10. Who played David Bliss in the 1960 sitcom *A Life of Bliss*?
11. Which writing duo created TV's *Goodnight Sweetheart*?
12. In which year was comedian Mel Smith born?
13. In which year did composer Sir Edward German die?
14. Who directed the 1963 film *8 and a Half*?
15. Who directed the 1962 film *Cape Fear*?

ANSWERS **1.** Ben-Hur **2.** Edward D. Wood Jr. **3.** A two-headed drumstick **4.** Glinka **5.** S.P. Eagle **6.** Anthony Page **7.** Brian Wilde **8.** Geoffrey Hinsliff **9.** Brian Aherne **10.** George Cole **11.** Laurence Marks & Maurice Gran **12.** 1952 **13.** 1936 **14.** Federico Fellini **15.** J. Lee Thompson.

ART AND LITERATURE

1. Who wrote the novel *The Devil Rides Out*?
2. What is the subtitle of the play *Twelfth Night*?
3. Who wrote the novel *Westward Ho!*?
4. Which artist won the 1995 Turner Prize?
5. Which comedian wrote the 1991 novel *The Liar*?
6. Who wrote the children's book *The Owl Service*?
7. In which 1932 comic novel did Great Aunt Ada Doom appear?
8. Which artist worked from 1795 until his death on drawings concerning the comparative anatomy of *Man, Tiger, and Fowl*?
9. What is the name given to the bottom layer of a painting, such as the canvas?
10. Which painter's subjects included Winston Churchill in 1954 and Somerset Maugham in 1949?
11. Who wrote *Captain Corelli's Mandolin*?
12. What was the title of William Golding's novel about a shipwrecked group of schoolboys?
13. Whose autobiography was *Goodbye to All That*?
14. Who wrote *Jude the Obscure*?
15. "Hale knew they meant to murder him before he had been in Brighton three hours." The opening lines to which novel?

ANSWERS 1. Dennis Wheatley **2.** What You Will **3.** Charles Kingsley **4.** Damien Hirst **5.** Stephen Fry **6.** Alan Garner **7.** Cold Comfort Farm **8.** George Stubbs **9.** Support **10.** Graham Sutherland **11.** Louis de Bernières **12.** Lord of the Flies **13.** Robert Graves **14.** Thomas Hardy **15.** Brighton Rock, by Graham Greene.

POP

1. Sonya Aurora Madan is the lead singer with which group?
2. In which city was the electronic band 808 State formed?
3. Who were the three members of the group E.L.P.?
4. Who had a No. 1 single with the song *Orinoco Flow*?
5. Vince Clarke and Andy Bell - which electronic duo?
6. Dave Stewart and Annie Lennox - which duo?
7. What are the forenames of the Everly Brothers?
8. Who are Ben Watt and Tracey Thorn?
9. Which band recorded the 1971 album *A Nod's as Good as a Wink...to a Blind Horse*?
10. In which city was Marianne Faithfull born?
11. *Bingo Master's Breakout* was the first single from which Manchester band?
12. Whitney, Grech, Townsend, King and Chapman - which band?
13. From which city does the group The Farm hail?
14. Who was the lead singer in the group Frankie Goes to Hollywood?
15. Rodgers, Kirke, Fraser and Kossoff - which group?

ANSWERS **1.** Echobelly **2.** Manchester **3.** Emerson, Lake and Palmer **4.** Enya **5.** Erasure **6.** Eurhythmics **7.** Don and Phil **8.** Everything but the Girl **9.** The Faces **10.** London **11.** The Fall **12.** Family **13.** Liverpool **14.** Holly Johnson **15.** Free.

GEOGRAPHY

1. Which mountain range is known as the 'backbone of England'?
2. In which U.S. state is the town of Albuquerque?
3. In what is Bounty Island, New Zealand, covered?
4. What is the capital of the Central American republic of Panama?
5. On which river is Newport, Isle of Wight?
6. Montevideo is the capital of which South American country?
7. What is the name of the garden suburb S.W. of Birmingham founded by George Cadbury in 1897?
8. On which river is Alloa in Scotland?

9. What is the name of the strait separating the Isle of Wight from Hampshire?
10. On which river is the Pennsylvania port of Pittsburgh?
11. In which county of the southwest is Portishead?
12. What is the chief island of the Society Islands in French Polynesia?
13. What is the seaport capital of the Falkland Islands?
14. In which ocean is the Sargasso Sea?
15. Which is longer - the River Rhône or the River Rhine?

ANSWERS **1.** The Pennine Range **2.** New Mexico **3.** Guano (it is uninhabited) **4.** Panama City **5.** Medina **6.** Uruguay **7.** Bournville **8.** Forth **9.** The Solent **10.** Ohio River **11.** Somerset **12.** Tahiti **13.** Stanley **14.** Atlantic Ocean **15.** River Rhine.

GENERAL KNOWLEDGE

1. Which horse racecourse is 9 miles south-east of Glasgow?
2. Which country's police force is named after the phrase 'guard of the peace'?
3. Who created the fictional detective Mike Hammer?
4. In which U.S. city is the flatiron building?
5. Who was the third son of David in the Old Testament?
6. What is the nickname of West Ham F.C.?
7. In which year was the Battle of Bannockburn?
8. HKJ is the international car registration of which country?
9. For which constituency did the entertainer Lenny Beige stand at the 1997 election?
10. Which Irish political party was formed by De Valera in 1923?
11. In which year did Robert Louis Stevenson die?
12. Which creature is also called a fitch?
13. What was the poet W.H. Auden's first name?
14. In which year did the musician Frank Zappa die?
15. Who composed the opera *Cavalleria Rusticana* ?

ANSWERS **1.** Hamilton Park **2.** Republic of Ireland **3.** Mickey Spillane **4.** New York **5.** Absalom **6.** The Hammers **7.** 1314 **8.** Jordan **9.** Putney **10.** Fianna Fail **11.** 1894 **12.** Polecat **13.** Wystan **14.** 1993 **15.** Pietro Mascagni.

ENTERTAINMENT

1. Who directed the 1997 film *Seven Years in Tibet*?
2. Who played Dr. Watson in the 1929 film *The Return of Sherlock Holmes*?
3. Who played Sherlock Holmes in the 1946 film *Dressed to Kill*?
4. Who does Diane Burke play in the television show *Brookside*?
5. Who does John Bardon play in the television show *EastEnders*?
6. In which Mozart opera does the aria *Una voce sento al core* appear?
7. Who played the character Sheila in the 1979 film *Hair*?
8. Who directed the film *Hail the Conquering Hero*?
9. What was the character name of Meg Tilly in the film *Valmont*?
10. Who directed the 1941 film *Western Union*?
11. Who directed the 1970 film *The Ballad of Cable Hogue*?
12. Who directed the 1978 film *Fedora*?
13. What was Christopher Lloyd's character name in the film *One Flew Over the Cuckoo's Nest*?
14. Who does Sue Jenkins play in the television show *Brookside*?
15. Which comedian was a house member in the celebrity version of *Big Brother* in March?

ANSWERS 1. Jean-Jacques Annaud **2.** H. Reeves-Smith **3.** Basil Rathbone **4.** Katie Rogers **5.** Jim Branning **6.** La Finta Giardiniera **7.** Beverly D'Angelo **8.** Preston Sturges **9.** Tourvel **10.** Fritz Lang **11.** Sam Peckinpah **12.** Billy Wilder **13.** Taber **14.** Jackie Corkhill **15.** Jack Dee.

WORDS

1. What would you do with a sarangi?
2. What does the phrase ‘ecce homo’ mean?
3. What were Switzers?
4. What would you do with a surrey - ride in it or drink it?
5. What method of transport is a PSV?
6. What is an oenophile?
7. What is the 23rd letter of the Greek alphabet?
8. How many are there in an ogdoad?
9. What is a ‘lyke-wake’?
10. What in ancient Rome was a scutum?
11. Why might being hit with a ‘salt eel’ hurt?
12. To what creature does the adjective lupine refer?
13. What sort of creature is a longspur?
14. What is the U.S. name for a courgette?
15. A parka is a type of coat. What does the word mean in the Aleutian language?

ANSWERS **1.** Play it **2.** Behold the man **3.** Swiss mercenaries **4.** Ride in it **5.** A public service vehicle **6.** A lover of wines **7.** Psi **8.** Eight **9.** A watch over a dead person **10.** A large shield **11.** It is the end of a rope **12.** A wolf **13.** A bird **14.** Zucchini **15.** Skin.

POP

1. Lynval Golding, Neville Staples and Terry Hall - which band?
2. In which year did Peter Gabriel leave Genesis?
3. In which year was Emmylou Harris born?
4. Ian Craig Marsh, Martyn Ware and Glenn Gregory comprised which early 1980s band?
5. Which guitarist recorded the 1976 album *Cry Tough*?
6. Which band recorded the 1967 album *Da Capo*?
7. Which country singer was married to actress Julia Roberts?
8. Which U.S. band is associated with the songs *Freebird* and *Sweet Home Alabama*?
9. Candida Doyle is the keyboard player in which group?
10. Who was bass player in the group Queen?
11. Thom Yorke is lead singer in which band?
12. Johnny, Joey, Dee Dee and Tommy - which band?
13. Who was leader of the 1970s band The Raspberries?
14. Which group recorded the 1969 album *Let it Bleed*?
15. Which guitarist's first solo album was 1974's *Slaughter on 10th Avenue*?

ANSWERS 1. Fun Boy Three **2.** 1975 **3.** 1947 **4.** Heaven 17 **5.** Nils Lofgren **6.** Love **7.** Lyle Lovett **8.** Lynyrd Skynyrd **9.** Pulp **10.** John Deacon **11.** Radiohead **12.** Ramones **13.** Eric Carmen **14.** The Rolling Stones **15.** Mick Ronson.

ENTERTAINMENT

1. Who directed the 1989 film *Mississippi Burning*?
2. In which city was Susan Sarandon born?
3. Who played Joe Orton in the film *Prick Up Your Ears*?
4. Who played Grushenka in the 1957 film *The Brothers Karamazov*?
5. In which Italian city was Pier Paolo Pasolini born?
6. Who played nightclub manager Danny Kane in the TV drama *The Paradise Club*?
7. Which U.S. actress was born in Quincy, Massachusetts in 1935?
8. Who played Nicola Freeman in the soap *Crossroads*?
9. Who directed the Marx Brothers in *A Night at the Opera* and *A Day at the Races*?
10. Who played Holly Harwood in *Dallas*?
11. Who directed the 1965 comedy thriller film *Mirage*?
12. In which year did Westward TV come into being?
13. Who directed the 1984 film *City Heat*?
14. Who played Paul Buchet in the TV series *The Protectors*?
15. In which year did the actor Anthony Perkins die?

ANSWERS 1. Alan Parker **2.** New York **3.** Gary Oldman **4.** Maria Schell **5.** Bologna **6.** Leslie Grantham **7.** Lee Remick **8.** Gabrielle Drake **9.** Sam Wood **10.** Lois Chiles **11.** Edward Dmytryk **12.** 1961 **13.** Richard Benjamin **14.** Tony Anholt **15.** 1992.

GENERAL KNOWLEDGE

1. What is the nickname of Sheffield Wednesday F.C.?
2. Who is the Conservative M.P. for Billericay?
3. What would you do with Atholl brose - drink it or plant it?
4. Who composed the opera *Porgy and Bess*?
5. In which book by Charles Dickens does the Fat Boy appear?
6. What location was the setting for the hotel-based soap opera *Crossroads*?
7. In which department is the French tourist resort St. Tropez?
8. In which year did the dancer Martha Graham die?
9. What sort of animal is a bufflehead - a snake or a duck?
10. For what does the abbreviation HGV stand?
11. How many are in a gross?
12. What was the first book in the Father Brown series?
13. Who directed the 1993 film *Manhattan Murder Mystery*?
14. Which ancient Egyptian goddess is usually depicted as having cow's horns?
15. Which naval officer marries *Madame Butterfly* in Puccini's opera?

ANSWERS 1. The Owls **2.** Teresa Gorman **3.** Drink it - it's whisky and honey **4.** George Gershwin **5.** Pickwick Papers **6.** King's Oak **7.** Var **8.** 1991 **9.** A duck **10.** Heavy goods vehicle **11.** 144 **12.** The Innocence of Father Brown **13.** Woody Allen **14.** Isis **15.** Pinkerton.

ENTERTAINMENT

1. Who directed the 1974 film *The Front Page*?
2. Who directed the 1941 film *Man Hunt*?
3. What was the character name of Moses Gunn in the film *Ragtime*?
4. Who directed the film *The Miracle of Morgan's Creek*?
5. Who does Stan Richards play in the television show *Emmerdale*?
6. Who played Sherlock Holmes in the 1978 film *The Hound of the Baskervilles*?
7. Who directed the 2000 film *Thirteen Days*?
8. Who played Dr. Watson in the 1931 film *The Speckled Band*?
9. Who directed the 1951 film *Fourteen Hours*?
10. Who directed the 1955 film *The Seven Little Foys*?
11. Who does Tony Caunter play in the television show *EastEnders*?
12. In which Mozart opera does the aria *Padre, germani, addio* appear?
13. Who directed the 1972 film *Junior Bonner*?
14. What was Clark Gable's character name in the film *Saratoga*?
15. What was the character name of Colin Firth in the film *Valmont*?

ANSWERS **1.** Billy Wilder **2.** Fritz Lang **3.** Booker T. Washington **4.** Preston Sturges **5.** Seth Armstrong **6.** Peter Cook **7.** Roger Donaldson **8.** Athole Stewart **9.** Henry Hathaway **10.** Melville Shavelson **11.** Roy Evans **12.** Idomeneo **13.** Sam Peckinpah **14.** Duke Bradley **15.** Valmont.

GEOGRAPHY

1. On which river is the French city of Metz?
2. The Salmon River of Idaho is only navigable downstream. What is it also known as?
3. In which European country is the port of Setubal?
4. Part of the boundary between which two U.S. states runs down the middle of the main street of Texarkana?
5. Taipei is the capital of which island in Asia?
6. In which county of the Republic of Ireland is the village of Shillelagh?
7. In which U.S. state is Lake Okeechobee?
8. On which river does Munich stand?
9. In which European country is the publishing centre of Lund?
10. On which river is the village of Beaulieu in Hampshire?
11. What is Bedloe's Island in New York harbour also known as?
12. Which is larger - Tasmania or Bahrain?
13. In which African country is the airport town of Entebbe?
14. In which U.S. state is the seaport of Galveston?
15. Bad Homburg is a spa city in which European country?

ANSWERS **1.** Moselle **2.** The River of No Return **3.** Portugal **4.** Texas and Arkansas **5.** Taiwan **6.** Wicklow **7.** Florida **8.** Isar **9.** Sweden **10.** River Beaulieu **11.** Liberty Island **12.** Tasmania **13.** Uganda **14.** Texas **15.** Germany.

POP

1. Which group had a Top 30 single in 1997 with *A Prisoner of the Past*?
2. Which Goth group's debut single was *Ignore the Machine*?
3. What was the only No. 1 single, in 1979, by The Pretenders?
4. Which group recorded the 1986 album *Spreading the Disease*?
5. How many solo No. 1 singles has Alan Price had?
6. Who was the lead singer in the group Any Trouble?
7. Which group charted in 1996 with the single *Lump*?
8. What was Elvis Presley's last U.K. No.1 single, in 1977?
9. On which studio L.P. by Tom Waits does the song *In the Neighborhood* appear?
10. Which group had a Top 30 single in 1972 with *Conquistador*?
11. What was the title of Neil Young and Crazy Horse's 1997 live album?
12. Which celebrity learner driver had a minor Christmas hit in 1997?
13. Who was the vocalist in punk group The Dead Boys?
14. What was R.E.M.'s first U.K. chart single entry?
15. In which country did the group Dead Can Dance form?

ANSWERS **1.** Prefab Sprout **2.** Alien Sex Fiend **3.** Brass in Pocket **4.** Anthrax **5.** None **6.** Clive Gregson **7.** Presidents of the United States of America **8.** Way Down **9.** Swordfishtrombones **10.** Procol Harum **11.** Year of the Horse **12.** Maureen Rees **13.** Stiv Bators **14.** The One I Love **15.** Australia.

WORDS

1. Oster-monath was the Anglo Saxon name of which month?
2. What would you do in Russia with a kissel - use it for building or eat it?
3. On which part of the body would you wear a larrigan?
4. What is liquidambar - a tree or an artificial language?
5. What sort of creature is a luderick?
6. What in English is a WH question?
7. What was an oriflamme?
8. Which part of the body is also known as the genu?
9. What would you do with a lava-lava - cook it or wear it?
10. What does the Latin phrase loco citato mean?
11. What would you keep in a lota - fruit or water?
12. What is the name of the astronomical toy showing the relative movements of the planets?
13. What sort of food is a kneidel in Jewish cookery?
14. What is a lazy Susan?
15. What in the circus is a liberty horse?

ANSWERS **1.** April **2.** Eat it - it is a dessert **3.** The foot, it is a boot **4.** A tree **5.** A fish **6.** One requiring other than a yes-no answer, i.e. why, where, when etc. **7.** A scarlet flag adopted as the national banner of France in the Middle Ages **8.** The knee **9.** Wear it - it's a skirt **10.** In the place quoted **11.** Water **12.** An orrery **13.** Dumpling **14.** A revolving tray for holding condiments **15.** A riderless horse that moves to verbal commands.

GENERAL KNOWLEDGE

1. In which year did Finland join the European Union?
2. What is the UPU within the United Nations?
3. What is the official language of Slovenia?
4. In which European country is the port of Varna?
5. Of which country is the letter M the international car index mark?
6. In which European country is Politiken a national newspaper?
7. In which year was the cookery writer Elizabeth David born?
8. Who was king of France from 1610-43?
9. Who was the Japanese emperor from 1926-89?
10. Which city has the larger population - Athens, Greece or Barcelona, Spain?
11. What is the symbol for the element rhodium?
12. Which saint's feast day is February 27th?
13. Who wrote the 1948 novel *The Golden Hawk*?
14. In Norse mythology, of what is Bragi the god?
15. What does the forename Zoë mean?

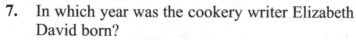

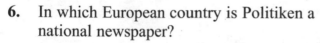

ANSWERS **1.** 1995 **2.** Universal Postal Union **3.** Slovene **4.** Bulgaria **5.** Malta **6.** Denmark **7.** 1913 **8.** Louis XIII **9.** Hirohito **10.** Barcelona **11.** Rh **12.** Leander **13.** Frank Yerby **14.** Poetry **15.** Life.

ENTERTAINMENT

1. In which year did comedian Larry Grayson die?
2. Which actor in *Coronation Street* played Tippy the Tipster in the children's show *Bright's Boffins*?
3. In which city was the composer Georges Bizet born?
4. How much in dollars was Julie Andrews paid for the film *Mary Poppins*?
5. Who directed the 1953 film *Albert R.N.*?
6. In which year was the newsreader Peter Sissons born?
7. Who played Melanie in the film *Gone with the Wind*?
8. What was the name of the pet pig in the U.S. comedy *Green Acres*?
9. Who composed the song-cycle *The Heart's Assurance*?
10. Who directed the 1960 film *Ocean's Eleven*?
11. What was ITV's disastrous version of the sitcom *The Golden Girls* called?
12. Who scripted the 1977 film *The Goodbye Girl*?
13. What is the middle name of film director George Lucas?
14. Which member of The Grumbleweeds was Wilf 'Gasmask' Grimshaw?
15. What was the U.S. title of the 1952 film *The Card* which starred Alec Guinness?

ANSWERS 1. 1995 **2.** Johnny Briggs **3.** Paris **4.** $125,000 **5.** Lewis Gilbert **6.** 1942 **7.** Olivia de Havilland **8.** Arnold **9.** Michael Tippett **10.** Lewis Milestone **11.** Brighton Belles **12.** Neil Simon **13.** Walton **14.** Carl Sutcliffe **15.** The Promoter.

GENERAL KNOWLEDGE

1. How many people partake in a game of mahjong?
2. Who wrote the novel *A Small Town in Germany*?
3. What would you do with a barong?
4. What profession is indicated by the letters FRCVS?
5. In which European country is the town of Fribourg?
6. Who was American vice president from 1969-73?
7. What type of fruit is a Doyenne du Comice?
8. According to the Bible, at what age did Methuselah father Lamech?
9. Which unit of measurement was originally defined as one ten-millionth of the distance from the Equator to the North Pole?
10. In which African country is the market town of Yola?
11. How many galleries are there in the Metropolitan Museum of Art?
12. In which year was the Yom Kippur War?
13. What is the standard monetary unit of Afghanistan?
14. How old was the travel writer Dame Freya Stark when she died?
15. In which year did John Hinckley Jnr. shoot Ronald Reagan?

ANSWERS 1. Four **2.** John Le Carré **3.** Cut with it - it's a knife **4.** Vet **5.** Switzerland **6.** Spiro Agnew **7.** Pear **8.** 187 **9.** Metre **10.** Nigeria **11.** 248 **12.** 1973 **13.** Afghani **14.** 100 **15.** 1981.

POP

1. Which group recorded the 1976 Top Ten album *King Cotton*?
2. Which Texas group recorded the album *Everything You Thought Was Right Was Wrong Today*?
3. What is the significance of the title of the album *Zenyatta Mondatta* by the Police?
4. What age was Sid Vicious, the former bass player with pop group Sex Pistols, when he died?
5. Which duo released the 2000 single *Could I Have This Kiss Forever*?
6. Which pop group had a 1990 No. 1 single with the song *Hangin' Tough*?
7. At which festival in Denmark in 2000 did nine fans die during a set by Pearl Jam?
8. Who recorded the 1993 album *Dream Harder*?
9. Which art form have Pink Floyd's members Roger Waters, Rick Wright and Nick Mason all studied?
10. Which group comprise Kenneth Stephenson, Bill Taylor, Scott Myers and Ryan Richardson?
11. Who wrote Jimmy Nail's hit single *Cowboy Dreams*?
12. In which two years did Tom Jones reach the Top 20 with the song *It's Not Unusual*?
13. Which group did Donal Lunny join after leaving Planxty?
14. With which instrument is Jean-Luc Ponty associated?
15. What are the forenames of musician Damon Albarn's mother and father?

ANSWERS 1. Five Penny Piece **2.** Slobberbone **3.** It is Sanskrit for 'top of the world' **4.** 21 **5.** Enrique Iglesias and Whitney Houston **6.** New Kids On The Block **7.** Roskilde **8.** The Waterboys **9.** Architecture **10.** The Kingsbury Manx **11.** Paddy MacAloon **12.** 1965 and 1987 **13.** The Bothy Band **14.** Violin **15.** Keith and Hazel.

ENTERTAINMENT

1. Which singer/actor was born Dino Paul Crocetti?
2. Who was the announcer on the sitcom *Soap*?
3. In which country was the actress Lilli Palmer born?
4. Who played P.C. Henry Snow in the TV drama *Softly, Softly*?
5. Who played Mary Bailey in the 1946 film *It's a Wonderful Life*?
6. Who directed the 1990 film *Awakenings*?
7. Who wrote the 1992 sitcom *Sitting Pretty*?
8. Who directed the 1987 film *The Princess Bride*?
9. In which Marx Brothers' film does Groucho say "Love flies out the door when money comes innuendo"?
10. Who directed the 1985 film *Revolution*?
11. Who played Nicola Marlow in the TV drama *The Singing Detective*?
12. In which European country was the film director Karel Reisz born?
13. In which city was the actor George Sanders born?
14. In which year did the actor Lee Marvin die?
15. Who directed the 1983 film *Carmen*?

ANSWERS **1.** Dean Martin **2.** Rod Roddy **3.** Germany **4.** Terence Rigby **5.** Donna Reed **6.** Penny Marshall **7.** John Sullivan **8.** Rob Reiner **9.** Monkey Business **10.** Hugh Hudson **11.** Janet Suzman **12.** Czechoslovakia **13.** St. Petersburg **14.** 1987 **15.** Carlos Saura.

GENERAL KNOWLEDGE

1. What do you do to a whale if you flense it?
2. In which year was the Battle of Pearl Harbor?
3. Which Old Testament book comes between Joshua and Ruth?
4. What is the computing programming language Fortran a corruption of?
5. In which U.S. city is Logan airport?
6. What type of creature is a matamata?
7. TAP is the chief airline of which country?
8. What is Fletcherism?
9. What does ASLEF stand for?
10. In which South American country is the plateau region the Mato Grosso?
11. Who in history was 'the Bloody Butcher'?
12. In architecture, what is a camponile?
13. What was the pseudonym of the artist and editor of Punch magazine Kenneth Bird?
14. Which comedian's real name is Joseph Levitch?
15. What nationality is the composer Heinz Hollinger?

ANSWERS **1.** Strip it of blubber or skin **2.** 1941 **3.** Judges **4.** Formula translation **5.** Boston **6.** A turtle **7.** Portugal **8.** The practice of chewing food thoroughly and sipping liquids to aid digestion **9.** Associated Society of Locomotive Engineers and Firemen **10.** Brazil **11.** The Duke of Cumberland **12.** A bell tower **13.** Fougasse **14.** Jerry Lewis **15.** Swiss.

ENTERTAINMENT

1. Who played Billy Bibbit in the film *One Flew Over the Cuckoo's Nest*?
2. Who directed the 1974 film *Bring Me the Head of Alfredo Garcia*?
3. Who played the character Sarah in the film *Ragtime*?
4. Who directed the 1964 film *Seven Faces of Dr. Lao*?
5. Who is the presenter of the television quiz show *Fifteen To One*?
6. Who played Dr. Watson in the 1988 film *Without a Clue*?
7. Who played Sherlock Holmes in the 1965 film *A Study in Terror*?
8. Which boxer was a house member in the celebrity version of *Big Brother* in March?
9. Who does Shaun Williamson play in the television show *EastEnders*?
10. What was Clark Gable's character name in the film *San Francisco*?
11. Who directed the 1940 film *The Return of Frank James*?
12. Who directed the 1944 film *Double Indemnity*?
13. Who directed the 1999 film *Seven Girlfriends*?
14. Who does Steven Pinder play in the television show *Brookside*?
15. In which Mozart opera does the aria *Biancheggia in mar* appear?

ANSWERS 1. Brad Dourif **2.** Sam Peckinpah **3.** Debbie Allen **4.** George Pal **5.** William G. Stewart **6.** Ben Kingsley **7.** John Neville **8.** Chris Eubank **9.** Barry Evans **10.** Blackie Norton **11.** Fritz Lang **12.** Billy Wilder **13.** Paul Lazarus **14.** Max Farnham **15.** The Dream of Scipione.

WORDS

1. What would you do with a salmi - eat it or ride it?
2. What in Ireland was the 'Hanging Gale'?
3. Which word meaning a toady do we derive from the Greek phrase meaning 'fig-blabbers'?
4. What would you do with a sarrusophone - play it or say it?
5. What is to 'slick off'?
6. To which part of the body does the adjective sural apply?
7. What would you do with an ocarina?
8. What, architecturally, is an 'oeil-de-boeuf'?
9. What was a sutler?
10. Which finger is the 'ear-finger'?
11. How long, in feet, is Gunter's Chain?
12. What bird is also known as a plantain-eater?
13. Where were the nymphs known as hamadryads supposed to live?
14. What does pps stand for at the end of a letter?
15. What is the name of the Japanese dish consisting of small rice cakes topped with fish?

ANSWERS 1. Eat it - it's a ragout of game **2.** The custom of taking 6 months' grace in the payment of rent **3.** Sycophant **4.** Play it **5.** To finish a job in hand without stopping **6.** The calf of the leg **7.** Play it - it's a musical instrument **8.** A circular window **9.** A merchant who accompanied an army in order to sell provisions **10.** The little finger **11.** Sixty-six **12.** A touraco **13.** Forest-trees **14.** Post postscriptum **15.** Sushi.

POP

1. Which group charted in 1995 with *I'll Be There for You (Theme from Friends)*?
2. On which studio album by David Bowie does the song *Joe the Lion* appear?
3. With which single did Cliff Richard have a Top Ten in 1998?
4. Which group recorded the 1972 album *Machine Head*?
5. What was Renee and Renato's 1983 follow-up to their No. 1 *Save Your Love*?
6. What was the surname of Delaney and Bonnie?
7. Which pair duetted on the 1981 Top Ten single *Endless Love*?
8. In which U.S. city did the group Destroy All Monsters form in 1973?
9. What was Andrew Ridgeley's only solo chart hit, in 1990?
10. What was the title of Dexy's Midnight Runners 1985 album?
11. How many No. 1 singles did Right Said Fred have?
12. What was Prince's first Top Ten single in the U.K.?
13. Which group recorded the1973 album *Toulouse Street*?
14. Which group backed Kate Robbins on the 1981 hit *More Than in Love*?
15. Which band recorded 1969's *Kip of the Serenes* L.P.?

ANSWERS 1. The Rembrandts **2.** Heroes **3.** Can't keep this feeling in **4.** Deep Purple **5.** Just One More Kiss **6.** Bramlett **7.** Diana Ross and Lionel Richie **8.** Detroit **9.** Shake **10.** Don't Stand Me Down **11.** One **12.** When Doves Cry **13.** The Doobie Brothers **14.** Beyond **15.** Dr. Strangely Strange.

PEOPLE

1. Which actress plays *Xena: Warrior Princess* on TV?
2. What is the singer Sporty Spice's real name?
3. Which Swedish model played Mrs. Freeze in the film *Batman and Robin*?
4. Which American stuntman was born in Butte, Montana, in 1938?
5. Who was executed for the kidnapping and murder of aviator Charles Lindbergh's son?
6. In which year was Marie Antoinette guillotined?
7. In which year was the spy Mata Hari executed?
8. By what name was the American gambler Nicholas Andrea Dandolos known?

9. On which island was the Duke of Edinburgh born?
10. Who was the famous sister of writer Lee Radziwill?
11. In which country was fashion designer Yves St. Laurent born in 1936?
12. Which US actress had a romance with Prince Andrew in 1982?
13. Which American TV evangelist was sentenced to a 45 year jail term in 1989 for defrauding his followers?
14. Which Dublin-born social reformer opened his 'Homes for Boys' in 1870?
15. By what name was US murderer David Berkowitz known?

ANSWERS **1.** Lucy Lawless **2.** Mel Chisholm **3.** Vendela **4.** Evel Knievel **5.** Bruno Hauptmann **6.** 1793 **7.** 1917 **8.** Nick the Greek **9.** Corfu **10.** Jackie Onassis **11.** Algeria **12.** Koo Stark **13.** Jim Bakker **14.** Dr. Barnardo **15.** Son of Sam.

GENERAL KNOWLEDGE

1. What in New Zealand is hokonui?
2. Which author built Fonthill 'Abbey' in Wiltshire?
3. In which year was the Battle of Crécy?
4. Who wrote the historical novel *Musk and Amber*?
5. What was the name of the Prince of Wales's home near Sunningdale from 1929-36?
6. Where on a horse would you find hocks?
7. As what does the Latin phrase *nota bene* translate?
8. What was the name given to the feudal code of the Japanese samurai?
9. What type of wood is acajou, which is used by cabinet makers?
10. In which South American country is the city of Avellaneda?
11. What was the name of Oliver Cromwell's son, who was born in 1626?
12. In education, what did the initials CSE stand for?
13. Who in mythology was the first wife of Aegeus?
14. Who was the arch enemy of comic character Dan Dare?
15. In which year was the QEII launched?

ANSWERS **1.** Illicit whisky **2.** William Beckford **3.** 1346 **4.** A.E.W. Mason **5.** Fort Belvedere **6.** Legs **7.** Mark well **8.** Bushido **9.** Mahogany **10.** Argentina **11.** Richard **12.** Certificate of Secondary Education **13.** Meta **14.** The Mekon **15.** 1967.

ENTERTAINMENT

1. Which was the Best British Film at the 1965 British Academy Awards?
2. Who directed the 1932 film 'Air Mail'?
3. Which comic actress played Cynthia Bright in the 1985 sitcom *The Bright Side*?
4. Who played Catherine of Aragon in the 1970 drama series *The Six Wives of Henry VIII*?
5. Who played Sinbad in the 1974 film 'The Golden Voyage of Sinbad'?
6. Who directed the 1976 film *Obsession*?
7. Who wrote the 1970 TV comedy drama *The Gravy Train*?
8. Which actor won the 'Most in Need of Retirement' title at the 1944 Harvard Lampoon Movie Worsts Awards?
9. What section of Mendelssohn's hymn 'Hear my prayer' is often performed separately?
10. Who starred in the 1980 action film *The Octagon*?
11. Which comedian was born Eddie McGinnis in 1942?
12. Who starred in and directed the 1942 film *The Gold Rush*?
13. Who played *Captain Kidd* in a 1945 film?
14. In which year was the composer Harrison Birtwistle born?
15. Who played the Reverend Elton in the 1996 film *Emma*?

ANSWERS 1. The Ipcress File **2.** John Ford **3.** Paula Wilcox **4.** Annette Crosbie **5.** John Phillip Law **6.** Brian De Palma **7.** Malcolm Bradbury **8.** Paul Muni **9.** O for the wings of a dove **10.** Chuck Norris **11.** Eddie Large **12.** Charles Chaplin **13.** Charles Laughton **14.** 1934 **15.** Alan Cumming.

PEOPLE

1. What is the name of Camilla Parker Bowles's son, who was involved in a 1999 drug scandal?
2. Which politician wrote the 1880 novel *Endymion*?
3. Tejan Kabbah is president of which African country?
4. Which star of the sitcom *Diff'rent Strokes* died in May 1999 of a drug overdose?
5. Which Labour M.P. opened the National Assembly in Cardiff in 1999?
6. Who wrote the 1999 novel *Score!*?
7. Who resigned from the cabinet in December 1998 over a mortgage loan?
8. Which child's death landed nanny Louise Woodward in court in 1998?
9. British yachtsman Glynn Charles was killed during which race in December 1998?
10. Which comedian turned actor starred in the film *Enemy of the State*?
11. Which economist wrote the book *The Crisis of Global Capitalism*?
12. Who played Marion in the 1998 remake of the film *Psycho*?
13. In which country is Jean-Claude 'Baby Doc' Duvalier of Haiti living?
14. Which U.S. radio talk-show host planned Nixon's Watergate break-in?
15. What was the name of the British foster parents who went on the run in January 1999?

ANSWERS **1.** Tom **2.** Disraeli **3.** Sierra Leone **4.** Dana Plato **5.** Alun Michael **6.** Jilly Cooper **7.** Peter Mandelson **8.** Matthew Eappen **9.** Sydney-to-Hobart **10.** Will Smith **11.** George Soros **12.** Anne Heche **13.** France **14.** G. Gordon Liddy **15.** Jeff and Jennifer Bramley.

POP

1. What was the name of Eagle-Eye Cherry's debut album?
2. Who duetted on the 1974 hit *Mockingbird*?
3. In which year did The Fall have a hit single with *There's a Ghost in my House*?
4. Which group's L.P.s include *Ma Kelly's Greasy Spoon*?
5. Which U.S. vocalist recorded the 1986 album *Three Hearts in the Happy Ending Machine*?
6. What was David Bowie's '70's album of cover versions called?
7. Which reggae artist recorded the 1979 album *Forces of Victory*?
8. Jilted John was the alter ego of which actor?
9. Cleo, Zainem and Yonah Higgins comprise which vocal group?
10. Who recorded the 1980 album *Songs the Lord Taught Us*?
11. Which group recorded the 1979 album *Replicas*?
12. Who recorded the 1999 album *Ffrr*?
13. William Reid and Jim Reid comprise which group?
14. On which record label did Led Zeppelin record *Physical Graffiti*?
15. Which electronic duo recorded the 1979 L.P. *The Bridge*?

ANSWERS 1. Desireless **2.** James Taylor and Carly Simon **3.** 1987 **4.** Status Quo **5.** Daryl Hall **6.** Pinups **7.** Linton Kwesi Johnson **8.** Graham Fellows **9.** Cleopatra **10.** The Cramps **11.** Tubeway Army **12.** Orbital **13.** The Jesus and Mary Chain **14.** Swan Song **15.** Thomas Leer and Robert Rental.

ART AND LITERATURE

1. Painter James Tissot's London house was near which cricket ground?

2. What was the painter Augustus John's elder sister called?

3. On which island was the bird illustrator John James Audubon born?

4. Whose novels include *Rabbit Run* and *Rabbit at Rest*?

5. In which 1947 novel did the character Geoffrey Firmin appear?

6. What are the names of Shakespeare's *Two Gentlemen of Verona*?

7. Who painted 1859's *Absinthe Drinker*?

8. Whose fables include 'Asleep with one eye open' and 'Crying wolf too often'?

9. Which German Expressionist painter was killed in the Battle of Verdun in 1916?

10. Whose books include *Vox* and *The Mezzanine*?

11. In which year did the artist Henri Matisse die?

12. Which Scottish author wrote *The Wasp Factory*?

13. Who was the painter of 1878's *Snow at Louveciennes*?

14. Who wrote the poem *The Twa Dogs*?

15. What nationality was the painter Ando Hiroshige?

ANSWERS 1. Lord's **2.** Gwen **3.** Haiti **4.** John Updike **5.** Under the Volcano **6.** Valentine and Proteus **7.** Manet **8.** Aesop **9.** Franz Marc **10.** Nicholson Baker **11.** 1954 **12.** Iain Banks **13.** Alfred Sisley **14.** Robert Burns **15.** Japanese.

GENERAL KNOWLEDGE

1. Of what is Gaillard Cut a part?
2. Who wrote the play *The Night of the Iguana*?
3. For which 1979 film did Peter Sellers receive an Oscar nomination?
4. On which sea does the town of Morecambe stand?
5. Which mountain range contains the volcano Cotopaxi?
6. Who wrote the play *Noises Off*?
7. Which Verdi opera was first performed in Venice in 1853?
8. Who was the England cricket captain in the 1986/7 Ashes series?
9. Who was German chancellor from 1930-32?
10. How much did it cost to post a standard first class letter in 1977?
11. What does the Latin phrase 'crambe repetita', meaning an old story, translate as?
12. Which of the Ten Commandments is 'Thou shalt not kill'?
13. What is the standard monetary unit of Albania?
14. In which year was the actor Spencer Tracy born?
15. What is the approximate population of Cairo in millions - 7, 10 or 13?

ANSWERS 1. The Panama Canal **2.** Tennessee Williams **3.** Being There **4.** Irish Sea **5.** Andes **6.** Michael Frayn **7.** La Traviata **8.** Mike Gatting **9.** Heinrich Brüning **10.** 9p **11.** Cabbage repeated **12.** Sixth **13.** Lek **14.** 1900 **15.** 13 million.

ENTERTAINMENT

1. Who does Chris Chittell play in the television show *Emmerdale*?
2. Who played Sherlock Holmes in the 1988 film *Without a Clue*?
3. Who directed the 1942 film *Seven Days' Leave*?
4. Who directed the 1960 film *Ocean's Eleven*?
5. Who played Dr. Watson in the 1946 film *Dressed to Kill*?
6. Who directed the 1953 film *Stalag 17*?
7. Who directed the 1978 film *Convoy*?
8. Who directed the 1955 film *Moonfleet*?
9. What was Clark Gable's character name in the film *The Tall Men*?
10. What was Danny De Vito's character name in the film *One Flew Over the Cuckoo's Nest*?
11. Who directed the 1995 film *Twelve Monkeys*?
12. Who does Alexandra Fletcher play in the television show *Brookside*?
13. Who does Charlie Brooks play in the television show *EastEnders*?
14. In which Mozart opera does the aria *Batti, batti, o Bel Masetto* appear?
15. Who played Tateh in the film *Ragtime*?

ANSWERS **1.** Eric Pollard **2.** Michael Caine **3.** Tim Whelan **4.** Lewis Milestone **5.** Nigel Bruce **6.** Billy Wilder **7.** Sam Peckinpah **8.** Fritz Lang **9.** Ben Allison **10.** Martini **11.** Terry Gilliam **12.** Jacqui Dixon **13.** Janine Butcher **14.** Don Giovanni **15.** Mandy Patinkin.

PEOPLE

1. Which Chancellor of the Exchequer nationalised the Bank of England in 1946?
2. Who wrote the music for the film *Genevieve?*
3. What was the middle name of US vice-president Spiro Agnew?
4. Which saint was known as the Apostle of Northumbria?
5. Which astronaut walked in space for over 5 hours during the Gemini 12 mission?
6. Which Chilean politician won the presidency in 1970?
7. Which German neuropathologist lends his name to the disease of presenile dementia?
8. Who is the chief executive of Channel Four television?
9. Which religious leader was appointed to the Order of Merit in May 1999?
10. Rudolph Guiliani is the mayor of which US city?
11. Whose final film as director was *Eyes Wide Shut?*
12. Who was the second wife of Tom Cruise?
13. Who was made Secretary of State for Wales in May 1997?
14. Which Norwegian explorer's ships included *Fram* and *Maud*?
15. In which year was the photographer David Bailey born?

ANSWERS 1. Hugh Dalton **2.** Larry Adler **3.** Theodore **4.** St. Aidan **5.** 'Buzz' Aldrin **6.** Salvador Allende **7.** Alzheimer **8.** Michael Jackson **9.** Cardinal Basil Hume **10.** New York **11.** Stanley Kubrick **12.** Nicole Kidman **13.** Ron Davies **14.** Roald Amundsen **15.** 1938.

ENTERTAINMENT

1. *The Ambushers* was the third in a series of films starring Dean Martin as which spy?
2. Who played Simon Templar in TV show *The Return of the Saint?*
3. Which actress plays the widow of a US president in the 1994 film *Guarding Tess?*
4. On whose novel is the 1989 film *Cat Chaser* based?
5. What was awarded the Best Film accolade at the 1970 Cannes Film Festival?
6. Who played Zoe Herriot in *Doctor Who?*
7. Who composed the 3-Act opera *Treemonisha?*
8. Who played Adam Chance in *Crossroads?*
9. Which duo starred on TV as *The Odd Couple?*
10. Which comic actress starred in the 1977 sitcom *Come Back Mrs. Noah?*
11. Who played Lou Beale in *EastEnders?*
12. Who was musical accompanist on TV comedy *Hello Cheeky?*
13. Which member of the Monty Python team co-wrote and starred in the 1991 film *American Friends?*
14. In which US city is the Juilliard School of Music?
15. Which country singer co-stars in the 1971 film *A Gunfight?*

ANSWERS **1.** Matt Helm **2.** Ian Ogilvy **3.** Shirley MacLaine **4.** Elmore Leonard **5.** M*A*S*H **6.** Wendy Padbury **7.** Scott Joplin **8.** Tony Adams **9.** Tony Randall & Jack Klugman **10.** Mollie Sugden **11.** Anna Wing **12.** Denis King **13.** Michael Palin **14.** New York **15.** Johnny Cash.

GEOGRAPHY

1. Which is the largest of the Channel Islands?
2. To which European country does the island of Lampedusa belong?
3. Which islands lie 45km SW of Cornwall?
4. Which strait lies between the Italian mainland and Sicily?
5. Mount Palomar is in which U.S. state?
6. The Pevensey Levels is a marshy area of which English county?
7. In which Australian state is the former uranium site of Rum Jungle?
8. Kigali is the capital of which African republic?
9. In which U.S. state is Lake Winnebago?
10. In which county of the Republic of Ireland is the Twelve Pins mountain range?
11. Cardiff stands on the mouth of which river?
12. Which is the smallest of Japan's four main islands?
13. Melbourne, Australia, is at the mouth of which river?
14. In which eastern European country is the city of Lodz?
15. On which river does Norwich stand?

ANSWERS **1.** Jersey **2.** Italy **3.** Isles of Scilly **4.** Messina Strait **5.** California **6.** East Sussex **7.** Northern Territory **8.** Rwanda **9.** Wisconsin **10.** Galway **11.** Taff **12.** Shikoku **13.** River Yarra **14.** Poland **15.** River Wensum.

GENERAL KNOWLEDGE

1. What was the Toy of the Year in 1967?
2. Which actress was the *Girl with the Million Dollar Legs*?
3. What is the name of the alcoholic drink consisting of half burgundy, half champagne?
4. Who succeeded Ahab as king of Israel?
5. Who led the Paramount Jazz Band?
6. From which illness did author Katherine Mansfield die?
7. Which Radio D.J. won the Pipe Smoker of the Year award in 1982?
8. What is the brightest star in the constellation Scorpius?
9. Who played Father Dougal in the TV show *Father Ted*?
10. Which actress was 'The Vamp'?
11. What is the most famous work of sculpture by Gutzon Borglum?
12. Who wrote the 1922 story collection *Tales of the Jazz Age*?
13. Who authored the 1938 novel *The Yearling*?
14. Of what is an Elsan a portable variety?
15. What type of creature is a guan - a lizard or a bird?

ANSWERS **1.** Spirograph **2.** Betty Grable **3.** Cold duck **4.** Jehu **5.** Acker Bilk **6.** Tuberculosis **7.** Dave Lee Travis **8.** Antares **9.** Ardal O'Hanlon **10.** Theda Bara **11.** The carved busts of the U.S. presidents on Mount Rushmore **12.** F. Scott Fitzgerald **13.** Marjorie Kinnan Rawlings **14.** Lavatory **15.** Bird.

ENTERTAINMENT

1. Who played Sherlock Holmes in the 1959 film *The Hound of the Baskervilles*?
2. Who played Dr. Watson in the 1959 film *The Hound of the Baskervilles*?
3. Who does Steven Cole play in the television show *Brookside*?
4. Who directed the 1984 film *Sixteen Candles*?
5. Who directed the 1957 film *The Spirit of St. Louis*?
6. What was Clark Gable's character name in the film *The Call of the Wild*?
7. Who directed the film *Christmas in July*?
8. In which Mozart opera does the aria *Vedrai, carino* appear?
9. Who does John Middleton play in the television show *Emmerdale*?
10. Who does Jack Ryder play in the television show *EastEnders*?
11. What was the character name of Fairuza Balk in the film *Valmont*?
12. Which two female television presenters were house members in the celebrity version of *Big Brother* in March?
13. Who directed the 1954 film *Seven Brides for Seven Brothers*?
14. Who played Sherlock Holmes in the 1979 film *Murder By Decree*?
15. Who played Dr. Watson in the 1979 film *Murder By Decree*?

ANSWERS **1.** Peter Cushing **2.** André Morell **3.** Leo Johnson **4.** John Hughes **5.** Billy Wilder **6.** Jack Thornton **7.** Preston Sturges **8.** Don Giovanni **9.** Rev. Ashley Thomas **10.** Jamie Mitchell **11.** Cecile **12.** Anthea Turner and Vanessa Feltz **13.** Stanley Donen **14.** Christopher Plummer **15.** James Mason.

ART AND LITERATURE

1. The painting *Do Not Go Gentle Into That Good Night* by Ceri Richards was inspired by a poem by whom?
2. Which Scottish painter's works included *Village Politicians*?
3. Who created Winnie-the-Pooh?
4. Who wrote the novel *Hemlock and After*?
5. Who wrote the play *A Streetcar Named Desire*?
6. Vladimir and Estragon are tramps in which play?
7. In which Thomas Hardy novel does Eustacia Vye appear?
8. From which country did artist Kurt Schwitters flee to England from the Nazis in 1940?
9. Which British painter is associated with the village Cookham?
10. Which Paris-born artist lived in Tahiti from 1891?
11. Which Russian author's stories included *The Death of Ivan Ilyich*?
12. Which female author wrote the 1982 novel *The President's Child*?
13. Whose thriller books include *Executive Orders*?
14. Who wrote the crime novel *Road Rage*?
15. What was the title of Irvine Welsh's 1998 novel about a corrupt policeman?

ANSWERS 1. Dylan Thomas **2.** Sir David Wilkie **3.** A.A. Milne **4.** Angus Wilson **5.** Tennessee Williams **6.** Waiting for Godot **7.** The Return of the Native **8.** Norway **9.** Sir Stanley Spencer **10.** Paul Gauguin **11.** Tolstoy **12.** Fay Weldon **13.** Tom Clancy **14.** Ruth Rendell **15.** Filth.

PEOPLE

1. Which circus clown, born in 1910, was a star attraction of the Blackpool Tower Circus for 39 years?
2. What was frontierswoman Martha Jane Burke better known as?
3. Which English speedboat racer died in 1967 when his hydroplane Bluebird crashed on Lake Coniston?
4. In which year did the gangster Al Capone die?
5. In which Italian city was French fashion designer Pierre Cardin born?
6. Who is the Artistic Director of the National Theatre?
7. What was the name of the chief schools inspector embroiled in controversy in 1999?
8. Which folk musician was recovering in hospital in April 1999 when told of his obituary in the Daily Telegraph?
9. Who is the leader of the political group Plaid Cymru?
10. Who is Chairman of the BBC?
11. Who is the president of Sinn Fein?
12. Which former newspaper editor runs Talk Radio?
13. Which young leading actor had to swim for his life whilst filming *The Beach* in 1999?
14. Who did Ted Hughes succeed as poet laureate?
15. In which London suburb was Elizabeth Hurley born?

ANSWERS 1. Charlie Cairoli **2.** Calamity Jane **3.** Donald Campbell **4.** 1947 **5.** Venice **6.** Trevor Nunn **7.** Chris Woodhead **8.** Dave Swarbrick **9.** Dafydd Wigley **10.** Christopher Bland **11.** Gerry Adams **12.** Kelvin MacKenzie **13.** Leonardo DiCaprio **14.** John Betjeman **15.** Basingstoke.

ART AND LITERATURE

1. Who wrote the thriller novel *Birds of Prey*?
2. Who wrote the thriller books *Black Market* and *Midnight Club*?
3. Whose novels include *Other People's Children*?
4. Which American artist's works include 1960's *People in the Sun*?
5. Whose works of art include 1956's *Just What Is It That Makes Today's Homes So Different, So Appealing*?
6. What are the forenames of art duo Proesch and Passmore?
7. Whose books include *The World According to Garp*?
8. In which novella by Henry James do the characters Mrs. Grose and Miss Jessel appear?
9. Which French author wrote *Bel-Ami*?
10. Which Cubist artist made the abstract film *Le Ballet Mechanique* in 1924?
11. With which visual art movement is the American Roy Lichtenstein associated?
12. Which Scottish portrait painter's works include *Rev. Robert Walker skating*?
13. Which horror writer penned *The Green Mile*?
14. Which poet's volumes include *Birthday Letters*?
15. Which novel inspired Jean Rhys's *Wide Sargasso Sea*?

ANSWERS 1. Wilbur Smith **2.** James Patterson **3.** Joanna Trollope **4.** Edward Hopper **5.** Richard Hamilton **6.** Gilbert and George **7.** John Irving **8.** The Turn of the Screw **9.** Guy de Maupassant **10.** Fernand Léger **11.** Pop Art **12.** Sir Henry Raeburn **13.** Stephen King **14.** Ted Hughes **15.** Jane Eyre

GENERAL KNOWLEDGE

1. In which European country is Avriani a national newspaper?
2. Of which country is the letter C the international car index mark?
3. Which major city does Benito Juarez airport serve?
4. In which European country is the port of Sundsvall?
5. In which year was the cookery writer Gary Rhodes born?
6. Who was Australian prime minister from 1949-66?
7. What is the official language of Pakistan?
8. What is the WMO within the United Nations?
9. The element krypton derives its name from the Greek word for what?
10. In which U.S. state is the Mackinac Bridge?
11. Which saint's feast day is June 5th?
12. Who wrote the 1971 novel *The Winds of War*?
13. In which year was the pop singer Julian Cope born?
14. In Norse mythology, of what is Aegir the god?
15. Of which country was Jean-Luc Dehaene prime minister from 1992-9?

ANSWERS 1. Greece **2.** Cuba **3.** Mexico City **4.** Sweden **5.** 1960 **6.** Bob Menzies **7.** Urdu **8.** World Meteorological Organization **9.** Hidden **10.** Michigan **11.** Boniface **12.** Herman Wouk **13.** 1957 **14.** Sea **15.** Belgium.

ENTERTAINMENT

1. Which comic actor played Dr. Rex Regis in the 1994 sitcom *Health and Efficiency?*
2. Who was named Best Actor at the 1978 Cannes Film Festival?
3. Who directed the 1989 film *Always?*
4. Which actress plays Kat in the 1995 film *Casper?*
5. Who played Ivy Tilsley in *Coronation Street?*
6. Who plays a cynical weatherman in the film *Groundhog Day?*
7. What was Wolfie's girlfriend called in the show *Citizen Smith?*
8. Who played Jim Wilkins in the one-off 1975 TV comedy show *Milk-O?*
9. Who composed the opera *The Ice Break*, produced at Covent Garden in 1977?
10. Who won the Best Actress award at the 1975 Cannes Film Festival?
11. Who directed the 1955 film *House of Bamboo?*
12. On whose book is the 1987 film *Castaway* based?
13. Who played Jamie McCrimmon in *Doctor Who?*
14. Who composed the series of percussive works entitled *Imaginary Landscape?*
15. What was the profession of *Clarence* in the Ronnie Barker sitcom?

ANSWERS **1.** Roger Lloyd Pack **2.** Jon Voight **3.** Steven Spielberg **4.** Christina Ricci **5.** Lynne Perrie **6.** Bill Murray **7.** Shirley **8.** Bob Grant **9.** Michael Tippett **10.** Valerie Perrine **11.** Samuel Fuller **12.** Lucy Irvine **13.** Frazer Hines **14.** John Cage **15.** Removal man.

SPORT

1. Who won the Olympic men's 400m in 1960?
2. Which animal was the official mascot of the 1984 Summer Olympics at Los Angeles?
3. Which woman won the 1996 Boston Marathon?
4. Which country won the 1994 Uber Cup in badminton?
5. Which baseball team won the 1948 World Series?
6. Which horse won the 1984 1000 Guineas?
7. Which Miami Dolphins quarterback was the 1984 NFL Most Valuable Player in American Football?
8. Who was the 1976 and 1980 Olympic women's balance beam champion in gymnastics?
9. In which year was the former England Test cricket captain Alec Stewart born?
10. Who scored 109 for England in the 1st innings of the 2nd Test against Sri Lanka in March, 2001?
11. Who won the Olympic men's 800m in 1968?
12. What were the names of the two child mascots of the 1994 Winter Olympics at Lillehammer?
13. Which horse won the 1984 2000 Guineas?
14. From which club did Ipswich Town sign the defender Chris Makin in March, 2001?
15. Which football club did George Burley manage from June-November, 1994?

ANSWERS 1. Otis Davis **2.** Sam the Eagle **3.** Uta Pippig **4.** Indonesia **5.** Cleveland Indians **6.** Pebbles **7.** Dan Marino **8.** Nadia Comaneci **9.** 1963 **10.** Nasser Hussain **11.** Ralph Doubell **12.** Kristin and Haakon **13.** El Gran Senor **14.** Sunderland **15.** Colchester.

POP

1. In which year was Adam Faith born?
2. Which group recorded the album *Arthur, or the Decline and Fall of the British Empire*?
3. Which group had a 1994 Top 40 single with *Millennium*?
4. Which duo had a 1998 Top 20 single with *Burning*?
5. Under which name did Jonathan King record the 1971 hit *Sugar Sugar*?
6. Which group had a 1998 Top 20 single with *The Dope Show*?
7. Which band backed Neil Young on the 1995 album *Mirror Ball*?
8. Which duo comprise The Pet Shop Boys?
9. Which group charted in 1998 with the single *Bad Old Man*?
10. In which year did John Lennon release the live album *Some Time in New York City*?
11. Which group recorded the album *Larks' Tongues in Aspic*?
12. What was the 1962 singles chart entry for the Clyde Valley Stompers?
13. *Laughing All the Way to the Cleaners* was the debut single of which band?
14. Which punk singer guested on Leftfield's single *Open Up*?
15. Which group had a 1998 hit single with *God is a D.J.*?

ANSWERS **1.** 1940 **2.** The Kinks **3.** Killing Joke **4.** Baby Bumps **5.** Sakkarin **6.** Marilyn Manson **7.** Pearl Jam **8.** Chris Lowe and Neil Tennant **9.** Babybird **10.** 1972 **11.** King Crimson **12.** Peter and the Wolf **13.** The Lemonheads **14.** John Lydon **15.** Faithless.

ART AND LITERATURE

1. In which century did the Dutch painter Jan van de Cappelle live?
2. Who wrote the 1932 novel *Tobacco Road*?
3. Who were the co-authors of the 1931 book *1066 and All That*?
4. Who wrote the 1958 novel *The Darling Buds of May*?
5. Which crime writer authored the books *Dead Souls* and *Let It Bleed*?
6. Which comedian wrote the novel *Whatever Love Means*?
7. Who penned the 1704 literary work *A Tale of a Tub*?
8. Which artist won the 1997 Turner Prize?
9. Who wrote the novel *Spilt Milk*?
10. Who wrote the novel *Millie's Fling*?
11. Who wrote the thriller novel *Beneath the Skin*?
12. Who wrote the whodunnit *Mr. X*?
13. Which country music artist authored the novel *The Mile High Club*?
14. Whose paintings include *The Fighting Téméraire*?
15. Who authored the novel *Cutter and Bone*?

ANSWERS 1. 17th century **2.** Erskine Caldwell **3.** R.J. Yeatman and W.C. Sellar **4.** H.E. Bates **5.** Ian Rankin **6.** David Baddiel **7.** Jonathan Swift **8.** Gillian Wearing **9.** Lana Citron **10.** Jill Mansell **11.** Nicci French **12.** Peter Straub **13.** Kinky Friedman **14.** J.M.W. Turner **15.** Newton Thornburg.

GENERAL KNOWLEDGE

1. Around which island do a group of Brittany sailors fish in a famous series of novels by Pierre Loti?
2. Who was the Best Actress winner at the 1992 Laurence Olivier awards?
3. What was the pseudonym of the crime writer Edith Pargeter?
4. How many packs of cards are used in the game boston?

5. Which conductor arranged Sinatra's album *Songs for Swingin' Lovers*?
6. In which year did Oklahoma join the Union?
7. What was the Toy of the Year 1987-89?
8. Which green alcoholic drink has a high wormwood content?
9. What is the hedge sparrow also called?
10. Which English poet and critic authored *Seven Types of Ambiguity* in 1930?
11. Who was the legendary wife of King Arthur?
12. What is the standard monetary unit of Nicaragua?
13. What type of bird is a lanner - a swan or a falcon?
14. On which bay is the Cyprus port of Limassol?
15. What is the Land of the Long White Cloud?

ANSWERS **1.** Iceland **2.** Juliet Stevenson **3.** Ellis Peters **4.** Two **5.** Nelson Riddle **6.** 1907 **7.** Sylvanian Families **8.** Absinthe **9.** Dunnock **10.** William Empson **11.** Guinevere **12.** Cordoba **13.** Falcon **14.** Akrotiri Bay **15.** New Zealand.

ENTERTAINMENT

1. What was Karl Howman's character name in the TV comedy *Brush Strokes*?
2. Who composed the theatre piece *Blind Man's Buff*?
3. Who played *Shoestring* on television?
4. What nationality was the composer Max Bruch?
5. How much, in dollars, was Dustin Hoffman paid for the film *The Graduate*?
6. Who scripted the 1966 film *Alfie* from his own play?
7. In which year was the comedian George Burns born?
8. What is the actress Jane Seymour's real name?
9. Who directed the 1979 film *Escape from Alcatraz*?
10. About whom was the 1988 film *Gorillas in the Mist*?
11. Who wrote the 1983 sitcom *Hallelujah!* which starred Thora Hird?
12. Who wrote the 1971 sitcom *Lollipop Loves Mr. Mole*?
13. In which year did the pianist Dame Myra Hess die?
14. Who played Bill Sikes in the 1948 film *Oliver Twist*?
15. Who directed the 1996 film *Carla's Song*?

ANSWERS 1. Jacko **2.** Peter Maxwell Davies **3.** Trevor Eve **4.** German **5.** $17,000 **6.** Bill Naughton **7.** 1896 **8.** Joyce Frankenberg **9.** Don Siegel **10.** Dian Fossey **11.** Dick Sharples **12.** Jimmy Perry **13.** 1965 **14.** Robert Newton **15.** Ken Loach.

PEOPLE

1. Which American bank robber penned the poem 'The Story of Suicide Sal'?
2. Which American wit died alone in her apartment with her dog Troy by her side?
3. Which Conservative politician had an affair with his secretary Sara Keays?
4. Which French film pioneer produced the cliff-hanger series *The Perils of Pauline*?
5. Which U.S. soldier was known as 'Old Blood and Guts'?
6. Which French soldier's defence of Verdun in World War I made him a national hero?
7. In which country was British double agent Kim Philby born?
8. Which Canadian-born film actress was known as 'the World's Sweetheart'?
9. Which detective foiled a plot in 1861 to assassinate Abraham Lincoln?
10. Which American Indian princess married John Rolfe in 1613?
11. What was the French entertainer Joseph Pujol known as?
12. Which member of the royal family presented the Best Video Award at the 1998 MTV Europe Awards?
13. Which pop singer changed his name to Abdul Rahman in 1998?
14. Which Canadian socialite wrote the book *Beyond Reason* in 1979?
15. Which son of Theodore Roosevelt wrote *War in the Garden of Eden* in 1919?

ANSWERS **1.** Bonnie Parker **2.** Dorothy Parker **3.** Cecil Parkinson **4.** Charles Pathé **5.** George Patton **6.** Henri Pétain **7.** India **8.** Mary Pickford **9.** Allan Pinkerton **10.** Pocahontas **11.** Le Petomaine **12.** Sarah Ferguson **13.** Mark Morrison **14.** Margaret Trudeau **15.** Kermit Roosevelt.

POP

1. Which boyband released the single *Shape of my Heart* in 2000?
2. Which group's debut L.P. is entitled *Internal Wrangler*?
3. In which year did the singer Jason Donovan have a No. 1 single with *Any Dream Will Do*?
4. Who recorded the 2000 album *Halfway Between the Gutter and the Stars*?
5. Which group recorded the 2000 album *Black Market Music*?
6. At which college did the musician Badly Drawn Boy study classical music and jazz?
7. Who was the leader of the group Dream City Film Club?
8. From which U.S. city do the group The Shazam hail?
9. Which group's second album, released in 2000, was called *Madonna*?
10. In which year did the punk rock group The Damned have a Top 10 single with the song *Eloise*?
11. Which pop group recorded the 2000 album *No Strings Attached*?
12. Which female singer had a No. 2 single in 1985 with the song *That Ole Devil Called Love*?
13. Which girl group recorded the 2000 single *Holler*?
14. Which pop group had a 1979 No. 1 single with the song *Video Killed the Radio Star*?
15. Which former soap actress recorded the 2000 single *I'm Over You*?

ANSWERS 1. Backstreet Boys **2.** Clinic **3.** 1991 **4.** Fatboy Slim **5.** Placebo **6.** Leeds College of Music **7.** Michael J. Sheehy **8.** Nashville **9.** ... And You Will Know Us By The Trail Of Dead **10.** 1986 **11.** 'N Sync **12.** Alison Moyet **13.** Spice Girls **14.** Buggles **15.** Martine McCutcheon.

ENTERTAINMENT

1. Which Oscar-winning actress was born in Walton-on-Thames in 1935?
2. Which comedian discovered the Swedish actress Ann-Margret when she was a nightclub singer and dancer?
3. What was silent film star 'Fatty' Arbuckle's real first name?
4. Who replaced Gene Kelly in the 1948 film *Easter Parade* after he was injured?
5. Which film director won the Bancroft Medal at RADA in 1942?
6. *A.J. Wentworth, B.A.* was thc last TV series of which comedy star?
7. In which TV show did the character Captain 'Howling Mad' Murdoch appear?
8. Which comedian's characters included secret agent Basildon Bond?
9. Which comedians were *Mr. Don and Mr. George* in 1993?
10. Which music-hall perfomer born in 1851 was billed as the 'Vital Spark'?
11. What was Sir Laurence Olivier's middle name?
12. Which comic actress made her New York debut in 1947 as Lady Bracknell in *The Importance of Being Earnest*?
13. Which music-hall performer born in 1866 is associated with the songs *Boiled Beef and Carrots* and *Hot Tripe and Onions*?
14. Which Dublin theatre reopened in 1977 with *John, Paul, George, Ringo... and Bert*?
15. What is the middle name of the playwright Peter Shaffer?

ANSWERS 1. Julie Andrews **2.** George Burns **3.** Roscoe **4.** Fred Astaire **5.** Sir Richard Attenborough **6.** Arthur Lowe **7.** The A-Team **8.** Russ Abbot **9.** Jack Docherty and Moray Watson **10.** Jenny Hill **11.** Kerr **12.** Margaret Rutherford **13.** Harry Champion **14.** Olympia Theatre **15.** Levin.

GENERAL KNOWLEDGE

1. What is the official language of Liechtenstein?
2. *Kicking in the Wind* is a 1996 book by Derek Allsop about which football club?
3. In which country is the Lion's Gate bridge?
4. The element bromine derives its name from the Greek word for what?
5. Lovech and Varna are provinces of which European country?
6. In which year did Portugal join the European Union?
7. In which country is the Bakun dam?
8. In which year was the cookery writer Keith Floyd born?
9. In which European country is the port of Toulon?
10. Which major city does Ciampino airport serve?
11. Of which country is the letter H the international car index mark?
12. In which European country is Ethnos a national newspaper?
13. What does the forename Virginia mean?
14. In which year was the award the Légion d'Honneur established in France?
15. Which saint's feast day is December 6th?

ANSWERS **1.** German **2.** Rochdale **3.** Canada **4.** Stench **5.** Bulgaria **6.** 1986 **7.** Malaysia **8.** 1943 **9.** France **10.** Rome **11.** Hungary **12.** Greece **13.** Maiden **14.** 1802 **15.** Nicholas.

ENTERTAINMENT

1. How much in dollars was Marlon Brando paid for the 1951 film *A Streetcar Named Desire*?
2. Who starred as *Al Capone* in a 1959 film?
3. Who were the actors Paul Barber and Philip Whitchurch in a 1980's sitcom?
4. In which country was the comedy actress Carmen Silvera born?
5. Who directed the 1996 film *The English Patient*?
6. Which duo co-scripted and starred in the 1997 film *Good Will Hunting*?
7. Of which female political figure was Joyce Grenfell the niece?
8. Who composed the 1883 opera *Henry VIII*?
9. Which Australian comedian created the character Norman Gunston?
10. Who won the Worst Single Performance - Male for his role in the film *The Stranger* at the 1946 Harvard Lampoon Movie Worsts Awards?
11. What musically are 'bleeding chunks'?
12. Which jazz artist wrote *At the Woodchoppers Ball*?
13. How much in dollars was Clint Eastwood paid for the 1964 film *A Fistful of Dollars*?
14. Who directed the 1955 film *Oklahoma!*?
15. What was the U.S. title of the 1964 film *The Caretaker*, based on Harold Pinter's play?

ANSWERS **1.** $75,000 **2.** Rod Steiger **3.** The Brothers McGregor **4.** Canada **5.** Anthony Minghella **6.** Ben Affleck and Matt Damon **7.** Nancy Astor **8.** Saint-Saëns **9.** Garry McDonald **10.** Orson Welles **11.** Operatic extracts played out of context in the concert-hall **12.** Woody Herman **13.** $15,000 **14.** Fred Zinnemann **15.** The Guest.

ART AND LITERATURE

1. Who was the author of the thriller novel *10lb Penalty*?
2. Who painted the portrait *Mme Gautreau* which was exhibited in 1884?
3. Who wrote *Madame Bovary*?
4. "To begin at the beginning: It is spring, moonless night in the small town, starless and bible-black..." Which poem?
5. Who wrote the novel *Oranges Are Not the Only Fruit*?
6. Who painted 1642's *The Night Watch*?
7. What was the name of the 1956 art exhibition at the Whitechapel Art Gallery which was influential in the development of Pop Art?
8. Who was the author of the novel *My Legendary Girlfriend*?
9. Which English woodcarver, born in 1648, became Master Carver in Wood to the Crown under Charles II?
10. Which detective writer's books include *LaBrava* and *Cat Chaser*?
11. What was Helen Zahavi's controversial 1991 novel called?
12. Which American novelist wrote 1963's *Cat's Cradle*?
13. What is the name of the brown pigment made from the ink of cuttlefish?
14. In which decade was the art movement The Brotherhood of Ruralists conceived?
15. Which French painter worked with the Paris Customs Office from 1871-93?

ANSWERS **1.** Dick Francis **2.** John Singer Sargent **3.** Gustave Flaubert **4.** Under Milk Wood **5.** Jeanette Winterson **6.** Rembrandt **7.** This Is Tomorrow **8.** Mike Gayle **9.** Grinling Gibbons **10.** Elmore Leonard **11.** Dirty Weekend **12.** Kurt Vonnegut Jr. **13.** Sepia **14.** 1970s **15.** Henri Rousseau.

POP

1. Which singer featured on Melanie B's No. 1 single *I Want You Back*?
2. Which single by the Police reached No. 1 in both the U.K. and the U.S.?
3. Which duo had a 1987 Top Ten hit with *Rise to the Occasion*?
4. Which group recorded the 1998 album *Munki*?
5. Which female vocalist had a 1997 Top 30 hit with *100%*?
6. Which group's debut L.P. was 1996's *At the Club*?
7. Which group recorded the 1975 album *Handsome*?
8. Which 1978 hit was subtitled *The Telephone Answering Machine Song*?
9. In which town was the singer Robert Palmer born?
10. What was Kicks Like A Mule's 1992 Top Ten hit single?
11. Which group had a No .1 hit in 1998 with *Rollercoaster*?
12. What was the debut L.P. of the group Graham Parker and the Rumour?
13. Which pop singer was born Barry Pincus in 1946?
14. From which European country do the group Clubhouse come?
15. What was Elvis Presley's first single to reach No. 1 in both the U.S. and U.K. charts?

ANSWERS **1.** Missy 'Misdemeanour' Elliot **2.** Every Breath You Take **3.** Climie Fisher **4.** The Jesus and Mary Chain **5.** Mary Kiani **6.** Kenickie **7.** Kilburn & the High Roads **8.** Hello this is Joanie (by Paul Evans) **9.** Batley **10.** The Bouncer **11.** B*Witched **12.** Howlin' Wind **13.** Barry Manilow **14.** Italy **15.** All Shook Up.

PEOPLE

1. Who became Chairman of the Conservative Party in October 1998?
2. How did the restauranteur and chef Alain Ducasse become unique in March 1998?
3. Sinclair Beecham and Julian Metcalfe are founders of which sandwich shop chain?
4. Who was the women's Modern Pentathlon gold winner at the 2000 Olympics?
5. In which year was the choreographer Siobhan Davies born?
6. In which year did the ballet dancer Galina Ulanova die?
7. In which country was the conductor Paul Angerer born?
8. Which actress did David Thewlis marry shortly before appearing in the film *Naked*?
9. In which year was the choreographer Jerome Robbins born?
10. Ade Blackburn is the frontman of which rock group?
11. Who was the 27th president of the U.S.A.?
12. Who was the 1974 Commonwealth pentathlon champion?
13. Which king of Lydia was noted for his great wealth?
14. Which U.S. cavalry general was killed at Little Bighorn in 1876?
15. Which U.S. songwriter collaborated with Frederick Loewe on the stage show *Camelot*?

ANSWERS **1.** Michael Ancram **2.** He became the only chef at that time to hold six Michelin stars, three stars each for two of his establishments in Paris and Monte Carlo **3.** Pret A Manger **4.** Stephanie Cook **5.** 1950 **6.** 1998 **7.** Austria **8.** Sara Sugarman **9.** 1918 **10.** Clinic **11.** William Howard Taft **12.** Mary Peters **13.** Croesus **14.** George Armstrong Custer **15.** Alan Jay Lerner.

GENERAL KNOWLEDGE

1. Which saint's feast day is April 23rd?
2. In Norse mythology, of what is Mimir the god?
3. Who wrote the 1925 novel *Mrs. Dalloway*?
4. In which year was the award the Bronze Star established in the U.S.A.?
5. In which European country is El Pais a national newspaper?
6. Of which country is the letter B the international car index mark?
7. In which European country is the port of Genoa?
8. Who was queen of the Netherlands from 1890-1948?
9. What is the official language of Cambodia?
10. In which year did Austria join the European Union?
11. The element neon derives its name from the Greek word for what?
12. In which country is the Guavio dam?
13. In which country is the Gladesville bridge?
14. Of which European country is Lapland a province?
15. What is the real name of the singer Alice Cooper?

ANSWERS **1.** George **2.** Wisdom **3.** Virginia Woolf **4.** 1944 **5.** Spain **6.** Belgium **7.** Italy **8.** Wilhelmina **9.** Khmer **10.** 1995 **11.** New **12.** Colombia **13.** Australia **14.** Finland **15.** Vincent Furnier.

ENTERTAINMENT

1. In which year did TV animal trainer Barbara Woodhouse die?
2. What was the subtitle of Mahler's Symphony No. 2 in C minor?
3. In which year was football commentator Kenneth Wolstenholme born?
4. Which comedian and pianist was born Borg Rosenbaum in Copenhagen in 1909?
5. Who directed the 1984 comedy *Ghostbusters*?
6. Who composed the 1840 comic opera *King for a Day*?
7. Who played Ron Glum in the 1978 sitcom *The Glums*?
8. Which film won the award for Best Original Score at the 1967 Golden Globes?
9. Who played the title role in the 1972 film *Lady Caroline Lamb*?
10. Who starred as *The Admirable Crichton* in a 1957 film?
11. Who played Ronnie Barker's son Raymond in the sitcom *Going Straight*?
12. Who starred as Lester in the 1982 sitcom *L for Lester*?
13. Who directed the 1956 film *Giant*?
14. Which musician played a Mexican gardener in the 1968 film *Candy*?
15. Who scripted the 1983 film *Educating Rita* from his own play?

ANSWERS 1. 1988 **2.** Resurrection Symphony **3.** 1920 **4.** Victor Borge **5.** Ivan Reitman **6.** Verdi **7.** Ian Lavender **8.** Camelot **9.** Sarah Miles **10.** Kenneth More **11.** Nicholas Lyndhurst **12.** Brian Murphy **13.** George Stevens **14.** Ringo Starr **15.** Willy Russell.

PEOPLE

1. Who became the Duke of Edinburgh's first woman equerry in 1999?
2. What is the name of the former deputy prime minister of Malaysia sentenced in 1999 to six years in jail for misuse of power?
3. Which film director presided over the international jury at the 1999 Cannes Film Festival?
4. Which celebrity married Anna Ottewill in 1999?
5. Which Scottish bacteriologist discovered penicillin in 1928?
6. Which comedy duo host the surreal TV game show *Families at War*?
7. Which British actress played Mel Gibson's wife in *Braveheart*?
8. In which country was the industrialist and philanthropist Andrew Carnegie born?
9. Which Conservative politician was secretary general of NATO from 1984-88?
10. Which Norfolk-born Egyptologist discovered the tomb of Tut'ankhamun in 1922?
11. Who won a place in the Guinness Book of Records for writing 26 books in 1983?
12. Which supermodel had a cameo role in Spike Lee's film *Girl 6*?
13. Which talk-show host was the mayor of Cincinatti?
14. Who played *Peyton* in Aaron Spelling's TV saga *Savannah*?
15. In which year did the industrialist Howard Hughes die?

ANSWERS 1. Lynda Johnson **2.** Anwar Ibrahim **3.** David Cronenberg **4.** John McCarthy **5.** Alexander Fleming **6.** Bob Mortimer and Vic Reeves **7.** Catherine McCormack **8.** Scotland **9.** Peter Carrington **10.** Howard Carter **11.** Barbara Cartland **12.** Naomi Campbell **13.** Jerry Springer **14.** Jamie Luner **15.** 1976.

POP

1. Which group had a 1997 Top 40 Christmas hit with *I Want an Alien for Christmas*?
2. Which irony-laden group had hits in 1996 with *Rotterdam* and *Don't Marry Her*?
3. Which singer had a 1992 hit with *Feed my Frankenstein*?
4. Which female singer featured on D.J. Milano's 1998 hit *Santa Maria*?
5. Which veteran singing group had a 1997 Top Five single with *Alone*?
6. Which singer had a minor hit in 1996 with *I Come From Another Planet Baby*?
7. Which singer had a 1995 Top Five hit with *Total Eclipse of the Heart*?
8. Niki Sullivan, Jerry J.J. Allison and Joe B. Maudlin comprised which band?
9. In which city was Jimi Hendrix born?
10. *(We Don't Need This) Fascist Groove Thang* was which group's debut single?
11. In which city was Isaac Hayes born?
12. In which year did Hawkwind release their debut L.P.?
13. Which member of the Beatles released the 1981 solo L.P. *Somewhere in England*?
14. Which singer/songwriter penned *When An Old Cricketer Leaves the Crease*?
15. Who wrote the song *If I Were a Carpenter*?

ANSWERS **1.** Fountains of Wayne **2.** The Beautiful South **3.** Alice Cooper **4.** Samantha Fox **5.** The Bee Gees **6.** Julian Cope **7.** Nicki French **8.** The Crickets **9.** Seattle **10.** Heaven 17 **11.** Memphis **12.** 1970 **13.** George Harrison **14.** Roy Harper **15.** Tim Hardin.

ART AND LITERATURE

1. Who painted the *Garden of Earthly Delights*?
2. In which century did the French painter Francois Boucher live?
3. Who was Poet Laureate from 1968-72?
4. Which French author wrote the novel *Germinal*?
5. Who painted *Sunday Afternoon on the Island of the Grande Jatte*?
6. In which city was the artist Egon Schiele born?
7. Which British writer and illustrator wrote the 1946 manual *The Craft of the Lead Pencil*?
8. In which European city did the Phalanx group of artists form in 1901?
9. Which famous artist was born at Caprese, Italy, in 1475?
10. Which 19c English artist painted 1850's *Christ in the House of His Parents*?
11. Which Spanish artist designed the ballet *Jeux d'enfants* in 1932?
12. Which Irish author wrote the novellas *First Love* and *The Expelled*?
13. Which Russian author's books include *The Idiot* and *The Devils*?
14. Which U.S. author's children's books include *Superfudge*?
15. What was the controversial 1991 book by Bret Easton Ellis?

ANSWERS 1. Hieronymus Bosch **2.** 18th **3.** Cecil Day-Lewis **4.** Emile Zola **5.** Georges Seurat **6.** Vienna **7.** Mervyn Peake **8.** Munich **9.** Michelangelo **10.** Sir John Millais **11.** Joan Miró **12.** Samuel Beckett **13.** Dostoevsky **14.** Judy Blume **15.** American Psycho.

GENERAL KNOWLEDGE

1. What drink is the legendary Flemish king Gambrinus said to have invented?
2. Who wrote the novel *Cry, the Beloved Country*?
3. Which king of England was known as Farmer George?
4. From which football club did Coventry City sign Liam Daish?
5. Farringford was the home of which poet?
6. Argent is the poetic name for which metal?
7. On which bay is the town of Aberystwyth?
8. FIDE is the world federation of which sport?
9. As what is 'herpes labialis' better known?
10. What is the capital of the Netherlands?
11. Who wrote the book *Uncle Silas*?
12. What is the name given to the red ring on an archery target?
13. Who was the 1978 British Open golf champion?
14. Who wrote the play *The Zoo Story*?
15. Which farmyard animal suffers from the disease gapes?

ANSWERS **1.** Beer **2.** Alan Paton **3.** George III **4.** Birmingham City **5.** Lord Tennyson **6.** Silver **7.** Cardigan Bay **8.** Chess **9.** A cold sore **10.** Amsterdam **11.** Sheridan Le Fanu **12.** Inner **13.** Jack Nicklaus **14.** Edward Albee **15.** Domestic fowl.

ENTERTAINMENT

1. Who directed the 1952 film *Actors and Sin*?
2. Which actor was born Cyril Louis Goldbert?
3. Which comedian wrote and starred in the 1994 comedy series *My Blue Heaven*?
4. Who directed the 1995 film *Get Shorty*?
5. Which actor won the Cecil B. DeMille Award at the 1966 Golden Globe Awards?
6. Who composed the opera *Gianni Schicchi*?
7. Who co-wrote and directed 1995's *The Glam Metal Detectives*?
8. Who directed the 1961 comedy film *The Ladies' Man*?
9. What was Angus Deayton's character name in the sketch show *KYTV*?
10. Who directed the 1994 film *Ladybird Ladybird*?
11. Which comedian was known as 'The Little Waster'?
12. Which private eye did Frank Sinatra play in the film *Lady in Cement*?
13. What nationality is the harpsichordist and organist Kenneth Gilbert?
14. Who directed the 1990 film *Ghost*?
15. Who played *The Candidate* in a 1972 film?

ANSWERS **1.** Ben Hecht **2.** Peter Wyngarde **3.** Frank Skinner **4.** Barry Sonnenfeld **5.** Charlton Heston **6.** Puccini **7.** Peter Richardson **8.** Jerry Lewis **9.** Mike Channel **10.** Ken Loach **11.** Bobby Thompson **12.** Tony Rome **13.** Canadian **14.** Jerry Zucker **15.** Robert Redford.

ART AND LITERATURE

1. Whose romance books include *The Ranch* and *The Ghost*?
2. Who wrote the novel *Armadillo* about loss adjustor Lorimer Black?
3. What in the world of art is a polyptych?
4. Which British gallery houses *When Did You Last See Your Father?* by W.F. Yeames?
5. In which year did the sculptor Elisabeth Frink die?
6. Which British artist's collages include 1961's *The First Real Target*?
7. Who wrote the poem *The Wreck of the Hesperus*?
8. In which novel do the characters William Dobbin and Rawdon Crawley appear?
9. In which year did the artist Jackson Pollock die?
10. Which London-born artist's forenames were Joseph Mallord William?
11. Who wrote *Moby-Dick*?
12. '1801 - I have just returned from a visit to my landlord' are the opening lines of which book?
13. Which U.S. thriller writer's books include *The Postman Always Rings Twice*?
14. Napoleon and Snowball are creatures in which satirical novel?
15. Which English playwright wrote the comic novel *Head to Toe*?

ANSWERS 1. Danielle Steel **2.** William Boyd **3.** A picture consisting of four or more leaves or panels **4.** Walker Art Gallery in Liverpool **5.** 1993 **6.** Peter Blake **7.** Longfellow **8.** Vanity Fair **9.** 1956 **10.** Turner **11.** Herman Melville **12.** Wuthering Heights **13.** James M. Cain **14.** Animal Farm **15.** Joe Orton.

ENTERTAINMENT

1. For which singer was the 1994 film *Angie* originally written?
2. Who played *Irma La Douce* in a 1963 film?
3. What was the 1987 follow up to the sitcom *Up the Elephant and Round the Castle*?
4. Who played Ding Bell in the film *It's a Mad, Mad, Mad, Mad, World*?
5. Who won a Best Actor Oscar for his performance as *Charly* in 1968?
6. Who played Teddy Barnes in the 1985 film *Jagged Edge*?
7. Who played the Earl of Essex in the 1971 BBC TV drama *Elizabeth R*?
8. What was James Stewart's character name in the film *It's A Wonderful Life*?
9. What was the conductor Annunzio Paolo better known as?
10. Who played the villainess Rosa Klebb in the film *From Russia With Love*?
11. What is the French national anthem?
12. Who directed the 1988 film *Frantic*?
13. In which year was the comedian Jack Dee born?
14. Who played Carr Gomm in the 1980 film *The Elephant Man*?
15. Who played Tim O'Hara in the 1960s sitcom *My Favourite Martian*?

ANSWERS **1.** Madonna **2.** Billy Wilder **3.** Home James! **4.** Mickey Rooney **5.** Cliff Robertson **6.** Glenn Close **7.** Robin Ellis **8.** George Bailey **9.** Mantovani **10.** Lotte Lenya **11.** La Marseillaise **12.** Roman Polanski **13.** 1962 **14.** John Gielgud **15.** Bill Bixby.

GEOGRAPHY

1. Which ancient city of Italy, at the mouth of the River Tiber, was once the port of Rome?
2. On which river does Nottingham stand?
3. Which strait separates the Isle of Anglesey from mainland Wales?
4. In which U.S. state is the iron and steel town of Bessemer?
5. Which Asian republic's chief rivers are the Helm and Kabul?
6. In which Australian state is Alice Springs?
7. Which dog is the largest state in Mexico?
8. Ennis is the county town of which county of the Republic of Ireland?
9. What is the French name for the English Channel?
10. In which country is the cheese-producing region of Emmental?
11. What is the highest mountain of Japan?
12. As what is Lake Tiberias better known?
13. Amman is the capital of which Asian kingdom?
14. In which European country is the River Lek?
15. Which island of New York contains the borough of Brooklyn?

ANSWERS 1. Ostia **2.** River Trent **3.** Menai Strait **4.** Alaska **5.** Afghanistan **6.** Northern Territory **7.** Chihuahua **8.** Clare **9.** La Manche **10.** Switzerland **11.** Fujiyama **12.** Sea of Galilee **13.** Jordan **14.** The Netherlands **15.** Long Island.

GENERAL KNOWLEDGE

1. Which saint's feast day is February 23rd?
2. In which year was the cookery writer Graham Kerr born?
3. Who was Australian prime minister from 1983-91?
4. Burgenland and Voralberg are states of which European country?
5. In which year did Spain join the European Union?
6. The element lithium derives its name from the Greek word for what?
7. In which country is the Kishau dam?
8. In Norse mythology, of what is Loki the god?
9. In which year was the award the Purple Heart established in the U.S.A.?
10. Of which country is the letter F the international car index mark?
11. Which major city does Arlanda airport serve?
12. In which European country is the port of Bourgas?
13. What does the forename Andrew mean?
14. In which year was the Canadian singer Bryan Adams born?
15. In which U.S. state is the Commodore Barry bridge?

ANSWERS **1.** Polycarp **2.** 1934 **3.** Bob Hawke **4.** Austria **5.** 1986 **6.** Stone **7.** India **8.** Mischief **9.** 1782 **10.** France **11.** Stockholm **12.** Bulgaria **13.** Manly **14.** 1959 **15.** Pennsylvania.

ENTERTAINMENT

1. What was the belated follow-up, in 1992, to the show *Are You Being Served?*?
2. Who directed the 1985 film *After Hours*?
3. Who played Vincent in the 1990 film *The Godfather Part III*?
4. Who won Best British Actor at the 1962 British Academy Awards?
5. Whose opera *The Rape of Lucretia* reopened Glyndebourne after World War II?
6. In which city was the composer George Gershwin born?
7. Who played *Lassiter* in a 1984 film?
8. Who directed the 1930 film *L'Age D'Or*?
9. Which comedian was born Cyril Mead in 1942?
10. Who directed the 1991 film *The Last Boy Scout*?
11. What nationality was the composer William Billings?
12. Which movie was judged Best Film at the 1963 British Academy Awards?
13. Who scripted the 1965 film *The Agony and the Ecstasy*?
14. Who wrote the sitcom *Bread*?
15. Who played an ex-rodeo champion in the film *The Electric Horseman*?

ANSWERS 1. Grace and Favour **2.** Martin Scorsese **3.** Andy Garcia **4.** Peter O'Toole **5.** Benjamin Britten **6.** New York **7.** Tom Selleck **8.** Luis Bunuel **9.** Syd Little **10.** Tony Scott **11.** American **12.** Tom Jones **13.** Philip Dunne **14.** Carla Lane **15.** Robert Redford.

SPORT

1. Which animal was the official mascot of the 1988 Summer Olympics at Seoul?
2. Who won the Olympic men's 400m in 1984?
3. Which horse won the 1972 1000 Guineas?
4. Which golfer was the runner-up in the 1998 world matchplay championship?
5. Which country won the 1998 Uber Cup in badminton?
6. In which year did Jim Jefferies take over as manager of the football club Hearts?
7. What nationality is the tennis player Harel Levy?
8. What nationality is the tennis player Magnus Norman?
9. In which year did the golfer Isao Aoki turn professional?
10. What is golfer Billy Casper's middle name?
11. What nationality is the boxer Mads Larsen?
12. Which horse was ridden by Captain Becher in the 1839 Grand National?
13. Which horse won the 1998 2000 Guineas?
14. Who was the men's 110m hurdles champion at the 1999 World Championships?
15. What nationality is the boxer Jesus Rojas?

ANSWERS 1. Hodori the Tiger **2.** Alonzo Babers **3.** Waterloo **4.** Tiger Woods **5.** China **6.** 1996 **7.** Israeli **8.** Swedish **9.** 1964 **10.** Earl **11.** Danish **12.** Conrad **13.** King of Kings **14.** Colin Jackson **15.** Venezuelan.

GENERAL KNOWLEDGE

1. Who wrote *The Rime of the Ancient Mariner*?
2. Which of the Canary Islands is known for its *Mountains of Fire*?
3. In which year was the first Aldermaston march?
4. Alan Saldanha was 1993 British champion at which board game?
5. Which musician won the Pipe Smoker of the Year award in 1981?
6. Who was the world professional snooker champion in 1982?
7. What was the 1981 TV Show of the Year in the Melody Maker Polls?
8. In which county is Bosworth Field, site of a 1485 battle?
9. In which year was the U.S. battleship Maine blown up in Havana Harbor?
10. Who was the Best Actor award winner at the 1986 Laurence Olivier awards?
11. Which magician won the 1993 Carlton Award for Comedy?
12. What was the first name of the French tyre manufacturer Michelin?
13. Who composed the opera *Eugene Onegin*?
14. Who wrote *Tess of the D'Urbervilles*?
15. In which play does Algernon Moncrieff court Cecily Cardew?

ANSWERS 1. Samuel Taylor Coleridge **2**. Lanzarote **3**. 1958 **4**. Scrabble **5**. James Galway **6**. Alex Higgins **7**. Tiswas **8**. Leicestershire **9**. 1898 **10**. Albert Finney **11**. Ali Bongo **12**. André **13**. Tchaikovsky **14**. Thomas Hardy **15**. The Importance of Being Earnest.

PEOPLE

1. Who is disc jockey Zoë Ball's father?
2. Who was the first Madam Speaker of the House of Commons?
3. Which soap actress and singer once worked as an assistant in the store 'Knickerbox'?
4. Who captained England's cricket team for the 1999 World Cup?
5. Which model and actress is the daughter of singer Steve Tyler and model Bebe Buell?
6. Which *Blue Peter* presenter was sacked in 1998 after allegations of drug use?
7. Who was the female star of the film 'Clueless'?
8. What nationality is the actress Famke Janssen?
9. Which Irish patriot and author of 'the Black Diaries' was hanged for high treason in 1916?
10. Who murdered John Lennon in 1980?
11. Charles the Fat was king of which country from 884 A.D.?
12. Which English publisher compiled a famous *Peerage of England, Scotland and Ireland*?
13. Which French general wrote the 1940 book *The Army of the Future*?
14. Which judge held the inquiry into the resignation of politician John Profumo?
15. Kindred is the middle name of which American science fiction author?

ANSWERS 1. Johnny Ball **2.** Betty Boothroyd **3.** Martine McCutcheon **4.** Alec Stewart **5.** Liv Tyler **6.** Richard Bacon **7.** Alicia Silverstone **8.** Dutch **9.** Sir Roger Casement **10.** Mark Chapman **11.** France **12.** John Debrett **13.** Charles de Gaulle **14.** Lord Denning **15.** Philip K. Dick.

GENERAL KNOWLEDGE

1. Who created the fictional private eye Matt Helm?
2. In Greek mythology who succeeded Oedipus as King of Thebes?
3. For what would you use a hibachi in Japan?
4. BD is the abbreviation for which postcode area?
5. Which pope succeeded John XXIII in 1963?
6. What is the standard monetary unit of Belarus?
7. What is the approximate population of Nairobi in millions - 1.4, 2.4 or 3.4?
8. The ABC chain of teashops first opened in 1884. What did ABC stand for?
9. What does the Latin phrase 'ab initio' mean?
10. During which war were the two Battles of the Bull Run?
11. What is the Italian name for the city Florence?
12. In which novel by Charles Dickens does Jerry Cruncher appear?
13. In which year was the composer Aaron Copland born?
14. In which novel by Turgenev does the character Bazarov appear?
15. Which actor played Sigmund Freud in a 1962 film?

ANSWERS 1. Donald Hamilton **2.** Creon **3.** Heating and cooking food **4.** Bradford **5.** Paul VI **6.** Rouble **7.** 1.4 million **8.** Aerated Bread Company **9.** From the start **10.** American Civil War **11.** Firenze **12.** A Tale of Two Cities **13.** 1900 **14.** Fathers and Sons **15.** Montgomery Clift.

ENTERTAINMENT

1. Which actress won the Cecil B. DeMille Award at the 1969 Golden Globes?
2. Who did Barbara Bain play in the TV show *Space: 1999*?
3. What nationality is the choreographer Antony Tudor?
4. Who played Dave Deacon in the 1980s sitcom *Bottle Boys*?
5. Which film won the Best Motion Picture (Drama) accolade at the 1972 Golden Globe Awards?
6. Who directed the 1997 film *G.I. Jane*?
7. What nationality is the composer Louis Glass?
8. Which actress starred in the sitcom *The Labours of Erica*?
9. What was the sequel to the U.S. sitcom *The Golden Girls*?
10. Who played Lady Jane Grey in the 1986 film *Lady Jane*?
11. Who played the inventor in the 1940 film *Edison, the Man*?
12. Who composed the symphonic fairy-tale *Peter and the Wolf*?
13. What is the subtitle of the 1995 film sequel to *Candyman*?
14. Who directed the 1989 film *The Adventures of Baron Munchausen*?
15. Who composed the 1937 cantata *In Honour of the City of London*?

ANSWERS 1. Joan Crawford **2.** Dr. Helena Russell **3.** English **4.** Robin Askwith **5.** The Godfather **6.** Ridley Scott **7.** Danish **8.** Brenda Blethyn **9.** The Golden Palace **10.** Helena Bonham Carter **11.** Spencer Tracy **12.** Prokofiev **13.** Farewell to the Flesh **14.** Terry Gilliam **15.** William Walton.

ART AND LITERATURE

1. *Down the Rabbit-Hole* is the opening chapter in which book?
2. The author of Booker Prize-winning novel *The Sea, the Sea* died in 1999. Who was she?
3. Whose novels include *Nostromo*?
4. Who wrote the novel *Absolute Beginners*?
5. In which century did Rembrandt live?
6. Who painted 1864's *Symphony in White No.2: Little White Girl*?
7. Which portrait painter was born the son of a clergyman in Plympton St. Maurice, Devon, in 1723?
8. In which century did Vincent van Gogh live?
9. In which book does Mr. Worldly Wiseman appear?
10. In which Shakespeare play does the petty constable Verges appear?
11. In which novel by Charles Dickens does Mr. Wopsle appear?
12. Who was Phileas Fogg's valet in the novel *Around the World in Eighty Days*?
13. What nationality was the Pop Artist Jim Dine?
14. Which artist's studio was known as 'The Factory'?
15. In which museum and art gallery is the statue *Venus de Milo* housed?

ANSWERS **1.** Alice's Adventures in Wonderland **2.** Dame Iris Murdoch **3.** Joseph Conrad **4.** Colin MacInnes **5.** 17th **6.** James Whistler **7.** Sir Joshua Reynolds **8.** 19th **9.** Pilgrim's Progress **10.** Much Ado About Nothing **11.** Great Expectations **12.** Passepartout **13.** American **14.** Andy Warhol's **15.** The Louvre.

GENERAL KNOWLEDGE

1. Which secretary-general of the United Nations won the 1961 Nobel peace prize?
2. What was the name in Roman mythology for the gods who guarded the store cupboard?
3. Which English businessman was associated with the 1982 Skytrain project?
4. In which year did the Belgian songwriter Jacques Brel die?
5. Who wrote the poem *Gunga Din*?
6. What is the name for an eighth part of a circle?
7. Who was elected MP for Berwick-upon-Tweed in 1997?
8. What is the approximate maximum depth in feet of Loch Ness?
9. Which zodiac sign is also called the Water Carrier?
10. In which year was the Lockerbie disaster?
11. What type of creature is the congo eel?
12. What was the nationality of the architect Arne Jacobsen?
13. In which year did the postcard artist Donald McGill die?
14. Which female singer recorded the 1971 album *Tapestry*?
15. Which actor directed the 1992 film *Hoffa*?

ANSWERS 1. Dag Hammarskjöld **2.** Penates **3.** Freddie Laker **4.** 1978 **5.** Rudyard Kipling **6.** Octant **7.** Alan Beith **8.** 755 **9.** Aquarius **10.** 1988 **11.** Salamander **12.** Danish **13.** 1962 **14.** Carole King **15.** Danny DeVito.

WORDS

1. What is the name given to a person who makes cutlery?
2. What in Russia is a droshky?
3. Why might you display famille?
4. What in Australian rhyming slang is a 'Joe Blake'?
5. What is a young swan called?
6. In the American legal system, what does D.A. stand for?
7. What, in the military, is a D.S.C.?
8. What sort of garment is the Indian dupatta?
9. Fango is used in the treatment of rheumatic disease. What is it?
10. What is the two-piece cotton costume worn in judo?
11. What type of fish is a kelt?
12. What in the U.S. is one's fanny?
13. What vegetable is also known as jibbons?
14. In chess, what does the symbol KBP stand for?
15. Parts of which animal were formerly cooked and eaten in a humble pie?

ANSWERS 1. A cutler **2.** A four-wheeled horse-drawn carriage **3.** It is a type of porcelain **4.** A snake **5.** Cygnet **6.** District Attorney **7.** Distinguished Service Cross **8.** A scarf **9.** A type of mud **10.** A judogi **11.** A salmon **12.** The buttocks **13.** Spring onion **14.** King's Bishop's Pawn **15.** Deer.

GENERAL KNOWLEDGE

1. In which year did Sweden join the European Union?
2. Which saint's feast day is March 1st?
3. The element helium derives its name from the Greek word for what?
4. In which U.S. state is the Ravenswood bridge?
5. Of which country is the letter A the international car index mark?
6. In which European country is Ya a national newspaper?
7. What was the real name of the singer Marc Bolan?
8. In which European country is the port of Constanta?
9. Who was queen of Portugal from 1777-1816?
10. What is the official language of Angola?
11. Setubal and Evora are regions of which European country?
12. What is the WIPO within the United Nations?
13. Who was Japanese emperor from 1912-26?
14. Of which South American country was Belisario Betanur president from 1982-6?
15. In which Scandinavian country is the Order of the Elephant awarded?

ANSWERS **1.** 1995 **2.** David **3.** Sun **4.** West Virginia **5.** Austria **6.** Spain **7.** Mark Feld **8.** Romania **9.** Maria I **10.** Portuguese **11.** Portugal **12.** World Intellectual Property Organization **13.** Taisho **14.** Colombia **15.** Denmark.

ENTERTAINMENT

1. In which year was the comedian Tony Slattery born?
2. Who directed the 1998 film *Godzilla*?
3. Who played *Grandad* in the early 1980s children's TV series?
4. In which city was composer Berthold Goldschmidt born?
5. Who played gangster John Smith in the 1996 film *Last Man Standing*?
6. What nationality is the composer Colin Brumby?
7. Who directed the 1980 film *The Elephant Man*?
8. Which duo produced the 1978 film *Lemon Popsicle*?
9. Who directed the 1944 film *Laura*?
10. Who directed the 1960 film *Let's Make Love*?
11. Who played *The Elusive Pimpernel* in a 1950 film?
12. Who was the male lead in the 1945 film *Objective, Burma!*?
13. In which city was Rory Bremner born?
14. Who directed the 1978 film *Goin' South*?
15. Who directed the 1997 film *Air Force One*?

ANSWERS **1.** 1959 **2.** Roland Emmerich **3.** Clive Dunn **4.** Hamburg **5.** Bruce Willis **6.** Australian **7.** David Lynch **8.** Golan and Globus **9.** Otto Preminger **10.** George Cukor **11.** David Niven **12.** Errol Flynn **13.** Edinburgh **14.** Jack Nicholson **15.** Wolfgang Petersen.

WORDS

1. What is the name of the weight in bowls which makes them deviate from the straight line?
2. A billy is a name for a pocket handkerchief. What then is a ‘blue billy’?
3. To be ‘stabbed with a Bridport dagger’ is to be killed by what method?
4. What is the literal meaning of the word candidate?
5. When are one’s ‘cap-and-feather’ days?
6. What sort of fish is a Severn capon?
7. What metal is named after the German word for ‘gnome’?
8. What sort of animal is a saiga?
9. What is the name of a person who manufactures salt?
10. What would you do with a sampan - fly it or sail it?
11. What sort of animal is a sassaby - a kangaroo or an antelope?
12. From what is the Chinese drink samsara made?
13. What is the motto of the U.S.A.?
14. What is guano?
15. What was a ‘guinea pig’ on a ship?

ANSWERS **1.** Bias **2.** A blue pocket handkerchief with white spots **3.** Hanging **4.** Clothed in white **5.** Childhood **6.** A sole **7.** Cobalt **8.** An antelope **9.** A salter **10.** Sail it **11.** An antelope **12.** Rice **13.** E Pluribus Unum **14.** Bird droppings **15.** A midshipman.

PEOPLE

1. Who is the president of the World Professional Billiards and Snooker Association?
2. Who in May 1999 became the first Briton to climb 11 of the world's 14 highest mountains?
3. Who is the Metropolitan Police Commissioner?
4. Which singer won the 1999 Eurovision Song Contest?
5. What is terrorist Ilich Ramirez Sanchez better known as?
6. Which Australian ballerina created the role of *Pineapple Poll* in the 1951 ballet?
7. Which actor did German director Werner Herzog plot to kill on the set of the film *Fitzcarraldo*?
8. What is the nickname of James Gardner, friend of the footballer Paul Gascoigne?
9. Former Walt Disney studio chief Jeffrey Katzenberg now works for which studio?
10. Which actress played the younger Diana Dors in the 1999 TV film *The Blonde Bombshell*?
11. Which actress played the older Diana Dors in the 1999 TV film *The Blonde Bombshell*?
12. Who was the French presenter of TV's *Le Show*?
13. Who became the new Poet Laureate in 1999?
14. Who was appointed first minister of Scotland in 1999?
15. Which large Scottish island was formerly owned by Keith Schellenberg?

ANSWERS 1. Lord Archer **2.** Alan Hinkes **3.** Sir Paul Condon **4.** Charlotte Nilsson **5.** Carlos the Jackal **6.** Elaine Fifield **7.** Klaus Kinski **8.** Five Bellies **9.** Dreamworks SKG **10.** Keeley Hawes **11.** Amanda Redman **12.** Antoine de Caunes **13.** Andrew Motion **14.** Donald Dewar **15.** Eigg.

WORDS

1. In Australia, what is a woodchop - a type of bird or a wood-chopping competition?
2. The German phrase meaning ‘world pain’ is used to denote melancholy. What is the phrase?
3. On a ship, what did the phrase ‘to paint the lion’ mean?
4. What is the plant deadly nightshade also called?
5. What is belomancy?
6. What is a corroboree?
7. What is the Swiss equivalent of John Bull, the typical Englishman?
8. What is the name given to the tail of a fox?
9. What does the Latin term ‘Bona fide’ mean?
10. Which alcoholic drink is known as ‘blue ruin’?
11. What is ‘black strap’ to a sailor?
12. What does the phrase ‘beside the cushion’ mean?
13. ‘Cucumber Time’ is the dull season in which trade?
14. What type of animal is a grivet - a monkey or an antelope?
15. What would you do with a sackbut - play it or drive it?

ANSWERS 1. A wood-chopping competition **2.** Weltschmerz **3.** To strip a person naked and then smear the body with tar **4.** Belladonna, or dwale **5.** Divination by arrows **6.** An Australian wardance **7.** Colin Tampon **8.** Brush **9.** In good faith **10.** Gin **11.** Bad liquor **12.** Not to the point **13.** Tailoring **14.** A monkey **15.** Play it - it is a musical instrument.

GENERAL KNOWLEDGE

1. Harry A. Atkinson was the first prime minister of which country?

2. Which writer was also the 1st Baron Tweedsmuir?

3. How much did it cost to post a standard first class letter in 1990?

4. What is the former Leeds Polytechnic now known as?

5. Who was elected Labour M.P. for Exeter in 1997?

6. In which country was Indian politician Sonia Gandhi born?

7. What is 157 x 300?

8. In which year did Grace Darling and her father rescue the shipwrecked off the Farne Islands?

9. Which African river joins the River Zaïre at Irebu?

10. Who wrote the 1980 novel *How Far Can You Go?*?

11. What is the name given to the bottommost plank of a vessel's hull?

12. In which century did Hideyoshi Toyotomi unify Japan under one rule?

13. Who bccame archbishop of Canterbury in 1928?

14. In which city is the Robert Gordon University?

15. Which wine bottle holds the equivalent of 16 normal bottles?

ANSWERS 1. New Zealand **2.** John Buchan **3.** 22p **4.** Leeds Metropolitan University **5.** Ben Bradshaw **6.** Italy **7.** 47,100 **8.** 1838 **9.** Ubangi **10.** David Lodge **11.** Garboard **12.** 16th **13.** Cosmo Lang **14.** Aberdeen **15.** Balthazar.

ENTERTAINMENT

1. Who played Maid Marian in the 1938 film *The Adventures of Robin Hood*?
2. What was the alternative title to the 1968 film *The Girl on a Motorcycle*?
3. In which year was the comedian Max Boyce born?
4. Who played Marsha Stubbs in the TV drama *Soldier, Soldier*?
5. Who played Alf Larkins in the 1950s sitcom *The Larkins*?
6. Which movie won the Best British Film accolade at the 1958 British Academy Awards?
7. What nationality is the trumpeter Edward Tarr?
8. Who directed the 1962 film *Advise and Consent*?
9. What was the title of the 1973 Xmas Special by The Goodies?
10. In which year was the current affairs presenter Peter Snow born?
11. Who did Jeffrey Tambor play in the TV comedy *The Larry Sanders Show*?
12. Who played the lead in the 1954 film *The Glenn Miller Story*?
13. Who directed the 1991 film *Edward II*?
14. Which comedienne started by billing herself *The Sea Monster*?
15. Who played *The Canterville Ghost* in a 1944 film?

ANSWERS **1.** Olivia de Havilland **2.** Naked under Leather **3.** 1943 **4.** Denise Welch **5.** David Kossoff **6.** Room at the Top **7.**American **8.** Otto Preminger **9.** The Goodies and the Beanstalk **10.** 1938 **11.** Hank Kingsley **12.** James Stewart **13.** Derek Jarman **14.** Jo Brand **15.** Charles Laughton.

ART AND LITERATURE

1. In which century did US sculptor Hiram Powers live?

2. In which European city is the Prado museum of art?

3. Who wrote the novel *The Woodlanders*?

4. What kind of animal is the Empress of Blandings in stories by P.G. Wodehouse?

5. Which French artist's studies of ballet dancers include *The Rehearsal* of 1873-4?

6. Which Romania-born sculptor created 1907's *The Kiss*?

7. Who created the character Moll Flanders?

8. "Now, what I want is, Facts". The opening line of which novel by Charles Dickens?

9. Which book takes place in Laputa and Brobdingnag, among other places?

10. Who wrote the novel *The Mosquito Coast*?

11. Which female British artist born in 1931 is associated with the Op Art movement?

12. Which sculptor's only equestrian statue, *General Lynch*, was destroyed by a revolution in Chile?

13. Who painted *The Raft of the Medusa*?

14. Whose thriller books include *Best Laid Plans*?

15. Who is the author of the *Harry Potter* series of books?

ANSWERS 1. 19th **2.** Madrid **3.** Thomas Hardy **4.** A pig **5.** Edgar Degas **6.** Brancusi **7.** Daniel Defoe **8.** Hard Times **9.** Gulliver's Travels **10.** Paul Theroux **11.** Bridget Riley **12.** Rodin **13.** Théodore Géricault **14.** Sidney Sheldon **15.** J.K. Rowling.

GENERAL KNOWLEDGE

1. Aqua fortis is an obsolete name for which liquid?
2. In chess, what does the abbreviation e.p. mean?
3. What was the annual boarding fee in 1997 at the Oratory School, Woodcote, Berkshire?
4. Who wrote the story collection *You Know Me, Al*?
5. To which genus does the cobra belong?
6. From which football club did Chelsea sign Gianluca Vialli?
7. In which country is the parliament called the boule?
8. In which U.S. state is the Comstock Lode, an extensive gold and silver vein?
9. On what date is Hallowe'en?
10. In which year was Russian author Mikhail Lermontov killed in a duel?
11. Who wrote the novel *Psycho*?
12. Which blind soothsayer in Greek mythology disclosed the crimes of Oedipus?
13. Which position did Manny Shinwell hold from 1950-51 in the Labour Government?
14. Which European coastal plant's Latin name is *Crambe maritima*?
15. Who was artistic director of the Ballet Rambert from 1981-6?

ANSWERS 1. Nitric acid **2.** En passant **3.** £13,635 **4.** Ring Lardner **5.** Naja **6.** Juventus **7.** Greece **8.** Nevada **9.** October 31st **10.** 1841 **11.** Robert Bloch **12.** Tiresias **13.** Minister of Defence **14.** Sea kale **15.** Robert North.

PEOPLE

1. Which comedian and actor in *EastEnders* penned the autobiography *T'rific*?
2. In which South American country was the French rugby union player Serge Blanco born?
3. In which year did the ballet dancer Alexandra Danilova die?
4. In which year was the English composer Simon Bainbridge born?
5. In which city did the composer Ludwig van Beethoven die?
6. In which year did the English conductor Basil Cameron die?
7. Which jazz pianist born in 1929 joined Miles Davis's sextet in 1958?
8. In which year did the composer Ralph Vaughan Williams die?
9. To which Brazilian supermodel did the actor Leonardo DiCaprio become engaged in 2001?
10. Actress Kate Hudson's husband Chris Robinson is a musician in which rock group?
11. Rande Gerber is the husband of which model-actress?
12. What is the forename of pop singer Ronan Keating's wife?
13. What nationality was the composer Ferdinando Paer?
14. In which year did the French composer Jules Massenet die?
15. Which actress-singer recorded the 2000 album *Wishing*?

ANSWERS 1. Mike Reid **2.** Venezuela **3.** 1997 **4.** 1952 **5.** Vienna **6.** 1975 **7.** Bill Evans **8.** 1958 **9.** Giselle **10.** The Black Crowes **11.** Cindy Crawford **12.** Yvonne **13.** Italian **14.** 1912 **15.** Martine McCutcheon.

GENERAL KNOWLEDGE

1. Which major city does El Alto airport serve?
2. In which European country is the port of Gijon?
3. Of which country is the letter K the international car index mark?
4. What does the forename Patricia mean?
5. In which year was the award the Iron Cross established in Germany?
6. In which year was the British singer Joan Armatrading born?
7. Which saint's feast day is March 19th?
8. In which country is the Chivor dam?
9. The element xenon derives its name from the Greek word for what?
10. Burgos and Avila are provinces of which European country?
11. What is the official language of Ethiopia?
12. Who was president of Austria from 1986-92?
13. Who was Roman emperor from 117-138 A.D.?
14. Who was king of Belgium from 1909-34?
15. In which US state is the Wheeling bridge?

ANSWERS **1.** La Paz **2.** Spain **3.** Cambodia **4.** Noble **5.** 1813 **6.** 1950 **7.** Joseph **8.** Colombia **9.** Stranger **10.** Spain **11.** Amharic **12.** Kurt Waldheim **13.** Hadrian **14.** Albert I **15.** Virginia.

ENTERTAINMENT

1. Who played Dr. Watson in the 1978 film *The Hound of the Baskervilles*?
2. Who does Deena Payne play in the television show *Emmerdale*?
3. In which Mozart opera does the aria *Tu fosti tradito* appear?
4. Who played the orderly Turkle in the film *One Flew Over the Cuckoo's Nest*?
5. Who played Sherlock Holmes in the 1985 film *Young Sherlock Holmes*?
6. Who directed the 1936 film *Fury*?
7. Who directed the 1965 film *Major Dundee*?
8. Who wrote the 1995 play *Dealer's Choice*?
9. Who replaced Johnny Carson as host of *The Tonight Show*?
10. Who directed the 1997 film *Career Girls*?
11. *Nun's Life* is a spoof magazine title read by a child passenger on an aircraft in which 1980 film?
12. Who played Sherlock Holmes in the 1931 film *The Speckled Band*?
13. Which television cook is rector of Aberdeen University?
14. Who plays *Rachel* in the television drama *Cold Feet*?
15. Which French actress returned to the stage after 17 years absence in Paris in 2000, playing the lead in *La Dame aux Camélias?*

ANSWERS 1. Dudley Moore **2.** Viv Windsor **3.** La Clemenza di Tito **4.** Scatman Crothers **5.** Nicholas Rowe **6.** Fritz Lang **7.** Sam Peckinpah **8.** Patrick Marber **9.** Jay Leno **10.** Mike Leigh **11.** Airplane! **12.** Raymond Massey **13.** Clarissa Dickson Wright **14.** Helen Baxendale **15.** Isabelle Adjani.

PEOPLE

1. In which city was Walt Disney born?
2. Which British statesman was the 1st Earl of Beaconsfield?
3. Which Plymouth-born naval commander died at Porto Rico in 1595?
4. What is the polar explorer Sir Ranulph Fiennes' full name?
5. Actresses Madonna and Kim Basinger walked out on the making of which 1993 film?
6. Who was the father of Jemima Khan?
7. Which footballer is married to the actress Leslie Ash?
8. In what subject does the actress Mira Sorvino have a degree from Harvard?
9. With which illusionist was Claudia Schiffer romantically linked in the mid 1990s?
10. On which day of the year was model Helena Christensen born?
11. What was the stage name of the sharpshooter Phoebe Anne Oakley Moses?
12. Who was the second wife of actor Laurence Olivier?
13. What was the middle name of Greek ship owner Aristotle Onassis?
14. Which Australian media proprietor created World Series Cricket?
15. What was the name of the Swedish prime minister assassinated in 1986?

ANSWERS **1.** Chicago **2.** Disraeli **3.** Sir John Hawkins **4.** Ranulph Twisleton-Wykeham-Fiennes **5.** Boxing Helena **6.** Sir James Goldsmith **7.** Lee Chapman **8.** Chinese **9.** David Copperfield **10.** Christmas Day **11.** Annie Oakley **12.** Vivien Leigh **13.** Socrates **14.** Kerry Packer **15.** Olof Palme.

POP

1. Which pop group had a Top Twenty hit in 1976 with the song *Little Does She Know*?
2. What was the B-side of *Boney M*'s 1978 No. 1 single *Rivers of Babylon*?
3. Which Austrian group had a 1985 Top Ten single with the song *Live is Life*?
4. Which female singer recorded the 2000 album *Gotta Tell You*?
5. Which member of the quartet Wondermints played on the 1996 album *Wondermints* but not the 1998 album *Bali*?
6. Which group recorded the November 2000 single *One More Time*?
7. Which girl group recorded the 2000 single *Independent Women*?
8. In which year did the group Sham 69 have a Top Ten single with *Hersham Boys*?
9. Which singer won the 1972 Eurovision Song Contest with the song *Après toi*?
10. Which female singer recorded the 2000 single *Can't Fight the Moonlight*?
11. Which singer recorded the 2000 single *She Bangs*?
12. Which group had a chart hit in 2000 with the single *Gravel Pit*?
13. Which folk group recorded the album *Hark the Village Wait*?
14. In which year did E.M.I. first market L.P.s in the U.K.?
15. Which country singer recorded the 1982 live album *Last Date*?

ANSWERS 1. Kursaal Flyers **2.** Brown Girl in the Ring **3.** Opus **4.** Samantha Mumba **5.** Jim Mills **6.** Daft Punk **7.** Destiny's Child **8.** 1979 **9.** Vicky Leandros **10.** LeAnn Rimes **11.** Ricky Martin **12.** Wu-tang Clan **13.** Steeleye Span **14.** 1952 **15.** Emmylou Harris.

ART AND LITERATURE

1. What was Luke Rhinehart's 1971 cult novel called?
2. Who wrote the 1937 novel *Dead Man Leading*?
3. Who wrote the 1990 novel *L.A. Confidential*?
4. Which Russian author wrote the novel *The Master and Margarita*?
5. What nationality was the painter Mary Cassatt?
6. In which year did the artist Paul Cézanne die?
7. Which co-founder of the Pre-Raphaelite Brotherhood died in 1882 in Birchington-on-Sea?
8. Which American artist's *Death and Disaster* series featured train wrecks and electric chairs?
9. Tobias Tweeney and Ickey the Pig were the creations of which U.S. short story writer?
10. Who wrote *Gentlemen Prefer Blondes*?
11. Which Leghorn-born artist said 'I am going to drink myself dead'?
12. Which Dutch artist's paintings include *Boogie-Woogie*?
13. In which city was the artist Paula Rego born?
14. Who was the king's jester in the play *Hamlet*?
15. Who created the character 'Berry' Pleydell?

ANSWERS **1.** The Dice Man **2.** V.S. Pritchett **3.** James Ellroy **4.** Mikhail Bulgakov **5.** American **6.** 1906 **7.** Dante Gabriel Rossetti **8.** Andy Warhol **9.** Damon Runyon **10.** Anita Loos **11.** Modigliani **12.** Piet Mondrian **13.** Lisbon **14.** Yorick **15.** Dornford Yates.

GENERAL KNOWLEDGE

1. Who are the male and female stars of the film *84 Charing Cross Road*?

2. Which darts player won the 1975 British Open?

3. In which English county is the town of Bideford?

4. What is the home ground of Bradford City F.C.?

5. Who plays police chief Brody in the 1978 film *Jaws 2*?

6. Which singer recorded the 2001 album *Hot Shot*?

7. Which Billy Joel song did the pop group Westlife cover in 2001?

8. Which writer was born at 393 Old Commercial Road, Portsmouth?

9. What is the official name of the city of Hull?

10. In which year did Queen Elizabeth I grant a charter to the city of Leicester?

11. Who was elected M.P. for Birmingham Ladywood in 1997?

12. Who is the Sovereign Head of the Order of St. John?

13. In which year was the British yachtsman John Merricks killed in a car crash in Italy?

14. Who resigned as chief executive of the Rugby Football League in January 1998?

15. What was the real name of the actress Lily Langtry?

ANSWERS 1. Anthony Hopkins and Anne Bancroft **2.** Alan Evans **3.** Devon **4.** Valley Parade **5.** Roy Scheider **6.** Shaggy **7.** Uptown Girl **8.** Charles Dickens **9.** Kingston upon Hull **10.** 1589 **11.** Clare Short **12.** HM The Queen **13.** 1997 **14.** Maurice Lindsay **15.** Emilie Charlotte Le Breton.